ECONOMIC HISTORY OF EUROPE

1760–1939

LONGMANS ECONOMICS SERIES

GENERAL EDITOR

ERNEST L. BOGART

———

ECONOMIC HISTORY OF EUROPE, 1760–1939
By ERNEST L. BOGART

ECONOMIC HISTORY OF THE AMERICAN PEOPLE
By ERNEST L. BOGART

WORKBOOK IN ECONOMIC HISTORY OF THE
AMERICAN PEOPLE
By ERNEST L. BOGART *and* ROBERT D. BROWNE, *University of Illinois*

MODERN INDUSTRY
By ERNEST L. BOGART *and* CHARLES E. LANDON, *Duke University*

A HISTORY OF ECONOMIC IDEAS
By EDMUND WHITTAKER, *University of Illinois*

MONEY AND BANKING, NEW EDITION
By FREDERICK A. BRADFORD, *Lehigh University*

QUESTIONS AND PROBLEMS IN MONEY
AND BANKING
By ROBERT W. MAYER, *Lehigh University*

FOUNDATION OF ACCOUNTING
By ALFRED D'ALESSANDRO, *Northeastern University*

THE MODERN RAILWAY
By JULIUS H. PARMELEE, *Bureau of Railway Economics*, Washington, D. C.

PRINCIPLES AND PROBLEMS OF ECONOMICS
By OTHO C. AULT, *George Peabody College for Teachers, and*
ERNEST J. EBERLING, *Vanderbilt University*

INVESTMENTS AND INVESTMENT POLICY
By FLOYD F. BURTCHETT, *University of California, Los Angeles*

PUBLIC FINANCE
Edited and annotated by ELMER D. FAGAN, *Leland Stanford University*
and C. WARD MACY, *Coe College*

ECONOMIC HISTORY OF EUROPE

1760–1939

BY

ERNEST L. BOGART

LONGMANS, GREEN AND CO.

LONDON · NEW YORK · TORONTO

1942

LONGMANS, GREEN AND CO.
55 FIFTH AVENUE, NEW YORK
221 EAST 20TH STREET, CHICAGO

LONGMANS, GREEN AND CO. LTD.
OF PATERNOSTER ROW
43, ALBERT DRIVE, LONDON, S.W. 19
17, CHITTARANJAN AVENUE, CALCUTTA
NICOL ROAD, BOMBAY
36A, MOUNT ROAD, MADRAS

LONGMANS, GREEN AND CO.
215 VICTORIA STREET, TORONTO

BOGART

ECONOMIC HISTORY OF EUROPE

FIRST EDITION

PRINTED IN THE UNITED STATES OF AMERICA

PREFACE

To attempt single-handed to write an economic history of Europe since the Industrial Revolution may be considered a proof of rashness or ignorance. I plead guilty to both indictments. My excuse must be that at the time I began work there was no satisfactory text on the subject. Although this lack has since been corrected, I am hopeful that this volume may prove a useful addition to the growing literature. An effort has been made to give a functional account of economic institutions during the past 175 years, and to explain the consequent changes in the economic activities and structure of society. The Industrial Revolution ushered in a new material era in the world's history which has been marked by conquest of natural forces and of distance, expansion of human and international relationships, and the substitution of an economy of abundance for one of scarcity. The story of these developments is complex but dramatic. For obvious reasons the narrative ends with the year 1939. Economic factors were not the only ones that determined Europe's history during this period, but they were important enough to warrant separate study.

This volume gives a narrative and chronological account of the major economic activities of Britain, France, and Germany during the whole of the period covered, with a side glance at Russia and Italy for recent years. It is hoped that the student may be helped to understand the genetic character of economic development and may be stimulated to further reading. Considerable use has been made of statistical tables, which present in compressed form a body of information whose description in the text would be tiresome. An effort has been made to assemble in these tables widely scattered material. Annotated bibliographies have been provided which list books found most useful. They testify faintly to the extent of my obligations to other authors.

My greatest obligations are to the various libraries that generously made their books and facilities available to me — those of the universities of Illinois, Columbia, Vienna, Munich, Paris, and Cambridge. My special thanks must go to the two first-named institutions for co-operative consideration and patience in the face of many demands.

ERNEST L. BOGART

New York City
January 3, 1942

CONTENTS

Part I. 1760–1870

THE RISE OF THE MACHINE

vii

CONTENTS

GENERAL BIBLIOGRAPHY

I. EUROPE

An increasing number of books on the economic history of Europe has appeared in the past decade, of which the more important may be listed. The earliest and most scholarly was J. H. Clapham, *The Economic Development of France and Germany*, 1815–1914 (Cambridge, 1921; 2nd ed., 1923). This was succeeded by H. E. Barnes, *An Economic History of the Western World* (New York, 1937), an able review of development since the stone age; A. Birnie, *An Economic History of Europe*, 1760–1930 (New York, 1930), a useful outline; W. Bowden, M. Karpovich, and A. P. Usher, *An Economic History of Europe since* 1750 (New York, 1937), containing much good material badly organized; S. B. Clough and C. W. Cole, *Economic History of Europe* (Boston, 1941), succinct summaries from 600 A.D.; C. Day, *Economic Development in Modern Europe* (New York, 1933), covering only agriculture and manufactures; E. Eyre (Ed.), *European Civilization, its Origin and Development*. Vol. V, *Economic History of Europe since the Reformation* (Oxford, 1937), a sketchy account; H. Heaton, *Economic History of Europe* (New York, 1936), a clear and concise review since prehistoric times; M. M. Knight, H. E. Barnes, and F. Flügel, *Economic History of Europe in Modern Times* (New York, 1928), a keen analysis; E. Lipson, *Europe in the Nineteenth and Twentieth Centuries*, 1815–1939 (New York, 1941), an excellent survey; F. L. Nussbaum, *A History of the Economic Institutions of Modern Europe* (New York, 1933), a summary of W. Sombart's *Der Moderne Kapitalismus*; F. A. Ogg and W. R. Sharp, *The Economic Development of Modern Europe* (rev. ed., New York, 1926), a useful summary; G. F. Renard and G. Weulersse, *Life and Work in Modern Europe* (New York, 1926), a thin account; R. H. Soltau, *An Outline of European Economic Development* (London, 1935), brief but suggestive. Of German treatises three deserve mention: H. Cunow, *Allgemeine Wirtschaftsgeschichte*. 4 Bde. (Berlin, 1931). Vol. IV provides a good summary since 1800; J. Kulischer, *Allgemeine Geschichte des Mittelalters und der Neuen Zeit*. 2 Bde. (München, 1929). Vol. II covers the recent period in useful fashion; W. Sombart, *Der Moderne Kapitalismus*. 4 Bde. (5. Aufl., München, 1922–27), deservedly a classic. Vol. IV covers the nineteenth century. Of French books two should be named: H. Sée, *Les Origines du capitalisme moderne* (Paris, 1926. Translated by H. B. Vanderblue and G. Doriot as *Modern Capitalism, its Origin and Evolution*, New York, 1928), suggestive; E. Théry, *L'Europe économique* (Paris, 1911), good for statistics.

The leading encyclopedias and official publications will be found most useful for particular topics, but may be listed here. Among the former five are outstanding: R. H. Palgrave, *Dictionary of Political Economy*. 3 vols. (rev. ed. by Henry Higgs, London, 1923–26); *Encyclopedia of the Social Sciences*. 15 vols. (New York, 1930–35), a monumental work edited by E. R. A. Seligman and Alvin Johnson; *Handwörterbuch der Staatswissenschaften*. 6 Bde. (June, 1890–94; 4. Aufl. 1926, mit Engänzungsband), a memorial of German scholarship, edited by J. Conrad and associates; *Dictionary of Statistics*, compiled by M. J. Mulhall (London, 1899; revised by A. D. Webb. London, 1911); *Die Welt in Zahlen*, by W. Woytinsky. 7 Bde. (Berlin, 1925–28), with critical comment. The leading government publications for the economic historian are *Annuaire statistique* (Paris, annual); *Statistisches Jahrbuch für das Deutsche Reich* (Berlin, annual); *Statistical Abstract for the United Kingdom* (London, annual).

2. GREAT BRITAIN

There are many economic histories of Britain, but only those useful for the recent period need be cited. An excellent collection of source material from 1060 to 1846 is A. E. Bland, P. A. Brown, and R. H. Tawney (Eds.), *English Economic History: Select Documents* (2nd ed., London, 1915). The standard work is J. H. Clapham, *An Economic History of Modern Britain.* 3 vols. (Cambridge, 1927–33), based on exhaustive research and ripe scholarship. W. Cunningham, *The Growth of English Industry and Commerce in Modern Times* (4th ed., Cambridge, 1904) long held the field, but has been superseded by more recent studies. A suggestive survey is C. R. Fay, *Great Britain from Adam Smith to the Present Day* (London, 1928). H. O. Meredith, *Outline of the Economic History of England* (London, 1908) is a reflective analysis for advanced students. G. A. Perris, *An Industrial History of Modern England* (London, 1914) is strongly biased. G. R. Porter, *Progress of the Nation* (London, 1846. Rev. ed. by F. W. Hirst, London, 1912) contains much interesting information. A good though brief introduction is A. Redford, *The Economic History of England, 1760–1860* (London, 1931). J. F. Rees, *A Social and Industrial History of England, 1815–1918* (New York, 1920) is a thoughtful survey. A. P. Usher, *An Introduction to the Industrial History of England* (Boston, 1920) emphasizes the technological factors. W. M. Waters, *An Economic History of England, 1066–1874* (London, 1925) is useful, though frankly based on secondary sources.

3. FRANCE

The outstanding authority on French economic history is Henri Sée, whose *Französische Wirtschaftsgeschichte* (Berlin, 1936) is the most exhaustive and scholarly work. This largely supersedes his earlier books: *Esquisse d'une histoire économique et sociale de la France depuis les origines jusqu'à la guerre mondiale* (Paris, 1929), and *La vie économique de la France sous la monarchie censitaire, 1815–1848* (Paris, 1927). An interesting study in English is S. B. Clough, *France: A History of National Economics, 1789–1939* (New York, 1939). Some attention is paid to economic history in the ambitious work of E. Lavisse, *Histoire de la France contemporaine depuis la Révolution jusqu'à la paix de 1919.* 10 vols. (Paris, 1920–22). A useful survey is G. Martin, *Histoire économique et financière de la nation française* (Paris, 1927). G. Renard and A. Dulac, *L'evolution industrielle et agricole depuis cent cinquante ans* (Paris, 1914) is a mere sketch. A. Viallate, *L'activité économique en France de la fin du XVIII⁰ siècle à nos jours* (Paris, 1937) covers the field rather inadequately.

4. GERMANY

The books on the economic history of Germany are legion. Of those in English the most useful are J. E. Barker, *Modern Germany* (London, 1909; 6th rev. ed., 1919); W. H. Dawson, *The Evolution of Modern Germany* (London, 1938), both sympathetic studies by Englishmen; H. Lichtenberger, *Germany and its Evolution in Modern Times* (trans. from the French by R. M. Ludovici; New York, 1913), objective and scholarly; W. F. Bruck, *Social and Economic History of Germany from William II to Hitler, 1888–1938* (Cardiff, 1938). Of German books the best one is Sartorius von Waltershausen, *Deutsche Wirtschaftsgeschichte* (Jena, 1923) though it is biased in favor of state activity. R. Häpke and E. Wiskemann, *Wirtschaftsgeschichte.* 2 vols. II. Teil, 1800–1933 (Leipzig, 1933) is excellent. G. G. Neuhaus, *Deutsche Wirtschaftsgeschichte im neunzehnten*

Jahrhundert (München, 1919) is a useful introduction. L. Pohle, *Die Entwicklung des deutschen Wirtschaftsleben im letzten Jahrhundert* (2nd ed., Leipzig, 1898) is excellent. E. Rude, *Die Geschichte der neuesten Zeit* (Berlin, 1939) presents the newer point of view. A sparkling account, written for popular consumption, is W. Sombart, *Die deutsche Volkswirtschaft im 19. Jahrhundert und im Anfang des 20. Jahrhundert* (Berlin, 1903; 6. Aufl., Leipzig, 1927). A scholarly work is W. Wygodzinski, *Wandlungen der deutschen Volkswirtachaft in XIX. Jahrhundert* (Köln, 1912).

Economic and social history may often be illuminated by historical novels. An excellent critical introduction to English novels is Louis Cazamian, *Le roman social en Angleterre* (London, 1904). E. A. Baker, *A Guide to Historical Fiction* (London, 1914) covers British, American, French, and German fiction in English, with annotations and description. J. A. Buckley and W. T. Williams, *A Guide to British Historical Fiction* (London, 1912) is also annotated and descriptive. Jonathan Nield, *A Guide to the Best Historical Novels and Tales* (London, 1911; 5th ed., 1928) states the subject matter. J. R. Faye, *Historical Fiction, Historically and Chronologically Related* (Chicago, 1920) summarizes important novels. John Marriott, *English History in English Fiction* (New York, 1941) gives critical estimates.

ECONOMIC HISTORY OF EUROPE

1760–1939

ECONOMIC HISTORY
OF EUROPE

1760–1939

Part I: The Rise of the Machine. 1760–1870

CHAPTER I

AGRICULTURE

1. THE AGRICULTURAL REVOLUTION IN ENGLAND

It is difficult for a person living today to picture conditions as they existed one hundred and fifty years ago in western Europe and to realize the extent to which the agriculture, manufactures, and commerce of the countries located there were shackled by custom, by tradition, and by legal arrangements. The contrast with the present in all these respects was profound. "The economic conditions of modern life," wrote Alfred Marshall,[1] are marked by "the emancipation from custom, and the growth of free activity, of constant forethought and restless enterprise." Freedom of industry and enterprise, which Marshall considered the special characteristic of economic life in the modern age, could not be achieved until industry was liberated from the old restrictions. This movement of liberation may be considered as the first great economic achievement in the transition from the eighteenth to the twentieth century.

The movement of liberation in agriculture presents three main forms: first, the liberation of the person of the rural laborer, or the emancipation of the serfs; second, the liberation of the ownership of land from legal restrictions, that is, greater mobility in land transfers; and third, the release of agricultural technique from ancient custom and usage, or greater freedom in the management of land. These different steps proceeded at different rates of speed in the various countries, but in all of them there was a movement along these lines.

Liberation of the person. In England the legal emancipation of the workers had already been fully effected. The Black Death

[1] *Principles of Economics* (London, 1898), 5.

I

in 1348 had given the death blow to serfdom, though it still lingered on in places until the sixteenth century, when it was finally ended. The system was an anachronism in an age which no longer knew the manor or the feudal land organization, and to its early disappearance in England must be ascribed in no small degree the superior character of English labor and the pre-eminence which that country later assumed over her continental rivals.

In one respect, however, there was a restriction upon the freedom of the person, and this was in mobility of movement. The free circulation of labor from one employment to another was obstructed by the Statute of Apprentices of 1563, and the free movement from place to place was restricted by the Law of Settlement of 1662.

The poor law of 1601 imposed upon each parish the duty of providing for its own poor. Who were to be considered the poor of each parish became, therefore, a question of some importance. This matter was defined by the Settlement Law of 1662, which placed the primary obligation upon the parish in which the individual was born, unless he acquired a new settlement in another parish by uninterrupted residence there for forty days. Since no parish wished to be saddled with dependent persons who might apply for relief, the overseers of the poor either refused to admit such persons or removed them before the expiration of the forty day period to the parish where they were last settled, unless they could give security that they would not become a public charge. Although these provisions were somewhat modified later by a system of granting to workers certificates which enabled them to leave a parish without losing settlement and forbidding other parishes from ejecting workers until they actually became public charges,[2] they always constituted an obstacle to the free movement of labor from place to place. "It is often more difficult," exclaimed Adam Smith, "for a poor man to pass the artificial boundaries of a parish, than an arm of the sea or a ridge of high mountains." The tendency of this legislation was to immobilize the unskilled workers in the parishes of their birth.

Agricultural labor was little affected by the legislation concerning apprentices, but its freedom of movement in seeking the most remunerative employment was seriously curtailed by the laws of settlement. In the north there was a migration from the fields to the developing factories, but there was no migration from the agricultural south to the industrial north, which would have adjusted the supply of labor to the demand. This was prevented not only by the law of settlement, but also by inertia and the difficulty and expense of travel before the railway era. Such a journey would

---

[2] 35 Geo. III. c. 101. *An Act to prevent the removal of poor persons until they shall become actually chargeable.* (1795.)

have been more difficult than migration to Canada a hundred years later.

Mobility in land transfer. A second step in the movement of liberation as it relates to the land was the freeing of ownership from legal restrictions, so that agricultural land could be freely bought and sold. The orthodox economic theory is that, if there were perfect mobility in land transfer, land would tend to come into the possession of those users who could pay the highest price, that is, those who could make the most productive use of it.

Land was emancipated from its feudal burdens in England more than a century before similar reforms were effected in France, Prussia, and other European states. Thereafter, the only restrictions to which land was subject were those which might be created by will or deed. This early emancipation of the land gave to English landlords an advantage in agriculture over their European rivals which provided an opportunity for outdistancing them. Unfortunately, however, this advantage was largely sacrificed to family pride by the introduction in the seventeenth century of modern family settlements, by which primogeniture was placed on a firm basis. This custom of primogeniture, strongly entrenched among the nobility, was given the sanction of law in cases of intestacy. The effect of custom and law together was effectively to keep the great estates intact, and this was enforced by the practice of entail.

While certain political and social advantages have been claimed for this system, it is clear that the restrictions on the alienation of land must frequently have kept it in the hands of landlords who were ignorant of the best principles of agriculture, who had no interest in the subject, or who were without adequate capital to utilize their property to the best advantage. Mobility in land transfer was further restricted by the complicated land titles and by the legal difficulties in the way of obtaining a clear title by purchase. From an economic point of view the perpetuation of entail and primogeniture placed a handicap on English agriculture and prevented the most productive use of the land.

The bad effects of an uneconomic system were, however, modified in England in the eighteenth century by two circumstances, namely, the social responsibility of many English landlords, and the introduction of fresh capital by the marriage of impecunious eldest sons with the daughters of wealthy merchants and manufacturers. When these hereditary landlords were alive to the duties that went with their estates, they exemplified high ideals of social service, in public office, as agriculturalists showing the way to better practices through costly experimentation, or as landlords building model cottages or schools and improving the condition of their tenants.

Not only did the city merchants intermarry with the landed aristocracy, but many of the former also bought land for the sake of social prestige and political power which ownership conferred. These business men treated land as a source of profit and did much to improve agricultural practice. Rents came to be determined by the returns from the land rather than by custom. There was a steady tendency toward concentration of ownership in fewer hands, especially in the eighteenth century. By the nineteenth century there was undoubtedly also an increase in the size of the average agricultural unit, though on both these points there is lack of precise evidence. Economic, social, and legal forces were all working in this direction, among which one of the most important was the enclosure movement.

Enclosures.[3] The enclosure movement may be viewed from several standpoints, but for some purposes it is desirable to regard it as a phase of the greater mobility of land. The arrangement of the land under the open field system was disadvantageous for its best use, and a redistribution or rearrangement was greatly needed. Under this system the arable land of each village was usually divided into three great fields, one of which lay fallow each year, while the other two were cultivated. The land of every farmer would be distributed in these fields in acre strips, not in a compact holding, but intermingled with the strips of the lord and of other tenants. Outside the cultivated open fields lay the meadow which was held in common, and the waste on which all the farmers had rights of pasturage. Such a system did not permit individual initiative or enterprise, but held agriculture to traditional methods and practices. Before any real progress could be made there would have to be a transfer of property and a consolidation of scattered holdings in the hands of individuals. That such a step was necessary is evidenced by the fact that in 1758 less than one-third of the townships of the typical county of Oxford were entirely enclosed, which may fairly be taken as representative of conditions generally.

Enclosure might be carried out in two ways, either by mutual agreement of all the owners, or by private act of Parliament. Voluntary agreements called for almost more unanimity than might be expected, yet many were apparently made, which were carried through by the parish authorities and subsequently ratified in chancery. These gradually merged in enclosure by private act, which made the reallotments compulsory upon the dissident minor-

[3] The writers on the subject of enclosure fall into two groups. Curtler, Gonner, Johnson, Levy, and Prothero (Lord Ernle) contend that the movement was inevitable, necessary, and in the national interest, though the consequent reorganization was hard on the small holder. The Hammonds, Hasbach, and Slater question the inevitability and advantages, which they believe were outweighed by the harm done the small holder. I have in general followed the first group.

ity. The former might leave the meadows and commons as before and would simply reallot the scattered strips; no serious social changes would therefore be involved. Where, however, the comprehensive enclosure of all the lands of a village was brought about by Act of Parliament the consequences might be far-reaching. The rapid increase in the number of these acts after 1750 possesses therefore great significance. The following table gives the figures:

ENCLOSURES IN ENGLAND

Decade	Enclosure rate	Acres enclosed
1720–30	33	
1730–40	35	
1740–50	38	337,877
1750–60	156	
1760–70	424	704,550
1770–80	642	1,207,800
1780–90	287	450,180
1790–1800	506	858,270
1800–10	906	1,550,010
1810–20	771	1,560,990
1820–30	186	

The movement became important after 1750, reached the high point in the two decades 1800–20, and thereafter declined. By 1845 practically all the open fields in England had been enclosed and the rearrangement of the holdings was completed.

To carry out a scheme of enclosure fairly, allotting to each small tenant a plot of ground approximately equivalent to his scattered strips and embracing compensation for the loss of grazing and meadow rights, called for a degree of care and disinterestedness which was not to be found in a Parliament controlled by the landed gentry. Even when enclosure was carried out with due recognition of the rights of all, the costs were extremely heavy, and, to the small owners, ruinous. The charges for commissioners, lawyers, surveyors, valuers, and other officials, the outlay for hedges, roads, gates, bridges, drainage, and other expenses, placed a burden on the land which sometimes swallowed up the value of a small allotment. In order to reduce costs and promote uniformity a general enclosure act was passed in 1801, which simplified procedure somewhat, though private acts of Parliament were still necessary. This act applied mainly to commons, and a new impetus seems to have been given to this form of enclosure. The fundamental reason for enclosure, which these legal measures merely facilitated, was the increasing profitableness of arable farming, the growth of population, and the consequent enlarged demand for foodstuffs.

While the enclosure movement must be regarded as a necessary step in the process of freeing the land from antiquated and complicated burdens, the social consequences were most unfortunate. The yeomen farmers were often adversely affected, but the most serious injuries were inflicted on the copyholders or on owners of common-right cottages, who had rights of ownership or pasturage in the common fields. These groups were separated from the soil and were made wholly dependent upon their wages as hired laborers. They had often had a right, or were permitted, to graze a cow upon the commons. But when the common land was enclosed their ill-defined right was disallowed or they were granted a plot of ground too small to support a cow. In defence of the enclosure of the commons, it may be said that only in this way could pasturage be protected from over-stocking. Moreover, only on enclosed land could pedigreed stock be raised or cattle fattened for the market. This was especially necessary in the Midlands and southern counties, where cattle raising went hand in hand with arable farming and the growing of fodder in a scientific rotation of crops. Nevertheless there was great discontent over the results of this policy. A popular piece of doggerel stated that

> The law locks up the man or woman
> Who steals the goose from off the common;
> But leaves the greater villain loose
> Who steals the common from the goose.

Arthur Young, who was an advocate of enclosure on economic grounds, concluded that "by nineteen enclosure bills in twenty they are injured, in some grossly injured." The arbitrary power of the commissioners in fact left the poor with very little protection against injustice. His words on this point are wonderfully trenchant: [4]

"Go to an alehouse kitchen of an old enclosed county, and there you will see the origin of poverty and poor rates. For whom are they to be sober? For whom are they to save? (Such are their questions.) For the parish? If I am diligent, shall I have leave to build a cottage? If I am sober, shall I have land for a cow? If I am frugal, shall I have half an acre of potatoes? You offer no motives; you have nothing but a parish officer and a workhouse! Bring me another pot."

"The poor in these parishes," he added, "may say, and with truth, *Parliament may be tender of property; all I know is, I had a cow, and act of Parliament has taken it from me.* And thousands may make this speech with truth." Young urged the reservation

[4] Arthur Young, *An Inquiry into the Propriety of Applying Wastes,* etc. (London, 1801), 13.

of sufficient common land to provide pasturage for a cow for each cottager, such land or right to be inalienable and to be attached to each cottage. This was not done, and the number of dairy cows diminished to such an extent that the children of the poor could not be furnished with milk to drink. Altogether the enclosure policy must be held to have contributed to the increase in poverty and social degradation of a peculiarly unfortunate group, which was wholly unable to adjust itself to the changes in the economic organization.

Release of agricultural technique. The third step in the reorganization of agriculture was the release of agricultural technique from ancient custom and usage and the development of greater freedom in the management of land. Before any great improvement could be made it was necessary to get rid of the old open field system, and to give each farmer the opportunity to manage his land in his own fashion. This leads to a reconsideration of enclosures, but from another angle, namely that of the economic productivity of the land. The open field system involved waste along at least four lines.

In the first place there was a waste of land. It was estimated by the Board of Agriculture in the last decade of the eighteenth century that there were still over 6,000,000 acres of waste or uncultivated land in England out of a total of 22,000,000 acres in Great Britain. So long as the population was relatively stationary and there was no pressure on the land for additional food the economic loss involved in this uncultivated land was not felt, but after 1760, when the population increased rapidly and the demand threatened to outrun the supply, more effective utilization of the land became imperative. Under the open field system much arable land was wasted in balks and footpaths. Drainage was almost impossible, and erosion of the rich top soil was difficult to prevent.

The system involved also a waste of labor. The grouping of the farmers in a village meant a long trip each morning to their land, and as each man's strips were scattered throughout the open fields there was further loss of time and labor in moving his tools and in all the processes of manuring, plowing, planting, and harvesting at remote points. The opportunities for dishonesty offered by the slight boundaries and the unfenced lands necessitated constant watchfulness and led to frequent quarrels and litigation.

There was also a waste of capital. Under a system of small scattered strips the use of improved implements, of selected seed, of more profitable crops, or of better live stock was practically impossible for the more progressive farmer. The common rights of pasture on the stubble fields prevented the growing of winter crops. The manure of the pastured cattle was wasted. The promiscuous herding of cattle and sheep on the commons precluded the breeding of improved live stock and exposed the animals to disease. Where the commons were unstinted they were overrun with stock, which in good years were half fed and in bad years died of starvation.

But the greatest wastes were those of management owing to the obstructions to efficient utilization of the land which were presented by the open field system. All the occupiers were bound by custom and were compelled to carry on the same operations at the same time and by the same methods. Individual initiative was impossible, and improvement by co-operative action was unthinkable. And yet the growth of the population required more productive use of the land. Since at that time no adequate source of supply was available in other countries it was necessary to increase home production. This could be obtained in two ways — the amount of land under cultivation could be increased, or the land in use could be so managed as to produce more. It is a matter of historical record that both methods were used.

The abolition of the wasteful three (or two) field system with its unproductive fallow, and the substitution therefor of a system of rotation, brought a considerable amount of land under continuous cultivation. If, as has been estimated, over 6,000,000 acres of the cultivated land of the country were still farmed in open fields in 1760 and another 6,000,000 acres were in waste lands, then the inclusion of the fallow and the waste in the cultivated area was roughly equivalent to a fifty per cent increase of the land under cultivation.

Even more important were the changes in technique, by which the production from a given amount of land was increased. These may be conveniently grouped under the two heads of management and breeding.

Better management or technique. This took several forms, which were gradually developed. Better methods of cultivation were introduced by Jethro Tull, who invented a grain-drill, planted the seed in rows at just the right depth, and insisted upon frequent cultivation to kill the weeds and conserve the moisture.[5] Tull's principles were put in practice by large landlords in various parts of the country and became the fashion among the more progressive of the landed gentry. New implements were produced, better ploughs, drills, reaping, mowing, and winnowing machines, horse rakes, turnip slicers, and other tools; in 1784 a crude threshing machine was invented.

New crops were also introduced, such as swedes, mangel-wurzel, kohl-rabi, turnips, clover, and other plants from Europe. The land was improved by marling, drainage, manuring, and in other ways.

[5] His *Horse Hoeing Husbandry*, which advocated those principles, was published in 1733.

But still more important was the skillful rotation of crops, which both increased the yield and improved the land. A pioneer in this respect was Lord Townshend, whose insistence upon the importance of turnips gained him the nickname of "Turnip" Townshend. He introduced the famous Norfolk course, a rotation of four crops: turnips, barley, clover, or clover and ray-grass, wheat.

This rotation not only permitted complete and continuous utilization of the land, but, by alternating deep root crops with grain, introduced nitrogen into the soil and restored its fertility. The turnips and clover, moreover, provided winter feed for stock from which more manure could be obtained with which further to enrich the soil. In promoting this and other improvements the work of Arthur Young was of great importance. Young traveled widely, recording faithfully his observations, and urged the necessity of abandoning obsolete methods and introducing better methods. He advocated enclosure and large farms, because in them he saw greatest hope for advancement.

Breeding. There does not seem to have been much conscious effort in England to develop the best types of animals or plants prior to the eighteenth century. Indeed the effect of the open field system and of common grazing grounds had led rather to their deterioration. A pioneer in breeding was Robert Bakewell, whose success in developing new types of sheep was especially noteworthy. Until the middle of the eighteenth century sheep had been valued chiefly for their wool and cattle for their milk and their powers of draft, but with the growth of population a demand was soon to be created for meat. Fastening his attention on desirable features in a meat animal Bakewell sought to produce these by breeding from selected individuals which most nearly possessed these characteristics. His New Leicesters, compact in form, small in bone, with good fattening propensities and early maturity, soon replaced the former lean, long-legged, and large-boned sheep. He was less successful with cattle, but he had shown the way, and his many successful imitators soon improved the breeds of cattle and horses as well as sheep.

Breeding of plants progressed more slowly. Although the Dutch had achieved extraordinary success in the development of new varieties of tulips, the principles used there seem not to have been applied to farm crops. Coke of Holkham, however, toward the end of the eighteenth century greatly improved his hay crop by more careful selection of seed.

Agrarian reorganization. The changes which have been described are frequently called the agricultural revolution in England, and taken as a whole they brought about a thorough reorganization of agrarian methods and mode of life. The results contained both good and bad features. On one hand there was more land under cultivation, more efficient methods of farming, lowered costs, and larger crops and better meat to supply the increasing demand of the expanding population. Against these undoubted benefits must be placed social losses such as attend any process of economic reorganization. The class of yeoman farmers, who worked their own lands, was gradually extinguished, many small tenants were deprived by the enclosures of pasturage for their cows, while the accompanying industrial revolution destroyed the domestic industries upon which they depended as by-industries. It was difficult for men displaced from familiar environments and accustomed occupations to adjust themselves easily, and much hardship resulted. In agricultural practice a double change occurred: from open fields and common pasture to enclosure, and from freehold or customary tenure to tenancy at a money rent. The French system of share rent (*métayage*) never came into vogue in England. The matter was briefly summed up by Lord Ernle:[6] "The divorce of the peasantry from the soil, and the extinction of commoners, open field farmers and eventually of small freeholders, were the heavy price which the nation ultimately paid for the supply of bread and meat to its manufacturing population."

From the readjustment there gradually emerged the tenant system which was characteristic of the nineteenth century. Landed proprietors let their lands in large farms to tenants, the former supplying permanent improvements and the latter the circulating capital. With long leases such a system induced the tenant to farm the land carefully, while the right to all the profits beyond the fixed rent stimulated the largest possible production. The system worked best in the production of staple crops like cereals, but it lacked elasticity. Below these two groups of land owners and tenant farmers stood the agricultural laborers, who constituted a permanent class of wage-workers without hope of becoming land owners or even tenant farmers.

The expanding demands of a rapidly growing population, increasingly urban, stimulated agricultural production. From 1780 to 1813 prices rose steadily, and after 1790 rents kept pace with prices. Enclosures brought more land under cultivation, improved transportation opened wider markets to the farmers, and improvements in methods and technique aided larger production. Agricultural societies were formed in most of the counties of England during the last two decades of the eighteenth century, and did much to disseminate the best results. The application of science to agriculture

---

[6] R. E. Prothero (Lord Ernle), *English Farming, Past and Present* (London, 1912), 149.

was first made by Humphry Davy in 1803 through his lectures on "The Connection of Chemistry with Vegetable Physiology," but thereafter scientific knowledge was combined with practical experience. Large farms operating with considerable capital could meet the new requirements best, and were thus able to obtain the large profits realizable by those who were successful in expanding production. In good seasons it was a struggle to keep pace with growing national needs, and in periods of deficient home production importations were necessary. After 1792 England was definitely dependent on foreign supplies of food.

The continuous rise in prices in spite of expanding production was unprecedented and has been variously explained. Aside from the growing demand, there were not infrequent years of bad harvests which reduced the available supply of grain. But it was the Napoleonic wars which drove prices up to famine heights. Imports from the Baltic region — then the granary of Europe — were curtailed by the Continental system, while those from the United States were made costly by high charges for freight and insurance. But the most general cause of high prices was inflation of the currency, which occurred after the suspension of specie payments by the Bank of England in 1797. Relieved of the necessity of redeeming its notes in gold the Bank overissued its notes, which soon depreciated. Since Bank of England notes constituted the money of account, prices were stated in terms of this depreciated currency and consequently rose as the value of the notes fell.

The depreciation of the pound, combined with deficient harvests, served to raise the price of wheat to unprecedented heights in 1812. In that year the country stood on the very verge of famine and the price of wheat went up to 155 s. per quarter,[7] or over $4.50 a bushel. Fortunately, better harvests during the next three years brought relief, and in 1815 the price of wheat was down to 65 s. 7 d.

The Corn Laws. With the cessation of the Napoleonic and American wars in 1815, British agriculture was exposed to the depressing effects of international competition. A serious agrarian depression set in, which seemed to threaten speedy ruin to landlords and farmers, if not to laborers. During the wars landlords had brought under cultivation submarginal lands, such as uplands and wastes, in which they had invested considerable capital. Tenant farmers, presuming upon the continuance of high prices, had leased lands on terms which could not be met if prices fell. Some farmers threw up their leases and abandoned the cultivation of the land, and laborers found it difficult to get employment at even nominal wages.

[7] A quarter is about eight bushels.

Under these conditions Parliament hurriedly passed the Corn Law of 1815. This provided that foreign wheat could not be imported into England unless the domestic price was 80 s. or more a quarter (about $2.50 a bushel). Other cereals received similar protection.[8] The purpose of this act was avowedly protective, to shut out imports and to maintain the prices of home-grown grain above a level regarded as necessary. The Corn Law of 1815 has frequently been represented as selfish class legislation of a small but powerful group which dominated Parliament. There were, however, plausible grounds upon which it was defended. The country had just emerged from a war in which it had more than once been threatened with starvation, and it was held on military grounds that the country must not be dependent on foreign supplies of food. A vigorous soldiery was, moreover, assured by a widespread agriculture. Heavy taxes, both national and local, had meanwhile been imposed upon land, and it was agreed that these could not be borne unless the income from land were maintained at the prevailing level. The tenant farmers, too, who had contracted to pay high rents, would be ruined if prices fell; since taxes were heavy and interest rates high, they could do little to reduce costs. And finally agricultural employment would diminish and wages fall. These arguments prevailed and the policy of making England self-sufficient with respect to grain was adopted. The protests of the manufacturers and of their operatives were disregarded.

A great deal of controversy ensued over the actual effects of the corn laws, but the verdict of history has condemned them. The prices of agricultural produce were on the whole higher than they would have been if these laws had not been in force, but they fluctuated wildly. In good years they were so low as to be ruinous to the farmers, while in times of deficient harvest prices ran far higher than the import level before the rise could be checked. Since importation was not a regular business considerable inertia had to be overcome before needed supplies could be diverted into unaccustomed channels, and there was normally no regular surplus in the foreign countries for export.

Dissatisfaction with the operation of the corn laws led to considerable experimentation in the next twenty years. In 1822 the limit price for wheat was reduced to 70 s., but as the market price remained below this point it had no practical effect. In 1828 and again in 1832 this restrictive legislation was modified by the adoption of a sliding scale of duties, which varied with the price of grain, being lower as the price rose. A new speculative element was now introduced, for importers of grain combined to raise domestic prices

[8] Thus for barley the limit price was 40 shillings, and for oats 26 shillings.

in order that they might bring in foreign supplies at lower rates of duty. The experience of these years with the sliding scale was unsatisfactory to the farmers, to the landowners, and most of all to the consumers, especially the working classes.

The repeal of the corn laws was first seriously urged by the Anti-Corn-Law League, founded in 1838 under the leadership of Richard Cobden and John Bright, both cotton manufacturers. Their arguments were partly humanitarian, urging the need of cheaper food and a higher standard of living, and partly selfish in that cheaper food could mean lower wages. A desire to retaliate upon the landed interest, by whose help the factory acts had been passed, may also have played a part. They also pointed out that the land owners alone profited by the monopoly conferred by this legislation, while every other group was harmed. The League was a most effective organization and soon roused public opinion but Parliament, under the control of the landed interests, would not move. Sir Robert Peel, the prime minister, finally announced his conversion to repeal; he had become convinced that wages did not rise automatically with a rise in the cost of food, as the landlords claimed, but that the workers suffered privation and even starvation if grain prices were high. The bad harvests of 1844 and 1845 in England and the potato famine in Ireland in 1845–46 definitely turned the scale and repeal became inevitable. Famine proved a powerful ally and repeal was finally accomplished in 1846.

The repeal of the corn laws was a formal recognition of the fact that Great Britain had changed from an agricultural and commercial to an industrial and commercial state. Manufacturers and trade profited by the introduction of free trade, but agriculture was not ruined, as the opponents of repeal had prophesied. Instead, during the next quarter century agriculture enjoyed a period of great prosperity. Foreign grain supplemented but did not displace that grown at home. Only the agricultural laborer failed to reap the advantages that had been promised him. The price of wheat averaged 57 s. a quarter during the twenty years 1828–1847, and was 52 s. in the period 1848–1867; [9] the price of bread, still the staple in the laborer's diet, therefore declined but little. But wages fell and machinery displaced many workers. In one way, however, they, in common with all other consumers, gained. As supplies were drawn from a wider area the former price fluctuations disappeared and fear of scarcity vanished.

Agricultural progress. One of the bad effects of the corn laws had been to protect the less efficient farmers who had neither the energy nor the capital to adopt improved methods. These were

[9] J. S. Nicholson, *The History of the English Corn Laws* (London, 1904), 156.

followed by a small minority only, and only gradually spread.   Before 1837 "farming was still terribly backward.   Little or no machinery was used, implements were often bad, teams too large, drilling little practised, drainage utterly inefficient." [10] James Caird, who made a careful survey of British farming in 1850, concluded that the majority of landowners, under the influence of protection, had neglected their land, for they felt no stimulus to make improvements.   Pasture farming and market gardening not only failed to progress, but actually deteriorated.   A turn for the better now took place and improvements were introduced.   In 1837, said Prothero,[11] "the age of farming by extension of area had ended, that of farming by intension of capital had begun."

The most pressing need was drainage, for the prevailing method of ridging the land led to erosion.   The pioneer of the new drainage was a Scottish engineer, James Smith, who in 1823 drained his farm by trenches filled with stones, which were covered over.   This practice was widely adopted, but in the forties John Reade, a gardener, produced a clay tile and Thomas Scragg invented a machine for making them.   These were a great improvement and by their use much heavy clay and wet land was reclaimed.   Restoring and maintaining the fertility of the land was even more important, but this had to wait until the science of agricultural chemistry had been developed. Sir Humphry Davy had emphasized the effect of the character of the soil and manures upon vegetable life in 1812, but the correct principles were introduced into England by the German Justus von Liebig, who in 1840 made a report to the British Association for the Advancement of Science on organic chemistry and its application to agriculture and physiology.   This revealed the connection between plant growth and the composition of the soil.   In 1843 J. B. Lawes began his field experiments on his estate at Rothamsted, which became the most famous agricultural experiment station in Britain. The use of artificial fertilizers, as distinct from the barnyard manure, bones, and similar things up till now available to the farmer, began to spread and was generally followed by 1870.   Superphosphates, nitrate of soda, ammoniacal manures, Peruvian guano, mineral phosphates, and other products were applied to the land in increasing quantities.   Since these were costly and produced their best results on well-drained land, their use led to better farming generally. They also rendered the farmer comparatively independent of the alternate system of cropping.

At the same time the list of field crops was extended by the addition of Italian rye-grass, Belgian carrots, mangel-wurzel, winter

[10] W. H. R. Curtler, *A Short History of English Agriculture* (Oxford, 1909), 231.
[11] *English Farming, ut supra*, 361.

beans, and alsike clover; swedes, cabbages, and kohl-rabi, already known, were given renewed attention. Nearly half of the land was, however, in permanent pasture. The rearing and breeding of live stock were carried on more scientifically. Old breeds of cattle, such as shorthorns, Herefords, and Devons, were improved, and new breeds, such as Ayrshire, Sussex, and Channel Island, were introduced and perfected. In sheep growing the progress was even more marked and new breeds like Lincolns and Shropshires were developed. The improved stock was, moreover, disseminated more widely throughout the country, and an earlier maturity was obtained in the process of fattening. At the same time the practice of stall-feeding with oil cake increased and enriched the supply of barnyard manure. Only dairying lagged behind. The growing interest in scientific agriculture was greatly promoted by the establishment of the Royal Agricultural Society in 1838 and of the Royal Agricultural College and the Agricultural Chemistry Association in 1842. Farmers' clubs were established and cattle shows were held.

Agricultural implements were improved as a result of mechanical advance and new ones were invented. Specialized plows, adapted to particular uses and suited to different soils, such as the subsoil plow, became common; iron harrows, cultivators, seed drills that sowed in even lines and permitted intertillage, horse-hoes, and horse-rakes came into general use. Even more important than implements for preparing the ground, and sowing and cultivating the crops, was the introduction of reaping and mowing machines which facilitated harvesting without loss of time when the grain was ripe. A reaper had been invented in 1812, and improved in 1822, but was not commonly adopted until after 1850. Harvesting by hand was universal before 1837 and only gradually gave way to machinery. Grain was cut by scythes, threshed by flails, and winnowed by hand fans.

In general, it may be concluded that there was serious agricultural depression for twenty years after 1815, which was aggravated by a disordered currency, bank failures, bad seasons, labor difficulties, and agrarian discontent. This was a period of readjustment and elimination of inefficient practices and farmers, which brought distress, but also progress. After 1837 there was a slow revival of agriculture, which was especially marked after 1853.

About this time several external events came to the aid of the farmer. The gold discoveries in California and Australia, between 1848 and 1851, greatly increased the world supply of gold and started an upward movement of prices which continued for a quarter century. The Crimean War of 1854 shut off supplies of Russian grain and still further stimulated the price rise. The great commercial and industrial expansion of this period gave employment at good wages and provided large home markets for agricultural produce even at enhanced prices. And finally new methods had increased the productiveness of the land, while the costs of production and marketing had been reduced by improvements in agricultural machinery and in transportation facilities. Good harvests were characteristic of this period, and prices of grain and live stock remained fairly high until about 1870 while that of wool doubled. It was an era of prosperity for agriculture.[12]

2. PEASANT PROPRIETORSHIP IN FRANCE

Abolition of feudal claims. At the end of the eighteenth century France was more truly an agricultural country than either England or Germany. In 1790 the rural population was officially estimated to form 78 per cent of the total population.[13] It is not easy to trace the development of French agriculture during the period of the Revolution, for it was influenced so deeply by the political and social changes of that event that it can scarcely be considered apart from them. Before the Revolution the French agriculturalist was unfree in many respects and the methods of agriculture were bound by tradition. Agriculture could not develop until it was liberated. In describing this process of liberation it will be well to begin with the actual cultivator of the soil and to ascertain what his status was.

There was little actual serfdom in France in 1789. Estimates vary between 300,000 and 1,500,000 [14] persons out of a population of 26,000,000 who were legally in this class, most of these being in the eastern regions near the German border. The vast majority of the cultivators were free peasants. Few of these, however, owned outright the land they tilled but held it as tenants.[15] But these peasants, while legally free, were subject before 1789 to various feudal payments which effectively limited their independence.

Opinions differ as to the number of peasants who might fairly be called proprietors, though there was probably a considerable number. Legally they were few, but as the feudal claims upon them were in many cases virtually extinct they may be considered as actual owners of the land which they cultivated. Much more numerous was the class of customary hereditary tenants, the *censiers*, who held land by an ancient fixed quit-rent or *cens*. Possibly half the land in

---

[12] It has not been possible to submit statistical material in support of statements made in this chapter, for statistics of acreage, crops, and livestock were not collected before 1866, and were not complete enough to be reliable until 1870.

[13] G. Renard and G. Weulersse, *Life and Work in Modern Europe* (New York, 1926), 355.

[14] The latter figure is given by Lavisse, *Histoire de France*, 255.

[15] Kovalesky in his *France économique et sociale à la veille de la Révolution*, denies that any considerable number of peasants were real owners of the land; he asserts that they were practically all tenants or hereditary holders.

France was in the hands of this group. They could bequeath or sell their lands but were obliged to pay certain dues. In the case of the most favored *censiers*, the payment of the quit-rent and of the fine when the land changed hands at the death of the holder might constitute the whole burden. Since the quit-rent and fine had been fixed long ago when money had a much greater purchasing power, these payments were now trifling. Most *censiers*, however, must meet much heavier payments in the form of *banalités*, tithes, and taxes. Among the *banalités* was the obligation of the peasant to take his grain to the lord's mill to be ground, his bread to be baked in the lord's oven, or his grapes to the lord's wine-press to be made into wine, for all of which services a heavy toll was exacted. The tithe — about a seventh of the produce — must be paid to the church, while the state took from a third to a half in the heavy direct taxes and also required, at least down to 1787, compulsory labor on the roads — the *corvée* — equivalent at the maximum to about fifteen days in the year. A recent study estimates that out of each hundred francs of a peasant's income these exactions absorbed about 60 francs, leaving the peasant only 40. Out of this share the peasant was, moreover, to pay the salt tax and other indirect taxes. The French peasant, though not legally bound to the soil, was in actual fact as much fixed by taxation and feudal obligation to one spot as was the German serf east of the Elbe.

At the bottom of the scale stood the serfs, who could not sell their land and could pass it on only to their children if they lived and worked there. They owed manual services to the lord and were bound to the soil. There was also a small class of agricultural laborers, who worked for a wage, but this group existed mostly in those few provinces where an attempt was made to carry on large scale farming on the English model.

The creation of large farms seems to have occurred for the most part on church land which was rented to substantial farmers who could pay a money rent. In the formation of these farms commons were enclosed and the peasants were thus deprived of their winter pasture, a change which threatened their very existence. Knowles[16] believes that the agricultural discontent thus engendered was one of the potent causes of the Revolution, but Professor Clapham[17] contends that such large farms were limited to a small area and that not more than twenty per cent of the land in this area was farmed on the English model. All conditions were unfavorable to the large enterprise and to rational exploitation of the land; the economic life

[16] L. C. A. Knowles, "New Light on the Economic Causes of the French Revolution," *Econ. Journal*, April, 1919, 1-24.

[17] J. H. Clapham, *Economic Development of France and Germany* (Cambridge, 1923), 17.

of the country, its social and political conditions, and its fiscal regime placed unsurmountable obstacles in the way.

The French Revolution began with the proclamation of the National Assembly in June, 1789. The burning of the châteaux and other acts of violence by the peasants showed the necessity of revising the feudal economy before it was too late, and on the night of August 4 the clergy and the nobility, in what Mirabeau called "an orgy of sacrifice," surrendered their privileges and exemptions. A slight study of the proceedings leads one to suspect that the so-called "sacrifice" was rather an effort on the part of the privileged classes, by surrendering what they had already lost, to save what might perhaps be rescued. The peasants had already seized the pasture lands and forests and divided these among themselves. The lords hoped, by legitimatizing by legislation the forced destruction of certain feudal rights, to obtain a money indemnification of others. The Assembly, as a matter of fact, after declaring that all persons should be free and that certain "usurped" seigneurial dues should be abolished without compensation, appointed a committee to fix the terms of compensation of the remainder. This committee submitted its report on August 6 and it was enacted into law by the Assembly. The clergy protested against the abolition of tithes, but it was voted. Some of the nobles opposed the abolition of serfdom, which still existed in some places, of feudal personal services, and of feudal dues, but it was carried. Most of the nobles opposed bitterly the abolition of hunting rights and the keeping of dove-cotes and rabbit hutches, but this was urged by the clergy. Each group was willing to sacrifice what belonged to someone else.

The destruction of the old feudal rights was not accomplished in a single night, but gradually, step by step, and was not completed until 1793. In 1790 church tithes were abolished and in 1792 feudal dues were to be bought up by paying an indemnity to the lords affected, but in 1793 they were abolished without indemnity. It was also provided that all tithes and records must be burned. These acts marked the complete and final abolition of the feudal system, and by them the peasants became entirely free. Without the revolutionary movement of these years the complete disappearance of feudalism might have been as tedious and expensive for the French peasant as it was for the serfs of Germany and Russia, but the freeing of their property from feudal burdens gave them real freedom for the first time.

Ownership of the land. Probably no question has given rise to more acrimonious debate than the subject of the ownership of the land at the time of the Revolution. Two opposing views have been held. The first one claimed that before the Revolution most of the land was owned by the clergy and the nobility, and that the small peasant holdings of today were a result of the sale of the national domains at the time of the Revolution. They based their position upon an assertion of Target, deputy to the National Assembly, who in 1789 boldly declared that nineteen-twentieths of the population possessed no property.[18] This view was first challenged by de Tocqueville, who showed conclusively in his book, *L'ancien régime et la Revolution,* that peasant proprietorship existed on a large scale during the eighteenth century. The correctness of this latter view has been confirmed by the careful researches in local records by a Russian writer, J. Loutchisky.[19]

Arthur Young, a trained British observer, had been impressed during his travels in France in 1787–1789 with the many instances of peasant proprietorship, and concluded that about one-third of the land was tilled by peasant owners. Although there were wide variations between different regions and even between parishes, Loutchisky concludes that about half of the land held by some 4,600,000 proprietors was in the hands of peasants; in the north they held a little more than one-third, in the center almost one-half, in the *Midi* more than one-half, and in the east two-fifths. Even during the sixteenth and seventeenth centuries there had been considerable mobility in land transfer and the peasants had added to their possessions land sold by impoverished nobles; in the eighteenth century these sales had become more frequent, reaching a maximum in the decade preceding the Revolution. Changes in the ownership of land usually worked to the advantage of the peasants and to the detriment of the nobility. In the rural districts of France there were few persons who were entirely detached from the land or who did not possess land. France differed in this respect from other countries of Europe, where a concentration of ownership of land was taking place in the hands of the privileged classes. This was especially noteworthy in England, and also in Germany.

The peasant holdings were increased, though not to the extent claimed by early writers, by the sale of the crown lands and those confiscated from the church and the nobility. On November 2, 1789, the church lands were nationalized, and were sold at auctions in order to meet the pressing financial needs of the government. Citizens and peasants, and some nobles, eagerly bought these properties. The small purchasers were favored by a decree authorizing a down payment of only 12 per cent and the amortization of the bal-

[18] Paul Briteau, *L'état de la France en* 1789 (Paris, 1860), 47.

[19] *La petite propriété en France avant la Révolution et la vente des bien nationaux* (Paris, 1897).

L'état des classes agricoles en France à la veille de la Révolution (Paris, 1911).

La propriété paysanne en France à la veille de la Révolution (Paris, 1912).

ance in 12 annual instalments. Peasants united in associations of 40 to 50 persons or even more to purchase large properties which they afterwards divided among themselves. In 1793 this practice was forbidden. By these acts and sales the old church property disappeared completely and forever.

The lands of the *émigrés* were confiscated in 1792 and offered for sale at very low prices. This policy seems to have been dictated partly by fiscal considerations, to bring in needed revenues as rapidly as possible, partly by political, to win new supporters for the Revolution, and partly by economic, to increase the number of agriculturalists and thus avoid the danger of famine. These lands were not bought so largely by the peasants, who feared later claims from their former lords. Much of this property — perhaps one-half — was regained by the nobles, either by buying it at the auctions, by restoration later, and to a smaller extent by the "*émigré milliards*" of 1825.

A moot question is that of the distribution of these confiscated properties among the different groups of the third estate. It has often been asserted that the larger portion came into the possession of the merchants and bourgeois of the towns.[20] The records seem to show, however, that the peasants obtained a larger share of the land except in the vicinity of the cities and especially of the large cities. "In the districts where no important municipal center existed," concludes Loutchisky, "the peasants were able to obtain by the sale of these lands often half, often even three-fifths, and very often two-fifths." There is no doubt, on the other hand, that much of this property passed into the possession of land speculators, who paid for it in the depreciated *assignats* which the government accepted at par, and that there was thus created a new territorial aristocracy alongside the peasant democracy. The conclusion seems warranted, however, that the holdings of the peasants were increased by the land sales of the revolutionary period, and that the number of peasant proprietors was augmented.

Types of holdings. It was one thing to free the peasant and his property; it was quite another to provide for the redistribution of the land. The law of June 10, 1793, stated that all common lands of every description belonged to the communes in which they were situated. All claims of the nobles to those lands, unless based on forty years' occupancy, were declared to be void, and lands thus held must be given back. Many communes gained by this law hundreds of acres in arable land, forests, pastures, and meadows. The law further prescribed the condition of division among the peasants, pro-

---

[20] This view is held by P. Sagnac, "La propriété foncière et les paysans," in *L'oeuvre sociale de la Révolution française* (Paris, 1901), 254. I have followed Loutchisky and H. Sée, *Esquisse d'une histoire du régime agraire en Europe* (Paris, 1921), 205.

viding that all persons over 21 years of age had a share, and stating that the land should be divided if two-thirds of the votes favored it. The land thus acquired was actually divided in comparatively few cases, for the most part in the departments where vegetables and grain were grown for sale in near-by towns, especially in the north and northeast of France, and in the wine regions of the Rhine valley. In most of the departments and especially in those where animal husbandry was widespread, the acquired land was added to the existing communal holdings. Where division occurred it was usually confined to the arable land; only infrequently were the meadows and pasture land divided. In 1803 the further distribution of the commons was forbidden. Not until the second half of the nineteenth century, under changed economic conditions, were the commons finally divided through distribution, sale, and rental, and devoted to productive use.

By these various methods the larger peasants were enabled to increase or consolidate their holdings, while the smaller ones, who had previously held mere scraps of land, managed to add a little to their possessions. Few of these peasants, however, had enough to constitute a productive agricultural unit and they were compelled to rent other land. Before the Revolution independent farmers had rented land from their seigniors, for which they paid a money or grain rent. This type of holding was found principally in the grain producing regions of the northwest. The most prevalent type of tenancy was *métayage,* or share tenancy, which was especially characteristic of the central highlands. The landlord under this system contributed half the cattle and seed, and usually half the taxes, and sometimes a share in the cost of implements; the produce was shared equally between landlord and cultivator, though sometimes the landlord's share was larger if he furnished a larger proportion of the working capital. Arthur Young conjectured that seven-eighths of the land of France was held by this form of tenure,[21] but Professor Clapham estimated that "three-eighths or a half would probably be nearer the mark." [22]

The Revolution made no change in these types of holdings. Some of the independent peasants enlarged their holdings, but for those with insufficient land of their own the system of *métayage* remained the favorite method of tenancy. The redistribution of lands at the time of the Revolution had also created a new class of owners, some of whom undertook the work of commercial farming on more rational lines, but most of whom probably preferred to rent their lands. With the inadequate statistics available it is impossible to say how much of

[21] This estimate is repeated by Loutchisky, *L'état des classes agricoles,* 75.
[22] Clapham, op. cit., 15.

the land was cultivated by owners and how much by tenants, either before or after the Revolution. The conclusion may be hazarded, however, that most of the land continued to be farmed by tenants, and that within his group the proportion of the cash tenants grew at the expense of the share tenants.

Methods of agriculture. The open-field system prevailed over the northern and northeastern part of France at the time of the Revolution, and was to be found to a lesser degree in other regions. Under this system the arable land was divided into three great fields, in each of which the villager held scattered strips. He also had rights of pasture on the common and on the stubble after the grain was cut, as well as the right to wood in the forests for fuel or building purposes. The customary rotation in the cultivation of these open fields was winter wheat, summer barley or oats, and fallow. No essential change seems to have been made by the Revolution in this system of land holding or use by the peasants, not even by the distribution of the commons, though the larger owners were able through the land sales both to enlarge and to consolidate their holdings.

The Revolution not only gave liberty and land to the peasants, but it also removed the old restraints on cultivation. By the act of June 5, 1791, compulsory methods of land use were abolished and the cultivator was free to plant what he wished, in the order that he pleased, and could harvest his grain at the time and with implements of his own choosing. Few changes were, however, made in the conduct of agriculture during the Revolution. Improvements, such as the draining of marsh land, were authorized, but were not carried out. The internal disturbances, the war, the changing prices as a result of the paper money regime, and the compulsory delivery of foodstuffs all introduced disorder in agriculture. Many of the young men were drafted into the army and there was a lack of labor, as there was also of horses, of implements, and of manure.

Napoleon proclaimed that agriculture was the soul (*l'âme*) of the national economy, but he was too much influenced by political considerations to serve its best interests. His main purpose was to keep grain prices low in order to placate the city proletariat, and in doing this he sacrificed the interests of the grain growers. But along other lines his needs promoted agriculture. Wool was necessary for soldiers' uniforms, and Napoleon had merino sheep imported from Spain in 1795. The tobacco monopoly stimulated tobacco growing at favorable prices. Madder, woad, and chicory were encouraged by premiums and loans, and by the prohibition of imports. But above all it was necessary to replace colonial sugar, the importation of which was cut off by the British fleet. This problem was solved by chemists Barruel and Ismard, and in 1811 Napoleon ordered that 79,000 acres should be planted in sugar beets. By the following year 40 factories were grinding 10,000 tons of beets, but the high hopes entertained for this enterprise were not fulfilled, and none of these factories survived the Napoleonic regime. The real development of this industry came later.

Agriculture prospered less through artificial intervention of the state than from other causes. The improvement of roads and the building of canals, carried out though they were by Napoleon for military purposes, widened the domestic market. The continental system excluded foreign competition, and order ruled within France. Grain prices were fairly steady, wine culture increased, and animal husbandry showed an improvement. But there was no thorough-going change in agricultural methods up to 1815 and agriculture was still very backward.[23]

The agricultural reports of 1814 [24] give a vivid view of conditions, and picture an agriculture little changed since pre Revolutionary days. They describe the primitive implements and methods of cultivation, and the continuation of the wasteful fallow, though they note some advance through the abolition of grazing rights. But a distinction must be made between the backward districts, like Brittany, and rich regions, like Normandy. In the former the farms were poorly equipped with implement, stables badly kept, breeding neglected, manure insufficient, continued use of fallow, natural meadows scarcely known. On the other hand districts like upper Normandy give clear evidence of progress; commercial crops like rape-seed and sugar beets were introduced, hay was grown, and other improvements made. Yet even here the complaint was heard: "Rural economy has made no progress, the method of cultivation is always the same." Apparently the French peasant was not easily moved to change his ways.

The period 1815–50 witnessed the greatest development of French agriculture, which was especially marked after 1817. It began inauspiciously with harvest failures in 1816 and 1817, which not only increased the price of bread, but caused a shortage in feed for stock. The high prices led the farmers to increase their acreage and plant more, and when the following years brought bumper crops, prices fell precipitately. The agricultural crisis of these years affected France less than most of her neighbors, since the peasants could

---

[23] There seems to be little basis for Chaptal's enthusiastic description in 1815 (J. A. C. Chaptal, *De l'industrie française*, Paris, 1819, I, 152):

"If one compares agriculture with what it was in 1789, one is astonished at the improvements that have been made—Harvests of all kinds cover the soil, numerous strong animals labor and manure the land, food is wholesome and abundant, houses are clean and comfortable, there is simple but decent clothing; such is the share of the inhabitants of the fields. Misery has been banished and ease has been born of the power of the free disposal of all products."

[24] *Statistique agricole de* 1814. Edited by Comité des Travaux Historiques (Paris, 1914).

adjust their economy, largely self-sufficing, to changing conditions. And most of the land was in the hands of the peasants. There did not exist in France in 1815 a landed aristocracy, who managed their own estates, as did the Junkers in Germany. Nor did the large owners rent their land to great farmers, as in England, but to peasants in small units. France was a nation of small farms. A slight change in this respect was noted after the July Revolution of 1830, when the large owners frequently withdrew to their estates and devoted themselves to agriculture.

But peasant farming had its disadvantages. The peasants clung to their old methods and introduced improvements very slowly. And even if they wished to practice more rational agriculture they lacked the necessary capital. The old three-field system was still usual, though there was a tendency to shorten the fallow period. Wheat was supplanting rye, even in Brittany. The potato was winning recognition as an article of food, though in most districts it was used only for cattle or the very poor. But by 1862 it ranked in importance next to wheat and oats, and three-quarters of the crop went into human consumption. Increasing attention was paid to commercial crops like rape (for oil) in the south and sugar beets in the north. The production of raw silk was greatly increased. A steady though slow development is indicated by these changes.

The weakest point in French agriculture was the large amount of fallow and of waste land, which still persisted. In 1841 13 per cent was still in fallow, nearly 17 per cent was waste land; only about 37 per cent was under cultivation. This resulted from the continuance of the three-field system, which necessitated the fallow, and the maintenance of old grazing rights, which required the use of waste land as pasture. But such a system made very difficult the growing of fodder, which the natural meadows could not supply in sufficient quantity. Hay was scarce and high-priced, though the growing of such crops as clover, sainfoin, lucerne, and similar green crops gave some relief and also introduced needed deep root crops in the old three-field course. Backward as French agriculture was, it yet showed improvement over conditions at the time of the Revolution.

Implements. The character of the tools used indicates that agriculture had become only slightly mechanized at the end of this period. Clear evidence of the backward state of French agriculture at the beginning is furnished by the primitive character of the farm implements. Little change had been made in this respect since the Middle Ages. The peasant clung to his hoe, his long shafted spade, and that short scythe, the *pique*, which Arthur Young had allowed to be one of the most useful implements that can be seen.[25] The

25 Clapham, op. cit., 26.

plow was made of wood with a metal coulter; sometimes it was placed between two cumbrous wooden wheels. Such a plow would be pulled by from 2 to 6 oxen, or by 2 oxen and 2 or 3 horses. It seldom penetrated the ground deeper than 5 or 6 inches. As time went on the plows were improved, metal replacing the wood parts and wheeled plows the wheelless types. The harrows were inadequate and the sickle was in more frequent use than the scythe. The grain was threshed with a flail or trodden out by oxen on open air threshing floors but after about 1830 simple threshing machines began to be introduced. As late as 1862, however, there were only 2849 steam threshing machines in all France, and 98,000 managed by hand. All told there were some 27,000 steam hay-making, mowing, reaping, and threshing machines. Of the 3,200,000 plows only 795,000 were improved; the others were ordinary "country" implements. French farmers relied almost exclusively upon their spades, plows, and harrows (of which there were 1,000,000 in use) for cultivation of their land. Writing in 1850, an American observer stated that "many of the French farmers sow their wheat in drills, and by a machine, but not of a very improved character." [26] Of all other specialized agricultural implements there were only 262,000, or 1 to every twelve farms. If all agricultural implements had been distributed equally in 1862 the average farm would have had two-thirds of a plow, a quarter of a harrow, and a total of one and one-third implements. [27]

Under such circumstances it is evident that the average holding could be only a small one; more than half of the holdings in 1862 were less than $12\frac{1}{2}$ acres and three-quarters of them contained 25 acres or less. The cultivation of such a small farm resembled horticulture more than agriculture and involved much hand labor. The returns from the land were obtained at the cost of an incredible outlay of human labor. A Frenchman, Dupin, writing in 1827 and using, it is true, rather shaky estimates, figured an average of 13.5 human labor units per 100 acres in France, an average of 2.5 in England. An Englishman (Lord Lovelace, writing in 1848 but using earlier figures) estimated 9.5 labor units per 100 acres in France, 3 in England. "No one believes these figures to be exact; no one can contest the general truth of the contrast which they indicate." [28] But the contrast between the earlier and later date in France shows improvement in that country, although it lagged far behind England.

Only a peasantry accustomed to hard work and thrifty to the point of "pinching meanness" could have achieved the results which

[26] H. Colman, *Agriculture and Rural Economy* (New York, 1857), 453.
[27] Based on tables in *Statistique de la France. Agriculture* (Résultats généraux de l'enquête décennale de 1862. Strasbourg, 1868), CXXVI.
[28] C. Day, *Economic Development in Modern Europe* (New York, 1933), 162.

French agriculture showed. French economic organization and the laws of inheritance favored widespread holdings of small properties and a comparatively even distribution of wealth. The French peasant had little capital with which to operate, and what he saved he was inclined to apply to the purchase of additional land rather than to improve his equipment. He was conservative to the point of obstinacy, individualistic, cautious in spending, and little given to display or luxury. Under these circumstances peasant agriculture was strongly traditional, characterized by a predominance of manual labor, and little given to change. About 1860 it began to be affected by economic changes going on in other parts of the economic organization, and after 1870, as capital became more plentiful, it became more mechanized and industrialized.

After about 1850 agriculture shared fully in the economic progress of the period. The building of roads and canals and later of railways opened new markets, permitted specialization, lessened transportation costs on agricultural products and on manure, and gave a stimulus to improved and increased production. The industrial expansion and the growth of cities absorbed the larger supplies and prices were good. Profitable markets abroad for French products, especially wine, were opened up by the liberal commercial treaties between 1860 and 1870; losses in the vineyards through insects in the early fifties were offset by higher prices. At the same time improvements were being made in agricultural practice and production was increasing. The yield of wheat was raised from an average of 11 bushels per acre in 1815–20 to 16.4 in 1862–71, and that of rye, barley, potatoes, and oats, in equal or even larger proportions. Leguminous crops or esculent vegetables for human consumption were but little cultivated.[29]

Animal husbandry was also given more attention, and with the conversion of the wasteful common pasture into arable it was possible to support larger numbers. A few selected years may be given.[30]

LIVESTOCK IN FRANCE
(in millions)

Year	Horses	Cattle	Sheep	Swine
1812	1.9	6.7	27.0	4.5
1820	2.4	9.1	28.9	4.9
1840	3.6	9.9	24.8	4.9
1862	3.5	11.0	24.5	6.0

The greatest increase was to be found in horses, which were used not only on the farm but also in the enlarged internal commerce.

[29] Colman, op. cit., 373.
[30] E. Levasseur, La France, II, 44; Stat. de la France. Agric., 1862, LXI.

Sheep, on the other hand, showed a considerable decline. This was partly offset by a gain in weight, but animal husbandry made slow progress and was far below the capacity of the land. Some improvement was made in breeding, primarily by importing blooded stock from other countries. Lafayette called renewed attention to merino sheep and in 1825 the first pure-bred Durham shorthorn cattle were imported from England; they stood at the head of all blooded stock at the Paris Exposition in 1855.

3. THE AGRARIAN MOVEMENT IN GERMANY

The agrarian movement in Germany, like the prior developments in England and France, must be regarded as one of liberation from legal and economic institutions that had survived since feudal times and had long outlived their usefulness. In tracing the developments which occurred in Germany, we may note (1) the emancipation of the peasantry from serfdom or its equivalent, (2) the freeing of the land and the growing ease of transfer, and (3) the progress in agricultural technique.

Condition of the peasantry before 1807. It is difficult to make any generalization about the peasants in Germany, for their position varied greatly from state to state and even within a single state. Still, a broad distinction may be made between the areas east and west of the Elbe, although the line of demarcation is not a sharp one.

The inhabitants of the western section were almost of pure Teutonic blood and wholly Teutonic in civilization. East of the Elbe the rural population was predominantly Slavonic in blood and largely so in speech and custom. But more important than the racial differences were the differences in social and economic organization. The Germans who settled in the eastern region conquered the Slavs and gradually extended their dominion over them until they reduced them to practical slavery (*Leibeigenschaft*). The position of the peasants in these two districts was quite different, that of the western peasant being much better, though the economic position of the German peasantry as a whole was probably lower than that of the French on the eve of the French Revolution.

The position of the peasant in *western Germany* was tolerable, though there were numerous gradations. At the head stood peasants who held their land quite securely in return for a definite quit-rent, which was paid in money or kind. In addition they would probably owe certain duties to the lord and would pay a fine when the land changed hands. At the bottom of the scale stood a class of peasants whose tenure was not fixed, who owed the lord labor dues (ploughing, harvesting, etc.), and who were subject also to various *banalités* (the obligation to have their grain ground at the lord's mill, to bake their bread in the lord's oven, and to put their grapes through the lord's wine-press, for all of which they paid). Between these two extremes were to be found all the peasants of western Germany.

Irksome though some of these services might be, and heavy the taxes, the position of the peasant was on the whole a secure one. He was in effect a renter, usually holding his land hereditarily, paying his rent in services and in kind, or in cash, or both. It is true that "the peasant can not leave his holding; his marriage rights and those of his children are in degree subject to the lord's will; there is forced domestic service; and he gives unpaid labor on the lord's land for a number of days not to exceed three per week." [31] While these disabilities indicate that he was not free in the modern sense, it must be noted that these obligations were fixed by law or by the peasant's tenure. In addition to the peasant farmers there was a class of small landholders, who could not live by their holdings but were compelled to work as agricultural laborers on the larger estates of the landlords or the "big peasants."

The landowners in western Germany did not possess such large estates as those in the east, nor did they dominate agriculture or politics to such an extent. Their attitude towards the peasantry was not unfriendly and in some states a policy of peasant protection (*Bauernschutz*) was prevalent.

In describing the position of the peasant in *eastern Germany* it will help to an understanding if that of the lord is first stated. The key to an understanding of this is the remembrance that the manors in the east had been acquired by conquest and that the lords —holders of a knight's fee, commonly called Junkers—were the descendants of conquerors. There was therefore a wide gulf between the lord and the peasant, which was constantly widened by the prevalent policy of expropriation or "putting down the peasants" (*Bauernlegen*). By eviction, by addition of arable land from moor, marsh, and forest, and in other ways the lords had come into possession of vast estates, often of 1000 acres or more. But the Junkers differed from the French seigneurs of the old regime and from the English landlord of the eighteenth century, who also owned large holdings, in one important respect. The French lord had seldom farmed his estate and the Englishman usually rented out his land. The East Prussian Junkers, however, became capitalist cultivators, at least after 1800, and farmed their land with the help of peasant labor. Their power over the peasant was, moreover, strengthened by the military and administrative functions which they exercised.

Free peasants were to be found in a few places, but the great mass

[31] G. S. Ford, "The Prussian Peasantry before 1807," in *Amer. Hist. Rev.*, April, 1919, 363.

of the peasants in eastern Germany were servile. It is estimated that upwards of two-thirds of the population was to some extent unfree. Of these unfree peasants there were three groups, which corresponded roughly to the cotters and villeins of the old English manor. Lowest in the scale were the cotters (*Häusler*) and gardeners (*Gärtner*), who owned little patches of ground, insufficient for their support, and had some rights of pasture on the stubble and the common. These two groups constituted the day laborers who worked on the estates of the lords or "big" peasants for wages.[32] The true peasant, the man who held land in the fields, was distinguished by the power to harness his own beasts to the plough. He was called *spannfähig*, or capable of harnessing his yoke of oxen.

Since they were servile all of the groups owed services to the lords, which are reminiscent of medieval agrarian conditions. But the burdens had grown heavier, not lighter, with the passage of time, as the lords had increased the holdings which they were having farmed on their own account.

Emancipation of the serfs. The emancipation of the German peasantry did not take place, as it had in England, as a result of a long historical evolution, nor, as in France, as a result of a political revolution which suddenly removed all remaining feudal burdens from the peasants. In Germany the movement was initiated and carried through by the government, often meeting with resistance not only from the lords but even from the peasants themselves. The process of liberation was, moreover, a protracted one, dragging on in some features for almost half a century.

Early steps towards emancipation were taken in Bavaria as early as 1779 by the King, but the most conspicuous movement was that in Prussia two decades later.[33] The first measures adopted were in the interest of the peasantry on the *Crown* domains. In 1799 the obligations to provide horses and carts (*Spanndienste*) and manual services (*Handdienste*) were abolished to a large extent, and it was enacted that peasants should be allowed to become owners if they would renounce their rights of use in the state forests and claims to certain grants of relief. In this way 30,000 peasants in East and West Prussia and Lithuania became proprietors of their holdings.

The next step was to provide for the villein peasantry on *private* lands. The King had shrunk from emancipating them, out of respect for the rights of the nobles. After the defeat of Prussia by Napoleon at Jena (October 24, 1806) and the humiliating treaty of Tilsit (June 25, 1807), in which the Czar consented to the dismem-

---

[32] G. F. Knapp, *Die Bauernbefreiung und der Ursprung der Landarbeiter in den älteren Theilen Preussens* (2 vols. Leipzig, 1887), I, 12.

[33] For a good account see *Handwörterbuch der Staatswissenschaften*, s.v. "Bauernbefreiung."

berment of Prussia, it was evident that a thorough overhauling of the political and economic organization of German society was in order. If the German nation was to be united it must be by abolishing feudal privilege and creating a free people. Among the numerous reforms which were undertaken was the famous emancipation edict of October 9, 1807, under the leadership of Freiherr vom Stein. The purpose of the edict was declared in the preamble to be the removal of "all the hindrances which hitherto prevented the individual from attaining the prosperity which, according to the measure of his powers, he was capable of reaching." The principal reforms introduced may be summarized as follows:[34] Villeinage was abolished after 1810, and also caste in land, and in occupations.

Caste in land is so foreign to our modern conceptions that it requires a fuller explanation. According to the code of Frederick, which came into force in 1794, noble estates could be held only by nobles, and citizens (*Bürger*) could acquire them only by permission of the sovereign. So, too, peasant land could be held only by peasants and town lands only by citizens. Here the idea of caste was extended from human beings to the land which they owned, which was thus given a rank as noble or citizen or peasant land. This curious and obstructive institution was cancelled by Stein's edict.

The edict also abolished caste in occupation. The code of Frederick prohibited the nobleman from engaging in any occupation properly belonging to the citizen; only under certain conditions could citizens perform work belonging to peasants, or peasants engage in citizen pursuits. To each of these three groups was assigned its special activity. The noble supervised cultivation of his estate and exercised civil and military duties; the citizen carried on trade and industry in the town; and the peasant tilled the soil and performed military service.

Such an organization of society is wholly foreign to modern ideas, and is reminiscent of Plato's Republic. A system which assigned every man's occupation to him from his birth prevented initiative and produced stagnation. There was no opportunity for a man to become an agriculturist if he disliked trade, or to enter industry if he failed in agriculture; natural aptitudes were stifled and both human and material resources remained undeveloped. The edict accordingly abolished caste in occupation and permitted free choice.

The emancipation of the serfs soon followed in other German states: in Bavaria in 1808, in Nassau 1812, in Wurtemberg 1817, in Hesse-Darmstadt and Baden 1820, and Kurhessen 1821. By the

---

[34] The edict is conveniently found in B. Rand (Ed.), *Selections Illustrating Economic History since the Seven Years' War* (4th ed., New York, 1903), 97.

latter date the non-existence of serfdom had been officially recognized in all the remaining German states.

Freeing of the land and the ease of transfer. The second great step in the liberation of German agriculture had to do not with the person of the cultivator but with the land itself. A move had been made in this direction by Stein's emancipation edict, which, as has been pointed out, removed some of the disabilities on landholding and opened the way for a freer exchange. All land could now be held indiscriminately by any person; but it was still held under old forms of feudal tenure. It was necessary to substitute allodial ownership — ownership in fee simple — for feudal tenure. The peasant must be helped to become a landowner.

This positive step was taken by Stein's successor, Hardenberg, by two decrees of September 14, 1811. The first of these, entitled "an Edict for the Regulation of the Relations between Lords of the Manor and their Peasants," dealt with peasant holdings. Peasant tenants fell into two classes: (1) those who cultivated hereditary holdings, and (2) those who held at will or for a term of years and whose holdings were therefore terminable.

The relations between the lords and the tenants consisted of a number of rights and obligations on each side which may be stated in tabular form as follows: [35]

Rights of landlord	*Rights of tenant*
(1) Ownership of land	(1) Claim to assistance in misfortune
(2) Claim to service	(2) Right to gather wood, etc., in forests of manor
(3) Dues in money and kind	(3) Claim for repair of buildings
(4) Equipment	(4) Assistance if unable to pay taxes
(5) Easements or servitudes	(5) Pasturage rights on common lands and in forests

After balancing these claims and obligations against one another, it was declared that (1) the hereditary tenant should obtain two-thirds of his holding in absolute ownership upon surrender of one-third to the lord, and that all claims of either of the two parties upon the other should be cancelled. In the case of small holdings (under 35 acres) the peasant might continue to cultivate all the land and pay the lord a grain rent upon the one-third, title to which was surrendered to the lord.

(2) The tenants who held at will or for a term of years received one-half of the land in absolute ownership but were required to surrender the other half.

[35] These are listed, though not in tabular form, in *Handwörterbuch der Staatswissenschaften,* s.v. "Bauernbefreiung" (Preussen).

The second edict of September 14, 1811, was entitled "An Edict for the Better Cultivation of the Land," and dealt with agrarian reform. The purpose of this was to permit entire freedom in buying and selling and bequeathing land—in a word, unlimited right of disposal. Freedom of trade in land seems natural enough today, but it was an innovation in Germany at that time. The object was to get the land into the hands of those best able to use it, now that the restrictions on ownership had been broken down by Stein's edict. Such was the theory, but it worked out badly for the mass of the peasants.

The decree of 1811 on the redemption of manorial rights in East Prussia was interpreted and modified by the royal declaration of May 29, 1816, in a manner unfavorable to the peasants. These were divided into two groups: those who had the right of redemption and those who did not. In the first group were included the true peasants, who were *Spannfähig*, or capable of harnessing their yoke of oxen, and who had a share in the village fields. These constituted, however, only the upper stratum of the peasantry, and thus, by a single stroke, the number of those who could redeem their land and become owners was greatly reduced. Moreover, among the *spannfähigen* peasant holdings only those were redeemable which had already existed in 1763.[36]

All peasants below this group—and they were the great majority—were excluded from the right to take advantage of the edict of 1811. These "regulated" peasants, as the tenants of non-hereditable holdings came to be called, had received their personal liberty and were no longer serfs, but the government was unwilling to make them peasant proprietors. They remained under the control of the noble landlords, who needed them to cultivate their domains. These "small folk," whom Hardenberg's edict so ostentatiously took under its protection, were therefore placed at a great disadvantage; where their services were hereditary they continued to be burdened with feudal services and dues, and where these were not hereditary they were evicted wholesale.[37] Even if these small holders were not pushed out, the lords made their rights of possession worse by changing them into time renters, with whom rent contracts were made for fixed periods.

The *cotters*, and the *gardeners*, with their little scraps of land, together with some of the bought-out peasants, became agricultural laborers, in much the same situation as contemporary laborers in England. Although their legal freedom conferred a limited right

[36] J. Kulischer, *Allgemeine Wirtschaftsgeschichte des Mittelalters und der Neuzeit* (2 vols. Munich, 1929), II, 437.

[37] R. B. B. Morier (Ed.), *Systems of Land Tenure in Various Countries* (London, 1870), 385.

of migration this was of slight value, owing to the particularism of the small German states, which did not welcome strangers, and the inertia of the peasants. They therefore remained in the villages and worked on the lord's domain. Here they subsisted in a wretched way, partly on the products of their little holdings, partly on money earned as day laborers, but their position was miserable.

Reforms of 1850. The revolutionary movement of 1848 introduced a new and more sympathetic spirit into the handling of the peasant problem. Two important laws were passed in Prussia, on March 2, 1850, which indicated the new spirit. The purpose of this legislation was to rectify the injustice done to the small cultivators whom the royal declaration of 1816 had excluded from the benefits of the Hardenberg edict.

The first of these laws finally determined the relations between the lords and peasants by abolishing twenty-four different kinds of feudal rights, mostly survivals of early vassalage, without indemnity. All those peasants who had hereditable rights of use in the land were made absolute owners of such land. The commutation of such services as still remained, manual and with plough oxen, was made easier and less expensive. The legislation came too late, however, to effect any but a small remnant. All those peasants who had become meanwhile renters for fixed periods and had surrendered their lands, and those who had sold out, or who had been evicted and had become agricultural laborers—all these were excluded from the operation of the law of 1850. This applied only to those who had remained under the old agrarian constitution as it existed before 1807 and who had hereditable rights in the land; but these were only a negligible part of the peasantry.

Much more important was the law providing for the establishment of rent banks. The peasants had already been given the right to redeem the rent-charges on their holdings by a single capital payment representing eighteen times the annual sum due. As few were wealthy enough to avail themselves of this privilege a new method was devised by which they might purchase their lands on more convenient terms. Rent banks were set up in each province and into these the peasants paid their annual rents; the rent banks then gave to the lord of the manor a bond for the value of the capital charges. As the credit of the rent bank was better than that of the individual peasant it was able to borrow the necessary funds at a low rate of interest, so that the payments by the peasants were sufficient not only to pay the interest charges but also to amortize the capital. In this manner they were able to pay off their indebtedness in $41\frac{1}{2}$ years; or, if they paid in only nine-tenths of their previous rent each year, they could pay out in $56\frac{1}{12}$ years. This legislation put the capstone on the agrarian reforms, though the final transformation of these tenants into peasant proprietors was not completed until a number of years later.

Rent banks were established in other German states, such as Bavaria (1848), Saxony (1852), Wurtemberg, Baden, etc. In some of these the state government assumed the function of organizing and managing the rent banks, though the method was the same as where voluntary co-operative institutions existed.

The number of persons who were released from services and other dues in Prussia down to 1865 was 1,386,280; this was about 75 per cent of all who might have been affected. The number of plough days abolished was 6,344,569, and of manual service days 23,540,331.[38]

In this Prussian legislation three steps may be observed. The first task was to establish the personal freedom of the peasants, second to abolish the obligations of service, and third to alter the uncertain conditions of possession into absolute ownership. The smooth development of these reforms was, however, made impossible by the strong opposition of the lords, who did not wish to have the old agrarian organization disturbed, nor to lose the services of the peasants which were necessary to conduct their large holdings. The great defect in the Prussian agrarian legislation was the failure to assure the peasant an assignment of land.[39] It was too easy for the lords to take advantage of the ignorance or necessity of the peasants and to possess themselves of their holdings. The division of the land by the edict of 1811 was too favorable to the lords, and under this and subsequent legislation the great estates grew steadily at the expense of the small peasant holdings. But more responsible for this movement than the favorable legislation was the greater productivity of the larger farms under the new systems of agriculture that were being developed.

Progress in agricultural technique. The third step in the transformation of German agriculture lay in the freeing of agricultural technique from the antiquated methods which prevailed at the beginning of the nineteenth century. In 1800 the peasants lived in the villages and not, as in the United States, on single farms. The territory about the village consisted of cultivated land, which was divided among the owners in well-recognized holdings, and of undivided land like pastures, meadows and forests. The situation may be pictured by thinking of the village as a nucleus; here were situated the manor house and peasant cottages, near each of which was a house garden which was cultivated by the spade. Outside of this

[38] T. v. d. Goltz, *Geschichte der deutschen Landwirtschaft.* 2 Bde. (Stuttgart, 1902–03), II, 155.

[39] *Handbuch der Landwirtschaft.* Ed. by F. Aeroboe, J. Hansen, and T. Roemer (5 vols. Berlin, 1930), I, 69.

was a narrow ring of land, divided into field gardens (*Würthen*), used for vegetable raising and also grain, of which one belonged to each peasant; this he cultivated as he pleased. About this circle there lay another ring, the so-called *Binnenland*, which was divided into three fields, which were cultivated in common according to the three-field system. Here the holdings of the peasant, and even of the lord himself, were scattered into dispersed strips among the three fields. The cultivation of these fields was regulated in common, and was said to be subject to *Flurzwang* or compulsory cultivation; the proceeds of each particular holding belonged, however, to the owner. Around this ring of cultivated fields lay finally the *Aussenland*, consisting of pasture, forest, and waste land. Here, too, the rights of usage were regulated according to ancient custom, in that each peasant was permitted to drive his cattle to the pasture, to get wood for building or fuel, etc. The territory upon which the lord and his peasants lived was thus a complicated affair: some of the land divided and some undivided; the divided land in individual use or in common use; a part of the acres belonging to the peasants and another part to the lord.[40]

Under the primitive conditions of agriculture based on grain and grass the inconveniences of the open field system with its compulsory common cultivation had probably not been felt as a limitation. The system had been adopted to avoid interference with cultivation through the passage of cattle or to protect rights of pasture. But after the introduction of clover and potatoes in the last third of the eighteenth century, and of the more rational systems which Thaer and his followers developed, there was need for a freer economy. German agriculture remained behind that in England and even in France until well into the nineteenth century. The first half of the nineteenth century, therefore, witnessed a movement for the abolition of common cultivation, the bringing together of scattered strips, the enclosure of common lands, and above all an improved agricultural technique. Each of these changes may be briefly described.

Before improved methods of cultivation could be introduced it was necessary to get rid of the compulsory uniformity imposed by intermingled holdings in the three-field system, and permit each individual to farm his own holding as he saw fit. A step in this direction was taken by the Prussian law of 1820, which provided a method by which individual holdings could be assembled in one compact area. The bringing together of scattered pieces of land was called "separation" in Prussia, but in other states was known as "uniting," "coupling," "consolidation," etc. This could be done if one-fourth of the sharers favored it. But progress along this line

[40] The arrangements are well described by Knapp, *Bauernbefreiung*, 4-11.

was painfully slow among the peasants.   By 1866 only 38,000,000 acres (out of 69,000,000 in Prussia), belonging to 1,600,000 peasants, had undergone the process of repartition and consolidation.

In 1821 a further ordinance was passed providing for the division of the common land.   The purpose of this was to abolish the existing rights of usage, which belonged to each holder of lands in the fields, on the pasture, meadow, and stubble, and also to get rid of existing rights of usage in forest and moor.   The result was similar to that which followed like legislation in England, and many a peasant found himself unable, after the division, to keep his cow, or even his pigs and geese, on his small individual holding.   There was therefore a tendency for these peasants to sell their holdings to the lords and become agricultural laborers or to move to the growing towns.   The following table shows the changes in peasant holdings in Prussia between 1810 and 1859:

PEASANT HOLDINGS *

Year	No. of peasant holdings	Amount of land (acres)
1810	351,607	21,688,210
1816	354,610	22,213,846
1859	344,737	21,104,013

* A. Meitzen, *Der Boden und die landwirtschaftlichen Verhältnisse des Preussischen Staates* (Berlin, 1868), I, 501.

The changes in other German states were on the whole more favorable to the peasants.   In the south and southwest the peasants were free and fairly prosperous, and had no desire to see their fields rearranged or to have the commons enclosed.   Little was therefore done along these lines in the first half of the nineteenth century. In the northwest, especially in Hanover, the commons were generally divided and enclosed, and an opportunity was given for more rational methods of agriculture.   Even here, however, most of the legislation came after the middle of the century.   While these changes did not of themselves improve existing systems of land utilization, they made possible the improvements in agricultural technique which followed.

Until the beginning of the nineteenth century the three-field system prevailed in Germany, in which grain was the only crop raised, though in some places grass was cultivated.   Winter grain, summer grain, and fallow followed in regular successions, though sometimes when the fields were far removed from the village or were infertile only rye would be grown in alternation with fallow.   The three-field system was a true picture of misery in many parts of Germany.   A fair return was 8 or 9 bushels of wheat per acre and somewhat more of rye and barley. As late as 1816 the average return of rye in the Mark Brandenburg was only 5.2 times the amount of seed sown. This was now changed.

Improved methods. A leader in the movement was Albrecht D. Thaer (1752–1828),[41] whose classical work, *Grundsätze der rationellen Landwirtschaft* (4 vols. Berlin, 1809–12), introduced and laid the foundation for rational agriculture. Under the influence of English experience he emphasized the importance of rotation of crops, the planting of potatoes, the raising of sheep and cattle, and the value of stall-feeding. If these ideas were to be carried out, the old three-field system must be destroyed and fodder grown in addition to grain. For this the fallow, making up one-third of the arable land, offered the best opportunity. In most of the villages, accordingly, the former fallow was planted wholly or partly with leguminous and leaf plants, among which the most important were red clover, potatoes, and beets. The other two-thirds of the land was not affected by this change, and upon it summer grain and winter grain were planted in the old style. Extensive cultivation still prevailed, and any increase in production was obtained rather by an extension of arable land than by improved methods. This new system of cultivation was called by Thaer the "combined" three-field system; later it was given the name of "improved" three-field system, and the old system was called the "pure" three field system.

This "improved" system was a great advance over the "pure." The fallow was partly or wholly abolished and much land, hitherto unused, came to be devoted to the production of plants. Clover, turnips, and potatoes served for winter and summer feeding of animals. As animal husbandry increased the cattle were better fed, manure was more abundant, and the fields were better fertilized; in consequence the crop yield was increased. At the same time the introduction of green and deep root crops helped to restore the fertility of the soil by introducing the needed nitrogen, which further increased the yield. The improved system of crop rotation thus produced larger crops and at the same time provided animal food without any increase in the amount of land under cultivation. An additional advantage of this change was the more equal distribution of labor throughout the year. Under the old three-field system there was a great demand during the harvest quarter (between the end of June and the end of September) and little at other times; but now the work was spread more evenly.

In the first half of the nineteenth century the traditional methods

---

[41] For an account of Thaer's life and work see T. v. d. Goltz, *Geschichte der deutschen Landwirtschaft*, II, 3-86; *Handbuch der Landwirtschaft*, I, 111; *Handwörterbuch der Staatswissenschaften*, VIII, 217; Wilhelm Knorte, *Albrecht Thaer* (Leipzig, 1839).

of agriculture underwent a complete transformation. The "pure" three-field system, which had prevailed for a thousand years, disappeared entirely, and in its place came some system of alternation of crops. Nor was the improved agriculture confined to the large farms; it transformed the peasant economy as well. In the more genial regions west of the Elbe the change was from the grain and fallow system to one of a rotation of plants and grain. But in the higher regions and in the less fertile districts of the east the change from the old three-field system embodied the cultivation of grass. There were variations, however, and it was often difficult to say what system was being followed. The "improved" system really consisted of a number of experiments, largely empirical. Moreover, the lack of capital and of scientific knowledge prevented radical and wholesale innovations, so that the transformation was spread over half a century.

It is impossible to say just how much of the former fallow land was regularly planted to crops at any one time, but an eminent German authority [42] estimated that at the beginning of the nineteenth century the arable land comprised 52,000,000 acres, of which one-third, or 17,000,000 acres, was fallow. By the middle of the century he estimated that 15,000,000 acres of this former fallow were growing cultivated crops. The greatest advance was made in southwestern Germany. In the northwest improvements in the existing system were made somewhat more slowly. In the east progress was still tardier.

Along with the changes in methods of cropping there went also improvements in the technical operations in farming and also in agricultural implements. At the beginning of the nineteenth century plowing was seldom deeper than three to four inches. By the middle of the century there was scarcely a half-way rationally conducted farm that did not work seven or eight inches deep in the ground on the average. The deeper working of the soil could, however, not be done with the hitherto existing tools. It was necessary to have better implements, not only for the better working of the soil with plow, harrow, and roller, but also for the cultivation of intertilled crops during their growth. Accordingly horse-hoes, drills, weed-killers, subsoil plows, improved rollers and harrows, and other specialized implements were introduced. The models for these came from England and the Netherlands, but they were made for the ordinary farm by the local blacksmith or wheelwright. Made of wood, for the most part, they were much too heavy and clumsy for effective use. Only gradually, as machine industry developed during the first half of the nineteenth century, were lighter and stronger im-

[42] T. v. d. Goltz, op. cit., II, 257.

plements made of iron. New machines were also introduced, as fodder-cutting machines, threshing machines, etc., which were also obtained from the factories.

With the better cultivation of the crops there went hand in hand a richer manuring of the fields, the possibility for which was given by the larger production of fodder and the practice of stall-feeding. The application of manure was also improved.[43] Previously it had been applied evenly to the land according to its quality, but now the needs of the various plants were studied and different amounts applied according to their requirements. Improvements were also made in the selection of seed and in the cultivation and harvesting of particular plants. Experiments were continuous along these and other lines, and as a result the total farm produce was greatly increased.

In the second third of the century there was a remarkable spread of sugar beet growing. Although Germany has the honor of having invented the production of sugar from beets and of having built the first beet sugar factory in the world in 1798, this factory went bankrupt and the industry languished until Napoleon gave it new life. In the thirties there was a rapid growth of sugar beet factories in Saxony and Silesia. The number of beet sugar factories in the area of the Zollverein grew from 156 in 1836–37 to 234 in 1851–52, while the annual quantity of beets used by all factories during this period increased from 200 to 3900 tons.[44] The growing of beets led to deep plowing, drilling, and the use of better implements generally in eastern and central Germany. As a result of all these improvements the yield of the land was greatly increased.

Animal husbandry was also transformed, especially in the case of cattle and sheep. Horse-raising already stood on a high level, especially of workhorses in Holstein, and of saddle horses for the nobility and the rich, while swine husbandry was as yet of relatively minor importance, and the breed very indifferent. The great obstacle to improvement had been the insufficiency of fodder, so that the feeding of cattle had been inadequate as to amount and kind. In the warm weather the cattle had managed to exist on the stubble and common pasture, and in the winter were insufficiently nourished with straw. The cattle had been given as much fodder as was available, but generally not as much as they needed if they were to yield per-

[43] The difficulty of change is illustrated by a remonstrance of an old official to the management of the domain Lobositz in Bohemia, which began to introduce rational methods in the first decade of the nineteenth century — "That it is done with shameless, disgraceful hand, for it is a crime against God to improve nature, even though it is only by a different system of manuring than has been used since the beginning of time." — W. Sombart, *Der Moderne Kapitalismus* (5th ed., Berlin), II, 632.

[44] A. Meitzen, *Der Boden und die landwirtschaftlichen Verhältnisse des Preussischen Staates* (Berlin, 1869), IV, 558.

formances corresponding to their size and character. And until the growing of root crops such as clover, potatoes, etc., the composition of the fodder was defective.

The following table shows the increase of livestock in Prussia between 1816 and 1861.

ANIMAL CENSUS OF PRUSSIA *
(000 omitted)

Year	Total	Horses, mules and donkeys	Cattle	Goats	Sheep	Swine
1816	15,155	1243	4014	143	8,260	1494
1840	25,438	1520	4976	360	16,344	2239
1849	26,275	1575	5372	585	16,297	2466
1861	28,275	1687	5634	806	17,438	2710

* G. W. Viebahn, *Statistik des zollvereinten und nordlichen Deutschland.* 3 Thle. (Berlin, 1858–68), III, 174.

Sheep and goats increased faster than the population, which about doubled during this period, swine kept about even, while horses and cattle fell behind. Better and more capable breeds of animals were also introduced. Of special significance was the rapid spread of sheep raising, and particularly of merino sheep, especially in Saxony and Prussia. At the beginning of the nineteenth century some merinos were introduced into Germany from Spain, but most of them were descendants of animals imported in the previous century. The total number of sheep doubled, but the proportion of merino and half-improved (*halbveredelte*) sheep grew from 38 to 76 per cent. As a result the yield in wool greatly increased, practically doubling during the first half of the nineteenth century. Dieterici estimated that at the beginning of the century the average yield of wool per sheep was $1\frac{2}{3}$ pounds, and that this had increased to between 2 and 4 pounds in 1846.[45] The same authority estimated a practical doubling in the weights of animals in Prussia between 1800 and 1836.

The great improvement in animal husbandry is equally well illustrated by the increase in the yield of milk per cow. The average yield per cow in good regions near Berlin increased from 1525 quarts in 1805 to 1818 quarts in 1846.[46] Dairy husbandry was one of the lines next to sheep raising along which the greatest advance was being made.

All of these changes spelled prosperity for the German farmer. Prices were rising, while wages remained low, or at least did not rise so rapidly. The natural gross returns probably increased on the aver-

[45] C. F. W. Dieterici, *Der Volkswohlstand im Preussischen Staate* (Berlin, 1846), 134.
[46] T. v. d. Goltz, op. cit., II, 263.

age about 50 per cent, and on the especially well-managed farms they reached 100 per cent. But this differed from place to place and depended largely on the character of the farmer. The greatest advances took place in the forties and fifties, when the growth of cities created new markets for agricultural produce.

Down to the middle of the nineteenth century agriculture was still largely self-sufficing and each individual farm consumed a large part of the produce which it raised. Viebahn estimated for this date that on the average about two-thirds of the products of agriculture were consumed where grown. Only on the large estates east of the Elbe did commercial farming prevail. As capitalistic farming spread and land was cultivated more rationally owing to better markets, prices of land rose and sales became frequent.

One other factor, which contributed to the agricultural advance of this period, remains to be considered; this was agricultural education. Beginning in the 1830's a number of agricultural colleges was established in Prussia, and in the older universities scientific courses in agriculture were added to the curricula. Exhibitions of cattle and of farm machinery were also held, and improvements were demonstrated to doubting farmers. Agricultural societies spread the latest information. But the new equipment was expensive and experimentation might prove costly. Moreover, the new scientific knowledge could be applied only on large concentrated holdings. As a result the leadership in agricultural progress was assumed at this time by the Junkers in East Prussia.

BIBLIOGRAPHICAL NOTE *

1. *Britain.* The best book on the agricultural history of England is Lord Ernle (R. E. Prothero), *English Farming, Past and Present* (London, 1912; 5th ed., rev. by A. D. Hall, London, 1936), by a well-informed scholar. Not so clear, but full of useful detail, is W. H. R. Curtler, *A Short History of English Agriculture* (Oxford, 1909); his *Enclosure and Redistribution of our Land* (Oxford, 1920) is a comprehensive account of the enclosure movement. This is also discussed in two other careful studies: E. C. K. Gonner, *Common Land and Enclosures* (London, 1913) and G. Slater, *The English Peasantry and the Enclosure of the Common Fields* (London, 1907). W. Hasbach, *A History of the English Agricultural Labourer* (London, 1908) is impartial, but gloomy. A. H. Johnson, *The Disappearance of the Small Landowner* (London, 1909) is a sympathetic survey. L. G. de Lavergne, *Rural Economy of England and Scotland* (Edinburgh, 1855) is an interesting contemporary picture. J. Orr, *A Short History of British Agriculture* (London, 1922) is useful.

2. *France.* The only history of agriculture in France is M. Augé-Laribé, *L'évolution de la France agricole* (Paris, 1912), which is useful but sketchy.

* For general works on the economic life of the people as a whole and also in special fields the reader is referred to the General Bibliography (pp. xi-xiv). The chapter bibliographies contain specialized treatises.

L. G. Lavergne, *Économie rurale de la France depuis* 1789 (4th ed., Paris, 1877) contains useful information. H. Sée, *Esquisse d'une histoire du régime agraire en Europe aux XVIIIe et XIXe siècles* (Paris, 1921) is a suggestive outline. Most of the writers confine themselves to the period of the French Revolution and to the land sales. Among these are A. Gain, *La restauration et les biens des émigrés* (Nancy, 1928); M. Kovalevsky, *La France économique et sociale à la veille de la Révolution* (Paris, 1909); G. Lecarpentier, *La vente des biens ecclésiastiques pendant la Révolution française* (Paris, 1908); J. Loutchisky, *L'état des classes agricoles à la veille de la Révolution* (Paris, 1911), and *La petite propriété en France avant la Révolution et la vente des biens nationaux* (Paris, 1897); M. Marion, *La vente des biens nationaux* (Paris, 1908).

3. *Germany.* The best book on the history of agriculture in Germany is T. von der Goltz, *Geschichte der deutschen Landwirtschaft*, 2 vols. (Stuttgart, 1902–03). Vol. II covers the nineteenth century and is authoritative and comprehensive. E. Michelsen, *Geschichte der deutschen Landwirtschaft* (Berlin, 1911) is a useful survey. Most writers are more concerned with the peasantry than with agriculture. Among these the following may be named: G. S. Ford, *Stein and the Era of Reform in Prussia*, 1807–1815 (Princeton, 1922) and J. R. Seeley, *Life and Times of Stein*, 3 vols. (Cambridge, 1878), both of which describe the emancipation of the serfs. The classic work on this subject is G. F. Knapp, *Die Bauernbefreiung und der Ursprung der Landarbeiter in den älteren Theilen Preussens*, 2 vols. (Leipzig, 1887). H. Gerber, *Geschichte des deutschen Bauernstandes* (3rd ed., Leipzig, 1928), continues the story in interesting fashion. The most ambitious and detailed study is A. Meitzen, *Der Boden und die landwirtschaftlichen Verhältnisse des preussischen Staates*, 8 vols. (Berlin, 1868–1908). R. B. B. Morier (Ed.), *Systems of Land Tenure in Various Countries* (2nd ed., London, 1881) is a useful survey.

CHAPTER II

INDUSTRY

I. THE INDUSTRIAL REVOLUTION IN ENGLAND

Towards the end of the eighteenth century there occurred in England a change in economic organization and industrial technique which has been called the Industrial Revolution. In order to understand the changes which are implied in this name, it is desirable to portray conditions as they existed prior to this event.

The old type of industry can best be pictured in the woolen industry, for this was the oldest and the most thoroughly British trade that was to be found in the country. Certain features at once stand forth, which show a very different form of organization than that existing today. In the first place, the industry was widely diffused over the whole country. From Yorkshire in the north it stretched to Norfolk in the east and to Devonshire in the southwest. These were the main regions, but between these regions and within each district there was a further dispersion. Defoe, who gives the most vivid picture of this form of industry in his "Tour," describes the "innumerable villages, hamlets, and scattered houses, in which . . . the spinning work of this manufacture is performed." [1]

A second feature was the fact that the workshop was the cottage in which the worker and his family lived. From this fact it has frequently been called "cottage industry." The cottage was a small house, frequently little better than a hovel, in which the loom occupied the best room, where the family life centered. Here the weaver worked at his loom, while his wife and daughters prepared the yarn at the spinning wheel and the boys carded the wool. Since, however, it required the labors of six to ten spinners to provide enough yarn to keep one weaver busy, there were households that devoted themselves exclusively to spinning.

The most striking characteristic of modern industry, namely division of labor, was present only in the most rudimentary form in this primitive organization. In each of these numerous and scattered cottages the same products were turned out by the same methods in endless repetition. Some specialization there was, of course, among the different processes of carding, spinning, weaving, dyeing, pulling, and other stages of manufacture, but it was functional specialization rather than division of labor, that is the splitting up of a process into minute parts.

[1] Daniel Defoe, *A Tour through the Whole Island of Great Britain* (3 vols. London, 1724–27), II, 43.

43

Capital played only a small part in this domestic stage of industry. The loom was the only appliance that required any considerable investment, the others being of the simplest character. The spinning wheel, either hand or foot, which dated only from the sixteenth century, was generally used for spinning. Hand cards were used for carding. For washing or dyeing the wool a tub was sufficient. Since such a small capital investment was required any young man of good character could ordinarily obtain credit sufficient to enable him to set up as a small manufacturer. Capital and labor were embodied in one person, and some modern problems of industry did not present themselves.

Finally, industry was seldom carried on as the sole occupation, but the worker usually possessed a small plot of ground which he cultivated, and perhaps he kept a cow on the commons. Agriculture was thus a by-industry practiced by these small household manufacturers, and afforded a part of the family income. Industry was highly decentralized and most workers lived in small villages, where they had access to the land.

Domestic system. The organization of production thus described has usually been called the domestic system. A description contained in the Woolen Report of 1806 sums up the salient features as follows: "In the domestic system . . . the manufacture is conducted by a multitude of master manufacturers, generally possessing a very small and scarcely ever any considerable amount of capital. They buy the wool of the dealer and, in their own houses, assisted by their wives and children, and from two or three to six or seven journeymen, they dye it, when dyeing is necessary, and through all the different stages work it up into undressed cloth." Under ideal circumstances the master worker was represented as owning his workshop and his tools, purchasing his raw materials, and disposing directly of his finished products. Such an ideal was, however, probably never fully realized.

The first departure from it occurred when spinners ceased buying their own wool, and received it from traveling merchants, being paid piece-work wages (in modern parlance) for their work of spinning it into yarn.[2] Master manufacturers sometimes owned the looms at which the weavers worked, and sometimes workers were even gathered for convenience in central buildings. Adam Smith stated with some exaggeration in 1776 that in every part of Europe twenty workmen served under a master for one that was independent. For industry organized in this fashion perhaps a better name than domestic would be the "putting-out" system, for a chief characteristic was the

---

[2] See A. E. Bland, P. A. Brown, and R. H. Tawney, *English Economic History: Select Documents* (London, 1914), 484, 500.

putting out of the work in its different stages to artisans working in their houses, the collection from them of the wool, the yarn, or the cloth, and carrying these to the next group for processing. The merchant capitalist or middleman stood in the midst of a vast web of interlacing activities, which he organized and directed. A long step toward capitalistic organization of industry had been taken before the factory system with power machinery was introduced.

In the north of England the workers were more independent. Here the weavers, working in their own cottages, still owned their own tools and raw materials; the latter they bought as they needed them and sold the finished goods in a near-by market or sent them to London for sale. This system was known as the "cottage" system, and differed from the "putting-out" system only in allowing somewhat greater freedom to the worker.

Until the invention of machinery, there was no particular advantage in moving the workers into factories. The appliances used in the textile industries were simple and, since they were operated by human power, they did not require a central plant. To do this more capital would have been required and capital was scarce. In the absence of developed markets the elasticity of the system was an advantage over the hiring of a permanent body of workpeople. Employment and output were easily adjusted to market conditions. Facilities of transportation were, moreover, too bad to permit the centralization of production in single localities or in large establishments, or the concentration of population in large cities.

The domestic system has been idealized by some writers, who see in it a system of independence and contentment which it probably did not possess. But whatever its virtues as a social system, as a scheme of economic production it had undoubted imperfections. The employment of the housewife must have interfered with home duties, and that of children at long hours — "scarce anything above four years old, but its hands were sufficient for its own support," approvingly wrote Defoe — finds no support today. The product was uneven in quality, irregular in output, and low in standard. The hours were long, the conditions of work often unwholesome, and the pay usually small. Under the scattered system of production supervision was impossible, there was a waste of time and labor in passing partly finished goods from one group of handworkers to another, and the system was incapable of adapting itself rapidly to meet the requirements of an expanding market.

During the latter part of the eighteenth century all of these conditions changed and the economic organization was completely altered. The domestic system gave way to the factory system.

The Industrial Revolution. The older idea, given currency by the term "industrial revolution," that a sudden and revolutionary change was wrought in English industry by a dramatic series of new inventions, has been replaced, as a result of more careful study, by the view that the old economic system was modified only gradually by a series of changes which took a long time to work out. "Economic history is not catastrophic," said F. W. Maitland; the economic eighteenth century lasted in some aspects beyond the middle of the nineteenth century. There were really two stages in the evolution. During the first period far-reaching changes in organization occurred, but few in the methods of production, while, during the second, revolutionary improvements were made in the technique of production. The former may be traced briefly before describing the second.

One of the first improvements in the dispersed domestic system just described was the drawing together of the operations under the control of a merchant capitalist. In order to ensure a steady supply of yarn, for instance, he found it advantageous to buy raw material and distribute it among the spinners in their homes, and from them to collect weekly the spun yarn. The yarn in turn was distributed among the weavers, from whom was gathered the woven cloth. The cloth was handed over to other craftsmen for further processing, such as dyeing, pulling, etc. Economies in the cost of production were effected by this system, and better control was obtained. But the merchants' interest in production was limited to savings in marketing; he did not seek to improve technique or to regulate labor. The work of production was left entirely to the domestic worker.

Further steps in the firmer control of the materials of commerce and in better methods of marketing were taken when the merchants became owners of the tools and finally of the workplaces. They were then in complete charge of production, and could regulate the amount produced and therefore the price.

This movement was stimulated by the position of British trade, both foreign and domestic. International competition began and there was a pressure to reduce costs of production. In other countries any such effort would probably have taken the direction of lowering costs by reducing the return to labor, which after all was the major factor. But in England, where personal freedom and security of property were most developed, where the geographical position favored both the obtaining of raw materials and marketing of the finished products, and where a new industry — that of cotton — had arisen free from gild and legal restrictions, the movement to reduce costs took other directions. The most important of these was the invention of labor-saving and thus cost-reducing machinery. This was the second stage in the Industrial Revolution.

Two interesting questions present themselves in this connection: (1) Why did the Industrial Revolution take place just at the end of the eighteenth century? (2) Why in England?

(1) "Necessity is the mother of invention," says an old proverb, and this is the best answer to the first question. Productivity in almost every line was limited by inefficient methods and ineffective tools. In the textile industry there was a disequilibrium between spinning and weaving, for it took six to ten spinners to furnish yarn for one weaver; in mining there was constant difficulty with water, which had to be pumped out lest it flood the mines; water power, almost the only motive power other than human muscles, was irregular and failed altogether when the stream was frozen or in time of drought. The processes used in the iron and steel industry were crude and inefficient. Supply was held down by prevailing methods. Demand, on the other hand, was expanding. There was a steady extension of the market for British goods, especially after 1760, and exports increased. But a larger supply of goods, at cheaper prices, could be produced only if something better than the slow and expensive hand methods were developed.

An important factor in making possible the invention of labor-saving machinery at the end of the eighteenth century was the development of natural science. In the fields of heat, light, electricity, and chemistry, pure science had been carried further on the continent than in England, though the contributions to scientific knowledge by such Englishmen as Davy, Faraday, Herschel, Cavendish, and others were original and noteworthy. But the English excelled in the application of scientific knowledge to practical affairs, and this knowledge had passed beyond the realm of speculation and was ready for application to industry. Perhaps the best illustration of this was the invention of the steam engine by James Watt. Acquainted with the theories of the expansive power of steam, and profiting by the advice of Joseph Black, Professor of Physics at the University of Glasgow, Watt discovered the principle of the modern steam engine while trying to repair an old engine of Newcomen. The need for a good steam engine was definite and urgent, for the coal mines had been dug down to depths from which the old hand pumps or those driven by water power or even by Newcomen's crude engine could no longer keep them clear of water. The danger of flooding was always imminent and the pressure was strong for improvement.

Another factor in promoting the invention of machinery was the superior character of the English patent law. This dated back to the Statute of Monopolies of 1624, which prohibited monopolies but excepted patents granted for a limited period to the true and first inventor "of any new manufactures." [3]   Similar legislation was not passed in France until 1791, nor for the whole of Germany until 1842.   The number of patents granted in England after 1760 grew markedly, from an annual average of slightly over 6 in the period 1700–60, to 31 in the period 1760–85.   The expense and difficulty in obtaining and asserting patent rights give added significance to these figures.   There was a general interest in mechanical improvement; new inventions were not the work of a few individuals, but rather the expression of economic forces.

Political, social, and legal conditions in England were also favorable to industrial development.   The people of England enjoyed a larger degree of political liberty than those of any continental country.   The system of constitutional government ensured political immunity of person and also protected property rights and encouraged the accumulation of capital and its productive investment.

Legislation was enacted to guarantee the security of property and the freedom and sanctity of contracts.   Arbitrary royal interference with economic activities or property rights had been largely ended by the Revolution of 1688.   After that event the merchant class had influenced if not dominated commercial policy; the danger of excessive and unjust taxation was greatly reduced; the consular service was inaugurated, and English diplomats were acquainted with business conditions and commercial needs of the country.   Religious freedom existed and a considerable emphasis had already been given to freedom of industrial and commercial action.   Especially important was the fact that in England the social and economic ladder was more open and accessible than in any country in Europe.   There was also developing a commercial and financial mechanism adapted to the furtherance of business, such as joint stock companies, a banking system, and business houses having commercial connections with the continent.

England becomes the workshop of the world.   (2) The question as to why the Industrial Revolution should have occurred in England rather than in some continental country, like France, or Holland, or Switzerland, has already been partially answered.   England had reached a riper stage of industrial development and was in a better position than other countries to exploit scientific knowledge as well as natural resources.   But there were other factors which gave England a distinct advantage over her rivals.

England possessed, either at home or in her colonies, practically all the raw materials necessary for the development of capitalistic machine industries.   At home she had wool, coal, and iron; from the colonies she obtained iron, cotton, dyewoods, lumber, and naval

[3] Bland, Brown, and Tawney, op. cit., 465.

stores. She also possessed at home good water power and a humid climate. These resources furnished the basis for industrial development, particularly in the textile and iron industries. Their nature, moreover, impressed a definite character upon English industry. Since the chief wares were bulky and cheap, their market must be found in the consumption of the masses; they must therefore be processed on a large scale, in the mass, if they were to be produced at a low price and yet be profitable. This requirement of cheaper costs necessitated the use of machinery and non-human power. The two industrially most advanced nations in Europe at the end of the eighteenth century were France and Holland, but both differed from England in this respect. France produced raw silk and other products, which called for careful workmanship and artistic skill in the making of quality goods for the wealthier consumers. Holland lacked raw materials, though her people were industrious and science was highly developed there. On this score England had the advantage. •

A second factor was the existence in England of considerable supplies of free capital. The rapidity with which London was rebuilt after the fire of 1661, the wild speculation in the South Sea Bubble in 1720 and the resulting panic — panics do not occur in a poor country, — and the existence of a large and wealthy merchant class with capital to invest, show this. Prior to the Industrial Revolution capital had been of significance only in agriculture and commerce. Sheep raising and later improved agriculture called for considerable expenditure of capital, as did commerce for ships and stores of merchandise. The rise of middlemen and the putting-out system required the concentration of fairly large sums even in the domestic system. With the development of the factory system the capitalist control, already established in the domestic system, was intensified.

On the subject of labor, both as to its quantity and quality, there is less agreement. During the seventeenth and eighteenth centuries some of the best artisans of Europe had sought in England a refuge from intolerable conditions at home. The technological quality of labor in England was therefore high. Political and social conditions tended also to develop in the laboring class qualities of ambition, enterprise, and initiative. On the other hand, relative to the demand for labor and the opportunities offered by the expanding market, the supply was inadequate. With the inefficient hand processes that existed under the domestic system the demand for English manufactured goods could not be met. It was clear that labor must be supplied with effective implements if more goods were to be produced. Strong pressure therefore existed to improve prevailing processes and to invent better machines with which to process the abundant and cheap raw materials. In the later stages of the Industrial Revolution, when the new machinery made labor more productive, and when the agrarian changes filled the towns with former agricultural workers, labor became relatively abundant, and the new factories found plenty of unemployed to draw upon. But, at the beginning, the scarcity of efficient labor was one of the strongest forces leading to the invention and introduction of labor-saving machinery.

Finally, it may be pointed out again that the co-ordination of industry under the control of merchant-manufacturers had already proceeded far. In the woolen industry the combers, spinners, weavers, dyers, and other home workers were practically only piece-work artisans, who worked on materials furnished by their employer and often with tools owned by him. It was a simple step to concentrate these various workers in a single building, the factory, when the new machinery displaced the hand tools. The same situation existed in the small metal and some other industries.

The factors thus far mentioned were on the side of supply and describe the favorable conditions which made possible and logical the transition in England from the domestic to the factory system. The real driving force must, however, be sought on the side of demand. It was the expansion of the market, especially after 1760, that called forth the efforts of British producers and led them to seek better and cheaper methods of production. France, Holland, and the Scandinavian countries were developing during the eighteenth century and the European demand for English goods expanded; the American colonists were buying increased quantities; and other parts of the world provided good markets. The British had the greatest merchant marine in the world and controlled much of the commerce. Maritime enterprise opened up new markets in Asia and America, and led to a profitable extension of trade with those two continents. Exports from Great Britain doubled between 1720 and 1760 and doubled again between 1760 and 1795.

At the same time, owing to the growth of the home population and improvements in transportation, the domestic market stood ready to absorb larger quantities of goods. Even more important than the actual market was the potential one — the market that would come into being if cheap supplies of commodities could be produced for the masses. It was no accident that this market was first realized for cotton goods, crockery, and iron wares, for those three branches were based on cheap raw materials, mass production, and popular demand. There was here an interaction of cause and effect: the potential market stimulated improvements in processes of production; these in turn cheapened costs and tapped new levels of consumer demand;

and the expanded market permitted further improvements. This is well illustrated by such a small item as the production of stockings. "Two centuries ago not one person in a thousand wore stockings; one century ago not one person in five hundred wore them; now not one person in a thousand is without them." [4] The production of goods in bulk, at low cost, for mass consumption, was found to be more profitable than the production of small quantities of luxury goods at high prices.

The great inventions. Thus far the discussion has centered for the most part about the economic factors, that is those having to do with the price determining factors of supply and demand. But there was another important group, namely the technical and engineering improvements in the technique of production, which made possible the Industrial Revolution. For purposes of description the textile and the iron and coal industries are usually selected, and there are good reasons for this choice. Not only were they the most important industries in England, but each made a unique contribution: the textile industries moved the workers from their homes into the factories, and the iron and steel industries provided materials for many other lines and also for the new machines and above all the steam engine.

The technical inventions which are usually included under the Industrial Revolution fall into two main groups: (1) new machines which took over the work formerly performed by hand tools; and (2) machines which generated applied power — water or steam — in place of human muscles or animals.

The cotton industry was the first to be mechanized and the one that set the pace for the others. It was apparently introduced into England by the Flemish about 1585, but remained on a small scale for two hundred years; in 1760 the consumption of raw cotton was only about 1,000,000 pounds. The two chief branches of the textile industry were spinning and weaving; these were both carried on by hand, but of the two spinning was so much slower that from six to ten spinners were necessary to keep one weaver busy. This disproportion was made still greater when John Kay in 1733 invented the so-called flying shuttle by means of which a weaver was able by an automatic spring to propel unaided the shuttle carrying the cotton weft back and forth through the upright linen threads composing the warp. One weaver could now operate a loom that formerly required the labor of two, and at the same time could weave a broader cloth.

The demand for cotton thread increased and led to a series of in-

[4] *The Results of Machinery* (London, 1831), quoted by J. L. and B. Hammond, *The Rise of Modern Industry* (5th ed., London, 1937), 210.

ventions for mechanical spinning. In 1764 James Hargreaves, a weaver, invented the spinning jenny, a simple machine that turned eight spindles instead of the one of the spinning wheel; before his death he had increased the number of spindles on his machine to eighty. The jenny was light and inexpensive, but it had the serious defect that it spun a loose and coarse thread, which had to have flax mixed with the cotton in order to make it strong enough for use.

Much more important and original was the water frame, patented by Richard Arkwright in 1769. Credit for the invention seems to belong to a mechanic named Highs,[5] whose ideas were appropriated by Arkwright, a barber. But the latter had ability and made it a practical success. This machine introduced a new principle, having two sets of revolving rollers, of which one set turned more rapidly than the other, thus pulling out the yarn into a finer thread; by introducing additional sets of rollers the thread could be made of any desired fineness, and at the same time made tighter. The yarn could now be made of unmixed cotton. The machine was so cumbersome and heavy that it could not be turned by hand, but required water power to run it; hence it was called the "water frame." Because of this fact it could not be used by the domestic worker, but only in factories. The spinning jenny continued to be used in the cottages.

As yet no fine, firm yarn was produced in England that could compete with the hand-spun yarn of India. This was first made possible by Samuel Crompton, who invented his spinning mule in 1779. It was given this name to indicate its hybrid origin, comprising as it did the best features of the jenny and the water frame. The first machine had 20 spindles; a number of improvements were made and the machine was enlarged. By 1790 there were mules with 400 spindles, and by 1835 there were 1100 spindles. Much finer cotton, that was at the same time firm and hard, was now spun at a much lower cost.

The former situation was now reversed: there was a surplus of yarn and not enough weavers. Attention was directed to the need of mechanical weaving, and in 1785 Edward Cartwright, a clergyman, patented a power loom. This was very clumsy, and did not come into general use until it had been worked over and improved in the early nineteenth century by Radcliffe and Horrocks. In 1813 there were only 2300 power looms in England; between that date and 1820 it obtained a firm foothold, and by 1820 there were 12,150 looms; in 1830 there were 45,120. But there were still 250,000 hand looms. The decade of the thirties saw their final defeat, how-

[5] There has been much discussion over the origin of this invention. Edward Baines, Jr., *History of the Cotton Manufacture in Great Britain* (London, 1835), credited John Wyatt with the idea, but R. Guest, *Compendious History of the Cotton Manufacture* (Manchester, 1823), claimed the honor for Thomas Highs.

ever, as a boy could manage two power looms and weave three and [machine tending] a half times as much as the best weaver on a hand loom.

It was not enough to provide the machinery; a plentiful supply of cheap raw material was also necessary. This was assured when Eli Whitney invented the cotton gin in the United States in 1793. Before this event short-staple cotton had been imported from India, Egypt, and the Far East, but it was expensive and met the demand inadequately. Little cotton had been grown in the United States because of the high cost of separating the seed from the lint; by hand a man could clean about one pound of lint of short-staple, or about ten pounds of sea-island, cotton in a day. By Whitney's machine 300 pounds of cotton could be cleaned in a day by one person, an amount which was later greatly increased. The production of cotton now became highly profitable and its growth and exportation showed extraordinarily rapid expansion, while at the same time the price declined. The imports and consumption of raw cotton in England proceeded with equal rapidity; the consumption grew from 54,-000,000 pounds in 1801 to 273,000,000 in 1831, and 1,260,000,000 in 1860. The following table shows the steady expansion that took place:

IMPORTS OF COTTON *

Year	Quantity of cotton imported (thousand pounds)	Exports of manufactures (thousands of pounds sterling)
1785	17,993	....
1790	31,448	1,662
1801	54,203	5,406
1811	90,310	....
1821	137,402	16,000
1831	273,250	17,200
1841	437,094	23,400
1851	757,380	30,000
1861	1,261,400	46,800
1871	1,676,100	72,800

* W. S. Jevons, *The Coal Question* (London, 1865), 251.

Iron and steel industries. The second field which was being transformed by inventive genius was the production of iron and steel. The smelting of iron ore was one of the oldest industries in England, but, in spite of a great increase in demand, it remained stagnant, largely because of the exhaustion of the forests which had provided the charcoal for smelting. By the middle of the eighteenth century England was importing some 20,000 tons of iron a year from Sweden, which was slightly more than the domestic production. Prices were going up, and England turned to the American colonies for relief. By the Act of 1750 colonial bar and pig iron were admitted free of duty, while iron and steel manufactures were forbidden in the colonies; in 1771 the importation of colonial iron amounted to about 7,000,000 tons.

The first improvements of a permanent character in English metallurgical processes seem to have been made by the Darbys, of whom there were three generations. The first Abraham Darby experimented with the use of coke as fuel, but it remained for his son to make a commercial success of it, about 1735. Another step forward was made when John Smeaton invented the air-blast furnace in 1760, which produced a very hot fire and permitted the iron ore to be thoroughly smelted. By the end of the century the smelting of iron by coal or coke instead of charcoal had been almost universally adopted. The application in 1828 of the hot air blast to smelting concluded the first cycle of the inventions that dealt with the production of raw iron.

The first stage in the manufacture of iron and steel wares had now been successfully met; pig iron could be cheaply and systematically produced. But the economical conversion of cast iron into wrought iron or steel presented a further metallurgical problem, the chemistry of which was not then understood. Cast iron contains a high percentage of carbon, which renders it brittle and unsuited for purposes where tensile strength is desired. Malleable or wrought iron is iron that is largely freed from carbon and other impurities; if it contains more than two per cent carbon it cannot be made into steel.

In the years 1783–85 two important improvements were introduced by Peter Onions and Henry Cort. The first of these was "puddling" in a reverberatory furnace. The conversion of pig iron into malleable iron or steel required reheating, but it was necessary to do this without bringing the iron into direct contact with the fuel, as this would only introduce additional carbon of which there was already too much. The reverberatory process smelted the pig iron in a shallow furnace which threw back from the ceiling the heated gases from the burning coal. The carbon and other impurities were eliminated by stirring or puddling the molten iron in the furnace. This left a high-grade product, known as wrought iron.

The second great improvement was the shaping and cutting of the malleable iron by means of rollers. Before the use of the roller process, the iron taken from the puddling furnace had been beaten into the desired shape by hammers, which also cleaned it of cinders and other impurities. Now the hot iron was run through grooved and notched rollers which gave it any form desired. Especially valuable was the making of sheet iron, which was used for the construction of tanks, boilers, and iron barges; rods and bars, bolts, plates, and other shapes were also made in quantity.

By 1800 these developments had brought into existence what has been called "The Malleable Iron Period." Several important consequences flowed from these changes. In the first place the use of coal had freed the producer of pig iron or of manufactured iron wares from the necessity of locating his works near forests, and had transferred the iron industry to the vicinity of the coal fields. In the second place entirely new industries were now made possible. "During the charcoal period it was impossible to make light pots and utensils by the casting process, because charcoal iron ran very thick; but coke-smelted iron was free from this disadvantage, and its quality made possible the rise of a new industry, viz. the manufacture of cast-iron hollow ware. Meanwhile the rise of the steam engine gave a stimulus to the production of heavy castings." [6]

The coal industry. The new metallurgical processes in the making of iron called for additional supplies of coal. The mining of coal had been carried on in England since Roman times, and was quite extensive in the sixteenth and seventeenth centuries. It had long been used for domestic heating and for certain industrial processes, such as forging iron. But the demand for these purposes was small, as wood was preferred for fuel and was used in the form of charcoal for smelting and refining. About 1740 the oak forests of England were near exhaustion and the remaining trees were reserved for shipbuilding. At about the same time the method of using coked coal for fuel in smelting was discovered. A great impetus was thereby given to the coal industry.

Coal mining was handicapped by two difficulties, namely the presence of water and the danger from flooding the mines, and the presence of gas and the danger of explosion. The early mines were usually opened by an adit, or nearly horizontal tunnel, through a side hill to the coal seam; the vertical pit was then dug from the surface to the end of the tunnel. The water which seeped through the walls was drained off through the adit and the shaft provided ventilation. The coal was worked out around the foot of the pit and was hauled up the shaft in baskets. Owing to the difficulties of ventilation it was not possible to work the coal more than about 200 yards from the bottom of the shaft, and the limit of depth was about 180 feet. A coal mine had only a comparatively short life; sooner or later water or gas got the mastery. Newcomen's engine,

[6] J. C. Allen, *The Industrial Development of Birmingham and The Black Country*, 1860–1927 (London, 1929), 22. By permission of the publishers, George Allen and Unwin, Ltd., London.

which was used to pump out the water, pushed the depth down to about 300 feet, but this increased the difficulty of ventilation and the danger of explosion from various gases. The latter was finally met by the invention of the safety lamp in 1815. Sir Humphry Davy, the famous chemist, invented a lamp in which the flame was guarded by a mantle of wire gauze from direct contact with the gases and so did not ignite them, and at about the same time George Stephenson, later the promoter of the steam locomotive, invented another in which a metal casing with fine holes took the place of the wire gauze. Neither lamp was quite safe, but their use greatly reduced the number of explosions and permitted mines to be dug deeper and wider. After about 1780 Watt's steam engine was used to hoist coal to the surface. The output of coal increased enormously, from a few thousand tons in 1700 to about 10,000,000 tons in 1800, and 28,000,000 tons in 1830. The pre-eminence of England in this respect is indicated by the fact that the total consumption of the rest of the world at the beginning of the nineteenth century was probably not in excess of 100,000 tons.

The steam engine. Although James Watt is usually credited with the invention of the steam engine, this was really the culmination of a long series of inventions. The expansive power of steam was understood by the Greeks, but the first practical application of this principle which led to the modern steam engine was made in 1690 by Denis Papin. His machine generated steam in a cylinder, one end of which was open. Thomas Savery in 1698 invented a "fire engine" with a separate boiler for generating steam. Those ideas were combined in a more practical but cumbersome engine about 1705 by Thomas Newcomen. His engine had a cylinder from four to six feet in diameter, with a piston making from six to twelve strokes a minute, hand-operated valves, and a lever beam for transmitting the power. In spite of its cumbersomeness and wastefulness — it consumed more than 12 tons of coal a day and three-fourths of the fuel was wasted — it was largely used in mines, waterworks, blast furnaces, and for other purposes.

It was while repairing one of these engines, in 1763, that James Watt, an instrument maker at the University of Glasgow, developed the true principles of the modern steam engine. He closed both ends of the cylinder and applied steam to force the piston back and forth in the cylinder instead of trusting to atmospheric pressure, as had been done in the earlier types. Successive improvements brought a separate condensing chamber, in 1782 the "double-acting" principle, and finally automatic control of the steam pressure by a governor. The early steam engines, with their straight line motion, were attached to pumps. It was still necessary to transform the straight line or back-and-forth motion of the cylinders into circular motion, in order to make the steam engine available for driving machinery, but this was patented in 1781; the usual device for this purpose was a crank and shaft.

While credit must be given to the genius of James Watt for inventing the steam engine, the contributions of other men must not be overlooked. Matthew Boulton, with whom Watt formed a partnership in 1769, supplied financial backing and also the mechanical resources of his Soho plant near Birmingham. Even these were scarcely sufficient to produce cylinders so accurately bored that the pistons would fit in them without waste of steam. Cylinders bored by hand were distressingly irregular; there was an error of three-eighths of an inch in one such cylinder made for Watt. Not until John Wilkinson invented his cannon-boring machine in 1774 was Watt able to produce a workable steam engine. Still further improvements in accuracy and precision were made possible when Henry Maudslay in 1794 invented the slide rest, a device in which the cutting blade or boring tool was held steadily against the work by a slide block instead of by hand. In 1800 he made his first screw-cutting lathe. The modern steam engine was now realized.

The chief, and as it seemed to Watt, the only demand for these engines was to pump water and to hoist coal out of the Cornish mines. Their use in the Lancashire cotton mills began about 1785, but they were frequently employed only to pump water to a higher level to feed the water wheel which drove the machinery. Gradually, however, the "rotative" engine was used for driving the machinery directly, and they were more generally introduced. By 1800, 289 Watt engines, with 4543 horse power, were in use, and after this their introduction and use in manufacturing was rapid. These engines were, for the time, unusually capable, cheap, simple, and free from danger, and soon won supremacy not only in the coal mines, but also in the textile industry. In this respect England was far ahead of her continental rivals. In 1810 England had 5000 steam engines, France 200, while in Germany they were scarcely introduced before 1830.

Significance of the Industrial Revolution. The new system of industry involved not only technological and economic changes, but it occasioned also profound political and social alterations in the structure of society. On the political side it created and placed in the saddle a new middle class, and eventually led to the enfranchisement of the workers. It broke down the remnants of feudalism and accomplished for Britain what the political revolution did for France, but by peaceful change. The social effects were more far-reaching, for it transformed Britain from a rural to an urban country, called into being a large dependent wage class, widened the gulf between capital and labor, introduced greater instability in employment and trade, and permitted evils which may have been the pains of readjustment but were nevertheless serious. On the other side, it greatly enlarged output and made possible a higher standard of living, it opened up new social and economic opportunities, and widened the intellectual horizon of the whole people. The Industrial Revolution has been variously appraised according to whether the emphasis was laid on material progress or on the more elusive element of human happiness; from the former standpoint its achievements have been exalted, from the latter its effects have been condemned. The truth probably lies between the two extremes. Like any dynamic change it brought in its train both evil and good, but from the point of view of the economic as distinguished from the social historian it must be regarded as introducing a new era in human affairs.

2. GROWTH OF THE FACTORY SYSTEM IN ENGLAND

Transition to the factory system. The economic and technological improvements which have been described contained the seeds of revolutionary changes in industry, but the transition to the factory system was gradual. There was an acceleration of tempo, but the complete transformation was spread over the lives of two or three generations. As a matter of fact the changes in the economic organization of the period between 1760 and 1815 were not due primarily to the invention of the steam engine or of machines, but rather to improvements in agriculture and transportation. Enclosure and improved agricultural technique increased the supply of food and released many workers from the land, while improved transport facilities widened the markets and facilitated the movement of the population into towns. Until 1800 the steam engine was confined almost entirely to the mining and iron industries, but here it cheapened fuel and iron products, both of which were essential in the expanding transport industry.

The establishment of the factory system came later than used to be supposed by those who dated it from the first invention of the new machines. Early machinery was clumsy, costly, and expensive to operate because of the large fuel consumption. Stoppages for repairs were frequent, and it was difficult to find skilled workers. It is therefore not surprising to find that in most industries the introduction of machinery was relatively slow. The first change occurred in the cotton industry, which was, however, not typical, for it was a new industry and readily adopted innovations. The woolen industry was more stubborn to change: the spinning of wool was not revolutionized until 1830, carding not until 1860, there was no power loom for weaving wool (as opposed to worsted) until 1839, and it was 1870 before weaving was wholly done on the power loom. Even in the cotton industry the power loom was not generally used until 1815, and Crompton's spinning mule was not perfected until it was made self-acting nearly fifty years after its first invention. In the spinning of fine muslins, machinery did not displace hand work until the decade 1850–60.

The second great industry to be affected by these changes was the mining industry, but here too qualifications must be made. By its very nature this had never been carried on by domestic workers, and the technological improvements which were introduced increased production without essentially altering the structure and organization of the industry. The really great expansion in the iron and steel industry did not occur until the invention in 1856 of the Bessemer process of making steel. Even the steam engine, the very soul of the new factory system, only supplemented water power until about 1850. In other words, the so-called Industrial Revolution was part of a development which began before the great inventions and which required almost a century in which to work out completely its transforming effects.

It is necessary to insist, however, that a revolution had been begun which was to have profound effects upon the production of wealth and on human relations. The really revolutionary change was the substitution of non-human for human power. So long as the motive force was human muscles and the correct performance of productive processes depended on human skill, the production of wealth was strictly limited. When, however, the forces of nature were harnessed to drive machines and tireless iron machines took over the work of flagging human hands, then limitless possibilities were opened up. That it took a long time fully to realize these opportunities does not detract from the importance of the change. A new era began with the invention of the steam engine.

Long before the steam engine was invented water power had been used for numerous industrial purposes, such as pumping water, hoisting coal, grinding grain, operating bellows, and acting as the motive force for driving machines of various kinds. But the use of water power was attended by serious disadvantages: it restricted industry to the vicinity of streams, and to regions often remote from raw materials, markets, or supplies of labor; it was, moreover, fluctuating and subject to interruption from drought in summer and ice in winter. The steam engine was essential if industry were to be freed from these restrictions and given mobility. The factory with machinery worked by steam power was the outcome of the various improvements already described.

The technical apparatus of the new industry required other features: improved transportation facilities, which were soon provided by canals and railways, the development of credit facilities to care for the expanded operations, and improved organization of the processes of production and marketing. Only the last named will be described at this point.

Organization of industry. The first steps in the closer integration of the various processes of production and marketing under the domestic system have already been described. With the invention of machinery and the steam engine the forces making for integration became stronger and industry came to be concentrated in larger establishments and under centralized control.

The first step in this process had been the establishment of central workshops, which, as we have seen, antedated the factory. This possessed two great advantages. In the first place, the workers were now under supervision and could be controlled and disciplined. Such an organization was even more necessary in the factory, where punctuality and regular continuous work were essential. In the second place, it permitted the division of labor. Adam Smith's famous account, published in 1776, of the making of pins in a workshop employing ten men shows the increase in productivity arising from the division of labor. By dividing the work and specializing on parts of the process ten men produced 48,000 pins, whereas if each had carried through the whole process "he could not have made twenty, perhaps not one pin in a day." The division of labor was the first step toward the invention of machinery. When a process was broken down into a series of simple acts, often mechanical and repetitive in character, the opportunity was presented of making a mechanical appliance or machine to take over this work. The factory rested upon the division of labor and in turn encouraged it.

The new machinery was too expensive for the domestic worker to buy. At first the spinner did buy his own machines, mortgaging them to obtain the necessary funds. But improvements were so rapid that he might be left with an obsolete machine before he finished paying for it.[7] If the machinery was driven by water or steam power its concentration in a factory became essential. But to equip a factory with machines, and to provide the new motive power required considerable capital. Even in those industries not yet transferred to the factory larger investments were required to pay the increased number of domestic workers and the larger stocks of goods required by

[7] R. Gaskell, *The Manufacturing Population of England* (London, 1833), 43.

the expanding market. The control of industry came therefore more and more into the hands of a new group of capitalists.

The new industry called for management quite as much as for capital. Increasing competition required that costs be kept down; production for a market that was international in scope necessitated knowledge and judgment; and the larger scale of industry called for men of force and driving power. These requirements were met by the rise of a new class of shrewd, hardworking, and ambitious enterprisers, many of them coming up from the ranks of the workers. Such men were Richard Arkwright, William Radcliffe, John Wilkinson, Josiah Wedgwood, and a host of others, less well known, but each contributing his part to the making over of English industry.[8]

The most striking change in the integration of industry was the transference of domestic workers into factories. When this change was effected the ownership of raw materials, tools and machines, and workplace was centered in the capitalist employer, and in his hands rested the control of the whole productive process. The large investment of capital necessitated by the new technological processes tended also to concentrate industry in the hands of men able to command capital as well as to direct its use profitably. The concentration of all the processes under a single roof, moreover, saved the cost of carrying materials and partly finished goods from one set of workers to another. The factory did not at once supplant household industry, handicraft work, or the domestic system, but it tended to become the dominant type.

Another change, closely linked with the growth of the factory system, was the increase in the size of the average plant. The articles which English industry was producing were staple goods, designed for mass consumption. For the most part their production was carried on under conditions of decreasing cost; that is, the cost per unit of a large output was less than that of a small output. As the market grew and larger quantities could be sold there was strong economic pressure to meet this additional demand by increasing the size of existing plants rather than by building additional ones. All

[8] An interesting comment on the growth of such a class is made by Professor Pirenne: "I believe that, for each period into which our economic history may be divided, there is a distinct and separate class of capitalists. In other words, the group of capitalists of a given epoch does not spring from the capitalist group of the preceding epoch. At every change in economic organization we find a breach of continuity. It is as if the capitalists who have up to that time been active recognize that they are incapable of adapting themselves to conditions which are evoked by needs hitherto unknown or which call for methods hitherto unemployed. They withdraw from the struggle and become an aristocracy. . . In their place arise new men, courageous and enterprising . . . there are as many classes of capitalists as there are epochs in economic history. That history is not an inclined plane; it resembles rather a staircase." — H. Pirenne, "The Stages in the Social History of Capitalism," in *American Historical Review*, April, 1914, 444. By permission of the Editor.

the advantages lay with the large scale producer. The size of the average plant tended therefore to become steadily larger.

The new system of industry has sometimes been called the capitalistic system because of the large use of capital involved. The origin of this new industrial capital is therefore a matter of some significance. Before the middle of the eighteenth century capital had been used primarily in agriculture and in commerce. Some of the profits from these industries were invested in manufacturing, either directly or through marriage portions. Little was obtained from the banks, for they were accustomed to finance commerce and not industry. Industry itself furnished most of the new capital from its profits, which were plowed back into the plants. James Watt, for instance, allowed himself a bare minimum for living expenses, and returned to the business conducted by him and Boulton all above this sum. Josiah Wedgwood, starting with £20, put back his earnings into his pottery works and at his death left one of the largest industries in England. When Arkwright died in 1792 his son and daughter each received £200,000 and his cotton factories were estimated to be worth as much more. In this process the capitalist employers acted, unconsciously, as social trustees of the surplus earnings of industry and used them to build up the industrial plants rather than to distribute them as dividends or in the form of higher wages. Whatever may be thought of the equity of this system of distribution, the fact remains that needed capital was produced and saved and directed into the expansion of English industry.

Growth of the factory system. From what has been said it is evident that the factory system was of slow growth. The typical town laborer in 1830 was not yet a factory operative in a large establishment fully equipped with power-driven machinery. Increasingly, however, with each passing decade, he conformed to this type and by 1870 the transition was pretty well completed in the leading industries. Except for cotton most of the industries using machines in 1830 were relatively small; the machines themselves, including the steam engines, were diminutive. Even in the great industries the very small independent producer continued to dispute the mastery of the factory. Professor Clapham [9] has gathered an array of statistics which illustrate the size of the average industrial establishment at this time. Concentration was greatest in the textile industry; here the average cotton mill employed 175 hands, silk 125, linen 93, and wool only 45. A second industry in which large establishments were to be found was iron-working. A few of the

[9] J. H. Clapham, *An Economic History of Britain*, 1820–1850 (2nd ed., London, 1930), 184-198.

greater English and Welsh works employed from 1500 to 2000 persons, but there were many small works to offset these; the average Scottish iron foundry had only about 20. A third industry which was usually organized in comparatively large units was glass-making, but for this no employment figures were available.

Although the factories remained small an increasing proportion of the workers was moving into them from domestic and handicraft industries. Thus, by 1841, it was estimated that over two-thirds of the cotton operatives were employed in factories, and about half of those in linen and silk; but only 40 per cent of the woolen operatives were to be found there. The movement went on steadily and by 1870 the factory had become the dominant type, not only in the textile industries, but in all those using power machinery. These included not only the textile industries, but also iron, machinery, small metal industries like screws and pins, pottery, and others. In those lines, however, in which hand labor was important, the factory system made little progress. Such were the clothing and leather industries, tailoring, millinery, shoemaking, watchmaking, cutlery, some metal industries, and a few others. The factory system meant direct supervision of workers concentrated in buildings equipped with power-driven machinery, and conducted on a large scale; none of these conditions was universal before 1870, though some industries had nearly reached this stage.

Textiles. During this period the textile industries progressed beyond all others, and of the various branches cotton became the leading one. Down to about 1830 the woolen industry had held first place, with cotton steadily pushing ahead of linen. In that year cotton led, with wool in third place, but by 1860 linen had been pushed out of use by cotton and had fallen far behind; cotton mills produced two-thirds of the combined products of the three textiles, whether measured by quantity or value.[10] The expansion was, however, jerky and was affected by dear food and depression at home and by civil war in the chief land of supply.

Spinning was the first branch in which machinery was adopted and by 1830 most of the processes had been mechanized. The self-actor was patented by R. Roberts in 1830, and was improved by other inventors in subsequent years. The early machines were clumsy affairs, made of wood, but metal machines were gradually introduced and by 1870 were in general use. This permitted the spinning of much finer counts and also an increase in output. The total number of spindles was increased from 10,000,000 in 1830 to 30,000,000 in 1860, and the number per operative from 71 to 122.

[10] T. Ellison, *The Cotton Trade of Great Britain* (London, 1886), 117.

With the greater use of machinery and the speeding up there was an increase in the production per operative and per spindle and a reduction in the cost.   This is shown in the following table: [11]

PRODUCTION OF COTTON YARN IN ENGLISH MILLS

Period	Annual production (1000 lbs.)	No. of operatives	Annual production per operative (lbs.)	per spindle (lbs.)	Cost of labor per lb. of yarn (d.)
1819–21	106,500	111,000	968	......	6.4
1829–31	216,500	140,000	1546	21.6	4.2
1844–46	523,300	190,000	2754	26.8	2.3
1859–61	910,000	248,000	3671	30.0	2.1

Weaving was mechanized much more slowly than spinning, and in 1870 there were still a few hand weavers fighting a losing battle against power looms.   The outcome was, however, not open to doubt for a weaver on a power loom accomplished about as much as forty good hand weavers.[12]   In 1830 there were about 55,000 power looms as against 240,000 hand looms.   By 1850 the figures were reversed, with 250,000 power looms and perhaps 40,000 hand looms.   Twenty years later there were 440,000 power looms, but the hand looms had practically disappeared.   These figures show both the expansion of the industry and the progress of its mechanization.   The rapid substitution of power for hand looms — at the rate of 10,000 a year between 1830 and 1850 — meant a continuing dislocating of the handworkers and brought great suffering upon a helpless group.   The speed of the machines was increased and yet a single operative tended two looms in 1870 as opposed to one in 1830.   Other betterments, such as the improved loom, gave further advantages to the power weaver and increased the output absolutely and per operative.

PRODUCTION OF COTTON GOODS *

Period	Production (1000 lbs.)	No. of operatives	Annual production per operative (lbs.)	per loom (lbs.)	Cost of labor per lb. (d.)
1819–21	80,620	250,000	322	....	15.5
1829–31	143,200	275,000	521	470	9.0
1844–46	348.110	210,000	1658	1234	3.5
1859–61	650,810	203,000	3206	1627	2.9
1870	991,000	449,000	2208	2252	....

* Schultze-Gavernitz, op. cit., 112.   Based on Ellison, op. cit., 66, 69.

[11] G. v. Schultze Gavernitz, *The Cotton Trade in England and on the Continent* (London, 1895), 99.   Based on T. Ellison, op. cit., 66, 68.

[12] S. Andrew, *Fifty Years of the Cotton Trade* (London, 1887), 7.

Similar changes occurred in the woolen industry, though they proceeded much more slowly. The opposition of vested interests, whether embodied in hand skill or fixed capital, as well as tradition, stubbornly resisted change. Spinning yielded first to power machinery, but the transformation was barely accomplished by 1870. It was hastened by technical improvements in the mule, by the invention of combing machinery, and by other changes. Weaving by hand held its own much more successfully in the woolen industry than in cotton; as late as 1866 the hand weavers managed about a quarter of the looms in the trade.[13] Statistics of the changes in the woolen industry during this period are scattered and not very dependable, for they were none of them official. The following table, taken from Mulhall, gives at least a picture of the rate of progress:

THE WOOLEN INDUSTRY *

Year	Factories	Operatives	Spindles	Looms
1838	1313	71,300	....	5,000
1850	1998	154,000	2,500,000	42,000
1870	2579	239,000	4,950,000	113,000

* M. G. Mulhall, *Dictionary of Statistics* (London, 1899), 602.

The changes in the textile industries were not confined solely to mechanical improvements and the substitution of power machinery for hand labor. There was a great concentration of the cotton industry in Lancashire,[14] where the presence of power — water at first and later coal — and of a moist climate offered great advantages, and of the woolen industry in Yorkshire. The localization promoted the development of a class of highly trained and efficient workers. The mills grew in size and a high degree of specialization and division of labor was introduced. This facilitated the use of improved and specialized machinery, which was substituted for human labor where possible. So rapidly did the cotton industry grow that the displaced labor was quickly absorbed and there was a steady increase in the number of operatives. In the woolen industry, however, the market for whose products was not so elastic, there was a decline after 1830 in the number of workers as machines were introduced. While the effects of these changes were tragic in the cases of many of the older handworkers, who could not rapidly readjust themselves, they did not proceed much more readily than the death-rate in these industries.

In 1830 Great Britain had a practical monopoly in the cotton in-

[13] J. H. Clapham, *An Economic History of Britain*, 1850–1885 (Cambridge, 1932), 83.
[14] Twenty per cent of the cotton operatives were in Lancashire in 1841. H. D. Fong, *Triumph of the Factory System* (Tientsin, 1930), 4.

dustry, especially in the production of yarn. In 1843 the prohibition of the export of cotton machinery was removed and a more rapid extension of mill building abroad took place. Partly by reason of this and even more because of other factors Germany and the United States expanded their cotton industries even more rapidly than did Great Britain. This country retained its pre-eminence in the woolen and worsted industries, however, just as France did in the silk industry.

Iron and steel. In the process of converting iron ore into finished products there are several steps. The first stage is the reduction of iron ore to pig iron; the second is the conversion of the pig iron into steel or refined iron; the third is the shaping of the steel into the desired forms; and still the fourth may be the fashioning of highly finished articles, like cutlery or hardware.

Progress in the process of smelting iron ore involved several improvements. First, there was a change in the fuel from charcoal to coal and coke. Quite as important were the changes in the mechanical processes and in the technique of the blast furnace. A new epoch was introduced by the invention in 1828 of the hot blast by James B. Neilson. This not only greatly increased the production of iron but it permitted the smelting of ores irreducible under earlier processes and regarded as useless; it also rendered unnecessary the coking and roasting of the coal and greatly reduced the consumption of fuel.[15] A further improvement was made in 1845 by J. P. Budd, who utilized the waste gases of the furnace to heat the blast, and thus still further economized the use of fuel. Furnaces were built higher in order to ensure a hotter and stronger draft, and with the growth in size went an increase in efficiency and output. In 1840 the better works had blast furnaces of from 40 to 60 feet in height, with a weekly output of perhaps 100 tons; by 1870 the best plants had 80-foot stacks, which produced a weekly output of about 500 tons.

Under the impetus of these changes a great increase in the production of pig iron took place. Official statistics were not gathered until 1854 and figures before that date are estimates, but at least they show the upward trend.

PRODUCTION OF PIG IRON (in tons)

Year	Output	Year	Output
1810	250,000	1850	2,250,000
1820	400,000	1860	3,830,000
1830	680,000	1870	5,960,000
1840	1,390,000		

[15] W. Fairbairn, *Iron, its History, Properties, and Processes of Manufacture* (new ed., Edinburgh, 1865), 11.

As it comes from the blast furnace the smelted product is cast iron, whose uses in this form are strictly limited. It lacks the toughness, ductility, elasticity, and all-round strength which are required of most industrial iron products. This condition is owing to the excessive amount of carbon, phosphorus, sulphur, and other impurities which are present in the metal. Iron freed from these impurities was called malleable or wrought iron. Until the middle of the century mechanical means were usually used to get rid of these elements, but during the latter half of the century several chemical methods were invented, which completely revolutionized the industry.

The earliest mechanical methods had been to hammer the pig iron, so as to beat out the impurities. A great improvement was puddling, which consisted in stirring the molten iron. These methods had been worked out by the end of the eighteenth century and no vital improvement took place for over fifty years. The puddling furnace produced a good quality of malleable iron, but not steel; the manufacture of this latter was so slow and expensive that it could be used only for edged tools and high-priced cutlery. Crucible steel cost about $250 a ton in 1850. But iron did not meet the requirements of the expanding industrial system and efforts were being made to produce steel cheaply. The story of the inventions which made this possible is dramatic.

The metallurgical problem presented in the conversion of pig iron into steel was in reality an intricate chemical problem rather than a mechanical one. Its solution was effected by Henry Bessemer, a self-taught genius, who invented all manner of things before he finally devoted himself to the making of steel. In 1856 he patented the so-called Bessemer process, though his claim to priority was disputed by the American William Kelly. The process consisted in driving a blast of cold air through a molten mass of iron in a cylindrical vessel called a converter. The oxygen of the air combined with the carbon and other impurities of the iron and set up a violent combustion which burned out the impurities in ten or fifteen minutes, leaving nearly pure iron. To produce steel, however, a certain amount of carbon is necessary. Bessemer originally planned to stop the process of decarbonization at the point where the proper amount of carbon still remained in the iron, a point which could be determined by the color of the flame. Later it was found that more accurate results could be obtained if all the elements were burned out and then the requisite amount of carbon or other ingredients was added to produce the kind of steel that was desired. A great improvement was the application by Mushet in 1857 of spiegeleisen (or cast iron rich in manganese) to the finished steel produced by the Bessemer process. It has been estimated that it took 10 days to make steel by the charcoal process, 6 hours by puddling, but only 20 minutes by the Bessemer process.

Bessemer's experiments, which were highly successful, had been made with very pure Swedish iron, but the method failed when it was applied to British ores which contained a large amount of phosphorus. Some British ores, however, were non-phosphorus-bearing, and upon these as well as imported Swedish and Spanish ores was built the new Bessemer-steel industry. From them steel could be produced at a "cost not exceeding £6 or £7 per ton." [16]

During the sixties some of the railways replaced their iron rails with steel ones, a few ships were built of steel plates, and tools, shafts, rods, steel wire, and other articles were manufactured of the new metal. But the transition from iron to steel was a slow one. British iron had an excellent reputation and builders and manufacturers clung to it. The War Office and the Admiralty were particularly obstinate in refusing to use steel for armament on ships. Vested interests, represented by a vast investment of capital and skill in puddling, opposed change. The Age of Steel came after 1870.

Meantime, at the very end of this period, another inventor developed the open hearth method of making steel, which was soon to become the rival of the Bessemer process and ultimately to displace it. This was William Siemens, who in 1865 invented the regenerative gas furnace, which was really a twofold process. In the first place the "regenerative" furnace heated the air supply, so that it reached the hearth at a very high temperature, and secondly the gas was used as fuel. By this method the consumption of fuel per ton was reduced from $2\frac{1}{2}$ tons of coke to $1\frac{1}{2}$ tons of coal. The great advantage of the open hearth system lay in the fact that the manufacturing process could be more carefully controlled as the process of conversion was much slower than in the Bessemer converter and permitted the withdrawal of samples of steel, which could be analyzed and tested during the process of manufacture. The process was still further improved by the Martin brothers, who fed scrap iron or other ingredients into the molten pig and thus obtained the desired composition of the metal. The field was divided, the Bessemer process being used for steel rails and heavy rolled sections, while the Siemens process was used for plates and forgings. The general adoption of the Siemens process, however, did not take place until after 1870, and it belongs rather to the next period. In that year the total production of steel was 240,000 tons, of which 225,000 tons were made by the Bessemer process.

[16] H. Bessemer, *Autobiography* (London, 1905), 189.

The third stage in the iron and steel industry is the shaping of the metal into the desired forms. The early process was by hammering, and for this purpose tilt or trip hammers were early used. In 1842 James Nasmyth invented the steam hammer, which was raised by the pressure of steam and fell of its own weight. Much more important was the application of grooved rollers to the shaping and rolling of iron and steel products. The principle of this dates back to the eighteenth century, but now it was more generally applied and permitted the use of iron and later steel for structural purposes. The fourth stage, that of fashioning highly finished articles out of steel by machinery, had to wait until the earlier processes had been perfected. Its history comes after 1870.

These various inventions and improvements had made Great Britain the leading producer of iron in the world. Between about 1850 and 1870 one-half of the total world product was smelted there. At the latter date Great Britain produced 5,960,000 tons of pig iron and 215,000 tons of steel, as against Germany's 1,390,000 tons of iron and 126,000 tons of steel, and France's 1,180,000 tons of iron and 84,000 tons of steel. The reasons for this pre-eminence were many, but foremost among them must be placed the genius and enterprise of the leaders in the industry. Most of the great inventions were of British origin. The economic situation encouraged the development. Demand for cheaper and better iron and steel existed in the advancing mechanical industries and especially in the railways, while an adequate supply of raw materials was guaranteed by the discovery and exploitation of great ore fields. The last of these, the Cleveland district, was opened up in 1850. At that time neither Germany, France, nor the United States had developed their important iron ore fields, which indeed were for the most part unknown. In spite of this all of these countries imposed inordinately high tariff duties on imports of steel and steel products. Hence the English output had to find its market at home or in areas outside the three countries named.

Coal. Basic for the iron and steel industry was the production of coal. "Coal commands this age," wrote Jevons in 1865 in his classic book;[17] "coal alone can command in sufficient abundance either the iron or the steam." The proof of this statement was to be found in the rapidly mounting production. Until 1854 only guesses existed as to the facts, but in that year the system of mining records was begun. The following table presents Jevons' estimates [18] for the early years and official statistics for 1854 and following:

[17] W. S. Jevons, *The Coal Question* (London, 1865. Third ed., rev. by R. W. Flux, London, 1906), viii.
[18] Op. cit., 270.

PRODUCTION OF COAL
(in tons)

Year	Output	Year	Output
1801	10,255,000	1854	64,500,000
1831	28,700,000	1861	83,600,000
1851	57,100,000	1871	117,000,000

It is impossible to say how this growing output was consumed, for no reliable information was obtained on this subject. The curve of production makes a sharp upward curve after 1831, a period marked by the development of the steam railway, of the iron and steel and other metallurgical industries, of gas production, and of domestic consumption for heating. There was indeed no branch of industry, which used power machinery, which did not make its levy. With the growth of commerce and of industrial development in other countries exports took an increasingly larger proportion, from about 2 per cent at the beginning of the cenutry to 10 per cent in 1871; a rapid increase in exports took place after the repeal of the coal export duty in 1850. But the ultimate explanation of the vast growth in coal production must be found in the industrial development of Great Britain.

In spite of the importance of coal and of the growing demand for it, coal mining remained largely a handicraft industry, almost unmodified by the technical changes which were revolutionizing other parts of the industrial structure. Pits were sunk deeper as supplies near the surface gave out, but a limit was always placed by the stage of progress of mining engineering. From about 1000 feet in 1830 a depth of 2448 feet was reached in 1869. As the shafts penetrated further the problem of ventilation became more serious, and the danger of explosion greater. Sir Humphry Davy's safety lamp of 1815 had mitigated the latter danger, but it was not effectively grappled with until better ventilation was provided. This did not come until after 1849.

A second problem was that of mechanical haulage. In some of the earlier mines the coal had been carried in baskets on the backs of women, who climbed incredible distances up ladders. Winding machines took their place, but down to 1840 they were small affairs of about 30 h.p., and the receptacles for the coal were usually wicker baskets. In the thirties a metal cage with wire rope was substituted for the baskets, with increased safety to the miners who traveled down and up and greater speed and efficiency in lifting the coal. By 1870 mechanical haulage had completely replaced the old manual methods.

Combination. Competition rather than combination was the characteristic feature of British industry during this period. The nascent industries needed freedom in which to develop new methods and processes and find wider markets. And yet almost from the beginning there were instances of industrial and commercial combinations. Integration began early in the iron and coal and pottery industries and railroads amalgamated almost from the beginning, as road and canal transport services had already done. The number of banks was being steadily reduced by amalgamation. Most of these instances were of integration or absorption rather than of co-operation of competing interests. Cases of combination of independent concerns for the purpose of controlling prices or trade were to be found among dealers rather than among manufacturers, but in the field of selling they were common. The movement was, however, not sufficiently dominant in British industry to permit fuller treatment at this point.

To emphasize unduly the slow development of the factory system and the persistence of domestic work along some lines would be to overlook the really revolutionary effect of the new system. With the expanding markets and the opportunities opening up to enterprising manufacturers there developed a new economic and social philosophy. The old restrictions on trade and industry were found to be unduly restrictive and the new capitalistic classes began to demand greater freedom in the conduct of their enterprises. For this they found welcome support in the new economic doctrines of natural liberty and *laissez faire* that were formulated by Adam Smith in his famous book, *The Wealth of Nations*, and were carried forward by the so-called classical economists. These declared that the greatest economic benefits resulted from permitting each individual to pursue his own interests without restriction of any sort. "The simple system of natural liberty," as Smith called it, would result in the best possible functioning of economic enterprise. Government activities should therefore be restricted to a minimum. Competition would stimulate individuals to put forth their best efforts and would protect commerce by holding prices down. The fallacy in such reasoning lay in not perceiving that individual self-interest did not always harmonize with the interest of society and that the weaker classes would not be able to protect themselves against predatory power. The new doctrines gained such ascendancy, however, that the latter half of the nineteenth century may well be called the period of *laissez faire*. To be sure, there never was wholly unregulated competition, for evils were checked by restrictive legislation as they showed themselves; such were the factory acts. But the underlying spirit of the new age was economic individualism, with its brilliant achievements in freeing men from economic scarcity, in spite of the costs in human suffering. The need of intelligent social control was only slowly recognized, and was not fully applied until the next century.

3. SMALL INDUSTRY IN FRANCE

Persistence of old methods. The Revolution brought a great improvement in industry with the introduction of industrial freedom. Before this time the gilds had practically controlled industry, at least in the towns. Turgot had made an unsuccessful attempt to dissolve the gilds in 1776, but after his fall they were reconstituted with an elaborate system of national control. Stringent rules as to quality and other features were set up and royal inspectors were appointed to enforce them. The gilds controlled apprenticeship and attempted to limit numbers and gain a monopoly of industry by admitting only town boys and excluding country workers. They also opposed the introduction of new methods. In 1789 the memorials from domestic workers in the country and in the suburbs of the towns demanded the abolition of the gilds, while the gild masters of the cities defended the system. Industrial freedom was, however, an essential feature of the new liberalizing spirit and on March 17, 1791, the Assembly declared that every person was free to exercise any craft or profession, provided only that he obtain the necessary license (*livret*) from the public authorities and comply with the police regulations. At the same time the system of governmental inspection was swept away. As the licenses were inexpensive and easily obtained, the gild monopoly was effectually broken. Only goldsmiths, druggists, apothecaries, and brokers were kept under gild control.

The Revolution, by establishing the principles of freedom and equality in the sphere of industry, opened the way to individual initiative, and this was further encouraged by Napoleon in his recognition of *la carrière ouverte aux talents*. Upon the ruins of the Revolution it was therefore possible to build up a new economic structure. The first great requisite, however, was security for persons and property, and this was secured by Napoleon. The next step was to revive industry along the new lines of industrial freedom. The old gild system was not restored, though those of the bakers and butchers were set up in order better to control the provisioning of the cities.

Positive measures were taken in many directions for the purpose of building up the French economic system; the Code Napoleon was drawn up, which co-ordinated the scattered laws; roads and canals were extended and improved; the monetary system was placed on the decimal basis, and the metric system of weights and measures was established;[19] invention was encouraged and rewards given to Jacquard for his silk loom, to Lenoir for his cotton machines, to Leblanc for his method of making soda, and to the chemists who extracted sugar from beets; engineering and mining schools were established; and every effort was made to extend French markets. Napoleon was no economist but he saw the importance of the new machine technique that had developed in England, and tried to develop technical improvements in France. His economic theories were based on a crude mercantilism whose fallacies underlay his misguided Continental System and a policy of high tariffs.

The downfall of Napoleon had a surprisingly slight effect on French economic development and this proceeded with little interruption along the lines he had laid down. The period of peace between 1815 and 1848 was favorable to industrial development, output increased, savings were possible, and capital accumulated. Next to Great Britain, France was the most important industrial nation in Europe, and was progressing steadily, if slowly. After 1825 England permitted the export of machinery and France was able to equip itself with improved machines. In certain fields, as in bleaching and dyeing, and in the application of chemistry to industry, France was pre-eminent.

The Revolution of 1848 brought about a temporary setback, but the next twenty years were probably the most brilliant period of French economic development. During this time industry made rapid strides, aided by an extended railway system and an improved banking and credit organization. Cheapened transportation was probably more effective in reducing costs of production than were improved productive methods. Through this influence the isolation of small industrial centers was broken down and they were exposed to international competition. The Paris Exposition of 1855 presented to the world a vast array of French products, showing technical efficiency as well as artistry and careful workmanship. Under the liberal commercial policy of the sixties foreign trade grew and industry expanded to provide the wares of commerce.

A clearer idea of the progress of French industry may be obtained if the development of particular lines is traced; for this purpose the two most important branches may be selected, namely, textiles, the

[19] "At the end of the eighteenth century, when France undertook needed reforms, there were still in Europe 391 different units of weight corresponding to the term pound, 370 of which were superseded by the kilogram, while the word foot applied to 282 units of length. . . In 1797 the new system of weights and measures was adopted with the meter as the fundamental unit of length and the franc as the unit of coinage. . . In 1840 other systems were outlawed." — *Encyclopedia of the Social Sciences,* XV, 390. By permission of the publishers, The Macmillan Company, New York.

outstanding consumption goods industry, and iron and steel, the most important capital goods industry.

Textile industry.   The textile industry is one of the oldest in history, and the *woolen* industry was one of the earliest divisions. It had long existed in France and was based on native wool of rather poor quality.   Merino sheep were imported from Spain in the late eighteenth century and by 1827 supplies of fine wool were almost adequate to domestic needs; in that year only 17.6 million pounds were imported.   Sheep raising was, however, a declining industry in France and after 1835 imports of foreign wool steadily increased. Improvements in marine and railway transportation after 1850 brought in large supplies from Australia and Argentina, which were still further stimulated by the free admission of wool under the tariff of 1860.   The expanding industry had outgrown the inadequate domestic clip.

The mechanization of the industry and the introduction of the factory system went forward slowly.   The French woolen industry rested upon well-established traditions.   On the eve of the Revolution it was organized on the putting-out system, under which the various processes were carried out by domestic workers in their homes, the finished goods being supplied to the capitalist employer, who supplied the raw materials and sometimes the implements, and paid for the products by the piece.   Spinning was widely dispersed and was carried on in most country homes; weaving was scarcely less so, though it was mostly in the hands of small independent masters working in their own workshops.   The processes, but not the organization of the industry, were changed between 1792 and 1815 by the use of machinery.[20]   Jennies on the Hargreaves model, but adapted to the use of wool, were introduced into France soon after their invention in England.   These machines could be used by home workers in their cottages, and they therefore continued the tendency to dispersion.   Mechanization proceeded rapidly after 1815, but at uneven rates for different branches; it was more rapid in spinning than in weaving.   By the middle of the century the jenny had been replaced by the mule; as this latter machine cost more and required power, there was a tendency, with its steady spread, toward concentration of the industry in factories.

Various factors in France prevented the rapid introduction early in the century of the new machinery which was transforming English industry.   Protected by high tariffs from foreign competition, and with an assured domestic market, the manufacturers did not feel the spur of competition and were not inclined to embark on new methods.   There was a tendency to remain in the old ruts.   This

[20] Charles Ballot, *Introduction du machinisme dans l'industrie française* (Paris, 1923), 35.

conservative attitude was shared by the general public and especially by the workers. Among the latter there were riots and smashing of machines several times in the early twenties.

About 1830 changes began in the textile industry as a whole, but especially in the woolen industry. The consumption of wool more than doubled in the next twenty years, and the home workers began to move into the factories, especially the spinners. The work of preparing the wool for spinning the yarn was also handed over to machines. Carding for the manufacture of woolens had been a machine operation since the beginning of the century, but the combing of wool for the worsted industry was performed by hand until Josué Heilman invented an improved wool-combing machine in 1845. The worsted industry in France was revolutionized by this invention; the quantity of combed wool was increased fifty per cent, the quality was improved, and at the same time the cost was cut in half. By 1870 all yarn, whether carded or combed, was spun by machinery.

Weaving remained primarily a hand industry until 1860, when British competition, admitted by the commercial treaty of that year, forced French manufacturers to adopt improved methods. Fancy cloths which were subject to changes in fashion and very fine ones like muslins could still be made on hand looms, but for the manufacture of plain cloths the victory of the power loom was assured. A certain concentration of different branches of the industry in particular localities had meantime worked itself out. Coarse woolen cloth was produced in Elbeuf, Carcassonne, and Lodève, fine cloths in Louviers and Sedan, army cloth was turned out in Mazamet.

The *cotton* industry was already well developed before the Revolution, and cloths of pure cotton, obtained from the Levant, or of cotton mixed with wool, flax, or silk were produced. Its growth followed the same lines as the woolen industry, but it suffered from competition of the more advanced English production, though the Hargreaves spinning jenny was introduced within a few years after its invention. This machine was simple and inexpensive and could be used in the cottages of the domestic workers; it therefore met with little opposition. Quite otherwise was it with Arkwright's water frame and Crompton's mule, for these were expensive and required power and could consequently be set up only in mills; as a result they gained ground only slowly. The industry received a great impetus when Napoleon's Continental blockade prevented British imports, though the heavy duties laid on imported cotton in 1806 and 1810 and the British control of the seas interfered with the necessary imports of raw cotton.

The establishment of factories was made easier by the purchase at low prices of the secularized monastery buildings. Cheap labor in the persons of women and children could be had in abundance. Only capital was difficult to get because of its diversion to the needs of the state and the poor organization of the money market. The use of machinery in spinning was firmly established during the Napoleonic regime, and in a few instances large enterprises developed such as the factories of Richard Lenoir which in 1810 employed 14,000 workers. The center of the industry was in upper Normandy, the neighborhood of Paris, and Alsace (especially Mulhouse). The location was determined in part by costs of transportation of the imported raw material, and in part by the availability of power, which at this time was water power. A widespread home spinning industry also existed in the country districts, and weaving was as yet done entirely by hand. The number of spindles increased from 3,500,000 in 1845 to 6,000,000 in 1867; the loss of Alsace reduced the number to 4,500,000 in 1871.

Between 1815 and 1860 heavy duties were imposed on imports of foreign yarn, and the importation of foreign cloth was prohibited. Behind this tariff wall the French cotton industry prospered, though progress was undoubtedly slower than it would have been if the industry had been compelled to meet British competition. Hand spinning had nearly disappeared by 1820, and thereafter the mills grew steadily larger and were equipped with improved machinery. In 1850 the self-acting mule was introduced from England and by 1860 had passed the older type of mule-jennies in numbers. Since the cost of installing these was very high their increase points to the growth of concentrated capitalistic industry. And this tendency was accentuated by the crisis resulting from the cutting off of American cotton during the Civil War in the United States (1861–65), during which the weaker mills disappeared and the better ones grew larger. This was in the cities, for in the country many small mills persisted, using water power.

Mechanical weaving developed more slowly. The power loom seems to have been introduced from England in the twenties, but it spread slowly until the fifties when its adoption was more rapid; by 1860 mechanical weaving was supreme in Alsace, the most important center of the cotton industry. Even here, however, the small mill held its own, for it had the advantage of cheap power, so long as it used water power, and of cheap labor, especially in those regions where work in the mills could be combined with agriculture. The number of power looms grew from 31,000 in 1848 to 80,000 in 1865; in 1871 it was down to 55,000 owing to the cession of Alsace.

The commercial treaty of 1860, which lowered the duties on imported machinery, led to the bringing in of improved machines from

England, both in spinning and in weaving. But even more important was the introduction of competition and the breaking down of the monopoly behind which French cotton manufacturers had maintained themselves. By 1870 the cotton industry had recovered from the shortage of American supplies of raw cotton and was on a fairly firm basis. It was never able to rival the British industry, however, owing to a certain technical inferiority and to high costs, both in raw material, in power, and in capital.

The *silk* industry had rested upon the luxury demand of an extravagant court during the eighteenth century. Although it suffered under the Revolution it revived under Napoleon as a result of a renewal of official luxury and of a widened market in Central Europe that extended far beyond the old boundaries. The raising of silk worms was also carried on in France but the home production of raw silk could not keep pace with the increasing demand. In 1853, when the maximum production was attained, half the raw silk used was imported from Italy. In that very year the silk worms were attacked by a disease (pébrine or oïdium) which greatly reduced production and from which the industry never fully recovered. With improvements in ocean transportation increasing competition from Chinese and Japanese silk followed, but the silk manufacturing industry profited from the enlarged supply. About 1860 the manufacturers had to face a new danger: changes in fashion favored cheaper silks or mixed fabrics made by mixing silk with cotton or other fibers instead of pure silks of fine quality in which the French were pre-eminent. British manufacturers were producing mixed silk goods and offered effective competition in this line. Throughout their history both the silk raising and the silk manufacturing industries were exposed to a series of mischances which made them fluctuating and hazardous.

The strength of the silk industry lay in the careful and artistic workmanship of French artisans. Owing to the risks and the considerable amount of capital required the business was in the hands of so-called manufacturers, who bought the raw silk, had it spun, and disposed of the finished wares. The weaving was done by small masters who owned their own looms and worked in their homes on orders and on designs furnished by the manufacturers. This was the familiar putting-out system. Power machinery never played so important a part in this as in the other textile industries. There was nevertheless a continuous development along this line.

Silk throwing, that is twisting the fibers into yarn strong enough to withstand the strain of weaving, had been performed by machines driven by water power even in the eighteenth century; this now made progress. Spinning, however, remained in large part a hand industry carried on in the homes of the workers. Weaving was revolutionized by the invention by Jacquard in 1805 of a silk power loom, which was later perfected. By 1812 there were 12,000 Jacquard looms in operation and in 1835 over 35,000; but they were not driven by water power until the forties and did not come into general use until about 1850. Steam power does not seem to have been applied for another decade. Only those processes which required power machinery were carried on in factories, but the number of these grew steadily; the power was derived primarily from water until the end of this period. With the spread of machine methods and the cheapening of prices, particularly of mixed goods, silk became available to the masses. The seat of the industry was Lyons.

Those branches of the textile industry, like the *linen* industry, which found their market principally in foreign countries, suffered severely under the blockade during the Napoleonic wars. It was also hurt by the competition of the artificially fostered wool industry. By 1811 the production was only half what it had been in 1789. Technical difficulties in machine spinning kept the industry overwhelmingly a house industry as late as 1850. Not until 1838 was a power loom for linen invented. The real reason for the decline of the industry was, however, not its mechanical backwardness, but the irresistible competition of the cheaper cotton goods and the changes in fashion. Saint Quentin was the center of this branch.

Iron and steel industry. A better test than textiles of industrial progress in the modern age is to be found in the coal and the iron and steel industries, and to these we may now turn.

At the beginning of the nineteenth century only two fields of France's inconsiderable coal resources had been discovered and were being exploited. These were the Valenciennes field in the extreme northeast, near the border of Belgium, of whose more valuable holdings it is only an extension, and the Loire field between Lyons and St. Etienne. Of the two the latter showed more activity, its production being double that of the other. But the whole industry was limited by lack of convenient markets, high costs of transportation, the smallness of undertakings which consumed the coal, and especially the character of the coal deposits. In the Valenciennes district only about a dozen seams were thick enough to be worked, and even they seldom exceeded 2 feet 4 inches. The Loire basin contained seams varying from 3 to 18 feet in thickness, but irregular in form. In 1789 the total output had been 700,000 tons; in 1815 it was about 880,000 tons. After this date it expanded fairly rapidly, attaining an output of 1,774,000 tons in 1828, of 5,153,000 in 1847, and of 13,180,000 in 1870; but this was only slightly more than two-thirds of the domestic consumption, which was much less than that of either Greater Britain or Germany. In addition France imported at the latter date 5,650,000 tons. Production was always inadequate for home needs.

The iron and steel industry may be separated into its two main branches, first, the primary work of smelting iron ore and the recovery of crude iron, and second, that of working up the crude iron into finished and semi-finished products for further processing.

At the beginning of the century iron was smelted in hundreds of little charcoal furnaces which were situated in the neighborhood of scattered ore deposits, and also near forests, which furnished the fuel. The lack of good transportation forced the ironmasters to use fuel that was close at hand. But the primitive methods consumed too much fuel to make the product available for general use. Experiments were made with coal and coke, notably at Le Creusot, before 1800, but the use of these fuels spread very gradually. Until 1821 iron was smelted almost exclusively with wood charcoal, and the number of small charcoal furnaces continued to increase until 1839 when they numbered 445; after this they fell off. The number of coke furnaces meanwhile increased from 29 in 1830 to 106 in 1846, and 147 in 1865. It is not possible to say exactly how the production of pig iron was divided between these two types of blast furnaces, but it has been estimated that at the last date given nearly three fifths was still smelted by charcoal. Although the coke furnaces numbered only about one-fifth of all, they were larger and better equipped and turned out proportionately more.

The industry operated, however, under serious disabilities. A law of 1830, forbidding ironmasters to own coal mines, in order to prevent monopoly, prevented efficient organization. Heavy taxes and transportation charges also raised the cost of coal to the ironmaster. The French iron industry always suffered from the wide separation of iron and coal, which in Britain lay so conveniently near each other. In the middle of the century the French iron industry ranked second to that of England, but it was far behind its insular rival. The production of pig iron grew very slowly, from 60,000 tons in 1800 to 220,000 in 1830, 570,000 in 1850, and 1,180,000 in 1870; at the last date British production was 5,960,000 tons. France, however, remained ahead of the United States until 1866 and of Germany until 1868. Marshall[21] estimated that the price of a ton of pig iron was $18 in Glasgow and $23 in France. Such a difference, maintained only by a high protective tariff, placed a heavy burden on the national economy, and one that bore with especial severity on the building of railroads, which began about this time.

[21] F. Marshall, *Population and Trade in France in 1861–62* (London, 1863), 192.

The production of finished iron and steel goods kept pace with the pig iron industry. Rolling mills were greatly improved, the output of rolled plates doubling between 1834 and 1844. Building iron was turned out and iron bridges built, but these latter suffered from the preference given to stone bridges. In 1840 a steam hammer was set up in Rive-de-Gier, the weight of which, originally 550 pounds, was soon increased to one ton. This invention was of especial significance for the armament industry. But the branch of the iron and steel industry which best measures the mechanical progress of a people is the manufacture of machinery. The early textile machinery — the first to be developed — was made of wood with metal fittings, both in England and on the continent. These early machines were very simple, many of them driven by hand and the others by water power. The real test was the construction of all-metal machines and the building of machinery to make these machines. Down to the middle of the century French manufacturers had made indifferent progress along these lines and were far behind the British. The explanation was to be found in the higher cost of iron in France, in the higher cost of fuel, greater transportation charges to bring the iron and coal together, inferior equipment of the plants, and the technical inferiority of French labor. The industry was reorganized and improved in the fifties and an English observer,[22] writing in 1862, was able to speak of the great success and perfection of the manufacturing and construction branches.

The greatest progress was made in the installation of improved rolling machinery, which turned out rolled and wrought iron plates, bars, angles, and other parts at prices to compete with imported British products. In spite of expensive raw materials, French ironmasters were able to meet domestic requirements for engines, locomotives, bridges, and similar constructions. Rails were, however, imported from England, as was spinning and weaving machinery, in the production of which the French were backward. In the manufacture of steel they were at a serious disadvantage, for French iron ore contained a great deal of phosphorus, and was therefore not adapted to the Bessemer process. This consequently made slow progress in France until the Siemens-Martin process made it possible to use phosphoric iron in a converter. In 1869 France produced 110,000 tons of Bessemer steel, more than any other country except Britain, but the great expansion along this line came later.

The factory system. The factory system may be said to have developed in France between 1830 and 1848, but it did not dominate

[22] F. Marshall, op. cit., 199.

industry at any time down to 1870. There was a gradual shift from house industry to factory production in most lines, but it progressed at unequal speed in the different branches and was complete in none. Without attempting to define the term factory, the tendency to large scale undertakings using power driven machinery can be gauged by noting the number of employees, the extent of mechanization, and the amount of power.

The census of 1851 throws light on the size of the average establishment. The "great industry," which included textiles, iron and steel, mining, and some other manufacturing industries, claimed 1,331,260 and the domestic industries 4,713,026. The former group comprised 124,133 employers and 1,207,127 workers; that is to say, each "great" establishment had about 10 employees. The domestic group comprised 1,548,334 masters and 3,164,692 journeymen, apprentices, and women workers, or an average of about 2 for each master. The typical concern was therefore a small shop, and even the average so-called large establishment was small compared with standards of today. Only the textile industry showed a considerable degree of capitalistic organization: the average number of workers in silk and cotton establishments was over 100, and in wool 60.

A second test is the extent of mechanization. If this be applied to the most developed industry, that of textiles, the slow progress of the industrial revolution in France is again illustrated. The victory of machine over hand methods occurred first in the wool industry. House spinning had already disappeared in Normandy in the thirties. By 1840 the prefect of the lower Seine could write: "The displacement of hand weavers by machines makes thousands unemployed. The country weavers, who earn barely 1 franc or 1.25 francs daily, disappear more and more." In cotton hand spinning had nearly disappeared by 1820, but mechanical weaving had barely won a belated victory over hand looms by 1870. In the silk industry house spinning declined slowly, and the hand weavers persisted only by accepting lower wages. The linen industry remained a domestic hand industry until the middle of the century. In all branches a domestic industry survived in the mountainous and remote regions to the end of this period. There was evidently no such sweeping victory of the large scale highly mechanized factory over the hand processes of the domestic industry in France as had occurred in Britain.

The use of power in industry is an extremely difficult test to apply because of the lack of information. The following table gives such statistics as are available:

Year	Number of steam engines	Total horse power
1815	15	....
1820	65	....
1830	625	10,000
1840	2,591	34,350
1850	5,322	66,642
1860	14,936	180,555
1869	26,221	320,447

Unfortunately it is not possible to say what proportion of these engines were used in industry and what in other lines. The engines listed in 1820 were all used in mining and probably all of those in 1815. Statistics published in 1845 for the years immediately preceding listed 22,500 water installations, with a total power output probably two and a half times as great as that of the steam engines. Not until after 1857 did steam power pass water power. The average horse power per steam-driven machine averaged between 10 and 15 during practically all this period. From these various facts the conclusion is irresistible that the establishments using these engines must have been small affairs. It is evident that the factory system had not displaced the innumerable small artistic industries which were still carried on in little workshops.

4. HANDWORK IN GERMANY

Primitive conditions. German industry in 1800 was almost as medieval as German agriculture, and for much the same reasons. Production of goods by a distinct class of artisans for sale in a market had not proceeded very far. Three-fourths of the people lived in the country, and these rural households were nearly, if not entirely, self-sufficing. Most necessaries were made in the home. Not only was food sufficient for the family needs raised on the land of the peasant or larger proprietor, but also raw materials for clothing and other necessities. Clothing was made of home-grown flax and wool, which was carded, spun, woven, and often dyed at home. The itinerant tailor was called in only to make the cloth into garments. Soap and candles were made, leather was tanned, feathers for bedding were pulled from the geese, and beer was brewed by the rural household. Most of the furniture was home-made, and even the house, constructed of wood with a thatched roof, was built by the owner with the help of neighbors. Only the paid thatcher would be called upon to thatch the roof, and the mason to put up the chimney and build the fireplace. If the skill of the house father was insufficient to work over the home-grown raw material, he called a handworker into the house as a wage-worker, as the tailor, cobbler, or cabinet maker. Only in those cases where special appliances were needed was it necessary to go outside the home, as for blacksmithing or grinding grain. For an American reader this is highly reminiscent of colonial or frontier conditions in the United States, but it persisted in Germany until the middle of the nineteenth century.

Even in the towns the households preserved a rural character and were largely self-sufficing. Every family, from handworker to nobility, had its own cattle and swine. The horn of the shepherd called the city cows daily to the herd, which during the day pastured on the common meadows. It is estimated that in Prussian towns in 1802 there were over 63,000 barns. Sombart states that butcher shops were almost unknown because people killed and salted their own meat. In Berlin, the only large city in Germany, the houses on the principal streets had great gardens behind where fruits and vegetables were cultivated.

Industry as such, that is the production of goods or the sale of specialized craftsmanship in the market, was confined principally to the towns, in which a quarter of the population lived. It is true that the larger estates had their own smiths, millers, saddlers, and builders, but these artisans were few in number and had to receive permission from the state government to work there, and even then remained under gild regulations. Industry cannot be treated as a unit, however, for various branches were differently organized and were confronted with their own special problems. Three main forms may be distinguished, namely handwork, domestic industry, and manufacturing in factories or under the factory system.

Handwork. Handwork was the basis of practically all industrial production in 1800, but it was technically crude and backward. Prior to 1806 a town artisan was prohibited from plying his trade in the country districts. Although this restriction was abolished by Stein's Edict of Emancipation in that year, little economic change followed this introduction of industrial freedom. Workers were organized in gilds which were narrow and petty and were still run on medieval lines. They were associations of masters who controlled admission to the gild and also administered municipal police regulations and industrial legislation. They therefore exercised compulsory powers and practically controlled the town government. The gilds in Germany, where there was no strong central government to hold them in check, as there was in France and England, had become arbitrary and largely irresponsible. They limited the number of members in a trade, they imposed difficult examinations upon journeymen in order to keep the number of masters small, and they endeavored to restrict their privileges to a close corporation of gild masters. The power of the old gild constitution rested firmly on two points, compulsory membership in the gild and proof of capacity by an examination.

The worst of these abuses were remedied in Prussia in 1810 when the principle of industrial freedom (*Gewerbefreiheit*) was introduced. The gilds were not abolished, but their exclusive monopoly position was destroyed. The other states followed this example slowly. In Wurtemberg reform began in 1828, but for another quarter century a man in that state was not free to practice any trade he pleased. In Bavaria the first serious attempt at reform was made in 1848, but was not completed until 1868. Only in the southwest, where the whole gild system was swept away by the enlightened French administration prior to 1815, did real industrial freedom exist during this period. In one respect, however, the principle of industrial freedom was fully applied, and this was to the journeyman during his *Wanderjahre*. "About 1820 a wandering journeyman, provided only with the permit of his local official, could seek work in the whole of Germany, without any one bothering himself about his gild or non-gild connections." [23] In other respects work was still closely regulated by the gilds, which were recognized as the only existing agency for educating young workers along vocational lines. Backward as they undoubtedly were, the gilds seem to have fitted into the general economic and social organization of the country without serious friction, and were probably not felt to be unduly burdensome.

An explanation of this fact is to be found in the primitive industrial system. Because of the large number of separate states — some 360 in 1800 and 38 in 1806, after Napoleon's reforms — each with its tariff barriers, poor and expensive means of transportation, poverty and low purchasing power of the mass of people, and other considerations, the market was small and restricted. The unit of production was frequently a master working alone, or a master with a single journeyman or apprentice. Thus in Prussia in 1816 there were only 56 workers for each 100 masters. Nearly half the tailors and hatters worked alone; the tanners averaged one assistant each, and the dyers two.[24] Further light is thrown on the picture if we note the size of the towns in which these masters carried on their work. Of the 1016 so-called towns in Germany in 1802 only 18 had more than 10,000 inhabitants. The master craftsmen in the smaller places were merely jobbing workmen, most of whom worked directly for the

[23] Sartorius von Waltershausen, *Deutsche Wirtschaftsgeschichte, 1815–1914* (Jena, 1923), 22.
[24] K. F. W. Dieterici, *Der Volkswohlstand im Preussischen Staate* (Berlin, 1846), 353.

purchaser of his services, and with antiquated tools and methods.

In spite of his unprogressiveness the small handworker maintained his economic position fairly well until the middle of the century; after this he was threatened by the enlargement of the market through railroads and by the rise of factories. The following table shows the situation for selected years in Prussia, for which alone statistics are available, but which may be accepted as fairly typical of Germany:

SMALL INDUSTRY IN PRUSSIA, 1816–1861 *

Year	Number of masters	Number of helpers	Total	Percentage of total population in small industries	Number of apprentices and journeymen to 100 masters
1816	258,830	145,459	404,289	11.6	56.2
1825	315,118	187,176	502,294	12.0	59.4
1834	356,515	215,650	572,165	12.4	60.5
1843	408,825	311,458	720,283	12.8	76.2
1852	553,107	447,502	1,000,609	16.1	80.9
1861	534,556	558,321	1,092,877	14.9	104.4

* Gustav Schmoller, *Zur Geschichte der deutschen Kleingewerbe im* 19. *Jahrhundert* (Halle, 1870), 65, 331. The fifth column includes the families of the handworkers as well as the workers.

The first quarter of the nineteenth century was not favorable for economic development. The great losses and disturbances of the Napoleonic wars, the famine of 1816–17, and the agricultural crisis of 1820–25, all held back progress. By 1830 these obstacles had been overcome and economic conditions began to improve. The growth in the number of handworkers reflects these changes. Between 1816 and 1834 there was practical stability: although the number of small masters and their helpers increased it kept fairly even with the growth of population. During the twenties the new industrial freedom conferred by Stein gave to the master a chance to spread out and hire more workers, to the journeyman an opportunity to set up his own business, and to each of them the possibility of opening a store for the sale of his products. By the thirties the vacant spots were pretty well filled and it was not so easy to establish an independent business. Some trades went forward and some back. Those that were adversely affected by the competition of large industry fell off, as the soap makers, the glove and hat makers, pottery and stone workers. Those, on the other hand, who found employment in the larger industries, as mechanics, locksmiths, and stone grinders, increased. A third group, which was little affected by the development of capitalistic industry, as bakers, shoemakers, and butchers, did not change much.

The first crisis in German handwork began in 1840, after the commercial crisis of 1839. The gild organization was breaking down; apprentices and journeymen did not wish to follow the old rules of training and service. During the forties and fifties railroad building began, internal trade barriers were removed, markets were widened, international relationships grew, and larger enterprises with better technique, more capital, and abler management came into being. Most of these changes spelled disaster to the small industry, but nevertheless the number of small masters grew. Soon there were too many and they could not all keep busy. The masters complained of the encroachments of the developing factories, and especially of the putting-out system, which was reducing many of them to the status of wage-earning piece-workers. The Prussian government endeavored to meet this situation by the industrial ordinance of 1845, which restored some of their privileges to the gilds; in some forty-two industries the right of a master to have apprentices was made dependent upon his possession of a certificate of competence. But this was insufficient to safeguard the hand-workers.

Their plight is sufficiently disclosed by an extraordinary series of demands made by a congress of German handworkers in Hamburg on June 2, 1848: [25] Limitation of the number of masters in one place, prohibition of peddling, prohibition of association with non-gild members, subjection of all handwork of factories to the gild master of the place, limitation of gild members to one industry, allocation of small trades in hand-made wares to the gild masters, prohibition of the letting of public works to the lowest bidder and distribution of these among the masters by an industrial council, prohibition of public auction of new wares, prohibition of keeping more than two apprentices, taxation of factories for the benefit of handwork, and finally compulsory training of apprentices and the passing of a theoretical and a practical examination.

The tailors' congress also passed resolutions in which they urged the abolition of stores, the limitation of women's work, and the prohibition of the importation of foreign-made clothing.

The complaints of the gilds boiled down to the fact that one could become a master and open a business too easily. The principle of industrial freedom was challenged, and more regulation was demanded. The so-called "handicraft Parliament" yielded to this

[25] See *Handwörterbuch der Staatswissenschaften*, s.v. "Handwerk."

shortsighted and selfish class interest and passed the reactionary ordinance of February 7, 1849. This act prescribed again fixed limits for the more important industries, and for their practice required membership in a gild after proof of ability before the gild or through an examining committee. A rigid course of training as apprentice or journeyman was prescribed; master workmen only could use apprentices or journeymen in technical work; and these could engage in handwork only with a master or with a factory owner. If the conduct of a store for retail or hand-made wares was held disadvantageous for a place, the local ordinances could restrict its conduct to masters.

These regulations held down the number of masters, which fell off considerably between 1852 and 1861, but they laid chains on the handworkers, and limited the number of small trades, without interfering with the large industry or the stores, the regulations concerning which were not enforced. The provision for examinations seems also to have been liberally interpreted. On the other hand, the gilds arranged for the better education of the apprentices — continuation schools and vocational schools, often supported by the state, appeared; and free associations, such as trade organizations, credit unions, workmen's education unions, became frequent.

The master had meantime sunk to a lower position in the industrial organization. He became increasingly dependent on the merchants or dealers (*Verleger*), who had the right after 1810 to accept orders for handwork or repairs as well as to sell finished goods. The customer who wished a coat or a pair of shoes did not need to go to a tailor or shoemaker; he could go to the dealer in clothing or shoes, and if he did not find what he wanted in stock, he could order it from the merchant. The merchant had the goods made, not in his own shop, but by a handworker of the city who did not have a sufficient clientele of his own and was therefore willing to work cheaply for the merchants. In many of the cities, especially in Berlin, this organization of industry developed rapidly. A greater part of the handworkers under this system were only nominally independent. Often the handworkers were nothing but home-working wage-earners employed by a dealer, and who, wholly dependent upon this single employer, were mercilessly exploited by him.

Changes in technique also lessened the domain of former handworkers, as of cabinet makers, coopers, tinkers, and rope makers, for wooden and other utensils were replaced by zinc, copper, bronze, porcelain, and similar materials; changes in fashion also, as in wearing wigs, destroyed the trades of still others.

House industry. House or domestic industry was the second form of organization of German industry during this period. This was scattered over the whole country, wherever raw materials of wood, clay, metal, and fibers were to be found, although here and there a concentration occurred in certain favored regions, as spinning and weaving in Saxony and Silesia. It is certainly erroneous to regard household industry as a middle stage between handwork and the factory, and to speak of the successive reduction of the handwork master first to domestic worker and later to dependent factory wage-earner. The single illustration of this is the textile industry. In other industries the three systems existed side by side as independent forms, each having its unique place. The house industry prevailed where demand was irregular or subject to change, as in embroidery, wood carving, leather and paper industries, and similar lines. It was practiced partly in the cities and partly in the country, as in middle and south Germany, while in Silesia and Saxony it was more characteristic of the mountainous regions, and gave employment to spinners, weavers, nail-, key-, and knife-smiths, wood carvers, straw plaiters, watchmakers, potters, and many others. Mining was carried on in the mountains and little iron furnaces were conducted near the forests, since the ore was still smelted by charcoal.

Similar to the strict control of the gilds there existed also for house industry at the beginning of the century governmental regulations which were to care for the technical and industrial supervision of the many scattered workers and for the satisfactory quality of the wares, and also to protect the home workers against exploitation. After the introduction of the principle of industrial freedom, however, the house workers were exposed to new forces of competition and organization, especially to the advancing division of labor and the increasing use of expensive machines by the developing factories. The merchant capitalists sought to organize them in those lines where decentralization did not prove too much of a handicap, and a vast amount of spinning and weaving was done under their leadership in the cottages of the country districts. These home workers often owned their looms and other appliances and usually bought their own raw material. The goods thus produced were sold by the merchants in the towns, and considerable quantities were exported. But the variety in lines of production, the technical backwardness of the house workers, and the lack of capital proved almost insurmountable obstacles. The home workers were able to maintain their position somewhat only within certain restricted lines of industry, and in some larger cities and rural districts. Here they were gradually reduced to the status of sweated wage-workers for the merchant capitalists, or, like the poor weavers of Silesia, carried on a protracted but hopeless struggle against the factory system. The industrial position of these domestic workers can be best traced in the textile and metal-working industries.

The stronghold of the domestic system was the linen industry, which was carried on almost exclusively as a by-industry by peasants who at the same time cultivated their land. The linen industry had held high rank in the eighteenth century and had received royal support. Everywhere the peasants grew their own flax and hemp, which they always spun and frequently wove at home. Dyes were often raised and the cloth was dyed by the peasant, and made into garments by the housewife. Only for the more difficult processes, like "heckling" and sometimes dyeing, were the services of a professional craftsman utilized. In the case of outer clothing, beyond the skill of the housewife, the itinerant tailor would come to the house, where, in return for his board and a small wage, he would dress and patch up the whole family. All the statistics of this industry tell the same story, namely the persistence of the domestic system of manufacture. In Prussia in 1831, out of a total of 252,000 linen looms, only 35,500 belonged to linen weavers who depended exclusively upon weaving for their livelihood. The others belonged to peasants or village weavers who worked them in their spare time, not required for the cultivation of their land.[26] Even as late as 1855, out of some 46,000 looms, only 3000 were in factories.[27]

The linen industry declined in the nineteenth century. Partly responsible was the adherence to antiquated hand methods both in spinning and weaving. The situation was aggravated by a lack of raw materials, as farmers refused to plant flax, for which there was no longer a steady demand. The industry was adversely affected by the removal of internal trade barriers under the Zollverein and the greater freedom of trade which exposed it to new competition. This was met by adding cotton to the linen and producing poorer and shoddy wares. The hand weavers of Silesia were reduced to destitution, which was aggravated by the hunger typhus of 1846 and 1847 resulting from bad harvests. The old linen hand spinning and weaving were also depressed by the new machine industry, though this remained backward. In 1839 there were only 11 machine spinning establishments in all Prussia.

The woolen industry had its chief seat in southwestern Germany. The spinning was primarily a domestic industry, and, like linen spinning, was carried on largely by peasant families in their homes. But weaving was more professional and tended to become more capitalistic as more expensive looms were introduced. This was in

[26] J. H. Clapham, op. cit., 92.
[27] H. Cunow, *Allgemeine Wirtschaftsgeschichte*. 4 Bde. (Berlin, 1926–31), IV, 82.

the hands of gild masters and was usually located in the towns. But, as already pointed out, the masters became more and more dependent on the merchant capitalist, both for supplies of yarn and for the sale of their products, until they came to be virtually only piece workers, earning a scanty wage. As the market grew their dependence increased. By the end of the thirties German woolen goods were being exported to Switzerland, Italy, Turkey, the United States, and even penetrated to the highly protected markets of Belgium. It remained a small scale industry and was exposed to the competition of the English machine-made products.

The cotton industry was located principally in Saxony and the Rhenish provinces, though it was also to be found in Prussia. It was handicapped by heavy costs of transportation of the imported raw material, which were much higher than those paid by British manufacturers. As a consequence, most of the yarn was imported, chiefly from England, and the Germans confined themselves largely to cotton weaving. The silk industry was also dependent upon imported raw material, which was drawn from Italy and Austria. The chief center of silk manufacture was Crefeld. As a result of the dependence of the workers on merchant capitalists for their yarn and for the marketing of their products, these industries were highly organized. But the organization did not take the form so much of the factory system as of the *Verleger* or putting-out system. The workers were trained handicraftsmen, but they worked for an entrepreneur and were mere wage-earners.

An idea of the extent to which the various branches of the textile spinning industry were carried on in the home or the factory about 1845 may be gained from the following table:

NUMBER OF SPINDLES, 1845 *

Industry	Total number of spindles	Number of spindles in large mills
Cotton	150,000	130,000
Wool	450,000	140,000
Linen	28,000	26,000

* Banfield, op. cit., II, 233.

From these figures it would appear that linen and cotton spinning was carried on for the most part in factories, but that the wool-spinning industry was still largely in the hands of domestic workers. Weaving remained a small industry, carried on by hand labor, for a much longer time than did spinning. This is shown in the following tabulation for 1855:

NUMBER OF LOOMS, 1855 *

Industry	In small home-industrial establishments	In factories
Silk weaving	13,800	15,340
Cotton weaving	50,680	18,888
Wool weaving	12,617	15,755
Linen weaving	43,129	3,268

* H. Cunow, op. cit., IV, 82.

From this it is clear that linen weaving had remained almost exclusively a domestic industry, that silk and wool were passing out of the home into the factory, and that cotton weaving was still largely carried on in small establishments.

Iron and steel. Of greater importance than the textiles in measuring the industrialization of Germany during this period are those industries which yield fuel and metals. The same persistence of small scale production is seen in them. Wood was used at the beginning of the nineteenth century not only for domestic use, but also for industrial purposes. After the middle of the thirties the depletion of the forest resources forced a larger use of coal. The great Ruhr coal field had been effectively worked since 1815, but the important Silesian field was producing only enough for the needs of its citizens in 1840, while north Germany was dependent upon English coal, which penetrated inland as far as Magdeburg. "The whole Prussian output," records Clapham,[28] "including that of the Saar, was only about 3,200,000 English tons a year in 1846. At that time France was mining 4,500,000 tons, Belgium a great deal more, and London was consuming more than Prussia raised."

An explanation of the small use of coal as fuel or as a source of power is to be found in the primitive state of the metal-working and machine-using industries. The iron and steel industry really consists of two distinct processes: (1) the smelting of iron ore in blast furnaces, and (2) the working over of the iron thus won into steel and finished products.

Smelting was carried on at the beginning of the nineteenth century in small furnaces with charcoal as fuel. It was generally a by-industry of peasants living near the extensive forests and obtaining their iron ore from small mines in the neighborhood. The average yield of a blast furnace was incredibly small; even as late as 1851 it was less than a ton a day.[29] By this time, however, the industry

[28] Op. cit., 91.
[29] A comparison of the productivity of blast furnaces in different countries emphasizes the smallness of the German furnaces. The average annual production in England was 3500 tons, in the United States 2500, in Belgium 1500, in Russia 600, in France 450, and in Germany 350. — Peter Mischler, *Der Deutsche Eisenhüttengewerbe* (1852), I, 150.

was beginning to be modernized: the coke blast furnace was supplanting the charcoal furnace, and the bloomery and iron hammer were giving way slowly to the method of puddling. But as late as 1846 there were in Upper Silesia only 9 coke alongside of 52 charcoal furnaces, and only 9 puddling works beside 240 bloomeries. The production of pig iron increased from 40,000 tons in 1800 to 120,000 in 1830, to 402,000 in 1850, and 1,330,000 in 1870.

The working up of the crude iron was carried on by handworkers, who refined and wrought the metal in primitive forges, blown generally by a hand bellows, and on equally primitive anvils where they hammered and shaped the material. By the forties machines had taken over some of these processes: tilt-hammers for the making of wrought iron and steel; slitting mills which cut the sheets of iron into rods suitable for nail making. But all the machines were small and were worked by water power. The further processes of manufacture, as of cutlery, were entirely in the hands of independent handworkers. The decade of the sixties, however, was one of rapid development for the steel industry, the output increasing from 25,000 tons in 1860 to 161,000 in 1869.

Emergence of the factory system. It is difficult to fix the beginning of the factory system in Germany, for it came in very slowly and was a matter of gradual growth. Much depends, moreover, upon the definition of the word factory. Machinery was used at an early date, but industry was not organized to any considerable extent under the factory system until the middle of the nineteenth century. Germany was still primarily an agricultural country, in which handwork and home industry found wide scope and persisted even after the machines had established themselves.

The first jenny machines seem to have been introduced from England into Saxony as early as the end of the eighties of the eighteenth century, and after 1790 each jenny carried 10 to 20 spindles; after 1800 water power was used to drive them. A further development came with the offer of a state subsidy of one thaler for each spindle brought into use in the year 1807. By 1813 there were already 22 spinning establishments with 107,283 spindles. The principal effect of this was to hurt the home spinning. Only weaving and embroidery remained to the home workers, organized under the putting-out system. In other parts of Germany, however, the development was somewhat different.

These first early tender blossoms of the German factory system — mostly small spinning mills and sugar facories — were in great part again destroyed in the second decade of the nineteenth century. After the end of the Napoleonic wars and the lifting of the Continental System, which had given effective protection to the struggling

German industry, English competition set in and, except in south Germany, where the gild system still persisted, almost destroyed these hot-house products. Other factors made it difficult for Germany to compete: the lack of industrial capital, the backwardness of the continent in the field of industrial technique, the famine of 1816–17, and the agrarian crisis of 1820–25. Only in the thirties did conditions substantially improve. The Prussian government in 1831 created the *Gewerbe Institut* (Trade Institute), for the purpose of spreading the knowledge of new industrial methods and of encouraging experiments. The removal of internal barriers by the Zollverein, the modernization of the agrarian constitution and the introduction of the principle of industrial freedom, and a larger degree of local self-government all enlarged the sphere of free undertakings, while a change in the industrial taxes made these less burdensome than formerly. In addition to all this the decade of the thirties and forties ushered in the great improvement of transportation and trade through the building of better roads, railroads, the postal system, and finally the telegraph. By the fifties the cumulative effect of all these changes had laid the foundation for a factory system in the modern sense.

The period 1833–48 witnessed a considerable expansion in manufacturing and the introduction of many improvements. The transition from hand to machine work made steady progress. Technical schools were opened, manufacturers traveled abroad, especially in England, in order to study the methods employed there. Machines were imported from England, and also from France and Belgium; only infrequently were they built in Germany, though steam engines had been constructed in Berlin as early as 1812.[30] The first trustworthy count of steam engines in Prussia was made in 1837 when it appeared that there were in all Prussia only 423 steam engines with 7513 h.p. Saxony was even more backward, for in 1846 it contained only 197 steam engines for industrial and agricultural purposes with 2446 h.p. In 1855 the number of those in industry alone was 3050 with 61,965 h.p. Most of these were employed in mining, then followed metal working, machine making, textile industry, etc.

The first stage in the development of industry was the shift from hand tools and human power to simple machines moved by water power. This began at the end of the eighteenth century and was pretty well completed by 1835. The next decade saw the beginning of the second stage, the transition from small machinery and water power to large factories with steam. The Rhenish manufacturing district was in this stage about 1845.[31]

[30] W. Sombart, *Der Moderne Kapitalismus* (3te Aufl.), I, 868.
[31] T. C. Banfield, *Industry of the Rhine* (London, 1846–48), II, 23.

For industry as a whole, however, the dominating form of business was still the home industry. Spinning was the first branch to be affected by the new machinery, but a Prussian writer reported, under date of 1846, "spinning has remained hitherto essentially hand-spinning, although there exist already some larger enterprises, mainly of recent date." [32] A count at this time of some 16 cotton spinning mills in the Rhenish district showed that 10 of them used only hand power, 3 were worked by water power, and 3 by steam power. The size of the establishment was, however, growing, and a certain amount of concentration was taking place; thus, between 1846 and 1861 the number of cotton and linen spinning mills declined from 209 to 69, but the number of spindles per operative grew from 1126 to 5783. [33]

Weaving was almost entirely a hand industry and was, moreover, carried on largely as a by-industry in the workers' homes. Here, in 1846, were still to be found 585,835 looms as compared with 217,388 in "establishments." [34] It would be a mistake, however, to think of these establishments as factories, for weaving was as yet almost untouched by machinery. Less than four per cent of the looms in Prussia in that year were driven by power, and in Saxony there were no power looms at all.

In some other industries the movement to large scale operation was more apparent. This is shown for three important German industries of this period in the following table:

GERMAN INDUSTRIES, 1846 AND 1855 *

| | | 1846 | | | 1855 | |
Industry	No. of estab.	No. of workers	No. of workers per estab.	No. of estab.	No. of workers	No. of workers per estab.
Paper	394	6,393	16.2	335	8,164	24.3
Wagon	45	1,269	28.2	70	3,823	54.6
Sugar	83	7,668	92.4	176	25,595	145.4

* Cunow, op. cit., IV, 83.

In conclusion it may be said that industrial freedom had abolished untenable conditions, had stimulated change, and had brought about improvements in technique and in industrial organization. Inevitably, however, these processes of change weakened, if they did not destroy, the small hand industry and opened the door to the factory with steam power and to associational methods of production. But the transition was not completed for another quarter century. A

[32] Dieterici, op. cit., 254.
[33] Schmoller, op. cit., 162.
[34] Sombart, *Der Moderne Kapitalismus* (1902 ed.), I, 429.

considerable impetus was given to German industry by the international expositions in London (1851), Paris (1855), and London (1862), in which Germany made a good showing and from which her industrialists received a needed stimulus.

BIBLIOGRAPHICAL NOTE

1. *Industrial Revolution.* The Industrial Revolution is still a controversial subject and its discussion has brought out various points of view. Down almost to the World War the text books presented the view that a sudden and violent "revolution" had occurred, but more recent research has discredited that conclusion. Modern scholars also hold that each industry and region had its special history and that generalizations based on one are not applicable to others. And finally the social and economic results of the Industrial Revolution have been differently interpreted, some holding that they were largely evil and others that they were beneficent. The term Industrial Revolution was given currency by A. Toynbee, *Lectures on the Industrial Revolution* (London, 1884), who at the same time emphasized the view of a cataclysmic change. This book may still be read with profit, but should be corrected by later works.

The social consequences are painted in dark colors by J. L. and B. Hammond, *The Rise of Modern Industry* (5th ed., London, 1937), but minimized by L. C. A. Knowles, *The Industrial and Commercial Revolutions in Great Britain during the Nineteenth Century* (4th ed., London, 1926). Both books should be read. Other studies are H. L. Beales, *The Industrial Revolution,* 1750–1850 (London, 1929), a brief sketch; E. C. Fairchild, *Labour and the Industrial Revolution,* 1760–1832 (London, 1923), a broad survey; W. Bowden, *Industrial Society in England towards the End of the Eighteenth Century* (New York, 1925) gives the background, and his *The Industrial Revolution* (New York, 1928) carries on the story with an excellent collection of contemporary documents; R. W. Cooke-Taylor, *The Modern Factory System* (London, 1891) is by a factory inspector; H. D. Fong, *The Triumph of the Factory System in England* (Tientsin, 1930), is a careful study; P. Mantoux, *La Révolution Industrielle* (Paris, 1906; English trans. *The Industrial Revolution in the Eighteenth Century,* London, 1927) is the best account of the changes to 1800.

2. *Factory system.* The further development in Britain may best be traced in the separate industries. Of the voluminous literature on the textile industry the following are especially useful: (1) Cotton: E. Baines, *History of the Cotton Manufacture of Great Britain* (London, 1835) is a valuable contemporary account; S. J. Chapman, *The Lancashire Cotton Trade and Industry* (Manchester, 1904) gives a good general picture; T. Ellison, *The Cotton Trade of Great Britain* (London, 1886) contains full statistical tables; L. S. Wood and A. Wilmore, *The Romance of the Cotton Industry in England* (Oxford, 1923) is a good popular account. (2) Woolen and Worsted: J. H. Clapham, *The Woollen and Worsted Industries* (London, 1907) is especially good on the technical side; E. Lipson, *History of the Woollen and Worsted Industries* (London, 1921) is incomplete for the nineteenth century; James Burnley, *History of Wool and Wool Combing* (London, 1889) is a standard history. (3) Silk: F. Warner, *The Silk Industry of the United Kingdom, its Origin and Development* (London, 1921).

Coal and Iron and Steel. R. N. Boyd, *Coal Pits and Pitmen* (London, 1892) and R. L. Galloway, *The Annals of Coal Mining and the Coal Trade,* 2 vols. (London, 1898–1900) are discursive and anecdotal but useful. J. S. Jevons, *The*

Coal Question (London, 1865; 3rd ed., 1906) is a classic. T. S. Ashton, *Iron and Steel in the Industrial Revolution* (Manchester, 1924) is the best book on this subject. Lowthian Bell, *The Iron Trade in the United Kingdom* (London, 1886) is a well-informed technical account. Henry Bessemer, *An Autobiography* (London, 1905) is an interesting picture of the struggles of an inventor; William Fairbairn, *Iron: its History, Properties and Process of Manufacture* (Edinburgh, 1869), is largely technical. W. T. Jeans, *The Creators of the Age of Steel* (New York, 1884) describes the work of the leading inventors. J. H. Roe, *English and American Tool Builders* (New Haven, 1916) is the best book. S. Smiles, *Industrial Biography: Iron Workers and Tool Makers* (London, 1863) is popular and interesting. On the discovery of the steam engine and its gradual introduction the best account is J. Lord, *Capital and Steam Power*, 1750–1800 (London, 1923); this may be continued in S. Smiles, *Lives of Boulton and Watt* (Philadelphia, 1865) and T. H. Marshall, *James Watt*, 1736–1819 (London, 1925), both concise and readable.

3 and 4. *France and Germany*. There are scarcely any books devoted specifically to industry in France and Germany during this period, owing probably to the fact that both countries were overwhelmingly agricultural. An excellent essay, covering the period 1789 to 1815, is Chas. Ballot, *Introduction du machinisme dans l'industrie française* (Paris, 1923). The story is carried forward by G. and H. Bourgin, *Le régime de l'industrie en France de 1815 à 1848*, 2 vols. (Paris, 1912–21), a careful and comprehensive work. The final chapter for this period may be found in A. L. Dunham, *The Anglo-French Treaty of Commerce of 1860 and the Progress of the Industrial Revolution in France* (Ann Arbor, 1930). R. Lévy, *Histoire économique de l'industrie cotonnière en Alsace* (Paris, 1912) is a special study of an important industry.

A good introduction for German industrial history is the scholarly work of G. Schmoller, *Zur Geschichte der deutschen Kleingewerbe im neunzehnten Jahrhundert* (Halle, 1870). The gradual transition to the factory system is well portrayed in P. Benaerts, *Les origines de la grande industrie allemande: Essai sur l'histoire économique de la periode du Zollverein*, 1834–1860 (Paris, 1934). Less connected is H. Grothe, *Bilder und Studien zur Geschichte der Industrie und Maschinenwesen* (Berlin, 1870). A comprehensive account of an important industry is L. Beck, *Die Geschichte des Eisens in technischer und kulturgeschichtlicher Beziehung*, 5 vols. (Braunschweig, 1884–1903).

CHAPTER III

COMMERCE AND COMMERCIAL POLICY

I. FREE TRADE IN BRITAIN

Mercantilism. Until the breakdown of mercantilism the prevailing commercial philosophy had held that monopoly was essential to success in trade. The economic and commercial expansion of the leading European nations during the seventeenth and eighteenth centuries was therefore attended by incessant strife. Commerce and war went hand in hand. Chartered commercial companies were at first employed by all countries for distant trading enterprises, but as economic nationalism developed colonies became more important. The trade of these could be monopolized by the mother country. At first prized as sources of supplies, they later were valued also as markets for manufactured goods. This was especially true after the Industrial Revolution. The earlier trade was confined largely to articles of small bulk and high value, but with every improvement in transportation and reduction in costs, bulkier articles of less relative value were moved in increasing quantities. The range and value of foreign commerce were steadily extended.

With the growth of population and of economic development colonies had become increasingly important and commercial relations between the mother country and colonies were carefully regulated in accordance with mercantile theories. These regulations proved galling to the expanding and liberty-loving English colonies in North America, which revolted against such treatment and achieved their independence in 1783. It was confidently expected that the loss of the colonies by England would mean the loss of trade with their inhabitants, but to the surprise of mercantilist statesmen the political rupture did not interrupt commerce. After independence as before Great Britain enjoyed most of the trade with America. A fatal blow was thus struck at one of the most cherished doctrines of mercantilism.

As a result of these and other factors the foreign trade of England increased about sixfold during the eighteenth century, from £12,000,000 in 1700 to £62,640,000 in 1800.[1] At the beginning of the eighteenth century the trade with Europe comprised about three-fourths of the total, but by the end it had fallen to one-half.

[1] Down to 1854 the values of imports and exports are official, not real, values. That is, the prices were calculated according to those originally fixed when the office of inspector-general of imports and exports was instituted in 1697; so that these figures do not represent the real value of the foreign trade. They are of relative but not absolute significance. The practice of publishing the real or "declared" values was not begun until 1798 and then only for exports.

The trade with America, on the other hand, grew from about 13 to 32 per cent, constituting at the close of the century the most important single branch of commerce. At that time woolens, cottons, and manufactures of iron and steel made up nearly one-half of the exports. England was already making herself not merely the "workshop of the world," but also the commercial leader. From other countries she drew increasing quantities of raw materials and foodstuffs that could not be produced at home. The leading imports at the end of the eighteenth century were sugar, tea, grains, Irish linen, raw cotton, and coffee. These six articles made up almost half of the total imports.

The great increase in foreign trade came after 1780, when the first effects of the Industrial Revolution began to be felt. This event gave a great stimulus to foreign commerce, for by it greater emphasis was placed upon specialization. The significant feature of nineteenth-century trade was the division of the world into countries producing raw materials and those manufacturing them. England was the first country to profit by this territorial specialization, and had already begun this process in the eighteenth century. The complete adjustments were, however, made slowly. Every effort was made to build up industry, but definite limits were set by the supply of raw materials. For these, as well as for markets for the finished goods, England was becoming increasingly dependent on foreign countries. The expansion of industry was, therefore, conditioned by the development of trade. Both were hampered, however, by the persistence of old customs, antiquated methods, the resistance of vested interests, and the persistence of mercantilistic ideas.

The economic policy of mercantilism had rested upon the desire to strengthen national power, and interference with business and industry had been justified on the ground that private interests could not be trusted to promote that end. Adam Smith gave a new turn to commercial policy by placing the emphasis upon national wealth instead of power and by pointing out that wealth could best be increased by permitting each individual to pursue his own gain without state interference. The notion of freedom of enterprise and of individual initiative was all important for domestic industry and business, but for international trade it was revolutionary. By showing that each party to an exchange may benefit, Smith proved the profitableness of foreign trade and the needlessness of regulation.

Development of free trade. The reaction against the mercantile system was not so definite in England as it was in France, but was a gradual growth and depended more on political conditions. During most of the eighteenth century a policy of high protection prevailed, but toward the end of the century this was somewhat modified. The so-called Eden treaty of 1786 reduced duties on French wines, vinegar, and brandy and on English hardware, cotton goods, and woolen manufactures. The complaints on each side of the channel that the other country profited most suggests that the exchange of benefits was fairly equal. In the next three years trade between the two countries was doubled. This movement in the direction of freer trade was unfortunately interrupted by the French Revolution.

In the tariff system of England certain definite achievements were, however, accomplished. The customs duties were greatly simplified in 1787 by abolishing all existing imposts and consolidating into a single duty upon each article taxed the various duties with which it was loaded. The extent of this reform is indicated by the fact that Parliament passed about 3000 resolutions to give it effect. Duties were also reduced in order to discourage smuggling. Thus the duty on tea was lowered from 120 per cent to $12\frac{1}{2}$ per cent; under the higher rate scarce a third — five or six million pounds out of eighteen million [2] — of the tea consumed passed through the customs. The cost of collecting the customs revenues was at the same time reduced.

The Continental wars. Upon the outbreak of the revolution in France in 1789 the Eden treaty ceased to be effective and soon afterwards it was abrogated. In 1793 war was declared against England by France, which spread until it involved practically all of Europe, and all commerce was thereafter thrown into confusion. The struggle between France and England at this time has been compared to a fight between an elephant and a whale, for the two adversaries, each supreme in its own sphere, could not come to grips. Consequently they endeavored indirectly to embarrass each other by interfering with commerce. England had gained control of the sea and the monopoly of trade and industry which attended it, and intended to maintain it. But such interference threatened the rights of neutral states and they objected vigorously. In 1794 Denmark and Sweden entered into a convention for the defense of their neutral rights, and five years later were joined by Russia. The United States, whose carrying trade was now second only to that of England, was another neutral whose rights were flouted. These powers insisted upon the maintenance of certain principles of international law, that free ships make free goods, that only contraband goods defined as such should be forbidden to neutral trade, and that "paper" blockades were not valid. To all these principles England took exception, for she wished to prevent the carrying on of trade

[2] G. L. Craik, *History of British Commerce* (London, 1844), III, 125.

with France by neutrals, to exclude from France non-contraband though essential articles such as wheat, timber and hemp, and by treating all French ports as blockaded to prevent the entrance of neutral ships. By the battle of Copenhagen in 1801 England crushed the northern confederacy of Russia, Sweden, and Denmark, but the United States still carried on the forbidden trade.

To put a stop to American trade England issued various Orders in Council, which declared all ports belonging to France or her colonies or allies to be in a state of blockade. While this was largely in the nature of a "paper" blockade it made neutral vessels trading with such ports liable to capture. The English government hoped in this way to deprive France of needed supplies from her colonies and those of her allies, and to end the neutral trade. Napoleon retorted with similar extravagant decrees, declaring the British Isles to be in a state of blockade and forbidding all trade with them; he also prohibited all commerce in English merchandise. This mad exchange of orders and decrees was climaxed by Napoleon's tariff of Trianon in 1810 which ordered the seizure and burning of all British goods found in France, Germany, Holland, Italy, Spain or other places occupied by French troops.

The issue behind this struggle was clearly drawn. Napoleon sought to bring England to terms by ruining her commerce and industry; this was the vulnerable spot in a "nation of shopkeepers." The prohibition of the importation of British goods into Europe, whether by combatants or neutrals, would close to England her best markets and deprive her of valuable commercial privileges which she had hitherto enjoyed. The British on the other hand would allow no trade to be carried on with France and her allies except by themselves. By virtue of their command of the sea they were able to enforce fairly well the Orders in Council, though it brought them into conflict with neutrals. It was necessary for Napoleon, on the other hand, to obtain the co-operation of practically all of Europe to carry out his Continental system. The hardships which this system imposed upon the people of Europe created widespread opposition to Napoleon, and his inability to bring Spain and Russia within its prohibitions led finally to its breakdown.

The restrictions upon commerce by Great Britain and Napoleon were somewhat mitigated by the system of licenses, which sanctioned contraventions of the orders and decrees. The result was to make smugglers out of all European traders.

Foreign commerce, 1793–1815. The actual trade carried on by Great Britain during the course of the war did not suffer so much as might have been anticipated. The first effect was to destroy the trade with France, and next that with Holland, which was invaded by France. That with Italy, Spain, and Russia fell off, but these losses were more than counterbalanced by the gains in trade with Prussia, the German free ports, the Scandinavian countries, the British East and West Indies, the United States, and after 1810 with Spanish South America. The Peace of Amiens permitted a still further though brief expansion, but after 1803 foreign trade remained pretty steady for a decade. Beginning with 1814 there was a sudden jump in exports to £53,573,000 and in imports to £37,-755,000, and they stayed at about these figures until 1826. Imports, which in 1790 were nearly equal to the exports, continually lagged behind and an ever greater disparity developed. The reasons for this were the payment for a large part of the exports with cash, which does not appear on the merchandise balance sheet, and especially the grants of subsidies to British allies. These are estimated at £57,000,000 between 1792 and 1817 [3] and were generally paid in the form of British manufactures. Although the Continental War undoubtedly retarded British commerce, it did not destroy it. New channels of trade, lawful or otherwise, were found about as rapidly as the old ones were closed, and after the downfall of Napoleon Great Britain regained her former markets and added to them by territorial expansion. In 1815 the commercial supremacy of the country was on an even more secure basis than it had been in 1793.

Although peace brought the resumption of maritime communication, trade did not at once move forward. On the contrary, a severe depression set in; aggravated by the disorganization attendant upon a return to peace-time activities and the cessation of war demands, thousands of artisans were thrown out of work, and suffering became general. The old trade connections and business methods had been disrupted by the long wars, and various industrial regulations had been abandoned. The agricultural and industrial revolutions worked themselves out with a minimum of restriction. The result was the opening of large opportunities to men of enterprise and ability, and a great growth in the volume of trade and a corresponding increase in shipping. The commercial prosperity was, however, frequently purchased at the expense of the well-being of the workers, trade became more speculative, and the industrial and agricultural base was less stable. The truth of Hume's dictum, that a nation cannot be rich and busy when all its neighbors are idle and poor, was abundantly illustrated. So long as the Continent was exhausted the activity of Great Britain was limited, in spite of the new markets which had been opened up in other parts of the world. Agriculture, and even industry, can recover quickly from the waste

[3] H. de B. Gibbins, *History of Commerce in Europe*, 180.

of war, but trade connections, once destroyed, are not so easily re-established.

At the end of the eighteenth and through part of the nineteenth century the history of foreign trade, according to Bowley,[4] "is the history of the division of the world into new countries producing raw materials and old countries manufacturing them." England was the seat of woolen and cotton manufactures, the United States and the Baltic regions exported wheat, timber came from Scandinavia, hemp from Russia, wine from France. There was thus laid the basis for a profitable interchange of products.

Growing importance of foreign trade. It may have been true, as Bowley claimed, that the foreign trade of Britain contributed only slightly to the development of the country in the eighteenth century, but in the nineteenth it was becoming increasingly essential to the industry and even the existence of the people. Foreign trade grew more rapidly than the population, showing a greater dependence upon outside contacts. The expansion was particularly rapid after 1846, owing to improvements in transportation which widened the area of profitable commerce, and also to the adoption of free trade and the repeal of the navigation laws. The development may be indicated by giving the figures for a few selected dates.

AVERAGE ANNUAL TRADE OF THE UNITED KINGDOM
(millions of pounds sterling)

Period	Imports	Exports	Total	Excess of imports
1801–05	28	33	61	5 *
1826–30	33	35	68	2 *
1846–50	72	60	132	12
1855–59	146	116	262	30
1865–69	237	181	418	56

* Excess of exports. It should be noted that the old system of "official" valuation of imports was changed in 1854 to real or declared valuations. The figures before and after that date are, therefore, not comparable. The figures of imports before 1846 are, moreover, undoubtedly too low because of the large amount of smuggling. On the other hand, the figures after 1850 reflect the higher price level resulting from the influx of gold from America and Australia.

Exports. The basis of trade is to be found in the resources and industries of a country, and an account of the growing export trade of Britain during this period is therefore largely a reflection of its industrial development. Raw materials did not contribute largely, even at the beginning of the century; in 1830 they made up only about 17 per cent of the total exports. This group comprised coal, tin, copper, lead, a little iron, and even less china clay. As the century wore on, and British foreign commerce and shipping developed, most of these materials were consumed at home, but coal came

[4] A. L. Bowley, *England's Foreign Trade in the Nineteenth Century* (London, 1905), 3.

to be an important article of export, occupying a unique place in that trade. Since most of the imports, such as timber, wheat, sugar, cotton, iron, and tobacco, were bulky, they required many vessels with large cargo capacity for their carriage. If these vessels left British ports loaded merely with equivalent or even considerably greater values in light but valuable manufactured goods they would have much unused cargo space, which would be filled in part with unprofitable ballast. Coal was a commodity which was in general demand in other countries and of which Great Britain had large supplies. It was, therefore, exported as ballast at extremely low rates of carriage, since anything above the bare cost of handling contributed to the lessening of freight charges on the rest of the cargo. This is well shown by taking the weights of imports and exports. In 1860 the imports weighed 12,776,000 tons and the exports, exclusive of coal, 3,000,000 tons; to offset this, coal to the amount of 12,891,000 tons was exported.[5]

Manufactured goods, wholly or partly finished, made up the bulk of British exports throughout the whole of this period, and increasingly so as time went on. Woolen manufactures and yarn, which in 1800 were the great staple of the export trade and formed one-quarter of the total, gradually lost their pre-eminence; by 1870 they were about one-tenth of the total. Woolen manufactures had been thrust into second place by the rapidly growing exports of cotton manufactures and yarn, which increased from £17,000,000 in the decade of the twenties to £71,000,000 in 1870. It was the leading export with no close second. The textile group — woolens, cotton, silk, and linen manufactures — together accounted for over two-thirds of all the exports in the earlier period, but only slightly over one-third in 1870. By this date they were being overshadowed by the growth of a vast array of miscellaneous manufactured products, including iron and steel, cutlery, hardware, machinery, and pottery.

The export of machinery offers an interesting illustration of the commanding position of British manufactures and of the changes in commercial policy. From the very beginning of the Industrial Revolution England had sought to secure to her manufacturers a monopoly of the new inventions by forbidding their export. This prohibition began in 1774 with tools used in cotton or linen manufacturing, and was steadily extended to cover machinery used in woolen and silk manufactures, printing cotton goods, the iron and steel industry, and others. It became less effective with the passing years and the secure position of the country as the "workshop of the world," and both machinery and plans therefor were exported in growing quantities. Until 1843, however, when the restrictive legislation was repealed,

[5] W. S. Jevons, *The Coal Question* (London, 1865), 315.

such exports were seldom declared although a system of licenses permitted a few returns to be made to the customs. According to these the machinery and millwork exported in 1830 were worth only £208,000, and half that the following year; by 1870, when the customs returns reported the truth, they amounted to £5,000,000.

Imports. The principal imports around 1830 were the textile raw materials — cotton, flax, hemp, and wool — timber, iron, and foodstuffs such as grain and flour, sugar, coffee and tea, wine and spirits, and tobacco. This group probably made up three-fourths of the whole import trade, both in bulk and value, at this date. As the textile industries grew there was an enormous increase in the importation of raw cotton, from 200 million pounds annual average in 1821–30 to over 1000 million in the decade 1861–70. At the same time domestic supplies of home-grown wool proved quite inadequate to the expanding woolen and worsted industries and after the development of the Australian wool-growing industry increasing supplies were drawn from this quarter. From an average annual import of 25 million pounds in 1821–30 there was a tenfold increase to 1870 when 263 million pounds were brought in. Great Britain also became increasingly dependent upon foreign foodstuffs, and after the repeal of the corn laws larger amounts of breadstuffs found their way into the British markets. Until the seventies, however, domestic agriculture succeeded in meeting fairly adequately the increased demand caused by the growing population and the higher standards of living. After 1870 imports of foodstuffs grew enormously.

Demand for foreign products did not express itself freely during this period, for restrictive legislation and heavy import duties distorted the pattern. The Napoleonic wars left a heavy burden of taxation whose incidence was particularly heavy on such semi-luxuries as sugar, tea, coffee, and tobacco. Until the introduction of free trade the import figures of these commodities remained low, though smuggling undoubtedly permitted a larger consumption than official records show. After 1850 there was a considerable increase in all these items, and import statistics record accurately the needs and desires of the British people for foreign commodities.

The balance of payments. Before 1830 merchandise exports exceeded imports, but after that time the balance swung in the other direction and the disparity between the two sides of the international balance sheet became ever greater.[6] By 1870 the excess of imports over exports was over £50,000,000 a year. This excess was paid for by invisible or "concealed" exports. These included the earnings of British ships in carrying goods and passengers for other nations,

[6] See table on p. 102.

commissions and profits of British commercial and financial institutions in conducting world trade, and interest and dividends from capital invested abroad. Information on all these points is fragmentary and unreliable, but it has been estimated that British investments abroad in government securities and private undertakings probably amounted to £300,000,000 in 1850, and £800,000,000 in 1870, from which the returns at the later date would have been not far from £40,000,000. Taken together, these various items would not only have liquidated the adverse merchandise balance, but provided additional sums for further investment.

Distribution of foreign trade. In 1830 over 40 per cent of British exports found their way to European markets, but thereafter the proportion declined as the continental states imposed restrictions in order to build up their own industries. The great expansion of British trade after this date was in more distant markets. The United States was Britain's best customer and from that country she drew an increasing proportion of her raw materials and foodstuffs. About three-quarters of her raw cotton came from southern cotton fields in the middle of the century. India, once the exporter of fine cotton goods, became England's best customer for the expanding British cotton manufactures. The Far East was opened up and after the abrogation of the monopoly of the East India Company in 1834 private merchants developed a vigorous trade. This was unhappily promoted by the Chinese opium war, at the end of which in 1842 Hong-Kong was ceded to Britain and other Chinese ports were opened. A treaty with Japan in 1858 opened that country also to British trade. The immediate profits were large, but they were obtained at a heavy ethical cost, to be discharged later. The discovery of gold in Australia and the even more important development of wool growing were followed by a phenomenal increase in trade with that country both in imports and exports. Africa remained largely undeveloped, but the South American states and Mexico drew most of their supplies of manufactured goods from Great Britain.

This vast increase in trade called for corresponding improvements in port and dock facilities. In 1800 London was practically without docks, Liverpool had only a few small ones, and Manchester had not yet been connected with the sea; Glasgow, the leading port of Scotland, was little better off until the middle of the century. Up to this time most ships discharged their cargoes either directly on to the wharves or into lighters and barges. In tidal rivers, like the Thames, the first method was difficult, and the second was inefficient and gave endless opportunity for pilfering. During the nineteenth century, however, the dredging of the harbors and the building of docks and landing places went on apace. London led the way with the construction of a comprehensive dock system between 1802 and 1828, and other seaports followed suit rather tardily. Liverpool had ten docks by 1834, Southampton built its first dock in 1842. By 1870, however, the port and dock facilities were adequate to the commerce and shipping of that time.

Commercial policy. In 1815 commerce was burdened with a multitude of imposts and restrictions; foodstuffs, raw materials, and manufactured goods alike were subject to import duties. As trade increased, the evils of the system were accentuated. Reform took place along three lines: (1) the moderation and eventually the abolition of protection to manufacturers; (2) the repeal of the corn laws; and (3) the repeal of the navigation acts.

The free trade movement is usually dated from 1820, when a group of London merchants petitioned Parliament that all restrictive regulations and all duties except for revenue be repealed at once. The House of Commons reported favorably on the proposal, and Thomas Huskisson, president of the Board of Trade, began a series of reforms, which simplified the customs laws, reduced the duties on raw materials, especially wool and silk, lowered those on most foreign manufactures to about 30 per cent, and removed most of the restrictions on exports. These measures were tentative, but they constituted a breach in the protective system.

A second stage in the work of tariff reform came in the forties. Joseph Hume's report of 1840 showed that 46 articles paid 98 per cent of the customs revenues and that 350 articles produced less than £100 each. Two years later Sir Robert Peel, the prime minister, brought in his first budget for financial reform. After assuring himself adequate revenues by reimposition of the income tax — estimated to bring in £5,000,000 a year — Peel attacked the customs duties. He abolished or reduced the duties on 750 articles, especially on raw materials. A further step was taken by William Gladstone, as Chancellor of the Exchequer, in 1853, when he obtained the abolition or reduction of duties on 260 articles. The final step in the movement to free trade was effected by Gladstone in 1860 when the number of dutiable articles was reduced to 44, and the last duties on manufactures (wool and silk) were removed. The following table shows briefly what was accomplished between 1841 and 1862:

Year	No. of dutiable articles	Gross customs yield
1841	1163	£21,898,845
1853	466	22,373,662 *
1862	44	24,036,000

* 1851.

To the surprise of both friends and foes of tariff reform, the anticipated deficits did not appear, but more revenue was obtained from 44 articles in 1862 than from 1163 in 1841. This was, however, not so much a triumph of free trade principles as it was a result of the simplification of the customs laws and a wise selection of revenue articles. The changes were followed by a considerable expansion of British trade, which free traders have usually ascribed to the adoption of their principle. Other things being equal, there would naturally be a larger international exchange of goods if all barriers were removed and each country devoted itself to the production of those goods for which it was best suited. This was done by Great Britain, which concentrated on a relatively small range of industries — textiles, iron, machinery, and coal. Her people bought increasingly articles which were not produced in Great Britain or for whose production they were unsuited, and paid for them with those in which they enjoyed especial advantages. It was roughly an exchange of manufactured goods and coal for raw materials and food. This meant an increase of both imports and exports. An event of especial importance was the negotiation of the Cobden-Chevalier treaty of commerce between Great Britain and France, by which each country granted considerable concessions to the other. The result was a great increase in Anglo-French trade. This was followed by numerous other treaties with other nations and in the extension of the "most favored nation" principle, as a result of which Europe came closer to freedom of international trade than ever before or since.

The second great change in England's commercial policy was the repeal of the corn laws, but as this has already been described, a reference to the earlier chapter is sufficient.

The third group of restrictions — the navigation acts — was designed to prevent the competition of foreign shipping, and dated for the most part from the seventeenth century. The old colonial theory had in the meantime been largely overthrown by the American Revolution, by the establishment of the independence of the Spanish American republics, by the Napoleonic wars, and by the decline of mercantilist ideas. An attempt by Great Britain to revive the old system after 1815 led to reprisals by the United States and other countries. Consequently Huskisson began in 1824 a series of treaties which placed foreign ships on an equality with British ships, except in the coasting and colonial trade. In 1830 the latter was made available to nations which granted reciprocal privileges, and finally, in 1849 and 1854, even the coastwise trade was thrown open and the colonial trade was made free to all. In spite of the removal of protection, British shipping showed a vigorous growth, corresponding to the expansion in trade.

Merchant marine. At the beginning of the nineteenth century foreign commerce was carried on in wooden sailing vessels. Judged by modern standards they were small. A few East India ships ran to 1500 tons, but the average trading vessel was about 300 tons. During the Napoleonic wars larger ships were built and by 1815 vessels of 3000 tons were not infrequent. Built primarily for safety rather than for speed, with the length only four times the beam, they would today be considered tubs. Shipping was exposed to serious risks — wrecks on uncharted seas, lack of lighthouses along the coasts, piracy, privateering during the wars down to 1815, and high mortality rates among the sailors due to bad food and unhealthful quarters.

Trade and shipping were diverted from their normal channels during the Napoleonic wars, and after peace in 1815 there ensued a difficult period of adjustment, but by 1830 they had recovered. Capital and enterprise, however, found more profitable employment in the development of the country's internal resources, in building and equipment of factories and the construction of railways, than in shipping and foreign trade. It was a period of rapid industrial development, not merely in Great Britain, but in other countries as well. The growth of the population, the opening of new markets in North and South America, and the expansion of production created, in the long run, a demand for increased tonnage and improved facilities. The United States had taken advantage of the situation and had greatly increased its merchant marine, establishing lines between that country and England after 1816 and by 1840 advertising regular sailings. Between 1835 and 1845 British shipping took an upward spurt, and at the same time began experimenting with the steamboat.

Two revolutionary changes occurred in shipbuilding which destroyed the supremacy of the wooden sailing vessel. In the first place, steam gradually took the place of sails, and in the second, iron replaced wood in construction. The first successful steamboat for passenger travel was launched on the Clyde by Henry Bell in 1812. During the first quarter of the nineteenth century steamboats were used chiefly in inland navigation and the coasting trade. Not until 1819 did a steamboat venture across the Atlantic; this was the *Savannah,* which made the voyage in 29½ days under sail and steam, mostly sail. The first real steamers came in 1838 when four ships crossed to New York in 15 days. The following year the Cunard Line was established with four paddle-wheel wooden steamers, which, however, carried auxiliary sails. It adopted a fixed schedule for sailings, which the sailing vessels, depending on variable winds, could not do.   These early vessels, with an average speed of $8\frac{1}{2}$ knots an hour, were very economical, consuming only 450 tons of coal for the trip from Liverpool to Boston.   The introduction of the steamboat relieved water transportation from reliance on the wind. It was now possible to travel in a dead calm, or even in moderately boisterous weather.   At the same time the cost of water transportation was only one-third of that by land.

The use of steamers for ocean voyages was delayed by the lack of coaling stations.   The consumption of coal was so large for a long trip that if a vessel carried enough fuel for the entire voyage little space would be left for cargo, and there were, moreover, few harbors where steamers could coal.   In consequence the early ocean-going steamers carried masts and sails and made only part of the voyage under steam.   Even as late as the eighties Atlantic liners carried spare masts with yards.   By 1850, however, coaling stations were generally established and vessels no longer needed to carry such large quantities of coal.   But steamboats did not at once supplant sailing vessels; the process was a slow and gradual one.   Indeed, for a time the sailing vessels seemed invincible.

The iron, and later the steel, ship possessed two great advantages. In the first place, much larger vessels could be built of iron than of wood.   The structural limit of a wooden vessel was about 300 feet, owing to the impossibility of finding large enough ship's timber, but there was no such limit for an iron one.   To the end of the nineteenth century 2000 tons was the limit of wooden sailing vessels. In the second place, the great strength of iron and steel permitted a reduction in the thickness of the shell, so that, although iron is heavier than wood, an iron ship weighed less than a wooden one and could carry more cargo.   A curious prejudice, fostered by the builders and owners of wooden vessels, delayed the general adoption of iron ships: it was contended that they would ruin the fruit and meat and spoil the flavor of the tea, if loaded with these articles.   But their advantages were so great that their superiority was ultimately recognized.   The real victory of the iron ship was won, however, not through structural advantages but by the use of steam power. But this, in turn, had to wait for improvements in the engines, driving methods, and other factors.

The first improvement came when, in 1839, the screw propeller was substituted for paddle wheels, with which the first steamers had been fitted.   The second was the compound engine with four cylinders, which was introduced in the late fifties.   The compound engine greatly lessened the consumption of coal and thus increased the cargo capacity.   At the same time the adoption of mechanical appliances for loading and unloading and the building of larger ships economized on labor. Britain had great advantages in constructing iron ships, as her iron and steel industry was well developed, and lost little time in turning to the iron steamer instead of wooden sailing vessels. The following table shows both the growth in the merchant marine and the gradual shift in the type of vessel:

MERCHANT MARINE OF THE UNITED KINGDOM *

(gross tons)

Year	Sailing vessels	Steamers	Total
1840	2,680,330	87,930	2,768,260
1850	3,337,546	167,398	3,504,944
1860	4,134,390	452,352	4,586,742
1870	4,506,318	1,111,375	5,617,693

* W. S. Lindsay, *History of Merchant Shipping and Ancient Commerce* (4 vols. London, 1883), IV, 114.

The number of iron steamers grew from 159 with a tonnage of 68,368 in 1861 to 382 with a tonnage of 222,922 in 1870. The crucial date in the struggle between sail and steam is usually given as 1869 when the Suez Canal, built by Ferdinand de Lesseps with the aid of French capital, was opened. This gave the steamer a shorter route to the East, a route, moreover, which was studded with coaling stations at convenient intervals. The distance from London to Bombay as compared with the route around the Cape of Good Hope was shortened by 4500 miles, and to Yokohama by 3000 miles. The change to the iron steamer was, however, a slow one, and the real triumph over its older rival came in the next period.

2. LIBERALISM IN FRANCE

Liberal commercial policy. A breach was made in the French system of prohibitions and high duties in 1786 when the liberal Eden treaty of 1786 was arranged between France and England. This made mutual concessions — to French wines and to English manufactures — and was followed by a considerable increase of trade between the two nations. The outbreak of the Revolution reversed this liberal policy and the tariff of 1793 prohibited the importation of all English commodities. For the next twenty years the commercial policy was determined almost entirely by hostility to Britain, and a highly protective system was fastened upon the country — a usual result of war. During the war the prohibitory system was systematically directed against Great Britain and reached its culminating point in the Continental System of Napoleon.

The Continental System. This is the name given to Napoleon's attempt to crush Great Britain by means of commercial war. Since the latter was supreme on the ocean and France on land they could not come to grips, so Napoleon determined to attack Britain in what seemed to him her most vulnerable spot — her commerce and industry. This would serve both military and economic ends. By excluding from the Continent — Britain's best market — all British ships and goods, especially colonial produce, British industry and commerce were to be suffocated, "vanquished by excess." The economic principle underlying the plan was the mercantilistic idea of the balance of trade. Unable to export goods Britain would be drained of gold and thereby weakened. At the same time Napoleon hoped that labor disturbances in England would endanger her position at home. French producers, on the other hand, would profit from the exclusion of British goods from the Continent and would gain new markets for French products. The means for the accomplishment of these aims was to be a self-blockade of the Continent.

There were two periods in the Continental System. During the first, 1806–10, the severity of the absolute prohibition was mitigated by smuggling and by the issuance of licenses, both by Napoleon and by the British government. Owing to the general demand for British and especially colonial wares, such as sugar, tea, spices, and similar articles, smuggling was carried on to an enormous extent. To meet this situation Napoleon promulgated the Trianon tariff, which admitted colonial goods at customs rates just below the cost of smuggling. Licenses were also granted to individual ships to disregard the prohibitions upon payment of stiff fees. Napoleon is said to have made 400 million francs by the sale of licenses, and in 1810 over 18,000 British licenses were issued. They brought in much-needed revenue to both sides.

Meanwhile, the carrying on of this commercial warfare by means of blockade had borne heavily on neutral nations, especially the United States, which alone had a considerable merchant marine capable of carrying on trade with the belligerents. Napoleon, by the Berlin and Milan decrees, and Great Britain, by Orders in Council, endeavored to prevent neutral ships from supplying the enemy's needs.

The second period of the Continental System, 1810–12, was marked by strict enforcement. Smuggling was suppressed and British goods were definitely excluded; when found they were seized and burned. But the system was incompatible with the economic interests of Russia and that country refused to carry out Napoleon's mandates. Russia might forbid the export of her goods to England, though it weakened her foreign exchange, but she could not do without colonial goods, such as sugar and tea. She therefore allowed such wares to come in freely if brought by neutrals, and at the same time excluded French luxury articles, such as silks, lace, and porcelain. All this was doubly contrary to the Continental System and inevitably led to war between France and Russia. The failure of the Russian campaign was decisive in Napoleon's downfall, but the complete breakdown of the Continental System hastened it. Just as disorder and economic insecurity had led to Napoleon's rise, so now the reappearance of the same evils caused his decline.

The Continental System constituted a system of extreme protection for French indusries, and there came into existence during the war years powerful groups of ironmasters and textile manufacturers, who exercised great influence in continuing the policy of high protection in peace times. Producers of grain and cattle obtained a practical monopoly in these articles as they were too bulky and low-priced to be imported from any distance by land, although they were duty free. The only important new industries set up during the prohibitory period were some chemical branches, notably the Leblanc soda process, and the production of sugar from beets.

Commercial policy, 1815–1860. With the restoration of the Bourbon monarchy (1815–30) the question of tariff reform came up. The government removed the obstacles placed on maritime commerce and replaced the prohibition on imports by moderate duties on colonial products, like sugar and coffee, and on raw materials like cotton. But the great landowners and industrialists, who had a monopoly of political power under the restricted franchise of 1815–48, objected to any change. The arguments advanced during the different debates show the extent to which the protectionists were prepared to go. The cotton manufacturers wrote in 1814 that unless protection was granted an immense population would be reduced to despair, that prohibition of imports was a "political and social right," and that from manufacturer to laborer all had the right of providing for the consumption of the country which they inhabit. They demanded an indemnity of 30 million francs and the prohibition of the import of cotton yarn and cloth. They got the prohibition. The iron manufacturers made further demands. After the peace the price of their products had fallen 30 to 40 per cent of the former price, and they now demanded, if not an indemnity, at least the prohibition of foreign iron. They obtained a quadrupling of the tariff on imported iron. Imported coal was taxed, and thereby an inducement was given to French manufacurers to continue to use wood and retain primitive processes. Finally the agriculturists also asked for protection, and could not well be denied. Corn laws on the English model were passed in 1819 and 1821, designed to exclude foreign grain except in times of scarcity, a duty was placed on wool and that on cotton retained, fresh and salt meat and cattle were taxed, and rates on colonial sugar were raised. The only interest that was overlooked was that of the common people, for whom bread was the common food. It is true that one deputy maintained that the dearness of bread was a benefit to the workers, because it obliged them to work with more ardor in order to live. But this singular theory found little echo.

The Orleanist monarchy (1830–48) was too dependent upon the support of the industrialists and landowners to initiate any far-reaching changes in the tariff, but a few modifications were made. The duties on wool, linen, cotton, iron, coal, and a few other commodities were reduced, and the absolute prohibitions were changed to duties in other cases, such as fine cotton yarn. In the forties a free-trade movement developed, stimulated by the work of the Anti-Corn Law League in England, but it never succeeded in establishing a powerful organization like its English prototype. An able leader appeared in Frédéric Bastiat, whose *Economic Fallacies* was a series of popular and caustic free trade arguments. He once petitioned the government on behalf of the candlemakers, demanding protection against the intolerable competition of the sun "in flooding the national market with light at a marvelously low cost." Outside of the commercial interests in the larger ports and the wine and silk industries, whose chief markets were abroad, the movement won few converts. The main result was rather to unite the manufacturers in firm resistance to all change. The protective edifice remained virtually intact.

Under Napoleon III (1852–70) came the nearest approach to free trade that France ever experienced. The revival of industry was one of the most important points in his program and this he thought could be attained only by reducing the protective duties. A proposal in 1852 to abolish all prohibition on exports, and to abolish or reduce over 300 import duties, was rejected by the Chamber of Deputies, and thereafter the Emperor decided to regulate customs by decree, which he could do without legislative approval. In 1852 the sliding scale on grain, the prices of which had risen considerably, was replaced by a small fixed duty, and those on cattle were lowered. Tariff reductions on wool, cotton, oil, and tobacco followed. Coal and iron duties were reduced and materials for shipbuilding were made free. The success of French industries at the Exposition of 1855 showed how little they had to fear foreign competition, and in the following year the Chamber unanimously approved these various decrees. But attempts to abolish the prohibitions or to moderate the general tariff met with the determined resistance of the protectionists, who were unwilling to sacrifice any advantage. The manufacturers threatened to close their establishments if further tariff changes were made.

Anglo-French Treaty of 1860. A plan was formulated in 1859, presumably by Michel Chevalier, for a series of economic reforms which included the repeal of prohibitions, the admission of free raw materials, better communications, reduction of canal dues, and the loan of capital to industry at low rates of interest. Since it was clear that the Chamber of Deputies would not approve such a program, Napoleon decided, under the influence of Chevalier, to make the transition to free — or freer — trade through a commercial treaty with Britain. A clause in the constitution of 1852 gave the executive the power to alter the tariff as part of a treaty with a foreign nation without requiring ratification by the Chamber, and Napoleon determined to use this method. A draft was prepared by Chevalier and preliminary negotiations were carried on principally between him and Richard Cobden. Extreme precautions were taken to keep the matter secret in order to avoid obstructions from the protectionists, and in January, 1860, the Anglo-French Treaty of Commerce was signed. France promised to remove all prohibitions and to reduce duties on English goods; England, on the other hand, reduced its duties on manufactures and wines and brandies. Both countries renounced export taxes, and agreed to grant each other any favor granted any other country. The treaty was to last ten years.

The heavy industries and agriculture were greatly dissatisfied, but the shock of transition to a more competitive system was eased by allowing an interval before the new duties were put into effect, and by government loans to industries. Over 38,000 million francs were granted to 200 applicants, mostly in the textile and metal industries. The reduction of duties on manufactures was followed by the free admission of raw materials and coal, and foreign ships were admitted on an equality with French. Manufacturers were thus enabled to accommodate themselves to British competition with a minimum of difficulty, but drastic scrapping of primitive and obsolete methods was in order.

The importance of the Anglo-French Treaty of 1860 lay not so much in its effect on French industry and upon the trade between the two countries as in its far-reaching influence upon European commercial policy. It set an example which other states were compelled to follow, and became the starting point of a general movement toward free trade. Since Great Britain had already embraced the policy of free trade she had little bargaining power, so it was left to France, which still could make valuable concessions, to be the leader in the direction of commercial reform.   A commercial treaty was made by France with Belgium in 1861, with Prussia in 1862, which three years later was accepted by the Zollverein; Italy followed in 1863, Switzerland in 1864, Sweden, Norway, Holland, Spain, and the Hanseatic cities in 1865, Austria in 1866, and Portugal in 1867.[7] All these treaties contained, like the Chevalier-Cobden treaty, the most-favored-nation clause, so that all Europe was bound together in a network of mutual concessions.

Foreign commerce. The Eden treaty of 1786 had been followed by an increase of foreign trade, but this declined greatly during the long war period and as a result of the Continental System.   Although it revived somewhat after 1815, the repressive tariff policy prevented any considerable growth.   After 1850 the reform of the tariff by Napoleon III led to a remarkable expansion.   In the decade 1850–60 trade with England quintupled, and that with other neighboring European countries grew only a little less rapidly.   By the latter date France ranked next to Great Britain as a trading nation.   After the commercial treaty of 1860 with Britain and the similar treaties with other countries, which introduced almost unrestricted intercourse, the foreign commerce of France expanded still more rapidly.   There was a great increase in the importation of raw materials and a some-what smaller growth of exports of specialized French manufactures. The statistical basis for these statements follows.

FRENCH FOREIGN TRADE *
(in millions of francs)

	General commerce		Special commerce	
Year	Imports	Exports	Imports	Exports
1789	577	441	59	1
1800	323	372	28	1
1810	339	336	45	10
1820	335	543	109	89
1830	638	573	489	453
1840	1052	1011	747	695
1850	1120	1435	791	1068
1860	2657	3148	1897	2267
1870	3498	3456	2867	2802

* A. de Foville, *La France économique* (Paris, 1887), 220. The figures for 1789 are un-doubtedly too high; the total trade for this year was probably between 600 and 700 million francs.

The special commerce includes only those things which were wholly French in their origin or were destined for domestic con-sumption; the general commerce comprises all wares that enter or

[7] O. Noël, *Histoire du commerce extérieur de la France depuis la Révolution* (Paris, 1879), 214-20.

leave France. Broadly speaking, both groups show the same general tendencies — a steady growth during the nineteenth century and a preponderance of imports down to 1850, after which exports were larger. The difference between the special and the general commerce measures the re-export trade, which grew *pari passu* with the other branches of trade. France is situated on the cross-roads of European traffic and there was a continuous stream of foreign commerce entering and leaving her ports. The excess of exports during the latter part of this period marks the entrance of France into the world financial markets and the investment of French capital savings in other countries. By 1870 these foreign investments amounted to between 12 and 14 million francs.

It will be noticed that the decades of the fifties and sixties show an extraordinary advance over the previous period. Various factors combined to produce this result. The modification of the prohibitory tariff systems was of course a prime factor, but the improvement and cheapening of transportation, both on land and sea, were of scarcely less importance. The great increase, measured in monetary values, was in part illusory, owing to the gold discoveries and the general rise in prices throughout the western world. Measured in quantities, the growth was not so great. This becomes apparent when the few cases are examined in which quantities were recorded. Thus the export of wines, measured in millions of gallons, was as follows: 1820, 320; 1840, 340; 1859, 660; 1869, 920; this was a threefold increase from 1820 to 1869. But the value for the same dates jumped from 48 million francs to 261, or a fivefold gain. The exports of textiles were as follows in millions of francs:

Year	Woolens	Silks	Cottons
1831	27	119	55
1846	44	122	107
1859	181	500	67
1869	268	447	70

It is difficult to draw any satisfactory general conclusions from the fragmentary statistics, for each industry was subject to its own peculiar mischances, such as phylloxera in the vineyards, the shortage of cotton due to the Civil War in the United States, and changes in fashion and technique which affected both the woolen and silk industries. But in general the period after 1850 was one of general trade expansion. The exports of toys, haberdashery, and small articles of luxury showed a particularly marked increase, jumping from 56 million francs in 1852 to 175 million in 1868. This was the field in which French manufacturers met with least competition in foreign markets. Trade with Great Britain showed the greatest increase, more than doubling in the decade of the sixties, but that with other countries expanded rapidly as liberal commercial treaties were made with them.

Ocean shipping. The French merchant marine failed to share adequately in the expansion of this period, and even showed a relative decline when compared with competing services. Economic disadvantages and legislative disabilities both contributed to this end. The cost of shipbuilding was higher in France than in most other countries. It was about 6 per cent higher than the cost in Britain in 1860 for wooden ships and 20 per cent higher for iron ships.[8] This was in spite of free admission of raw materials for shipbuilding by a decree of 1855. Equal disadvantages in manning the ships were imposed by French law, which subjected all sailors, fishermen, and workers on ships to the system of "maritime inscription," according to which they were at the disposal of the navy at any time. Uncertainties in construction resulted from this possibility of having the mechanics in a private shipyard called without notice to government services, and an additional hazard was added for seamen in being forced to serve in the navy without warning and for an indefinite time. On the other hand the system of prohibitions and protection was extended both to shipping and to cargoes. By a law of 1793 all vessels flying the French flag must be French-built, and at least three-fourths of the crew must be French. Foreign ships could bring in only goods of their own countries. The coastal and colonial trade was absolutely closed to foreigners. The latter monopoly was abolished in 1826, but no further change was made in this legislation until 1860, when foreign-built ships were admitted to French registry upon payment of stiff duties; at the same time the proportion of the crew that must be French was reduced to one-half. A discriminatory tax had been imposed in 1814 on foreign vessels entering French ports, but in 1866 this was abolished. There was thus a gradual liberalization in the treatment of such ships. The growth of the merchant marine may be briefly shown.

TONNAGE OF FRENCH MERCHANT MARINE

Year	Sailing	Steam	Total
1840	652,000 *	10,000 *	662,000
1850	674,228	13,925	688,153
1860	928,099	68,025	996,124
1870	917,633	154,415	1,072,048

* Estimated.

[8] F. Marshall, *Population and Trade in France in* 1861–62 (London, 1862), 276.

The story of the French merchant marine is much the same as that of other countries. At the beginning of the nineteenth century it was composed exclusively of wooden sailing vessels. In the twenties steam made its appearance, but the early steamships were of the mixed type, with auxiliary sails. The early steamers were engaged primarily in the river trade, and remained very small—an average of 107 tons in 1847 and 205 in 1858. Until 1860 the sailing vessel was not seriously menaced and the supremacy of steam was considered doubtful by many. The great obstacle to the use of steam was the cost of fuel and the space absorbed in carrying it, for the early engines made extravagant use of coal. Gradually, however, improvements were made in the engines and machinery. The first screw steamer was the Napoleon in 1839 with an engine of 220 h.p., which attained a speed of 10 knots an hour; in 1862 the double screw was introduced.[9] About the same time compound engines were built, with triple and even quadruple expansion. Parallel with improvements in machinery went a revolution in construction: iron was substituted for wood. But the introduction of iron vessels on any considerable scale had to wait for metallurgical inventions which should make iron cheap. For whatever reason the French were very slow in building steamers. Between 1838 and 1860 the tonnage of English steamships grew from 80,000 to 500,000, while that of the French increased only from 10,000 to 68,000.

The French merchant marine was never adequate even for the carriage of her own commerce, and most of the foreign carrying trade was done by the British and other vessels. In 1820 over half of the tonnage entering French ports was foreign; in 1840 it was almost three-quarters, but after that sank to about two-thirds. Even the trade between French ports, which had been retained exclusively for the home fleet, showed a falling off. The building of railways cut in half the traffic between the northern ports and those on the Mediterranean, but the shorter coastal trade showed a steady gain. Marseilles was the leading port at the beginning of the century; but, as the center of trade moved to the Atlantic, Havre took its place. The latter ranked only after London and Liverpool in 1870. Many of the French ports were river ports, which were adequate in the days of small sailing vessels, but as larger iron ships with deeper draft began to be built these ports fell into disfavor. They were shallow, there was constant silting, they lacked sufficient dock space, and they were not rebuilt to meet new demands.

[9] A. Colin, *La navigation commerciale au XIXᵉ siècle* (Paris, 1901), 43.

3. ZOLLVEREIN IN GERMANY

Particularism. In 1815 the 350 states of Germany were reduced by the Congress of Vienna to 38.[10]   Although this was an improvement over the former chaotic situation, the greatest lack of unity and particularism still existed among the separate states.   Each state was allowed to retain its fiscal autonomy.   The numerous taxes and customs duties which were levied at each border seriously hampered trade.   In Prussia alone there were sixty-seven different tariff systems in operation, separating district from district and cities from the surrounding country district.   These customs and taxes were, moreover, so complicated and required the filling out of so many forms that merchants who carried on considerable regular shipments had to employ one or two clerks just to fill out the forms.   Wares had to be packed in prescribed fashion, sealed and signed, and the route and destination must be stated, from which no deviation was permitted.   It was against such conditions that Frederick List protested in 1819.   "Thirty-eight tariff walls impede internal commerce and have much the same effect as if every limb of the human body were tied up so that the blood could not circulate.   To go from Hamburg to Austria, from Berlin to Switzerland, ten states must be traversed, ten tariffs studied, ten customs duties paid."

Such a system was extremely expensive to maintain, and it bore with especial severity upon the small states.   An enormous number of officials was necessary to administer the customs and guard the frontiers, and on the average from 10 to 18 per cent of the revenues went for costs of administration.   In Bavaria and Wurtemberg the costs in 1829–31 absorbed 44 per cent of the gross receipts.   Baden, with its far-spreading boundaries, realized the impossibility of maintaining such a system and went over almost to free trade.

Under these conditions the industry which flourished most was smuggling.   So profitable was it that it had become a widespread and well-organized business.   It was impossible to guard adequately the extensive boundaries which were sometimes, as between Baden and Wurtemberg, situated in the mountains.   Many small state governments winked at the smuggling and based their customs policy upon this profitable trade.   Thus, although the population of Anhalt was less than one per cent of that of Prussia, the tax-free importation upon the free Elbe River was seven times as much per capita for Anhalt as for Prussia.   Some of the states were too small and without adequate financial resources to set up customs houses, and through such regions smuggled goods flowed freely.   This was true also of the thirteen little states wholly enclosed in Prussian territory, the

[10] In 1817 the number was increased to 39.

enclaves, which had been permitted to receive imports subject to very low transit duties or even none at all.

Leadership of Prussia. Such a confused situation obviously called for reform, and efforts had been made as early as 1797 to find a remedy; but the first decisive step was the Prussian tariff of 1818. This established freedom of trade within Prussia; it abolished all internal duties of the separate districts and all customs limitations of the provinces, and also all prohibitions of exports and imports, except the importation into Prussia of salt and playing cards, since these were government monopolies. In order to produce revenue and to prevent smuggling, low duties were imposed on imports of grain and manufactured goods. These were specific duties, so much on the pound, the bushel, or the yard, but averaged about 10 per cent when calculated on an *ad valorem* basis. Moderate export duties were also imposed on needed domestic raw materials, while those produced abroad were admitted free or at very low rates. On colonial wares, whose entrance could be controlled most easily, rather heavy revenue duties of 20 per cent were laid.

The fiscal policy upon which this measure of Maassen was based was thoroughly sound and enlightened. Low duties are more easily collected than high, and offer less temptation to smuggling. Specific duties can be more accurately computed than *ad valorem*, which offer opportunity for evasion by undervaluation. And because of these facts the receipts would be increased. Political and geographical factors impressed upon Prussian — and that means German — commercial policy from the very beginning certain features which have ever since characterized it and which made it at the time the most liberal in all Europe.

But quite as important for immediate ends was the fact that the new law was strictly administered. The transit dues were raised and collected. The little *enclaves*, which saw their profitable smuggling trade vanish at one blow, protested vigorously but in vain. In 1819 the little principality of Schwarzburg-Sondershausen yielded to the pressure and by 1828 all these little states had surrendered their fiscal independence. The terms were, however, very liberal: trade between Prussia and the *enclaves* was made entirely free, all duties were collected at the Prussian frontier by Prussia, and the customs revenues were divided *pro rata* on the basis of population.

The Prussian transit dues were resented by other states, but they were helpless, for most of the main trade routes of Germany ran across Prussian territory. Under the circumstances the other states had only two choices: they could form unions among themselves in opposition to Prussia or they could unite with Prussia. The former course was taken by two groups of states. In 1828 Bavaria and

Wurtemberg formed a customs union which comprised the essential features of the larger Zollverein of 1834. Freedom of trade between the two states was provided for, and the customs duties were to be collected by each state on its own frontier, but were divided *pro rata* on the basis of population. In the same year in which this southern union was formed a central league was organized of Saxony, Hanover, Brunswick, the Thuringian states, the free cities of Hamburg and Bremen and other units. Each state retained its old tariffs, as they could not agree on a common system. They did, however, arrange to facilitate trade in foodstuffs and to build some roads.

The second alternative was taken by Hesse-Darmstadt, which in 1828 made a treaty with Prussia. This was important, for it indicated clearly the terms on which further union was to proceed, which were similar to those agreed upon by the southern union. Freedom of trade between the two states was provided for, each state was to administer the customs on its own frontier, but the Prussian tariff of 1818 was to be adopted by Hesse, and the customs revenues were to be divided according to population.

The Zollverein. It is unnecessary to recount the political and economic struggles among these various groups in the next half decade. It is sufficient to state that after much maneuvering the northern and southern unions finally came to terms in 1833. The central league had already broken up and no longer offered an obstacle to a larger union. The result was the formation for eight years of a customs union or Zollverein, which came into force on January 1, 1834, and comprised the states of Prussia, Bavaria, Wurtemberg, Saxony, the two Hesses, the Thuringian states, and some others. The Zollverein included seventeen states with a population of 25,000,000, and an area about two-thirds that of the future German Empire.

There was, however, still a considerable group that remained outside, made up of Hanover (still an English possession), Luxemburg (Dutch), Schleswig-Holstein (Danish), and states whose advantage lay in free trade rather than in the moderate protection of the Prussian tariff, as Baden, Nassau, the Hanse cities, and other northern states. These states, together with Austria, continually opposed the closer union of the Zollverein states and especially objected to the basic Prussian tariff of 1818 — Austria because it was too low, the other states because it was too high. England and France exerted themselves to prevent a German union. The French government offered the little states commercial treaties and endeavored to prevent the customs union. A member of the British House of Commons declared that Prussia had "no right to make treaties with other German states which disadvantageously affect English trade." Austria, which disputed with Prussia the leadership of the smaller German states, always opposed any measures which would strengthen the position of Prussia.

The provisions of the Zollverein followed the lines of the arrangements already in existence. All internal duties and staple rights were abolished, river dues and road taxes were lightened, and equal rights were given all members at markets and fairs. Coinage, weights, and measures were to be standardized by future agreements. A common tariff was set up at the border, to be administered by each state on its own territory, but the revenues were to be pooled and distributed according to population. Each state was to retain its own commercial code, its own patent laws, and its fiscal monopolies, and any change should require unanimous approval.

The Zollverein may be regarded from two standpoints. First, it was a movement for free trade within Germany, and, second, it was a union of German states against the outside world. Although it has generally been discussed from the point of view of foreign commercial policy, its great importance, both political and economical, lay in the establishment of fiscal unity and the abolition of internal barriers to trade. The Zollverein, wrote Dr. John Bowring, who made a report on it in 1840 to Palmerston, "derived its first and strongest influence from a desire to get rid of those barriers to intercommunication which the separate fiscal legislation of the various states of Germany raised. . . [It] was the substantial expression and effect of a general desire among a great nation, split into many small states, but still of common origin, similar manners, speaking the same language, educated in the same spirit, to communicate, to trade, to travel, without the annoyance and impediments which the separate fiscal regulations of every one of their governments threw in the way."

It is easy to exaggerate the influence of the Zollverein in bringing about the undoubted industrial and commercial development which occurred in Germany after 1835, for it was only one of many factors. The improvement of roads and later the building of railways, the influx of British capital, the spread of new techniques in manufacturing and agriculture, and the gradual improvement in the standard of living, all contributed to its prosperity. Smuggling was suppressed, internal trade grew, manufactures developed in favorable locations, and agriculture prospered as a wider domestic market opened up.

On the other hand, wrote Bowring, "the Zollverein was advocated as a measure of self-defence against the hostile legislation of foreign nations." Now, for the first time, the member states had a common tariff and could adopt a uniform commercial policy with regard to foreign trade.   The Prussian tariff of 1818 formed the basis of the Zollverein in 1834.   This imposed moderate duties on many manufactured goods, but admitted raw materials or materials serving the needs of agriculture and manufactures free or with very low duties. In order to prevent smuggling and to simplify the administration, the duties were specific and not *ad valorem*.   The result was that they bore most heavily on coarse, low-priced, and heavy articles. Foreign articles of low quality and general consumption were thus generally excluded and the home market for goods of this character was reserved for the home producer.   And with every cheapening in cost, this effect became more noticeable.

Commercial development.   In 1842 the eight year period for which the Zollverein was first organized came to an end, and the question at once arose as to the terms upon which it should be renewed. Several of the states which had stood outside had in the interval joined the union, which now represented a number of divergent interests.   The north and east in general favored free trade, for there were centered the shipping, trading, and exporting interests. The eastern districts produced large quantities of grain for export, which found an outlet through the Baltic ports; neither agriculturalists nor shippers needed protection.   On the other hand, the landowners needed agricultural machinery, which they could buy cheaply abroad; protection to the iron industry would force them to pay more.   The Baltic ports carried on a vigorous trade with England and the United States, and the interior market towns of Leipzig and Frankfort were *entrepôts* for foreign goods.   The textile industry of Saxony and Prussia represented two diverse interests: the spinners and the weavers.   The latter obtained two-thirds of their yarn from England and did not wish the price increased.   Against them stood the spinners, many of them home workers, who were finding it increasingly difficult to compete with the machine-made spun yarn of England.   Improvements in manufacturing technique and reductions in costs of transportation through the building of railroads had, moreover, made the competition more serious.   But the weavers were more powerful.

In the iron industry there was a contradiction similar to that in the textile.   A considerable iron-working industry had been built up in the Ruhr, in Aachen, and in the mountainous districts upon the basis of cheap raw iron which came in duty free.   Until 1849 there was not a coke oven in the Ruhr territory for the primary production of iron.   But the German iron industry was meeting increasing competition.   Technological improvements had led to a great expansion in England, and after the panic of 1837 and resulting depression there was over-production.   Prices fell and an outlet was sought on the continent. Imports of iron into Germany, which were only 45,000 short tons in 1839, increased to 130,000 tons in 1842, and 210,000 tons in 1843. The absence of blast furnaces left the coal miners in the Saar district without a market for their product except as they found an outlet in France. But while France admitted German coal it would not admit German iron manufactures. It was decided therefore to build up the primary iron industry by a moderate duty on raw iron. The duties on bar, wrought, and rolled iron, and on rails were raised proportionately.

The protectionist movement found its strongest support in the south, though here also were divergent interests. At the head stood Wurtemberg, whose cotton-spinning industry was expanding, but which was unable to meet English and Belgian competition. It therefore favored protection. Baden and Hesse supported this view. Bavaria had to decide between the cotton-spinning industry, which demanded protection, and the weaving industry, which wished to make use of the cheap foreign yarn, but it finally voted for protection. The duties on cotton yarn were raised fifty per cent and those on linen doubled. In spite of the conflict of interests, the Zollverein was renewed in 1842 for another ten years.

When the ten year period expired in 1852 the question of a renewal of the Zollverein came up again. Three problems presented themselves: the question of protection, of the admission of Austria, and of Hanover. After protracted negotiations these were solved by including free-trade Hanover and excluding protectionist Austria. A commercial treaty was made with the latter, however, designed to promote mutual trade and to prepare for eventual union. The attitude of the different industrial groups to commercial policy at this time may be briefly stated. The commercial groups, shippers and traders, of the ports on the north and east seas with their followers inland favored free trade, for that brought them the greatest profits. The exporting agriculturalists took the same position, for they gained from the increasing sale of their grain, cattle, brandy, and lately sugar, while they bought agricultural machinery, fertilizer, and other supplies cheaply from abroad. During the 1850's and 1860's, after the repeal of the English corn laws, they supplied about one-quarter of the English imports of these commodities. After 1860, however, they yielded first place to the United States and after 1865 to Russia. The bankers stood by the large traders. The wage-earners had no voice politically and showed no interest. The liberal professions, the railroad men, and public officials favored free trade and followed the teachings of Adam Smith. Free trade was taught in the universities.

On the other side were the large and medium manufacturers in the iron and textile industries, the owners of coal and iron mines, the manufacturers of machines, the makers of railroad supplies, and many groups of handworkers.   In England the large manufacturers, who were exporters, advocated free trade, but the reverse was true of German industrialists who wished to retain for themselves the growing home market.   This group swore by Frederick List and found valuable support in his doctrine of historical development.

Benefits from the Zollverein.   The advantages of the Zollverein were both economic and political.   Domestic commerce and industry grew rapidly by the application of the principle of free trade within Germany.   A real national unity in economic matters was created at a time when politically Germany was only a semblance of a union. The Zollverein is generally considered to have constituted the first step toward German national unity.   A common system of weights and measures and a common currency, which had been pledged in 1834, were finally attained about 1870.   A common law regulating bills of exchange was adopted by the various states about 1850; a joint postal service was established about 1868.   Bowring concluded in 1840 that "by directing capital to internal improvements in preference to external trade," it had "already had a great influence in improving the roads, the canals, the means of travelling, the transport of letters — in a word in giving an impulse to inland communication of every sort."

From a fiscal point of view too the Zollverein was important, for it brought into the depleted exchequers of the constituent states much-needed revenues.   The receipts from customs were as follows (in thousand dollars):

Year	Imports	Exports	Transit	Total
1834	10,400	300	380	11,080
1839	14,800	380	520	15,700
1844	19,200	380	520	20,100
1849	17,800	300	380	18,280
1854	17,200	14	300	17,514
1859	17,600	14	300	17,934

The disappearance of smuggling has already been mentioned, but the reduction in costs of administration as a result of the simplification of the tariff and the establishment of a common frontier must also be emphasized.   The tariff frontier which Prussia had to guard in 1819 stretched over 1073 miles; by the end of the year 1837 the Zollverein, with a population of 26,000,000, almost double that of Prussia eighteen years before, had a tariff frontier of only 1064 miles in all.

Growth of commerce.   The course of foreign trade during the first half of the nineteenth century reflected less the changes in German commercial policy than it did the developments in ocean transportation, the growth of new countries overseas, and the increasing territorial division of labor. At the beginning of the century exports were almost entirely those of the extractive industries, as grain, building wood, and wool, together with linen and some other textiles. Germany was primarily an agricultural country with some home industries. The imports were largely tropical foodstuffs, as sugar, coffee, tea, dyes, and similar items. The continental blockade interrupted this trade, which, however, quickly recovered after 1815. After the fall of Napoleon the German markets were flooded with British goods, and the shipping and trading interests prospered though the domestic German industries were hard hit. Some rather unsatisfactory trade statistics for the period 1825–31 showed a moderate increase in the exports of grain, a considerable increase in those of manufactures, and a falling off in cattle; other items were mostly unchanged. By the middle of the century the principal business of the Hanseatic ports was the importation from overseas of luxuries, sugar, coffee, tobacco, spices, and raw materials for industry. Exports were still largely those of the extractive industries; manufactures played a small part.

With the establishment of the Zollverein in 1834 more trustworthy statistics of foreign trade were gathered. The external commerce of the constituent states showed a steady expansion after this date, both absolutely and per capita. The following table is taken from Rau: [11]

Year	Imports	Exports	Imports	Exports
	(in million dollars)		(in dollars per capita)	
1834	76	103	3.20	4.40
1842	135	116	4.80	4.15
1846	158	122	5.35	4.13
1854	192	239	5.90	7.40
1857	253	250	7.65	7.55
1860	261	333	7.80	9.90

The merchandise balance of trade was unfavorable in three out of the six years cited, and probably represents an investment of foreign — largely British — capital in Germany during this period. The steady increase reflects not merely the low tariff policy of the Zollverein, but also a gradual improvement in the standard of living of the German people. The small amount of foreign trade per capita shows, however, that the country was still largely self-sufficing.

[11] H. Rau, *Vergleichende Statistik des Handels der deutschen Staaten* (1863). Converted into dollars.

The composition of this foreign trade was given as follows by a German writer [12] for 1864:

Articles	Imports	Exports
	(per cent)	
Articles of consumption	26.7	22.9
Raw materials	38.1	15.1
Partly manufactured and materials for manufacture	22.6	9.0
Manufactures	9.2	52.6
Others	1.3	1.4

The striking feature of this table is the large importation of raw materials and partly manufactured articles, making up together over 60 per cent of the imports, and the almost equally great export of manufactures, over half of the whole. The picture presented is that of a highly industrialized state, but this is misleading, for German so-called manufactures in 1864 were still largely the product of handwork; the developed factory system was to come later. Imports comprised tropical products, raw cotton and silk, yarn, crude iron, machines, and numerous other items. Exports comprised grain, flour, brandy, lumber, wool, and other agricultural products, but most important were the manufactures. Chief among these were textiles, largely home spun and woven, which competed with English and Belgian fabrics mainly by reason of low wages and long hours, though partly because of better designs. Next came a multitude of metal wares, wrought and cast, such as the fine steel and cutlery of Solingen, the copper and brass wares of Nuremberg, fine instruments and other things. Chemicals, paper, earthenware, porcelain, and a great range of minor specialties concluded the list.

4. DOMESTIC TRADE IN GERMANY AND FRANCE
(a) GERMANY

Obstacles to trade in Germany. At the beginning of the nineteenth century a self-sufficing economy prevailed generally in Germany. Three-quarters of the people were engaged in agriculture, and these people produced, in addition to their food, most of their own clothing, furniture, housing, and other simple necessities. Industry was carried on almost entirely by handworkers or in the home, and the circle of exchange was usually limited to the village or town with its supporting agricultural population. Under these circumstances there was little opportunity or scope for domestic trade. Goods were seldom brought to market, but were consumed

[12] A. Bienengraber, *Statistik des Verkehrs und Verbrauchs im Zollverein* (1868). There are errors in the original in the columns of imports and exports, which add up 97.9 and 101 respectively. The whole table must be viewed with some doubt.

within the producing group. Not until territorial division of occupations existed, and a surplus of goods beyond the needs of the workers was produced, did exchange on any extended scale take place. But these conditions did not exist in the Germany of 1800.

The development of a market, and the production of goods for that market, depend on three factors: (1) The productivity of agriculture, that is the ability of the agricultural population to produce a surplus beyond their own needs, which they can exchange for manufactured goods. (2) The existence of a separate group of urban workers, who find it possible and profitable to devote all their time to the production of non-agricultural goods. (3) The existence of a marketing mechanism which facilitates the exchange of these two groups of goods. The more productive agriculture is, the larger becomes the number of urban workers, and the greater the share of the national products which are brought to market.

The backwardness of agriculture and the small size of the towns, both of which have already been described, furnish evidence, if such were needed, of the lack of an economic basis for a vigorous internal trade. The entire absence of any statistics of domestic trade is therefore not surprising.

In addition to these economic difficulties there existed political interferences with the movement of goods which hindered commercial development. River trade, which was the easiest and cheapest method of transportation, was almost destroyed by the medieval institution of the staple. "It was impossible to travel far on any German river without reaching a staple, where the boatman was subject to delay, inconvenience, and considerable expense. On the Rhine, for instance, there were thirty-two stations of this character where dues were still levied in 1800. As far as regarded the effect on commerce the flow of the rivers might as well have been interrupted by cataracts." [13]

Germany in 1800 was, moreover, not a united country politically, but was split up into 360 small states, each of which was intensely jealous of its rights. Some of these states were themselves split into pieces; even a small state might consist of eight or ten fragments, interspersed among its neighbors. Each state had its own system of customs duties and some had internal tariffs as well. A network of tariff barriers covered the whole country, restricting if not preventing the movement of goods. Prussia alone had sixty-seven tariffs, covering almost 3000 articles of trade. To reach an interior point from the frontier meant the crossing of many tariff boundaries, with payment of duties at each custom house.

[13] Clive Day, *A History of Commerce* (New York, 1907), 347. By permission of the publishers, Longmans, Green and Company, New York.

The whole apparatus of trade and exchange was burdened with yet other inconveniences due to this political separation. The more important states had their own systems of moneys, weights, and measures. There were seventeen different postal systems in the country, and nearly sixty different laws on bills of exchange. It seemed as though every device of which human ingenuity was capable had been applied to prevent the development of internal trade. And yet, in spite of all these hindrances, some domestic commerce existed. Its growth parallels the removal of the obstacles just described.

A notable step in the direction of removing some of these restrictions was taken by Prussia in the tariff law of May 26, 1818. Before this time different fiscal systems had existed in the various small states making up Prussia; thus the import duties in Brandenburg were three times as heavy as those in Silesia. The new law allowed the unrestricted movement of all foreign products which had once passed the frontier and the free transit of all home products. All internal customs were abolished and free trade was established throughout Prussia. The Zollverein, or Customs Union, among the different German states extended this free home market to some 25,000,000 people in 1834, and to nearly 35,000,000 in 1861. Steps were also taken toward a common system of moneys, weights, and measures, but this was not fully achieved until the establishment of the Empire in 1871.

Marketing agencies. The distribution of goods, or marketing, was carried on by a variety of agencies, which changed in character and relative importance from the beginning to the end of the first half of the nineteenth century.

Peddling was the oldest form, having existed for centuries. The peddlers wandered from place to place and from house to house, offering articles that had a large value in a small bulk and which found ready sale. Some of them were specialists, trading perhaps in the products of their relatives or fellow-villagers, and carrying brooms and pictures from Weissenfels, tinware from Saxony, Black Forest clocks, Bielefeld linen, or Nuremberg metal wares over the whole of Germany. These were produced by handworkers in their homes beyond the needs of the neighborhood, and for them it was necessary to find a wider market. Some of the goods found even an international market; thus fruit trees were sold in Norway and brooms in London.[14] For all parties concerned—small producers without market connections, peasant consumers who were illy served or not served at all by shops, and the peddlers them-

---

[14] W. Roscher, *Nationalökonomik des Handels und Gewerbefleisses* (7th ed., Stuttgart, 1899), 113.

selves — this form of sale was a necessity and has persisted to the present day wherever similar conditions are met. In Prussia in 1861 there were 44,410 peddlers.

The lack of permanent stores was met by markets and fairs. Weekly markets were held in every town, when the peasants brought their products for sale, and the housewife purchased the weekly supply of provisions. But these were local affairs and were merely agencies for the exchange of agricultural and manufactured products within a small area. More important and on a much larger scale were the yearly markets, where colonial wares and other goods not produced locally were assembled by peddlers and merchants. Here handworkers and foreign traders could display their wares in comparative freedom from local restrictions. Trade on the yearly markets was encouraged by reduction or suspension of duties, excises, and other fiscal and industrial burdens. Since they occurred so infrequently the housewife and other purchasers must lay in supplies adequate for a whole year. Sometimes cattle markets were held or markets for the sale of wool or flax or other products. There were other attractions, too, to draw and hold the crowds, such as puppet shows, rope-walkers, and similar diversions. The economic basis for the yearly market disappeared with the abolition of the old industrial organization, which had shut off the town from the country and one city from another. By 1840 they had ceased to be an important factor as a distributing agency except in remote regions and small places. Here outmoded goods and cheap wares still found a sale to the peasants.

Still higher in the scale of distributive agencies stood the fair. Of these only four attained national importance in Germany, namely those of Frankfort-on-the-Main, Leipzig, Frankfort-on-the-Oder, and Braunschweig. Although the oldest was that of Frankfort-on-the-Main, it ranked third in importance at the beginning of the nineteenth century. In 1842 it had only 16 per cent of all the goods displayed at these four fairs, and by 1854 its share had sunk to 10 per cent. With the coming of the railroads its significance as a center for the distribution of goods declined. Frankfort-on-the-Oder, serving an industrially and commercially less developed section in eastern Germany, retained its importance longer than the others. It showed a rapid development to 1840, and reached its height about 1855; in the year 1854 it had about 38 per cent of the trade of these four fairs. The fairs at Leipzig, though the youngest of all, soon outstripped the others, as it was centrally located. Three important fairs were held there each year, each visited by from 30,000 to 40,000 customers; goods worth about $4,000,000 were exchanged annually at each. In 1854 it boasted 45 per cent of the fair trade, and continued to grow until the sixties, after which its importance, together with all the others, showed a rapid decline. The fair at Braunschweig was the smallest of all, having only 7 per cent of the trade in 1854. These fairs were for the most part meeting places for dealers, where collectors of the products of hand-workers and domestic workers, *Verleger* who employed home workers on a piece-rate system, and foreign merchants, exchanged their products and redistributed them to the retail markets. The commercial significance of the fairs declined as freedom of trade developed and exchange ceased to be restricted to particular times and places.[15]

Retail trade. Retail trade, carried on in stationary stores, was only slightly developed in the first half of the nineteenth century. In Germany especially, where handwork prevailed in a number of industries — that is, where finished goods were produced for immediate use — there were many kinds of wares for whose sale absolutely no stores existed, since these wares were almost exclusively made by handworkers. Such were bakers, butchers, shoemakers, tailors, hat makers, saddlers, cabinet makers, coopers, furriers, and tinkers.[16] Sometimes these artisans had small shops for the sale of goods produced by them and of similar purchased manufactures.

The oldest form of stationary retail trade was the mixed products or general store, in which all varieties of goods were found together. Colonial wares were the first to be separated out, for these articles could not be supplied locally. A trade in fresh foods also appeared early, together with establishments for the sale of glass, porcelain, and crockery wares, small iron and brass wares, fancy goods and toys, and colonial wares.[17] Finally, second-hand stores appeared. Until the thirties there were not yet stores for the sale of furniture, clothing, shoes, hats, and similar goods. The early stores were very small affairs, as is shown by the following statistics: in 1801 Berlin had 1992 independent retail establishments with 932 helpers; in 1858 there were in all Prussia 39,329 stores with 22,907 employees.[18] That is, in nearly half of the stores the proprietor did not employ even a single clerk.

Between 1840 and 1860 marked changes occurred in the organization of trade. A greater specialization set in and the general store gave way to establishments which concentrated on particular types of

---

[15] K. Rathgen, "Märkte und Messen," in *Handwörterbuch der Staatswissenschaften* (Jena, 1892), IV, 1124.

[16] J. Kulischer, *Wirtschaftsgeschichte des Mittelalters und der Neuzeit* (München, 1929), II, 511.

[17] J. Kirsch, "Handel," in *Grundriss der Sozialökonomik*, V. Abt. (2. Aufl., Tübingen, 1925), 229.

[18] *Handwörterbuch der Staatswissenschaften*, s. v. "Kleinhandel" (4th ed., 1926), 498.

goods. As manufacturing enterprises grew larger the producer sought to reach the retailer directly and to eliminate the middleman. For this purpose he turned again to the peddler, but a peddler of an entirely different type, namely the commercial traveler, who went from city to city with his wares. Then arose the mail-order houses (*Versandgeschäfte*), at first especially for those articles which were influenced by fashion, as for women's clothes from Leipzig and Baden, but also for articles of more general consumption as for sausage and ham in Westphalia, Braunschweig, and Gotha, butter in Friesland and Schleswig-Holstein, wash goods in Silesia, paper collars, men's wear, and a thousand other articles in Leipzig.[19]

In the large and middle-sized cities there developed another type of retail trade on a large scale, namely the department store (*Warenhaus*). These threatened particularly the small retail trade. They sold articles cheap because of direct purchases, large turnover, and sometimes cash sales. The first store of this sort seems to have been established in Berlin in 1842; this sold principally women's clothing and excited great interest. A decade later 120 to 140 workwomen were employed in its workshop and 150 masters with 10 helpers outside. By the end of the forties whole classes of society in Silesia bought their clothing in clothing stores. In 1850 the first women's clothing store appeared in Munich.[20] Here, however, the government endeavored to save the small retail establishments and imposed taxes on the *Warenhäuser* amounting to $7\frac{1}{3}$ per cent of their turnover. In other places similar legislation was passed, though not so extreme; in Saxony the communities were forbidden to take in taxes more than $2\frac{1}{2}$ per cent of the turnover.

All of these changes brought about economic and social shifts. The peddlers and domestic industry were especially hard hit; handwork and the small retail trade somewhat less so; but all felt the effects. In the higher branches of trade the expansion of the railroads toward the middle of the century also made changes. Formerly the large producers had sought the markets, as at the fairs, but now this ceased. Instead they sent commercial travelers to their customers. Illustrations of this practice were to be found among producers of iron and steel, of glass and porcelain, and of colonial wares. This was a blow to the merchant middleman, but the full effects of this and of the other changes just described were not felt until the second half of the century.

Wholesale trade. The wholesale trade stands between the competing producers and retail dealers. At the beginning of the nineteenth century the manufacturer or importer seldom sold directly

[19] Lamprecht, *Deutsche Geschichte der jüngsten Vergangenheit*, 358.
[20] Jos. Kulischer, op. cit., II, 482.

to the retailer. Rather they delivered their wares to a wholesaler, who then held the purchases on his own account in storage and sought to dispose of them in small portions to the retailers in the different cities of his district. This he did through the aid of an agent or he himself went on a journey and offered the retailers his wares. Often he wrote to the retailers who traded with him regularly that he had wares of this or that kind and asked for an order. Since the retailer usually had only a small store and was, moreover, compelled to carry in stock the most varied articles, he could take from the wholesaler only a few kinds of wares. If his stock of a particular good was exhausted he ordered more or took from the wholesaler something similar. The whole trade was carried on in a primitive and leisurely fashion. Even trade in important colonial wares, as tea, coffee, and spices, moved along these lines, only the series of middlemen was increased by one or two persons. Only infrequently did the German importer draw his colonial wares direct from the distant regions of production; for the most part he bought them in England or Holland from a colonial house which stood in direct commercial relations with the colonies.[21]

(b) FRANCE

Artificial barriers. The larger part of France is a great plain with numerous rivers. The natural physical conditions were favorable to internal trade. But artificial barriers prevented it. Although France, toward the end of the eighteenth century, was politically a centralized state, the scattered fragments out of which it was composed had never been unified commercially and old tariffs and local tolls still remained. Three commercial areas may be distinguished. In the northern provinces internal trade was free except for local tolls, but goods coming into or going out of this area even to other parts of France paid duties. In the south was a group of provinces "reputed foreign," which was similarly shut off from the rest of France by tariff barriers. And in the east were provinces "foreign in fact," which had never been incorporated in France commercially, for they were outside the national customs frontier; they might have free trade with other countries but paid duties on goods sent into or received from France.

But in addition to these provincial tariffs there were thousands of local tolls exacted by lords, towns, or the church, which required an army of collectors and seriously interfered with trade. "It was estimated that a hogshead of wine travelling from Roanne to Paris (260 miles) paid no less than twenty tolls, in addition to two in-

[21] Cunow, op. cit., IV, 95.

ternal custom duties at Valence and Lyons." [13]   The amount of the tolls often exceeded the original cost of the goods.

The evil effects of such interferences with exchange had called forth the criticism of the Physiocrats and Turgot had endeavored to abolish some of the worst of them. But the reactionary forces were too strong for him, and relief had to wait for the Revolution. One of the first effects of the Revolution was to sweep away this cumbersome mass of provincial tariff and local tolls, and to establish freedom of internal trade. In 1791 the General Assembly declared "The territory of France in all its extent is free, as also the persons who inhabit it." The country was thus, for the first time, given commercial unity. At the same time the gilds were abolished and the burdensome price and market regulations came to an end. During the Napoleonic era, however, this commercial freedom was again restricted. In 1800 the old police regulations over trade in butter, cheese and eggs were reintroduced, and it was forbidden to sell these articles except in the market halls, on certain days and at prescribed hours. Everywhere strict supervision was instituted, not only in the municipal market halls, but also at the markets and fairs. The gilds of the printers, of the bakers, and of the butchers were also in part re-established. The ostensible purpose of these restrictions was to regulate prices and quality of goods and to assure cheap food.

Early French trade. Information about the internal trade of France in the first half of the nineteenth century is almost entirely lacking. That it was growing seems to be clearly indicated by the increased traffic on roads and canals and on the early railroads, especially after 1830. At the beginning of the century the commercial organization was probably not very different from that existing in Germany. Few permanent stores existed, except perhaps a few in the large cities which sold luxury goods. The immediate needs of the rural population for manufactured wares — and it must be remembered that over three-quarters of the people lived in the country — were served by peddlers, while markets in the country towns and occasional fairs in the larger centers provided opportunity for purchasing staple goods and colonial wares. But the great fairs had lost their importance in the eighteenth century: they had become almost purely agricultural markets. Only in exceptional instances were manufactured goods, especially cloth, brought to sale at these places. On the other hand, the rise of large cities like Paris, Lyons, and Marseilles necessitated a regular trade in foodstuffs drawn from a wide area. Various French products, moreover, such as wine and silk, found markets outside of France. Such a trade undoubtedly called for commercial organization on a considerable scale and a

[13] A. Birnie, *An Economic History of Europe*, 1760–1930 (New York, 1936), 65.

merchant class to care for it.   But details are wholly lacking.   The
peasantry supplied most of their own wants and made few demands
on any market.

Retail trade.   Retail trade scarcely existed outside the larger
towns.   The master craftsman made goods to order for the consumer, though sometimes he undoubtedly collected a stock from
which he sold ready-made wares.   But, in addition to these craftsmen's shops, a new type, the modern store, began to appear, kept
by a dealer and not by a producer.   At the close of the eighteenth
century there are records of such stores in Paris.   The earliest examples of these were general stores, handling a variety of merchandise,
but in time specialized stores for particular lines appeared.   With
their growth the traveling salesman, the *commis voyageur*, came
upon the scene, a type made famous in Balzac's *Illustrious Gaudis-
sant*.   His rise shows clearly the existence of a permanent class of
retail storekeepers whose orders he took and who distributed to local
consumers the goods which they bought.   These retail dealers were
unprogressive, waiting quietly behind their counters for customers,
and doing little to expand their operations.   Prices were fixed, profits
coming from wide price spreads rather than from a large turnover.

This period witnessed also the development of the large store and
of the department store, both in Paris.   In the thirties Parissot, who
had a small store for the sale of dry-goods, began to specialize in
the sale of ready-made clothing and soon built up a flourishing business.   When he retired in 1856 his fortune was estimated at 3,000,-
000 francs.   This was the first of the great stores, but the real development along this line came in the second half of the nineteenth
century.   The rapid economic development under the Second Empire, the rise of Paris as the leader of fashion for the world, and the
emergence of new strata of consumers opened undreamed-of opportunities for far-sighted merchants.   A pioneer among these was
Aristide Boucicaut, a penniless salesman who went into partnership
with a storekeeper named Vidau, and decided to sell at low prices
with a small profit, hoping by large sales to do better than those
merchants who made a large profit on a small turnover.

Until this time the public had had a choice between good stuffs
which were dear or cheap stuffs which were bad.   Boucicaut's orig-
inality consisted in selling guaranteed merchandise at low prices.
The prices were clearly marked on the goods, a daring innovation
in place of the customary haggling; customers were, moreover, permitted to return their purchases; and the employees were paid by
commissions on their sales.[22]   The name of the store, the *Bon
Marché*, expressed the aims of the founders.   Their faith was justi-

---

[22] G. d'Avenel, *Le mécanisme de la vie moderne* (Paris, 1922), I, 13.

fied, the sales for the first year amounting to 450,000 francs; by 1863 they were 7,000,000. Vidau withdrew and was replaced by Maillard, who had grown rich as a restaurant keeper in New York, and who contributed not only additional capital, but valuable experience. When Boucicaut died, in 1877, the sales were 67,000,000; 1893, 150,000,000; 1910, 227,000,000 francs. In 1880 the firm was converted into a stock company and the ownership of the shares was confined to the employees, of whom there were 6000 in 1910. The *Bon Marché* has been called the employees' republic.

In contrast to this the second great Parisian store, founded in 1855, was organized as a financial oligarchy. This was the *Louvre*, established by two young salesmen, Chaucard and Hériot, together with a capitalist Faret, who formed a connection with Periére, founder of the *Société Immobilière*. They set up their store in a building owned by the latter company. Although they began business in the year of the World Exposition in Paris, their profits amounted to only 1500 francs the first year. Faret withdrew but was replaced by Payen. The profits were put back into the business and after a hard struggle it was made a success. In 1876 the sales were 40,000,000 and in 1912 they were 200,000,000 francs. The *Louvre* extended its sales into the provinces, perhaps a third of its sales being made by post.

The success of these enterprises led to the establishment of others. The *Printemps* was founded in 1865, the *Samarataine* in 1869, and the *Galeries Lafayette* in 1889. None of these was as successful as the first two, but all of them showed steady growth and large sales; the sales for these three were as follows shortly before the World War, in the order named: 93,000,000 francs (1910); 110,000,000 francs (1909); 140,000,000 francs (1914).

All these establishments were the product of intelligence and hard work. The founders were all men from the ranks of the workers; capital played a small and sometimes an insignificant role in their success. They recognized the emergence of new groups of customers and set themselves the task of serving *au Bonheur des Dames*.[23] By democratizing luxury they opened up new fields; they were the first to make silk available to the masses. A shrewd knowledge of feminine economic psychology enabled them to appear convincingly to housewives, in whose hands lay usually the control of the family purse; their system of fixed prices and cash payments had a valuable educational influence. But the great department stores catered only to the average customer. Room was left therefore in Parisian

[23] This is the title of Émil Zola's novel describing the growth of the Parisian department stores.

trade for the special store which served the needs of more dis-
criminating and well-to-do clients.

For trade in the provincial cities another type of store existed, the
so-called Bazaar, which, however, also strove to meet mass demand.
The first of these was the *Nouvelles Galeries,* founded in 1861.
Others followed, and in 1906 they were united in a Bazaar trust, the
Société Française des Magasins Modernes.   Most of the trade,
however, still remained in the hands of the great Parisian department stores, which distributed their illustrated catalogues broadcast
and sold their goods by post.   The sales of the two types have been
estimated as follows: [24]

Cities	SALES (in million francs)	*Dept.* stores	*Bazaars*
Paris		270.0	.5
Cities with more than 100,000 inhabitants		10.4	2.7
Cities with more than 50,000 inhabitants		2.2	1.8
Cities with more than 20,000 inhabitants		1.5	.6

Instalment buying.   Department stores and bazaars rested upon
the principle of cash payment.   But not all customers were able to
pay in full, especially for larger purchases, and the next step was to
provide for instalment buying.   This was undertaken by Crépin,
who began by selling photographs on instalments and then extended
his business to clothing and underwear.   The business expanded
greatly when G. Dufayel took it over in 1871.   He erected his
own sales house, which offered all the advantages of the department
stores without a demand for full immediate payment.   Dufayel
demanded a payment of one-fifth on all purchases up to 50 francs,
of one-quarter up to 150 francs, of a third up to 200 francs, and of
one-half for all over 200 francs; the balance must be paid in instalments of not less than 3 francs each.   The number of customers grew
to over 600,000.

The success of Dufayel not only led to the rise of other credit
houses, but also compelled the retailers to unite in the formation of
their own instalment institution.   In 1901 the *Union économique*
was established as a corporation of retailers of all kinds in one place;
by 1914 there were 150 such unions in existence.   The procedure
was the same as with Dufayel.   The Union collected the instalments,
for which it charged 10 to 15 per cent, but in turn paid to the members dividends of 12½ per cent.

The small retailers demanded also that the state come to their
assistance to protect them against the great department stores.   Ac-

[24] Sée, op. cit., 513.

cordingly in 1889 and again in 1905 special taxes were imposed upon the large establishments, proportioned to the number of the employees and the rental of the sales rooms. These have been estimated at about 16 per cent of the gross sales.

The department stores and bazaars limited themselves to meeting the seasonal needs of their customers for clothing and similar articles, but did not undertake to sell food. This branch of trade was in the hands of a large number of small grocery stores (*épiceries*). Their methods of trade were, as Vicomte d'Avenel [25] points out, absolutely dishonest. Short weight and short measure were given the servants who carried home the purchases, and who received, as their share of the fraud, a sou a pound. This system was revolutionized by Bonnerot, who, about 1840, determined to give exactly what he sold and to be satisfied with a small profit. His competitors were furious, but he persevered and made a small fortune.

Felix Potin came to Paris from the provinces in 1844 and continued the same methods as Bonnerot, selling fair measure at a small profit. In order to have better wares to sell he began to manufacture on his own account, beginning with cocoa, and laid down the principle that a grocer should be a cook and also a chemist. He added to his reputation in 1870 by refusing to profiteer and disposing at the old prices by small sales to long queues of customers, of a stock of merchandise worth 2,000,000 francs which might have brought 6,000,000 francs. Potin died in 1871, but his business was carried on by his widow and his sons-in-law. The sales were 6,000,000 francs in 1869, 30,000,000 in 1897, and 45,000,000 in 1914.

BIBLIOGRAPHICAL NOTE

1. *Britain.* A good introduction to this period is A. L. Bowley, *A Short Account of England's Foreign Trade in the Nineteenth Century* (London, 1893). C. Day, *History of Commerce* (4th ed., New York, 1936) gives a general survey. L. C. A. Knowles, *Industrial and Commercial Revolutions in Great Britain during the Nineteenth Century* (4th ed., London, 1926) provides the historical setting. The best book is still Leone Levi, *History of British Commerce*, 1763–1870 (London, 1872), poorly organized but with a wealth of detail. W. Page (Ed.). *Commerce and Industry*, 1815–1914. 2 vols. (London, 1919); Vol. I is based on Parliamentary debates, and Vol. II contains excellent statistical tables. Interest in this period centers about the repeal of the corn laws and the adoption of free trade. On the former may be mentioned D. G. Barnes, *A History of the English Corn Laws from 1660 to 1846* (London, 1930); C. R. Fay, *The Corn Laws and Social England* (London, 1932); and J. S. Nicholson, *History of the Corn Laws* (London, 1904). On the latter the best general survey is P. Ashley, *Modern Tariff History* (3rd ed., New York, 1920), careful and impartial. The controversial period in the introduction of free trade is covered in B. Holland, *The Fall of Protection*, 1840–1850 (London, 1913). On shipping the fullest account is W. S. Lindsay, *History of*

25 Op. cit., I, 172.

Merchant Shipping and Ancient Commerce. 4 vols. (London, 1883). A. W. Kirk-aldy, *British Shipping, its History, Organization, and Importance* (London, 1914) carries on the story. F. C. Bowen, *A Century of Atlantic Travel,* 1830–1930 (Boston, 1930) is a gossipy narrative. J. Kennedy, *History of Steam Navigation* (Liverpool, 1903) is more specialized.

2. *France.* E. Levasseur, *Histoire du commerce de la France de* 1789 *à nos jours* (Paris, 1912) is a detailed account, as is G. Weill, *Histoire du commerce de la France* (Paris, 1913). Two books favoring free trade are L. Amé, *Étude économique sur les tarifs de douane* (Paris, 1876) and O. Noël, *Histoire de la France depuis la Révolution* (Paris, 1881). A. L. Dunham, *The Anglo-French Treaty of Commerce of* 1860 (Ann Arbor, 1930) describes an important event. E. F. Hecksher, *The Continental System, an Economic Interpretation* (Oxford, 1922) is a study of Napoleon's attempt to blockade England, and J. W. Horrocks, *A Short History of Mercantilism* (London, 1925) supplies the theoretical background. Merchant shipping is adequately treated in R. Colin, *La navigation au* 19e *siècle* (Paris, 1901) and in J. Tramond, *Histoire Maritime,* 1815–1914 (2e ed., Paris, 1927). A still longer survey is P. J. Charliot, *Trois siècles d'économie maritime française,* 1631–1931 (Paris, 1931). F. E. Melvin, *Napoleon's Navigation System* (Philadelphia, 1919) is an original interpretation.

3. *Germany.* The Zollverein was the main topic of interest in Germany during this period. A valuable picture of its early stages is given by John Bowring, *Report on the Prussian Commercial Union* (Parliamentary Papers, 1834, and also in his *Autobiography,* London, 1877). The most scholarly and detailed study of its beginning is R. W. von Eisenhart and A. Hitthaler, *Vorgeschichte und Begründung des deutschen Zollvereins,* 1815–1834. 3 vols. (Berlin, 1934). Another good account, written at the end of its life, is W. Weber, *Der deutsche Zollverein* (Leipzig, 1869). A more recent study is W. O. Henderson, *The Zollverein* (Cambridge, 1939). More general is W. H. Dawson, *Protection in Germany: A History of German Fiscal Policy during the Nineteenth Century* (London, 1904).

CHAPTER IV

TRANSPORTATION

I. BEGINNING OF THE RAILWAY AGE IN BRITAIN

Water transportation. Until the inland means of communication were improved, transportation between different points in Great Britain was carried on largely by water. Coastwise vessels transported most of the heavy freight, and coal was brought by water from Newcastle to London and other points so generally that it was known as "sea-coal." The sea served as a trunk line of commerce and united England with the continent and other parts of the world. The main rivers were channels of retail distribution of goods brought to the important seaports, as few of them were navigable for ocean-going vessels. Only six rivers in England are navigable for more than sixty miles even today. In the early eighteenth century improvements were made in the more important streams, but capital was scarce and when it became more abundant it was directed into the more profitable canals. The excellent ocean transportation served the needs of external commerce but the great expansion which followed the Industrial Revolution called for improvement in modes of internal trade.

Cheap and rapid transportation is essential to industry and, as this expanded, improved methods of inland traffic became increasingly important. The efforts to meet this need led to three successive movements: the construction of improved roads, of canals, and of railways.

Roads. The Romans, during their occupation of Britain, had built some excellent roads, but after their withdrawal in 407 the roads fell into disuse and the art of road building was forgotten. The early English roads were bridle paths about four feet wide which meandered across the countryside and were used by travelers on horses or mules or afoot. The sixteenth-century advent of coaches — as all sorts of carriages were at first named — called for something better. The wheeled vehicles dug deep gullies on either side of the bridle paths, which became bogs after a rain. An effort was made after 1663 to bring about the construction of improved highways by the turnpike acts, which authorized those who built turnpikes to levy tolls on the users. But little was done during the next hundred years. The principle followed was that of forcing the road users to accommodate themselves to the roads, and much legislation was passed regulating the width of tires, the weight of the loads, and similar acts designed to prevent too rapid wear. That the condition of the roads was bad may be shown by the complaints of travelers, one of whom may be quoted. Arthur Young, probably the most traveled Englishman of his day, wrote in 1770 of a road in Lancashire as follows: "I know not, in the whole range of language, terms sufficiently expressive to describe this infernal road . . . let me most seriously caution all travellers who may accidentally purpose to travel this terrible country to avoid it as they would the devil, for a thousand to one but they break their necks or their limbs by over-throws or breakings down. They will meet here with ruts which I measured, four feet deep, and floating with mud. . . The only mending it receives in places is the tumbling in some loose stones, which serve no other purpose but jolting a carriage in the most unbearable manner."

Even as Young wrote, however, improvements were being made. The national government undertook the building of roads instead of the lax parish officials. Under this centralized system rapid progress was made. Writing in 1767 Henry Homer speaks of the vast improvements: "Dispatch, which is the very life and soul of business, becomes daily more attainable by the free circulation opening every channel which is adapted to it. . . There never was a more astonishing revolution accomplished in the internal system of any country than has been within the compass of a few years in that of England. Everything wears the face of dispatch."

Judged by present standards, however, dispatch was still leisurely. From London to Manchester, 200 miles, was a journey of five days; from London to Edinburgh, 400 miles, was one of ten to twelve days. Inland commerce was held down by the cost and delays of transportation. It cost 2½ s. a bushel to convey wheat 100 miles by roads, while the expense of transporting coal by packhorse from the mines at Worsley to Manchester, a distance of 11 miles, doubled the selling price.

With the increase of internal commerce the need for a better system of inland communication was strongly felt. An ever-growing stream of goods was being conveyed by wagons and carts, the developing postal service was hampered by bad roads, and the rapid multiplication of public coaches, particularly in the "palmy days" of coaching between 1820 and 1835, all created a demand for improvement. The high cost and slow speed of transport show why the demand was so urgent. Passengers could travel by fast mail or stage coach in 1830 at a rate of 10 miles an hour, at a cost of from 2½ to 4 d. per mile for an inside place. Freight did not travel so fast; 2½ miles an hour, or 30 miles for a 12-hour day were a typical journey, and for this the cost was between ½ and ¾ d. per hundredweight per mile.

Pressure for improvement came from three sources: from the government, for postal and military reasons; from merchants and producers in inland counties, who wished access to markets; and from landowners and farmers, interested in the advancement of their locality.

Scientific road making began with the work of John Metcalfe, the blind surveyor, who for the thirty years after 1765 constructed roads in the north of England. He was followed by two Scotchmen, Thomas Telford and John L. McAdam. Metcalfe graded his roads carefully and laid good foundations, but was never able to build a good surface. Telford dug out the roadbed, placed on it a layer of carefully chosen large stones, which were covered by smaller ones, carefully tamped down by hand; on top of these was another layer of smaller crushed stone, covered with a binder of gravel. The roads were carefully graded, with a curved surface to shed the water, and broad enough so that two vehicles could pass each other. McAdam did not employ so expensive a system as Telford, but used irregular large stones for the base, covering this with a series of layers of progressively smaller stones, and covered the whole with a road binder. He trusted to the heavy traffic to produce a hard surface. For the work of construction he employed unskilled local labor. The simplicity and cheapness of McAdam's roads made them the favorite type, and today macadamized roads are found wherever stone is available for road making. By 1815 over 20,000 miles of improved turnpikes had been constructed, but by 1830 the grand period of road building was concluded.

The engineering problems connected with road building were solved more quickly and successfully than were the political. The administration of the roads was in the hands of local boards of turnpike trusts. The trustees were empowered to construct and maintain a specified piece of road and to levy tolls upon certain kinds of traffic for the upkeep and improvement of the turnpikes. These boards were inefficient, wasteful, and occasionally corrupt. Each little trust managed 10 to 20 miles of road, and among them there was no co-ordination. In the 1820's there was considerable consolidation of these petty projects into through lines, and the weak links in the chain were strengthened. Baron Dupin, writing in 1835, had only praise for the English roads, which he compared with those of France, to the latter's disadvantage. "During my travels in England," he wrote,[1] "I everywhere admired the superior excellence of the roads, as compared with the generality of our own." This applied, however, only to the 20,000 odd miles under the turnpike

[1] Baron Charles Dupin, *The Commercial Power of Great Britain; exhibiting a Complete View of the Public Works of this Country* (2 vols., London, 1835), I, 181.

trusts. In addition to these were over 100,000 miles of roads under parochial control, which remained unimproved and unco-ordinated. The Highway Act of 1835 introduced a better system by abolishing compulsory labor and empowering local authorities to levy a rate for the upkeep of the roads. The multiplicity of local boards — there were 16,000 in 1846 — prevented efficient administration until the control was centralized.

Beginning with the sixties there developed a public determination to get rid of the turnpike trust and its tolls. Road tolls had been abolished in Ireland in 1858 and the roads maintained out of taxes. There seemed to exist no reason, except the opposition of the trusts themselves, why the same course should not be followed in England. Parliament took the matter in hand and proceeded to end the turn-pike trusts. The Act of 1871 ended tolls in London; by 1883 they were abolished in Scotland. By 1890 there were only two trusts left and the last one was abolished in 1895. After 1888 the burden of supporting the main roads was placed upon the county.

Canals. The period of canal building in England coincided with that of improved roads, and was caused by much the same factors, especially the need for opening up interior points to markets. The long coast line and the excellent river system gave to England exceptional advantages for the development of water transportation. The first canal was built in 1761 by James Brindley for the Duke of Bridgewater, in order to facilitate the carriage of coal from his mines in Worsley to Manchester, seven miles away. The Bridge-water Canal was very profitable for its owner, and at the same time cut in half the price of coal in Manchester. This canal was next extended from Manchester to the mouth of the Mersey, which greatly reduced freight charges between Manchester and Liverpool, and in addition introduced greater speed and regularity in the transport of goods.

Other canals were soon built, linking up the main rivers and opening up the interior districts. The pioneer work of the Duke of Bridgewater was continued by a group of Midland manufacturers, who built the Trent and Mersey Canal. This gave access to the potteries district and facilitated the bringing in of the bulky and cheap raw material and the export of their valuable wares. A group of canals — the Birmingham Navigations — was built west and north of Birmingham and served the needs of the iron industry. The cost of transport between Liverpool and Birmingham was cut from £5 by road to £1 by water. The Thames and Severn Canal, built in 1789, constituted the final link between these two rivers. Other canals were built which furnished a complete network of waterways in inland England. The peak of this movement was

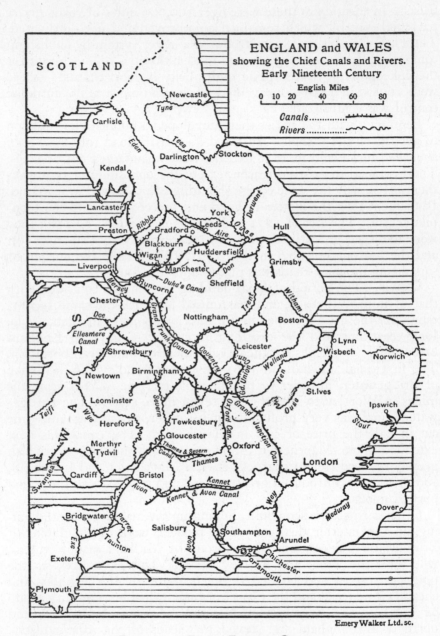

FIGURE I. EARLY ENGLISH CANALS

From D. W. Roberts' *An Outline of the Economic History of England* (Longmans, 1931). Reprinted by permission of the publishers.

reached in 1792–93, when there was a canal-building mania; but after its collapse, the building of canals declined somewhat.

Other canals were built between this date and 1830, when the canal system was practically complete and the advent of the railway stopped further construction. By 1830 there were some 3000 miles of canals and canalized rivers; and they represented an investment of about £14,000,000. It must not be thought that this great system of inland waterways was built without objections. The hostility of the interests vested in road transportation was vigorous and prolonged. The landed classes claimed that needed water would be drained off, their estates cut in two, and the quiet of the country disturbed; mill owners, who relied upon water power, objected to the deflection of the water; road trustees, carriers, and allied groups protested the diversion of traffic.

But the existing modes of land transport were so inadequate and costly that the canals were a necessity. They broke up the prevailing monopoly of land carriage, they afforded the farmer a wider and steadier market for his produce at lessened cost, they helped the manufacturer both in cheapening his raw materials and in distributing his goods, and they led to a great increase in trade, both domestic and foreign. The canals were especially useful in providing cheap transportation for heavy and bulky goods, which could not be moved — certainly not at a reasonable cost — on the poor roads then in existence. The movement of coal was of outstanding importance for the inland routes. London and other ports had obtained seaborne coal from Newcastle and Durham, but the interior counties had suffered from lack of fuel. On the through canal systems there was also a large movement of general merchandise — manufactured goods, agricultural produce, building materials, lumber, and many other things.

Not all of these canals were financially successful, the most profitable being those of the coal producing and iron manufacturing regions, especially in the district around Wolverhampton and Birmingham. Dividends of 10 per cent and upwards were paid on canals in the manufacturing districts, where a dense traffic was waiting to be moved, but in other less favored regions the investors received little or nothing. For this there were several reasons. Engineering difficulties necessitated the sinking of too much capital in some undertakings. Others were built with the expectation of traffic that did not develop. There was no unified system, and the depth, width, size of locks, and other features differed from one canal to another. This involved transhipment of goods and added cost. The canal boats were long, narrow barges, which moved at a rate of about $2\frac{1}{2}$ miles an hour. The canal companies were not public carriers. They were chartered, like the turnpikes, to provide a way which canal boat owners might use on payment of tolls. But the carriers provided poor facilities; they were unpunctual and charged extortionate rates.

And yet, with all their faults, the canals rendered great service to British industry. The cost of transportation by canal was from a half to a quarter of that by road.[2] Jackman estimates that the cost of carriage by fly boats — express service — was from 5 s. to 6 s. per ton per mile; heavy goods moved by slow boats for $\frac{1}{2}$ d. per ton per mile. New areas were opened up, outlets were provided for agricultural produce, population was rendered more mobile, the growth of towns was stimulated, new industries were called into being, and the general expansion of business was facilitated. In 1830 the question of canal versus railway transportation was still an arguable one. But the canal companies were unenterprising and made no efforts to improve their facilities and to forestall railroad competition.

The canals seem to have reached the acme of their success about 1838. After this date, the traffic fell off, the value of their shares declined, and the railways bought up many of them at low prices. Between 1845 and 1847 about 950 miles of canal came under railway control; but there still remained 2750 miles of independent canals and canalized rivers. These continued to carry bulk freight, which the railways were slow to take over. Except on the coal roads, the early railways found the passenger traffic more profitable, and left the heavy goods to the canals. After 1852 the railways made no further attempt to gain control of the canals, as they were able to attract their traffic by superior facilities. The decline of canal transportation was due to the inadequacy of such a system to meet the needs of the rapidly developing industry and commerce, rather than to railway control.

Railways. Neither the turnpikes nor the canals fully met the growing demand for cheap and rapid transportation to which the Industrial Revolution had given rise. Even at its best, traffic by coach or wagon was slow and expensive. Canals were cheaper, but were slow and could not reach all points. The railway marked a new era in the development of transportation.

There were two stages in the development of the railway: the first was the construction of a tramway or railed road, and the second the application of steam as a motive power. The early tramways were built to aid the coal and iron industries, and the first ones were built near the coal mines of Newcastle and the metallurgical works of South Wales. These were used for the conveyance of coal and

[2] Jackman, op. cit., I, 449; II, 8.

iron. But the success of these tramways led to the idea of building longer stretches for the transport of general merchandise and passengers. A tramway with iron rails was opened as a toll road for public use in 1803 between Croydon and Wandsworth, in the suburbs of London — the first chartered line of rails. This was a great success, one horse being able to draw a load of 50 tons, or fifty times as much as could be hauled on an ordinary dirt road. Tram-roads began to be generally built, especially in the northern counties.

The next step was the use of steam engines in place of horsepower. The first steam-propelled carriage seems to have been built by a Frenchman, Nicholas Joseph Cugnot, in 1729. This traveled at the rate of $2\frac{1}{4}$ miles an hour on a common road. Experiments with steam-propelled carriages were made in England during the 1780's by R. Robison and Murdock and somewhat later in the United States by Oliver Evans. Credit for first using a steam engine on iron rails belongs to Richard Trevithick. He built a locomotive in 1803 which operated on the tramway at Merthyr Tydvil in South Wales, and drew a load of ten tons at the rate of nine miles an hour. The engine proved too heavy for the cast iron rails and it was taken off. Other engines were built, but none of them was satisfactory, as they proved more costly than horse-power.

The real pioneer of the modern railway was George Stephenson. In 1814 he constructed an engine which was used to draw coal on a tramway at the coal mines in Kenilworth. By this experiment he discovered that cars could be propelled by the adhesion of a smooth wheel to a smooth rail. Rail transportation was thus shown to be feasible, but the problem still remained of generating adequate power in a locomotive engine. Two things were necessary for a practicable engine — sufficient draft to maintain a hot fire, and a large heating surface in small compass by which to generate sufficient steam. The first of these was met by Timothy Hackworth, who led the exhaust steam into the smokestack and thereby greatly increased the draft. The second problem was solved by Stephenson with his multitubular boiler. In 1821 the Stockton and Darlington railway was authorized, and Stephenson, who had been appointed engineer, prevailed upon the directors to lay iron rails instead of wood and to use steam instead of horse-power. When the line was opened in 1825 an engine, driven by Stephenson, hauled a train of thirty-four little cars, some filled with passengers and others loaded with coal, at the rate of ten to twelve miles an hour.

The Liverpool and Manchester Railway was the first line of any magnitude that was designed to carry passengers.[3] It was opened in 1830 and in a contest between competing locomotives Stephen-

[3] Harry Scrivenor, *The Railways of the United Kingdom* (London, 1849), 11.

son's *Rocket* won the prize, making the trip of thirty miles in slightly over two hours. At the same time malleable iron rolled rails were substituted for cast iron rails, thus permitting the use of heavier engines. Stage coaches were put on trucks for the convenience of passengers and impressed a permanent form on English passenger cars. The practicability of steam transportation by rail was now clearly demonstrated, and after this many railway projects were undertaken. These early railways were short local lines, serving the interests of already existing industrial centers, but they formed the foundation of most of the trunk lines which were later developed.

The new means of transportation was not developed, however, without a struggle. Owners of turnpike trusts, canal owners and carriers, as well as stage-coach drivers and carters, hostlers, innkeepers, in short all whose interests were adversely affected, united in opposing the building of railways.[4] It was argued that to travel at a rate of speed faster than four miles an hour was dangerous, while a speed of fifteen miles an hour was suicidal. When the London and Birmingham Railway sought to obtain its charter in 1830 a well-known engineer deprecated "the ridiculous expectations, or rather professions, of the enthusiastic speculator that we shall see engines traveling at the rate of twelve, sixteen, eighteen or twenty miles an hour." Farmers were told that they would be ruined, since there would be no demand for their horses. The railways would prevent cows grazing and hens laying, while the poisonous emanations from the locomotives would kill the flying birds. The locomotive was styled "an engine of the devil to lead immortal souls to hell." So strong was the opposition of vested interests that it cost the London and Birmingham Railway £70,000 to obtain a charter from Parliament.[5] The opposition of the turnpike trusts and canal companies to the newfangled railway becomes intelligible when it is noted that each stage-coach journeying daily between London and Manchester paid £1700 a year in tolls. When the coaches were driven off the roads the loss of this revenue forced the trusts into bankruptcy and their bonds became almost worthless. The canal companies suffered only a little less severely.

In the struggle between the canals and turnpike trusts on the one hand and the railways on the other the shortcomings of the former disposed shippers, manufacturers, and merchants to welcome the relief which the railways promised. Although at first the railways were regarded as feeders to the canals and destined to occupy a rather subordinate position in a co-ordinated system of road, canal, and rail

[4] Samuel Smiles, *The Life of George Stephenson* (London, 1881), 90.
[5] An account of the various objections made is given in Smiles, op. cit., 91; Findlay, 47; and J. S. Jeans, *Railway Problems* (London, 1887), 7.

transportation, after 1830 the steam railway made steady progress over its rivals. And yet even as late as 1836 a contemporary writer advocated the laying of tramways on the common roads, on which horse-drawn vehicles could proceed.[6] "The cost of transport by steam," he wrote, "is so very expensive that little merchandise is carried upon the railroad; and excepting for the rapid transport of passengers, the work may be said to be of no benefit to trade. . . Horse power, in the present state of our knowledge of the principles of motion, is, therefore, much cheaper than any of which we are possessed." As a matter of fact it was not until 1852 that the receipts from freight on the railways of England and Wales as a whole exceeded passenger receipts.

During the thirties railway construction made steady progress; in the forties there was a railway boom and expansion became feverish. Most of the important lines then constructed had been financially successful; dividends were from 10 to 15 per cent, and shares were quoted at 100 per cent premium. The extent of the mania is illustrated by the number of acts passed by Parliament authorizing new roads.

Year	No. of acts	No. of miles authorized
1844	57	805
1845	120	2700
1846	270	4538
1847	190	1354
Total	637	9397

Such reckless speculation, attended by many wild and fraudulent issues, resulted in a crash.[7] Of the 9400 miles sanctioned during this period, some 3600 were abandoned. This was followed by a period of reaction, yet the length of railroads open in 1850 was treble what it had been in 1843; by 1855 it was fourfold. The mileage was 500 in 1838, 2036 in 1843, 6635 in 1850, 10,470 in 1860 and 15,310 in 1870.

The task of developing a railway system in England was left to private enterprise. Parliamentary sanction was necessary before a new project could be launched, but the committee which examined applications for charters were chiefly concerned with the protection of individual property rights against invasion by the railways. As a result the railway companies were forced to pay huge sums for their rights of way and especially for the terminals in populous cities, to which must be added extravagant expenditures for legal fees and

[6] Henry Fairbairn, *A Treatise on the Political Economy of Railroads* (London, 1836), 31, 38.
[7] D. M. Evans, *The Commercial Crisis, 1847–48* (London, 1849), 2.

preliminary surveys. A writer in 1849 placed the cost of construction per mile of track in various countries as follows: [8]

COSTS OF RAILWAYS PER MILE

Great Britain (selected lines)	£56,915
Austria	11,300
Prussia	10,000
United States of America	5,000

The early railways were built as short local lines to carry coal, to connect interior areas with tide-water, or to unite industrial centers. They were dominated by local interests and did not provide through communication between important points. Gradually, however, the small links were united into longer lines, but down to the panic of 1847 there was little consolidation; after that event it proceeded rapidly. In 1846 there were 200 railways, but in 1848 only 22 large and a few small ones. During this period the great railway systems were born: The Midland (1844), the London and Northwestern (1846), the Great Northern (1850), the Northeastern (1854), and the Great Eastern (1862).

The individualism that characterized English enterprise at this time found expression in methods of railway building. The early colliery roads had a gauge of about 4 feet 8 inches, and this was adopted by Stephenson for the Stockton and Darlington Railway. I. K. Brunel, the engineer of the Great Western Railway, thought to obtain a monopoly of the western territory, as well as to promote speedier and safer transportation, by adopting a seven-foot gauge. When, however, roads with the different gauges met in 1845 the inconvenience was so obvious that Parliament intervened to compel uniformity. In 1846 the standard gauge of 4 feet 8½ inches was adopted for all of Great Britain, but it was 1892 before the Great Western converted the last of its tracks.

Railway legislation and railway policy. Parliament always exercised a certain control over the railways by refusing to allow any project that did not obtain a charter. The earliest charters, modeled on the turnpike and canal acts, prescribed that the tracks should be available to any user, upon payment of the designated tolls. This method was soon shown to be impracticable and the railways, in contradistinction to the canal companies, took over the entire operation of their lines. Railways were something new and Parliament was in doubt as to the best legislative principles to adopt; it wished to safeguard the public interests but not to stifle the development of

[8] Quoted by A. P. Usher, *An Introduction to the Industrial History of England* (Boston, 1930), 449.

railways. The position which it took was dictated by the prevailing doctrines of *laissez faire*. The policy adopted by Parliament toward the railways was the maintenance of competition, and for a time this attitude seemed to be justified. The railways broke the monopoly of the canals and brought down rates of transport. Down to 1840 there was little competition among the railways themselves, for each line was developing in its own territory, and Parliament, in the granting of charters, avoided unnecessary duplication of lines. The suspicion of monopoly could not be avoided, however, and in 1844 Parliament, after careful inquiry, passed an act providing for optional state purchase of the railways in twenty-one years.

The same Act of 1844 provided for "Parliamentary trains," to be run at least once each way every week-day, with seats protected from the weather, at a rate of not less than twelve miles an hour, and at a maximum charge of a penny a mile. Each of these provisions pointed to an existing abuse. Third-class passengers had been carried in open box cars, without a roof or seats; such cars had been attached to freight trains and moved at a snail-like pace; and there was no assurance of even such transportation.

The early railways were small and disconnected lines, the average length in 1843 being less than thirty miles. As the railway net filled in there was a strong tendency to consolidate these short links into longer systems. A Board of Trade report in 1845 concluded that combinations were beneficial if they were of continuous and not competing lines. Two decades later, in 1864, the Railway Companies' Power Act specifically authorized railway companies to formulate agreements among themselves in practically all matters of common interest. A Royal Commission the following year reported that amalgamations were going on and would continue, even to the point of monopoly, and advocated the publication of their agreements as a safeguard.

In 1865 the twenty-one year period set by the Act of 1844 came to an end and Parliament was faced again with the question of the relation of the state to the railways. In the meantime the railways had consolidated and grown stronger; their paid-up capital amounted to £455,000,000, which it would be necessary to add to the national debt in case of state purchase. The Royal Commission which considered the matter recommended "leaving the construction and management of railways to the free enterprise of the people, under such conditions as Parliament may think fit to impose for the general welfare of the people." [9] The report showed that competition was still regarded as an effective regulatory force, though the tendency to consolidate was recognized. Practically the only conditions imposed

[9] *Final Report*, p. 37.

during this period were certain measures of protection to the general public contained in the Act of 1854. This enunciated two principles: All railway companies were ordered (1) to give reasonable facilities to the public, to accept and forward through traffic from and to the lines of other companies, and (2) to grant no undue preference. This was the first really important effort to correct the abuses which had grown up and to protect the public against obnoxious practices and to harmonize the relations of competing railways with each other.

Economic advantages of the railways. The effect of the railway on the structure and functioning of English industry was transforming. Many of the economic changes following the Industrial Revolution usually attributed to improvements in the technique of industry, are in fact traceable to the speeding up of transportation. Several important effects may be briefly stated.

The railways reduced the cost of transportation below what the turnpikes and canals had formerly charged. When the Liverpool and Manchester Railway was opened the rate on light goods on the canal between these two cities was 15 s. a ton; the railway cut it to 10 s. Between Manchester and Hull the railway rate was half that charged by the canal. But there was plenty of traffic for both. Only in the north of England, where there were no canals, and on the short coal-carrying lines, did the railways receive the greater part of their revenues from freight; in other sections the passenger traffic was more important, and this was diverted from the turnpikes, which now lost all importance for through traffic. The canals which were well situated and had not too many locks expanded their business. The railways enabled Great Britain to distribute raw materials in bulk, to engage in mass production, and to dispatch finished goods with a speed and punctuality unrivalled by any country up to 1870. They were particularly valuable for the handling of heavy and awkward products such as machinery, railway rolling stock, gas and drain pipes, in the production of all of which the English iron industry took the lead at that time. Together with the ocean steamships they greatly facilitated the export of such articles.

The traffic of the railways was not wholly diverted from the canals and turnpikes; it was largely new business. Their construction gave employment to many more persons than those who lost their business with the disappearance of coaching on the turnpikes and the related industries. At the height of the railway boom in 1848, it was estimated that 188,000 men were engaged in construction work.[10] Another 56,000 were reported for the lines then in operation. The railways opened new markets and made old ones more accessible.

[10] D. Lardner, *Railway Economy* (London, 1850), 58.

They carried perishable foodstuffs and other agricultural products to the cities, and in return took coal, fertilizer, farm implements, and other supplies to the farmers. They conveyed raw materials to manufacturing centers and distributed the finished goods. Territorial specialization already existed in British industry, but the railways promoted it by reducing costs of transportation. New towns were developed at strategic points, and older cities expanded industrially. The growth of centralized, large scale production was promoted.

Railway transportation profoundly affected the commercial organization. The bagmen and chapmen of an earlier age disappeared, and commercial travelers took their place. Merchants carried smaller stocks because they could now count upon receiving regular supplies on short notice. Supply and demand were better equalized, and prices were rendered more stable. Most of the freight traffic was short-haul merchandise traffic in small amounts. This fact impressed upon British railways a feature which differentiated them, in common with the continental lines, from American railways. The typical car was a small wagon which could be left at a local station without depriving the railway of needed rolling stock.

Finally the railway made travel quicker and cheaper and thereby increased the mobility of the population. The complaint of Adam Smith that "of all species of baggage man is the most difficult to be moved" no longer held true. Men could now travel from areas of low wages to those offering high wages. A better distribution of the industrial population was effected. At the same time the speed of travel was increased. Professor Jackman [11] estimated that as a result of improved roads and mail coaches the speed of travel was doubled between 1750 and 1830; at the latter date it was nine to ten miles an hour. The railways at once doubled this, and by the middle of the century the best trains had a speed of over forty miles an hour. The innkeepers of the coaching days lost business, but the saving in time to the commercial classes was incalculable. The new facilities for travel and observation had, moreover, important social effects, and made for public enlightenment and national solidarity.

Communication. The post office was originally organized to carry the Sovereign's dispatches, but in 1760 it was surrendered by the Crown and became a national institution. It was, however, administered for profit rather than for public service and the rates were extremely high. Until 1839 letters were charged according to the number of sheets, the weight, and the distance, the rate from London to Edinburgh being 13 *d*. and others in proportion. The revenues were, however, large, reaching in that year £2,390,000, of which £1,633,000 was profit. In 1837 Rowland Hill published a

[11] W. T. Jackman, op. cit., I, 339.

pamphlet in which he showed that the main expense was the collection, weighing, and delivery of mail, and advocated a uniform rate irrespective of distance. This proposal was strongly supported by the public and in 1840 Parliament established uniform penny postage throughout the United Kingdom. At the same time postage stamps were introduced, so that the sender could prepay the charges. Although this involved a financial loss — not until 1874 did the net revenue of the post office again reach the level of 1839 — the social gain to the nation in the growth of private and commercial correspondence more than offset this. Other improvements followed. Postal money orders were legalized in 1839, postal savings banks were first introduced in England in 1861, and in 1864 postal life insurance and annuities were added.

One of the greatest means of the communication of ideas and the speed of knowledge in modern times, the newspaper, was repressed by the government in the early part of this period and only gradually assumed its rightful importance. In 1797 the duty on each issue was 3½ d. per paper, and as a result the price was high — about 7 d. — and the circulation small. Radical newspapers were checked by fines; in 1819 a bond was demanded of each publisher as security for fines. In 1836, when a more liberal attitude prevailed, the duty was reduced to 1 d., and in 1855 it was abolished.

The next step in the direction of quicker communication was taken by the introduction of the electric telegraph. Although W. F. Cooke and Charles Wheatstone applied for patents in 1837, the honor of making a practical success of the telegraph belonged to the American S. F. B. Morse, who put it into operation in 1844. Two years later the pioneer British company, the Electric Telegraph, was formed. At first it served primarily the railways, but after 1850 broadened its service for the general public. A demand for state ownership appeared about 1863, as a result of competitive and unco-ordinated operation, resulting in high rates, poor service, and failure to meet public needs. Finally in 1870 the state purchased the telegraph systems, paying the high price of £8,000,000 — and made it a governmental monopoly under the post office.

The final step in broadening the area of communication came with the laying of submarine cables, first to Calais (1851), to Calcutta (1865), to New York (1866), and finally to Australia (1871). The world was now knit together and international markets for securities and the great staple commodities were established.

2. TARDY DEVELOPMENT IN FRANCE

Roads. When Arthur Young visited France in 1789 he was full of praise for the French roads and canals. The old Roman roads had furnished a basis, which had been improved and extended during the previous two centuries. Since about 1750 labor for road building and repair had been obtained from the rural inhabitants, who had to give about thirty days a year to this service. In 1788 it was estimated that France had about 30,000 miles of made road. During the Revolution many of these fell into disrepair and were, moreover, beset by brigands. Toll gates were set up and users of the roads were taxed; this further reduced the traffic.

Napoleon realized the political and economic importance of good transportation, and under his leadership great improvements were made. He accomplished much with small expenditure, for prisoners of war were obliged to do most of the work. He made the roads free and laid out a comprehensive scheme designed both for military and economic purposes. From Paris to Mount Cenis in Italy, over the Simplon pass to Switzerland, to Hamburg, to Amsterdam, and to Madrid he built thirty great engineering works designed to make of his far-flung empire an economic unit. Numerous substantial bridges were also constructed. Between 1807 and 1812 over 300 million francs were spent, and some 32,500 miles of road were built or repaired. During the last years of his desperate campaigns, however, probably a third of the roads went out of repair.

Under the Restoration few new roads were built, but attention was directed rather to improving the local roads. Various factors had contributed to their bad condition. Since the industrial centers were so scattered a vast network was necessary, but the landowners were unwilling to be taxed for this purpose and labor was scarce. The worst roads were to be found in the rural districts or near industrial centers where the traffic was heavy. The July monarchy, with its strong economic interests, had a better understanding of the transportation problem. In 1831 a separate ministry of public works was established and the *École des ponts et chaussées* was made the outstanding institution of its kind in Europe. Under a law of 1836 a comprehensive program for land and water transportation was set up, and a decade later there had been expended 400 million francs for road building, 317 for canals, and 82 for river improvement. By 1848 over 21,700 miles of national roads had been constructed, 24,800 of departmental roads, and 434,000 of local (vicinal) roads. Many parts of France were now for the first time opened to contact and trade. The French road system was by the middle of the century the most extensive and finest in Europe, which meant in the world. After this there was a slowing up in road construction, as attention was diverted to railway building. In 1870 there were in use nearly 24,000 miles of national roads, 29,000 of departmental roads, and 338,000 of local roads, or a total of 390,000 miles. The very considerable decline in the mileage of local roads was due to the fact that many of these had been little better than paths and not suitable to the heavier traffic that was now developing; they were therefore no longer counted.

Although the roads were good the agencies of transport used on them were woefully antiquated in the early part of this period. In the east and south travel was mostly by horseback. Transportation by carriage was in the hands of two large private companies, which owned between 5000 and 6000 diligences, which was perhaps a third of all in France, each drawn by 2 to 5 horses. A trip from Paris to Bordeaux (about 430 miles) took 8 days in 1782 and from Paris to Lyons (about 290 miles) 5 days. With improvement of the roads and of vehicles the speed of travel was increased. By 1848 one could make the two trips just mentioned in 3 and 2½ days respectively by mail coach. By rail in 1870 the time was cut to about 7 hours by express train. At the same time the safety and punctuality of travel were greatly improved. This was for fast passenger service. Freight traffic was still painfully slow — about 2 to 2½ miles per hour in 1855 — though it increased somewhat in amount after the reduction of rates and tolls. The usual freight wagon was a two-wheeled cart, though after about 1840 four-wheeled carts drawn by eight horses were used; but these were hard on the roads. Rates were not high as measured by contemporary standards — perhaps 6 cents per ton-mile. For local traffic the omnibus was introduced in Paris in 1828. The total expenditures by the state on roads and bridges between 1814 and 1870 were 1362 million francs.

Waterways. The largest rivers in France — the Seine, the Loire, the Garonne, and the Rhone — are not as navigable nor so well situated as those of Germany, and did not serve the interests of commerce so well, with the possible exception of the Seine. Little had been done down to the end of the eighteenth century to improve them and shipwrecks were common. Some canals had been built by private initiative to link up the natural waterways, but ice in the winter and lack of water in the summer made them practically useless for eight months in the year.

The Restoration took up the work of canal building in earnest in 1818. The plan adopted called for the completion of 1711 miles of unfinished canal and 6696 of new construction. The costs were to be borne by the canal companies, which were authorized to charge tolls. By 1848 almost 2500 miles had been constructed, including the great links connecting the Rhine with the Rhone, and with the Marne. The beds of the commercially more important rivers were also deepened and improved. Traffic on the great rivers remained nevertheless very behindhand, and very slow; towed boats in the canals made only 26 miles per day on the average, and they were frequently hauled by men instead of by horses.

With the building of railroads the canal traffic fell off. It became clear that boats carrying less than 100 tons could not compete with the faster agency, especially in the carriage of valuable goods or of passengers. Only in the carriage of heavy, bulky, and cheap goods were the waterways able to hold their own. The small canals and rivers lost most of their business. This was partly due to the lack of modern improvements in the canals themselves and in their equipment. Locks, down to about 1870, were built mainly for the purpose of passing millraces; only after this date were they constructed for the purpose of equalizing the flow of water and making the canals available for shipping at all times.

After 1850, when the importance of the railway was recognized, renewed attention was directed to the water routes, which began to be looked upon as a valuable counterpoise to the monopoly of the great railway companies. Various canals were nationalized by being bought by the state, and after 1863 the private canals became insignificant. The system of tariffs was simplified, and those on the state canals were imposed on the private companies. In 1867 all canals were combined in a unified system, which included, in addition to the canals, 2000 miles of canalized rivers and 1900 miles of other navigable rivers. In spite of everything, however, traffic preferred the railways. One explanation might be found in the fact that the charges by rail were consistently lower than those by canal, and the time of carriage was of course much less. The development of the canal net is shown in the following table: [12]

EXTENT OF CANALS IN FRANCE
(in miles)

Year	Private	State	Total
1814	355	397	752
1830	1111	213	1324
1848	2429	377	2806
1870	562	2450	3012

Steamboats. An unsuccessful experiment was made with a steamboat on the Seine in 1803, but twenty years later regular traffic was established on the Saône between Lyons and Chalons with twelve steamers. These were, however, economically unprofitable. Not until 1829 was there regular steamship traffic on the Rhone, but here the rapid current offered a serious obstacle; although the trip from Lyons to Arles took only 13 hours downstream the return trip up-

[12] Sée, op. cit., 371.

stream required 7 days. After this the number of river steamers grew rapidly, so far as the insufficient water permitted, and by the middle of the century there were 364 steamers in the country, chiefly on the rivers, though some engaged in the coasting trade or crossed the Channel to England. Water transportation was helping to move goods in bulk, and, together with the excellent network of roads, provided France with a fairly adequate transportation system. Indeed, its very excellence delayed the introduction of railways until after they had been built in most other countries, and this delay retarded the full economic development of the country.

Railways. As early as 1823 a short line of railway was opened to the coal mines of St. Etienne, on which cars were drawn by horses. Almost a decade later (1832) the first locomotive was imported from England and placed upon a line between St. Etienne and Lyons; this drew passengers as well as freight. The following year the general council of bridges and roads was directed by the government to prepare a unified plan of railway building for the whole country. A short line was built from Paris to Saint Germain, but the Chamber hesitated between the Belgian system of state-owned railways and the English system of private companies. Three times, in 1835, 1837, and 1838, it rejected government proposals for state construction. In the last-named year it granted concessions to a few private companies to build needed roads, but the depression which followed the panic of 1837 prevented the carrying out of these plans. There were, however, about 350 miles of railway in France in 1841. By this time the scheme of state construction was no longer a possibility because of the large expenditures for armament, and the question became one of the extent of state participation and of control.

The law of June 1842 represented a compromise which gave a monopoly to large private companies under government supervision, with the proviso that the roads should become state property at the end of forty years. A national plan was adopted according to which seven trunk lines were to be built to the frontiers, radiating from Paris like the spokes of a wheel, together with a couple of shorter transverse lines. The state was to contribute the land and build the roadbed, including bridges and tunnels; this was estimated to amount to about 250,000 francs a mile. The private companies were to furnish the tracks, buildings, rolling stock, and working capital, amounting to about 200,000 francs a mile.

The carrying out of the railway program of 1842 was done by English firms. In 1840 the London-Southampton Railway obtained the concession of the line from Paris to Rouen and in 1842 that from Rouen to Havre. The work of construction was done by the firm of Thomas Brassey with English workers and English material. By 1845 fifty companies had been formed in England to finance French railway building and half of the capital of 625,-000,000 francs came from England. The administration of the railways was, however, retained in French hands.

The realization of this program did not take place without opposition. Agriculture pointed to the loss in value of its horses. The peasants, ship and canal boat owners, innkeepers, and coaching companies feared for their trade, and even the inhabitants of an industrial city like Lyons thought of the loss of the transit trade when Paris should have direct rail communication with Italy and Switzerland. But in spite of such shortsighted opposition the plan of 1842 was pushed forward. The line from Paris to Rouen was opened in 1843, and that between Rouen and Havre in 1847. By 1848 the railway net had grown to 1378 miles. The economic efforts of this expansion were soon apparent. Not only was the movement of freight and of passengers made faster, but rates were reduced. For the transport of freight the railways charged 2.6 and 5.2 cents per ton mile, while the express post wagons were still demanding 14.5 cents.

The panic of 1847 and the Revolution of 1848 put a temporary stop to railway building. Some of the companies gave up their concessions and others appealed to the state for assistance. Since the state already had a considerable stake in the roadbed it agreed to guarantee the interest on the capital invested. In the fifties it extended the period after which the roads were to revert to the state to 99 years instead of the 40 prescribed in the law of 1842. Under the leadership of Napoleon III railway building proceeded rapidly during this decade. The establishment of the *Crédit Mobilier* in 1852 made possible a greater participation by French capital in the building of railways. In order to lessen the cost the import duty on rails, which was about 100 per cent, was considerably reduced. All these measures bore fruit and by 1860 France was provided with a railway net of some 5900 miles, which connected Paris with the outlying districts and was beginning to revolutionize the transportation of freight and passengers.

The main features of the French railway system were now clearly discernible. Six great companies existed, five of them radiating from Paris, and the sixth operating in the south.[13] Each had a monopoly in its own district. But the companies built only the lines promising a profit, so that provincial towns often remained without railway connections. In order to remedy this situation the state next passed the Franqueville law of 1859, which required the build-

[13] These lines were the Paris-Orleans, Paris-Lyons-Mediterranean (PLM), the Northern, the Eastern, the Western, and the Midi.

ing of additional lines (*nouveau reseau*), to be financed by obligations on which the state guaranteed 4 per cent interest, but which the old lines (*ancien reseau*) were to amortize out of their earnings. In compensation the state retained the right of purchase after fifteen years. By 1870 about 11,000 miles were in operation. The growth of the railway net may be briefly indicated:

1828	14 miles	1860	5,854 miles
1840	268 miles	1870	10,835 miles
1850	1,865 miles		

The economic effects of the railway in France were noteworthy. A national economy was created rather than the provincial districts which prevailed before, and prices were leveled off. They hastened the territorial division of labor, concentrating industries in naturally favored localities; this in turn facilitated the growth of manufactures and of large scale production. The railway system bore the stamp, however, of the centralized state, since it was based centripetally upon Paris and neglected the transverse connections. All traffic converged in Paris and had to be redistributed from there.

Communications. The French postal service dates from the twelfth century, but for a long time it served the state rather than the general public. High charges prevented its general use. The Revolution did not include improvement of the postal service among its reforms, and no important change was made until the tariff of 1827 simplified the system. Until 1849 postal charges were calculated according to distance and weight, but in that year postage stamps were introduced and a single charge was made irrespective of distance but varying according to weight. The number of letters carried increased greatly and a reduction of rates in 1861 gave further stimulus. The post office handled 64,000,000 letters in 1830, 160,000,000 in 1850, and 358,000,000 in 1869.

3. PARTICULARISM IN GERMANY

The developing trade called for improved agencies of transportation, and the nineteenth century witnessed a revolution in this field not less noteworthy than the industrial revolution.

Land transportation: roads. At the beginning of the century there were few improved roads in Germany and these were mostly in the south; there were none in the provinces of Pomerania and Posen. The ordinary earth road was full of dust in summer and of mud in winter. Stones and holes were everywhere, and abandoned wagons were usual. Frequently there was no wish to improve the roads, for the longer the post coaches and freight wagons were forced to remain in a place so much greater were the profits of the land-lords and of the handworkers.[14]   The end of the eighteenth century saw the first attempts at macadamized roads, but these were narrow and with steep grades, provided with only the most necessary bridges, and built with too large stones.   Bad as they were, they constituted a great improvement over the ordinary earth road, especially for freight.   Before their construction heavy articles like wood, iron, and grain could not be transported by wagon far from their points of production because of the cost.   It was necessary to employ 25 horses to haul a wagon on the soft earth, 15 on the old country roads, and only 5 on the highways.

Passenger travel was attended not only by discomfort, but by posi-tive danger, and was painfully slow.   The average daily perform-ance of the post coach was six miles (German), "but one knew nothing better and was satisfied if he obtained a good seat, the horses trotted, and the landlords did not cheat too badly." [15]   In 1830 it took the express wagons of the royal Bavarian state post about $3\frac{1}{2}$ days for the journey from Munich to Berlin (51 miles), for which the fare was 81 marks.   In 1840 a journey from Hanover to Leipzig, of 169 miles, took 40 hours for the post wagon, while today it takes 5 hours by railway; there were then only 5 trips in each direction weekly.   To go from Berlin to Königsberg, 366 miles (English), where roads were especially bad, a week was required.   "Whoever has not patience," wrote one traveler, "should travel to the north of Germany; there he could learn it."   The wagons were as bad as the roads and the satirists of the day directed their wit at travel condi-tions.   "The postwagons are painted red, as the color of pain and of martyrdom," wrote one.   Sombart relates that it was proposed to convey corpses to the burial grounds in post wagons "in order that they might have time to awake at the resurrection."   A monograph was written on the "Post Snail."

During the Napoleonic war building of new roads stopped and old ones fell into disrepair, but when peace was declared the need of a road policy was recognized.   In 1816 there were in Prussia 420 miles (German) of roads maintained by the state, and 103 miles of other public roads, compared with 10,000 at the end of the century. This number was doubled in the next fifteen years, but the greatest growth took place after 1844.   In the next year an English trav-eler [16] reported that "not only good but luxurious roads . . . traversed those regions in all directions."   Germany was, however, far behind England and France; in 1860 for every square mile of territory

---

[14] H. Schnell, *Die wirtschaftliche Entwicklung Deutschlands im 19. Jahrhundert* (München, 1912), 5.

[15] Sartorius, op. cit., 23.

[16] T. C. Banfield, *Industry of the Rhine* (London, 1846), I, 24.

England had 4.72 (English) miles of road, France 4.84, and Prussia .98. The progress of road building in Prussia, which may be accepted as fairly typical, was as follows (in German miles):

Year	Roads supported by the state	Other roads	Total
1816	420	103	523
1831	829	299	1128
1848	......	......	1573
1862	1926	1865	3791

Railways. As in England the first proposal for a railway in Germany was for the purpose of obtaining access to coal. In 1826 Fritz Hardort urged a project to build a line from certain coal mines in Westphalia to the Rhine, but it was successfully opposed on the grounds that the wagoners engaged in hauling coal would be put out of business, that the revenues from road tolls would be reduced, and that coal mines not served by the railroad would be injured.[17] The first line actually constructed was one of 3.7 miles between Nuremberg and Furth. A count of 1833 showed that 720 persons traveled daily between the two places, so it was thought that a railway might be profitable. It took a couple of months to collect the needed capital of 224,000 marks, of which the state subscribed for two shares. Before entering upon such an untried project, however, it was felt that expert advice must be had and this was sought from the Bavarian higher medical college, which made the following celebrated report: "The rapid movement must produce in the travelers a brain disturbance, a special kind of Delirium furiosum. If, however, travelers wish to risk this terrible danger, the state must at least protect the spectators, or else they would fall victims to the same brain disturbance at sight of the rapidly moving trains. It is therefore necessary to shut in the roadway on both sides by a high thick board fence."

The rolling stock of this initial railway was at first one locomotive and eleven horses, and for some time horses were generally used. Coaches were fitted with flanged wheels for use on the rails. The road was originally designed for the transport of passengers and only in the second year was a modest amount of freight carried. The success of this line led to the building of others, but they were all short stretches, designed to serve local interests: 3 in 1838, 1 in 1839 between Leipzig and Dresden, which was later incorporated in the present railway net, 6 in 1840, 6 in 1841, and similarly in the following years. The decade of the forties was one of very rapid construction. Many of these early railways were built with private capital, some of which was obtained from abroad, largely in the form

[17] H. Lotz, *Verkehrsentwicklung* (Leipzig, 1910), 25.

of locomotives, rails, and other supplies. The southern states, Bavaria, Wurtemberg, Saxony, Baden, and others, were the first to build state railways, as they could then obtain the needed capital on better terms than could private capitalists, and private capital was scarce in the Germany of 1840. Brunswick has the distinction of building the first state railway in 1838. In Prussia, however, the roads were private until 1848, when the first state-built and state-operated road was built from Berlin to the Russian frontier, primarily for military purposes. But the state had meantime, since about 1842, imitated the French policy of guaranteeing the interest on railway bonds, up to $1,430,000 per annum.

During the fifties and sixties the current ideas of individualism and free trade, which found expression in the liberal commercial policy of this period, led to the sale or lease of state lines to private companies. Bavaria leased her state railways to a private company in 1856 and Brunswick sold hers in 1869. In 1870 there was a confused system, about 5600 miles being state-owned and 6500 private. In the south most of the railways were owned by the states, but in the north there were mostly private lines. There was no unity, as the political particularism of the various states prevented fusion of the small lines or the establishment of a unified policy. The building of railways went on apace, however, as the following table shows:

LENGTH OF GERMAN RAILWAYS

Year	Miles
1840	340
1850	3,747
1860	7,212
1870	12,137

These early German railways were built to serve local interests and consisted usually of short stretches between two towns. There was no national plan nor were the local lines linked together into through routes. In 1840 Baden built the first section of a north and south line and in 1848 Prussia began an east and west one, though List's dream of a co-ordinated system was far from realized. Owing to the scarcity of capital and the many projects among which it must be divided railway building was done as cheaply as possible. Land was cheap and, since the towns were small, terminals were not expensive. The extravagant pioneering of England had shown that it was not necessary to build absolutely level roadbeds, and the early German lines followed the natural level of the land as far as possible. The cost of the German railways per mile was thus about one-third of that of the English.

The economic significance of the railway in transforming the rural economy of Germany was enormous. With some exaggeration Treitschke [18] wrote: "It was the railways which first dragged the nation from its economic stagnation; they ended what the Zollverein had only begun; with such power did they break in upon all the old habits of life, that already in the forties the aspect of Germany was completely changed." In 1840 Germany was a country of peasants and handworkers. Owing to the bad roads, gild restrictions, and other causes, trade was limited, in spite of the freedom of exchange introduced by the Zollverein. Prices varied greatly for similar articles in different parts of the country; it was impossible before the railway to move products from surplus areas to deficit areas because of the high costs of transportation. Thus in 1817 a bushel of wheat cost 66½ Sgr. more in the Rhineland than in Posen, but in 1853 the difference was only 17 Sgr., although the price was higher. The railway leveled out prices and made of the whole country an economic unit. Before 1840 the towns were small and half rural; each city with its environs had constituted a sort of small economic unit, whose needs were practically covered by local production, and in which accordingly virtually every trade must be represented. After the building of railways there occurred a territorial division of labor and a concentration of the different branches of industry in those places where the most favorable physical and economic conditions of production existed, and exchange of goods among these different areas. An interesting estimate of the proportion of the province of Brandenburg that could be reached in a five-hour journey from Berlin gave the following results: in 1819, by post wagon, 8 per cent; in 1851, when the railway was beginning, 29 per cent; and in 1875, when the main lines were completed, 57 per cent. The railway united the country industrially and commercially. With some exaggeration Wilhelm Raabe later wrote: "The German Empire was founded with the first railway between Nuremberg and Furth."

Inland water transportation. The plain of Germany possesses an almost unrivalled system of internal waterways. Long navigable rivers, such as the Weser, Elbe, Oder, Vistula, and (though not wholly a German river) the Rhine, flowing in almost parallel courses from Central Europe to the North and Baltic seas, had for centuries been arteries of trade. Besides these main routes there was a score of minor streams, such as the Ems, Havel, Spree, Saale, Main, Neckar, Weichsel, and Memel, which formed indispensable links in the waterway system, especially after they were united by canals. At the beginning of the nineteenth century Germany possessed a more efficient network of waterways than any other continental country. The

[18] K. Treitschke, *Deutsche Geschichte*. 5 Bde. (Leipzig, 1879–94), IV, 582.

utility of these routes was, however, seriously diminished by the medieval system of tolls and staples at every turn. "In 1800 a cargo paid toll fourteen times on the Elbe between Hamburg and Magdeburg, and thirty-three times on the Main between Bamberg and Mainz." [19]   The unification of many of the petty states by Napoleon in 1803 somewhat improved matters, and the abolition in 1834 of all internal tolls within its boundaries by the Zollverein did still more.   But the abolition of the river tolls was not finally accomplished until after the middle of the century.   The Rhine, which the Treaty of Vienna had in 1815 declared to be free, was not finally cleared of all customs until the commercial treaty between Holland and the Zollverein in 1851, the ten customs stations on the Weser were abolished in 1856, and the fourteen on the Elbe were only partially removed in 1863 and not entirely until 1870.

More important in the development of the river traffic was the introduction of steamboats.   The first of these, the *Weser* and the *Princess Charlotte*, were built at Bremen in 1816.   The builder of the *Weser*, Fr. Schroder, received from the Bremen Senate a monopoly of steamship navigation on the Weser River for fifteen years.[20]   This boat was a side wheeler with a length of 84 feet and a breadth of 14 feet.   The engine, which was imported from England, was 14 h.p., and by it a speed of 6 miles per hour was attained. Other steamers were launched on the Danube in 1817, on the Elbe in 1818, and on the Rhine in 1820.

Passenger traffic was first sought by the steamers, which gave welcome relief from the jolting stage coaches, but it was not long before their value for the carriage of freight was recognized.   The first economic success with the steamboat was obtained on the Rhine.   In 1824 the *Seeländer*, a Dutch boat, steamed upstream for the first time and proved it could overcome the currents.   Three years later regular trips were begun between Mainz and Cologne by a Prussian company.   As improvements were made in the design of the boats and in the engines the speed was increased, more trips were made, and freight rates were reduced.   About 1830 tow-boats were introduced and a decade later companies were formed with their own vessels. The normal capacity of a Rhine boat was increased from about 100 tons to between 200 and 400.   In spite of opposition from small boat owners the larger companies soon obtained most of the business and the sailing vessels all but disappeared from the rivers.   In 1857 there were 2582 sailing vessels on the seven most important German rivers, compared with 13,769 steamers.   As the traffic developed improvements were made in the rivers, especially after 1831; towpaths

[19] Clapham, op. cit., 109.
[20] Oskar Teubert, *Die Binnenschiffahrt*, 2 vols. (Leipzig, 1922), I, 93.

were built, obstacles removed from the streams, and the river beds deepened. The rather uneven expansion of the river traffic may be seen from the following table (in 1000 tons):

RIVER TRAFFIC, 1836–60

	1836 Up-stream	1836 Down-stream	1840 Up-stream	1840 Down-stream	1850 Up-stream	1850 Down-stream	1860 Up-stream	1860 Down-stream
Customs office								
Emmerich (Holland boundary)	87.8	241.5	128.0	253.8	173.7	399.5	300.5	745.0
Coblenz (Prussia)	81.4	72.9	163.2	128.3	322.4	262.9	614.7	449.0
Kaub (Cassel)	76.3	69.0	160.8	113.9	336.8	230.7	600.9	335.2
Mainz (Hesse)	70.4	54.0	135.5	79.9	274.6	175.6	497.3	294.5
Mannheim (Baden)	42.4	61.8	43.0	48.7	58.8	83.8	49.6	171.8

During these twenty-four years the railway developed and began to offer competition to the river traffic. Although the first railways were regarded as feeders for the waterways and were so laid out, they began to divert traffic to themselves as they were extended. When the railway from Mannheim to Basle was built in 1844, it soon diverted the business from the upper Rhine, which was difficult and costly. Mannheim remained for the next fifty years the end point of traffic on the upper Rhine. Along the middle Rhine the outcome was somewhat different. Passenger travel and the carriage of valuable or perishable foods were taken over by the railways, while that of heavy and cheap goods, as coal, iron ore, and later petroleum and grain, was left to the river boats. Where conditions were distinctly unfavorable on account of changes in depth of water or the presence of locks, the river trade was diverted to the railways. This was true of the Main, Lahn, Mosel, Ruhr, Lippe, Ems, the upper Weser, Saale, and Oder. During the sixties the traffic on the smaller rivers almost completely ceased.

Ocean shipping. At the end of the eighteenth century German shipping consisted of small sailing vessels. In 1785 Prussian Baltic ports had 958 ships with a total tonnage of 68,784, while Bremen and Hamburg together had about 360 with some 38,000 tons. These were tiny boats. The states on the Baltic had more shipping than those on the North Sea (Hamburg, Bremen, Hanover, and Oldenburg). The continental wars stimulated the production and export of foodstuffs and other supplies, and German shipping, especially in the Baltic ports, experienced a rapid expansion. By 1805 the Baltic shipping was 250,000 tons and that of the North Sea 100,000. Napoleon's Continental System and the English blockade practically destroyed this lucrative business and also many of the ships.

German shipping was retarded not only by war, but also by the burdens placed upon it by surrounding nations, and even by some German states. Thus Denmark levied sound taxes on vessels passing through the Danish Sound, amounting to between 2 and 12 per cent of the value of the freight; these existed (with slight interruptions) from the 12th century to 1857, when she gave them up upon payment of a lump sum.[21] Antwerp also collected taxes on vessels passing through the Scheldt River until 1863. Hanover levied dues on the Stade River until 1861, although it had long since ceased to do anything to justify them, and they bore heavily on Hamburg shipping. Although the freedom of river trade from taxes had been declared by the Congress of Vienna in 1815, it took almost half a century to free shipping from these medieval shackles. Shipping was also exposed to dangers; German vessels did not dare venture into the Mediterranean for fear of the Barbary pirates.

The shallow waters and unmarked channels in most harbors kept the boats small and retarded shipping until the middle of the century. The normal vessel of the thirties was about 200 tons, and seldom exceeded 300. Its carrying capacity was even less than its tonnage indicated, for the deck was not covered and much space, nowadays used for cargo, was given to cabins, the commissary, etc. Nor were the vessels of this period provided with mechanical appliances for loading and unloading. These were sailing vessels. Not until 1848 did the first German steamer find its way to England, and the first transatlantic voyage came two years later. In ocean shipping Germany was distinctly backward.

Two different branches of German shipping must be distinguished, for their development was quite different. One branch sailed from the Baltic ports of Prussia, Mecklenburg, Lübeck, and Holstein, and the other from the North Sea ports of Hamburg, Hanover, Bremen, and Oldenburg. The former was at first more important, for it carried the grain and lumber from the eastern provinces to England and Holland. This trade was injured by the Continental System and all but destroyed by the British Corn Law in 1815. By 1825 it had declined to half its strength twenty years earlier, but after this it increased slowly to the middle of the century. The abrogation of the British Corn Laws in 1846 brought about an improvement, but now it had to meet the competition of the United States and later of Russia. When Germany became a grain-importing instead of a grain-exporting country, the final blow was struck at the Baltic shipping. The following table [22] of the Prussian merchant marine may be accepted as typical for the whole branch:

[21] E. Fitger, "Die wirtschaftliche und technische Entwicklung der Seeschiffahrt," in *Schriften des Vereins für Socialpolitik.* Bd. 103, Teil 1 (Leipzig, 1902), 9.

[22] Fitger, op. cit., 15.

PRUSSIAN MERCHANT MARINE

Year	Registered tons
1805	168,700
1815	115,700
1825	87,000
1836	106,500
1848	202,300

The North Sea shipping was practically confined to Bremen and Hamburg. While Baltic ships engaged in what was practically a coasting trade, the more enterprising and better-located shippers in these two ports found their opportunity in transatlantic trade. Hanseatic vessels had engaged in a profitable trade with the United States during and after the American Revolution at the end of the eighteenth century, and when the South American states declared their independence in the 1820's German vessels were among the first to trade with them. The ships which took German products to these countries, however, could not always obtain a return cargo, and were forced to pick this up along the coast or in the West Indies. The captain of such a vessel held a sort of roving commission, buying and selling and transporting goods to the best market according to his own discretion; if he were shrewd he could often make large profits. With the spread of the telegraph in the forties and fifties this sort of trade disappeared.

Gradually a division of labor developed between the two Hanseatic cities: Bremen became more important as a shipbuilding and Hamburg as a trading center. In 1840 Hamburg was already handling twice as much business as Bremen; it served a better hinterland than its rival. On the other hand, Bremen became the preferred point of departure for the thousands of emigrants who left their fatherland during this period. Between 1820 and 1850 about 1,600,000 emigrants left Germany and between 1850 and 1870 another 1,200,000, most of them to the United States. Important events were the founding of the H.A.P.A.G. in 1847, which opened business the following year with a fleet of four sailing vessels. It began a regular schedule to the United States in 1856, a decade behind the competing English and American lines. The following year the North German Lloyd Company was established. Germany still relied largely on foreign ships to carry her foreign trade. Half of all the vessels trading with Hamburg were British. Satisfactory statistics are lacking, but the following table of Hamburg shipping shows the course of development: [23]

[23] Sartorius, op. cit., 114.

Ocean-Going Vessels, Hamburg

Yearly average	Total number	Registered tons	Steamers	Registered tons
1836	146	25,722	..	......
1841–1845	211	39,570	3	895
1856–1860	483	139,236	18	10,282

The tardy adoption of steam is noticeable from this table. The old shipbuilders stood by their wooden sailing vessels. In the middle of the century the total number of steamers in Germany was only about 25, with an average capacity of 230 tons. After 1850 they increased fairly rapidly both in number and size; by 1870 there were about 100 steamers in Germany.

Means of communication: the post office. At the beginning of the nineteenth century the postal system was as backward as the roads along which the lumbering post wagons traveled. Post offices were to be found only in the cities, from which the rural inhabitants must fetch their own mail. The aim of the system was set forth by a royal instruction of 1808 in Prussia, that the post office had an economic rather than a fiscal purpose and the former was to guide its administration. With the development of the railroad there was a rapid expansion; the number of post wagons actually increased at the same time, as new rural routes were opened up. The number of miles covered in the postal service was as follows: [24]

Number of Miles Covered in Postal Service

	1852	1865
By roads	3,896,566	5,214,702
By railway	913,069	2,853,498

The postal system of the North German Confederation had 4340 post offices when it was founded in 1867; by 1871 there were 4927. The economic usefulness of the post is better indicated by the amount of mail carried than by the number of offices. Rather fragmentary data show a rapid development: [25]

	Prussia	No. Germ. Confed.
Year	No. of letters	No. of letters and postcards
	(in millions)	
1840	36	......
1851	90	......
1862	148	......
1868	......	274
1871	......	396

[24] K. Sautter, *Geschichte der Preussischen Post.* 2 Bde. (Berlin, 1928), I, 689.

[25] Sautter, op. cit., II, 11; G. Schmoller, *Zur Geschichte der deutschen Kleingewerbe* (Halle, 1870), 167.

A notable advance was made with the simplification of the Prussian postal tariff by the law of March 21, 1861, which reduced the number of classes from 6 to 2, and lowered the rates on printed matter, samples, and money shipments. This so stimulated the use of the postal facilities that in the following year the greatest surplus in the history of the post office to that time was achieved.

Telegraph. In the domain of communication the invention of the telegraph possessed an importance parallel to that of the railway in the field of transportation, to which it proved itself a useful adjunct. Almost simultaneously, in the United States, in England, and in Germany, the electro-magnetic telegraph was discovered. In 1837 Carl A. Steindeil put his apparatus into operation between Munich and Bogenhausen, but it remained for the American S. F. B. Morse to demonstrate the commercial practicability of the telegraph. During the forties most of the countries of western Europe were crossed with lines, and in the fifties submarine cables were laid in the shallow seas.

BIBLIOGRAPHICAL NOTE

1. *Britain.* The best book on road transportation is S. and B. Webb, *The Story of the King's Highway* (London, 1920). E. A. Pratt, *A History of Inland Transport and Communication in England* (New York, 1912) is a clear concise account of canal and railway history. W. T. Jackman, *Development of Transportation in Modern England*, 2 vols. (Cambridge, 1916) is particularly useful for canal and river transportation between about 1750 and 1850. The story is continued in C. R. Sherrington, *A Hundred Years of Inland Transport, 1830–1933* (London, 1934). For the early railways a contemporary account, J. Francis, *History of the English Railway, its Social Relations and Revolutions, 1820–1845* (London, 1851), is valuable, as is also H. G. Lewin, *Early English Railways, 1801–1844* (London, 1925). A. W. Kirkaldy and A. D. Evans, *History and Economics of Transport* (London, 1924) covers the later period. The commercial revolution brought about by mechanical transport is well described by L. C. A. Knowles, *The Industrial and Commercial Revolutions in Great Britain during the Nineteenth Century* (4th ed., London, 1926). Very interesting material is contained in the biographies by S. Smiles, *Lives of Metcalf and Telford* (roads), *Life of Brindley* (canals), *Lives of George and Robert Stephenson* (railways). A broader survey is R. S. Lambert, *The Railway King, 1800–1871, A Study of George Hudson and the Business Morals of his Time* (London, 1934). On communications J. C. Hammeon, *History of the British Post Office* (Cambridge, Mass., 1912) may be cited.

2. *France.* More attention was paid to railways than to roads or inland waterways. G. d'Avenel, *L'évolution des moyens de transport* (Paris, 1919) is a good introduction. Economic factors are emphasized in A. de Foville, *Les transformations des moyens de transport et ses consequences économiques* (Paris, 1880), still the best work. A short account of railway beginnings is given in L. J. Gras, *Histoire des premiers chemins de fer* (Saint Etienne, 1934). More thorough is Lord R. A. H. Monkswell, *French Railways* (London, 1911). A. Picard, *Les chemins de fer français* (Paris, 1884) is a well-known authority. A somewhat sketchy ac-

count is P. de Rousiers, *Les grandes industries modernes* (Paris, 1927), Vol. IV. Water transportation is covered in P. Léon, *Fleuves, canaux, et chemins de fer* (Paris, 1902).

3. *Germany.* A good introduction to railway history, popular but scholarly, is W. Lotz, *Verkehrsentwicklung in Deutschland,* 1800–1900 (2ᵗᵉ Aufl., Leipzig, 1906). The geographical setting is given in A. Mayer, *Geschichte und Geographie der deutschen Eisenbahnen* (1891). Inland waterways are adequately covered in T. Lenschau, *Deutsche Wasserstrassen* (Halle, 1906), and in O. Teubert, *Die Binnenschiffahrt* (Leipzig, 1912).

CHAPTER V

MONEY AND BANKING

I. THE CURRENCY VERSUS THE BANKING PRINCIPLE IN BRITAIN

Metallic money. During most of the eighteenth century England had a bimetallic standard, at a mint ratio of 15 to 1; the market ratio was about 15.21 to 1. The mint ratio therefore discriminated against silver, which was worth more as bullion than as coin; consequently little silver was presented at the mint for coinage. The full-weight silver coins were exported, in accordance with Gresham's law, and only the clipped and sweated coins remained in circulation. Partly because of the unsatisfactory condition of the silver coinage and partly because the expansion of commerce made the gold guinea [1] of 21 shillings more convenient for cash transactions, the legal tender quality of silver was limited to £25 by a statute of 1774; above this sum it could be tendered only by weight. This act really established the single gold standard in England, because it made gold coin the only legal money acceptable for all debts without limitation.

The formal adoption of the gold standard was made in 1816, which declared gold to be the sole standard of value, provided for the free coinage of gold at the mint price of £3 17 s. 10½ d. per ounce, and made silver coins legal tender in amounts up to 40 shillings only. Some technical changes were made at the same time: the guinea was discontinued and the sovereign of 20 shillings was declared to be the pound sterling; this coin contained 113 grains of fine gold. The silver content of the silver coins was reduced below their face value and they thus became mere token money, used for small change. The act of 1819 removed all restrictions upon the import or export of gold bullion or coin, and established a free gold market in England. The gold standard continued without change until August, 1914, when the outbreak of the World War swept it away over the whole of Europe.

Banking. The Bank of England was founded in 1694, and in 1697 it was given a monopoly by a provision that no other joint stock company should be permitted to carry on banking activities within the kingdom; in 1707 another act provided that no bank notes should be issued by partnerships consisting of more than six persons. From the language of these acts it is clear that Parliament understood by "banking" only the issue of notes, and that the monopoly of the Bank did not prevent the issue of notes by partnerships with six partners or less, nor the performance of other banking functions by joint

[1] Guineas were so called because the gold came from the Guinea Coast of Africa.

stock companies, or by partnerships with more than six partners.

A large number of private banks, organized as partnerships, existed in London and the provinces, some of them antedating even the Bank of England. After about 1772 the London bankers discontinued the issue of notes, finding the check system equally advantageous and more convenient; but the country bankers continued the issue of notes, subject only to restrictions later imposed by the Bank Charter Act of 1844. By 1797 there were 230 private banks in England. These banks did not hold large reserves of specie against their notes, as they found that they could obtain what they needed by keeping deposits with the Bank of England and drawing against them or by rediscounting their bills of exchange with that institution. The Bank of England thus became a bankers' bank and the holder of the specie reserve of the whole banking system, although for a long time its directors refused to acknowledge any special responsibility in this direction.

In 1793 war broke out between England and France, and soon involved the whole of Europe. The government borrowed heavily from the Bank and made use of its facilities for remittances to the Continent for military expenditures and subsidies to the Allies. So great was the drain on the Bank's resources that in 1795 the directors announced that they were compelled to restrict their loans to commerce and industry. The cash in the Bank was greatly reduced by the external drain to the Continent, to which was added in 1797 an internal drain due to the failure of a number of private banks. In February, 1797, the cash in the bank was only $1\frac{1}{2}$ million pounds while its liabilities amounted to $16\frac{1}{2}$ millions. Under these circumstances, and in order to avert more serious consequences, the Government authorized the Bank to suspend specie payments. Although designed as a temporary measure, it was continued by frequent renewals for twenty-two years.

The effect of the suspension was to exempt the Bank from the duty of meeting its obligations in specie, and it might have engaged in a policy of inflation. Instead it used great restraint, discounting only those bills which the public brought to it, and until 1808 no financial disturbance took place, although gold had disappeared from circulation. In that year, however, a serious fall in foreign exchange and a rise in the price of bullion in terms of the existing currency gave rise to a classic controversy. "The notes have not depreciated," said the directors of the Bank, "but the price of gold has risen." A Committee was appointed to inquire into the matter and they issued the famous Bullion Report of 1810, called by A. E. Feavearyear [2] "one of the most important documents in English currency history." The Gov-

[2] *The Pound Sterling: a History of English Money*, (Oxford, 1931), 182.

ernor of the Bank argued that there was an actual scarcity of gold and that its price had therefore risen, and that the fall in foreign exchange was owing to the condition of trade and the large payments by Great Britain to other countries; he further contended that there could not have been an over-issue of notes since these had been used only to discount "paper of undoubted solidity, arising out of real commercial transactions and payable at short and fixed periods." The Committee argued, on the other hand, that such an arrangement was not a guarantee against excessive issue, and pointed to the fall in foreign exchange as adequate proof that the notes were in reality depreciated. They called attention to the distinction between an advance of capital to merchants and an increased supply of currency, and pointed out that under the existing circumstances advances to merchants constituted additions to the money supply.

In order to restore the currency to par the Committee recommended that specie payments be resumed within two years. Although this proposal was rejected by Parliament, the discussion had contributed greatly to a better understanding of monetary theory. Credit and currency inflation by a central bank, now made familiar to all countries during the World War, was a new phenomenon then, and the monetary principles involved were not fully comprehended. Looking back on this episode from the vantage ground of the twentieth century, we may conclude that the general price level of 1814 was about double that of 1790 and that a very real inflation of the currency had taken place. In 1819 an act was passed obliging the Bank to resume specie payments, and in 1821 this was done without difficulty.

The growing demands of the country for banking facilities, which the Bank of England did not meet, caused an expansion of private banks; in 1814 there were 940 of them. These country banks usually grew out of the transactions carried on by merchants in financing their customers or discounting small acceptances and promises to pay of traders, manufacturers, and farmers in their neighborhood. They issued notes, but these had only a local circulation owing to the poor transportation system. Frequently the banking business became more important than the merchandizing business, and was separated from it. So long as they served purely local needs and were based on intimate knowledge of conditions they functioned well, but as they expanded many of them proved unsound. In 1826 an act was passed, giving to joint stock companies of more than six persons the right to issue notes, if established at a greater distance than sixty-five miles from London. The monopoly of note issue of the Bank was thus broken down. The Bank was also authorized to establish branches, and, acting on this authority, it established eleven branches, in the next few years, in Gloucester, Manchester, Birmingham, Bristol, Hull, Leeds, Liverpool, Newcastle, Norwich, and other important mercantile cities. A further breach was made in the supposed monopoly of the Bank in 1833. The joint stock banks had claimed that they had a right to open anywhere in England, even in London itself, if they did not issue notes, but the Bank of England contested their right to establish themselves in London. Their claim was, however, recognized in 1833, when the act renewing the charter declared that joint stock companies and partnerships of more than six persons might carry on the business of banking in London, or within the radius of sixty-five miles, provided that they did not issue notes.

In 1825 a severe crisis occurred. Excessive loans had been made to foreign governments, especially those of South America, which had recently obtained their independence, and to Denmark, Greece, and Naples in Europe, to a total amount of about £50,000,000. Speculation also took place in foreign mines, in cotton and other products, and in various chimerical schemes. Stock companies were formed with announced objects reminiscent of the South Sea Bubble; one of these proposed to drain the Red Sea to recover the gold lost by the Egyptians when pursuing the Israelites. The number of stock companies created was estimated at 624 with a nominal capital of £372,000,000. The most extravagant of these were the mining companies in South America; the shares of one of them, the United Mexican, on which only £10 had been paid, advanced from 35 to 1550 between December 10, 1824, and January 11, 1825. To meet the demand for funds the Bank of England and the country banks had increased their discounts and their note issues; at the same time the gold reserves had been reduced by the foreign drain to meet the borrowing of the foreign governments. These operations were brought to a halt by the failure of Sir Peter Pole and Co. in December. Sixty-three country banks were forced to suspend, and the Bank of England restricted its loans to protect its own shrunken reserve, which was down to little over £1,000,000. Later it enlarged its issues, and assistance was obtained from the Bank of France, but the process of liquidation could not be stayed and ran its course. The selfish policy of the Bank may be excused in part as the result of ignorance as to the proper policy to pursue,[3] and in part because the usury laws prevented raising the rate of discount above 5 per cent.[4]

[3] The proper policy for the Bank to pursue in a time of crisis — that of loaning freely but raising the rate of discount — was pointed out by Walter Bagehot in *Lombard Street* (London, 1873). It was scarcely feasible in 1825.

[4] The usury laws, so far as they applied to bills of exchange of three months and under, were repealed in 1833; the repeal was extended to bills of twelve months or under in 1837; and finally, in 1854, they were completely abolished.

A considerable extension of joint stock banks followed in the next few years. These early joint stock undertakings were only large co-partnerships with unlimited liability; not until 1856 was it possible to create corporate bodies with limited liability for any trading purpose. The London and Westminster Joint Stock Bank was established in London in 1834, followed by the London Joint Stock, the London and County, and the Union of London; and many banks began to issue notes outside the geographical limit. The expansion was, however, too rapid to be sound. The events leading up to the crisis of 1825 were repeated. There was a great deal of speculative lending to foreign governments, such as Russia, Spain, and some of the commonwealths in the United States. The drain of gold involved in these transactions reduced the metallic reserve of the Bank, which at the same time was lending freely to domestic borrowers and increasing its note issues. The principle upon which the Bank acted in regulating its note issue was apparently that of maintaining a reserve of coin and bullion equal to one-third of the liabilities, but this was seldom realized in practice. The panic of 1837 directed attention to the banking system, and especially to the question of note issue. The Bank was accused of having occasioned the crisis by over-issuing its notes. To this the directors replied that this was impossible so long as the notes were redeemed in gold. In addition to the Bank of England about 280 private or joint stock banks were issuing notes with little restriction. Out of this controversy there emerged two different theories, which came to be known as the banking principle and the currency principle.

The banking school argued that banks should be permitted to expand or to contract their issues in response to the demands of business. The necessity of redeeming their notes, they said, would be a sufficient guarantee against over-issue, for notes issued in excess of the requirements of the commercial community would be promptly returned to the banks for redemption, and thus the issues would be kept within bounds. The currency school retorted that mere convertibility was not enough to ensure prudence and restraint on the part of the bankers; that the unlimited power which the banks possessed of issuing notes was the immediate cause of commercial crises; and that the notes should be definitely tied to the amount of gold in the country. They urged therefore that the issue of bank notes should be strictly limited. The currency school won the debate and their ideas were incorporated in the Bank Charter Act of 1844.

By this Act Parliament undertook to make the notes of the Bank of England safe and to limit the issues of all other banks. To accomplish the first of these purposes the Bank of England was divided into two departments, the Issue Department and the Banking Department. The Issue Department was permitted to issue notes to the amount of £14,000,000 against government securities which it held; to this extent they rested on credit. But all other notes must be backed by an equivalent amount of gold coin or bullion. The Bank of England note was therefore practically destroyed as an instrument of credit and became a mere gold certificate. The Banking Department was entirely divorced from the issue of notes, but was free to carry on the banking functions of deposit and discount. The second object was met by limiting the issues of all other banks to the amount they then had outstanding, and to prohibit further issues by any new bank. If any existing issuing bank closed, failed, or discontinued its issues, then two-thirds of such issues should revert to the Bank of England, to be covered by securities. All profits accruing from such increase were to go to the treasury. The issues of these banks in 1844 amounted to £8,648,853. During the next eighty years amalgamation and other changes wiped out the issues of all these banks, and in 1921 the monopoly of the Bank of England over note issue became complete.

The Act of 1844 made the notes of the Bank of England safe and convertible, but in other respects it failed to fulfill the hopes of its supporters. When the notes were deprived of the credit feature a great stimulus was given to deposit banking and the use of checks. The use of notes came to be confined to small retail payments, but ordinary commercial transactions were carried on by drawing against credit accounts and using checks in making payments. The currency school had made a distinction between notes and deposits which does not exist, for both serve as money and credit expansion can take place through an increase of deposits even more easily than through additional issues of notes. Peel had expressed the hope that the Act would end commercial crises, but he was disappointed in this. Serious crises occurred in 1847, in 1857, and in 1866, and the Bank could do nothing legally to avert them. The Government accordingly in each instance suspended the Bank Act and authorized the Bank to increase its uncovered note circulation beyond the statutory limit; in 1857 such notes were actually issued to the amount of about £1,000,000. The question has frequently been raised as to the value of an act which had to be suspended in times of emergency, but it was not changed. It did, however, have the good effect of directing attention to the proper management of the metallic reserve.

The purpose of this legislation was to hold down the issue of bank notes and to ensure that there should be a large amount of gold in circulation. The smallest denomination which the Bank of England —and after 1829 any bank in England or Wales—was permitted to issue was for £5, which of course limited its use to the larger cash transactions. For general use a large circulation of gold sovereigns, with smaller silver coins, was called into being and remained the ideal of English monetary policy for the rest of the nineteenth century. In Scotland the banks issued £1 notes, which were convenient and safe, but this example was not followed south of the border. In 1800 the money in the United Kingdom amounted to £4.4 per inhabitant and consisted of £37,000,000 in gold, £8,000,000 in silver, and £25,000,000 in paper; in 1907 the amount per capita was 3.7 and the constituent parts were £117,500,000 gold, £24,300,000 silver, and £24,500,000 paper.

The panic of 1847 was caused in part by speculative railway promotions, but primarily by the deficient harvests in 1845 and 1846 and especially the potato famine in Ireland in those years. The purchase of large quantities of foreign grain, mostly in the United States, required the exportation of large amounts of gold, and the bullion holdings of the Bank of England fell below £10,000,000 in April, 1847, while the banking reserve was down to £2,500,000. A series of heavy failures occurred in August, and the Bank raised the discount rate to 5½ per cent and refused to make loans on public securities. This action precipitated a money panic and led to the hoarding of gold and bank notes. The reserve of the Bank dropped to £1,176,000. At this point the Government intervened and authorized the Bank to increase the issue of notes without a gold cover; that is, the Bank Act was suspended. At once the hoarded money came out of hiding and the panic was relieved, though inevitable liquidation of weakened business houses followed. It was evident that the Bank of England had not yet learned how to manage its operations so as to ward off a panic.

The panic of 1857 had its origin in the United States, but many English banks and business houses, which had extended credit to American institutions, became involved. This time the Bank of England tried to control the money market by drastically raising the rate of discount, which stood at 8 per cent on the first of November, 9 per cent on the fifth, and 10 per cent on the ninth. But by this time the joint stock banks and the private bankers had finally ceased discounting, so that the whole demand for loans fell upon the Bank of England. Several serious failures resulted in unprecedented demand for further accommodation. In the four days, November 9-12, the Bank advanced over £5,000,000 to the public, but without quieting the panic or stopping the drain of its reserve. On the evening of November 12 it held a banking reserve of only £581,000, against liabilities for deposits amounting to £13,000,000. The external drain of specie to the United States and the internal drain to the English banks and business houses had caught the Bank of England much as a run on any commercial bank might have caught such an institution with an insufficient banking reserve. Under the circumstances there was only one thing that could save the situation. The Government once more suspended the Bank Act of 1844 and authorized the issue of £2,000,000 of uncovered notes. This was effective in stopping the panic, and it was necessary to issue only about half of the notes authorized. This time the Bank had made more prompt and drastic use of the discount rate to curb expansion, but it had acted tardily. Manipulation of the bank rate alone was evidently insufficient.

A more scientific method than rigid rules of note issue, and one which became the permanent policy for the protection of its gold reserve, was taken by the Bank of England after the panic of 1857. This consisted in raising the rate of discount rapidly by degrees of one per cent when the reserve was threatened by a drain. The private and joint stock banks made no pretence of keeping coin reserves of their own, but relied wholly on the Bank of England for gold to meet emergencies. Under this "one reserve system" the entire responsibility of protecting the credit of the whole complex of banks and discount houses, and of the entire business community, devolved upon the Bank of England.

Although the Bank of England had established several branches after 1826 and threatened to enter the field of commercial banking, it gradually assumed its final position as a bankers' bank and the custodian of the bank reserves of the whole country. The Bank was the center of a complex of joint stock and private banks and discount houses, most of which kept chief reserves on deposit with the Bank. The position of the Bank was therefore one of great responsibility. Although it was organized as a private bank and still is, it came to recognize in time its unique position as a national institution and to assume the duties involved. But the lesson was learned only through experience. The Bank's changed position was emphasized by changes which were taking place in the English banking system.

The Acts of 1826 and 1833 had sanctioned the establishment of joint stock banks and they grew rapidly, especially in the country; by 1842 there were 118 in operation. At the same time the number of private banks declined from 940 in 1814 to 311 in 1842. Most of these failed because of unsound banking practices or were absorbed by the joint stock banks. The latter had the advantages of a superior type of organization, commanded greater confidence, had many branches, operated with a larger capital — after 1844 no bank could be formed with less than £100,000 of capital — and after 1856 had the advantage of limited liability. The most important reason, however, was the growth of deposit banking and the use of checks as means of payment, which made the loss of the right of note issue of lessened significance. The growth of world trade was so great during this period that it had quickly absorbed the new supplies of gold that were produced by America and Australia, and there was urgent necessity of providing a facile credit currency if economic progress were to be maintained. This was furnished by the check currency, which was more adaptable than notes, more elastic, economical, and safe. The number of joint stock banks did not grow as rapidly as their operations; in 1871 there were 1779 branches in England and Wales. By the 1860's the complete absorption of the private banks by their stronger competitors seemed to be only a matter of time. The amalgamation of joint stock banks with each other was also going on during this period. Country banks sought alliance with London banks, the joint stock banks wished wide geographical representation, and found in consolidation with existing banks the quickest method of expanding.

Economy in the use of cash had long been practiced by the private bankers in London, who in 1773 organized a primitive system of clearing checks and bills among themselves by having their clerks meet on the sidewalk. The size of the transactions soon led them to hire a room, but the private bankers retained exclusive control of the London Clearing House until 1854, when the joint stock banks were admitted. The Bank of England was not admitted until 1864. The clearing operations steadily expanded, from £954,000,000 for the year 1839 to £1,900,000,000 in 1857, and £3,425,000,000 in 1868. In addition to the London institution, clearing houses were established in the principal cities in the provinces, where local banks cleared the checks drawn on each other and on their branches in the immediate area.

2. ASSIGNATS AND THE BANK OF FRANCE

The assignats. At the end of the eighteenth century two noteworthy monetary experiments were made, which served to clarify economic thinking in this field and were long used as stock illustrations of monetary theory. These were the issue of assignats in France and the suspension of cash payments in England.

The financial difficulties of the French monarchy, with its extravagances, its mounting deficits, and its unequal system of taxation, undoubtedly contributed to the fall of the *ancien régime*. The failure of the crops in 1785 resulted in the highest prices for grain in half a century and the industrial crisis of 1787 brought about unemployment and unrest in the cities. The national debt amounted to about 5 billion francs, the interest on which absorbed a large part of the revenues. This was the situation which the National Assembly inherited with the Revolution. Its most immediate need was money with which to meet these various difficulties.

In November, 1789, the church lands had been confiscated and the following month their sale was decreed. There was a double reason for this speedy sale — a financial reason, to obtain money for the hard-pressed government, and a political one, to distribute the lands among as large a number of persons as possible and so commit them to the Revolution. The proposal was promptly made to establish a special fund from the sale of these lands and against this to issue treasury notes, called assignats. Objections were swept aside by Mirabeau, who declaimed: "We are told that paper money will become superabundant. Of what paper do you speak? If of a paper without a solid basis, undoubtedly; if of one based on the firm foundation of landed property, never." His argument prevailed and in December the government was authorized to issue these notes in the denomination of 10,000 francs up to a total of 400,000,000, to bear 5 per cent interest and to be redeemed systematically within five years, but without forced circulation. According to the original theory the holder of such a note would have so much land assigned to him, and some writers have regarded the notes as a means of distributing the confiscated church lands. As additional issues of assignats were authorized, an equivalent amount of land would be put on sale, so that they balanced.

In view of the condition of the treasury they must rather be viewed as a fiscal device. They were used in large part to pay the floating debt. When received in payment for land they were supposed to be burned, but enormous sums were left in circulation after the land was sold. Since they bore interest it was assumed that they would not enter into circulation as money; when interest was later abolished, this safeguard was removed. In April of the following year an additional 400,000,000 francs was authorized, the denomination was lowered to 200 francs and the interest to 3 per cent. The first issue had brought relief to the treasury and had apparently shown the fears of the objectors to be groundless, but this was a fatal step, for it was a move in the direction of pure fiat money, and from now on the movement to inflation was irresistible. It was argued that, since the notes were based on land, they could not fall in value. Later in the year the denomination was reduced to 50 francs, interest was abolished, and the total circulation raised to 1200 million. The assignats began to decline and metallic money to disappear from circulation. Retail trade was embarrassed by the lack of small coins, so the lowest denomination of the assignats was reduced to 10 sous in May, 1791. These issues of paper money brought little relief to the treasury, for they were received by the government in payment for the church lands at their face value. As the lands were sold the assignats accumulated in the treasury. The buyers of the land profited, especially as the depreciation became greater, but the government gained little.

In 1793 the lands of the *émigrés* were confiscated and placed on sale. Against these new issues of assignats were made, but the additional issues, which were not needed by business, choked the channels of trade and hastened their depreciation. The government decided to accept them for land at their current and not their face value. As this decree met with opposition, the sale of lands was finally stopped.

The issue of assignats did not stop, however, for the needs of the treasury were insistent and the fiction of basing their value upon land was given up. They were now pure fiat money, and issue followed issue in increasing amounts. By October, 1794, there were almost 7000 million in circulation; a year later over 17,000 million, and in September, 1796, when the issues stopped, 45,500 millions. By this time a hundred-franc note was quoted at one-third of a franc or $\frac{35}{10,000}$ of its face value. In 1797 the assignats were declared to be no longer legal money and the unfortunate possessor at the moment bore the loss. The total quantity of assignats in circulation at selected dates was as follows: [5]

Date	Millions of francs	Date	Millions of francs
June 1, 1791	912	July 1, 1795	12,338
Sept. 22, 1792	1972	July 1, 1796	34,509
Aug. 1, 1793	3776	Sept. 7, 1796	45,579
July 1, 1794	6082		

The value of the assignats showed on the whole a steady decline, though there were occasional periods when reviving confidence in the government or more energetic measures caused a temporary rise. Local figures, collected by Harris,[6] were generally higher than the official treasury quotations, but showed a wide variation from place to place. A few samples of the treasury figures will show the rapidity and extent of the depreciation.[7] (Par = 100.)

Month	1790	1791	1792	1793	1794	1795	1796
January	96	91	72	51	40	18	.46
July	95	87	61	23	34	3.1	

[5] A. Courtois, *Histoire de la Banque de France et des principales institutions françaises de crédit depuis* 1716 (Paris, 1875), 79.

[6] S. E. Harris, *The Assignats* (Cambridge, Mass., 1930), 166-86.

[7] Courtois, op. cit., 81.

The causes of the breakdown of the assignats were several. Most important of course were the excessive issues, which were augmented by forgeries, so that confidence was completely undermined. As the national lands were sold the security back of the notes declined, in so far as these were not retired. The usual explanation of the depreciation of the assignats, based on the quantity theory of money, was the immoderate over-issue, but there were other contributing factors. Among them were weakness of the government and unsound military, economic, and political conditions. There was also a reduced demand for money, owing to the curtailment of production and of business at the very time when the supply was increasing. As always in such cases the more the notes depreciated and their purchasing power fell, the more necessary became further issues of assignats in order to meet the demand for adequate media of exchange. A vicious circle was started which could end only in a breakdown. Efforts were made in 1793 to prevent depreciation by threats of severe punishment for any one who refused to accept assignats at par, which went to the extent of twenty years' imprisonment in irons, and finally death, though this was repealed after a year's trial. In spite of terroristic legislation depreciation continued and prices rose, so the method of fixing maximum prices was also tried. But as the prices fixed by legislation were always below the advancing market prices, this also proved ineffective. Persons who received assignats lost in proportion to the length of time they held them. The incentive to thrift disappeared; the way to fortune was to go into debt and to spend quickly. Normal economic principles were turned topsy-turvy. Prices rose to fantastic heights. A few illustrations may be given.[8]

	1790	1795
Boisseau of flour (1.4 pecks)	2 francs	225 francs
Boisseau of beans	4 "	120 "
Demi queue of Orleans wine (45 gals.)	80 "	2,400 "
Pair of shoes	5 "	200 "

Wages did not rise as rapidly as prices, and workers, public officials, and others with fixed salaries, or persons living on income from bonds or rents, all suffered. Manufacturers feared to produce or merchants to sell. Industry stagnated, unemployment grew, and relief works were started in the cities. In fairness it must be said that not all these disorders were caused by the assignats, but resulted from the reduction of supplies of food and other articles, as well as from the general chaos in France at the time.

Mandats. In spite of the breakdown of the assignats, the govern-

[8] E. Levasseur, *Histoire des classes ouvrières de 1789 à 1870* (2nd ed., Paris, 1904), I, 223.

ment in desperation again seized upon the device of paper money in 1796 to replenish the exhausted treasury. In March 2400 million francs of *mandats territoriaux* were issued; these were land warrants based upon the security of all the public lands. The old assignats were redeemed in these at the rate of about 50 to 1. The mandats experienced the same fate as the assignats, but in even shorter time. When, in February, 1797, the government withdrew the legal tender quality (forced circulation) from all the notes, the end of the paper money was signalized.

The government had not relied solely upon paper money to finance its administration, but had at the same time endeavored to raise revenue by taxation. The old system, with its inequality, corruption, and expensiveness, was rejected, and new taxes were decreed, which should be universal and proportional, levied according to external indices and not subject to bureaucratic whim. The laws of 1790 and 1791 established the *quatre contributions* which continued almost unchanged for over a century. At the basis was the land tax, which was assessed according to the net income; the tax on movable property proved unproductive and was replaced in 1797 by a tax on house rentals. The occupation tax or *patente* was levied according to the rent of the premises occupied and some other indicia. The door and window tax, the fourth of the series, was authorized in 1798 and was imposed according to the number of external doors and windows. Together these taxes constituted a simple and intelligible system in place of the complicated and unjust one that had prevailed. But on the other hand, the hatred of indirect taxes led to the abolition not merely of administrative fees but also of liquor, salt, and tobacco taxes, of transit dues, and of octrois. Only the duties at the frontier were retained. Returns from the new taxes came in slowly, the outbreak of the general European war in 1793 brought new disorder into the state finances, and the requirements of the government grew faster than revenue receipts. In spite of doctrinaire opposition it became necessary to resort in 1798 to the lucrative indirect tax on tobacco and at the same time the cities were permitted to re-introduce the octrois. Even with these additional sources of income expenditures exceeded receipts. The receipts from taxation reached nearly 50 per cent of the total revenues early in 1792, but during the years 1793–95 they fluctuated between 5 and 15 per cent. Under the circumstances a resort to paper money was almost unavoidable.

The national debt was a heavy burden, which it was decided to liquidate, and in 1797 the "two-thirds bankruptcy" law was passed which decreed that only one-third of the interest on the national debt and of pensions should be paid in cash; the other two-thirds were met by warrants which could be exchanged for public lands. These warrants soon fell to a tenth of their face value, so the creditors lost practically two-thirds of their holdings.

When Napoleon came to power as First Consul he saw as his first duty in domestic policy the creation of a system of sound national finance. A budget was set up in 1801, a thought foreign not only to the *ancien régime* but also to the Revolution. The existing direct taxes were retained, and indirect taxes on liquor (1804) and on salt (1806) were re-introduced. The tax on tobacco was replaced by a state monopoly. By 1812 the indirect taxes contributed 40 per cent of the revenues. The national debt was refunded. The one-third recognized by the law of 1797 was replaced by a 5 per cent consolidated issue, and the other two-thirds were funded at a rate which at least gave something tangible to the creditors though it represented a return of only one-quarter of one per cent on the original capital. By 1800 the financial chaos had been brought to an end. With the abolition of paper money the monetary disorders ended. Napoleon's financial policy was characterized by the effort to make his system felt as little as possible. This explains his preference for indirect in preference to direct taxes. He did not make use of public credit, partly because he did not fully understand the importance of credit, and partly because he did not wish to be dependent on financiers. On the other hand he exploited mercilessly the conquered lands. His finances shared therefore the fate of his military fortunes.

Coinage. Provision was made for a return of metallic currency in 1793 when a new coinage system was established on a decimal basis. Two years later the metallic currency was recoined to accord with the law, and the ratio between silver and gold was changed from 14.5 to 1 to 15.5 to 1. This was done by providing for a silver franc of 5 grams, $\frac{9}{10}$ fine, and gold pieces of certain weights, without designation of their value in francs, but which agreed with the ratio of 15.5 to 1. The franc was the unit and this was divided into 100 centimes. Between 1794 and 1803 silver coins in the amount of 106 million francs were struck off; no gold came to the mint. This system was not satisfactory and in 1803 provision was made for the free coinage of gold and silver at the ratio already set up, and the new coins were given unlimited legal-tender power. The ratio was nearly in accord with the market value of the two metals, and bimetallism was maintained by France for half a century with considerable success.

Under Napoleon the mint turned out 528 million francs gold and 888 million francs silver. A contemporary writer, Gaudin, asserted that France now had the best coinage system in the world; he estimated that gold made up one-third of the metallic currency. The existing ratio, however, undervalued gold and it began to be hoarded or exported; by 1848 it had almost disappeared. But the new gold from America and Australia in the fifties completely changed the situation. Gold was now cheaper and flowed into the mint, while silver began to disappear from circulation since it was now worth more as bullion than as coin. To domestic hoarding and use in the arts was also added the drain from the Orient, which was ready to absorb any quantity. Considerable inconvenience, especially to retail trade, resulted from the withdrawal of the silver coins, but the new gold was coined in large amounts and exerted a beneficial effect upon industry and trade.

The Bank of France. After the failure of John Law's *Banque Générale* in 1716 France had no central bank for over half a century until in 1776 the *Caisse d'Escomptes* was founded. This perished in the Revolution, but two other banks were soon established: the *Caisse des Comptes Courants* (1796) and the *Caisse d'Escompte du Commerce* (1797). These were absorbed in the Bank of France, founded under Napoleon's auspices in 1800. This at once took a leading position in French finance both because of the size of its capital (30,000,000 francs) and because of its close relation to the government. It became the depository of government funds, paid out the interest on the government debt, and in 1803 it was given a monopoly of note issue for 15 years. Since checks were unknown and most business was carried on by means of cash payments, this issue monopoly gave to the Bank of France a position of power. No limitation was placed upon the right of issue, except those dictated by sound banking principles, which were rigorously observed by the Bank directors. In addition to the public business the Bank discounted bills of exchange and other commercial paper of French manufacturers and merchants. Napoleon hoped by means of the Bank to furnish French industry with cheap and adequate credit. In 1806 the capital was increased to 90 million francs and two years later branches in the provinces were authorized. But only in Lyons, Rouen, and Lille were such branches established. The Bank remained primarily a Parisian rather than a national institution.

The close connection between the Bank and the government exposed the former to all the vicissitudes of Napoleon's military fortunes, for it was drawn upon heavily to help finance his campaigns. It is not necessary to trace the banking history of the years of war, from which the Bank emerged safely. Even in the final catastrophe of 1814 the Bank was able to avoid a suspension of cash payments. France was saddled with a war indemnity of nearly 2000 million francs at the end of the war, but was able, by floating a loan and with the aid of English and Dutch banks, to free the country of foreign troops by 1818. In financing the war indemnity the Bank of France rendered valuable assistance, but it was weakened by its close association with the government. In 1818 its capital was reduced to 68 million francs and dividends were limited to 6 per cent.

Private business was, however, not so well served by the Bank. Owing to its neglect of the provinces the branches in Lyons, Rouen, and Lille were suspended in 1817 by the government, which instead granted charters to independent or departmental banks in Rouen, Nantes, and Bordeaux. As these showed good results others were established, 1835–1838, in Lyons, Marseilles, Lille, Havre, Toulouse, and Orleans. These banks accommodated themselves to local conditions, and served successfully the commercial and industrial interests of the communities in which they were established. Their notes had, however, only a local circulation and had to be covered by a metallic reserve of at least one-third. Against this policy the Bank raised no objection, but in the thirties, stimulated by the success of the independent banks, it began again the practice of establishing branches in the provinces, which brought it into competition with the independent banks. In 1840 the charter of the Bank was extended for another 27 years, its capital was increased to 91,250,000 francs, and it was now provided that no independent note-issuing bank could be established except by law, whereas a ministerial order was enough to create a branch of the Bank of France.

The political crisis of 1848 established definitely the monopoly of the Bank. This had fifteen branches and there were also nine independent banks of issue. Cash payments were suspended by all the banks in this emergency but public confidence in the Bank of France remained unshaken, while the notes of the independent banks depreciated. The government took advantage of the situation to fuse the Bank of France and the independent banks, and thereafter the former had a complete monopoly of note issue. In 1850 it resumed cash payments. The denomination of its smallest notes was first reduced from the original 1000 francs to 500, then to 200 in 1847, and finally to 100 in 1850. Its notes, which had formerly been almost confined to Paris, thereby obtained a wider circulation and entered into retail trade. Owing to the fact, however, that it discounted only three-name commercial paper, one of which was usually that of a bank, it remained largely a bankers' bank.

The expansion of the note circulation reflects fairly accurately the prosperity of France and its steady commercial expansion during this period, while the metallic coverage indicates its conservative management. Commercial paper was discounted for only three months, but it could be renewed. The total sum of the discounted bills grew from 500 million francs in 1817 to 1617 million in 1846. At the same time it was able to reduce the rate of discount from 5 per cent in 1816 to 4 per cent for the period 1820–1850. The following table shows the essential facts concerning the note issues: [9]

Year	Average note circulation	Average metallic reserve (in millions of francs)	Coverage (per cent)
1816	69	50	85
1820	154	195	126
1830	223	145	65
1840	223	247	111
1850	496	458	92
1860	736	514	72
1870	1566	1131	72

The amount and management of the reserve were left entirely to the discretion of the Bank, and this was handled with the utmost caution and wisdom. Government legislation was limited to fixing the amount of the note issue, which was raised from time to time as need dictated. This was a strange rule, for the ability of a bank to grant credit and to maintain the convertibility of its notes does not depend upon their amount, but upon their relation to the metallic reserve. Owing to the good management of the Bank, however, the reserve, as indicated in the table, was always adequate.

During the period 1850–1870 the Bank rendered noteworthy services to the government. It assisted the conversion of the national debt in 1852 and 1862 by advancing large sums, and helped in financing the Crimean War. At the same time it served industry by aiding in financing the construction of railways and in the rebuilding of Paris. In 1852 it was able to reduce the discount rate to 3 per cent, though it was forced soon to raise it again. In 1857 the charter of the Bank, which would expire in 1867, was prolonged to 1897. As the price of this concession, however, the Bank was forced to advance 100 million francs to the government for the purpose of consolidating the floating debt. The capital of the Bank was increased to 182.5 million francs, and it was relieved of the limitation of its discount rate to a maximum of 6 per cent. This gave the Bank better control over the money market, which it exercised, in imitation of the Bank of England, by varying the discount rate; between this date and 1870 it changed its rate 66 times. Before this time the Bank had endeavored to control the amount of loans

[9] L. J. Loutchitch, *Des variations de l'intérêt en France de 1800 à nos jours* (Paris, 1930), 62; through 1840. After that the figures are taken from C. A. Conant, *History of Modern Banks of Issue* (4th ed., New York, 1909), 70.

by varying the length of time for which it would discount commercial paper. Thus, the normal time of 90 days was reduced in the stress of 1818 to 45 days, raised to 90 at the end of the year, and remained there until 1855, when it was again lowered to 75 days and in 1856 to 60; after the financial pressure was relieved it was gradually lengthened again to 90 days. The lowest denomination of notes was reduced to 50 francs, and the permission to establish provincial branches was changed into a requirement to do so. As a result the number of branches grew to 74 in 1870; but twenty-five departments still lacked representation by the Bank.

Other banks. Significant as were the services of the Bank of France, and powerful its position with a monopoly of note issue, it nevertheless stood removed from the business world. This was served by a number of other banking institutions, the number of which grew rapidly after 1830 in response to the commercial expansion of that period. At the head stood old firms like Lafitte, Périer, Hottinger, Rothschild, and others, most of them with foreign connections, who carried on international transactions. They constituted the so-called *Haute Banque* and had a practical monopoly of public loans and those of large organizations, as well as of international transactions in the precious metals. There were also more than 200 private bankers, who often combined banking with trade in textiles and colonial wares, and who were therefore to be found largely in the industrial and commercial cities. Some of these were more interested in speculation than in furnishing credit, and small industrial undertakings were forced to rely on private lenders at exorbitant rates.[10] The money market was, however, centralized almost wholly in Paris, and here in the Bank of France, so that the provinces were poorly supplied with banking and credit facilities. Those places where no branch banks existed were at a special disadvantage, for the Bank of France would not rediscount bills of exchange drawn on establishments located there, and the cost of credit was therefore very high to them. With the building of railways in the forties the demand for banking and credit facilities grew stronger and other institutions were developed to meet it, such as the *Caisse Central du Commerce et des Chemins de Fer* (1843). By 1847 five such credit institutions existed, which participated in industrial enterprises in addition to banking; but the panic year of 1848 brought them to an end. Industry was served less well by the banks in France than in either England or Belgium.

Since the government would not permit banks to organize as *Sociétés anonymes* or corporations with limited liability, they were

[10] B. Mahrens, *Die Entstehung und Entwicklung der grossen französischen Kreditinstitute* (Stuttgart, 1911), 12.

forced to take the form of *Sociétés en commandite*, which had un-limited liability for the management, but limited liability for the shareholders. The prohibition was based on the theory that bank-ing operations could not be rigidly prescribed by law, but rested largely in the discretion of the banker; he should therefore be made wholly responsible for his acts. The first bank which organized as a *Société anonyme* was the *Comptoir National d'Escompte*, founded in 1848 to provide credit to industry and commerce in the troubled days of the Revolution. Two-thirds of its capital was guaranteed by the state and the cities, and it was ordered to establish offices in all industrial and commercial cities. It was of great assistance and developed a widening sphere of influence until its failure in 1889.

A serious gap existed in the French banking structure in the absence of banks of deposit and in the use of checks. After 1859 several such institutions were established. It was a period of extraordinary development, brought on by the building of improved transportation facilities and by the industrial expansion, especially in the coal and iron fields. A higher standard of living and the spread of luxury also stimulated business. The system of discount banks and the use of cash in the settlement of transactions were inadequate in such a period of expansion and dangerous in times of emergency. Examples of credit banks already existed for financing railways and real estate, but business, especially the small business so character-istic of France, was inadequately provided with short-term credit. In spite of the efforts of Napoleon III, however, it did not prove possible to popularize the check and deposit system in France at this time.

In 1852 two credit institutions were founded which had a marked influence on the development of French banking. The *Crédit Mobilier* was organized by the brothers Isaac and Émile Pereire for the purpose of financing railways and industrial enterprises. They were financiers rather than bankers and thought of credit simply as a means of economic development. The company was authorized to issue its own bonds to ten times the amount of its capital, and al-ways tried to maintain high prices for its securities and also for those of enterprises which it financed. Its influence therefore encour-aged speculation. For a time it was very successful, building French, Austrian, Hungarian, Swiss and Spanish railways, assist-ing Haussmann in rebuilding the Rue de Rivoli, extending the har-bor at Marseilles, and financing mines, shipping companies, omnibus lines, and other similar enterprises. The *Crédit Mobilier* was op-posed by the more conservative bankers, headed by Rothschild, and when it collapsed in 1867 the government forced the resignation of the brothers Pereire, but let the Bank of France wind up its affairs

for the sake of the small investors. In 1871 it was reorganized under the same name.

The *Crédit Foncier*, also established in the year 1852, had as its
purpose the granting of loans upon land. It was given a government
subsidy of 10,000,000 francs, but most of the money needed for
loans was raised by the issue of its own bonds, against which it held
as security the mortgages on the land, which were to be repaid in
fixed annual instalments. Although it was empowered to lend
money on agricultural land it confined itself primarily to real estate
in Paris, which experienced a boom under the rebuilding operations
of Napoleon III. It was authorized to receive sums of money on deposit and to invest these in approved securities, but it was not a
commercial bank in the modern sense, though it met a need in the
credit field.

The savings banks should also be mentioned, though these constituted reservoirs of small capitals rather than granters of credit. The
first savings bank, the *Caisse d'épargne et de prévoyance*, was
founded in Paris in 1818; this was quickly imitated and five years
later eleven other cities had similar institutions. The Paris bank accepted deposits as low as one franc, but with a maximum of 50 francs
in a week (raised to 300 in 1835). Difficulties in investing the
deposits led to an association with the state, which accepted the funds
and guaranteed the deposits; this reduced the banks to mere de-
positories of savings without any active banking functions. The
growth of savings banks is shown in the following table: [11]

Year	No. of banks	No. of depositors	Total deposits	Deposits in Paris
1830	12	......	......	33,069
1840	278	351,807	192,383	70,355
1847	354	736,951	358,406	80,146
1849	355	561,440	73,918	23,094
1859	415	1,121,465	336,462	48,668
1869	508	2,130,578	711,175	54,181

3. BACKWARDNESS IN GERMANY

Money. At the beginning of the nineteenth century each of the
numerous separate states in Germany had its own system of coinage
and of weights and measures. When the Zollverein abolished the
internal barriers and trade and exchanges within the country increased, the inconvenience of such a lack of uniformity was clearly
perceived. The first step toward currency unity was taken in 1837.
A convention was concluded among the southern states of Bavaria,

[11] Sée, op. cit., 205n., 360n.

Wurtemberg, Baden, Hesse, Nassau, and Frankfort, providing for a common coin, the florin of 147.3 grains of silver. In the following year a similar union was made in the north, but here the common coin was the thaler: the Vereinsthaler was adopted, with 257.7 grains of fine silver. In 1857 these two systems were combined and at the same time the Austrian system was brought into conformity. Only Hamburg and Bremen retained their own coinage.

With the gold discoveries there came a rise of prices in the fifties. The gold from the United States and Australia found its way for the most part to England and France. Germany, which was on a silver basis, received silver from America and also from bimetallic France where it was displaced by the cheaper gold. The increase in currency came at a most welcome time, and was quickly absorbed by the expanding requirements of business. Industry was developing new techniques and growing in size with the opening up of wider markets, railroads were being built and, with steamships, were reducing the costs of transportation, and capital was being freed from burdensome legal limitations.

The rate of interest, which is a fair indication of the demand for and supply of capital, showed significant changes during this period. The destruction of capital and the urgent need of the governments forced it up during the Napoleonic wars, but after the middle of the twenties there was a steady fall for twenty years. The economic expansion of the forties created new demands for capital and the rate of interest, the price for its use, rose again. In the early fifties the usual rate on mortgages was 5 per cent, and on government bonds 4½ per cent, but it fell below these figures during the next decade. Prices in general followed much the same course as interest rates, with a marked acceleration after 1850.

Banking. At the beginning of the nineteenth century Germany was largely agricultural and agriculture was primitive and self-sufficing. Industry was carried on mainly by small handworkers, and trade was limited and small. Under such circumstances there was little demand for banking facilities. There was only one bank of issue, the Royal Bank of Berlin. This was a state institution, managed entirely by government officials, and it confined itself to loans on mortgages, the discounting of commercial paper, and advances on the security of commodities. Modern commercial banking, in the sense of credit deposits and checking accounts, was unknown.

In the twenties and thirties, when trade began to expand, a number of private banks sprang up, especially in the larger commercial cities, as Frankfort a. M., Berlin, and Leipzig, which carried on a profitable business and enjoyed good reputations. The most notable of these was the house of Rothschild in Frankfort. The early banks handled very largely government loans, dealt in bills of exchange, and acted as money changers.

In the twenties there emerged also so-called "knightly," agrarian, and municipal issue (*Zettel*) banks. Their purpose was primarily to furnish to trade and industry, but especially to agriculture, money loans at low rates of interest, but they could carry on other banking functions to a limited extent. In order to obtain the necessary capital they were permitted to issue notes (*Zettel*), limited in relation to their capital and under certain conditions, which must be covered to the extent of one-third by a metallic reserve and two-thirds by discounted paper. The first of these banks was the Knightly Private Bank of Pomerania, established in 1824; but after 1848 other similar banks were founded; by 1857 there were seven in Prussia.

Another type of issue bank was the Berlin *Kassenverein*, formed out of eight large private banks in 1831, which received the right, for the purpose of rendering easier the exchange of checks and deposits, of issuing so-called clearing certificates (*Kassenscheine*) in place of bank notes, which must be redeemed on presentation in metallic money and for whose redemption all members of the union were jointly responsible. When the ordinance of December 5, 1836, forbade the issuance of notes by all private institutions the union lost this privilege. But since the convenience of a common clearing house for the Berlin banks had been proven, the union continued and expanded its business. In 1850 it became the *Bank des Berliner Kassenvereins*, with a capital of 1,000,000 Thaler.

In 1847 the Bank of Prussia took the place of the Royal Bank of Berlin. Its capital was privately owned, but it was managed by government officials. It could establish branches and could issue notes up to a fixed maximum; the notes were redeemable on demand in Berlin and at the option of the bank in the branches. The other states also wished to have state banks of issue, in order to facilitate their financial objective. Accordingly Bavaria established in 1835 the Bavarian Mortgage and Exchange Bank, and Saxony in 1838 the Leipzig Bank. These institutions were well managed and helped finance the industrial and transportation development which began in the forties.

This development is clearly pictured in the growth of banks and of corporations. The existing money institutions could not meet the growing demands of business and after the "mad year" of 1847 one new credit bank after the other arose. Between 1848 and 1856 fourteen banks with a total capital of 183 million marks were established.[12] Sombart pictures the years after 1848 as a lively, profit-making period, in which the desire to win seized the widest circles

[12] Jacob Riesser, *Die deutschen Grossbanken und ihre Konzentration*, 647.

of the people and speculation took hold of the German people with a hitherto unknown power. In 1853 the Bank for Trade and Industry was established in Darmstadt, which place was selected in order to escape the limitations existing in Prussia; in 1857 was founded the Berlin *Handelsgesellschaft*, which thirteen years later became the Deutsche Bank.

As prices rose speculation spread to the agricultural classes. Many bought land, on which they paid only part, in order to have more capital free for the purchase of equipment, fertilizer, etc. Between 1850 and 1870 there was an increase in the number of mortgages not only on large but also on medium-sized properties. The mortgage loans granted by the Newmark Credit Institution (Kreditanstalt) grew from 4 million Thalers in 1815 to 11 million in 1835 and 17 million in 1865, but still the demand was not met. Other credit banks were formed: Leipzig 1858, Frankfort 1862, Prussia 1863, Bavaria 1864, and many others. These gave better credit facilities to agriculture than the private money lenders had done, for the latter made their mortgages for a definite term of years, while the state institutions were content so long as interest and amortization payments were regularly met.

Legislation followed this financial expansion. In 1849–51 a general law governing bills of exchange was introduced into the federal states instead of the 56 different ones then existing, of which the oldest dated from 1603. This was followed by the excellent work of the German *Handelsgesetzbuch*, which was introduced into all the German states in the sixties. There was similar confusion in the note issues, of which there were about 140 different types, and these were next brought into order. When the Empire was founded a single imperial currency was adopted in 1871 with the mark as the unit. Steps were taken after the foundation of the Reichsbank in 1875 to concentrate the note issues of the thirty-two issuing banks in this central institution, but this movement was a slow one and was not completed for another half century.

Germany had by now been unified, so far as foreign and even domestic policy was concerned, but its powers were strictly limited, especially in fiscal matters. Almost its sole source of revenue was the customs duties, supplemented by contributions from the states. The entire internal administration — education, police, judiciary, and taxation — was in the hands of the several federal states, and remained so until the World War. The particularism of the states prevented complete unification and centralization until this was forced upon them by the Revolution of 1918.

BIBLIOGRAPHICAL NOTE

1. *Britain.* An excellent history of British currency is A. E. Feavearyear, *The Pound Sterling: a History of English Money* (Oxford, 1931). The important Bullion Report of 1810 is reprinted in E. Cannan, *The Paper Pound of* 1797 *to* 1821 (2nd ed., London, 1919), with a valuable historical introduction. Somewhat distorted history is furnished in W. A. Shaw, *The History of Currency*, 1252–1894 (London, 1895). On banking a good general introduction is C. A. Conant, *A History of Modern Banks of Issue* (6th ed., New York, 1927). The most thorough study of the central bank is A. Andréadès, *History of the Bank of England* (London, 1909). Other banks and their operations are described in W. F. Crick and J. E. Wadsworth, *A Hundred Years of Joint Stock Banking* (London, 1936), which can be supplemented by Jos. Sykes, *Amalgamation Movement in English Banking*, 1825–1924 (London, 1926). A keen analysis of the British banking system is W. Bagehot, *Lombard Street: a Description of the Money Market* (London, 1873; new ed., 1917). On financial organization see W. R. Bisschop, *The Rise of the London Money Market*, 1640–1826 (translated from the Dutch, London, 1910); E. T. Powell, *The Evolution of the London Money Market* (London, 1915). Foreign investment is treated carefully in L. H. Jenks, *Migration of British Capital to* 1875 (New York, 1927). Government finance is well covered in S. Buxton, *Finance and Politics*, 1760–1885, 2 vols. (London, 1888), and S. Dowell, *History of Taxation and Taxes*, 4 vols. (London, 1884). A very useful sketch of the whole subject is J. F. Rees, *A Short Fiscal and Financial History of England*, 1816–1918 (London, 1921).

2. *France.* The interesting monetary experiments during the Revolution have been carefully studied by S. E. Harris, *The Assignats* (Cambridge, Mass., 1930) and by J. Morini-Comby, *Les assignats: Révolution et inflation* (Paris, 1925). More popular and less objective is A. D. White, *Paper Money and Inflation in France* (New York, 1879). Two books by A. Courtois are standard: *Histoire de la Banque de France et des principales institutions françaises de crédit depuis* 1716 (Paris, 1875), and *Histoire des banques en France* (Paris, 1881). An excellent economic survey is B. Mehrens, *Die Enstehung and Entwicklung der grossen französischen Kreditinstitute mit Berücksichtigung ihres Einflusses auf die wirtschaftliche Entwicklung Frankreichs* (Stuttgart, 1911). J. G. van Dillen (Ed.), *A History of the Principal Public Banks* (London, 1934), covers the Bank of France, as does G. Ramon, *Histoire de la Banque de France* (Paris, 1929). An interesting contemporary account is L. de Lavergne, *La Banque de France et les banques départmentales* (Paris, 1865). A more general study is R. Bigo, *Les bases historiques de la finance moderne* (Paris, 1933). A. Liesse, *Evolution of Credit and Banks in France from the Founding of the Bank of France to the Present Time* (London, 1909) gives a sweeping summary.

3. *Germany.* Until 1870 all banks in Germany were state banks, under various state laws. Consequently there are few books of general interest, and these deal with the end of the period. Coinage is described by A. Soetbeer, *Deutsche Münzverfassung* (Erlangen, 1874). On banking the following may be cited: O. Hübner, *Die Banken* (Leipzig, 1854); H. V. Poschinger, *Die Banken im deutschen Reiche, Oesterreich und der Schweiz* (Jena, 1877); A. Soetbeer, *Deutsche Bankverfassung* (Erlangen, 1875); M. Wirth, *Handbuch des Bankwesens* (3te Aufl., Köln, 1880). Another oft-quoted book by the same author is *Geschichte der Handelskrisen* (3te Aufl., Frankfort a. M., 1883).

CHAPTER VI

LABOR AND THE LABOR MOVEMENT

I. FACTORY LEGISLATION AND LABOR STRUGGLES IN BRITAIN

Growth of a factory population. Long before the advent of the factory system there had existed a wage-earning class. Under the "putting-out" system the textile workers were paid piece rate wages and retained only a semblance of independence. In other industries, such as mining, pottery, transportation, and agriculture, the payment of wages to persons who furnished only their labor was the dominant practice; there were few independent enterprises in these fields. It is incorrect therefore to say that the factory introduced the wage system. The spread of the factory system did, however, increase greatly the number of persons who worked for a wage, not only by moving many industries out of the home or workshop into the factory, but also by developing new industries. There was thus a great increase in the number of workers as well as in the proportion of those who worked for a wage. "It looks," wrote the Hammonds,[1] "as if the Peels and the Arkwrights had only to stamp on the ground to turn empty valleys into swarming hives of workpeople." Where did this factory population come from?

The new factory workers were assembled from many sources. Only a small proportion consisted of men, who probably constituted less than 20 per cent of the employees in textile mills in 1816; after 1835 the proportion was about 25 per cent. The indisposition of male adult workers to enter the factories seems to have been due in part to the dislike of discipline and in part to the bad reputation of the early factories. The cottage worker preferred his independence, even at lower wages, to the enforced discipline and compulsory hours of the factory. The same attitude operated to keep young women from going into domestic service. So long as there was some real freedom of choice, the workers preferred to work at home; but after the dominance of machinery the handworkers were finally forced into the factories. The early factories seem to have been confused with parish workhouses, as the same name was often applied to both institutions. Respectable workers were unwilling to take employment in an establishment that was not regarded as respectable. As a result the early factory masters were forced to obtain their labor from such other sources as were available.

One of these sources was the parish workhouses. From these were drawn adult labor, but more especially child labor. Under

[1] J. L. and B. Hammond, *The Town Labourer*, 11.

existing legislation, dating back to the Statute of Apprentices of 1563, it was provided that vagrant children might be bound out as apprentices. The overseer of the poor, standing in the place of the parent, was authorized to apprentice pauper children in order that they might learn a trade. The workhouses were overcrowded with children, for whom it was difficult to find a suitable occupation. When the early manufacturers discovered this supply of labor the parish authorities were eager to apprentice the children to them under ordinary industrial indentures. According to these the employers contracted to give board, clothing, and instruction for a certain number of years to the children who were apprenticed to them. In the cotton mills, where they were most largely used, the pretence of teaching the children a trade was soon abandoned and the child apprentices were practically slaves.

The early mills, run by water power, were established where power was to be had, usually along the rapid streams in the hilly districts of Lancashire, Yorkshire, Derbyshire, and Nottinghamshire. These were sparsely populated and it was difficult to attract workers there from other places. Moreover, labor was not as yet very mobile and did not move easily. The mill operators therefore seized upon this cheap mobile supply of child labor in the workhouses as a happy solution of their problem. Later, when steam power was used instead of water power to drive the machinery, the factories were established near the coal mines in the more densely settled areas. The use of apprentice children declined with this shift about 1816, but the employment of child labor did not lessen; now the children in the neighborhood were employed, whose parents were perhaps unable to find work. The condition of child labor throughout the whole period was so bad that it is unnecessary to distinguish between the pauper and the free children.

In addition to the children, women were drawn into the factories, especially the textile mills. In 1838 women constituted 55 per cent of textile operatives, and 57 per cent in 1856. Owing to the casual and subsidiary character of much of women's work it was not included in the census statistics of occupation, but Porter [2] estimated the number of women in gainful occupations in 1844 as 1,920,432.

Another part of the labor supply was drawn from industries in which labor had been displaced, or from handicrafts and home industries which were moving into the factories. Light on these changes is given in the testimony of a witness from Bolton before the Factory Commissioners in 1833, though the reference is to an earlier period. [3]

[2] G. R. Porter, *Progress of the Nation* (London, 1846), 29.
[3] Quoted by the Hammonds, *The Town Labourer*, 12.

"When power spinning came in . . . where were the spinners taken from?" — "A good many from the agricultural parts; a many from Wales; a many from Ireland and from Scotland. People left other occupations and came to spinning for the sake of the high wages. I recollect shoemakers leaving their employ and learning to spin; I recollect tailors; I recollect colliers; but a great many husbandmen left their employ to learn to spin."

The agrarian revolution and the enclosure movement had dispossessed a large number of small agriculturalists and had driven many of them into the towns. The long wars loosened large numbers of men from their accustomed moorings and at the end these men flooded the labor market. And improvements in transportation first provided new opportunities of employment in building turnpikes, canals, and railroads, and then gave a greater mobility to labor. The expansion of factories and other lines of industry came just in time to absorb this restless and rapidly growing mass of workers; but which was cause and which effect it is difficult to say.

One other group of recruits may be mentioned — the Irish. Their rapid increase at home sent many of them to England and Scotland, where they first performed menial tasks which called for little skill, but later they pressed into the industrial towns, where they became spinners, handloom weavers, and general laborers.

The growth of a distinct wage-earning class of factory operatives proceeded slowly but steadily. In 1760 Arthur Young had estimated that about 42 per cent of the population were engaged in farming; if to these are added the rural handicraftsmen, traders, and others who served the agricultural communities, we may conclude that about two-thirds of the population lived under rural conditions. By 1831 only 28 per cent of the families in Great Britain were employed in agriculture; possibly half of the population might still be classed as rural. But by 1870 England was thoroughly industrialized.

Industrial organization. It is difficult to picture the conditions under which labor was carried on during this period, for they were transitional and varied. Household production, domestic industry, workshop, and factory existed side by side, although the tendency was strong to bring them all under the last named system. It was a period of innovation, of expansion, and of continual readjustment, and these processes brought hardship and suffering to many who could not quickly adapt themselves to new conditions. Many of the evils attributed to the factory system were growing pains, and some of the worst abuses existed in industries that remained outside of the new industrial organization.

Household production of a primitive sort was to be found in Scotland and parts of northern England at the beginning of the nineteenth century and persisted in some lines for another thirty years. Clothing was made at home from flax or wool grown and worked up through the various processes to the finished cloth by members of the family, baking was domestic, and other work was carried on in the home. Custom weavers were to be found throughout most of the rural counties, who wove materials furnished by the customer.

The domestic system persisted in some lines, notably in weaving, and one of the most tragic chapters in this dynamic period was the unavailing struggle of the weavers to resist the encroachment of machinery. Small men working on their own account were common in the metal and cutlery trades. More frequently they were outworkers for a small master or shopkeeper. But even where these industries were not carried on in factories with the use of power, there was a strong tendency toward a capitalistic organization under the control of trading employers, or merchant capitalists, who owned the material and merely gave it out to workmen who received piece rate wages. This system prevailed in the textile industry in most of its branches, in the clothing industry, in button and glove making, and in many others.

Workshops, in which independent masters or handicraftsmen worked up their own materials by hand methods with the aid of tools, were to be found in many industries, especially in the metal trades. The position of these handicraftsmen ranged from complete independence to that of being a mere outworker for some merchant employer. As transportation improved and production came more and more to be carried on for distant markets, and as competition between different producing areas became keener, a steady pressure was exerted to bring all these workers under a capitalistic organization. The independent handicraftsman tended to become a dependent outworker, even though he was not brought into a factory. It was characteristic of British industry that many of the processes of manufacture were divided and subdivided and were then handed over to small entrepreneurs or handicraftsmen who carried on the work in their own little workshops.

The factory system may not have been the dominant type during all of this period, but it was growing at the expense of the other forms of organization and by 1870 was master of the field. The development was uneven in different lines. Where staple goods were made in large quantities for general consumption, as in the manufacture of cotton goods, it first demonstrated its efficiency. The progress can be best determined by noting the industries in which machinery driven by power was introduced. In 1800 the list was a small one: cotton and, to a less extent, the other textile industries, mining, and blast furnace work. By 1825 railroads and water transport were also using steam engines. After this the list grew rapidly. But the introduction of steam-driven machinery, so characteristic of the factory, took place slowly. This fact must be borne in mind in describing the conditions of work during this period.

Labor legislation. It was over the employment of children and women that the issue of state interference in private industry was raised, and settled. Protection was first granted, in 1802, to the most helpless class of all, the parish apprentice children: the minimum age of employment was set at 9 years, the working hours were limited to 12 a day, night work was to cease after 1804, the children were to receive two suits of clothing each year, and were to be given instruction during the first four years of apprenticeship; factories were to be whitewashed twice a year, and two visitors were to be appointed to inspect the factories. This act was designed to care for a particular evil and did not invoke the police power of the state in a general sense; it applied, moreover, only to cotton and woolen mills, and was inadequately enforced.

The shift of industry from remote districts to more populous centers reduced the dependence on pauper labor, but brought about the more general use of child labor. The investigation of 1816 showed the necessity for legislation to protect the interests of a group that could not protect itself, and the resulting Act of 1819 first applied the principle of state responsibility, though it was limited to children in cotton mills. The minimum age was fixed at 9 years, and children under 16 were restricted to 12 working hours; the administration of the act was placed in the hands of the justice of the peace, but it was not enforced.

Various events forced upon Parliament the question of a more comprehensive treatment of child labor. Richard Oastler published his first letter on Yorkshire Slavery in 1830, Michael Sadler introduced a ten hour bill in 1831, Lord Ashley and other reformers pressed for legislation. A Royal Commission, urged by the manufacturers, made a thorough investigation and disclosed such appalling evils that remedies were clearly called for. The resulting Act of 1833 applied to all textile mills, except lace and silk. The minimum age was still 9 years, but an important step was taken in classifying young persons into two groups, those between 9 and 13 and those between 13 and 18 years of age; for the former the working day was limited to 9 hours and for the latter to 12 hours. Children under 10 were to attend some school. But the most important provision was the appointment of salaried inspectors, responsible to the Home Office. Although these were too few for efficient service — only four being appointed under this Act — their systematic reports furnished valuable information for further reforms. The provisions were partly nullified by the use of a relay system, but this was met by further legislation in 1844. The effectiveness of the earlier Act is indicated by a decline in the number of young persons employed from 56,000 in 1835 to 41,000 in 1850.[4]

The Act of 1844 placed women under the same restrictions as young persons between 13 and 18 years of age and hence limited their work to 12 hours a day. By the same act the safety of operatives was regulated for the first time: children, young persons, and women were forbidden to clean or oil machinery while in motion and protective coverings were prescribed for dangerous machinery. The powers of the inspectors were also strengthened. In 1847 the Ten Hour Bill was passed and further laws in 1850 and 1853 required all work by protected persons to be performed between 6 a.m. and 6 p.m. The establishment of a normal working day had the practical effect of extending the ten hour day to male workers also, since the factory could not run without the women and children.

All the factory acts down to 1853 were limited to textile factories, but evils equally great existed in other industries and called for remedial legislation. In 1840 Lord Ashley obtained the appointment of a Children's Employment Commission to investigate the employment of children in mines and other branches of trade and manufacture. The conditions disclosed in the Commission's reports were shocking in the extreme: children harnessed to trucks of coal which they drew on rails through passageways so low they had to crawl on all fours; young girls carrying heavy baskets of coal on their backs up steep ladders; men and women half clothed or wholly naked working side by side. The Coal Mines Act was passed, almost without dissent, prohibiting the employment underground of women and female children and of boys under ten. This was the first Act which regulated the labor of adult women.

The decade of the sixties saw the extension of the factory acts to non-textile industries. Their provisions were now broadened so as to apply to children and young persons in bleaching establishments in 1860, to dyeing establishments in 1861, and to bakehouses in 1863. The following year saw the regulation of dangerous industries, such as the pottery and match industries, in which white lead and phosphorus were used, and industries in which grinding and polishing produced dust injurious to the lungs. Ventilation was required to remove dangerous gases, dust, and other impurities. The year 1867 saw two further important acts. The first, the Factory Extension Act, extended the provisions of the factory laws to all blast furnaces, iron and copper mills and foundries, brass foun-

[4] E. von Plener, *English Factory Legislation* (London, 1873), 35.

dries, printing mills, bookbinders' shops, and all other manufacturing establishments in which fifty or more persons were employed. The second, the Workshop Regulation Act, brought "workshops" under regulation, and abolished the artificial distinction hitherto made between smaller industrial establishments and the larger factories.

The early labor legislation was motivated by emotional, religious, and charitable ideas, but by the sixties more heed was paid to health and safety. The first factory acts were passed as a kind of exceptional legislation to remedy evils in a distinct branch of industry. From this they were gradually extended to the whole range of large and small industries. It was an empirical method and made progress slow and uneven. But by 1870 all work done by women and young persons had been placed under supervision and was subject to general regulations. Only the labor of adult men remained outside the exercise of the police power of the state. These acts had been violently opposed at first as an unwarranted interference by government in private business, but as the dire results prophesied did not materialize a gradual change occurred in public opinion. It had been argued that a reduction in hours would inevitably be followed by a diminution in output, but it was found that the product of eleven or even ten hours' work might be greater than that of twelve. The onerous school and register regulations, moreover, led the manufacturer to employ machinery rather than children. The strong tendency toward mechanization after 1840 must be attributed in no small degree to the operation of the factory acts. Not only was the productivity of industry increased by this change, but the most beneficial results in the health of the workers were soon evident; the so-called "factory leg" and other deformities disappeared and industrial diseases and accidents diminished.

Labor organization. Trade unions, that is continuous organizations of wage-earners, were common in the eighteenth century, long before the rise of the factory system. The forces which brought them into being were the separation of the independent artisan from his tools and materials and the divorce of agriculture and industry. They resulted, not from the introduction of machinery and the factory system, but from the capitalistic organization of industry under the domestic system, already described. Even in industries carried on exclusively by hand labor, as tailoring, or where simple appliances were used, as in the cutlery industries, a class of lifelong wage-earners came into being. In those lines in which larger capital was necessary, as in mining or in silk weaving, the workers could never hope to become independent masters, and here such wage-earners had long existed. But the divorce of the worker from the instruments of production became general in many lines with the introduction of the factory system, and the rise of labor organizations paralleled the development of the industrial revolution. The trade union movement was, however, a slow one, and beset with many difficulties.

In order to protect their standard of life against the upsetting changes that were occurring the craft workers first invoked the enforcement of existing legislation. Ever since the days of the gilds and of the Statute of Apprentices of 1563 the prevailing theory had been one of a static society in which wages should be held steady, profits maintained at a reasonable level, and consumers protected both as to quality and price. The old regulations had, however, been indifferently enforced and many of them were disregarded. Occupations grew up which were entirely outside the scope of these laws. Commercial companies were developing without government regulation, transportation and mining, new branches of manufacture, as cotton, and the new agricultural organization all broke through the protective ring surrounding the skilled crafts. Instead of a static society under governmental control, a highly dynamic society was growing up in which free initiative supplanted the ideal of social co-operation. The publication of Adam Smith's *Wealth of Nations* in 1776 set a stamp of approval on these changes. "In the meantime," wrote the Webbs,[5] "the workers were left to shift for themselves, the attitude of Parliament towards them being for the first years one of pure perplexity, quite untouched by the doctrine of freedom of contract."

The workers in the skilled trades, unable to obtain new protective legislation, turned to the enforcement of existing law. Statutes stood on the books which enabled justices of the peace to fix wages, limited the number of apprentices, or required journeymen to have served a full apprenticeship. The weavers in Yorkshire and the West of England in 1802 proceeded against their employers for infringing these old laws and asked that their wages be fixed by the magistrates. The net result of these suits was the suspension of the acts by Parliament in 1803. A few years later another effort along the same line was made, but this resulted only in the repeal in 1813 of the law empowering justices to fix wages.

The apprenticeship clauses of the great Elizabethan statute still remained, and the workers now petitioned that these be enforced and that they should be extended to new industries, not mentioned in the original statute. The system of apprenticeship had indeed broken down; under the cottage system of industry, and still more under the factory system, the requirement of a long and rigorous training before engaging in a trade had not been enforced or needed. Only

[5] S. and B. Webb, *The History of Trade Unionism* (1902 ed.), 47.

in those industries requiring great manual skill did it continue in a modified form. As the simplification of processes and the introduction of machinery rendered long training less necessary, the practice became general of using large numbers of apprentices. A seven year apprenticeship was no longer necessary. The response of Parliament for the enforcement of these acts was their complete repeal in 1814 as "against the natural rights and contrary to the common law rights of the land." This removed practically the last remnant of governmental protection of the laborer's economic position, which had come down from the gild period. The workers were now left to their own resources.

The eighteenth century saw the rise of trade unions, not among the unskilled class of permanent wage-workers, but among journeymen who also possessed the necessary independence to resist their employers. Trade unionism did not arise as a protest against intolerable living conditions, as is so often assumed, but among the superior workmen as a means of protecting their privileges. Trade clubs in the cities, half friendly societies and half journeymen's fraternities, were more apt to unite with their employers against interlopers than to join with their fellow workers of other industries in an attack upon the capitalist class. There was as yet no distinct cleavage between employers and wage-earners. This came with the divorce of the worker from the ownership of the means of production, and the trade union movement accordingly took place in those lines in which this separation was most complete, as among the cotton spinners, woolen workers, and the framework knitters. It paralleled the introduction of the factory system and the use of power.

Combinations among workingmen certainly existed all through the eighteenth century, frequently under the guise of benefit societies, secret orders, or sick clubs. Sometimes they were formed to carry out the purposes of existing legislation, as the enforcement of contracts, arranging for apprenticeship, or the fixation of wages. Such combinations were accepted as permissible, even if technically illegal under the common law and the statutes governing combinations and conspiracy.

The attitude of Parliament toward these combinations changed as time went on. At the beginning of the eighteenth century the policy had been one of protection, and Parliament had passed laws enforcing existing wages and practices at the request of the journeymen. In the middle of the century the doctrines of freedom of contract and competition began to influence legislation, and by the end of the century held full away. The technological changes which were revolutionizing British industry made the medieval apparatus of legislative protection unworkable. Unfortunately, nothing was put in its place, until the method of factory legislation was discovered in the nineteenth century.

Combinations of labor were contrary, with minor exceptions, to the principles of the common law. Workingmen might, as individuals, lawfully agree or refuse to work, but when two or more entered into an agreement to fix wages or other conditions they entered into a conspiracy, which was against the common law. There were also many statutes, some general and enacted primarily against political associations, some dealing specifically with labor organizations. The law of 1824, repealing these repressive measures, enumerated thirty-five such acts. Most of these laws applied to particular industries, but in 1799 Parliament passed a hasty act entitled "An Act to Prevent Unlawful Combinations of Workingmen," which expressly penalized all combinations whatsoever. This was replaced the following year by a more comprehensive measure, which required the concurrence of two magistrates for conviction and added some ineffectual arbitration clauses.

The effect of the Combination Acts on the organization of labor is a matter of dispute. Professor Clapham [6] warns "against attaching too much importance to Acts whose life was short, whose administration was ineffective, and whose aim every working man and some employers desired to circumvent." The Webbs,[7] on the other hand, cite numerous instances in which workers were convicted under these laws of unlawful combination. The truth seems to be, that, while associations of workers might be tolerated, they were technically illegal, and the employers had the power of meeting any unwelcome demands by a prosecution, or threat of one. "The main use of the law," wrote the Webbs,[8] "was to checkmate strikes, and ward off demands for better conditions of labor." The skilled handicraftsmen were able to resist the encroachment of the employers, but the workers in the new machine industries were practically helpless. The law, it is true, forbade combinations of employers as well as of workers, but there is no case on record of the enforcement of the acts against the former. On the other hand, we have the testimony of Adam Smith as to the "tacit, but constant" combination of employers to depress wages; people of the same trade seldom met, said he, even for diversion, but the conversation ended in "a conspiracy against the public or a contrivance to raise prices."

The injustice of these acts had long been recognized, and cannot be eliminated by pointing out the lack of enforcement. They put a weapon in the hands of the employers, which was used by the worst

[6] J. H. Clapham, *An Economic History of Modern Britain*, 205.
[7] S. and B. Webb, *History of Trade Unionism* (1902 ed.), 63-74.
[8] Op. cit., 70.

of them. It must not be thought that there were no humane or far-sighted manufacturers who deplored the low wages and long hours; but in a competitive market the price is set by the cost of production of the low-cost establishment. If this achieves its low cost by cutting wages, other competing establishments must follow suit or go under. When Parliament repealed the laws providing for the fixation of wages by justices of the peace it destroyed the machinery for coercing the bad employers and left the good ones helpless. And now the combination acts tied the hands of the workers and prevented collective action on their part.

The period following the Napoleonic war was one of industrial dislocation and political repression. The disbanding of the armies turned thousands of men into industry, which was deranged by the transition from war to peace-time activities; the extension of machinery displaced thousands of handicraftsmen; foreign trade recovered slowly; and agriculture was depressed by the fall in the prices of grain. A concerted movement was made by employers to cut wages, and these were reduced to starvation levels, although the cost of living was going up at the same time. Strikes and the destruction of property and other acts of violence were frequent. The agitations of the workers in 1818 were met by the use of troops to suppress a public meeting at Peterloo in 1819, and the passage of the notorious Six Acts, which practically prevented public meetings, tightened the law for seditious libel, authorized search for arms, and subjected working-class publications to the crushing stamp duty.

The leader in the movement for repeal of the combination acts was Francis Place, a prosperous master tailor, who, as a struggling journeyman, had experienced the hard lot of a worker and had been active in organizing associations. With the aid of Joseph Hume, a Radical member of Parliament, a Select Committee on Artisans and Machinery was set up in 1822 to investigate, among other things, combinations of workmen. Witnesses were brought from every part of the country and carefully coached by Place, who skilfully manipulated the whole movement. The result was an act in 1824, repealing all combination laws and legalizing trade societies. This was followed by a burst of trade union energy and many new unions were formed and existing ones came out into the open. Strikes and disturbances became general, and the employers were alarmed. Accordingly, in 1825, a new act was passed, which nominally re-established the prohibition of combinations, but specifically exempted from prosecution organizations to regulate wages or hours of labor. The common law of conspiracy was left in full force against all combinations in restraint of trade. Henceforth it was lawful for persons to meet together for the sole purpose of consulting upon and determining the rate of wages and the hours they would work; but the use of intimidation or molesting other workers would subject them to three months' imprisonment at hard labor.[9]   The effect of this legislation was to grant to trade unions the right of collective bargaining for their own members, and marked an important step forward in the trade union movement.   They were still without power, however, to establish wages or hours for persons not taking part in their meetings, or to strike on questions of piecework or number of apprentices or machinery or non-union workers.   The legal freedom of trade unions was therefore still far from complete.

The year 1825 was marked by a financial panic and was followed by four years of depression and commercial disaster.   Wages were lowered and thousands of workers were thrown out of employment. So great was the distress that many factory workers were kept from starvation only by charity.   The unions were too weak to fight successfully on a falling market, and strikes ended invariably in disaster. The discouraged workers turned from trade unionism, which seemed futile, to more ambitious programs of social reform, in which, from 1829 to 1848, the trade union movement became almost submerged.

The first effort was the inclusion of all manual workers in a single comprehensive trade union in place of sectional combinations of workers in single crafts.   In 1830 the National Association for the Protection of Labour was organized, and is said to have enrolled 100,000 members; but by 1832 it had disappeared.   A Builders' Union to include unions of all the seven building trades was formed in 1833 with 30,000 members.   And in 1834 Robert Owen organized a Grand National Consolidated Trades Union which is reported to have enrolled 500,000 members in a few weeks, including farm laborers and women.   The avowed aim of this union was a general strike of all wage-earners throughout the country, but its energies were dissipated by a series of local disputes, which the central organization was not strong enough to prevent.

The employers, thoroughly alarmed, countered with "presentation of the document," an agreement not to belong to any union.   In the "Derby turnout" 1500 men were locked out when they refused to sign.   The press opposed the Union, the middle class was exasperated by the inconvenience occasioned by the strikes, and the Government sided with the employers.   Workingmen were convicted under the common law for illegal combination.   The best known case is that of the six Dorchester farm laborers, who were sentenced to seven years transportation because they had taken a secret oath in their initiation ceremonies.   The legal basis was found in an old and

---

[9] The text of these laws is given in A. E. Bland, P. A. Brown, and R. H. Tawney, *English Economic History: Select Documents* (London, 1914), 636.

half-forgotten law passed at the time of the French Revolution. The Grand National Trades Union dissolved into fragmentary local societies, and the ideal for which it stood vanished in discredit.

The labor organizations of this period were profoundly affected by two movements which belong to social and political rather than economic history. These were Owenism and Chartism. Robert Owen, a manufacturer who had risen from the ranks, was a philanthropist and factory reformer, his New Lanark Mills were the first model factory. In his later years he turned to socialism. Owen impressed upon trade unionism the ideal of workers' productive co-operation and self-employment, which he thought would replace the existing competitive system. Some societies were organized to carry out these ideas, but they perished with the failure of the Grand National. The modern consumer's co-operative movement, however, remains as a permanent monument of Owenism, for it was an Owenite society, the Rochdale Pioneers, who started their shop in 1844.

The labor movement next reverted to the struggle for political power, which this time took shape in the Chartist movement. During the dark years 1837–1842, this completely overshadowed trade unionism, and did not finally quit the labor stage until 1848. It was not, however, a union movement, although many unionists supported it. Chartism was an effort to extend the franchise to the workers, and the People's Charter contained six points designed to achieve that end. These were universal manhood suffrage, vote by ballot, division of the country into equal representative districts, annual election of Parliament, and payment of members, so that poor men might serve. It is significant that all but one of these demands has since been granted. Meetings were held in all the important towns and a monster petition was prepared with 1,250,000 signatures for presentation to Parliament. This was overwhelmingly rejected by that body. Not only was it unwilling to discuss the introduction of a more democratic type of government, but it took severe measures against the Chartist leaders. The movement declined after 1839, but the continental revolution of 1848, combined with the severe panic of 1847, led to a revival of interest. A new petition for the Charter was drawn up, which was again rejected by Parliament. Dissension among the leaders weakened the movement, while the repeal of the Corn Laws satisfied many reformers. The workers turned from political reform to organization for industrial improvement.

With the revival of prosperity after 1848 the predominance of Chartism ended, and trade unionism revived. The surviving unions consolidated their organizations, took measures to defend themselves in the courts against legal oppression, limited the right to declare strikes, and placed more emphasis on education. A new type of organization appeared with the formation in 1851 of the Amalgamated Society of Engineers, which was a combination of seven smaller bodies of engineers,[10] machinists, smiths, millwrights, and pattern-makers. They accepted the economic axiom that wages depend upon the relation of demand and supply of labor in each particular trade; they therefore endeavored to keep out "illegal" men. They developed an elaborate financial and administrative organization, employing a paid secretary, and levying dues of one shilling a week, which they used for the payment of friendly benefits. In 1852 they demanded the abolition of piece-work and of systematic overtime, and though the employers, who formed the Central Association of Operative Engineers, won the struggle, the new society emerged unshaken.

The organization of the engineering societies was soon imitated by other crafts and a new model and spirit were introduced which marked a decided change in labor aims and tactics. Membership was restricted to legally apprenticed workmen in a particular craft, while the relatively high dues confined these to the elite of the labor world. The unions were thus exclusive protective organizations, without any of the impracticable all-embracing character of the Owenite and Chartist societies.

The main characteristics of this new type of union were as follows: (1) the amalgamation of allied trades into a strong central organization; (2) the maintenance of friendly benefits, the scope of which varied in different organizations; (3) the acceptance of the existing economic system, and concentration upon improving the conditions of their members in that system; (4) the employment of permanent salaried officials, in whose hands control was centralized.

The model of the Amalgamated Society of Engineers was closely followed by the Amalgamated Society of Carpenters and Joiners in 1860, and by the Amalgamated Society of Tailors and Tailoresses in 1866. In almost every other industry it exercised a profound influence, even if it was less slavishly imitated. This period witnessed also the rise of Trade Councils, or local federations of various unions, whose delegates met to discuss local conditions and agree upon uni-

[10] The Board of Trade Committee on Commercial and Industrial Policy (London, 1918) defined the "engineering trade" as consisting of the following four groups:

(1) Constructional steel work and the boiler and wagon trade.
(2) The machine-tool trade, including locomotives and cranes.
(3) The smaller auxiliary trades, such as small tools, gauges, and measuring instruments.
4) General trade, from motor cars and agricultural machinery to sewing machines, pianos, and watches.

Instead of "trade," an American student would use the word "industry."

form action. The final step was the organization of a central Trades Council, made up of the trade union officials who lived in close proximity in London; this was fairly representative of the labor movement as a whole and exercised great influence during the next two decades.

2. REFORMERS IN FRANCE

Economic organization. At the beginning of the nineteenth century the population of France was predominantly rural, and most of the agricultural workers were peasants who tilled their own land. The industrial workers in the towns and cities were still in the handicraft stage, and carried on their trades under the familiar organization of masters, journeymen, and apprentices. There did not exist therefore the group of propertyless factory wage-earners, who comprise what is called today the laboring class. There was no sudden industrial revolution and until 1848 no unbridgeable chasm separated employer and employee. Nevertheless changes were taking place which carried the seeds of more portentous events. House industry was declining and mechanized industry in the cities was growing. A new class of enterprisers, restrained by no tradition and little legislation, hard and resolute, came to the front. On the other hand, an industrial working class developed, different from the former handicraft workers. Industrial freedom and machine technique permitted the use of woman and child labor, which could be had cheap. The children received a trifling wage, and the women often only one-quarter as much as the men. They were most numerous in the textile industry, especially in the cotton branch.

The period from 1830 to 1870 was one of rapid economic development in France. A good index is the use of steam power: the number of steam engines grew from 600 in 1830 to nearly 19,000 in 1860. The textile industry showed the most rapid expansion, the number of spindles for flax and hemp spinning increasing from 57,000 in 1840 to 752,000 in 1865, and those for cotton from 2,600,000 in 1834 to 6,800,000 in 1867. After 1840 there was a much wider use of machinery and a growth in the number of large establishments. The rise of new forms of industry was paralleled by the development of new problems with respect to labor. There is no doubt but that the early large scale mechanized industry had an unfavorable effect upon the position of the worker.

The census of 1831 classified the total population according to the occupations of the workers, and, while there are undoubted inaccuracies in the census table and the meaning of the terms is unclear, it presents a broad picture of the economic activities of the people.

Categories	Number of persons	Percentage
Agriculture	24,000,000	66.7
Manufactures	2,500,000	7.0
Arts and trades	3,800,000	10.5
Liberal professions, Government employees, etc.	4,109,000	11.4
Domestic servants	905,500	2.5
Unclassified	683,500	1.9
	36,000,000	100.0

It is certain that the number of factory workers can have formed only a very small fraction of the total, and that the group engaged in manufacturing was small even if the handicraft workers are included.

Labor organization. Industry in France before the Revolution was centered largely in the gilds. These had persisted from the Middle Ages, when they had performed useful services, to the end of the eighteenth century, when they represented only obstacles to industrial progress. The gilds, with their familiar organization of masters, journeymen, and apprentices, were wholly under the control of the masters, who sought to maintain their position of local monopoly by preventing change. The ideal was the small shop with a few journeymen and apprentices working under the supervision of the master; in order to preserve this organization weavers were limited, for instance, to 4 or 6 looms each. No one could work at a trade unless he had served an apprenticeship; in order to maintain their monopoly the gilds in the towns limited the number of apprentices and excluded country workers. For the same reason they opposed new methods or changes in products or processes. There was also a widespread diffusion of home industry in the country districts over nearly every part of France. Under such a system labor was dispersed and almost unorganized.

Not the least of the positive reforms of the Revolution was the abolition of the gilds, a move which was thoroughly in accord with the destruction of privilege and the establishment of individual liberty. In March, 1791, it was enacted that every person was "free to do such business, exercise such profession, art or trade, as he may choose," on condition that he obtain a license from the government. As these licenses were easily had the monopoly of the gilds was effectively broken.

The introduction of liberty in industry seems to have been followed by a number of strikes and labor disturbances. The Assembly was urged to take measures to suppress them, and referred the matter to a commission, whose report, presented by Isaac Le Chapelier in June, 1791, was adopted. This forbade all meetings of industries, professions, or classes which aimed at a fixation of wages, working conditions, or demands, and prohibited all combinations of workers or employers, declaring all combinations, strikes, and agreements among workers to refuse to work or of employers to refuse to give work to be illegal. Clause 8 prohibited "all gatherings composed of artisans, workingmen, journeymen, or laborers, instigated by them and directed against the free exercise of industry and work to which all sorts of persons have a right under all sorts of conditions agreed upon by private contract." Such meetings were declared riotous and were severely punished. This decree remained officially in force until 1848, when it was repealed; but it was partially restored in 1851 and remained on the statute books until 1868.

Although on the surface this Chapelier decree made no distinction between workmen and masters, it operated in practice against the former. The legal equality set up proved to be illusory in the economic field. But it was in line with the philosophy of the Revolution, which was curiously individualistic in tone. In the Declaration of the Rights of Man more emphasis was laid upon the rights of property than upon those of men. "Property," it was declared, "is an inviolable and sacred right." The middle class in the cities and the peasant proprietors in the country gained by the Revolution, but the propertyless industrial worker profited little, even the freedom which the Declaration declared a natural right being seriously curtailed by the prohibition of joint action. Charles Gide could write "the situation of the worker in the first quarter of the nineteenth century was probably worse than at any other period of history; very much worse in every case than that of preceding centuries." The period from 1791 to 1848 was dominated by the conception of the individualistic organization of production, and was characterized by prohibitions of combinations, liberty of work, and a policy of *laissez faire* on the part of the state.

The legislation of Napoleon carried these principles a step farther, and limited still more the freedom of labor. A law of 1803 repeated the prohibition of labor combinations and required that all workmen equip themselves with a certificate (*livret*), which placed them under police control. In this *livret* were inscribed the names of the various employers, and no man could be hired unless his record with his last employer was satisfactory. In 1810 this law was incorporated in the Penal Code, which prohibited combinations of employers tending to force down wages "unjustly and abusively" and combinations of workers to regulate hours or otherwise to "suspend, hinder, or make labor dear." All societies or associations of more than 20 persons were declared illegal, and by a later act of

1834 associations of even 20 persons were forbidden if they were branches of a larger group.

It is clear that, during the first half of the nineteenth century, the legal position of labor was weak. Restrictive legislation and governmental antagonism kept the worker in an inferior position and strengthened the power of the employer. And yet, in spite of this situation, workers' organizations came into existence and exerted some influence. Chief among these was the ancient *campagnonnage*, composed of the unmarried journeymen in certain trades, especially those in which it was customary for the worker to make the *tour de France*, moving from town to town to find work and to perfect himself in his craft. In the handicraft stage of industry such an organization performed useful services, providing the wandering journeyman with food and shelter, assisting him to find work, aiding him in case of illness, helping him on his way if he could not earn enough, and cheering him with good fellowship after work was over. These were the most numerous and active of the old associations. As new trades developed, which were unknown to the eighteenth century, such as transportation and machine industries, these old handicraft organizations could not meet labor's problems. Quarrels among the rival associations and internal friction hastened a process of decay which was completed by the railway. This rendered unnecessary many of the facilities of the *campagnonnages*, and by 1848 their decadence was clear.

A second form of labor organization was the so-called mutual aid society — the *bureau de bienfaisance* or *caisse de secours mutuels*. These were formed, usually of members of some one trade, for the purpose of rendering aid to their members in cases of sickness, accident, retirement, or death. Since these organizations did not come under the ban of the Chapelier law they were not molested by government. By 1823 there were in Paris alone 160 such societies, and in 1840 over 200. Many of these groups carried on true trade union activities behind their innocent façade.

A third form was the "societies of resistance" (*sociétés de résistance*), which came into existence secretly between 1815 and 1845. These were the nearest approximation to trade unions of this period and were a product of the legal and industrial conditions. Lacking the fellowship features of the *campagnonnages* and the benefit arrangements of the friendly societies, they existed for the purpose of carrying on collective bargaining with employers, agreeing upon scales of wages, collecting strike funds, and forcing improvements in the general conditions of labor. In spite of their illegality these organizations carried on their activities more or less openly during this period.

The decade of the thirties was marked by industrial unrest. The leaders were, however, not factory workers, but handicraft journeymen, especially those in the building trades, shoemakers, hatmakers, and workers in the luxury trades, and the movement was more political than industrial. In the Lyons silk industry, which was especially sensitive to political and economic change, and where wages had been reduced, the workers organized great strikes in 1831 and 1834 and demanded a wage scale and piece rates. These were suppressed by the government. The Act of 1834, declaring illegal all associations of more than 20 members, was a direct blow at the combination of the Lyons weavers, one of the "societies of resistance," with about 3000 members. The years 1835–40 were quiet and little progress was made. But the unemployment resulting from the crisis of 1839–40 led to labor disturbances among the Paris workers. The tailors struck first, they demanded a 10 hour day and the abolition of the sub-contractor. The building trades joined the movement, with a demand for a 12 hour day and payment for overtime. The government crushed the movement and punished the leaders, but the experience left the workers more closely united, and the societies of resistance continued to grow.

Socialist influences. It is difficult to say how much the thinking of the workers was influenced during this time by the revolutionary and socialistic literature of this period, but it is easy to exaggerate the influence of the printed word. It is true that workingmen's papers appeared in Paris in 1830 and several were published during the forties, all conducted by workers. They demanded equal suffrage, the right to combine, and producers' co-operation, but opposed socialism. Their circulation was very limited and the workers were illiterate; in 1816 only 10 out of 25 million inhabitants could read. The utopian schemes of the French socialists of the first half of the nineteenth century must have confused the worker's thinking, insofar as they influenced him at all. Babeuf had advocated during the Revolution a thorough-going communism, in which absolute equality not only of incomes, but of housing, food, clothing, and all conditions of life, was to be the rule. Saint Simon, a member of the nobility, urged during the twenties a reorganization of society, with state ownership and operation of industry, but with distribution according to the contribution of each to the work of production. Fourier's doctrines came to the front in the thirties; he proposed the organization of society into small communities, each of which should be self-contained and in which a proper balancing of industry and agriculture, of work and play, and of other activities would make labor attractive by substituting novelty for monotony in work. An attempt to carry out this scheme in practice by establishing a

Fourieristic community in 1832 near Paris failed. Fourier's ideas were later carried to the United States where over 30 communities were established on his plan.[11] In 1840 Proudhon, who has been claimed both by the socialists and the anarchists, propounded his famous question in a book with the title: "What is Property?" (*Qu'est-ce que la propriété?*) His answer, "Property is Theft" (*La propriété c'est le vol*), was easily understood and remembered by the worker, who did not bother to read the qualification that property earned by labor was not theft.

These writers were social reformers, seldom drawn from the laboring class, and idealistic and utopian in their schemes. It remained for Louis Blanc, in his *Organization of Labor*, published in 1841, to give the workers a definite program and a catchy slogan. He advocated the establishment of co-operative workshops with state assistance, which he thought would ultimately supplant private competitive industry. He proclaimed the right to work (*droit au travail*) for labor, which it was the function of the state to make effective. These ideas were put into practice in the Revolution of 1848. Until that time the workers had not developed class consciousness. The labor movement was largely political, and it was led by handicraft workers rather than by exploited factory laborers. Hampered by social reaction and by legal disabilities the workers were limited in improving their condition largely to self-education and mutual aid.

The Revolution of 1848. The Revolution of 1848, like that of 1830, was essentially a middle-class movement, and was largely political in nature, but in 1848 economic and social grievances of the workers played a significant role. It was preceded by crop failure in 1847, which not only raised prices but made it difficult to carry on farm operations. The price of a bushel of grain in Lille, which normally cost 7-9 francs, reached 14 francs in January, 1847, and 17 francs in April. Floods were followed by the potato blight, which destroyed the chief food for swine. At the same time French industry was affected by the English financial crisis of 1847, which decreased the buying power of France's customer. Exports fell off, factories and workshops closed, unemployment increased, and in many cases wages were reduced just at the time that prices were going up. The suffering among the workers was terrible. It was estimated that in May, 1847, some 29,000 out of the 79,000 inhabitants of the city of Lille were on poor relief. A third of the population of Paris received relief and bread was distributed to 400,000 persons. The ruling classes were, however, blind to the deep-seated unrest and did nothing to change conditions. Early in

[11] See E. L. Bogart, *Economic History of the American People* (New York, 1935), 428.

1848 Louis Philippe was forced to abdicate and a provisional government was set up, pending the establishment of a republic.

The immediate problem before the Provisional Government was to provide employment, the more so as the workers who made the Revolution a success were still armed.   On February 25 the government pledged itself to guarantee the existence of the worker by labor, and it guaranteed work to all citizens.   Blanc demanded the creation of a ministry of progress, of which he should be the head, in order to carry out his socialistic plans.   When this was refused Blanc resigned from the Provisional Government, but he was persuaded to take the chairmanship of a Workers' Commission, which held its meetings at the Luxembourg Palace.   This Commission of about 500 was composed about equally of employers and workers, and represented the most diverse views.   It was, however, more than a debating society, for it accomplished something positive. Upon its insistent demand, the government decreed the reduction of the working day in Paris from 11 to 10 hours, and in the provinces from 12 to 11, and the abolition of exploitation of workers by middlemen.   It also arranged for arbitration and for the establishment of a few co-operative associations of producers.

But the unemployed workers demanded something more immediate and tangible, and in order to provide work the government set up national workshops (*ateliers nationaux*) in Paris, under Émile Thomas, an anti-socialist.   Although these were indignantly repudiated by Blanc, they were regarded by the populace as carrying out his doctrine of the right to work.   It is difficult to see how the organization of some such system of public work relief could have been avoided under the circumstances.   The difficulty was that no constructive undertakings were planned and those applying were set to work leveling off the Place de l'Europe and on similar unproductive projects.   Those who worked received 2 francs a day, and those for whom no work could be found got 1.50 francs.   Workmen flocked to Paris from the surrounding provinces and others deserted private employment to swell the ranks of the unemployed.   The number employed was about 6000 but those applying to the national workshops rose from 14,000 in March to 120,000 in May.   In order to spread the work, the number of working days in the week for any worker was reduced to two and the total weekly wage was fixed at a maximum of eight francs.   The drain upon the Treasury was enormous, though the relief to the unemployed was trifling.

In June the National Constituent Assembly abandoned the enterprise and gave the workers the choice of going into the army, working on the railways, or accepting work with private employers.   The workers in the national workshops refused and the sanguinary street fighting of the "June days" followed. This was forcibly suppressed by the government, but the national workshop project was dead. The disorders made a deep impression and when the elections were held the people voted overwhelmingly for Louis Napoleon, who announced as his platform: "order, nationality, and glory." Elected President, he became Emperor by the *coup d'état* of 1852, and devoted himself to the economic development of France. Many of the extreme radicals went into exile or were imprisoned, and the "garrulous forties" were succeeded by the political inertia of the fifties.

Position of labor, 1850–70. The period 1850–70 was one of rapid economic development. The railway mileage increased five-fold (from 2000 to 10,000 miles) and the number of ton-miles of freight increased tenfold. The building of railways created a demand for iron for their construction and opened up the mineral resources; they provided a wider market for agricultural products, and they stimulated industry by reducing costs of transportation. Above all, they facilitated the growth of cities and the concentration of industry. Improvements in banking and credit facilities aided manufacturers. The new gold from California and Australia raised prices and gave a fillip to business. The development of ocean transportation cheapened the cost of getting foreign raw materials and also opened wider markets for French products. These technical changes were accelerated by the lowering of the tariffs, first with England in 1860 and then with other nations, which greatly increased the foreign trade of France. The excellence of French products was abundantly shown at the London Exhibition of 1851 and the Paris Exposition of 1855.

But, while industry was making a brilliant showing, the position of labor remained weak. It is true that wages rose rapidly during this period, but this was owing more to the gold discoveries than to any strengthening of labor's economic position, and was, moreover, offset by a rise in prices. Combinations still remained illegal, and Article 1781 of the Civil Code, according to which the master's testimony was final in any wage dispute, continued in force, as did the provisions of the Penal Code outlawing concerted striking or picketing. The leaders were dispersed and labor was discouraged. The only stronghold of the workers was their benefit societies, of which there were 383 in Paris in 1860 with 80,000 members; these were frequently fighting organizations in disguise. The goal of labor was the right of combination, but to this the government of Napoleon III offered little encouragement.

While Napoleon refused this concession he tried in other ways to win the goodwill of the workers. He sought to provide employment by initiating a system of great public works, reconstructing Paris, and other projects. He assisted the benefit societies, admitted workers as well as employers to the trade tribunals, and permitted the workers to retain their workbooks instead of handing them over to the employers. When he lost the support of the clerical and conservative parties through the war with Italy he turned to the working class, and tried to win their alliance through charitable expenditures. In the crisis of 1862, occasioned by the cessation of cotton imports during the American Civil War, he personally contributed 100,000 francs to the sums voted by Parliament for the relief of the unemployed.

The decade of the sixties saw certain definite gains by labor, although no constructive legislation was passed. In 1862 the government sent to the World Exhibition in London a delegation of 200 workingmen, who were greatly influenced by the freedom of combination which they found in England, and which they now, with growing emphasis, demanded for themselves. In 1864 the first victory was gained when the right to strike was allowed, and strikers were punishable only if they used violence or deceit. Four years later the second victory came when the government announced that it would "tolerate" trade unions, though it was not yet ready to concede complete freedom of combination. At the same time the hated article 1781 of the Civil Code was repealed. A breach had at least been made in the individualistic system established after the Revolution of 1789.

Labor legislation. Although the factory system developed comparatively late in France, the industrial changes brought certain evils in their train. The first evil to attract attention and to call forth remedial legislation was the question of child labor. An Act of 1813 had prohibited the employment in mines of children under 10 years of age, and several laws had limited working hours in certain trades and on Sundays and holidays, but the individualistic philosophy of this period did not encourage restrictive or regulatory measures. The liberal element in the Catholic church, under the leadership of Lamenais, attempted to put through a social program, but without success. Official opinion opposed any interference with industrial freedom. But conditions finally called for action. The disclosures of the evils of the factory system and the passage of the factory act of 1833 in England were not without their effect in France. Between 1837 and 1840 Villermé conducted an investigation on child labor, which disclosed such evils, especially in the textile industries, that the Government submitted a bill to regulate them. This was opposed by the industrialists and by the economists, who argued for unfettered competition, but was supported by the clerical party and by the landed aristocracy, and became law on March 22, 1841.

This Act applied only to establishments with mechanical power or with more than 20 workers; it therefore did not cover the small shops of handicraftsmen or home industry. The employment of children under 8 years of age was absolutely forbidden; those between 8 and 12 could work 8 hours; and those between 12 and 16, 12 hours. Children under 12 years could not work at night, and must attend school.[12] This last provision was denounced as impracticable and was not enforced. But the greatest defect was the failure to provide for adequate inspection and enforcement; this was entrusted to honarary commissions consisting of public officials and ex-magistrates, but they did little or nothing. Demands were made for the appointment of paid inspectors, and in 1848 a bill providing for this and also raising the minimum age from 8 to 10 years was introduced into the Chamber. But before it could be passed the Revolution broke out, and the law remained unchanged for half a century longer.

The position of the worker differed as between various industries. Heavy industries and the sugar factories offered fair living conditions, but in the textile industries and mines the conditions were appalling, resembling those existing earlier in England. They were worst in the cotton mills, which were the latest comers in the industrial field and the most mechanized. According to a report made for the Academy of Sciences by Villermé in 1839 the average working day for all factory workers in the cotton and wool industries was from 15 to 15$\frac{1}{2}$ hours, less 1$\frac{1}{2}$ hours intermissions. At Mulhouse work began at 5 a.m. and continued until 8 or 9 p.m., the workers lived 1 to 1$\frac{1}{2}$ miles from the factory and had this weary walk in addition. At Lille the working day in the cotton mills was sometimes 17 hours; four year old children were found working in the mills.

There is no doubt that the development of mechanized large scale industry in France was attended by many of the same evils that developed in England. But there is danger in generalizing from these facts, for it must be remembered that the factory workers made up only a fraction of the total population. Conditions among the peasants and the handworkers were better; the house industry, on the other hand, could not meet the competition of the factory. In

[12] Illiteracy was widespread in France. In 1832 Baron Dupin estimated that the public schools were attended by 1 in 16 of the total population in Great Britain, by 1 in 18 in Prussia, and by 1 in 30 in France. Only about three-fifths of the communes maintained schools.

general, it may be concluded that the worker was better off than he had been before 1789, but that he was not sharing proportionately in the economic advance of this period.

3. GILD ORGANIZATION IN GERMANY

Growth of a wage-earning class. The number of persons working for a wage was very small in Germany in 1800, both in agriculture and in industry; but by 1870 there had developed large groups in both fields who were wholly dependent upon their daily labor.

In 1800 probably three-quarters of the people were engaged in agriculture, and even as late as 1868 Viebahn could write "about half the population busies itself with agriculture and perhaps a third with industry." As has already been pointed out, agricultural operations were carried on at the beginning of the century by peasant land owners or by serfs working on the estates of the lords. By the decrees of 1807 and 1810 in Prussia and by subsequent legislation in other states the serfs were emancipated and allotted a certain amount of land. Many of these received an insufficient amount for their entire support or they sold their holdings; in either case they became agricultural laborers. Under such conditions there was no organization of agricultural labor nor was there any specific labor legislation for this group.

Industry played a very small role in Germany in 1800, contributing perhaps 5 per cent of the national income. Although industry increased fivefold between 1800 and 1860 it was still very small at the latter date. Handwork, which served local needs, was the prevailing form of industrial organization. The handworkers comprised the majority of the industrialists, making up 82 per cent of all industrial establishments and 58 per cent of the personnel. Next to them came house industry, and last, and then only towards the end of this period, the factory system. The significant changes of this period are the change of the independent house industry into a putting-out or *Verleger* system, and the transformation of the master craftsman or handworker into a wage worker.

Organization of industry. In the simple rural economy of Germany at the beginning of the century house industry played an important role. The rural household was almost self-sufficing and even in the towns the family performed most of the work of processing raw materials into finished goods. Peasant families also carried on industries within the home, which produced goods in excess of domestic needs for sale outside. With the establishment of free trade within the limits of the Zollverein in 1834 and especially after the building of railroads, the markets widened, competition became more intense, and new forces, national and international, helped to determine prices. The small home worker was unable to buy raw materials or to sell the finished product advantageously, especially in luxury trades where it was difficult to get raw materials or dispose of the finished goods in the local market. In some lines these home workers remained independent, owning their own tools and buying their raw materials; only in the marketing of the product did they depend upon the *Verleger* or middleman who was in touch with the larger market now opening up. More and more however the tendency was for the whole business to become concentrated in the hands of the *Verleger* and for the home workers to become regular wage earners, working on a piece-rate system. In the textile industries, especially the export trades, where international competition was sharpest, the enterpriser had taken over the direction of practically all the processes of production, and the independent worker tended to become a paid wage worker. Even as late as 1850 the putting-out system prevailed in other industries, as machines were still relatively few, the country was poor and capital was lacking, and transportation and financial institutions were still backward. There was little opportunity for the organization of these scattered home workers into groups with common objectives and they remained unorganized and inarticulate.

At the beginning of the nineteenth century the gilds controlled industry. The familiar organization of these into master craftsmen, journeymen, and apprentices existed, and no one was permitted to carry on a handicraft as an independent master unless he had served an apprenticeship and been admitted to the gild. The technique of production was handwork. This system persisted almost unchanged until the forties. Each master had a small but stable clientele for whom he made goods on order, sometimes even working up materials furnished by the customer. Practically all production was carried on in this fashion by tailors, shoemakers, hatters, cabinet makers, butchers, saddlers, locksmiths, and other similar artisans. Only in the large cities did tailors, for instance, have supplies of ready-made cloth for the choice of their customers. Production was not carried on for the market, but was "bespoke."

In the forties a great change occurred. Under the impulse of liberal economic ideas, the privileges of the gilds were sharply curtailed and greater freedom of production and exchange was permitted. It was thought that the introduction of greater freedom, by getting rid of obsolete privileges, would open the way for small independent enterprises. But the advantages of freedom turned out to favor the large enterpriser because of changes in industrial technique, the widening of the market by improved transportation, and the better organization of credit. In Prussia an act of 1845 introduced a large measure of industrial freedom, but the handworkers saw in this a blow to their existence and in 1849 obtained the passage of a reactionary law which restored to them some of their former privileges.[13] But the forces of industrial change were too strong for them.

During the fifties and sixties the factory system gained ground, machinery was introduced, and industry was organized on a larger scale to meet the conditions of the expanding market. A struggle ensued between handwork and the large industry, which sometimes, as in the textile industry, led to the destruction of the independent handworkers. Spinners and weavers waged a protracted but losing battle against machinery, meeting competition by lowering their standard of living, but finally followed the machines into the factory. In some cases new techniques destroyed the very basis of the old handicraft, as when iron pipes replaced the wooden conduits for bringing water to the cities or inventions established new industries for which handwork was not suited, as in the manufacture of iron rails, locomotives, or machinery. In those lines in which the handworker retained his position as a master craftsman he became little more than a jobbing workman, or a repair man, as in the shoe and watch industries. Only in the villages was the handworker able to hold on. In the industrial towns there was a gradual transfer of work, and frequently of workers, from the small independent establishment to the factory. This was the case with spinners, weavers, cloth-makers, stocking knitters, silk workers, lace-makers, glove and cap makers, metal workers, rail and pin makers, rope makers, potters, dyers, and similar artisans. Those who served the personal or home needs of their customers were less affected; such were barbers, shoemakers, locksmiths, blacksmiths, tinners, and glaziers.

The rather unsatisfactory statistics seem to show that the handworkers were more than holding their own, for in Prussia they made up 5.9 per cent of the total population in 1861 against 3.9 per cent in 1816. The explanation is to be found in the fact that many trades, which by the sixties were accessory to factories, were included in the list. Among these trades may be mentioned those of machinists, masons, carpenters, cabinet makers, saddlers, locksmiths, and similar workers, who still retained a semi-independent position and could not be counted among the wage workers. Most of the master craftsmen were home-working laborers, who had a small shop where they worked alone or with one or two helpers, taking orders from the larger industrialist or merchant. Wholly dependent upon their

13 See page 87.

employers, they were exploited by the latter and were in a position almost worse than that of the wage-laborers.

German writers make a distinction between *Manufaktur* and *Fabrik*, which is essential in tracing the industrial changes of this period. *Manufaktur* exists when large-scale industry is carried on by means of tools and handwork; *Fabrik* exists when large-scale industry is carried on by means of machinery and non-human power. In both cases the workers are gathered under one roof, they work for wages, and the undertaking is under the direction of a capitalistic enterpriser. It must be said, however, that this distinction is not always observed by German writers themselves and the term *Fabrik* is loosely used to cover both types of industrial organization.

In the Germany of 1800 *Manufaktur* existed alongside home industry and the handicraft system. Under the prevailing mercantilistic philosophy the governments of the various states encouraged industries in order to render imports unnecessary, and many small businesses were started, such as calico printing in Saxony. During the continental blockade of the Napoleonic wars there was an increase in their number, but after 1815 English competition proved too much for most of these hothouse growths. In the thirties and forties changes occurred again and numerous large establishments made their appearance. Thus in Saxony between 1841 and 1850 there were 64 establishments with 50-100 workers, 70 with 100-500, and 11 with over 500. Sugar factories, cotton-spinning establishments, and similar enterprises were started. In Berlin the rate of growth of factory workers was more rapid than that of journeymen or of the total population; between 1816 and 1847 the factory workers increased 170 per cent and journeymen 50 per cent. By 1861 there were 4000 industrial establishments in the German Empire with more than 50 workers each.

The evidence is clear that the large establishment with dependent wage workers was growing, and also that it was slowly being transformed from *Manufaktur* to *Fabrik*. The best indication of this is probably the horse power used. At the beginning of the century power was usually furnished by water wheels, or by animals, but the need for continuous operation led to the introduction of steam. In 1837 there were 421 steam engines in Prussia, furnishing 7500 horse power; by 1846 there were 1139 with 28,000 h.p. After this their use spread more rapidly, growing to 62,000 h.p. in 1855 and over 600,000 h.p. in 1875. For the entire German nation these figures may fairly be doubled.

The workers for these establishments were drawn from various sources. The skilled workers were former masters or journeymen or perhaps home workers, who followed their trades as these were taken over by the factories. The unskilled labor was recruited from the children of this group who could no longer receive their training by apprenticeship, from the rural population, agricultural laborers, younger sons of peasants who had not inherited any land, and young unmarried women who did not wish to go into domestic service. The economic position of these workers was weak, for the supply exceeded the demand, they were wholly unorganized, and legislation prevented strikes. The position of the employer was correspondingly strong and this he used to exploit the workers. The transition from an agricultural to an industrial state in Germany was characterized by the same evils and abuses which had shown themselves in England a half century earlier — long hours, low wages, and unwholesome working and living conditions.

Equally unsatisfactory results were experienced in other states. Bavaria had passed legislation in 1840 and in 1854 restricting child labor, but had placed its enforcement in the hands of the local police and the school authorities, with the result that nothing was done. Baden, Wurtemberg, Hesse, and Saxony had equally unfortunate experiences. Really effective labor legislation was not obtained until after the formation of the Empire.

Industrial and economic changes. The period between 1830 and 1870 was one of transition, and was marked by profound and unsettling changes in economic organization. There was no sudden transformation, however, but rather a slow change from a rural to an industrial economy. The introduction of industrial freedom had abolished untenable conditions, stimulated change, and permitted the introduction of improved technique and organization. The establishment of freedom of trade within the Zollverein had widened the market. The building of railways and the introduction of steamers had reduced the costs of transportation and encouraged a better territorial division of labor. International relationships increased, great enterprises with better technique, more capital, and more efficient industrial and commercial leadership came into being. Many new inventions were made which improved the processes of production, and the ripened fruit of British experience was appropriated. The large industries which now appeared upon the stage were not the little industries grown big; there was a new kind of production with new functions and new techniques. The most important of these were the chemical and electro-technical industries, and the making of machinery, tools, and instruments. And hand in hand with these changes went specialization in production along with shifts in the location of industry. By the tide of this economic flux the laboring class was swept along, without possibility of organizing for their own defense. Workmen's combinations were illegal in all the states down to 1869. At the same time the old defenses of the workers, in the form of custom and usage, disappeared. The gilds, which had formerly exercised close oversight over production and the relation of apprentices and journeymen to the master, lost their power, and the members were exposed to the competition of the growing factory system. The patriarchal conditions which had once existed in home industry were replaced by a ruthless struggle for existence. In this period of change and readjustment the worker stood defenseless and unorganized.

Labor organization. The year 1848 is frequently hailed as marking the beginning of the "emancipation struggle of the fourth estate." It was not an uprising of exploited factory workers against their employers, but a protest of journeymen workers against conditions in the handicrafts. It had long been the custom for young journeymen, when they had completed their apprenticeship, to travel a year or two in search of employment and experience — the well known *Wanderjahre*. In the thirties some of these wandering journeymen brought back from Paris and Switzerland new ideas, in part democratic aspirations, in part derived from the communistic utopias of Cabet and Fourier. In the forties the German, W. Weitling, advocated in several books an ideal Christian communism, which spread these doctrines. These intellectual stirrings were, however, without much immediate effect on actual developments, though they doubtless influenced the thinking of some of the workers.

The real movement began with strikes in Berlin and Cologne during the Revolution of 1848. A congress of radical workers met in Berlin and made the following demands upon the government: a state guarantee of work, state support of industrial workingmen's associations, state care of all helpless and incapacitated workers, regulation and limitation of excessive hours of work, and reform of the system of taxation. Such a program evidenced less the spirit of self-help than of government protection. The German workers had not yet learned, as had the English, to fight their own battles against their employers. These demands were submitted, as were also those of the handworkers who held a meeting at the same time, to the National Assembly in Frankfort, but nothing came of them.

In Cologne the movement was more radical. Here the factory system was most developed and the workers were ripe for a proletarian uprising. This was given a political term by the Revolution of 1848, but the agitation which set it in motion was communistic. Karl Marx in his *Neue Rheinische Zeitung* advocated the cause of the workingman and of the democratic movement, which he regarded as the first step in the transfer of control of the instruments of production from the propertied classes to the hands of the proletariat. Together with Friedrich Engels he prepared the Communist Manifesto, which set forth in clear terms the aims of the communists. But the democratic revolution failed. Marx was banished from the country and his writings suppressed. The workers' movement was checked by the police, and the specter of communism was used as an excuse during the next decade to prevent all organization. The legitimate cause of labor was damaged by its association with communism.

Efforts to organize labor met obstacles, not only from adverse legislation and administrative opposition, but in the very structure of industry itself. Production was decentralized, home work and handwork kept the laborers scattered, and there did not develop a feeling of solidarity or of class interest among the wage earners. The technical backwardness and small scale of industrial establishments also prevented the creation of an urban proletariat.

The modern organized labor movement did not appear in Germany until the sixties — later than in any other industrial country. Unions of the printers and tobacco workers had existed since 1848, and some others were formed later, but there was no general organization of labor. The beginning of this is usually associated with the formation by Ferdinand Lassalle in 1863 of the Universal German Workingman's Association. Lassalle was a member of a well-to-do family but he adopted the democratic ideas of the Revolution of 1848 and from there moved on to socialism. He aimed to organize labor upon political lines, and demanded direct and equal universal suffrage in order to give the interests of the working class representation in Parliament. While he looked forward to a socialist commonwealth, he advocated as the first step the establishment of co-operative associations for production, to be subsidized by the state. These organizations were similar to the national workshops of Louis Blanc in France in 1848. Lassalle was killed in a duel in 1864, but the Association struggled on.

Meanwhile another type of labor organization had come into being in the sixties in Saxony and other states to the south. These were Workmen's Educative Associations (*Arbeiterbildungsvereine*) which were founded on the basis of the co-operative program of Schulze-Delitsch. These moderate organizations were gradually converted to socialism, under the skillful leadership of August Bebel and Wilhelm Liebknecht, who were later to become the leaders of the socialist movement in Germany. At a congress held in 1868 allegiance to the principles of Marxism was proclaimed, and the following year the associations organized the Social Democratic Workingman's Party. This demanded political equality in order to obtain economic equality. The specific demands set forth in their program were aimed at existing abuses and do not impress us today as radical; only the last one hints at socialism. They included equal and direct manhood suffrage, the secret ballot, the abolition of all privileges of birth, wealth, or religion, the separation of church and state, the secularization of education, freedom of speech and of the press, the establishment of a normal working day, the abolition of child labor, the suppression of indirect taxation, and the extension of state credit to co-operative enterprises.

The real beginning of the trade union movement in Germany is dated by some writers from 1868, when Max Hirsch and Franz Duncker organized trade unions on the English model. Dr. Hirsch had made a study of trade unionism in England and thought that the German workers could be similarly organized, and at the same time be made a political force for the radical branch of the Progressive Party. The trade union movement was thus given a political direction at its very inception, which has ever since been characteristic of it. These unions represented on the whole the elite of the working class, but grew very slowly. They accepted the existing economic system and repudiated socialism; in 1876 members were required to sign a declaration that they were not social democrats.

A final type of organization was the Christian unions, which were strongest in the industrial and mining districts of Catholic Westphalia. About 1870 Bishop Ketteler, a convert of Lassalle, organized associations of workingmen of a semi-religious character, in protest against the materialism and socialism of the Marxistic unions. These gradually assumed the features of the usual trade union, and accepted the existing political and economic order as "necessary and expedient."

There was little labor organization until Germany became industrialized. Even after the factory system was introduced the psychology of the worker remained for some time the same as that of the handworker journeyman, who looked forward to economic independence, and saw no need for organization. In this early movement there is no trace of a pure trade unionism, that is the formation of labor organizations devoted solely to the improvement of working conditions and the strengthening of labor's bargaining power. The German organizations were largely political or socialistic; many of them were formed by persons outside the working class, and all of them looked to the state for assistance in reforming conditions. Little trace was to be found of the individualistic self-help of the contemporary British trade union.

A distinction may, however, be made between the Social Democratic unions (*Gewerkschaften*) and the Hirsch-Duncker and Christian unions (*Gewerkvereine*). The latter were organized by middle-class leaders, generally for political purposes, but the former developed in innumerable little groups among the socialistically inclined workers and only gradually found a suitable form. This early formative period was one of restless experimentation, marked by the founding, decline, and reorganization of unions. By the end of 1870 there existed in all only 29 trade unions with 58,000 members, of which 18 had fewer than 1000 each.

The further history of these organizations belongs to a later period and will be described there.

BIBLIOGRAPHICAL NOTE

1. *Britain.* An excellent introduction to a study of this subject is G. D. H. Cole, *A Short History of the British Working Class Movement*, 3 vols. (London, 1925–27). Vol. I, 1789–1848; Vol. II, 1848–1900. A sympathetic contemporary account by two middle-class reformers is J. M. Ludlow and L. Jones, *Progress of the Working Classes*, 1832–1867 (London, 1867), which may be checked by F. E. Gillespie, *Labor and Politics in England*, 1850–1867 (Durham, N. C., 1927). The Chartist movement of this period is described in a number of books, but only two need be mentioned: Mark Hovell, *The Chartist Movement* (Manchester, 1918) is the best history, while F. Rosenblatt, *The Chartist Movement: Social and Economic Aspects* (New York, 1916) gives the economic setting. A special study is Ivy Pinchbeck, *Women Workers and the Industrial Revolution*, 1750–1850 (London, 1930). The standard history of trade unionism is S. and B. Webb, *History of Trade Unionism* (rev. ed., London, 1920). Also useful is C. M. Lloyd, *History of Trade Unionism* (3rd ed., London, 1929). More popular is R. M. Rayner, *The Story of Trade Unionism* (London, 1929).

2. *France.* The classic book is E. Levasseur, *Histoire des classes ouvrières et de l'industrie en France de 1789 à 1870* (2e éd., Paris, 1903). A popular account of the apprentices' organization is Jean Counay, *Le Campagnonnage; son histoire, ses mystères* (Paris, 1909). Two important contemporary accounts are L. R. Villermé, *Tableau de l'état physique et moral des ouvrières* (Paris, 1840) and A. Blanqui, *Les classes ouvrières pendant l'année 1848* (Paris, 1849). A good account of an interesting social experiment is D. C. McKay, *The National Workshops: a Study in the French Revolution of 1848* (Cambridge, Mass., 1933). The story is carried forward by E. Dolléans, *Histoire du mouvement ouvrier*, 1830–1871 (Paris, 1936), and by the excellent work of G. Weill, *Histoire du mouvement social*, 1852–1924 (3e éd., Paris, 1924). Equally good are two books by P. Louis, *Histoire du mouvement syndical en France*, 1789–1910 (3e éd., Paris, 1924), and *Histoire de la classe ouvrière en France de la Révolution à nos jours* (Paris, 1927). J. Kuczynski, *Labour Conditions in Western Europe*, 1820–1935 (London, 1937) is a somewhat biased account.

3. *Germany.* There was practically no labor movement in Germany before 1860, but an excellent introduction to the subject is Herrmann Müller, *Geschichte der Gewerkschaftsbewegung bis 1878* (Berlin, 1918). Also good is W. Kulemann, *Die Gewerkschaftsbewegung* (Jena, 1900). Stamm, *Geschichte der Arbeit* (2te Aufl., 1871) is a very general survey. L. Bamberger, *Die Arbeiterfrage* (Stuttgart, 1873) is one of a number of studies showing a realization that there was a labor problem in Germany.

CHAPTER VII

POPULATION AND WELFARE

I. SLOW IMPROVEMENT IN BRITAIN

Population. During the eighteenth century the idea was very generally held that population was declining. When a proposal was made in the House of Commons in 1753 for an official enumeration of the people, it met with violent opposition on the ground that it would disclose the military weakness of the country. One member exclaimed that the proposition was "subversive of the last remains of English liberty" and that it was "likely to result in some public misfortune or epidemical disorder." Interest in the subject led to many estimates of population growth, and a vigorous controversial literature on the subject developed. This was started by Dr. Price, who contended in his *Treatise on Annuities* (1780) that the population had been declining since 1688 and that it was then only 4,760,000. In 1798 Malthus directed attention, in his *Essay on Population*, to the possibility of the population increasing faster than the means of subsistence, and a new controversy began. The need for accurate information was strongly felt and in 1800 a bill for the first census was passed without opposition. This was taken in 1801 and at decennial intervals since that time. The growth of the population is shown in the following table:

GROWTH OF POPULATION, ENGLAND AND WALES *

Year	Total population	Urban	Rural
		(percentage)	
1801	8,892,536	40,6	59,4
1811	10,164,256	41,6	58,4
1821	12,000,236	43,4	56,6
1831	13,896,797	46,1	53,9
1841	15,914,148	48,3	51,7
1851	17,727,609	52,2	47,8
1861	20,066,224	53,4	46,6
1871	22,712,266	54,8	45,2

* As given in the Census Report of 1851 (*Accounts and Papers*, 1852–53, XXXV, p. xxxiii), with corrections by Rickman. After 1851 from *Enumeration Abstracts*.

The rate of growth between 1801 and 1811 was 14 per cent, and between 1811 and 1821 it reached the record height of 18 per cent. After 1821 the rate of growth declined somewhat and for the next five decades it was roughly 16, 14, 12, 12, and 13 per cent respectively. The causes of this rapid growth are complicated, but the main factor seems to have been a marked decline in the death-rate.

Medical education, scientific investigation, and sanitation were improved during the eighteenth century, and by 1800 such diseases as plague, leprosy, and scurvy were extinct, while dysentery, rickets, smallpox, and typhus were being reduced. Dr. Edward Jenner published his discovery of vaccination in 1798, and in 1840 this was made compulsory. The mortality of infancy and of early childhood showed the greatest reduction, but this was probably due as much to better feeding, improved dwellings, and less intemperance among parents as to improved medical attention. Greater personal cleanliness resulted from the substitution of cheap and easily washed cotton goods for the heavy and rarely washed woolen goods, and from the larger use of soap. These in turn were made possible by the industrial changes and the growing wealth.

These changes were reflected in the death-rate. This fell from the middle of the eighteenth century to about 1815, then rose slightly to 1830, after which it remained practically stationary until 1870. Aside from the period of dislocation and poverty following the Napoleonic wars, the general movement was downward. This may be held to represent a corresponding improvement in the lot of the common man. The rapid growth of towns and the concentration of population under unfavorable urban conditions was a factor adverse to public health, but this was offset, especially after 1850, by increasing prosperity and improvements in sanitation, drainage, and water supply. The beneficial effects of these were however obtained in the next period, when town life became healthier. But not only did the death-rate decline; there was also a steady increase in the birth-rate from 1838, the first year for which statistics are available, to 1870. The upward trend is clearly shown in the rates.

BIRTH-RATE AND DEATH-RATE IN ENGLAND AND WALES
(per 1000 of the population)

Year	Birth-rate	Death-rate	Excess of births over deaths
1840	31.8	22.4	9.4
1850	33.4	23.7	9.7
1860	34.3	22.2	12.1
1870	35.2	24.0	11.2

The statement is often made that the increase in population was caused by the industrial revolution and by the poor laws.[1] That the new system of industry, improved transportation, and more productive agriculture made it possible to support a larger popula-

[1] This question is critically discussed at considerable length by G. T. Griffith, *Population Problems of the Age of Malthus* (Cambridge, Eng., 1926), ch. v.

tion is indisputable. But it is less easy to prove, as some writers assert, that, since the early factories gave employment to children, the industrial revolution caused young people to marry early and raise large families, so that they could live on the labor of their children. The increase in the birth-rate alone, so far as can be judged from the doubtful statistics available, scarcely supports this contention, while the increase in the markedly industrial sections, such as Lancashire and the West Riding of York, was but little higher than for the country as a whole. Nor can the increase be attributed to the practice of giving poor-law allowances in aid of wages, as Malthus complained. He wrote of the "population raised by bounties," arguing that this practice undermined the independence of the laborer, promoted earlier marriages, and led to large families. Thus, in South Lancashire, where the Speenhamland system was in operation, allowances in aid of wages were made to able-bodied weavers who had more than two children. But it is dangerous to generalize from such instances, for the allowance system was more widespread in the agricultural than in the industrial counties, and these were the very districts where the population growth was smallest. It is more probable that the poor laws stimulated the growth of the population by providing medical attention and thus reducing the death-rate.

While it is clear that it is impossible to discover conscious purpose in the population growth, the fact remains that there was an increase. Not only did the increasing productivity of agriculture and industry provide a physical basis for a larger population, but various legal and industrial changes facilitated early marriages. The decay of apprenticeship removed a social and legal obstacle. The nature of many of the industries, especially those where machinery was used, permitted the worker to realize his full earning power early in life and therefore removed a financial obstacle. After all these allowances are made, however, it is clear that the explanation of the population increase is to be found more in the fall of the death-rate than in the rise of the birth-rate.

Growth of the towns. Not only was the population growing during this period, but it was being increasingly concentrated in the cities. By 1851 over half of the population was urban. The towns grew rapidly, haphazardly, and without regulation. No systematic town planning was attempted, streets and alleys were narrow, houses without sanitary conveniences and overcrowded, drainage bad, and conditions ripe for the spread of disease. In 1801 there were only 15 towns in England and Wales whose population exceeded 20,000, and of these only one — London — had over 100,000 inhabitants.

Less than 17 per cent of the people lived in these larger cities. The industrial changes that were taking place tended, however, to concentrate the workers in urban communities.

During the whole period from 1801 to 1871 the urban population grew faster than the average for the whole of England and Wales, and the greatest expansion took place in those cities which by the end of the period had over 100,000 inhabitants each. The smaller towns, with from 2000 to 20,000 inhabitants, grew more slowly, while the rural areas actually declined towards the end of the period. There were two periods during which there was a marked concentration in cities, namely 1821–31 and 1841–51. The first of these was characterized by the development of the textile industries, and the growing factory towns in the north showed a phenomenal expansion. In the decade 1841–51 occurred the most notable concentration of the century, the stimulus for which came from the opening of the railways, accompanied by an expansion of the iron industry. The cities which grew fastest during this decade were those situated near the coal fields and iron mines, like Merthyr Tydfil, Cardiff, Swansea in South Wales, or those in iron smelting districts like Newport. The expansion of domestic and foreign commerce, which followed the inauguration of practical free trade, also contributed to this growth, and ports like Grimsby and Birkenhead developed rapidly. After 1851 the rate of urban concentration slowed down, though it continued at a milder tempo. By 1871, 55 per cent of the population was urban, that is lived in towns of more than 2000 inhabitants.

The rapid growth of towns brought with it many serious problems. The streets were badly paved with rough cobblestones which were not only inconvenient and even dangerous for the growing traffic, but prevented effective cleaning. There was no such thing as town planning at the beginning of the nineteenth century and the expansion of the urban centers went on without control or arrangement. The old cities had been inconvenient and crowded, but the new factory towns produced still greater evils. Cheap and unsubstantial cottages were built in rows back to back, separated from other rows only by narrow alleys, in which ran open foul-smelling drains.[2] Public attention was seriously turned to conditions in the towns as a result of the cholera epidemic of 1831 and 1832, and a series of investigations were made which revealed a shocking state of affairs.

The prevalence of fevers was shown to be intimately connected with bad drainage. Originally, drainage was surface only, yet, as

---

[2] A terrible picture of conditions as they had developed in Manchester by 1844 was given by Friedrich Engels in *The Condition of the Working Class in England in* 1844 (London, 1892), 48 ff.

towns grew and a connected sewage system was needed, the old method continued. London was "seamed with open ditches," and as late as 1855 not a single large underground main had been constructed. The supply of water in the towns was inadequate. Even as late as 1850 it was estimated that 80,000 houses in London, inhabited by 640,000 persons, were unprovided with water. In the poorer districts the people could obtain water only from standpipes erected in the courts, and even here only at intermittent periods and for a short time each day; sometimes water was available only on alternate days, and not at all on Sundays. Under these circumstances recourse was had to pumps which drew their supplies from shallow wells — "slaughter wells" they were often called, as the water was badly contaminated.[3]

The connection between disease and impure water supplies and bad sanitation had long been recognized by physicians and the necessity of public control had been urged by reformers like Chadwick. "Associations for the Health of Towns" began to be formed in 1844, and two years later an important Act authorized local authorities to establish public baths and wash-houses. In 1848 the government established the General Board of Health, with powers to recommend and carry out health reforms. Local resistance and adherence to the doctrine of *laissez faire* proved insuperable obstacles, and the Board was abolished in 1854. A permanent central authority was not established until 1871, when the Local Government Board, with which the Poor Law Board was now merged, was empowered to carry out reforms. Sanitary legislation, at first confined to the towns, was extended to the rural districts in 1872. The Public Health Acts of 1871–75 and the Housing Acts of 1868–85 followed. The matters which received main attention were the provision of adequate supplies of water fit for human consumption, the regular collection and disposal of refuse, street cleaning, and housing. This last proved the most difficult problem, for property rights were all but untrammelled and were frequently enforced without regard to public health. Serious outbreaks of fever, however, such as those of cholera in 1831, 1855, and 1866, and of smallpox in 1871 aroused public apprehension, and vigorous steps were finally taken to abate the worst evils.

Ages and hours. Today it is generally held that it is socially undesirable and economically unsound to employ child labor. But in the first quarter of the nineteenth century one-half of all the children employed in the cotton factories were children under 16 years of age. Some of them began work at inconceivably early ages. Children of 5 and 6 were being employed when the first

[3] Henry Jephson, *The Sanitary Evolution of London* (London, 1907), 21.

factory act of 1802 was passed; and one-sixth of the workers were under 9 years of age. Thirty years later 7 or 8 years was a typical age. In 1839, after the Act of 1833 had forbidden the employment of children under 9 years of age, there were still 32,524 children between the ages of 9 and 13; and in spite of the act the Commissioners of 1833 found that while 9 was the most usual age of beginning work 7 or 8 was frequent, and 6 not uncommon. Even as late as 1856 children under 9 still formed 6.6 per cent of the whole number then employed.

Some of the worst abuses were to be found, not in the factories, but in the domestic industries, and it is doubtful if the factories lowered the age at which children began to work. Defoe had commented on this with satisfaction in 1724 — "scarce anything above four years old, but its hands were sufficient for its own support." [4] In the industries other than textiles and mining, where no age limits had been imposed by law, children generally began regular employment between 7 and 8. Parents seem to have been more prone to employ their own children at these early ages than were factory employers.

A partial explanation of these early ages for beginning work must be found in the continuation of old practices inherited from conditions usual in an agricultural economy and in the domestic system of industry. Carried over into a new economy they were retained partly through desire for profits on the part of the manufacturers and partly through the ignorance and apathy of the people at large. It was argued that if the children were not put to work they would grow up in idleness and learn bad habits. In this connection it must not be forgotten that there were no free public schools for the children of the laboring classes at that time; not until the General Education Act of 1870 were these established.

Not only was the age of beginning employment extremely low, but the hours of work were unconscionably long. A twelve hour day was prescribed by the first factory act of 1802, exclusive of the time required for meals; this provision was repeated in 1819 and 1833, so it may be assumed that the average working day was not shorter than this. For meals a half hour was usually allowed for breakfast and an hour for dinner, so that the actual time spent in the factory was 13 to 14 hours, though in many mills the time for meals was curtailed by various means. The working day was lengthened at times by the practice of making up lost time, caused by lack of water, by working an hour extra per day without extra pay until the lost time was made up; this was sanctioned in the Act of 1819. Cases were recorded where employers put the clocks forward in the

[4] D. Defoe, *A Tour through Great Britain* (London, ed. 1769), III, 146.

morning and back at night in order to filch a little more unpaid labor from the operatives.

The hours of labor in the cotton industry, which may be taken as roughly indicative of industry as a whole, were reported as follows: [5]

"In 1795 they are said to have been 'not infrequently 80 in the week.' From 1810 to 1825 they appear to have been 12 per day and 72 per week, and from 1826 to 1846, 69 per week. In 1847 the Ten Hours Act was passed, and the hours for young persons and women were fixed at 63 from July 1, 1847, and 58 from July 1, 1848. In 1850 another Act made these hours 60 weekly, and in 1853 the Acts were applied to 'children.' As no normal day was fixed for children until 1853 — though a normal day was fixed for young persons and women in 1850 — the Acts of 1847 and 1850 were evaded by the use of relays of operatives, and investigation indicates that 60 hours were usually worked from 1848 onwards. The trade was so depressed, however, in 1847–48, that any statutory duration of the normal week was only hypothetical, for very little full time was worked in Lancashire during this period. From 1853 until January 1, 1875, the legal normal week for operatives included in the Acts remained at 60, and this, of course, practically fixed the hours for male adults at 60 also."

Wages. Industrial wages in the first three-quarters of the nineteenth century showed a fairly steady, though slow, improvement in the conditions of the working classes, but the movement was not uniform. There were constant changes in methods of production, which caused industrial dislocations, destroying the acquired skills of some and giving others opportunity for improving their condition. In no industry was this more clearly seen than in cotton manufactures, where the hand-loom weavers suffered, while the machine workers gained steadily. Workers in the wool industry and carpenters did less well, but in mining and iron and steel work wages were more than average, and still more in the building trades.

Wage statistics alone, however, throw insufficient light upon the question as to the improvement in the standard of living of the laboring people. Previous chapters have shown that the productivity of the British people had been greatly augmented by the mechanical improvements and that there had been a vast increase in wealth. To whom had this gone? One answer to this question, covering the earlier part of this period, was given by the Hammonds, who stated that the wage earners employed in the developing industries "did not obtain any part of the new wealth." [6] This dark picture is not

[5] G. H. Wood, *The History of Wages in the Cotton Trade during the Past Hundred Years* (London, 1930), 2. By permission of the publishers, Sherratt and Hughes, London.
[6] J. and B. L. Hammond, *The Town Labourer*, 1760–1832 (London, 1917), 95.

borne out, at least for the greater part of this period, by the wage statistics gathered by other writers. The most authoritative of these [7] has summarized the money wage and price changes in the following table:

Period	Nominal wages	Prices	Real wages
1790–1810	Rising fast	Rising very fast	Falling slowly
1810–1830	Falling	Falling fast	Rising slowly
1836–1852	Nearly stationary	Falling slowly	Rising slowly
1852–1870	Rising fast	Rising	Rising considerably

The changes in money wages, retail prices, and real wages between 1850 and 1914 are shown in the graph opposite.*

The picture presented here is a very broad one, and does not throw sufficient light on the fortunes of the various groups of work-people. This is shown better by differentiating between the skilled and the unskilled, and between the town artisans and the agricultural laborer. For this purpose the following table constructed by A. L. Bowley,[8] which he considers "substantially correct," may be given:

TENTATIVE TABLE OF AVERAGE WEEKLY WAGES
(in shillings)

	1795	1807	1824	1833	1867
London type of artisan	25	30	30	28	36
Provincial artisan	17	22	24	22	27
Town labourer	12	14	16	14	25
Agricultural labourer	9	13	9½	10½	16

From this table it appears that the period of the thirties and the "hungry forties" was one of greatest hardships for all workers. The lot of the agricultural laborer was especially bad and was made worse by an ill-advised poor law down to 1834. His wages were below the subsistence level in 1795, and in that year a well-meant scheme, known as the Speenhamland system, was put into operation. According to this wages were to be supplemented by payments out of the poor rates; married men received more than bachelors and an additional allowance was made for each child. Early marriages were thus encouraged, and the illegitimate birth-rate rose. Farmers got their work done partly at the expense of the parish, but the taxes increased enormously. The effect on the laborers was thoroughly bad, for they were pauperized, while every motive for thrift, industry, or enterprise was seriously checked. Finally, in 1834, a Poor Law Amendment Act was passed, which centralized control

[7] A. L. Bowley, in Palgrave's *Dictionary of Political Economy* (London, 1918), App., 801.
[8] *Wages in the Nineteenth Century* (Cambridge, 1900), 70.

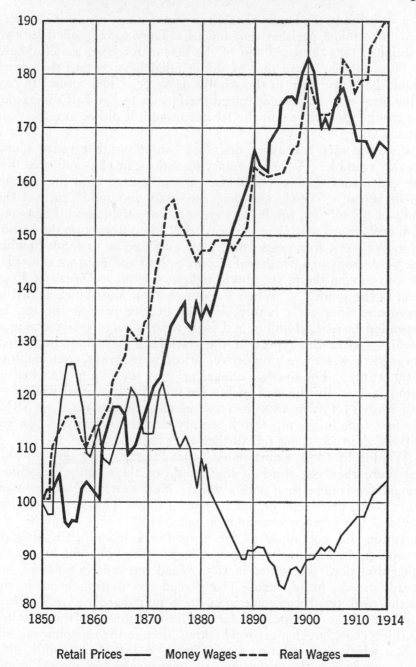

Retail Prices ——— Money Wages – – – Real Wages ———

FIGURE 2. PRICES AND WAGES IN GREAT BRITAIN, 1850–1914

* Based on statistics in G. D. H. Cole, *A Short History of the Working Class Movement,*
1789–1937 (London, 1937), II, 198; III, 228.

of poor relief in the hands of three commissioners, who were authorized to combine parishes into unions. They were guided by two principles: that the condition of the person receiving relief should be "less eligible" than that of the unaided laborer, and that relief should be given only to the wholly destitute. The refusal to pay allowances in aid of wages forced the farmer to pay full wages, but the change did not benefit the laborer though it did reduce the poor rates.

Contemporary testimony described conditions that today sound scarcely credible. A parliamentary committee in 1835 reported that the agricultural laborer "was often worse housed than the animals on the farm. 'Wattle and dab' (or straw and mud) formed the walls of his cottage, the floors were often of earth, and all ages and both sexes frequently slept in one room." The Report on the Hand-loom-Weavers, five years later, gave evidence as to food: "taking the whole body of agricultural labourers, beef and mutton, as articles of food among them, are almost unknown from the north of England to the south. . . When 8 s. out of 15 s. must be expended in bread and flour by a family, and the greater part of the rest be expended in rent, clothing, and fuel, what is there left for animal food?" After the repeal of the corn laws conditions improved, agriculture was more productive, prices were lower, and employment steady. The average annual price of the four pound loaf of bread — literally the staff of life for the British manual worker — fell from 15.3 d. in 1800 to 10 d. in 1840 and to 6.8 d. in 1850, the first time in the nineteenth century that it touched 6 d. It was still 6.8 d. in 1875, but fell further after that date.

Writing in 1878, Caird stated [9] that "thirty years ago probably not more than one-third of the people of this country consumed animal food more than once a week. Now nearly all of them eat it, in meat, or cheese, or butter, once a day. This has more than doubled the average consumption per head." This optimistic observation did not apply to the agricultural laborer, according to Joseph Arch, who might, however, be suspected of some bias in the other direction. He stated in 1872 "food was usually potatoes, dry bread, greens, herbs, 'kettle broth' made by putting bread in the kettle, weak tea, bacon sometimes, fresh meat hardly ever."

Most of the discussion so far has been confined to the so-called working class, but changes were taking place in the economic organization which were creating new groups. A large new middle class came into being; the professions, the managerial and clerical grades in industry, and middlemen of every sort increased rapidly. Industrialists and financiers prospered greatly. Profits were rising

[9] James Caird, *The Landed Interest and the Supply of Food* (London, 1878), 29.

faster than wages and the general level of comfort was decidedly raised. The period between 1850 and 1875 particularly was one of rapid and nearly continuous economic advance. That the standard of living of the mass of the people was steadily rising is indicated by the increased consumption of meat, sugar, tea, and other commodities. This is well shown in the following table:

QUANTITIES OF THE PRINCIPAL IMPORTED AND EXCISABLE ARTICLES RETAINED FOR HOME CONSUMPTION, PER HEAD OF THE TOTAL POPULATION OF THE UNITED KINGDOM *

Article	1840	1881
Bacon and ham, lbs.	0.01	13.93
Butter, lbs.	1.05	6.36
Cheese, lbs.	0.92	5.77
Eggs, no.	3.63	21.65
Potatoes, lbs.	0.01	12.85
Rice, lbs.	0.90	16.32
Corn, wheat, and wheat flour, lbs.	42.47	216.92
Raw sugar, lbs.	15.20	58.92
Refined sugar, lbs.	nil	8.44
Tea, lbs.	1.22	4.58
Tobacco, lbs.	0.86	1.41

* R. Giffen, *Essays in Finance* (London, 1886), 388.

In the case of some articles, which were produced at home, like butter, cheese, eggs, and potatoes, the increase in imports probably exaggerates the enlargement of consumption by the population, but in the case of those whose supply was drawn wholly from outside the evidence is clear. There was a distinct improvement in the dietary of the average British worker. Particularly significant was the increase in the consumption of meat, sugar, and tea. Before the middle of the century, says Porter, "the mass of the people scarcely ever tasted butcher's meat," but with higher wages its consumption expanded rapidly. Sugar in 1845 was still "a holiday luxury to the middle classes, and hitherto an unattainable one to the humble." [10] The increased use of sugar which came with its cheaper price encouraged the consumption of fruit, while tea served as a substitute for alcohol and led to increased sobriety. There also went on during this period, although not shown in the table, an increased use of vegetables and milk. To the enlarged and improved food supply must be attributed the improvement in public health, already noted, and the disappearance of such diseases as scurvy.

Co-operation. Among the efforts of the workers to help themselves the co-operative movement stands out as the most romantic and yet highly successful one. The plight of the working man was desperate in the thirties and forties. His wages were low, he was

[10] George Dodd, *British Manufactures* (London, 1845), V, 106.

frequently forced to accept poor and expensive goods in lieu of money wages, in spite of the Truck Acts of 1830–1831, and his prospect of setting himself up as an independent producer vanished with the advent of machinery. Several experiments had been made with co-operation by Owenites, Chartists, and others, but it remained for a poor group of weavers to apply a new method which enlisted the permanent interest of members. The Rochdale Society of Equitable Pioneers was founded in 1844 by 28 workers who raised a small capital by contributing 1 pound apiece. From the beginning they established two principles which have since been recognized as fundamental in their success. Democracy was assured by allowing one vote to each member, irrespective of the number of shares he might hold, and the self-interest of members was enlisted by returning the profits to them in proportion to their purchases. Capital received a fixed rate of interest, and goods were sold at market prices in order to avoid the hostility of private storekeepers. Full weight and measure were given and pure goods were furnished.

Beginning with a small stock of a few staple goods, the Society gradually added grocery, meat, and clothing departments and in 1852 began production of shoes and suits. A flour mill was acquired, but a cotton mill was less successful. In 1863 the Co-operative Wholesale Society was established to act as joint purchasing and distributing agency for all the retail societies. They were given a legal status by the Industrial and Provident Societies Act of 1852, "the charter of co-operators."

2. LOW STANDARDS IN FRANCE

Population. In 1789 France was the most populous country in Europe, with a population of 26,300,000. This was 5 million more than were in Germany and double the number in Great Britain; it was 16 per cent of the total estimated population of Europe, which was placed at between 160 and 165 million.[11] The first census of France, taken in 1801, showed a more accurate count and, together with subsequent statistics, is given in the following table:

Year	Population	Per cent urban	Per cent rural
1801	27,500,000		
1811	29,092,000		
1815	27,107,000		
1821	30,461,000		
1831	32,570,000		
1841	34,230,000		
1851	35,783,000	25.5	74.5
1861	37,386,000	28.9	71.1
1872	36,103,000	31.1	68.9

[11] E. Levasseur, *La population française* (Paris, 1892), 231.

The population received two setbacks during this period; the first, the losses inflicted by the Napoleonic wars, is recorded in the figures for 1815, which showed a population smaller even than that for 1801; the second, resulting from the loss of Alsace-Lorraine, is shown in the figures for 1872, which wiped out the gain of the preceding decade and a half. Partly for these reasons, and even more from other causes, the population of France grew more slowly during this period than that of either Great Britain or Germany, both of which countries passed France in numbers after 1860.

Except for the period of the Napoleonic wars the growth was fairly steady. Napoleon tried to stimulate it by offering favors to families with more than three children, but without avail. After about 1806 the birth-rate declined constantly, but a still greater fall in the death-rate permitted the population to grow, although the surplus steadily became smaller. The following table shows this relationship:

BIRTH-RATE AND DEATH-RATE IN FRANCE, 1801–1870
(per 1000 inhabitants)

Period	Birth-rate	Death-rate	Surplus
1801–10	33.0	29.0	4.0
1811–20	31.6	25.9	5.7
1821–30	31.0	25.2	5.8
1831–40	29.0	24.8	4.2
1841–50	27.4	23.3	4.1
1851–60	26.3	23.9	2.4
1861–70	26.3	23.6	2.7

Urban growth. The growth of cities, and the movement of population from rural to urban conditions, took place in France, in common with all other industrial countries, though in less marked degree than in either Great Britain or Germany. A document published by order of the Constituent Assembly in 1790 [12] estimated the population of the towns at 21.7 per cent and of the rural districts at 78.3 per cent. But this estimate was very vague and not until the census of 1846 fixed a precise limit of 2000 for towns, was it possible to give exact figures.

In 1801 there were in France, outside of Paris, only two cities (Lyons and Marseilles) with more than 100,000 inhabitants. By 1846 there were five altogether with 4 per cent of the population, and in 1870 there were eight with 8 per cent. The largest cities showed the most rapid urban growth, but the medium-sized ones grew faster than the population as a whole. In other words, the

[12] Quoted by Arthur Young, *Travels during the years 1787, 1788, and 1789* (Dublin, 1793), II, 374.

rural population was being drained off to people the cities. Military service acquainted the agricultural workers with the greater opportunities, the higher wages, and the better schools, and the discharged recruits were disinclined to return to the miserable conditions in the rural districts, which, moreover, remained unimproved. The movement was noticeable after 1830; and after 1845, when the railway increased the mobility of the population, it was especially strong. After 1850 there was an actual decrease of the agricultural population as a whole, and rural districts suffered greatly.

Levasseur described the movement as follows: [13] The rate of growth of the urban population is greater than that of the rural; that of cities of over 20,000 inhabitants is superior to that of the urban population in general; that of large cities of over 100,000 inhabitants is superior to that of smaller cities; and that of Paris is the greatest of them all. From these facts he deduced a so-called law of population: "the force of attraction of human groups, like that of matter, is, in general, proportional to the mass." France nevertheless preserved a predominantly rural character during the whole of this period. Even in 1846 three-quarters of the people lived in the country and twenty years later the proportion was still over two-thirds. There was no such disturbing agricultural or industrial revolution in France as depopulated the rural districts and filled the towns in England.

Other causes than mass attraction must, however, be noted to explain the growth of French cities. Topography had an important influence, for most of the important towns were seaports or were situated on navigable rivers, such as Marseilles, Bordeaux, Boulogne, Lyons, Lille, and Toulouse. Industry accounted for the growth of such centers as St. Etienne and Roubaix, while a few others owed their importance to their proximity to Paris, as Vincennes, St. Denis, and Neuilly. The movement of population was from the Alpine and upland districts and from the agriculturally more sterile regions.

Housing. Living conditions, even in the cities, were unprepossessing, judged by modern standards. Writing of Paris in 1787 Arthur Young said,[14] "this great city appears to be in many respects the most ineligible and inconvenient for the residence of a person of small fortune of any that I have seen; and vastly inferior to London. The streets are narrow and many of them crowded, nine tenths dirty, and all without foot pavements. . . I have been myself blackened many times with the mud from the kennels . . . all per-

---

[13] E. Levasseur, *Les populations urbaines en France* (Paris, 1887), 21.
[14] Quoted by M. C. Buer, *Health, Wealth, and Population in the Early Days of the Industrial Revolution* (London, 1926), 83.

sons of small or moderate fortune, are forced to dress in black with black stockings."

A half century later another English traveler gave similar testimony, but this time for the workers. "The homes of the working classes are for the most part dirty, comfortless, and evincing every symptom of bad management and poverty combined. Even those who have children in the cotton mills, do not keep up any appearance of comfort." [15] Villermé gives a picture of conditions in Lille which reproduces the essential features of Engels' description of Manchester. The workers slept on the floor and in cellars. Often the whole family had only a sack of straw for a bed. "In many beds," he reported, "I have seen persons of both sexes, of very different ages, lying together, mostly without clothing and very dirty." [16]

In view of the fact, however, that in 1846 less than a quarter, and in 1872 less than a third, of the people lived in towns of over 2000 inhabitants, it is more important to inquire as to the conditions in the rural districts. Here the evidence is even more unfavorable. Light is thrown on the character of the dwellings by the returns from the ill-judged door and window tax, which discouraged both forms of openings. Of 7,462,545 dwellings taxed in 1846, almost half had only two windows in addition to a door, 1,805,422 had only one window, and 313,691 were without windows. Not only were the dwellings inadequately lighted and ventilated, but they were overcrowded as well. "Many individuals are often crowded together in a small apartment, one room frequently containing the man and his wife, two or three children, and a workman and his wife." [17] Little improvement was made in these conditions during this period.

Wages. The explanation for the poor living conditions must be found largely in the low wages. The productivity of labor was low, and the per capita income was insufficient to afford more than a bare subsistence to the mass of the people. French wage statistics are notoriously inadequate, but a few scattering estimates will show the tendencies, which on the whole were upward. Chaptal, in 1819, estimated the average annual wage of the rural worker at 375 francs, but in 1827 Dupin placed it at only 358 francs; for the rural worker and his wife he calculated joint earnings of 477 francs, and for the urban worker (540) and his wife (180) he estimated 720 francs. Villermé estimated the average wage during the thirties at 2 francs per day for men, 1 franc for women, and $\frac{1}{2}$ to $\frac{3}{4}$ franc for children.

[15] J. C. Symons, *Arts and Artisans at Home and Abroad* (Edinburgh, 1839), 38.
[16] L. R. Villermé, *Tableau de l'état physique et moral des ouvriers* (Paris, 1840), I, 74.
[17] Symons, op. cit., 43.

The first official report was that of 1847, which gave almost the same figures as Villermé: men, 2.09 francs, women 1.03, children .73. These were averages; the extremes lay between 1 and 4 francs for men, and .75 and 2.50 francs for women.

A second investigation, conducted by the Labor Committee of the National Assembly in 1848, reported still lower wages, but this was because they included the rural areas around the cities. According to this report average wages for men were 1.78 francs, for women .79 franc, and for children .50 franc. Wages were highest in Paris, in mining, in iron and glass works, and in building trades. House industry in the country paid considerably less than factory work in the cities. There were, of course, great differences from region to region. In general, Sée [18] concludes that wages, after the sharp rise in the war period 1793–1815, remained practically unchanged until 1850. Between 1850 and 1870 they rose rapidly. Levasseur [19] estimated the rise at about 41 per cent for the provinces and 32 per cent for Paris. No allowance, however, was made in these statistics for unemployment, due either to crises, which were frequent, to strikes, or to illness, but the losses from all these causes were heavy throughout this period and bore with crushing weight upon the workers.

Real wages of course are more important than nominal wages, but they are especially difficult to reckon because of the lack of trustworthy statistics on the cost of living.[20] The price of bread, which absorbed $\frac{1}{3}$ to $\frac{1}{2}$ of the worker's budget, was stable, potatoes were plentiful, but meat went up in price during this period. Factory made products were cheaper and entered into general consumption, but wine, sugar, and coffee remained luxuries out of reach of the average workingman.

Standard of living. The standard of living improved during this period, but even at the close remained low. Sée [21] gives a picture of peasant economy in the thirties and forties. The peasants sold their wheat and contented themselves with rye and buckwheat,

---

[18] Sée, op. cit., 239.

[19] *Histoire des classes ouvrières de 1789 à 1870*, II, 872.

[20] A recent attempt to estimate the relative course of wages in France during this period yields the following results (1870=100):*

Year	Gross money wages	Cost of living	Gross real wages
1820	58	72	65
1830	61	75	68
1840	64	77	70
1850	68	77	73
1860	83	97	85
1870	100	100	100

* J. Kuczynski, *Labour Conditions in Western Europe*, 1820–1935 (New York, 1936), 105.

[21] Op. cit., 175.

though the city residents ate wheat bread.   Meat was seldom eaten, at most home-made sausage.   In remote sections conditions had changed little since the eighteenth century.   In many houses the light entered only through the door and a narrow window.   The furniture consisted of a bed, a wooden chair, and a table.   Usually all the people slept in one unplastered room.   The court, filled with manure, was a regular sewer.   Conditions in the rapidly growing factory towns were even worse, for there was a scarcity of houses, and the familiar phenomena of over-crowding, cellar dwellings, and unsanitary surroundings were everywhere to be found.   If a worker sought to escape from crowded quarters and unsanitary conditions he must find lodgings in the suburbs with wearying walks to and from work.   As time went on these particular evils were met by new building, but the standard of comfort remained low.   Insufficient nourishment, lack of bathing facilities, and open privies without ade-quate sewers created a favorable field for rickets and tuberculosis. Epidemics like the cholera of 1832 raged frequently, especially among the working classes.   The death-rate in the industrial cities, particularly of the children, was above the average for France. Physical degeneration was clearly visible.   In the 10 most industrial-ized departments almost half of those summoned for military serv-ice in 1840 were rejected.

In order to make the picture clearer the relation between earnings and cost of living may be given.   In 1832 it was estimated that an average worker, receiving 2 francs a day, might earn 600 francs a year.   The cost of supporting his family of self, wife, and three children would be 860 francs.   The budget could be balanced only if the wife and children also worked, but this made no allowance for unemployment or for illness.   Villermé, writing in 1840, concluded that a married couple without children could manage well and even save something if they had steady work; that no saving was possible with one child; and that outside relief was necessary with more than one child.   Other reports confirm these estimates.

The expenditure of a Paris workingman's household was esti-mated by Paul Louis,[22] for lodging, food, heat, and light, at 890 francs in 1810, 950 in 1820, 985 in 1830, 966 in 1840, and 950 in 1850.   After 1852 there was a rapid industrial development in Paris, and prices of everything shot up.   Rents doubled between 1846 and 1866, and the cost of food rose, though not so rapidly. Between 1844–53 and 1862 the price of beef rose from .44 to .59 franc per pound, that of mutton from .45 to .68, and that of pork from .45 to .67.   The report of the Paris workers delegated to the London Exposition of 1862 gives French working class budgets, of

[22] *Histoire de la classe ouvrière* (Paris, 1927), 52, 83.

which the following, for a Paris worker with wife and two children, is typical: [23]

	Francs
Lodging	300
Clothing	300
Heat and light	75
Laundry	100
Social insurance	36
School for one child	70
Food (except wine)	1100
Total	1981

The same report gave the highest daily wage in 1862 for a Paris worker as 6 francs, which, assuming 300 days of employment, would give annual earnings of 1800 francs. The balance would be met by earnings of the wife, or by charity. Although the latter subject lies outside the scope of this book, the student of French economic history cannot help being impressed by the frequency and extent of state and communal aid to French workers at various times.[24] Not until past the first third of the nineteenth century was any protective legislation passed on their behalf, and not until the end of the second third were they permitted to organize to enforce better conditions. In the interval they were thrown back on the goodwill of their employers or public charity. The two chief complaints of the industrial workers at the beginning of the Revolution were unemployment and low wages,[25] and these echo through the nineteenth century. The causes advanced in the *Cahiers* were two: one, old — too many holidays; [26] the other, which was just appearing — mechanization. This latter was a disturbing factor, which, in ever-increasing degree, upset the industrial equilibrium and necessitated constant readjustment.

Consumption. The budget of a working class family can be better understood if translated into actual commodities instead of money. Bread and potatoes were the staples of the French diet. Specimen menus for the 1830's, chosen from different districts, all show a low standard of living. An English traveler [27] reported in 1839

[23] Georges Weill, *Histoire du mouvement social en France* (2nd ed., Paris, 1911), 15. A similar delegation of workingmen was sent by the Government to the Exposition of 1867, and in their report discontent with existing conditions was expressed even more vigorously than in 1862. They demanded the abolition of poverty.

[24] Villeneuve-Bargemont declared in 1834 that of the 70,000 inhabitants of Lille 22,000 were paupers; and in the whole departement one-sixth of the population was registered at the *bureaux de bienfaisance.* — *Economic politique chrétienne* (Paris, 1834), II, 50.

[25] Roger Picard, *Les Cahiers de 1789 et les classes ouvrières* (Paris, 1910), 108.

[26] G. d'Avenel, *Histoire économique* (Paris, 1926), 352, states that before the Revolution there were 160 legal and obligatory days of idleness annually.

[27] J. C. Symons, op. cit., 46, 58.

that the peasants in Normandy "live chiefly on vegetable soup and the coarsest sort of bread. . . In other parts of southern France the peasantry live better. They eat wheaten bread, soup made with vegetable, and a little grease or lard twice a day, potatoes and other vegetables, but seldom butcher's meat; their drink is wine or piquette [made by pouring water over the pomace after the juice of the grapes had been extracted]. . . The luxuries of tea, etc., are quite unknown." The worst conditions were found in the textile districts of Alsace.[28] "In the 1830s the food of the workers consisted almost only of bread, potatoes and coffee. For breakfast they ate bread, which they dipped in coffee with milk, or a substitute. Others had soup, but this took time and fuel. At nine in the morning dry bread was eaten. At noon there were potatoes with pork fat, and vegetables for the better paid. At three in the afternoon dry bread again, and in the evening the 14-15 hours day, which was often followed by an hour's walk home, was concluded with bread and coffee. Meat was had only on Sundays. For a grown man at least one kilogram of bread was figured daily." These conditions improved somewhat during the next forty years, but never reached the standard of the contemporary British laborers.

But in spite of these evils, the standard of living of the French worker was slowly rising during this period. Scattered and unsatisfactory though they are, the statistics show a growing consumption of staples and the introduction of increased quantities of semi-luxuries into the dietary of the masses. The following table is submitted in evidence:

CONSUMPTION PER CAPITA IN FRANCE

Article	1831	1840	1852	1861	1870
Wheat (bu.)	5.0	7.7 *	6.6	......	8.1
Potatoes (lbs.)	352.0	574.2 *	......	......	536.8
Sugar (lbs.)	5.7	6.4 *	8.1	......	12.8
Beef (lbs.)	......	19.3	26.3	26.4	......
Mutton (lbs.)	......	5.3	6.5	6.7	......
Pork (lbs.)	......	18.8	18.3	22.1	......
Wine (qts.)	......	144.4	......	......	301.4 **
Beer (qts.)	......	20.2	......	......	29.8 **
Salt (qts.)	......	4.5	......	......	6.5 **

* 1841.
** 1867.

There was also an increased consumption of butter, cheese, eggs, milk, fresh and dry vegetables, and fruit. The consumption of colonial articles, all of which entered the country through French

[28] H. Herkner, *Die oberelsässische Baumwollindustrie und ihre Arbeiter* (Strassburg, 1887), 151.

ports, can be most exactly measured. Between 1820–22 and 1865–67 the net imports — that is the consumption — of sugar, coffee, cocoa, and tea increased as follows (in millions of tons): [29]

Article	1820–22	1865–67	Increase, per cent
Sugar	42.0	258.0	614
Coffee	8.1	45.3	559
Cocoa	688.0	6500.0	944
Tea	78.0	348.0	446
Population (millions)	30.4	38.1	127

Still one other index of well-being may be applied, namely the increase in wealth. The total wealth of the French people is estimated to have increased from 38,000 million francs in 1780 to 120,000 in 1820, and to 175,000 in 1870. At the same time the gross national income, a more correct measure of prosperity, increased from 4000 million francs in 1780 to 7860 million in 1820 and 18,000 million in 1866.[30] Even if these figures lack exactness the constancy of the progression shows a real improvement. This is borne out by statistics of deposits in savings banks, which quadrupled during this period, and of other similar indices.

Well-being. A final question presents itself. Did the workers share in the increase in national wealth? The peasant of 1789 received some of his wage in kind and in rights. The Revolution swept away many of these, and with the growing industrialization money wages took their place. Wage statistics therefore give an appearance of improvement, which does not always correspond to the facts. It is doubtful if in the first half of the nineteenth century the workers shared proportionately in the increase in wealth. In 1847 there existed in France, including the pawn shops, whose financial aid to the workers was of social and economic significance, 9242 charitable establishments with a total expenditure of 115 million francs. There were 7599 *bureaux de bienfaisance*, which assisted during the year more than a million poor, 1634 hospitals and hospices, which cared for more than 600,000 sick, and gave refuge to 120,000 abandoned children, to nearly 100,000 aged or infirm, and to 20,000 insane, and 40 institutions for deaf and dumb and blind.[31] After 1848 there was a steady improvement in the condition of the working class. In addition to an increase in both nominal and real wages, they received other advantages. Welfare organizations of various kinds were set up by employers, cheap lodgings and consumers' co-operative associations supplied essentials at lowest cost,

---

[29] E. Levasseur, *La population française* (Paris, 1892), 46.
[30] Levasseur, op. cit., 84-85.
[31] E. Levasseur, *Histoire des classes ouvrières et de l'industrie en France de 1789 à 1870* (2nd ed., Paris, 1904), 287.

and prices were held down by the free trade policy. Husson noted the increase in the amount spent for food and attributed it to an increase in personal consumption and higher standards of living.

Education. Among the more intangible benefits, in addition to an increase in leisure and improved living conditions, may be mentioned education. Primary schools had been in existence since the 16th century, and parish schools became common in the 18th century, but educational standards for the workers remained on a low level. The four rules of arithmetic, the catechism, and the calendar usually made up the curriculum. Master craftsmen could keep accounts and write letters, but documents written by the subordinate workman showed little practical knowledge. The leaders of the Revolution, under the influence of Rousseau, urged free public instruction and the abolition of church schools. But the official instruction was poor, and the religous orders continued their work.

The history of education in France is one of struggle between church and state over control of this institution. Napoleon set up an Imperial University with a practical monopoly of education: all candidates for the baccalaureate were required to attend certain classes, and the University alone had the right to confer degrees, which were required of all teachers. Church schools flourished, however, and after 1815 demanded liberty of instruction. The conflict was resolved in 1849 by the Falloux law, which aimed to break the monopoly in education by strengthening the position of the church without destroying the University. Provision was made for two kinds of schools: those founded or maintained by the communes, departments, or the state; and those founded or maintained by individuals or associations, which were called "free schools." That the latter were still an important factor in the educational system is evident from the fact that one-third of the 3,850,000 pupils in primary schools in 1857 received their instruction in the church institutions. Although illiteracy was decreasing, in 1859 over 36 per cent of the military recruits were unable to read and write; 44 per cent of the women could not sign their names to the marriage register. Nearly a quarter of the children between 5 and 13 years of age did not go to school; this was especially marked in the agricultural districts. The "public" schools of France were evidently not universal.

3. POVERTY IN GERMANY

Population. By 1800 Germany had scarcely more than recovered from the Thirty Years' War. In that year the population numbered about 22,000,000. The Napoleonic wars spelled another period of retardation, so that by 1816 the population, within the boundaries of 1871–1914, had grown to only 24,833,000. The period of peace which followed brought the numbers up to 29,-520,000 in 1830. This rapid increase of almost 20 per cent in fifteen years led to a cry of over-population. Under the influence of the doctrines of Malthus, which had penetrated to Germany, the authority of the state was invoked to limit marriages. In the southern states especially, as in Wurtemberg, Bavaria, Baden, Hesse, Hanover, and the Thuringian states, laws were passed requiring the prospective couple to prove that they had adequate property or income to support a family. One unfortunate result of this legislation was an increase in the number of illegitimate children.

Another result of this rapid growth in the population was a strong emigration movement. The year 1815 was the beginning of a series of crop failures, which reduced the German people to a condition of semi-starvation. In certain districts they made bread out of bark and ate weeds from the fields. The cessation of the wars threw thousands of soldiers out of work, who could not be readily re-absorbed into the economic organization, as industry was not developed and agriculture remained unprogressive. According to Engels the population of Prussia increased 13 per cent between 1816 and 1822, but hogs only 7 and cattle 6 per cent. It seemed as though the cry of over-population was justified. There had been little emigration during the Napoleonic wars, but after 1815 it assumed considerable dimensions. It is estimated that 20,000 Germans emigrated to the United States in 1816–17; five years later the number had fallen to 11,000, but by 1833 it was back to 20,000.

In spite of emigration the population continued to increase. By 1849 it was estimated at 35,128,000, by 1860 at 37,700,000, and in 1871, by a more accurate count, at 41,058,792. The average annual increase was about 275,000 between 1816 and 1871. In contrast with France the growth of Germany's population came from a very high birth-rate, which, in spite of a high death-rate, yielded a large excess of births over deaths. Statistics are not available for the early part of this period, but the situation was probably not very different from the latter part. The following brief table shows the relationship:

BIRTH-RATE AND DEATH-RATE IN GERMANY

Period	Birth-rate	Death-rate	Excess of births over deaths
1841–50	36.1	26.8	9.3
1851–60	35.3	26.3	9.0
1861–70	37.2	26.8	10.4

At the beginning of the nineteenth century the population of Germany was predominantly rural. In Prussia, which may be taken as typical, no less than 73.5 per cent were so classed in 1816. The proportion was still 71.9 in 1849, and in 1871 it was 63.9 for the German Empire. In 1800 there were 1000 places in Prussia with municipal status, but only 119 had more than 3000 inhabitants, while 881 had fewer than 3000. But the so-called cities were not only small, they retained a rural character, with agriculture and even cattle raising carried on within the town limits. There were only two cities — Berlin and Hamburg — with more than 100,000 inhabitants in 1800; Berlin had 172,023. By 1849 Prussia had six of these "great" cities. In Saxony, which was less industrialized, there were only three cities with more than 15,000 inhabitants at the middle of the century.

The distribution of the population is shown in the following table (persons living in places with fewer than 2000 inhabitants are classed as rural):

PERCENTAGE DISTRIBUTION OF POPULATION

Year	Rural	Urban
1816 *	73.5	26.5
1849 *	71.9	28.1
1867 **	64.2	35.8
1871 †	63.9	36.1

* Prussia.
** North German Confederation.
† German Empire.

The urban movement was a slow but steady one, slightly accelerated in the fifties, after the building of the railways. The urban population grew somewhat faster than the total population, and the rate of growth was greatest in the large cities; but even in 1870 only a third of the people lived in towns. If the growth of urban centers is an index of industrialization, we must conclude that this had not proceeded far in Germany. Any statement concerning the well-being of the people in Germany during most of this period must therefore deal primarily with the rural population.

Further proof of the predominance of agricultural interests during this period is furnished by the more rapid growth of East Germany, that is of the states east of the Elbe River, which were wholly agricultural in character. The industrial west also grew, though the great development of this section belongs in the period after 1870, but the south remained almost stagnant. This is shown in the following table: [32]

[32] P. Meuriot, *Des agglomerations urbaines dans l'Europe contemporaine* (Paris, 1898), 173.

POPULATION OF THE GRAND DIVISIONS OF GERMANY
(000 omitted)

Division	1825	1849	1871
West	10,436	13,202	15,695
East	8,973	11,889	14,764
South *	8,700	10,037	10,601
Total	28,109	35,128	41,060

* This comprised Hesse, Alsace-Lorraine, Baden, Wurtemberg, Bavaria, and Hohenzollern.

Conditions in these early towns were terrible. A report from Cologne in 1800 reads: "The refuse of the kitchen is emptied in the gutters and dead animals are thrown there, which cause an insupportable stench. In Berlin one must unceasingly hold his nose in his handkerchief, since in the morning there arise first the odors of the night stools emptied into the gutters, or the whole refuse of a home. Little care is taken to remove dead dogs and cats and I have often seen a dead horse lie half a day in a busy street." Streets were badly paved and unlighted. It was dangerous to go out after dark and theft and attacks were not infrequent. People carried their own lanterns. Watchmen patrolled the streets and blew their horns every hour, to the anger and nerve-wrecking of the inhabitants. Those conditions lasted until well into the nineteenth century. Such conditions were possible because the towns were still rural in character and collective action had not yet replaced individual self-sufficiency.

Condition of the peasants. The legal position of the peasant and his relation to the land have already been described. Here it will suffice to note the material well-being. But the peasant class was a large one, made up of various groups. Between the full peasant, with a sizable land holding and capable of driving his own yoke of oxen, and the landless hereditary serf, there was a wide gulf. At the beginning of the nineteenth century the position of the latter was miserable in the extreme. Bound to the soil, he received, in exchange for his services, a bare subsistence. The lord, it is true, owed the serf protection, and support in time of adversity, but the position of the serf was only a degree above that of slavery. Above him stood the free quarter- and half-peasants, and at the top of the hierarchy was the full peasant. Only the latter had enough land for his support, the others being compelled to eke out the returns from their small holdings by working for wages. These were pitiable, amounting to a few groschen a day, ten for men and six for women. Even the full peasant bore such heavy burdens in the form of dues to the lord and taxes that he had a struggle to make ends meet. The peasant, of whatever grade, worked hard, lived poorly, and was never able to raise himself in the economic or social scale.

Stein's Edict of 1807, abolishing serfdom, improved the legal position of the serfs and the later legislation removed some of the burdens from other groups, but the antagonism of the lordly land owners prevented the complete carrying out of this well-meant legislation. The raising of the material condition of the peasant had to wait for improvements in agricultural technique and organization, that made agriculture more productive and afforded the basis for better living.

The mode of life of the peasants was that of a self-sufficing economy. They were at the same time farmers, bakers, butchers, masons, carpenters, spinners, weavers, broom-binders, brushmakers, wood-cutters, and even soapmakers and beer brewers. On their holdings they raised the necessary food supplies and raw materials, and from the sale of surplus swine, and perhaps also milk, eggs, and geese, and, in case of the free agricultural laborers, from wages, they obtained a small money income with which to purchase articles not produced at home: house and kitchen utensils, pottery and glass, a few pieces of clothing, and colonial wares. The few free laborers were paid mostly in kind, and money was not often used in exchange.

These almost medieval conditions had changed very little by the middle of the century. A lively picture of life in the 1840's is presented by Sombart,[33] from whom the following facts are taken:

In the forties the industrial production of goods was still in force in all lines of the peasant economy. A German farm usually supported itself, care being taken to want as little as possible anything not supplied by the soil. Slaughtering and grinding meal were almost the only things done by outsiders. The meal was baked either at home or by a so-called community baker, who received a share or a few pfennigs. All drinks were made by the peasant in his household. The need for housing was slight, and the raw materials were gathered from communal forests and clay banks. If necessary, a carpenter, a mason, or a glazier, who wandered from village to village, gave his services for bread and room and a fixed wage. So too clothing was supplied from the farm and with labor of the family. "It is through the winter that they are busy dressing their hemp and flax, and the women all spinning and knitting. In an evening it is common custom for the women to take their wheels and meet together at their houses in rotation, where they tell endless stories, and make themselves very merry, while their husbands are at the wirth-

[33] *Der moderne Kapitalismus* (Berlin, 1902), Bd. II, Teil II, 664 ff. See also Bd. I, 433 ff.

house; and these, as in all other countries, are the short and simple annals of the poor." [34]

Town economy. Even in the towns at the beginning of the century a self-sufficing economy prevailed, the urban inhabitants frequently possessing gardens from which they obtained much of their food, and depending on outside help only in the case of locksmith and wheelwright. By the 1840's such a self-sufficing economy was no longer possible. By now wider separation of occupations necessitated a greater interdependence, and the independent craftsmen worked for a money wage. But even handwork was closely connected with agriculture. "They are hybrid creatures," wrote Sombart,[35] "these industrial individual workers in the villages of the old style, between handworkers and farmers, who often themselves did not know whether they belonged to the one or the other calling." Clothing and household utensils were produced for the most part in the home economy of urban households; bread and especially cake-dough were prepared at home and only the baking was done by the baker in return for payment. The city housewife also made soap, candles, and home brew. The women, wrote Howitt,[36] "busied themselves with working and sewing as though their lives depended on it." The growth of mechanization and of wider markets, however, soon brought the city industry and its workers within the circle of a more capitalistic economy.

The growth of the factory in Germany brought in its train the same undesirable conditions that followed the industrial revolution in England. By 1848 there was already a city proletariat. The conditions of the factory workers were like those of the handworkers a decade earlier — long hours, small pay, and bad living conditions. Many of the employers had risen from the working class and were ruthless and hard, without any social conscience. The old patriarchal relationships, which protected the worker, had been dissolved, and he was now exposed to the forces of a wider market.

Labor legislation. In contrast with poor pay, the work time was very long. In the 1830's in most workshops and factories the work day was 14 to 15 hours and in many 16. Pauses for breakfast, dinner, and vespers made up $1\frac{1}{2}$ to 2 hours, so that the actual work time was about 13 to 14 hours. An especially grievous evil was the overlong employment of little children in factories, and at night. There were no laws or ordinances which governed this. The law in Prussia determined only that children must attend school after their fifth year until they had attained "the knowledge necessary for every

[34] Howitt, 225.
[35] Op. cit., I, 438.
[36] Op. cit., II, 224, 233.

intelligent person of their class." What this knowledge was, how long they must attend school, and when they might begin work, were not stated but were left to the determination of officials. Consequently, the factory and workshop owners found no obstacle to employing children under 10 years of age for 13 and 14 hours a day, often at night.

As early as 1828 the military authorities drew attention to the extent of child labor and the resulting physical deterioration of the population; in the Rhenish industrial districts the army recruits were under par and were becoming worse. No action was taken, however, until April 6, 1839, when a royal decree ordered that children could not be "regularly" employed in factories before their ninth year, nor could older children be employed unless they could read and had made a beginning in writing. The work day for children under 16 was limited to 10 hours and night work was forbidden. These regulations were far behind the English act of 1833 and were not enforced. The enforcement of the law was entrusted to the local police, teachers, and clergymen, but these were unwilling or unable to compel obedience. In 1847 Prussia reported 13 children between 8 and 14 years of age per 1000 industrial workers; in Berlin there were 32 per 1000. Restrictive legislation did not yet have the support of public opinion, for it was feared that it would interfere with the economic expansion of the country. No legislation was passed to regulate woman's work or that of adult male workers. Outside of Prussia conditions were still worse, and children of 6 and 7 years of age were employed, while wages were so low that the diet was confined "largely to potatoes and salt and water."

The law of 1853 was the first labor legislation of practical significance, for this introduced factory inspection. This act fixed the minimum age for children at 12 years, limited the working day for children between 12 and 14 to 6 hours daily, and prescribed 3 hours of school instruction daily. But this must not be exaggerated, since only three inspectors were appointed for the whole of Prussia, inspection was applied only occasionally and employers threw every obstacle in the way of the inspectors. Parents sided with the employers by concealing the children, testifying falsely as to their ages, and in other ways. But the school provisions were more effective than military warnings and 80 per cent of the children of school age actually went to school in 1840. In the field of technical education Germany was in advance of the other countries, having established the first technical high school in Brunswick in 1745. In the 1860's a long step forward in this field was taken; the older schools were improved and several new polytechnic institutions were founded — Braunschweig in 1862, Darmstadt 1869, and Aachen 1870.

Wages. Wage statistics for this period are difficult to obtain. The following table, based on figures collected by J. Kuczynski, shows the trend: [37]

WAGES AND COST OF LIVING IN GERMANY
(1830–39 = 100)

Year	Gross money wages	Cost of living	Gross real wages
1830–39	100	100	100
1840–49	105	116	90
1850–59	118	140	86
1860–69	141	154	95

These figures, incomplete as they confessedly are, show that, while wages were moving upward during the period 1830 to 1860, prices were rising still more rapidly, so that the real wages of labor were steadily declining. While the decade of the sixties saw an improvement, in that wages rose faster than the cost of living, it was not sufficient to place the worker in as good a position as he had occupied in the thirties. A more realistic picture is presented in the following table, which shows agricultural wages paid on the domain Schlanstedt in Saxony:

DAILY WAGES FOR COMMON AGRICULTURAL WORK *

	(in pfennigs)			(in cents)		
Year	Men	Women	Children	Men	Women	Children
1840	50	37.5	25	12	9	6
1850	62.5	50	37.5	15	12	9
1860	75	60	40	18	14.4	9.6

* Von der Goltz, *Geschichte der Landwirtschaft*, II, 261.

In partial explanation of these incredibly low wages, it should be noted that the workers were paid partly in kind, and that the money

[37] Jurgen Kuczynski, *Labour Conditions in Western Europe* (New York, 1936), 92-95. The author writes depreciatingly of his studies: "The data on wages in Germany are considerably inferior to the collection made by Bowley and Wood for England. The collection for Germany made by myself does not contain as many data and the data are even more incongruous than those collected by Bowley and Wood because they are not only a mixture of trade union rates, general rates, and actual wages paid, but in addition they contain also average weekly wages actually paid, thus including wage losses, through short time, and average yearly wages. . . Especially bad are the data for agricultural wages, which are taken from a number of sources the reliability of which cannot be checked; many interpolations had to be made to arrive at an index. . . Even worse than the wage index is the cost of living index. For pre-War years it pertains only to food prices and to rents. . . Since many of the other factors taken into account for the computation of real wages are based on estimates, it is obvious that our figures are at best approximations. The trend of wages is shown roughly — but the year-to-year data should be regarded more as indefinite extension of the line along which wages moved than as the actual line itself." It was undoubtedly considerations such as these which led Sombart (*Deutsche Volkswirtschaft*) to reject incontinently all statistics of wages and consumption as indicia of economic progress. Nevertheless, I feel justified in using them, though with caution. By permission of the publishers, International Publishers, New York.

wage constituted only a part of their remuneration. There was a strong tendency, however, to substitute money wages for other means of payment, and with this change the position of the agricultural worker became worse, as money wages remained low. But money wages did not at once and entirely come into use. A widespread evil of this period was the truck system, especially in the house industry.[38] Here the workers were paid in liquor, tobacco, expensive colonial wares, unfashionable silk garments, and similar articles, or were compelled to buy in stores that were run by their employers or their relatives. It was estimated that twenty per cent of the wages were saved in this way. Against such abuses the worker was practically defenseless, for the Prussian government took the position that if the worker did not specify money in the wage agreement, he tacitly agreed to other methods of payment. Not until 1849 did Prussia pass legislation against the truck system. Other German states (Bavaria, Wurtemberg, Saxony) followed the Prussian lead between 1854 and 1861, but not until 1871 did the legislation against this evil cover all Germany. With the disappearance of payments in kind and in truck, money wages and prices became of paramount importance to the worker.

But prices were going up too. The following table shows the movement in some commodities which entered largely into the worker's consumption:

	Average price per ton in marks					Average price per lb. in pfg.	
Period	Wheat	Rye	Barley	Oats	Peas	Beef	Pork
1821–30	121.4	126.6	131.4	129.8	162.4	....	....
1831–40	138.4	100.6	76.6	79.8	97.0	26	34
1841–50	167.8	123.0	87.6	91.6	107.4	29	39
1851–60	211.4	165.4	111.2	100.6	130.0	32	50
1861–70	204.6	154.6	150.2	144.0	176.0	39	52

The poverty of the mass of the people at the beginning of the period is indicated by an inventory of the better class of peasants on several estates in East Prussia.[39] The peasants had average holdings of sixty-three acres, and an average capital equipment of four or five work horses, worth in 1800 about eleven thalers ($7.87) each, two work oxen worth about ten thalers ($7.15) each, two cows, two sheep, a few chickens and geese, and rarely some ducks. In addition he had a drag, two harrows, one or two sledges, forks, spades, axes, etc. The total money value of the inventory is estimated to have been seventy-five thalers ($53.53). The capital equipment of

[38] Jos. Kulischer, *Allgemeine Wirtschaftsgeschichte* (München, 1929), II, 486.
[39] K. Bohme, *Gutsherrliche-bauerliche Verhältnisse in Ostpreussen von 1770 bis 1830* (Leipzig, 1902), 3, 8, 9-11.

the lesser peasant (*Kossäthen*) is estimated to have been one-half this amount.

Incomes and consumption. Sombart estimated that in 1800, aside from the landed nobility, not over 1000 persons in all Germany had incomes over 10,000 marks ($2500). By 1853 there were counted in Berlin alone 1000 persons with incomes of over 9000 marks. Another writer gave the average money income in Prussia in 1802 as 27 Thaler ($20).[40] In view of what has just been said about the self-contained German economies of this period, such figures call for a great deal of interpretation. Perhaps a better light on the simple life of the people is afforded by an estimate of Dieterici that at the beginning of the nineteenth century the average annual consumption per capita in Prussia of certain commodities was as follows: 15 quarts of beer, 3 quarts of brandy, $\frac{3}{4}$ quart of wine, $1\frac{1}{2}$ pounds of tobacco, 1-$1\frac{1}{2}$ pounds of sugar, $\frac{3}{4}$ pound of coffee, spices for $\frac{1}{10}$ Thaler (7 cents), $\frac{3}{10}$ pound of rice, $\frac{1}{2}$-$\frac{3}{4}$ yard of woolen cloth, 4 yards of linen, $\frac{3}{4}$ pound of cotton yarn, $\frac{1}{4}$ pound of silk goods.

A description of the daily fare of a workingman's family in Wurtemberg in 1839 is given by an English traveler:[41]

"In the morning they eat soup, potatoes, or bread; dinner, vegetables or pudding; between dinner and supper, bread; supper, potatoes and milk, or soup; once or twice a week, meat. In the cold weather, the man would have a glass of inferior brandy before going to work in the morning. On Sundays, the man would have a little beer or wine, and the woman coffee, of which they are very fond."

Another writer[42] has pointed out that during this period the consumption of meat, sugar, tropical fruits, tobacco, wine, and books increased, while that of brandy fell off. The per capita consumption of sugar, for instance, grew from 4.69 pounds in 1840 to 9.89 pounds in 1865. This enlarged consumption of semi-luxuries indicates an improvement in the standard of living. In spite of such evidence of betterment the general picture of labor in Germany during the first half of the nineteenth century was one of a low standard of living, declining real wages, and increase of poverty and misery. Wages were on a subsistence level. If more were earned it was dissipated or the worker stopped working. This was called "seeking pleasure" or "laziness," and it was hardly anything else. In the middle of the fifties there began an upward rise of both money and real wages, but even then the general level of well-being was certainly lower in Germany than in England. At the beginning of the nineteenth century the consumption of even the most modest com-

---

[40] C. Day, *Economic Development in Modern Europe* (New York, 1933), 234.
[41] J. C. Symons, *Arts and Artisans at Home and Abroad* (Edinburgh, 1839), 79.
[42] K. Mass, *Deutsche Kultur- und Wirtschaftsgeschichte* (München, 1932), 108.

forts was astonishingly small. Consumption was held down by the poverty of the country and the prevailing inefficient methods of production to a standard not much above the level of subsistence. In years of scarcity, or among certain exploited groups like the Silesian weavers, it fell below even this. Accompanying the industrial advance of this period, however, there went on improvement and the standard was steadily raised.

BIBLIOGRAPHICAL NOTE

1. *Britain.* The best general history of labor legislation is B. L. Hutchins and A. Harrison, *History of Factory Legislation* (London, 1911). A concise account is E. von Plener, *English Factory Legislation* (London, 1873). An excellent account of various other reform movements is to be found in J. L. and B. Hammond, *Lord Shaftesbury* (3rd ed., London, 1926). Three other books by the same authors give a dark picture of early conditions: *The Town Labourer*, 1760–1832 (London, 1917), *The Skilled Labourer*, 1760–1832 (London, 1919), and *The Village Labourer*, 1760–1832 (4th ed., London, 1927). Even blacker is the description by the socialist Friedrich Engels, *The Condition of the Working Classes in London in* 1844 (London, 1892). Somewhat more cheerful are the conclusions as to the course of wages presented by two scholarly statisticians: A. L. Bowley, *Wages in the United Kingdom in the Nineteenth Century* (Cambridge, 1900), and G. H. Wood, *History of Wages in the Cotton Trade during the Past One Hundred Years* (London, 1910). Slow but steady improvement was shown also along other lines. The public health movement in its early stages is interestingly described in M. C. Buer, *Health, Wealth and Population in the Early Days of the Industrial Revolution* (London, 1926), and later developments in B. L. Hutchins, *The Public Health Agitation*, 1833–1848 (London, 1909). A more specialized but illuminating study is H. Jephson, *The Sanitary Evolution of London* (London, 1907). The pressure for popular education is described in A. E. Dobbs, *Education and Social Movements*, 1700–1850 (London, 1919). Population changes are shown in G. T. Griffiths, *Population Problems in the Age of Malthus* (Cambridge, 1926), and A. Redford, *Labour Migration in England*, 1800–1850 (Manchester, 1926). On the co-operative movement a discursive and popular account is G. J. Holyoake, *History of the Rochdale Pioneers*, 1844–1892, 2 vols. (10th ed., London, 1893). A semi-official history is Fred Hall and W. P. Watkins, *Cooperation: a Survey of the History, Principles, and Organization of the Movement in Great Britain and Ireland* (Manchester, 1934).

2. *France.* For this period of French history special studies in this field are scanty and one must rely on the general treatises. A. Audiganne, *Les populations ouvrières et les industries de la France* (2nd ed., Paris, 1860) is a careful study. G. Manco, *Les migrations ouvrières en France au début du* 19e *siècle* (Paris, 1932) is slight. E. Chevalier, *Les salaires au* 19me *siècle* (Paris, 1887) uses inadequate material skilfully.

3. *Germany.* A valuable contemporary book on population is K. F. W. Dieterici, *Ueber die Zunahme der Bevölkerung* (Berlin, 1857). G. Neuhaus, *Die Bewegung der Bevölkerung im Zeitalter des modernen Kapitalismus* (Tübingen, 1926) is a useful outline. Anna Neumann, *Die Bewegung der Löhne der ländlichen freien Arbeiter . . . in Preussen . . . bis* 1850 (Berlin, 1911) makes a desirable contribution in a difficult field. T. von der Goltz, *Die Lage der ländlichen Arbeiter im*

deutschen Reiche (Berlin, 1875) describes the condition of the least well-off class. Labor legislation is described by Th. Lohmann, *Die Fabrikgesetzgebung der Staaten des europäischen Kontinents* (Berlin, 1878), and the need of social insurance is emphasized by L. Brentano, *Die Arbeiterversicherung gemäss der heutigen Wirtschaftsordnung* (Leipzig, 1879). The movement of wages is carefully traced by J. Kuczynski, *Wages in Germany, 1820 to 1935* (Washington, Bur. of Lab. Stat., 1936). Two early studies of workers' budgets are: Ballin, *Haushalt der arbeitenden Klassen* (Berlin, 1883), and Ig. Gruber, *Haushaltung der arbeitenden Klassen* (Jena, 1887).

Part II: Economic Rivalries. 1870-1914

CHAPTER VIII

AGRICULTURE

I. AGRICULTURE SHIFTS FOR ITSELF IN BRITAIN

Agricultural depression. The decade of the 1870's was one of severe depression in British agriculture, and saw the beginning of a transformation of that industry which was spread over the next quarter century. The year 1875 introduced a series of unprecedentedly bad seasons, marked by rain, poor harvests, cattle plague, and sheep-rot. The worst harvest of the century came in 1879, when heavy rains ruined the crops. The Royal Commission on Agriculture in 1881 described the "great extent and intensity of the distress which has fallen upon the agricultural community." According to the testimony of James Caird, an outstanding agricultural authority, the five worst harvest years between 1852 and 1862 produced a yield of 24 bushels of wheat per acre, but the five years of bad harvests in the seventies — 1873, 1875, 1876, 1877, and 1879 — produced only 19 bushels. Short crops have usually been compensated by high prices, but in this instance prices fell. For the bad years of the sixties the price of wheat had averaged $1.90 per bushel, but in the seventies it was only $1.55. By the middle eighties it was down to $1.00 and by 1894 it had reached 70 cents, the lowest figure recorded for 150 years. Wheat is especially sensitive to price changes, but other grains shared in the decline, though not quite so disastrously. The Commission of 1881 [1] was inclined to attribute the depression to external causes, such as bad weather, but it was evident that the causes were deeper seated. Of these the most important was foreign competition.

Down to about 1870 the surplus of agricultural production of food and raw materials in other countries had not been sufficiently large to affect European prices, and the volume entering these markets had been held down by the cost of transportation. Caird held even in 1878 that the British farmer was fairly well guarded by the "natural protection" of distance. But after 1870 the transportation of bulky commodities was revolutionized. Railways, especially in the United States, opened up new areas of virgin soil and cheap production. The railway net in the United States grew from

[1] *Report of Royal Commission on Agriculture* (London, 1882), 12.

57,000 miles in 1870 to 156,000 in 1890. At the same time bigger and swifter steamships were being built, which could carry greater cargoes at cheaper rates. "In 1869 it cost 25 cents to transport a bushel of wheat, by lake and railway, from Chicago to New York, and 11.75 cents to transport it from New York to Liverpool — a total of 36.75 cents. In 1885 the charge from Chicago to New York was but 9.02 cents, and from New York to Liverpool 6.37 cents — a total of 15.39 cents, or considerably less than one-half. By 1905 the figures were reduced to 6.44 and 3.25 cents respectively, or a total of 9.69 cents." [2]

The impetus to these drastic reductions in rates was to be found in the expanding production of foodstuffs and raw materials, which was taking place not only in the United States, but also in Argentina, Australia, India, and, closer at hand, Russia. On the virgin land thus opened up, agricultural products were grown, with the aid of improved machinery, at low unit costs. Produced far in excess of home demand, they sought new markets, which now became world wide. The impact of these new forces on European agriculture was terrific. After some hesitation, France and Germany adopted policies of protection to home agriculture, but Great Britain, more thoroughly industrialized and wedded to a policy of free trade, left agriculture to adopt its own methods of meeting the storm. Cheap food and raw materials were held to be more important.

The burden of the new forces that were pressing on British agriculture may be estimated by noting the increase in the imports of some of the competing commodities. This was most serious in the case of wheat, as this bears distant transportation most easily, but was also marked in the case of wool, meat, and other items. The increase in wheat imports is shown in the following table:

AVERAGE ANNUAL IMPORTS OF WHEAT

Period	Bushels
1871–80	106,218,000
1881–90	144,741,576
1891–1900	179,714,856
1901–14	215,784,000

Meat from overseas entered the British market in the seventies. Live cattle, which had previously come from European countries, were shipped continuously from the United States after 1876 and exports of frozen meat date from 1874. A few years later shipments of frozen mutton from New Zealand began, followed by

[2] F. A. Ogg and W. R. Sharp, *Economic Development of Modern Europe* (New York, 1926), 158. By permission of the publishers, The Macmillan Company, New York.

chilled beef from Argentina. Wool also came in increasing volume, as Australian settlers turned from gold mining to sheep farming. The fall in wool prices was accelerated by changes in fashions. Even dairy products poured in; the imports of cheese rose by a third and those of butter were doubled. Only milk held its own fairly well, in spite of foreign competition even in this field. Other products which maintained themselves were hay and straw, the softer kinds of fruit that would not bear transportation well, and livestock of the finest quality.

Although the causes of the agricultural depression in Great Britain seem fairly obvious today, they were not so clear to contemporary writers. Brodrick,[3] writing in 1881, set down as the first of two causes, the second being foreign competition, "the depression in trade which prevailed throughout the year 1879, compelling the working classes to curtail their purchases of all articles, except the bare necessities of life, and manifesting itself most remarkably in the diminished consumption of alcoholic liquors." The Duke of Richmond's Commission, which sat from 1879 to 1882, attributed the prevalence of distress primarily to inclement seasons and only secondarily to foreign competition. Witnesses before the Royal Commission of 1895–97 asserted that the cause of agrarian distress was to be found in the demonetization of silver. Since Great Britain had not used silver, except for subsidiary coins, for a full century, this argument lacked conviction. It was, however, true that prices of all products fell during the last quarter of the nineteenth century. Writing at a still later period, Curtler[4] added as partial explanations of British agricultural depression the increased cost of production from higher wages, etc., the increased pressure of local taxation, and the excessive railway rates and preferential rates given to foreign agricultural produce. But difficult as it was to ascertain causes, it was still more difficult to find and apply remedies. It is consequently not surprising to find the first attempts of British agriculturalists to meet the new and hard conditions uncertain and fumbling. Indeed, Brodrick[5] complained that the farmer was "slow to discern the signs of the times, and to modify his old routine in accordance with new circumstances"; he thought American agriculture was much more elastic.

Shift in land utilization. Bewildered but not dismayed the British farmer first thought to hold his own by working harder along familiar and well-tried lines. As a matter of fact the distress was primarily felt in wheat-growing areas; where this was subordinate

[3] G. C. Brodrick, *English Land and English Landlords* (London, 1881), 378.
[4] W. H. R. Curtler, *A Short History of English Agriculture* (Oxford, 1909), 295.
[5] Op. cit., 294.

or where large towns offered a local market, the situation was tolerable, though it was clear that rents, which were based on more prosperous conditions, would have to come down. The decade of the eighties saw a readjustment along these lines, which was vividly portrayed by the Royal Commission of 1895:[6]

"Between 1880 and 1884 the number of farms given up either in despair or for reasons over which the occupiers had no control was stated to have been enormous. On poor estates no attempt was made to bring the land round, it was left alone and gradually "tumbled down" to such coarse and inferior herbage as nature produced. . . A regular panic set in; some tenants who had hitherto weathered the storm refused to renew their leases upon any terms, while others continued from year to year at large reductions. . . Rents were reduced between 1880 and 1886 from 25 to as much as 80 per cent."

The second way out of their difficulties lay in a shift from intensive to extensive cultivation, from the production of cereals to grazing. The extent to which this was done is best shown by statistics of land use in Great Britain.

Year	Arable land	Permanent grass
	(millions of acres)	
1871	18.4	12.4
1881	17.4	14.6
1891	16.4	16.4
1901	15.6	16.7
1911	14.6	17.4
1914	14.3	17.6

There is shown here a decline in arable land of over 4 million acres between 1871 and 1914. The decrease was greatest in the case of wheat, but it affected all corn crops[7] except oats. The area planted in wheat fell from 3,700,000 acres in 1870 to 2,500,000 in 1890, and 1,900,000 in 1911, or about one-half of the total acreage withdrawn from the plough. The lowest point in wheat acreage was reached in 1901 with about 1,600,000 acres, but after that there was a slight recovery to 1914.

The transition from arable cultivation to grazing took time and involved certain losses. Several years were needed to convert cultivated land to pasture, less home-grown food was produced, rents were reduced, and since fewer laborers were needed for the new type of farming a rural exodus to the towns took place. Cereal growing was given up except in areas of high productivity, and attention was

[6] *Royal Commission on Agricultural Depression, 1895, Final Report*, 8.
[7] These include wheat, oats, barley, rye, beans, and peas.

concentrated on the production of beef and dairy products, in which British farmers had almost a local monopoly. But even in these lines foreign competition made inroads on the British markets, except for raw milk. With improvements in refrigerating processes and the steady cheapening of transportation there poured in cheese from Wisconsin, poultry from Russia, butter from Denmark, the Cape, Australia, and New Zealand, and eggs from various quarters. Frozen meat and chilled mutton continued to arrive in increasing quantities.

A second crisis in British agriculture took place, which was only less severe than that of the seventies. The despair of British farmers led to the appointment of a Royal Commission on Agricultural Depression in 1893, whose report graphically depicts the situation. "It showed that the value of produce had diminished by nearly one-half (since 1882), while the cost of production had rather increased than diminished; that quantities of corn-land had passed out of cultivation, that its restoration, while the present prices prevailed, was economically impossible; that its adaption to other uses required an immediate outlay which few owners could afford to make. Scarcely one bright feature relieved the gloom of the outlook. Foreign competition had falsified all predictions. . . Yet the evidence collected by the Commission established some important facts. It proved that many men, possessed of ample capital and energy, who occupied the best equipped farms, enjoyed the greatest liberty in cropping, kept the best stock, and were able to continue high farming, had weathered the storm even on heavy land; that small occupiers employing no labour but their own had managed to pull through; that, on suitable soils, market gardening and fruit-farming had proved profitable." [8]

In the meantime some steps had been taken by Parliament to relieve agriculture of burdens, in so far as this could be done by legislation. Grants were made in aid of local taxation, and tithes were transferred from occupiers to owners (1891). Greater mobility was sought in land transfer in the Settled Lands Act (1882). Rates on the transport by railways of home and foreign produce were equalized. And in 1889 an Agricultural Department was established with a Minister of Agriculture. But legislation alone was powerless to meet the new conditions; this had to be done by the British farmer himself.

The third step in the readjustment of British agriculture was now taken. This consisted in more diversified and intensive farming with

[8] R. E. P. Ernle, *English Farming, Past and Present* (London, 1936), 383. By permission of the publishers, Longmans, Green and Company, New York.

a view to quality production. The raising of cattle proved to be profitable and farmers with adequate capital engaged in pedigree stock breeding. High prices were obtained for English pedigree rams and bulls, which were exported to Argentina and other countries, where deterioration of flocks and herds from inbreeding was feared. Dairying, market gardening, flower growing, and poultry keeping were substituted for cereal crops. In dairy farming the improvement was especially marked, stock-breeding societies were formed, and breeds of milk cows were differentiated from beef cattle. On the drained fens of Lincolnshire potatoes and bulbs took the place of wheat, while near every city market gardens supplied brussels, cabbages, peas, and other vegetables to urban consumers. Fruit growing was undertaken on a large scale on scientific principles. The cities proved good markets for fresh fruit; the surplus went into jam factories, which were exceptionally profitable at this time because of the low price of sugar. The rising standard of living in the nation also absorbed increasing quantities of milk, eggs, butter, cheese, and poultry. In spite of foreign competition in practically every one of these lines the British farmer found an adequate market for home-grown supplies among the wealthier purchasers; imported articles provided cheap food for the workers. By 1906 the transition in English farming had been practically completed and from then to 1914 agriculture enjoyed a period of solid if not brilliant prosperity.

Farm management. The necessity of reducing the costs of production gave an impetus to the larger use of farm machinery. "The most striking feature of agricultural progress within the last twenty years," wrote Caird [9] in 1878, "has been the general introduction of reaping machines, one of which can do the work of ten men." Owing to their high cost, however, these elaborate machines only slowly supplanted the inexpensive hand tools; indeed as late as 1895 the old-fashioned saw-edged shearing hook was still in use in Yorkshire. Machines for the preliminary work of ploughing and cultivating had been invented and generally introduced during the earlier part of the century, but these were now improved and adapted to specialized uses. Scarifiers, clodcrushers, steam diggers, and cultivators lightened the work of cereal production, while potato diggers, sheep-shearing machines, and power presses for hay and straw aided the worker in other lines. Haymaking was very late in the use of mechanical appliances, and it was not until the last quarter of the nineteenth century that the scythe, rake, and pitchfork were superseded. Then mowing machines, tedders, and horse rakes took

[9] J. Caird, *The Landed Interest and the Supply of Food* (London, 1878), 16.

their places. In 1894 the great sweep rake was introduced from the United States; this gathered up the hay and carried it to the stack, while an elevator hoisted it to the rick.

The dairy industry showed the most conspicuous improvement. The cream separator was introduced in 1879 and worked a revolution in butter and cheese making. Until this time all the processes of butter making had been carried on by hand, and as a result a regular supply of uniform quality was difficult to obtain; wholesalers therefore preferred standardized foreign products. Milking machines were never popular, as they were difficult to keep clean. British farmers did not record the butter-fat content of their milk and consequently had no dependable basis for improvement of their herds. Feeding was, however, improved with the general use of ensilage. Wire fencing and corrugated iron replaced the wasteful hedges and flimsy wooden farm buildings; the huge barn and numerous outbuildings were compressed into a single substantial barn. Power was increasingly furnished by internal-combustion engines and the number of horses declined, while oxen disappeared as draft animals on the farm.

Other improvements were made as the agricultural depression forced a reorganization of British agriculture. Drainage reclaimed much wet land; Caird estimated that some four or five million acres had been drained by 1878 out of some ten million that needed it. After that the work continued at a slower rate. There was much experimentation in the use of artificial fertilizers. Guano, which had been very popular, was replaced by nitrate of soda, and by ammoniacal, phosphate, and other fertilizers. With low prices for his crops, however, the farmer was inclined to economize on artificial fertilizers, which meant a cash outlay, and to rely upon farm manure.

British agriculture had shown considerable elasticity in adjusting itself to changing conditions, as shown by the shift from arable to pasture farming. Similar elasticity was exhibited in varying systems of crop rotation, although Brodrick thought that rent-paying farmers were encumbered by restrictive covenants. The backbone still remained Arthur Young's four-course Norfolk system (turnips, barley, clover, wheat), but this was modified in different districts according to local needs.

Rural depopulation. An important result of the shift in land utilization and of the greater use of machinery was the movement of agricultural laborers from the farms to the industrial towns. Owing to changes in the census classification the statistics are not strictly comparable, but the general trend is clear. This is shown in the following table:

PERSONS ENGAGED ON FARMS IN ENGLAND AND WALES

Occupation	1871	1881	1891	1901	1911
Farmers and graziers	249,735	223,943	223,610	224,299	208,761
Relatives of farmers and graziers assisting on farms	76,466	75,197	67,287	107,783	97,689
Farm bailiffs or foremen	16,476	19,377	18,205	22,662	22,141
Agricultural workers	962,348	870,798	780,707	620,986	643,117
	1,305,025	1,189,315	1,089,809	975,730	971,708

The causes of this migration were deep-seated and cannot be explained wholly by reference to foreign competition and agricultural depression. It is true that the shift from cereal growing to grazing lessened the demand for labor, while the larger use of improved machinery on the arable land which remained under cultivation also displaced labor. The workers who no longer found employment on the land sought this in industry. But the supply of agricultural labor fell off even more rapidly than the demand, so that in some parts of the country, at least at certain seasons, farmers were unable to obtain the necessary help. The explanation is to be found in social as well as economic factors. In the first place the position of the rural worker was unattractive; his wages, which had been rising fairly steadily from 1850 to 1874, fell again almost to the level of the sixties, after which they recovered somewhat. But both the money and the real wages were low even at the best, and were frequently eked out by the earnings of the wife, who worked at home for urban industrial establishments. "Everywhere," exclaimed Rider Haggard,[10] "they are flocking to the towns . . . chiefly owing to low wages." Housing was poor, in spite of low rents, and the whole standard of rural life was empty and low. In contrast with these drab conditions and the dreary monotony of the country the town offered bright lights, amusements, and social intercourse, and, for those who wished to take advantage of them, educational opportunities, access to art museums, libraries, and similar attractions.

But the most important reason for rural depopulation — and one that was peculiar to England — was the practical impossibility of social advancement. There was no economic ladder in rural areas such as existed in most other countries or in English cities; an agricultural laborer could not hope to rise in the scale, but must remain an agricultural laborer. This was a serious defect in the English agricultural structure. Closely connected with this was the almost

[10] H. R. Haggard, *Rural England* (2 vols. London, 1906), II, 569.

servile attitude of the workers to their employers, and the expectation if not the insistence upon such an attitude on the part of the latter. With the spread of education and of newspapers the more enterprising among the younger generation became extremely discontented and left the farms. "It seems safe to conclude," wrote Perris,[11] "that those left behind in the country were the older, weaker, more helpless, and servile members of a class whose ancient safeguards were now utterly destroyed, the most neglected and despised class in the population, and the one that had gained least by a century of material progress."

Concentration of land ownership. A striking feature of the agricultural structure of Great Britain was the concentration of the ownership of the land in the hands of a small number of persons. Just what the distribution was no one knew until the appearance of the so-called "New Domesday Book" in 1874, which was intended to furnish precise information on this point. Unfortunately, it contained so many errors of fact and interpretation that its figures call for a great many qualifications, but its general conclusions may be accepted. It appeared that in 1874 there were 972,836 proprietors, owning 33,013,514 acres; but 703,289, with 151,171 acres, were returned as possessors of less than one acre each. If these persons be subtracted there were left 269,547 owners of 32,862,340 acres. The distribution of the land within this group is shown in the following table:

Size of holding (acres)	Number of owners	Size of holding (acres)	Number of owners
1-10	121,983	500- 1,000	4799
10-50	72,640	1,000- 5,000	4534
50-100	25,809	5,000-20,000	804
100-500	32,317	20,000 and over	70

These figures were represented by the compilers as being only "proximately accurate," but a well-informed critic [12] contended that instead of being "a perfect record of 'owners,' the New Domesday Book is, at best, an imperfect record of estates." They did not include lands not taxed (which belonged to public bodies), nor common land, woods, and wastes (most of which were held by large landowners); and they counted men who held land in several districts as separate owners in each district. There was thus an exaggeration of the number of small owners. A careful analysis of the returns by Brodrick led to the conclusion that probably fewer than 4000 persons, owning estates of 1000 acres and over, possessed

[11] G. H. Perris, *The Industrial History of Modern England* (New York, 1914), 361.
[12] G. C. Brodrick, *English Land and English Landlords* (London, 1881), 163.

nearly 19,000,000 acres or four-sevenths of the area included in the returns; and that nearly half of the land belonged to 1½ per cent of all landowners.[13]   These conditions offered a striking contrast to those in France and Germany.

The large estates had been protected both by law and custom. Entail, that is the settlement of land inalienably on a person or his descendants, had long been obsolete, but a custom of family settlement had taken its place, whereby the heir, instead of receiving his estate with full power to sell or divide it, would be given a mere tenancy for life, his son being designated as the ultimate owner. If this arrangement were continued from generation to generation the estate would be held intact and would not come on the market. On the contrary, it would probably be enlarged by additional purchases.   To this must be added the right of primogeniture in case of intestacy.

The changes that took place in English agriculture after 1870, and other factors, gradually forced alterations both in legislation and in practice.   It had usually been possible to sell part of the estate, even under family settlements, to discharge mortgages, but not until the Settled Land Acts of 1882 to 1890 were tenants for life and other limited owners given the power of using the land to the best advantage by sale or lease.   Custom was strong enough, however, to prevent this legislation from having much effect for another quarter century, and little land came upon the market during this interval.

The effect of the great estates upon the efficient utilization of the land can easily be exaggerated.   Except for the devotion of certain areas to parks or as hunting preserves, little land seems to have been withheld from productive use by the large landowners.   Apologists for the English system have pointed to the expensive experimental work carried on by men of large capital and the unpaid social services rendered by the owners of large estates, which they considered sufficient justification.   Popular opinion would not be convinced, however, and there was much agitation for legislation to break up the concentrated holdings.   During the eighties the single-tax movement made considerable headway, but the fall in rents and in the value of land lessened the force of this agitation. Practically nothing was done to change the essentials of the prevailing system.

In the discussion of the land system, two problems were frequently confused.   One dealt with the question of ownership and the other with use.   Those who wished to break up the large estates pointed to the 5,600,000 small proprietors in France, or the yeomen farmers in eighteenth-century England, and insisted that outright ownership

[13] Op. cit., 165, 166.

of their land by small farmers was the only solution. The other group said that ownership was of less importance than right conditions of use. Reform was to be had by observing the three "F's" — fair rent, fixity of tenure, and free sale. The problem of fair rents would be met by providing for appeal to the courts and judicial decisions. Fixity of tenure presented a more perplexing problem. Annual leases were customary in England, though in Scotland the nineteen year lease was usual. It is probably true that landowners had no incentive to refuse to renew the yearly tenancy of satisfactory tenants and that many of these remained on the same holding from one generation to the next; but their status was uncertain. Their position was, moreover, complicated by another feature of the English land system, namely tenants' improvements. Except as he was protected by custom or by economic interest, the tenant had no legal right to notice to quit nor compensation for improvements other than the growing crops. But under the English system it was customary for tenants to make improvements, sometimes substantial ones, such as clearing, draining, fencing, and fertilizing the land, and they demanded legislation that would guarantee compensation for the unexhausted value of these improvements. The Agricultural Holdings Act of 1875 met these difficulties by legalizing compensation for tenants' improvements and regulating the notice to quit. This was merely permissive, but in 1883 another act made compensation compulsory and marked a turning point in land law. Landowners had resisted this movement since they regarded their property rights and freedom of contract as more important than tenant-rights, but Parliament did not agree and subsequently greatly extended the application of the compulsory principle.

Allotments. There was a growing feeling that land must be made available to the agricultural laborer, and that it should be possible for persons with limited capital to obtain small tracts for farming. To achieve these ends two devices were promoted, allotments and small holdings. Allotments were little pieces of land, less than an acre, designed to furnish a supplementary source of income to the agricultural laborer, or to urban artisans or shopkeepers. Small holdings, on the contrary, ranging from one to fifty acres, were intended to afford the sole means of support of the holder.

During the half century before 1870 a good many allotments had been made by private owners, but irksome conditions had often been attached to their use and the rents charged had been extremely high. It was urged that a regular supply of allotments should be furnished at reasonable rents and without conditions. Attempts to achieve this through administrative compulsion failed, but voluntary action by landlords produced better results. A Parliamentary Return in 1886, which can be regarded as only approximately correct, gave the following results: [14]

ALLOTMENTS IN GREAT BRITAIN, 1886

	Number
Under ⅛ acre	134,932
⅛ and under ¼ acre	117,766
¾ and under 1 acre	105,097
1 to 4 acres, both inclusive	36,712
Total allotments, detached from cottages	394,507
Gardens attached to cottages	272,567
Potato grounds	111,146
Cow runs	17,302
Grand Total	795,522

If the Scottish laborers be deducted, namely 46,223, there were some 750,000 workingmen in England and Wales who had the use of some land. At this date there were probably about 850,000 agricultural laborers, so it would seem that most of these were cared for. More than three-fourths of the detached allotments were stated to be within half a mile of the cottages. In addition to these, railway companies had furnished their employees with 45,567 allotments and gardens.

Parliament was not willing to trust this matter to the good will of the landlords, and extended the compulsory principle. In 1894 the newly created parish councils were empowered to acquire land compulsorily for allotments, and in 1907 the Small Holdings and Allotments Act made it obligatory on the council of any borough, urban district, or parish to provide allotments sufficient to meet the local demand. By the end of 1912 about one-fourth of these councils had acted.

Small holdings. The desirability of allotments was generally admitted, from both a social and an economic point of view. But, while they improved the condition of the worker, they contributed little to the solution of agrarian problems. From the time of Arthur Young reformers had urged the reconstitution of a class of small yeomen proprietors, and after the failure of the early allotment acts this movement was given new vigor under the leadership of Jesse Collings. In 1892 Parliament passed an ineffective permissive Small Holdings Act, which authorized County Councils to acquire land and to sell it in tracts of one acre to fifty acres. This

[14] W. H. R. Curtler, *The Enclosure and Redistribution of Our Land* (Oxford, 1920), 282.

act projected into the movement the much debated question of ownership versus lease. There may be, and undoubtedly are, social advantages in the existence of a class of cultivating owners, who would constitute a democratic agrarian middle class, but the permanence of such a group depends upon two circumstances: the comparative advantages of ownership as against a system of leasing, and the most profitable size of a farm. For a man with limited capital it might be more desirable to rent a farm and put all of his capital into equipment and improvements rather than to tie up a considerable portion in the purchase of the land. Given a fair rental and fixity of tenure, the lease system offered some real advantages, especially in a period of declining land values.

Further legislation proceeded along less doctrinaire lines and attempted to meet the problem in realistic fashion. Local authorities were given compulsory powers to acquire land, improve, and resell or lease it in small holdings. Between 1870 and 1914 the number of small holdings remained about stationary, showing that the demand was satisfactorily met. About a third of the holders were agricultural laborers, the other two-thirds being small village tradesmen or others. As a solution of the agrarian problem the movement fell far short of the hopes of its advocates.

Size of farms. The most desirable size of a farm from the standpoint of efficient operation is determined by economic considerations and not by land laws or ownership. Under a system of either proprietorship or tenancy the farm operator endeavors to obtain a holding which, under existing conditions of agricultural technique, prices, and costs, will yield the largest unit return. The English lease system permitted considerable elasticity in the arrangement of holdings, and it was generally believed that, with the introduction of improved agricultural machinery and more scientific methods, the size of the average farm had adjusted itself to changing conditions. Curtler stated that "The views of landowners on the advantages of the consolidation of farms, which had held the field until the agricultural depression about 1875," were greatly modified after that date and many reverted to smaller holdings where practicable. The census returns for 1885 and subsequent years for the first time showed the exact situation.

These figures show a falling off, between 1885 and 1913, of both the very small holdings of 20 acres or less and of the large farms above 300 acres. The middle group gained at the expense of the two extremes, though the total number of farms decreased. Large farms were most profitable where the land and the climate were specially suited to the growing of cereals, to mixed husbandry, or to the raising of pedigree stock, and where the topography per-

SIZE OF FARMS IN ENGLAND AND WALES

		Number of farms		Total acreage (in thousands)	
Acres	1885	1895	1913	1885	1913
1-5	114,273	97,818	92,302	325	285
5-20	126,674	126,714	122,117	} 3,889	{ 1,373
21-50	73,472	74,846	78,027		2,623
51-100	54,937	56,791	59,287	4,021	4,325
101-300	67,034	68,277	69,431	11,519	11,786
Above 300	16,608	16,021	14,513	7,955	6,737
Total	452,998	440,467	435,677	27,709	27,129

mitted the use of agricultural machinery. Otherwise, and particularly in the vicinity of large cities, small holdings with vegetable market gardens, fruit raising, and poultry breeding were more profitable. In other words, where an intensive use of capital was demanded, the large holding was superior; but where labor, and especially interested and intelligent labor, was required, then the small holding was successful. There was, however, insufficient mobility of land for purely economic considerations to have free play.

Other improvements. Certain agencies of agricultural improvement, such as co-operation and credit-banks, were much less developed in England than on the continent. The explanation is probably to be found in the conservatism and individualism of the British farmer. In 1913 there were only 478 co-operative agricultural societies in England and Wales; these had a membership of 48,000 and an annual turnover of nearly £2,000,000. Most of them were co-operative dairies, but even in this industry only a fraction of the producers were members. Even less developed were agricultural credit-banks, which had proved so valuable in Germany and France; there were only 45 such institutions in England and Wales in 1915.

Although the Rothamsted Experimental Station, established in 1837, was the first institution of its kind, agricultural education had been neglected. Until 1890 only one incorporated institution for agricultural education — the Royal Agricultural College of Cirencester — existed in Great Britain. In 1889 the Board of Agriculture was created and in the following year County Councils were empowered to provide for technical instruction. The more progressive Councils instituted lecture courses and classes, and some of them combined to set up colleges or agricultural departments in existing universities. A further advance was made possible by the Development Fund Act of 1909, which set aside £2,000,000 for agricultural research and other purposes. Farm Institutes were organized, which gave short courses with lectures, and other work. The number of persons who took advantage of these opportunities was, however, small.

The supply of food. However disastrous to the farmer and land-owner the importation of competing agricultural products may have been, the increased quantities and low prices of food were of great benefit to the mass of the people. Between 1851 and 1889 the total annual grain supply, both English and foreign, rose from 317 lbs. per capita to 400 lbs. and that of meat from 90 to 119 lbs. "The average value of the imports of food per head in the period 1859–65 was about 25s.; in the period 1901–07, 65s." [15] There was a growing dependence upon foreign supplies as the population grew beyond the productive capacity of British farmers to meet the demand. This was especially true of cereals; thus the imports of wheat more than doubled between 1870 and 1910 and those of barley and oats increased fifty per cent. Britain became increasingly dependent upon foreign trade for her food, while the means with which to purchase these supplies was obtained from expanding manufacturing industries.

Agricultural self-sufficiency was evidently impossible, but proposals were not lacking for legislation that would give agriculture a measure of protection against foreign competition. These came to a head in 1903, when Joseph Chamberlain launched a program of tariff reform, which included protective duties on agricultural products as well as on some manufactures. No action was taken in the period to 1914. The benefits of cheap food outweighed all the arguments of the agricultural interests.

2. GOVERNMENT EXTENDS A HELPING HAND IN GERMANY

Agricultural holdings. In common with other industrialized countries the agricultural population of Germany declined during this period. Including forestry and fisheries, agriculture claimed 19,225,455 persons in 1882, 18,501,307 in 1895, and 17,681,176 in 1907. This represented a decline from 42.5 per cent of the total population at the first date to 29.6 per cent of the last. A further analysis reveals that most of the loss occurred in the group of agricultural laborers, while that of operating farmers remained practically stationary. These devoted themselves increasingly to purely agricultural work, since such tasks as building, baking, slaughtering, cartage, and others formerly performed by the agricultural labor force were taken over by urban industry, which also provided tools, machines, wagons, and similar things. The decline indicated

[15] W. H. R. Curtler, *A Short History of English Agriculture* (Oxford, 1909), 330.

in the figures given above seems therefore to be partly statistical, due to increasing separation of occupations and reclassification.

German agriculture was carried on during this period primarily by land-owning peasants in the west and by large cultivating land-owners in the east. The size of holdings and the relative importance of each are shown in the following table:

Size	Per cent of holdings			Per cent of cultivated land		
	1882	1895	1907	1882	1895	1907
Under 1¼ acres	} 58.0	33.3	36.3	} 5.7	1.1	1.1
1¼-5 acres		24.9	22.6		4.5	4.3
5-12½ acres	18.6	18.3	17.5	10.0	10.1	10.4
12½-50 acres	17.6	18.0	18.6	28.8	29.9	32.7
50-250 acres	5.3	5.0	4.6	31.1	30.3	29.3
250 acres and more	.5	.5	.4	24.4	24.1	22.2

German statistics distinguish five rather clearly marked groups among these holdings. Those containing less than 5 acres are called small (*Zwerg*) holdings, those with 5 to 12½ acres "little" holdings, those with 12½ to 50 acres "middle" holdings, with 50 to 250 acres "big" holdings, and those over 250 acres large holdings. The total number of farms grew from 5,276,344 in 1882 to 5,736,882 in 1907. International comparisons are difficult, because of the different dates for which the various countries gather statistics, the different conditions, and for other reasons. Much depends on the kind of farming — whether market gardening and vineyards or cereal production and cattle raising — and on the agricultural policy. Nor are the limits of the various groups the same in all countries.

From these figures it appears that in 1907 about 59 per cent of the properties were in the hands of small holders of 5 acres or less, that the peasant holdings (5-250 acres) constituted about 40 per cent, and that the large holdings of over 250 acres were less than 1 per cent of all. When, however, we turn to the statistics of acreage the picture changes, for the small holders cultivated only 5 per cent of the farm land, the peasants about 72 per cent while the remaining quarter was in the hands of the great landowners. The last group had declined somewhat in this twenty-five-year period, though in the six eastern provinces of East and West Prussia, Brandenburg, Pomerania, Posen, and Silesia they still ruled supreme, running up over 60 per cent in Mecklenburg. On the other hand the smaller farms of under 250 acres made up 80 per cent of the holdings in Bavaria, and over two-thirds in Oldenburg, Saxony, and Wurtemberg. The size of the holdings stood in direct relation to the density of the population and also to the type of agriculture carried on in a particular district. In the southwestern part of Germany, where grapes, fruit, tobacco, or hops were raised, a small holding of 5 acres would support a family. West of the Elbe, moreover, were to be found the populous industrial districts, where urban centers furnished good markets for the products of small farmers and market gardens, and where transportation facilities were plentiful. Some of these small holdings were, moreover, cultivated by persons who combined agriculture with some other occupation.

East of the Elbe, on the other hand, the colder climate and the less fertile soil led to a concentration on cereal production. This was the grain zone, over two-thirds of the country's wheat and rye coming from this section. In the great even stretches of heavy soil such crops could be more economically raised by capitalistic methods and consequently large holdings were the rule. A typical estate might contain 2000 acres.

But natural conditions alone do not explain the differences in the size of holdings in the various regions. These resulted from a long evolution in which, along with climate, soil, machinery and prices, such factors as legal relations, political conditions, and training have been important. All these factors together resulted in the predominance of the large holding in the northeast, of the small and medium peasant holding in the west and southwest, and of the big peasant holding in the northwest.

Ownership and tenancy. Most of the land was farmed by peasant owners with the aid of their families or, in the case of the big peasants, with hired labor. In 1907 owners constituted 73 per cent of the smallest and 82 per cent of the largest holdings, but in the middle group they were predominant, holding 87 per cent of the medium peasant properties and 93 per cent of those held by the big peasants. The problem of tenancy scarcely existed in Germany during this period, the only real tenant farms being found in the large estates. The total rented area was only 18 per cent of the land devoted to agriculture. Germany differed in this respect from England, Belgium and most European countries and resembled the Scandinavian countries. Where land was leased the rent was practically always paid in money. Payment of a part of the produce (share-cropping in the United States, *métayage* in France) was so unimportant that it was not included in the agricultural census of 1907.

Land utilization. In 1913 only 61.5 per cent of Germany's 134,000,000 acres were cultivated. Over a quarter was in forest or woodland, for which land too poor for grazing was used, and a small fraction was mountain or poor grazing land. The rest was used for non-agricultural purposes. These figures are in striking contrast with those for England, where nearly three-quarters of the land was cultivated, or France where the proportion was even greater. The explanation must be found in adverse climatic conditions and the poor quality of the soil.

Of the land under cultivation in 1913 almost a third (32.2 per cent) was devoted to pasture, hay and green fodders for livestock, nearly a half (46 per cent) to cereals, about 18 per cent to potatoes, and the remainder to root crops, beans and peas, gardens, fruit and vineyards. During this period there was a slow but steady encroachment of arable upon grazing and pasture land, but a larger gain was made by the abandonment of the wasteful three-field system of cultivation and the utilization of land that had previously lain fallow. This was reduced from 9 per cent of the cultivated land in 1878 to 2 per cent in 1913.

The most striking feature of this period was the enormous increase in the productivity of German agriculture, especially in arable farming. This was obtained by better farming rather than by addition to the land under cultivation, as is strikingly shown in the following table, which gives the yield per acre of certain crops for two periods:

AVERAGE YIELD OF SELECTED CROPS
(in bushels)

Period	Rye	Wheat	Barley	Oats	Potatoes	Hay (cwt.)
1878–82	15.8	19.4	24.8	32.5	113.8	22.5
1909–13	28.9	31.9	38.6	55.0	203.6	33.7

The crops just given are those in which the greatest increases took place, but there was also a substantial growth of some other crops, such as sugar beets. On the other hand, some raw material crops, as flax and hemp, fell off. A broad view shows, however, that the average increase in agricultural production was about 65 per cent as against a population growth of about 41 per cent. In 1912 the yield per acre of all the crops mentioned was not only greater in Germany than in Russia, Austria or the United States, countries of extensive agriculture, but also in France, the typical land of intensive cultivation. The causes of this increased productivity will be discussed in a later paragraph; here we are concerned only with the facts. It may, however, be pertinent to ask the question at this point as to whether the improvement was to be found primarily on the peasant holdings or on those of the large landowners. Professor Clapham [16] answers this question.

"The peasant was slow to learn how he could get the maximum

[16] Op. cit., 219. By permission of the publishers, Cambridge University Press, and of The Macmillan Company, New York.

yield per acre out of what land he did cultivate. On the great estates this vital figure was improving steadily in the fifty years from 1860 to 1910. . . It was improving also on peasant land, but more slowly." For purposes of comparison Professor Clapham gives the yields of certain crops in Mecklenburg, where 60 per cent of the land were in large holdings of over 250 acres, and in Bavaria, where nearly 70 per cent of the holdings were under 50 acres.

AVERAGE YIELD PER ACRE, 1902–1911
(in bushels)

District	Rye	Wheat	Barley	Oats	Potatoes	Meadow hay (tons)
Mecklenburg	28.5	35.2	41.6	58.9	277.7	4.1
Bavaria	25.1	23.4	31.7	43.4	173.5	4.9

"These figures, if not exact, are telling. Where agricultural knowledge is least needed, in the hay field, Bavaria leads. Everywhere else it is hopelessly outdistanced, worst of all in the best crop — wheat. . . Even in potatoes the peasant fares badly."

The verdict seems to run heavily against peasant farming, but this is scarcely fair if it is counted in terms of personal efficiency, for many other factors combined to give the large farm an advantage in all these crops. Cereal farming was most economically carried on by large scale methods with improved machinery, which meant large capital and access to capital markets; in these respects the large landowner enjoyed undoubted advantages over his small peasant competitor. The same was true, in only slighter degrees, with the other crops. In intensive agriculture such as market gardening, fruit growing, and vineyards, the small peasant proprietor made a better showing. In view of the fact, however, that the leading crops were those calling for the contribution which the large scale operator could best make, the technical superiority of this type of holding must be admitted. The actual operation of the great estates was, however, unsatisfactory. Cereal production was subject to great fluctuations in yield and price and was essentially speculative. Wheat growers were especially hard hit by the great fall in the cost of ocean transportation. Thus the freight on a ton of wheat from New York to Liverpool (slightly more to Hamburg) declined between 1875 and 1910 from 30.7 to 6.3 marks. The great estates were heavily mortgaged, often beyond the capacity of the land to meet the charges. Altogether the economic position of the Junker in the northeast was a precarious one.

Livestock. It is surprising that in a country as densely settled as Germany, and where the population was growing so rapidly, the growth of livestock industry should almost have paralleled the increase in crop production. The expansion is shown in the following table: [17]

LIVESTOCK IN GERMANY
(in millions)

Year	Horses	Cattle	Sheep	Swine	Goats
1873	3.3	15.8	29.9	7.1	2.3
1883	3.5	15.8	19.2	9.2	2.6
1892	3.8	17.6	13.6	12.2	3.1
1900	4.2	18.9	9.7	16.8	3.3
1913	4.6	20.9	5.5	25.7	3.5

The really remarkable increase in meat production is not fully brought out in these figures, for not only were the numbers growing but the weight of the animals was increasing. Between 1883 and 1912 the live weight of cattle rose from 706 to 792 pounds, of swine from 255 to 277, and of sheep from 75 to 92. At the same time, by improvements in breeding and feeding, the animals were brought to maturity in a shorter time, and the quality of the meat was thereby improved. The amazing increase in the number of swine stood in close connection with the other branches of agriculture: first with the increase in the dairy industry, from which the buttermilk and sour milk served as feedstuffs; second, with the expansion of sugar beet production and potato distilleries where waste products also constituted animal fodder. Pigs were particularly popular on small farms.

In striking contrast with the increase in other lines stands the revolutionary decrease in the number of sheep. The explanation for this was to be found partly in the small demand for mutton and partly in the absence of protection to wool, which was opposed by the textile manufacturers. The price of wool fell disastrously, especially of the fine Saxony wool, as changes in technique permitted the wearing of coarser, cheaper grades, and changes in fashion lessened the demand. From sheep raising there was therefore a shift to the growing of potatoes and sugar beets, and to other branches of animal husbandry, which offered larger profits.

Writing in 1887, when the fierce international competition had rendered the position of the grain grower wellnigh hopeless, Professor Sering [18] proclaimed that the salvation of German agriculture lay in an extension of animal husbandry. The growing of vegetables, hops, wine, beets, and potatoes, he thought, offered little

[17] Von der Goltz, *Geschichte der Landwirtschaft*, II, 325.
[18] M. Sering, *Die Landwirtschaftliche Konkurrenz Nordamerikas in Gegenwart und Zukunft* (Berlin, 1887), 711.

hope, for any considerable expansion in the production of these would so greatly reduce the prices that they would prove unprofitable. The best promise was to be found in the development of the dairy industry. Although Professor Sering did not prove a particularly good prophet, the number of cows and goats ("the little man's cow") showed an increase, which, however, did not keep pace with the growth of the population.

The modern milk industry in Germany dates from the early seventies. The first journal devoted to this subject was published in 1871 and in 1874 the first dairy union was established in Bremen. Better breeding, feeding, and care led to an increase in milk per cow, from an annual average yield of 1900 quarts in 1883 to 2500 in 1906, and after 1890 greater attention was paid to cleanliness in production and marketing. Milk-control and cow-testing unions began about 1895. The dairy industry never developed in Germany as it did in neighboring Denmark. After 1900 certainly the relation between outlay and return, owing largely to the increase in the price of feedstuffs, favored grain growing and hog production rather than beef and butter.[19] So long as the farmer could get adequate prices for products which he could easily raise he was not going to turn to a line so technically difficult as dairying.

The development of the livestock industry as a whole was a result of the partial shift from arable farming to the production of animal products, which are more difficult to transport and in which international competition was therefore not so serious. This was further stimulated by an increase in the urban demand for meat, which was made possible by a rise in the standard of living of the factory workers. In 1913 the value of German animal products was almost twice that of vegetable products. German agriculture managed to fit itself into the international pattern of the agricultural market without essential sacrifice of its own development.

Forestry. As already noted, the forest covered in 1913 somewhat over a quarter of the agricultural land or 35,000,000 acres. This large area resulted from the forestry policy of the German states, which owned about a third of the forests and planted poor land with trees if it could be shown that the gross returns from timber were likely to exceed those from grazing. Somewhat less than one-half of the forests were owned by private individuals, but their administration was strictly controlled and followed the pattern of the government. Cutting must be replaced by new planting. The forests were regarded as essential to agriculture by the prevention of floods and the possible amelioration of the climate. They also

---

[19] M. Sering, et al., *Die deutsche Landwirtschaft unter volks- und weltwirtschaftlichen Gesichtspunkten* (Berlin, 1932), 9.

provided much winter employment for agricultural laborers who worked in the fields during the summer months. Their social significance was considerable, as they afforded opportunity for the walking trips of which Germans were especially fond.

Farm management. The mechanization of agriculture went on rapidly during this period. The essential facts for the more important machines are presented in the following table:

Year	Steam ploughs	Steam threshing machines	Other threshing machines	Sowing-planting machines	Reaping machines
1882	836	75,690	298,367	63,842	19,634
1895	1696	259,384	596,869	169,465	35,084
1907	2995	488,867	947,003	290,031	301,325

As might be expected, the large farms of 250 acres and over made the greatest use of labor saving machines, over 74 per cent of them using steam threshing machines in 1907, about 82 per cent having reaping machines, while the planting machines averaged over one to each farm. But the big peasants with farms of 100 to 250 acres also made large use of agricultural machinery, especially of threshers and reapers. Most of the machines were owned by the operators, only the steam ploughs and steam threshers being rented out. Other farm operations such as the harvesting of hay, the cultivation of root crops, and the digging of potatoes were also generally done by machines, especially on the larger farms. The ploughs, harrows, cultivators, drilling, threshing, potato-digging, and feed-cutting machines were mainly German made, but reaping and mowing machinery and horse-rakes were largely American importations.[20]

The small holder, with less than 5 acres, depended almost entirely upon hand labor. Handicapped by poverty and lack of fodder he was unable to make extensive use of animal power, and frequently his only cow was used to pull the plow or cultivator. Hand labor was extensively used in market gardens, vineyards, and in sugar beet growing, where the operations of thinning, topping and gathering were done largely by hand. For these purposes female labor was chiefly employed, to an extent unfamiliar in England and the United States.

The great increase of the productivity of German agriculture, already noted, is to be explained not so much by the use of machinery as by the skilful application of fertilizers. The science of agricultural chemistry had been founded by Liebig in 1840, but the full application of his principles had not been made. During this period,

[20] "Market for Agricultural Implements and Vehicles," *Special Consular Reports*, Vol. XXVII (Washington, 1903), 33.

however, a new impetus was given to the movement and the productivity of the soil was greatly improved. First among the resources to be applied, potash must be named. Germany was fortunate in owning enormous deposits of this salt, which were found to be especially valuable in maintaining the fertility of light sandy soil, which occurred over much of the country. Between 1890 and 1910 the use of potash, stimulated by the powerful Potash Syndicate, increased tenfold, from 220,000 to 2,220,000 tons.

A second essential fertilizer came from industry; this was phosphorus, which was obtained from basic slag of the steel industry. The impure Lorraine ores contained too much phosphorus to permit their use for steel making by the Bessemer process. In 1879, however, the basic open hearth method was invented by the Englishman Thomas, which utilized the phosphoric ores. It was discovered that the slag from the furnaces, if pulverized, constituted an effective fertilizer. The consumption of Thomas phosphate meal, as it was called, increased from 400,000 tons in 1890 to 1,430,000 in 1910. The third essential fertilizer in the agricultural trilogy was nitrate. This had been obtained in the form of guano from Chile, but now it was extracted in the form of ammonia from the gases of the coke ovens.

The necessary plant foods were thus obtained largely from industry with the aid of science. Their use was directed and stimulated by a well-organized system of technical education. Experiments were carried on at the agricultural experiment stations, and the results obtained there were carried to the farmers by printed instructions and by practical demonstrations. These methods proved successful and in 1910 the value of artificial fertilizers applied to the soil in Germany was nearly $100,000,000.

In explaining the development of agriculture during this period German writers lay a great deal of emphasis upon certain agricultural "by-industries," especially the distillation of alcohol from potatoes and of sugar. Potatoes entered largely into human consumption and as food for cattle. The average crop at the end of this period was estimated at about 45 million tons, of which some 16 million were fed to stock, 13 million were for human consumption, and 4 million tons were lost each year through rot and in other ways, as potatoes are a highly perishable product. At the beginning of the twentieth century an attempt was made to prevent this loss by the use of potato-drying machines. These proved successful and the number grew rapidly. With the outbreak of the World War they took on a new significance.

More important, however, in maintaining the fertility of the soil and in providing a cash crop for the farmers was sugar beet growing.

The area devoted to this crop increased steadily, as did the per acre yield of beets. The number of tons of beets worked up grew from about $2\frac{1}{2}$ million tons in 1870 to $15\frac{1}{2}$ million in 1911; at the end of this period somewhat over a million acres of land were planted with beets. The heavy excise tax on raw beets stimulated the selection of roots that would yield the largest percentage of sugar, with results that were astonishing. Whereas in 1871 it took 26 pounds of beets to produce one pound of sugar, by 1911 only 13 pounds were needed. In other words the percentage of sugar extracted from the beet almost doubled, while the sugar return per acre of land more than doubled. During this same period the production of sugar in Germany rose from 358,000 tons to 2,037,000 tons, which made this country the leading producer of beet sugar in the world. The number of sugar refineries decreased, however, from 456 in 1887 to 341 in 1914, as these adopted large scale capitalistic methods and improved machinery.

These two crops furnish an excellent illustration of the close connection in Germany between agriculture and scientific research. Their development was carefully studied and fostered, especially by the agricultural chemists. Each had an important place in a system of rotation. Beet growing especially called for deep plowing and careful planting and cultivation; it therefore led to better farming. Both furnished valuable fodder for cattle, and the increased supply of manure obtained from stall-fed animals in turn improved the fertility of the soil.

The organisation of agriculture. By 1870 there had been developed in Germany, partly by private agencies and partly under governmental control and assistance a well-planned system of credit and co-operation and education. Their combined effect in stimulating German farmers to improve their practice, and in providing the necessary resources for the increase of production, was noteworthy.

The most important agencies for lending money, secured by mortgages on land, were the land mortgage associations (*Landschaften*), which dealt primarily with large landowners, and savings banks, which served the interests of the peasant cultivators. In 1912 each of these had loans outstanding of about $850,000,000. The underlying principle was that of mutual co-operation with limited liability on the part of the members. When farmers wished to borrow money, they became members of an association, making payments in small annual installments; when they discharged their debts they ceased to be members. The association granting the loan issued its own bonds, which were sold on the open market; it was thus able to procure the necessary capital at lower rates than could the individual farmer by mortgaging his holding. Although the loans were usually made without requiring a declaration as to their purpose, the whole effect of such a co-operative system was a strong emphasis upon the business capacity of the borrower and an insistence upon the productive use of the funds advanced. Thus the credit system tended to raise the technical efficiency of the agricultural population. The inefficient farmer who was denied credit quietly yielded his place to others better qualified. There was thus a process of selection.

Two other groups of credit institutions may be briefly mentioned. The first consisted of land improvement funds and analogous institutions, which granted loans mainly for specific land improvement or building undertakings. The second group was that of the rent-charge banks, which were interested chiefly in the creation and equipment of small holdings.[21] By 1911 there were about 17,500 local co-operative banks with a membership of over 1,500,000 or about one-fifth of the agriculturalists, and with an annual turnover of about $2,000,000,000. Above the local banks stood regional central banks, which co-ordinated the small institutions and acted as intermediaries between them and the money market. The local co-operative credit associations were thus always assured of funds. At the apex of the system stood the state central bank. The organisation is reminiscent of the Federal Reserve System in the United States.

Co-operative societies, other than those for credit, developed much later and had not attained the importance of the co-operative banks. In this respect Germany lagged behind France but was ahead of Britain. Supply societies for the purchase of manures, feeding stuffs, seeds, machinery, and cattle handled about one-fourth of this type of business, with corresponding savings to the small peasants. Of these there were about 2000 societies with a membership of 200,000. A third type was selling associations, of which co-operative dairies were the most important; these numbered about 3000 with a membership of some 290,000. The first of these was established in Hesse in 1888 and during the nineties they spread rapidly, not only in the grazing sections of the Baltic provinces but also southwest to the Rhine district. They undertook the co-operative sale of milk and also the manufacture and sale of butter and cheese. Their existence eased the transition of many landed proprietors from unprofitable sheep raising to dairy farming. In 1912 these associations had an annual turnover of $100,000,000.

Of lesser importance were associations for things of common use, as of agricultural machines and breeding cattle, insurance, electricity supply, cattle selling, potato buying, and distillery societies. A few beet sugar factories were established on co-operative lines, but it was soon found that this form of organisation was not suited to such

[21] The origin of these was described on page 33.

capitalistic enterprises. Among the growers of grapes, fruit, and vegetables there were also co-operative societies, but these enrolled only a small proportion of the workers in these fields. Altogther, Sartorius [22] estimated that 3,500,000 persons out of an agricultural population of 5,736,000 belonged to some sort of a co-operative society.

Statistics of numbers and membership do not convey a just appreciation of the importance of the co-operative movement in the agricultural life of Germany. The associations for common purposes of the peasant cultivators — and it must be emphasized that this was primarily a peasant movement — had a great educational effect, and promoted improvements which the scientific experiment stations and the agricultural colleges had been unable to achieve. Dawson reached the conclusion that the co-operative societies had "done more for the small farmer than all the agrarian and protective laws together."

Agricultural education must also be given due credit for the promotion of better farming. Germany developed a most efficient system, reaching from the universities down to continuation schools. During the sixties and seventies the old agricultural academies were reorganized and attached to the universities; in 1913 there were nine such institutions, together with three academies which provided for higher education, primarily for the sons of large landowners. For the sons of peasants, who could not afford a lengthy course, winter schools were established; of these there were 279, and alongside them were 200 additional technical schools which gave practical instruction in a single branch, such as dairying or gardening. Below these came the agricultural middle schools, of which the first was established at Hildesheim in 1858; these numbered 43 and were especially designed to care for interests of the sons of big peasants. At the bottom of the agricultural educational system stood the continuation schools, which were attended by the sons of small peasants and laborers during the winter months. There were 3224 of these just before the outbreak of the World War. In addition to these should be mentioned the 70 agricultural experiment stations, which were scattered all over Germany.

The cost to the state of these various schools was considerable, but this was justified by Von Ruemker. "The great progress that agriculture has achieved in Germany during the last quarter of a century," he wrote, "is the result of the union of practice with science and proves that money spent on research and on education in every class brings in a high rate of return."

Protection of agriculture. Germans have always been accus-

[22] Op. cit., 460.

tomed to look to the state for guidance and assistance, and in the agricultural crisis of the period under review they turned to the government. The agriculturalists, especially the Junkers of the northeast, who had been free traders as long as they exported grain and wished to buy their agricultural implements and other supplies cheap, now turned to protectionism. After 1875 Germany became a grain-importing country; Russian rye and American wheat began to compete in the German markets with home supplies and seriously to depress prices. When proposals to increase the tariff were introduced in 1878 by Bismark the agricultural party, which held the balance of power in the Reichstag, was able to obtain a considerable measure of protection. The tariff of 1879 was, however, only a moderate protection to both manufacturer and agriculturalist. The importation of foreign foodstuffs, especially cereals, grew menacingly in the eighties. By 1884 the net imports of wheat into Germany were 778,000 tons, and the average wholesale price of wheat in Prussia fell from $1.46 a bushel in 1880 to $1.05 in 1886; after that it recovered somewhat. The recovery was attributed by the agrarians to the protective duties imposed by the tariffs of 1885 and 1887, although other factors contributed largely to that end.

In 1891, Caprivi, who had succeeded Bismark as prime minister, negotiated a number of commercial treaties, the basis of which was reciprocal most-favored-nation treatment and reduction of duties. The most important of these changes from the German side were reductions in the duties on agricultural products. Unfortunately the changes occurred just at a time when prices were falling. Thus the wholesale price of wheat in Prussia, which had reached $1.50 in 1891, fell to 90 cents a bushel in 1894, primarily because of bountiful harvests. The "accursed" policy of Caprivi aroused the fierce hostility of the agrarians, who ascribed the fall in price solely to the tariff. After 1893 the powerful Landlords' League (*Bund der Landwirte*) directed the demands for higher protection of agriculture, particularly as this affected the interests of the large landowners.

When a new general tariff was enacted in 1902 (effective in 1906) it contained important concessions to the agriculturalists and raised the duties on all cereals, live cattle, sheep and pigs, frozen meat, bacon, animal fats, meat of all kinds, margarine, macaroni, and other agricultural products. Meanwhile prices were rising, partly as a result of new gold discoveries and the general upward swing of the commercial cycle, and partly because of protection. Thus the price of wheat rose steadily to $1.42 per bushel, 1909–1913. The agrarians, however, gave full credit for the improvement to their policy.

It is not easy to determine the effect of the tariff policy on German well-being or even on agriculture itself. Even among German economists there was a difference of opinion. The free traders, led by Brentano, contended that the real causes for progress were improved technical efficiency, co-operation, and education, and that the rise in prices resulted from the growth in population and the increased prosperity of the working classes. The protectionists, on the other hand, among whom were Schmoller and Wagner, argued that agriculture must be protected for political and military reasons; that a one-sided industrialization, such as had taken place in England, was undesirable; and that protection was necessary to meet the agricultural emergency. In general it may be concluded that protection permitted many farmers to continue in business, who under free trade would have succumbed to the competition of cheap foreign supplies. Prices and the cost of living were raised. Most of the benefits went to the large landowners rather than to the peasant farmers.

But the tariff problem was not merely an economic one; it was also fiscal, social, and military. From the fiscal point of view it provided much-needed independent revenues to the imperial government. Socially it prevented a one-sided industrialization and maintained a vigorous agricultural population.[23] But the main argument was political and military. "It is my unshakeable conviction," said Caprivi to the Reichstag in 1891, "that in a future war the feeding of the army and the country may play an absolutely decisive part." This view found expression in all the tariff debates, which emphasized the necessity of making Germany as self-sufficient as possible in essential foodstuffs and raw materials. This very policy, moreover, gave a sense of security to the farmer, which encouraged him to continue in a business which would otherwise have been too speculative.

Self-sufficiency. Brilliant as was the progress in agriculture, the increased production of food did not keep pace with the demands of the expanding population. Germany was not self-sufficient at any time during this period and was least so at the end of it. From being an exporter of wheat she became a net importer in the late seventies and remained so uninterruptedly thereafter. Rye was raised at home in adequate quantities, but other grains were imported in varying amounts. In 1912 slightly over 85 per cent of all cereals was home grown and 15 per cent imported. A better showing was made for meat and meat products, of which 93 per cent was Ger-

[23] This view was presented by Prof. Adolph Wagner in his *Agrar- und Industriestaat. Die Kehrseiten des Industriestaates und die Rechtfertigung agrarischen Zollschutzes, mit besonderer Rücksicht auf die Bevölkerungsfrage* (Jena, 1902).

man. Potatoes provided not only for human consumption but yielded a surplus for feeding animals and for alcohol and starch manufacture. In the last year before the World War the total imports of live animals, foodstuffs and drinks were valued at 3000 million marks and the exports at 1000 million, leaving a net deficit of 2000 million marks. It was estimated that home production would take care of three-quarters of the total demand for food.

Rural labor. In spite of the growing mechanization of agriculture the number of agricultural laborers increased between 1882 and 1907 from 5,674,000 to 7,055,000. This was due in part to the transition from grazing to arable farming and more intensive cultivation, and in part to the growth of the population; relatively to other branches of industry the proportion in agriculture declined. While most of the laborers were to be found on the large estates east of the Elbe, it was just in that section that the loudest cry was raised as to the scarcity of labor. During the latter part of this period there was a land-flight of workers, which threatened to deprive the landowners of the needed labor. This phenomenon and the attempt to meet it call for explanation.

The conditions of agriculture in the cold northeast make it difficult to provide continuous work throughout the year. Formerly, the care of the cattle, threshing — with a flail — and by-industries in the home provided employment during the winter, but mechanized implements reduced the number of cattle, steam threshers supplanted the flail, and the by-industries were taken over by the factories. Consequently the landowner engaged his workers only for the busy planting and harvesting seasons. The permanent laborer became a seasonal laborer. Wholly dependent on his wages he was forced to seek employment elsewhere. His position was rendered worse by his inability to obtain land of his own. Not only was the laborer landless but his wages were low and housing and other conditions were miserable. Dawson presents as typical the following East Prussian wages contract for 1906: [24]

"The laborer receives free dwelling, 6 cubic meters of wood for fuel, half an acre of land for potatoes, forage for two or three goats, and straw. He receives per day from October 1 to April 1, one mark (25 cents), and from April 1 until mowing time 1 mark 25 pfennige (31 cents), and from then until October 1, 1 mark 50 pfennige (37½ cents). His wife receives 50 pfennige (12½ cents) per day all the year round."

The wages, both in money and kind, of this laborer were estimated at about $120 a year. Money wages for all agricultural labor, especially in the east, were incredibly low, probably three-quarters of the

[24] W. H. Dawson, *Evolution of Modern Germany* (Rev. ed., New York, n.d.), 271.

workers receiving less than $135 per annum. When to this are added the wretched housing, the social degradation, the inferior civil position, and lack of opportunity, the reason for the rural exodus becomes clear. Many of these persons emigrated from the country; the number of emigrants was very large in the early years — 221,000 in 1881 — but after 1885 the growing industrial towns absorbed them.

The large landowners proposed various measures to lessen the mobility of the population and to assure themselves a permanent labor force, some of which were enacted into permanent legislation. But their chief reliance was the importation of seasonal laborers from Polish-Russia and from Galicia in Austro-Hungary. In those districts wages were even lower and conditions worse than in eastern Germany and consequently many agricultural workers — 200,000 to 400,000 — streamed from these countries into Germany each year, returning home after the harvest season. These were the so-called *Sachsengänger* or Wanderers.

Such a foreign labor force was, however, not sufficiently dependable, and an effort was made to settle peasant proprietors and small holders in the Slavic provinces of the northeast in numbers sufficient to guarantee a supply of native labor and to assure the cultivation of the land. This was the so-called policy of "inner colonization," which was carried out in the Polish provinces. The Settlement Law of 1886 appropriated 100,000,000 marks to facilitate the settling of German peasants and workers in that district. Although the expenditures were steadily increased until they reached over 600,000,-000 marks in 1908, the results were disappointing. By 1910 some 32,175 families had been settled on 1,082,230 acres, which, as Sering pointed out, was four times as much as the great landowners had bought from the small peasants a hundred years earlier.

3. PEASANT PROPRIETORSHIP WINS THROUGH IN FRANCE

Agriculture still remained, during this period, the most important branch of industry in France, though it was slowly yielding place to manufactures and trade. Population as a whole grew slowly, and the proportion that remained on the land declined, so that there was not only a relative but also an absolute decrease in the rural population. The proportion of the population engaged in agriculture fell from forty-eight per cent of the gainfully employed in 1866 to forty-one per cent in 1911. The percentage of persons living in rural communities, that is with less than 2000 persons, fell from sixty-eight in 1871 to fifty-six in 1911. While not all of these persons were engaged in agriculture, they catered to its needs and lived on its returns.[25]

Twice only did the French census report on the organization of agriculture, in 1882 and 1892, but scanty as they are the statistics reveal clearly certain aspects of the French system. The number of operators was greater than that of the helpers in both years, showing the preponderance of one-man farms. The typical cultivator was a man working on a small holding with only family help. There was a small increase in the number of cash tenants, but the share-croppers (*métayers*) remained stationary. The number of day laborers and farm servants — the latter housed and fed by the employer and hired by the month, season, or year — fell off considerably, reflecting the increased use of farm machinery, but whether as cause or effect it is impossible to say.

The labor problem was called the central problem of French agriculture,[26] but it was not a new one. The movement of population from the land into the cities paralleled the building of railroads and the growth of manufactures and trade. But the agricultural depression that set in along the seventies gave it a new stimulus. The urban industries offered better wages while the towns provided opportunities lacking in the country. Enforced military service brought the young men into garrison towns where they acquired tastes and habits which they were unwilling to renounce. The dreary and monotonous life in the country no longer attracted them. Between 1896 and 1911 the number of males on the farms decreased 396,000, but their places were filled by an addition of 483,000 women. The character of agricultural labor was slowly deteriorating.

In one respect the position of the agricultural day laborer in France differed from that of his contemporaries in England and Germany. He was himself owner of a bit of land, perhaps some of the operating unit on which he worked as a laborer. The presence of this group shows the possibility of progress and the existence of an agricultural ladder. The day laborer might look forward to becoming a peasant proprietor on his own account some day.

Land holdings. There are no statistics of land ownership in France for this period, as the census reported only the size of operating units (*exploitations*). These covered only the years 1862, 1882, and 1892; since 1892 no agricultural statistics have been published which are comparable with the earlier ones, but in 1909 the Minister of Agriculture made a report for 1908, whose authoritativeness is less certain. The holdings were divided into five groups,

25 A complete table showing these changes is given on p. 475.
26 A. Souchon, *La Crise de la main d'oeuvre agricole en France* (Paris, 1914).

ranging from the very small (less than 2½ acres) to the very large (over 250 acres):

NUMBER OF AGRICULTURAL HOLDINGS

Categories	1862	1882	1892	1908
Very small (less than 2½ acres)	......	2,167,667	2,235,405	2,087,851
Small (2½ to 25 acres)	2,435,401	2,635,030	2,617,558	2,523,713
Medium (25 to 100 acres)	636,369	727,222	711,118	745,862
Large (100 to 250 acres)	} 154,067	142,088	{ 105,391	118,497
Very large (over 250 acres)			{ 33,280	29,541
	(not comparable)	5,672,007	5,702,752	5,505,464

An American, and even a British, reader is at once struck by the classification of this table, which lists holdings of 100 acres as "large," and enumerates four and a half million holdings (83 per cent of all) of less than 25 acres. According to Rowntree [27] the average size of a farm, excluding holdings under one acre, in the United States was 138 acres, in Great Britain 63, in Prussia 33½, and in France 24 acres. These differences were due to historical, climatic, and legislative factors, but they show the difficulty of making international comparisons, and of drawing too hasty conclusions. Perhaps the most striking feature about the table is the stability which is shown. Small changes occurred, but on the whole the picture of agrarian organization in 1908 was not very different from that of almost half a century earlier.

Broadly speaking, France could be divided into two regions: north of the Loire River the small holdings predominated, while south of that line the larger holdings ruled. Topography and climate played an important role; on the level plains, along the coast, and in the vineyard sections the small holding was profitable, but in the mountainous country, the forested regions, or where large scale operations with agricultural machinery were possible, large holdings prevailed. Market and flower gardening favored small holdings, cattle raising large. If by-industries were present, as fishing and household industries, additional support was given the small holding.

A somewhat different picture is presented if, instead of considering the holdings in each of the five classes, attention is directed to the amount of land involved. For this purpose the following table, showing the area, exclusive of uncultivated land and state forests, may be given:

[27] B. S. Rowntree, *Land and Labour* (London, 1910), 108.

AREA OF AGRICULTURAL HOLDINGS
(in acres)

Categories	1892	1908
Very small	3,070,700	3,034,600
Small	25,646,800	28,551,500
Medium	31,977,600	33,618,500
Large and very large	45,891,900	40,188,400
Total	106,587,000	105,393,000

Whereas 83 per cent of the holdings in 1908 were less than 25 acres, they covered only 29 per cent of the cultivated land; the large and very large holdings made up only 2.7 per cent of the total holdings, but contained over 37 per cent of the land. The tendency, so far as can be judged from the brief interval covered by this table, seemed to be for the medium-sized holdings to grow at the expense of both the very small and the very large ones. The well-to-do peasant added bit by bit to his holding. A discussion of this problem opens up at once a topic on which much has been written and little agreement reached. "The problem of land division," wrote Augé-Laribé, "is the Tower of Babel of economists."

Division of the land. The word division has been loosely used and may mean any one of three things:[28] a division of ownership (*morcellement*), a division of cultivation or management (*fractionnement*), and dispersion. *Morcellement* existed when there were a great many proprietors in a given district; it involved the question as to the relative advantages of small and large holdings. *Fractionnement* or parcellization occurred when a proprietor split his holding up into different fields or units for purposes of cultivation, using each for a different crop; or it might result from roads, railroads, rivers, hills, and other topographical features which broke the holding into several parcels. Dispersion signified that the holding was non-contiguous and was composed of scattered pieces of land that were physically separated from each other. These may be considered in reverse order.

Dispersion was of course the most inconvenient of the three forms. Cases cited by Sée[29] show an almost unbelievable situation. "In Limagne lay a holding of 12½ acres with 120 parcels in 7 communes. In Chaigny (Loiret) 5447 acres were split into 48,000 parcels. In Vaudremont (Upper Marne) the purchase of 447 acres required 116 deeds for 3000 pieces of land. In Voulangis in Brie,

[28] A. de Foville, *Le Morcellement* (Paris, 1885), 2.
[29] *Französische Wirtschaftsgeschichte*, II, 383.

a commune of 500 inhabitants, the area of 2395 acres, of which a quarter was forest, was broken up into 10,600 separate parcels."

To farm a collection of such parcels meant loss of time, impossibility of using agricultural machinery, difficulties of access, of fencing, of management, and of supervision. The little patches were manured only in the middle, since fertilizer on the edges might benefit neighbors' strips. So obvious were the disadvantages that one wonders how it could have developed. The usual explanations were sales and inheritance. The peasant regarded land as his savings bank and bought what came on the market, even if it were not contiguous to his previous holdings. In addition to this the egalitarian law of inheritance, which compelled the division of property equally among the children, split up holdings. In Germany, the law provided for compulsory rearrangement of the holdings if two-thirds of the farmers wished it. But in France, the distrust and jealousy of the peasants prevented such a sensible step, except in the east where the "powdering" of the land had gone farthest. Laws were passed in 1870 and 1884, offering tax reductions for rearranged holdings, but without result. An escape from an intolerable situation was found in renting the scattered parcels; this may be the explanation of the increase in cash renters. Where this was not done there was strong pressure to retain the antiquated three-field system of communal farming.

Parcellization was frequently bad farming. To avoid spending any money for the supply of his own wants the French peasant followed the practice of producing a little of everything — grapes, vegetables, wheat, oats, hemp, etc. — even though the soil was not suited to such crops. He did not manage his land as a unit to be utilized in the most productive fashion, but scattered his efforts unwisely.

Morcellement raised the question as to the relative merits of large and small holdings. In 1909 the Minister of Agriculture asked each department the question: "Is the small holding inferior, equal, or superior to the large?" The answer received may be tabulated as follows: [30]

	Inferior	Equal	Superior	Not Classified
In employments and methods	29	14	27	14
In economic results	16	8	47	13

If these returns be accepted at their face value, a strong case is made out for the small cultivator. His inferiority in the matter of

[30] Augé-Laribé, op. cit., 119.

implements and methods was apparently more than compensated for by his intensive hand work, while the economic advantages inherent in the large holding were lessened by the difficulty of obtaining the necessary supply of labor. Some allowance may, however, be made for the probable lack of full returns by the large proprietors because of fear of taxation. It was, moreover, possible for relatively inefficient enterprises to survive in the protected agricultural markets of France, for the margin of cultivation was pushed quite low and little competition existed. In other words the relative merits of small peasant proprietorship and large scale methods of agriculture were not put to the test; there was room for both and they lived on side by side.

Whatever conclusions may be drawn as to the relative merits of large and small holdings, French agriculture as a whole suffered in any international comparison. Clive Day [31] presents a table which gives in bushels per acre the yield of crops on the average for the decade 1903–12. In the last line the rank of France among European countries for the particular crops is given.

Country	Wheat	Rye	Barley	Oats	Maize	Potatoes
France	20	17	25	25	19	129
Germany	30	27	36	52	....	197
Great Britain	32	29	35	48	....	228
Russia	10	13	15	21	16	105
United States	14	16	25	30	27	96
Rank of France	9th	11th	10th	9th	5th	11th

"If the table were extended to include other products, France would still make a poor showing. In the product of sugar beets and in the amount of sugar obtained it was again 8th or 9th... Only in the culture of the vine did France stand high among European countries."

Land utilization. In the period under review a far-reaching shift took place in French agriculture. The railway reached its full development and broke up the narrow regionalism, which had hitherto held each community to a policy of self-sufficiency. Now specialization, based on peculiarities of soil, climate, location, and access to markets, became the rule. The development also of cheap ocean transportation and of the telegraph exposed French agriculture to foreign competition, and forced out of cultivation areas which were unsuited to the growing of the competing products. As a result there was a transfer of land from cereal growing to cattle raising; between 1882 and 1909 the former decreased 5 million acres and the latter increased 10 millions. The greatest change took

[31] *Economic Development in Modern Europe* (New York, 1933), 173.

place in the field in which the competition was keenest and in which prices fell farthest, namely wheat; the number of acres planted to this crop declined from 17,032,000 in 1873–77 to 16,277,000 in 1913. There was also a considerable reduction in the amount of land devoted to rye and barley, but oats showed an expansion owing to the increase in cattle and the demand for fodder.

The main cause of this shift was of course the fall in prices; wheat fell from $1.73 per bushel in 1871–75 to $1.21 in 1902–07. Even the poor crops of 1878–79 did not bring higher prices because of scarcity, for the vacuum was filled by increased imports, since per capita consumption remained fairly steady. For a France accustomed to supply her own needs for breadstuffs the imports of the seventies seemed portentous. These were 51,120,000 bushels in 1878 and 76,964,000 on the average for 1880–84, which was between one-sixth and one-seventh of the total domestic requirements. After this they fell off and France remained more nearly self-sufficing in respect to wheat than either Great Britain or Germany, being surpassed only by Russia in total production among European countries. The statistical basis for these statements is contained in the following table: [32]

PRODUCTION AND CONSUMPTION OF WHEAT

Period	Home grown	Imported	Total	Cons. per capita	Price per bushel
	(millions of bushels)				
1872–81	285	30	315	......	$1.59
1882–91	304	43	347	532	1.32
1892–1901	323	29	352	535	1.15
1902–1907	337	11	348	505	1.21

Closely connected with wheat growing, at least in the northwest, was the production of sugar beets, for much of the land formerly in wheat was now planted with beets. The area devoted to this crop expanded from 340,000 acres in 1862 to 825,000 in 1900, after which it declined slightly as a result of the abolition of sugar bounties by the Brussels sugar convention of 1902. Nonetheless the production of sugar increased as better beets were grown with a higher sugar content. Just as in Germany, the excise taxes on beets stimulated this movement, and the sugar content was raised from 10.1 per cent in 1868 to 18.1 in 1908. In addition to sugar, beets were largely used for the manufacture of alcohol and as fodder for cattle. They also constituted a valuable factor in a scientific system of crop rotation.

[32] E. Théry, *Les progrès économiques de la France* (Paris, 1909), 96.

Potatoes had come into general use as human food about the middle of the century, and during this period their consumption expanded rapidly, though France lagged behind both Germany and Great Britain in their production. Even more important was the use of potatoes for animal fodder and for the distillation of alcohol.

Grape culture had an eventful history, for no other crop underwent such fluctuations in annual yield nor did any other branch of agriculture suffer so much from disease. The production of wine grew steadily from the middle of the century, partly as a result of increasing domestic consumption and partly because of the foreign demand following the liberal commercial treaties of the sixties. The maximum output was reached in 1875 with 20,280,000 gallons. But the ravages of the phylloxera, a minute plant louse, were already beginning the destruction of the vines which during the next decade was to wipe out the industry in some departments. In addition to the louse, mildew spread everywhere, and black root began to appear. In Hérault, the leading vine district, four-fifths of the vines were destroyed. By 1885 the yield was only 6,760,000 gallons. Remedial measures proved ineffective until American rootstocks were imported, which were resistant to the disease, and chemical sprays were used. But not until the turn of the century were the vineyards restored. The climatically unsuitable regions were not replanted and the industry was confined to a smaller but more productive area.

Forests may be regarded as a crop and should be included in a discussion of land utilization. By the middle of the century the drain on the forest resources by charcoal iron furnaces had ceased, and in 1860 a legislative attempt at reforestation was begun, which was amplified in 1882. More important was the voluntary planting of poor land which the agricultural crisis and the destruction of the vineyards forced out of other use. Four-fifths of the 25,000,000 acres in forests belonged to private individuals. But French supplies did not cover the domestic demand and the imports grew steadily.

Animal husbandry was not affected as disastrously as was cereal production by the transoceanic competition of the seventies, and there was a considerable shift to the former from the latter. The movement was aided by other factors within the country. Between 1862 and 1909 the annual per capita consumption of meat increased from 57 to 125 pounds, and this increased demand had a favorable effect on prices. Cattle raising required less labor and thus offered an escape from the problem of the rural exodus. Especially on the light soils of central and northwestern France and in the mountainous regions pasture replaced the wheat fields and animal hus-

bandry grew in every line except sheep. This shift from extensive
field-crop production to intensive animal husbandry was initiated in
response to international economic changes which decreased the profits in grain growing and increased those in meat and milk production. But the movement was hastened by changes in the amount
and character of farm labor. The French farmer adjusted himself
to changing economic conditions with considerable ability.

NUMBER OF FARM ANIMALS IN FRANCE

Kind	1882	1892	1909	1913
Horses	2,837,952	2,794,529	3,236,130	3,222,080
Cattle	12,997,054	13,708,997	14,313,573	14,787,710
Sheep	23,809,433	21,115,713	17,357,640	16,131,390
Swine	7,146,900	7,421,073	7,305,850	7,035,850

Animals which did not fit into a more scientific agriculture, as
oxen, mules, asses, and goats, showed a great decrease. The lessened
demand for wool, coupled with foreign imports, led to a diminution
of sheep raising and a shift from the production of wool to that of
mutton. The French did not consume such quantities of pork as the
Germans, and this branch accordingly did not show any expansion.
Horses replaced oxen as draft animals and contributed at least one
noteworthy strain in the powerful Percherons. There was at the
same time an improvement in weight [33] which somewhat offset the
slow growth in numbers. A considerable increase in dairy cattle
and an improvement in quality may also be noted. When all is
said, however, France remained behind many of her neighbors in
animal husbandry, and the yield of milk was pitifully low. Thus
the average animal yield per cow in France in 1913 was only 2024
pounds; in Germany it was 4356, in Denmark, 5720, and in Switzerland 6556.[34] In cheese production, on the other hand, France enjoyed almost a monopoly in certain highly specialized lines. This
perhaps indicates the source of strength of the French peasant.
Where hand labor, hard work, and special skill were called for he
held his own, but was compelled to yield ground where large scale
methods were more profitable.

Mechanization of agriculture. The French peasant, who farmed
most of the land, had neither capital nor inclination to buy expensive
agricultural machinery. Until the crisis of the seventies he managed
to obtain satisfactory results with his traditional methods. The drastic fall in prices, however, compelled a reorganization along all lines.

[33] Between 1892 and 1913 the average dressed weight of beef cattle increased 104 pounds,
that of calves 60 pounds, and of swine 38 pounds.

[34] D. Rambaud, "Les progrès de l'agriculture en France et en Allemagne," *Revue d'économie
politique,* 1920, p. 314.

Unfortunately the only official statistics cover the period before any considerable changes had taken place, but they nevertheless show a movement toward the increased use of agricultural machinery, which grew stronger as time passed.

AGRICULTURAL MACHINERY
(in thousands)

Kind	1862	1882	1892
Plows	3,206.4	3,267.2	3,669.2
Horse-hoes	25.8	195.4	251.8
Threshers	100.7	211.0	234.4
Seed drills	10.8	29.4	52.4
Mowers	9.4	19.1	38.8
Reapers	8.9	16.0	23.4
Hay and horse rakes	5.6	27.4	51.5

Although French farms increased the number of their agricultural machines between 1862 and 1892, they were still inadequately equipped at the latter date. It will be remembered [35] that there were then about 3,500,000 holdings of over 2½ acres. There were thus barely enough plows to go round for these holdings and the 2,200,000 very small cultivators of less than 2½ acres apparently had to get along with spades. Even if we assume that only holdings of over 100 acres could afford the other machines, there would not be enough to meet the needs of the 139,000 holdings of this description, except in the case of horse-hoes and threshing machines. Sowing and reaping were evidently still done largely by hand. Even threshing was still performed in part by the flail and by treading.

Many factors militated against the use of agricultural machinery in France. In some regions grain and forage were grown on hills so steep that only hand labor could be used in preparing the land, and in planting, cultivating, and harvesting the crop. The division of the land into small holdings, which were frequently surrounded by hedges, made the use of mowers, reapers, binders, and similar machines impractical. And, finally, the nature of some French crops, as grape culture and beet growing, required hand labor rather than machine methods. The machines in use were French, English, German, and American.

By 1912 agriculture was becoming mechanized, though not to the same degree as industry. Not only had the number of agricultural machines increased, but they were greatly improved. Reports from some departments stated that mowers were so widespread that agricultural laborers no longer knew how to use the scythe, while threshing machines had almost completely driven out the flail.

[35] See p. 25.

Both Méline and Augé-Laribé thought that machines made their appearance on a farm only after the disappearance of the workers; it was a result, and not a cause, of the rural exodus. The employers, it is true, loudly voiced their lamentations, and even their fury, over the scarcity of labor, but the workers, both those who went to the city and those who stayed on the land, profited by higher wages. It is fairly clear that French farmers, conservative and poor, did not buy expensive machinery or adopt new methods until forced to. In the regions of more intensive agriculture, however, rapid progress was made after 1892. A French writer [36] supplies data for some departments which may serve as evidence.

Machine	Loir-et-Cher		Indre-et-Loire		Haute-Garonne	
	1892	1910	1892	1910	1892	1910
Mower	131	6800	200	10,800	450	15,000
Reaper	138	7100	130	4,000	180	25,000
Binder	......	......	......	......	60	1,280
Haymaker	131	7750	550	8,000	......	......

Other improvements. With the mechanization of the farm French agriculture entered into the modern economic system; rural self-sufficiency gave way to the production of products for sale, which involved specialization, increasing competition, and the dominance of capital. This transition was made possible, was even forced, by improvements in means of transportation, which broke down barriers of space and ignorance, and brought the French peasant into touch with the world market.

The work of the engineers revolutionized agricultural technique, but the physiologists, the chemists, and the physicists were also making contributions which were to render agriculture more scientific. These changes occurred in France during the latter half of the nineteenth century. The country was well supplied with phosphate, and the use of this artificial fertilizer became fairly general. Saltpeter from Chile and guano from Peru were imported, but potash was little used.

The output of agricultural products could be increased in two ways — by more intensive use of the land already under cultivation or my making unused land available. Both methods were employed, but for the results we shall have to guess, since French agricultural statistics do not record changes in all these lines. The wasteful three-field system had been common down to the middle of the century, but under the pressure of the new forces of competition more scientific methods of crop rotation were introduced, and the amount

[36] Pierre Régnier, *L'ouvrier agricole* (Paris, 1924), 144.

of fallow was reduced. How much, we are not informed, but the increase in the production of sugar beets and of fodder for cattle suggests that a more intensive system of rotation was replacing the fallow. At the same time the increase in fertilizers, both artificial, mostly imported, and natural, resulting from the expansion of dairying, removed the need for this practice.

The unused land made available for cultivation came from two sources. The census reported a reduction in the amount of "uncultivated land" from 15,368,000 acres in 1882 to 9,495,000 in 1909; most of this was probably reclaimed by drainage or irrigation. The figures correspond closely to the increase in pasture which took place at the same time, though shifts in the various categories undoubtedly took place.

The communal lands were estimated [37] in 1863 at 11,992,849 acres, of which slightly over 4,940,000 were forest, 4,001,000 productive land, and the remainder unproductive. By 1877 the total had fallen to 10,661,286 acres, as some of the productive land had been assimilated to the peasant holdings. The law of 1868 had laid down the principle that "the frozen lands, that is to say the communal property, should be attached to warm lands or cultivated lands." In 1884 the municipal councils were given power to regulate the affairs of the commune, and they proceeded to carry out the mandate of the law of 1868. By 1914 little productive land remained as communal property. The forest land was, however, retained largely in communal and state ownership and was improved by scientific forestation, though most of the forests of France belonged to private owners.

Agricultural co-operation. The modern co-operative movement in French agriculture is usually dated from 1884, when the restrictions in the penal code on professional associations were repealed, and it was provided that associations having exclusively for their object "the study and defense of commercial and agricultural economic interests" might be organized. The new co-operative societies which were organized after the legal obstacles were cleared away were known as agricultural syndicates. Their growth was very rapid. Gaumont [38] states that the large and medium landowners were active in organizing the peasants in order to meet the socialist agitation, which was causing them uneasiness. The socialists then endeavored to gain control of the co-operatives, the struggle coming into the open at the annual congresses. Since the statistics are not altogether trustworthy, it will be sufficient to give round numbers. [39]

[37] Paul Boiteau, *Traité de la fortune publique et des finances de la France* (Paris, 1866), I, 407.
[38] Jean Gaumont, *Histoire générale de la co-operation en France* (Paris, 1923), II, 597.
[39] A. Souchon, *Agricultural Societies in France* (San Francisco, 1915), 4.

Date	No. of syndicates	No. of members
1885	39	......
1895	1200	385,000
1905	3000	660,000
1913	6000	976,000

Membership in these societies was not restricted to farmers, and often included representatives of agricultural machinery and artificial fertilizer manufacturers, but most of them were cultivators of the soil. The syndicates were united in ten regional organizations, and finally in a central society, the *Union Centrale des Syndicates Agricoles*. In 1914 they claimed 1,000,000 members and an annual turnover of 1000 million francs.

The objects of the syndicates were varied. Most important was buying in large quantities at wholesale prices on behalf of the members. Fertilizers, farm implements, seeds, cattle, and a variety of other articles were handled in this way, with substantial savings to the peasants. Especially useful was the co-operative purchase of expensive agricultural machinery, like a threshing machine, which would then be rented to the members. The activities of the societies were, however, seriously limited by the restrictions of the law of 1884, which apparently prohibited the unions from performing commercial operations. These could be carried on only by the local societies, which were generally small. The selling function was even less successful. The first of these sales associations was founded in 1888 in La Rochelle. But it was soon found that selling agricultural products called for specialized knowledge of markets and wares, which the co-operatives seldom possessed. Co-operative sales societies were quite effective in disposing of fruits like strawberries and apricots, or of quality vegetables, but made little attempt to enter the wheat market. The wine growers of the Midi had a successful organization, establishing in Paris and other large cities depots with agents to take orders. Co-operation was found particularly well suited to the dairy industry, and syndicates were formed for the sale of milk, of butter, and of cheese. They succeeded best in the districts of small scale cultivation and in the wine-growing zone, that is, where a specialized industry was localized, and the members recognized a solidarity of interests.

Agricultural credit and insurance were natural developments in the co-operative movement, but were late in coming. Legislation in 1894 facilitated the organization of credit associations, and the following year Durand, a Lyons lawyer, organized the *Union des caisses rurales et ouvrières*, composed of mutual aid societies whose guarantee was the unlimited responsibility of the members. They were similar to the Raffeisen societies in Germany, and their idealism made them especially popular in the Catholic regions.[40] Legislation in 1894 and 1898 made the organization of credit associations easier and safer, but they lacked access to the capital market. This was provided in 1899 by the so-called Méline law, which provided that the non-interest-bearing credit, which the Bank of France granted the government as a condition of the renewal of its charter, should be placed at the disposal of the co-operatives and used to discount their notes. By 1912 the sums thus earmarked for agriculture amounted to 117,000,000 francs.

At the same date some ninety-seven regional banks had been set up, comprising about 4000 locals with 185,000 members, which made long-term loans to individuals and co-operative societies for such purposes as the purchase of land or the equipment of a dairy. In spite of state assistance the cost of credit to the members still amounted to 6-10 per cent. Short-term credit was also provided under laws of 1898 and 1906 for financing the harvests. Agricultural "warrants" were issued upon pledges of non-perishable products like grain, wool, wine, and similar commodities, which were discounted at the banks. These met a real need in view of the slight development of agricultural personal credit.[41] The wine industry made especial use of this form of credit. Development was, however, much slower than along similar lines in Germany, owing to the individualism and suspicion of the French peasant.

Co-operative insurance had a still slower growth, the first legislation on this subject being passed only in 1900. The most important branch of this was cattle insurance, which insured the cattle raisers against the death of their animals, up to four-fifths of their value, for a premium of one to two per cent. In 1910 there were 8500 such societies with a membership of 438,000. Fire insurance was provided by some 2000 societies, and hail insurance by not more than forty. Altogether there were in 1910 probably 11,000 co-operative insurance societies, carrying risks of perhaps 1000 million francs.

It is not easy to draw conclusions as to the value of agricultural co-operation in France. The high hopes of the early years, when the co-operatives were expected to replace the middlemen and reorganize the distribution of agricultural products, were not realized. The French peasants, who knew nothing of accounting, did not appreciate the work of the selling organizations and were slow to unite for this purpose. State-fostered credit associations were regarded

[40] Gaumont, op. cit., II, 579.
[41] A. Pfütze, *Die landwirtschaftlichen Produktiv- und Absatzgenossenschaften in Frankreich* (Tübingen, 1903), 33. The author gives in full the law of July 18, 1898.

with suspicion, the movement as a whole lacked spontaneity and certainly lagged behind the development in Germany.

Agricultural education. The state endeavored to advance the interests of agriculture by promoting education and spreading technical knowledge. The crisis years of the seventies especially directed attention to this method of improving French agriculture. In 1875 *écoles pratiques* were organized, which provided practical training for peasant children who could not afford to attend the agricultural colleges. They entered these schools at the age of thirteen, on completing their elementary schooling. A law of 1879 established agricultural instruction in the elementary schools themselves, with the double purpose of improving agriculture and combating the rural exodus, which was beginning to cause alarm. Higher education was provided by the National Agronomic Institute at Paris, dating from 1876, and by special schools for gardening, dairying, and other branches. Finally, the Ministry of Agriculture showed great activity in developing education and assisting agriculture by advice and state subventions.

BIBLIOGRAPHICAL NOTE *

1. *Britain.* Interest centered largely during this period on the question of land reform. A careful and critical early study of the land system is G. C. Brodrick, *English Land and English Landlords* (London, 1881). H. Levy, *Large and Small Holdings* (Cambridge, 1911) is a history of the rise of large holdings and the forces of disintegration. R. M. Garnier, *History of the English Landed Interest* (London, 1893) describes agricultural technique. Most of the writers decry the decline of ownership and applaud efforts to increase it: H. C. Taylor, *Decline of the Landowning Farmers in England* (Madison, 1904); L. Jebb, *The Small Holdings of England* (London, 1907); J. Collings, *Land Reform: Occupying Ownership, Peasant Proprietary, and Rural Education* (London, 1908); T. P. Whittaker, *Ownership, Tenure, and Taxation of Land* (London, 1914). A general outline is W. J. Claxton, *Brief Sketch of Agricultural and Commercial History* (London, 1934). A serious effort, following the example of Arthur Young, to describe agricultural conditions, is H. R. Haggard, *Rural England*, 2 vols. (London, 1902). Changing conditions are described in E. A. Pratt, *The Transition in Agriculture* (New York, 1906), and P. A. Graham, *Revival of English Agriculture* (London, n. d.). A radical account of labor conditions is F. E. Green, *History of the English Agricultural Labourer*, 1870–1920 (London, 1920). Less biased is O. J. Dunlop, *The Farm Labourer* (London, 1913). For careful, first-hand investigations the Royal Commissions on Agriculture, *Reports* of 1880–82, 1894, 1919, are excellent.

2. *Germany.* A textbook on agriculture and agricultural policy during this period is R. Buchenberger, *Agrarwesen und Agrarpolitik.* 2 vols. (Leipzig, 1892–93). An encyclopedia is K. Steinbrück, *Handbuch der gesamten Landwirtschaft*, 4 vols.

* Some of the books in the previous bibliography on this subject cover this period. The special bibliographies of all related chapters and the General Bibliography (pp. xi–xiii) should be consulted in every case.

(Jena, 1908). The history is covered in H. Dade, *Die Gesamtentwicklung der deutschen Landwirtschaft*, 1888–1913. 2 vols. (Halle, 1913); J. Croner, *Die Geschichte der agrarischen Bewegung in Deutschland* (Berlin, 1909); T. H. Middleton, *The Recent Development of German Agriculture* (Great Britain, Parliament, Common Papers, 1916, Vol. IV, Cd. 8305, London, 1916). The question as to whether agriculture should be protected or sacrificed to industry and cheap overseas foods was vigorously debated by Adolf Wagner, *Agrar- und Industriestaat* (2te Aufl., Berlin, 1902); L. Pohle, *Deutschland am Scheidewege* (Leipzig, 1902); K. v. Rümker, *Die deutsche Landwirtschaft* (Berlin, 1914). A careful report is J. H. Cahill, *An Enquiry into Agricultural Credit and Agricultural Co-operation in Germany* (Great Britain, Agriculture and Fisheries Board, London, 1913).

3. *France.* The question of small versus large holdings was debated by French writers during this period. A careful comparison of small, medium, and large properties is E. Flour de St. Genis, *La propriété rurale en France* (Paris, 1902); A. de Foville, *Le morcellement* (Paris, 1885) defends the small holding; M. Augé-Laribé, *Grande ou petite propriété* (Montpelier, 1902) weighs the merits of the two. A more specialized study is Comte de Tourdonnet, *Situation du métayage en France* (Paris, 1831); on the same subject see J. Couveilhier, *Essai sur l'évolution du métayage en France* (Paris, 1893) and A. Hermes, *Der Theilbau in Frankreich* (Jena, 1903). A statistical study is E. Michel, *La propriété* (Paris, 1911). The problem of farm labor is discussed in A. Souchon, *La crise de la main d'oeuvre agricole en France* (Paris, 1914); J. Méline, *The Return to the Land* (trans. from the French, London, 1906), a plea of a politician to stop the rural exodus; P. Régnier, *L'ouvrier agricole* (Paris, 1924). Agricultural credit and co-operation are carefully investigated in J. Gaumont, *Histoire générale de la coopération en France*, 2 vols. (Paris, 1923–24); Coulet, *Le mouvement syndical et coopératif dans l'agriculture française* (Paris, 1898); M. T. Herrick and R. Ingalls, *Rural Credits* (New York, 1914); and A. Souchon, French commissioner to the San Francisco Exposition of 1915, *Agricultural Societies in France* and *Agricultural Credit in France* (both San Francisco, 1915), and *Co-operation of Production and Sale in French Agriculture* (Evreux, 1915). A good general summary is G. Welter, *La France d'aujourd'hui: agriculture, industrie, commerce* (Paris, 1927).

CHAPTER IX

INDUSTRY

I. TRIUMPH OF MACHINE INDUSTRY IN BRITAIN

Structure of British industry. Of the countries covered by this study England was the only one that was thoroughly industrialized in 1870, that is, in which manufacturing had passed in importance all other activities, including agriculture. England already led the world in textiles, in iron and steel, in shipbuilding, in machine construction, and in other lines, and the leadership and prosperity of the nation seemed to rest upon an impregnable foundation. During this period, however, other nations, especially the United States and Germany, began to exploit their resources and to develop their industries on a scale which threatened this leadership.

Characteristic features of English manufactures after 1870 were the steady growth and expansion of industrial production, the greater specialization in the processes of manufacture, the movement towards large scale production and combination, the increasing search for markets coupled with the development of an unsurpassed merchant marine, and finally the growing competition of other nations not only in foreign but even in the domestic British markets. The momentum of an early start gave English manufacturers an advantage at first, but as time wore on certain disadvantages became apparent, such as the hardening of traditional methods into unchangeable practices, the building up of an industrial plant whose obsolescence was not readily recognized, and the development of labor and management attitudes that prevented quick adaptations and changes.

The place occupied by manufactures in the industrial life of the people is clearly brought out by the census tables of occupations:

OCCUPATION, ENGLAND AND WALES
(in thousands)

Category	1871	1881	1891	1901	1911
Industrial	5138	6,373	7,336	8,350	9,621
Agricultural and fishing	1657	1,383	1,336	1,152	1,322
Commercial	815	980	1,400	1,858	2,237
Domestic	1634	1,804	1,960	1,995	1,895
Professional	684	647	926	973	1,212
Total occupied	9928	11,187	12,958	14,328	16,287

The industrial group included manufactures, mining, and the building trades. Hobson concluded [1] that "though the whole class shows a considerable and continuous increase in proportion of employment, that increase is chiefly attributable to mining and building." In support of this contention he gave the following percentages of the total population over ten years of age engaged in manufactures proper: 1881, 21.5; 1891, 21.9; 1901, 21.7. It may be argued, however, that the proportion of the population employed in a given occupation is not the most accurate measure of its importance in the national economy. Manufactures made the largest use of labor-saving machinery and improved methods of organization, and was able to increase its output greatly even though the labor force remained relatively stationary. Other branches, which made smaller use of machinery and power, could expand only by increasing their personnel. A more correct view would be obtained if the statistics of output could be given, but they are unfortunately not available. That there was a great increase in production is, however, not open to doubt.

Factors of growth. The explanation of this growth in production must be sought first of all in increased demands for British wares. The expanding domestic market absorbed some of this, but the growth of population — about 13 per cent per decade — alone does not sufficiently account for the expansion. It is true that the standard of living was rising steadily though slowly during these years and that a more prosperous people demanded more things. But the domestic market could not consume the great mass of staple goods that characterized British manufactures. For these, foreign markets were needed. It seemed at times as though this foreign demand was not altogether spontaneous, but the fact remains that foreigners bought British wares, and that is the test of demand.

While factors of demand are fundamental in any explanation of industrial growth, a nation's industries can respond to these forces only if conditions of supply are favorable. In this respect England was well qualified. She was fortunate in possessing large beds of coal, which began to be exploited on a vast scale towards the middle of the century. Stanley Jevons alarmed the nation in 1865 when he estimated that at the then rate of production the best coal would be exhausted within 200 years, but the more optimistic Royal Commission of 1871 calculated that the supplies would last for 360 years. Later estimates in 1914 again reduced the life of the coal fields to 235 years.[2] "Improved methods and the tapping of new coal beds allowed the industry to meet the ever-expanding needs of

[1] J. A. Hobson, *Evolution of Modern Capitalism* (London, 1907), 387.
[2] H. S. Jevons, *The British Coal Trade* (London, 1915), 732.

industry and transportation. In Britain coal mining knit itself into the very fabric of economic life. In 1914 it employed more workers than any other industry except agriculture, and one-twelfth of the population was directly dependent on it. Iron and steel, ship building and engineering lived on cheap coal." [3] Domestic production grew from 120,000,000 tons in 1870–74 to 270,000,000 in 1910–14, while exports increased from 12,500,000 tons in 1871 to 90,000,000 in 1913. The metallurgical and manufacturing industries were the chief consumers of coal at home.

Next to coal, iron ranked as the most important raw material, and this too England possessed in abundance. Not until the United States and Germany developed their mines did Britain meet any substantial competition in this field. Other metals, as tin and lead, played a minor role in the country's industrial development.

An adequate system of transportation was of the first importance both for the organization of industry and for obtaining foreign supplies and markets. A splendid coast line and river system had been early supplemented by canal and railroad building, and after the middle of the century steamships began to supersede the slower sailing vessels. The tonnage built in British shipyards grew steadily, and in 1914 the merchant marine had 12,415,000 tons afloat.

Scarcely less in importance than the factors already mentioned was power. Statistical information on this subject is very scarce, for the census did not collect figures on production until 1907, and before that date only estimates are available. The following tentative table shows a great expansion in the use of steam motors in the early years of the twentieth century:

STEAM MOTORS IN GREAT BRITAIN
(capacity in 1000 h.p.)

Use	1870 *	1898–99 †	1907 ‡
Industry	900	5000-6000	8,000
Railways	2140	6,000	7,000
Merchant marine	} 1000 {	5,000	10,000
Navy		2,800	3,500
Total	4040	19,000	28,500

* M. G. Mulhall, *Dictionary of Statistics*, 546.
† W. Lexis, *Handwörterbuch der Staatswissenschaften*, 3te Aufl., Bd. VI, p. 613.
‡ *Final Report of the First Census of Production of the United Kingdom* (1907), 15, 16. This was the first census of this kind in Britain in 150 years of capitalistic development.

These figures show an enormous growth in the use of power and power-driven machinery. It is clear that the great development of

[3] H. Heaton, *Economic History of Europe* (New York, 1936), 527. By permission of the publishers, Harper and Brothers, New York.

the steam engine came, not with the Industrial Revolution, but with the end of the nineteenth and the beginning of the twentieth century. Of the energy produced to assist man in his operations, 91 per cent was produced by the steam engine, which in turn depended on coal. At the same time the efficiency and economy of the engines had been greatly improved. A witness stated to the Coal Commission of 1871 that the ordinary factory engine consumed about 10 pounds of coal per horse-power per hour, but the Royal Commission on Coal Supplies in 1905 reported that consumption was then about 5 pounds.

Clearly connected with the foregoing factors, the inventive genius of British industrialists may be noted in explanation of the developments of this period. The contributions of Bessemer, Siemens, Thomas, and Gilchrist in the iron and steel industry have already been described. Other men made notable contributions in other fields.

The textile industries. England's industrial strength rested upon a comparatively small number of manufactures, which were highly specialized. Most of them fell into two main groups — textiles and metal working. On the basis of number of workers and value of output, the former was more important, and may therefore be considered first; it was also the older and more thoroughly intertwined in the whole British economy.

The cotton industry has two distinct branches — spinning and weaving — and these progressed at rather uneven rates of speed. Spinning was the first to be completely mechanized. This had been pretty thoroughly effected by the middle of the century and thereafter the main changes were making the machines wholly automatic and speeding up. Ring-spinning on the frame, introduced in the seventies from the United States, where it was popular because it could be done by women and children, was used for the coarser counts, and twenty years later was finding general adoption. Mule spinning, performed by adult male labor, was used for the finer counts, but the hand mule yielded more slowly to the automatic, self-acting machine. By the eighties, however, the outcome was no longer in doubt; in 1883 there were only 80 hand mules in Lancashire. As they were perfected the machines were speeded up and the result of the two processes was a lessened use of human labor and an enormous increase in the output per operative. The expansion of this branch of the cotton industry is shown in the following table:

A similar movement was taking place in weaving, though here hand processes remained in use much longer than in spinning. But the movement towards mechanization was irresistible, and after 1870 the industry moved out of the homes and workshops into the

PRODUCTION OF COTTON YARN IN GREAT BRITAIN *

Year	Spindles at work	Operatives employed	Annual production per spindle (lbs.)	per operative (lbs.)
1870	38,000,000	449,000	28.9	2420
1880	41,900,000	487,000	33.5	2860
1900	42,640,000	529,000	38.3	3089
1910	48,088,000	571,000	32.0	2700

* Based on M. G. Mulhall, *Dictionary of Statistics* (London, 1899), 159, and Census.

factories, which were equipped with power looms. In these too there was observable the same tendency towards automatic machinery, which permitted the tending of more looms by each operative, and a speeding up of the rate of production.

PRODUCTION OF COTTON GOODS IN GREAT BRITAIN

Period	Looms at work	Operatives employed	Annual rate of production per loom (lbs.)	per operative (lbs.)
1859–1861	400,000	203,000	1627	3206
1880–1882	550,000	246,000	1806	4039
1891–1893	660,000	310,000	1866	3972

The cotton industry was characterized by extreme specialization and localization. As long as the industry was carried on under the domestic system, the whole process of manufacture was closely co-ordinated, but when spinning machinery was invented, this branch moved into the factories, while weaving still remained a cottage industry. After the general introduction of the power loom, spinning and weaving were united in the factories. Later, the partnership was dissolved again, and during the period 1870–1914 each branch showed a high degree of specialization and decentralization. Thus spinning was chiefly concentrated in South Lancashire, but this branch was itself further subdivided, the finer yarns being spun from Egyptian or sea-island cotton in Bolton near Manchester, while the coarser ones were produced in Oldham from American cotton. Weaving was conducted chiefly in North Lancashire, a similar differentiation again occurring among the different branches. Subsequent processes, such as printing, bleaching, dyeing, and finishing, were also separated and specialized.

The localization of the cotton industries — nine-tenths being found in Lancashire and the neighboring districts in Cheshire and Derbyshire — was due originally to geographical and climatic factors, such as a moist climate and proximity of coal for power. Even after these advantages were partly neutralized by new inventions, the nearness of Liverpool, with its excellent facilities for importation of raw materials and export of finished goods, anchored the industry to this region. The momentum of an early start was not easily overcome. With localization went specialization, which permitted the economies of large scale production. This was made possible by highly developed market facilities, centering in the Manchester Cotton Exchange and the Liverpool Cotton Association, which coordinated the business and handed over to other groups of specialists the intricate problems of marketing.

A striking feature of the British cotton industry was its complete dependence upon imported raw material. It suffered a severe depression as a result of the cutting off of supplies during the American Civil War (1861–65), but after this there was an expansion which became extraordinarily rapid towards the end of the nineteenth and the beginning of the twentieth century. Imports of raw cotton, which constitute a fairly reliable measure of expansion, increased from over 1200 million pounds in 1870 to 2438 million in 1913–14. By 1912 British mills were producing 12,700 miles of cotton cloth a day; this exceeded the production of all other European countries; and of this amount almost 85 per cent was exported to other lands.

The position of Great Britain in the international cotton trade, and gradual loss of its early dominance, are shown in the following table:

CONSUMPTION OF COTTON *
(million lbs.)

	1870–71	1880–81	1890–91	1900–01	1907–08
Great Britain	2410	2858	3,384	3,269	3,690
Continent of Europe	1570	2365	3,630	4,576	5,720
United States	893	1694	2,406	3,635	4,237
India	70	297	923	1,060	1,500
Total	4943	7214	10,343	12,540	15,147

* A. D. Webb, *New Dictionary of Statistics* (London, 1911), 166.

The consumption of raw cotton is, however, not a fair test, for England specialized in the finer products, which produced a much greater value from a smaller amount of material. Thus the yearly consumption of cotton per spindle was only 34 pounds in England in 1892, while it was 56 pounds in France and 86 in Germany.[4]

[4] G. v. Schulze-Gävernitz, *The Cotton Trade in England and on the Continent* (London, 1895), 86.

Other countries, protected by their tariffs, produced medium and lower grades.

The woolen industry had depended chiefly on home-grown wool down to about the middle of the century, and this had sufficed to meet the needs of an industry carried on largely by hand methods. But when the new power machinery was introduced the domestic supply proved quite inadequate and prices rose. New sources of supply were fortunately found with the development of wool growing in Australia, Cape Colony, and later South America. Imports of wool grew from 263,000,000 pounds in 1870 to 724,000,000 in 1908. In 1914 more than eight-ninths of the supply was imported.[5] British manufacturers profited by the stagnation on the continent during the Franco-Prussian war and a great expansion took place. A fall in prices towards the end of the seventies left the industry in an over-expanded and depressed state, which was accentuated by changes in fashion that lessened the demand for British woolens. The nineties saw a recovery and the decade before the World War witnessed the greatest expansion that had yet occurred. There was an even greater localization of the industry than in cotton manufacturing, 89 per cent of the mills being situated in the West Riding of Yorkshire. On the other hand a smaller proportion of woolen and worsted goods was exported, as the domestic market absorbed about three-fifths of the output.

WOOLEN, WORSTED, AND SHODDY FACTORIES IN THE UNITED KINGDOM

Year	Number of factories	Number of spindles	Number of power looms	Number of operatives
1870	2579	2,692,761	48,140	238,503
1885	2751	3,285,085	57,990	282,000
1890	2671	3,407,001	61,831	301,556
1904	....	6,685,000	104,500	264,021 *
1914	....	8,023,000	114,600	....

* 1907.

Iron and steel. By 1870 the 80-foot blast furnace was typical, and in the better plants was capable of producing 500 tons per day at an expenditure of about two tons of coal for one ton of pig iron. During the next half century great improvements were made in the scale of operation, furnace design, and economical use of raw materials, but the essential principles of the early blast furnace remained unchanged. The greatest advance was made in the preparation and use of fuel. Modern practice utilizes the gases generated in the

[5] The average annual clip of home-grown wool for 1909–13 was 95,000,000 lbs., while the imports were 800,000,000 lbs.

blast furnace for the purpose of heating the blast, but at the beginning of this period this was unusual, and the gases were discharged into the atmosphere or were at best burned for lighting. The same waste of by-products attended the making of coke, but by the twentieth century the more progressive plants had adopted more scientific procedure. Improved smelting efficiency lowered costs, consumption of coke and flux per ton of iron were reduced, and the output per furnace was raised. The annual average output per furnace in Great Britain increased from 10,-000 tons in 1875 to about 40,000 in 1913. The total make of pig iron was raised from 6 million tons in 1870 to 10 million in 1913; at the latter date Germany's output was 19 million, and that of the United States 31 million.

The most revolutionary change in the iron and steel industry occurred in the next stage of production, namely in the conversion of pig iron into steel. In 1870 a small amount of steel was being made by the Bessemer converter process, but the Siemens open-hearth method, invented in 1865, was only beginning to be introduced. Both of these processes, it will be remembered, were adapted only to the use of non-phosphoric ores. But most British ores contained phosphorus and for their utilization some other process was needed. Such

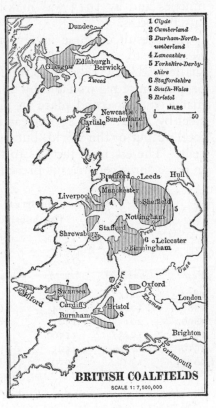

FIGURE 3. BRITISH COAL FIELDS

From C. C. Adams' *A Text-Book of Commercial Geography* (D. Appleton & Co., 1909). Reprinted by permission of the publishers.

a process was invented in 1879 by Sidney Thomas and Percy Gilchrist, who introduced in the converter a basic lining of limestone or dolomite which absorbed the phosphorus. A similar lining was also used in the Siemens-Martin open-hearth furnace, which eliminated the phosphorus even more satisfactorily than did the Thomas-Gilchrist converter. Both of these new processes were called basic, because of their use of a base lining. Phosphoric iron ore could now be used in the manufacture of steel, and in addition it was discovered that the slag from these ores made valuable fertilizer. The new basic open-hearth method was speedily adopted by the United States, which was thereby enabled to utilize enormous deposits of phosphoric ores. Germany, which had vast stores of phosphoric ores in Lorraine, preferred the Thomas-Gilchrist basic converter. Great Britain began to shift from Bessemer to open-hearth methods in the nineties and by 1913 was making 85 per cent of her steel by the latter process.

As a result of these inventions not only was there a shift from Bessemer to open-hearth steel, but the dominance of Britain was challenged. By 1890 the United States passed Great Britain in the production of pig iron and by 1887 in the production of steel. Germany gained second place in pig iron production by 1897 and of steel by 1902. In 1870 Great Britain produced 55 per cent of the total output of the world, but by 1910 its share had sunk to 15 per cent. The essential facts as to the expansion of the steel industries in these three countries is presented in the following table:

PRODUCTION OF STEEL IN LEADING COUNTRIES *
(in thousands of long tons)

	United Kingdom		Germany		United States	
Year	Converter	Open-hearth	Converter	Open-hearth	Converter	Open-hearth
1870	215	....	....	....	38	1
1880	1044	584	680	35	1074	101
1890	2015	1725	1815	382	3689	513
1900	1745	3156	4296	2013	6685	3,398
1910	1779	4595	8073	5033	9413	16,505
1915	1301	7050	6588	5583	8287	23,679

* Encyclopedia of the Social Sciences, VIII, 302.

It is clear from this table that, although the Bessemer converter had been invented before 1860, no great expansion of steel production occurred until the eighties. In view of the technical superiority of steel over wrought iron it seems strange that the transition should have been so long delayed. Partly responsible was the conservatism of engineers, partly the high cost of steel, and partly the huge vested interests of capital and skill in prevailing methods. But probably the most effective factor in preventing rapid change was the heavy capital outlay required to set up the large plant that was necessary for economical production. The depression of 1876–86 introduced far-reaching changes in the metal-working industries, and the decade of the nineties was marked by a new machine era based on cheap steel.

The demand for this great increase in production came from many sources. First were the railways. It was soon found that steel rails were much more durable than iron rails, that they stood up better under heavy traffic, and that they were more economical in the long run. During the decade 1870–80 there was a shift on the part of the leading railways to steel rails, in spite of their higher price. The next decade saw the beginning of steel shipbuilding, but iron ships still gave ample employment to puddling furnaces, for plates and angle bars of iron were much cheaper than steel. For marine boilers and propeller shafts, however, where quality was more important than price, steel completely supplanted iron. And finally there were the machine-making and numerous metal-working industries, in which steel began to supersede wrought iron. Machinery, now universal in industry, was built of steel.

The transition was hastened by the great advance that was being made in metallurgical knowledge and in its industrial application. New alloy steels were developed, which permitted the manufacture of high-speed cutting and boring tools; these in turn made for more rapid production and lowered costs. The materials and processes of the various metal-using industries were transformed. Standardization was tardily introduced in many lines, and mass production of cheaper and lighter articles took place. Machine parts were also made perfectly interchangeable, especially in textile machinery and in the newer engineering industries. The driven machinery was also made more completely automatic. As an illustration the bicycle industry may be named, starting in the sixties, expanding greatly in the eighties, and reaching its culmination in the nineties. Fortunately, its place was taken by the motor industry, which required light strong metals.

Industrial organization. In 1870 English industry was still organized on a comparatively small scale and was being carried on by a large number of competing units. Concentration in large scale establishments was carried farthest in the iron and steel industries, especially in shipbuilding and in blast furnaces, where large investment of capital in plant was necessary. The textile industries were also carried on in comparatively large establishments. But for the most part the industries were divided into many specialized processes, each of which was carried on by a large number of independent and dispersed plants. Under such a competitive system English industry had grown strong and had conquered the world's markets, and it yielded only slowly to the impact of new forces.

The new forces, compelling a different organization, became pressing during this period. The great improvement in and cheapening of transportation facilities extended the market and opened up new opportunities for mass production and mass distribution. But they also introduced new competitors and quickened the struggle for possession of the international markets. Changes in methods of production, especially the introduction of the gas engine for driving machinery, were made. Falling prices and foreign competition caused the more enterprising manufacturers to seek new ways of reducing costs, and it was found that the large undertaking could profit by the principle of decreased cost per unit for an increased output. The small undertaking was at a disadvantage under these conditions, and there was a strong tendency towards industrial combination as a method of escaping from the disadvantage of competition and of establishing greater control over prices. The combination movement began in the eighties with some temporary associations, and set in on a considerable scale about 1898–1902. The tardy development in England, as compared with Germany and the United States, may be attributed to the unfriendliness of the law and the courts to associations in restraint of trade, to the system of free trade, which made it difficult to gain control of the home market, and to the individualistic and specialized character of British industries.

Two kinds of combination are usually distinguished — vertical and horizontal — and both kinds were found in the English movement. Temporary combinations on the model of the German cartel were less frequent and usually took the form of sales associations. Vertical combination was a method by which all the processes of production, from that of providing raw materials to the sale of the finished products, were concentrated in one company as a result of the combination of hitherto independent firms. This was confined very largely to the iron and steel industry because of special conditions to be found there. In the United States this integration of processes frequently resulted from the expansion of a single company, reaching out backwards and forwards, until it was self-sufficient and complete. But in Great Britain, where many independent competing firms already existed at every stage of production, it was found simpler to combine existing firms into an integrated whole. Thus John Brown & Co., Ltd., of Sheffield, which manufactured rolled and heavy steel products and owned extensive iron-ore mines, combined with the Clydebank Engineering and Shipbuilding Co.[6] This combination, with its allied interests, thus controlled every step of production, from the mining of the ore to the construction of the finished vessels. Other similar cases were Cammell and Laird, Vickers and Maxim, and Hadfield's.

The compelling force leading to this new form of organization of the iron and steel industry was the changing position of Britain

[6] George R. Carter, *The Tendency towards Industrial Combination* (London, 1913), 81.

in the international market and the growing competition of the
United States and Germany. It was difficult to control prices, so it
became necessary to reduce costs if this new competition were to be
met. An essential condition of economical production in this industry is continuous operation. Enormous savings in heat energy are
possible if the red-hot ingot is conveyed directly from the blast
furnace to the rolling mill for further processing, or if the molten
iron is at once converted into steel, before cooling. There is, moreover, a great saving of time, by-products can be obtained, and waste
heat and gas can be utilized to heat the blast and drive the engines.
If separate firms carry on these operations independently, reheating
of the pig iron is necessary, and other economies are lost. The pressure towards integration in the iron and steel industry, especially in
the case of rolled products, became irresistible and, as before stated,
this took the form of vertical combination. Although temporary
combinations had appeared earlier, permanent organizations date
from about 1900.

In the textile industries permanent amalgamations began about
1895. Here the combinations were of rival firms at the same stage,
for the purpose of eliminating competition in favor of common action with respect to production and prices and labor. Industrial
enterprises had been growing in size in order to obtain the advantages
of large scale operation and the number had decreased. The competition among the surviving firms became more intense and even
disastrous. In order to escape the results of this competition, and
also to effect economies, combination was resorted to. Such a form
of industrial organization may be considered a natural development
under the conditions of the British market. Combination in the
textile industry may be dated from 1896 when J. and P. Coats, Ltd.
— the Thread Trust — was organized out of five independent
thread manufacturers. In the next five years about 20 combinations
were effected in the textile industry, or half of all those listed by
Carter for this period.[7] Some of these were formed from the fusion
of many firms, and others by the union of a few strong firms. Thus,
in the Bradford Dyers' Association, the firms numbered 30, and in
the Calico Printers' Association there were 60. They were at first
formed mainly in industries which were of a specialized type, and
therefore did not attract public attention. The statement in the
Report of the Committee on Trusts in 1919 that there were in
England 93 quasi-monopolist combinations regulating prices and
production, came as a surprise.

Combination was a method of adjusting the relation between production and demand, and, by limiting supply, of controlling prices.

[7] Op. cit., 25.

It occurred in the large industries, especially those in which the introduction of improved machine processes had increased productive capacity beyond normal needs. Competition introduced elements of instability, but industrial combination sought to organize business on a firmer basis. The vertical integration of iron and steel establishments in different stages of production into a co-ordinated whole must be regarded as a positive improvement in industrial technique, whose primary aim was to reduce costs. Horizontal combinations, however, which were organized to eliminate destructive competition and to control prices, tended towards monopoly. The monopolistic element was held in check in Great Britain by the free trade system, which permitted foreign producers to compete in British and foreign markets. International combinations existed, however, in rails, screws, sewing thread, bleaching powder, borax, nitrates, and tobacco, to which British firms were parties.[8]

2. GERMANY BECOMES AN INDUSTRIAL NATION

Industrialization. The period beginning about 1870 ushered in an era which saw the complete industrialization of Germany, and her transformation from a backward agricultural country to one of the leading industrial nations of Europe. This process in Germany was, however, very different from that which took place in England, where there had been a gradual development since the Industrial Revolution in technique and in liberal institutions. Germany, on the other hand, remained down to 1870 primarily an agricultural country, with industry largely in the stage of handwork and small shops, a semi-feudal political organization, and a mercantilistic commercial policy. She passed almost immediately from this stage to one of advanced capitalistic enterprise without the intermediation of a period of technical experimentation or of a *laissez faire* philosophy. Coming on the industrial stage at a time when technological and organizational methods were far advanced, Germany was able to appropriate the best that had already been worked out in other countries. She was unhampered by the existence of obsolete industrial plants or of old habits and prejudices on the part of labor or the employing class, which were already retarding English development. The industrial advance of Germany during this period was therefore extraordinarily rapid. Certain other factors should also be noted which facilitated the industrial transformation, especially in the early stages.

The formation of the Empire in 1871 and the establishment of political unity are cited by many writers as important causes of the

[8] H. W. Macrosty, *The Trust Movement in British Industry* (London, 1907), 342.

forward movement. While the effects of this were somewhat intangible they were nevertheless real. Political uncertainties and disagreements were lessened, and a unified policy replaced the former particularism. As a result of the successful war with France, the rich provinces of Alsace and Lorraine were added to German territory and a war indemnity of $1,000,000,000 was collected. Although the sudden acquisition of this new wealth led at the time to over-speculation and a rapid rise in prices, which were followed by a financial crash, the long-time effects were beneficial. But more important than any of these factors were the positive contributions made by the Germans themselves, in the building of an efficient industrial plant, adequate transportation facilities, a modern banking and financial system, and new inventions and improvements in familiar industries and the development of new and wholly German branches.

As an indication of the growing industrialization of Germany, there may be noted first of all the displacement of agriculture by industry as the leading occupation. The number of persons employed in the various branches, as given by the occupational census, is shown in the following table:

OCCUPATIONAL DISTRIBUTION OF POPULATION *
(including dependents; in thousands)

	Absolute numbers			Per cent		
	1882	*1895*	*1907*	*1882*	*1895*	*1907*
Agriculture, including forestry and fisheries	19,225	18,501	17,681	43	36	29
Industry, including mining and construction	16,058	20,253	26,387	36	39	43
Trade and transportation	4,531	5,967	8,278	10	12	13
Domestic and personal service	938	887	792	2	2	1
Public service and professions	2,223	2,835	3,407	5	5	6
Unoccupied	2,246	3,327	5,175	5	6	7

* Statistical and other material becomes more abundant and reliable during this period. And yet a German economic historian could complain "Für den grössten Teil des neunzehnten Jahrhunderts steht uns nur wenig vergleichbares Material zur Verfügung." A. Hasse, *Die wirtschaftliche Entwicklung des deutschen Reiches* (Jena, 1912). Three times the government undertook an occupational census, in 1882, 1895 and 1907, but the scope of this was limited.

Industry gained steadily on agriculture and about 1890 passed it. The transition from an agricultural to an industrial state was com-

pleted during this period, an event which evoked expressions of
alarm from some German economists, and proceeded at a rapid rate
until 1914. Although in 1860 industry contributed only about 40
per cent of the total production of goods, by 1913 the proportion was
70 per cent. There was a growth not only in quantity, but also
in variety, as new industries were developed and new wares were
produced. At the three dates given in the table of occupations the
census listed the following numbers of different occupations: 6000,
10,000 and 14,000. The growth in numbers reflects in part the
diversification that was taking place and in part the movement of
occupations out of the home and into the factory or workshop, such
as the making of clothing, preparation of food, laundry work, etc.
Industrial production increased almost sixfold between 1870 and
1913.

Geography of industry. The industrial centers of Germany in
1870 were situated in the western, central, and southern sections of
the country, and were still located there in 1914. The manufacturing districts were inland and for the most part at a considerable distance from convenient ports, but an excellent system of rail and
water transportation gave manufacturers their raw material and
fuel at reasonable prices, and also gave them access to the world
markets. Germany lies in the very heart of Europe and is very
close to all the important European countries. These conditions
made the home and European markets more important than those
overseas. There was a concentration of industry in particular localities of which the Rhineland was the most important, especially for
iron and steel. Other areas of concentrated production were Saxony
for cotton and woolen goods, Bavaria for leather and glass, Silesia
for linen, and Alsace for cotton goods.

Structure of industry. The census distinguished 16 great industrial groups, which in 1937 ranked in the following order, according to the number of persons employed: building, clothing, food and
food products, machines, instruments, textiles, metal working, mining, etc. The largest number of people was engaged in satisfying
the primary necessities in the form of consumers' goods; the making
of producers' or capital goods (with the exception of some building)
came farther down the list. More significant, however, in estimating the progress that Germany was making towards the capitalistic,
large scale system of industry, was the change in size of the different
undertakings. This is shown in the following table of industrial
establishments, including mining and building:

There is shown here a slight decline in the number of small industrial establishments and of the persons employed in them, a more
than doubling of the medium-sized establishments, and a trebling of

NUMBER OF ESTABLISHMENTS AND OCCUPIED PERSONS IN INDUSTRY
(in thousands)

Year	Small industries (1-5 persons)		Medium industries (6-50 persons)		Large industries (51 persons and over)	
	Establ.	Persons	Establ.	Persons	Establ.	Persons
1882	2176	3270	85	1109	9	1554
1895	1990	3191	139	1902	18	2907
1907	1870	3200	187	2715	29	4938

the large. It is evident that there was going on a shift from the little independent business to the large capitalistic establishment. The development of German industry during this period was primarily a growth of large establishments. Unfortunately, the German census does not give statistics of production, but there can be little doubt that by 1907 the major production of manufactured goods was being carried on in large establishments employing over 50 persons each. At this date there were 548 giant establishments each with over 1000 employees. Many of these establishments were, moreover, linked together in great enterprises with unified control. On the other hand, handwork and house industries were not destroyed, but persisted almost unchanged as to number, though their character altered greatly. Germany was not equally developed in all regions, but different sections showed different stages of economic development. Industry, therefore, even in 1907, exhibited diverse forms, ranging from primitive handwork to highly integrated capitalistic undertakings.

House industry. In 1870 the work of transforming raw materials into finished goods was still to a considerable extent carried on by handworkers in small workshops or by domestic workers in their own homes. Between this date and 1914 production was transferred largely to the factory, and by the end of the period this was the dominant form of industrial undertaking. It is difficult to present an accurate statistical or historical picture of these changes as the material is too uncertain, in spite of the fact that Germany was the first country, in the census of 1882, to separate clearly these different types of industrial organization. The salient facts may, however, be presented.

The number of domestic establishments, that is of house industry, declined from 386,000 in 1882 to 316,000 in 1907, and of persons involved from 545,000 to 482,000. Since these figures were probably too low, owing to the omission of many women, children, and old persons who undoubtedly assisted, the number at the last date may safely be placed at 500,000. This was approximately 5 per cent of those employed in industry.

The charactertistic feature of house industry was its organization, in spite of its decentralization, under the direction of a capitalistic entrepreneur, the merchant capitalist or *Verleger*. Seldom were the workers independent craftsmen and still more seldom did they sell their products directly to the consumer. House industry was a form of capitalistic undertaking, which had survived from the early system of rural domestic production and had been made over to meet the needs of a capitalist economy. Unorganized, poor, and ignorant, these domestic workers were usually exploited by the *Verleger*, and received miserable wages. The fact that over half of them were women probably made their exploitation easier. Owing to their wide dispersion, it was found very difficult to bring them under the protection of factory or education laws. They may be classified as (1) outworkers [9] for stores and factories, (2) rural home workers, who used their spare time for by-industries, and (3) sweated workers in the large cities. Probably 90 per cent of all home workers in 1907 were to be found in the textile and clothing industries.

German economists argued the question of domestic or home work with much heat, just as French economists did that of peasant proprietorship. Brentano, Philippovich, Sombart and others saw in it only a survival of an outgrown, primitive institution, and advocated its abolition. Arndt and a smaller number of apologists believed that it performed a useful function in the industrial structure and could not be spared. Although this latter group acknowledged the technical inferiority of domestic work as compared with the machine-made product of the factory, they contended that many branches of production did not lend themselves to machine processes. Some domestic work was creative and artistic, and even when it was crude and simple it was a necessary adjunct for many workers whose earnings from other sources were inadequate. The verdict of history meantime ran heavily against the institution, and with that verdict economists must be content.

Handwork. Down almost to the foundation of the Empire the handworkers in Germany had been able to retain the old gild regulations of apprenticeship, examinations, etc., but the development of the factory system made these limitations very irksome. During the sixties the individual states abolished most of these institutions and in 1869 the North German Confederation provided for complete

---

[9] Outworkers may be defined as workers doing work off the premises of the employer on materials furnished by him.

freedom of industry, which two years later was made imperial law. Although Germany was the last country in western Europe to take this step, it was opposed by the handworkers. In 1873 they formed the Union of Independent Handworkers and Manufacturers, which advocated the establishment of handworker chambers, industrial tribunals, obligatory continuation schools, reform of prison labor, of auctions, of peddling, etc. Annual congresses urged protective legislation, and finally, by the laws of 1884 and 1887, voluntary gilds (*Innungen*) were permitted which could make regulations for their own members.

This did not satisfy the handworkers, who continued to urge compulsory gilds, examinations, trade chambers, and other medieval trappings. Although these demands were not met, the restrictions were sufficiently burdensome to force many master craftsmen to join the modernized gilds; by 1890 probably a fourth of those in Germany were members. A further concession was made to the handworkers in 1897 when local officials were permitted to approve compulsory gilds, if asked for by a majority in the craft which all established master craftsmen in that locality must join, and provision was made for the organization of handworker chambers. Finally in 1908 a reactionary act was passed which gave to master craftsmen, who were not less than 24 years of age and had themselves passed a master's examination and served a three-year apprenticeship, the sole right to have apprentices — that is, to employ cheap labor. That these measures were not wholly successful is shown by the fact that in 1907 there were 3500 compulsory and 8500 free *Innungen*. The total membership of the gilds was about 500,000 or nearly half of the independent master craftsmen. Most of them were found east of the Elbe, in old Prussia and in Saxony.

In spite of legislative protection, the handworkers were waging a losing fight against the new industrial forces. They were strongest in industries where labor played an important part and which came least under the influence of machinery, such as butchers, bakers, barbers, smiths, painters, glaziers, plumbers, and personal service industries. But even in those industries their position altered for the worse. Many of them became mere outworkers for merchant employers or carried on repair work or accessory industries for factories, and were independent more in name than in reality. Although there was a decline in the number of handworkers, they did not disappear. It seldom happens in economic development that a new institution suddenly or completely displaces an old one, and in this case factory, workshop and house industry continued to produce side by side. That the handworkers persisted as long as they did, alongside the expanding factory system, was due to their acceptance of low pay, the small amount of capital required, and the possibility of quickly expanding and contracting their operations according to the state of the market. They certainly failed to solve the economic and social problems of modern industry, as their advocates hoped they would do.

The factory. The period between 1870 and 1914 witnessed the complete victory of the factory system over both home industry and handwork. The census does not define the factory, but if all establishments employing over 10 persons are assumed to have been factories rather than workshops, it appears that the number of factory workers grew from 39 per cent of all in 1882 to 66 per cent in 1907. If the same rate of growth prevailed during the whole period, it may be estimated that factory workers made up about one-quarter of all in industry in 1870 and three-quarters in 1914. This indicated a remarkable transformation in the organization and technique of German manufactures. The reasons for the superiority of the factory over its competitors were partly economic, in that it could produce at lower costs, and partly technological, in that it was more efficient.

In his stimulating book, *Der moderne Kapitalismus*, Werner Sombart lists the following conditions for the victory of industrial capitalism, which will serve as a guide in analyzing the advance in Germany: (1) a sufficient number of enterprising, energetic, superior men, who (2) control the necessary capital to introduce improvements in industrial production; (3) a profitable market; (4) a technique of production which permits output of goods of a finer quality; (5) a sufficient quantity of suitable workers; and (6) a sufficient quantity of the materials of production. Practically all of these conditions were met in Germany during this period, some of them with outstanding success.

Many of the successful industrialists in England and most of those in the United States rose from the ranks. The social constitution of Germany made this difficult, though there were some notable exceptions. Owing, moreover, to the military organization of the country, the army offered more attractions than did industry or trade, which were looked down upon.[10] The promising returns proved sufficiently alluring, however, to attract men of ability to organize and direct the new industries, and Germany did not suffer from any serious lack in this regard.

Modern industrialism requires large amounts of capital, and this, too, was forthcoming. As already indicated, German capitalistic industry started almost from scratch, unburdened by outmoded plants

[10] "There is here, in Germany, something which has great influence — it is the fact that trade and industrial pursuits are not honored. Industry and trade are only taken up as a pursuit, frequently, when no other calling can be found." Protokolle of the *Enquete*, 1878. Quoted in Schulze-Gävernitz, op. cit., 155n.

and obsolete practices. The new plants created in Germany during this period could therefore avail themselves of the latest techniques and represented a great economy in capital investment. At the beginning many of the new machines were purchased from England and with them came English engineers and skilled workmen to instruct the Germans in their use. But increasingly, as time went on, the capital equipment was constructed at home, improvements were made, and new methods and machines were invented. This process was facilitated by the excellent system of technical education that was developed. Capital formation usually takes place by the savings of the well-to-do or by corporate accumulations which are not distributed as dividends but are plowed back into industry. Both these sources were used. The incomes of those in the higher income brackets grew faster than the national income, and as a result the degree of saving and internal capital formation received an extraordinarily strong stimulus. Not only was the dependence of Germany on foreign capital markets reduced, but German investments were made abroad, especially in the twenty years before the war. By 1914 it was estimated that German foreign investments amounted to between 22 and 25 billion marks.

Profitable markets were found at home and abroad. The increasing well-being of the people permitted larger consumption, especially of staple goods of low cost and mass production. The export of capital, which was going on, took the form of goods, many of them of finer quality. The fuller discussion of this may be deferred to a later chapter.

Perhaps the most notable changes in the development of industrial capitalism were improvements in the technique of industry. These can be best described in connection with particular industries, but a few general statements will make their importance clear. If power-driven machinery be taken as a criterion, it may be asserted that the technical equipment, and at the same time the product per worker, had doubled in the period 1875–1907. Production was steadily becoming more capitalistic, that is, it was using more machinery and non-human power in the work of transforming raw materials into finished goods. The horse power of the motors used in industry increased from 1,056,000 in 1875 to 3,357,000 in 1895 and to 8,008,000 in 1907. If the capacity of one mechanical horse power be estimated as the equivalent of the physical labor power of ten men, then in 1907 each person engaged in industry had at his service two iron men. This was, however, only one-half the mechanical power per worker in Great Britain and one-fourth of that in the United States, though more than in France. That most motors were to be found in the factories is shown by the fact that only 233,000 estab-

lishments were equipped with motors at this date. As there were
only 216,000 establishments with more than 5 employees each, it
is fair to assume that the vast majority of the 1,870,000 small establishments — domestic workers and workshops — were without
mechanical power. Moreover, the larger the enterprise the greater
the use that was made of motors. If the larger industries are subdivided according to the number of workers this stands out clearly.

POWER IN LARGE INDUSTRIES, 1907

Size of establishment (no. of persons)	Number of establishments	H.p. per establishment	H.p. per 100 workers
51-200	21,782	80	84
201-1000	4,875	383	101
1001 and over	548	4177	1077

Most of this power was derived from steam engines, mostly direct, only 11 per cent being applied in the form of electricity.
Water power, wind and animals as sources of energy declined steadily in importance and at the end of this period played a very minor
role. Mechanical power was used primarily in the metal-working
and machine industries and in mining.

The important factor of labor will be treated fully in a later
chapter;[11] here only the quantity may be noted. The rapid growth
of the population from 41,000,000 in 1871 to 65,000,000 in 1910
was thought by Von Beckerath[12] to have been an important driving
force leading to increased production. Economic development is too
complex for any one factor to be given exclusive credit for progress,
but the pressure of an expanding population upon limited national
resources undoubtedly stimulated resourcefulness and invention,
while the larger numbers furnished the necessary labor supply. The
fact, however, that production increased more rapidly than population — 4 per cent as against 1.5 per cent per annum, 1860 to 1913 —
suggests that the causal relationship of these two factors might have
been in the other direction. Not merely the abundance, but also
the high quality of labor helps to explain the rapid forward movement of German industry.

Finally, the possession of adequate supplies of raw materials may
be noted. Between 1870 and 1914 Germany had half of the known
coal deposits of Europe and vast deposits of iron ore in Silesia and

[11] See Ch. XIII, sec. 2.
[12] H. von Beckerath, *Der moderne Industrialismus* (Jena, 1930), Bd. II, Th. I, p. 13.

Lorraine; her potash deposits were unrivalled. She drew upon France and other countries for additional iron, and was forced to rely upon outside sources of supply for cotton, silk, much of her wool, and numerous other articles. Since, however, modern capitalistic industry was based on coal and iron, Germany must be accounted as well equipped in those respects to develop her industries in competition with Great Britain and the United States.

Textiles. Down to 1870 the textile industry in Germany had been primarily a small scale domestic industry, with limited output, but the acquisition of Alsace the following year led to a considerable expansion, especially in the cotton industry, for 56 per cent of the spindles and 86 per cent of the power looms in the new Reich came from that territory. The cotton industry was relatively undeveloped, for cotton clothing was just beginning to come into popular use, and consequently no such social and economic revolution attended its development as had occurred in England earlier in the century. The expansion followed familiar lines — the substitution of machines for handwork, the concentration of the industry in large establishments, and gradual attainment of national self-sufficiency, followed by export to the international markets.

There was a steady concentration of the industry into a smaller number of establishments. Between 1895 and 1907 the number of establishments declined to one-half, while the average number of workers per establishment more than doubled. At the same time the total number of operatives increased. A few cottage spinners still survived, but the work had gone almost entirely into the factories, which were equipped with power machinery. Domestic weaving on hand looms persisted in considerable measure.

The German cotton industry was not so favorably situated as was the English industry in Lancashire. Except in Bavaria and Wurtemberg, where water power was used, most of the mills in Alsace, Baden, Saxony and elsewhere were far removed from their fuel supplies; they were also unfavorably placed with regard to raw materials by the distance from the cotton ports and cotton market, of which Bremen was the center. A crisis occurred in the industry when Alsace was included in the Empire, for the Alsatian mills had produced the finer counts under the protection of the high French duty. Now they were exposed to the competition of English and Swiss yarns under the low German tariff, and only gradually adjusted themselves to the making of the coarser yarns for the German market. But that meant competition with existing German mills. Finally, in 1879, the tariff raised the duties, making them higher for the finer yarns. This, however, called forth protests from the weavers, who contended that they could not compete in the world markets unless they had cheap yarns. Gradually Germany moved in the direction of special lines in which the workers developed exceptional aptitudes, such as hosiery and embroidery, or in which taste or ingenuity gave them advantages.

At the time of the cotton Enquete in 1878 it appeared that most of the spinning and almost all of the weaving machinery were imported from England. By 1914 Germany was not only making her own machinery, but was exporting it. A similar improvement took place in the skill and capacity of the workers. A German writer [13] in 1892 testified that English spinners tended twice as many spindles as a German, although the English machines ran faster. Consequently, English costs were less though the wages of the English spinner were double those of the German and the work day was seldom over 9 hours as compared with 11 to 11½ in Germany. By 1914 the conditions were fairly even, though England still led in the production of fine goods. The expansion of the cotton textile industry is indicated by the increased annual consumption of raw cotton, which grew from 116,000 tons in the period 1871–75 to 475,000 in 1911–13.

The woolen industry developed more slowly than the cotton, but in much the same direction. This was an old industry in Germany and was not so easily dislodged from its old moorings of domestic work under the direction of *Verleger*. Although the factory system had gained a foothold in 1870, there were still many domestic spinners and village weavers. By 1914 the domestic wool spinners had practically disappeared and only a few thousand domestic weavers still struggled against the power age. The number of hand looms in use declined from 47,000 in 1875 to 19,000 in 1907.

The woolen industry was in a prosperous condition in 1870, but the depression of 1873 and following years brought about a great fall in the prices of all wool products. This in turn led to a growth of large scale establishments, equipped with power-driven machinery, in an effort to reduce costs of production. The lower prices stimulated consumption, however, and the industry continued to grow. There was an increasing dependence upon foreign sources of supply, as the number of sheep in Germany steadily declined; in 1870 the domestic wool clip met about 60 per cent of the German consumption, but by 1910 it supplied less than 10 per cent. Not only did the imports of foreign wool grow, but those of foreign, and especially English, yarn increased.

The story of the other textile industries, linen and silk, may be briefly told. The former showed a steady decline. This was due in part to the shift in demand to cheaper cotton goods and more

[13] G. v. Schulze-Gävernitz, *Der Grossbetrieb* (Leipzig, 1892), 135.

recently to rayon, and in part to the lessened production of flax in Russia, from whom Germany had drawn her main supplies of raw material. The silk industry was still largely a domestic industry in 1870, especially weaving, and it continued along these lines until the late eighties. Power looms began then to replace hand looms and the silk industry became a true factory industry. Production increased, especially in part-silk staple goods for mass consumption, and by 1900 Germany's exports were second only to those of France and far ahead of Great Britain.

Iron and steel. The development of Germany's iron and steel industry was the most spectacular feature of the economic expansion which marked this period. Before 1870 Germany had a dispersed iron industry, which was localized in certain districts in Westphalia, the Siegerland, and the Ruhr, and was for the most part carried on in small establishments in primitive fashion. The acquisition of Lorraine provided the industry with enormous deposits of iron ore, which were well located for use with extensive stores of coal in the Rhine region. At the eastern edge of Germany, in Silesia, even better iron was to be found in close proximity to coal, though this was not of such good coking quality. There was thus the physical basis of an extensive iron and steel industry; all that was needed was an improved technology, capital, and organization. As J. M. Keynes wrote,[14] "The German Empire was built more truly on coal and iron than on blood and iron."

The first step in the production of the multifarious iron and steel articles which characterize modern industry — railways, ships, machinery, ordnance, and modern buildings — is the smelting of the ore. By 1850 Germany had already passed from the primitive charcoal furnaces to the use of coal and coke, though it was still far behind Great Britain in the use of improved processes. From this time on there was steady development, interrupted only by the depression years of the early seventies. The production of pig iron in Germany and that of her nearest rivals are given in the following table:

The increase in production was accompanied by a concentration of the industry into a smaller number of large establishments. These declined from an average of 218 in 1871–75 to 108 in 1889. At the same time the number of blast furnaces fell from 246 in 1880 to 213 in 1889, but the annual output of each increased from 11,000 tons to 22,000 at the same dates. In 1912 there were 313 furnaces whose annual output averaged 50,000 tons. In 1902 Germany passed Great Britain as a producer of pig iron and was exceeded only by the United States.

[14] *Economic Consequences of the Peace* (New York, 1920), 75.

PRODUCTION OF PIG IRON *
(in thousands of gross tons)

Year	Germany	United Kingdom	France	United States
1870	1,240	5,964	1178	1,665
1880	2,429	7,749	1725	3,835
1890	4,035	7,904	1962	9,203
1900	7,429	8,960	2714	13,789
1910	12,905	10,012	4038	27,304
1913	16,700	10,260	5130	30,650

* Encyclopedia of the Social Sciences, VIII, 301.

For the development of an iron industry it is essential that the ore and coal deposits should be in close proximity or that they should be united by cheap transportation. In 1830 a German writer prophesied that an iron industry could never be developed in Westphalia because coal and iron were fifty miles apart. This obstacle was met by the construction of railways, on which especially favorable rates were given after these were taken over by the state. Ruhr coal was made into coke near the mines and shipped to Lorraine; pig iron, as well as some ore and steel, was shipped back. This two-day utilization of rolling stock lowered transportation costs and made possible the union of these two resources. About 40 per cent of the pig iron produced in Germany was smelted in the Rhine-Westphalia district around Dortmund.

It was not enough to produce iron; this must be converted into steel if it were to meet the demands of the metal-using industries. Henry Bessemer had solved this problem for Great Britain, but his process was not suitable for the phosphoric ores of Lorraine or even those of Silesia. With these ores and the technical processes then prevalent, Germany had probably reached in 1870 the maximum development possible. The real beginning of the modern steel industry in that country is sometimes dated from 1881, when the rights to the English Siemens-Martin process were purchased. This basic open hearth process was well adapted to the elimination of phosphorus and was generally adopted in Great Britain and the United States.[15] In Germany, however, the Thomas-Gilchrist converter process, invented in 1879, was soon given preference, perhaps because the slag produced by this method was found valuable for use as an agricultural fertilizer. More than half of the steel made in Germany in 1915 was produced by the Thomas-Gilchrist converter

[15] See table on p. 314.

process. After the adoption of these improved methods, the final technical obstacle was removed to the phenomenal rise of the iron and steel industry. By 1914 Germany was the leading producer in Europe.

Chemical and electrical industries. Two other industries must be mentioned, though briefly, for they best illustrate that union of science and manufacture which was an important factor in the country's industrial progress. Germany possessed important stores of natural resources, which formed the basis of a heavy-chemical industry. She had almost a monopoly of potash, abundant supplies of salt, sulphur, sodium chloride, and coal, the last serving both as raw material and as a source of heat and power, upon which she built up an extensive production of heavy chemicals, especially of sulphuric acid. These were used mostly in domestic industries.

More spectacular was the development of fine chemicals, especially dyes, for these were the product of science and education. Although the discovery of aniline dyes from coal tar was made by an English chemist, W. H. Perkin, in 1856, they were developed in Germany. At that time dyes were all made from organic products, as cochineal, indigo, logwood, madder, woad and other vegetable products, and were limited and expensive. For the new synthetic dyes, which were made from the waste products of gas works and coke ovens, Germany was soon using all her own supplies and importing vast quantities from England, Belgium, and other countries in the form of benzole. Bayer succeeded in 1897, after twenty years of research, in making artificial indigo from coal tar, and destroyed the Indian production of natural indigo. In 1913 about three-fourths of the world's dyes were made in Germany. Haber invented a process for capturing atmospheric nitrogen to make synthetic ammonia, upon which was built up the explosives industry of the World War. Perfumes and medicinal drugs, of which the best known is aspirin, were also produced from coal tar, as well as a vast array of other diverse products.

These industries were due to the scientific work of a large number of university-trained chemists, who were employed by industry on a scale unequaled in any other country. In 1900 over 800 chemists were in the laboratories of eight large companies, which were employing 18,000 workmen.

The electrical industry was later in developing, for the industrial application of the epoch-making inventions in this field belong in the last decades of the nineteenth century and the first of the twentieth. The application of electricity in the heavy-current field, which produced a complete revolution in power and labor-saving machinery, had its origin in the invention of the dynamo by Werner von Siemens in 1867. The problem of power transmission took longer to work out, but in 1891 the possibility of transmission over long distances was demonstrated at the Frankfort Exhibition, when a water power of about 300 h.p. was transmitted 108 miles, with a current loss of only about 28 per cent. Siemens had already, in 1879, demonstrated the first electrical railway, but now the development of electric traction went forward on a large scale. Electricity began also to be increasingly used as a source of power for manufacturing, and as a source of light and communication. The expansion in production and the invention of new machines demanded an increase in motive power and especially of easily disposable power. By 1913 Germany was making intensive use of electric power in the heavy industries. In that year she produced one-third of the world output of electrical products and almost half of all exports.

The electrical industry showed the same tendency towards concentration that characterized other fields. "Like mushrooms in the woods after a warm summer rain," wrote Sombart, "plant after plant in this industry shot up in the eighties and especially in the nineties." In spite of the increasing demand, their capacity outran existing needs, and competition became severe. Combination began and by 1905 there emerged two large companies, which controlled basic inventions and patent rights, and dominated the industry. In the light-current field the leader was the Siemens and Halske firm. The most important enterprise in the heavy-current field was the *Allgemeine Elektrizitäts Gesellschaft* (A.E.G.), formed in 1883. Research laboratories were an essential feature of this industry and enabled inventors and industrialists to solve the technical and economic problems involved. In this field, as in that of industrial chemistry, Germany was a leader and had achieved a dominating position by 1914.

The combination movement. Allusion has already been made to the tendency towards concentration in large scale establishments which was manifesting itself in Germany as in other industrial countries, by the development of capitalistic undertakings employing large amounts of capital in mass production. This movement was especially strong in mining, iron and steel, the manufacture of machinery, and in the chemical and textile industries. But there was also taking place a combination of businesses in associations for concerted action. Two main forms may be distinguished, which correspond roughly to American pools and industrial consolidations.

The cartel was distinctively German. It was a contractual union of enterprises, which retained their identity and industrial independence, for the regulation of the market, either in purchasing goods for production or especially in selling their products. Their purpose was not to abolish competition, but to regulate it.

The other type was the so-called *Konzern*. The concerns had as their task the rationalization of the processes of production within a great industrial complex, and might take the form of horizontal or of vertical combinations. They aimed, not at the regulation of the market price structure, but rather at economies in production. Concerns were the result of technical improvements. When it was found more economical, for instance, to carry the molten iron from the blast furnace directly to the steel works or the foundry, thus avoiding the costs of reheating, the fusion into integrated combinations of plants on different levels of production which followed one another took place. Such were vertical combinations. Where establishments on the same level of production were united, horizontal combinations were formed. In neither case, however, did they aim at monopoly power over prices. This was a function of the cartels.

The first cartel was probably the rail association of 1864, but the cartel movement on a large scale dates from the seventies. The depression of those years, the low prices, and the intense competition forced the individualistically trained enterprisers to unite and, by regulating competition, attempt to improve the unsatisfactory market conditions. Cartels have been called by some German writers *Kinder der Not*, children of necessity. They were given a decided impulse by the protectionist policy after 1879, which, by shutting out foreign competitors, made it easier for domestic producers to combine. During the next two decades they were the ruling form of industrial combination. The number of cartels was estimated as 137 in 1890, but the first official count was made in 1905 by the Ministry of the Interior, which reported 385. Six years later Tschierschky estimated their number at 550 to 600. They were strongest in the potash, coal, iron and steel, textile, plate glass, cement, and chemical industries.

One of the oldest of these cartels was the Rhenish coal-selling syndicate, and its organization may be described as fairly typical. Formed of the Rhenish-Westphalian coal owners, it did not attempt directly to control production, but acted as a selling agency. Orders for coal from German industries and foreign consumers were accepted and prorated among the different producers according to their capacity, their location, and the place where the coal was to be sent, and the selling price was fixed. Under such a scheme the individual coal owner controlled his own costs of production and his profit depended on his ability to hold those down. On the other hand, it was contended that the result of such a method was to keep a number of marginal producers in the business.

The concerns developed for the most part after 1895. As long as prices of raw materials and half-finished goods were low, as they had been during the preceding years, there was no incentive for manufacturers of finished products to hook up with raw material plants. Nor had technology advanced sufficiently for such union to bring with it technical or economic advantages. After 1895, however, conditions changed and vertical and horizontal combinations were formed. The movement was characterized not only by a technical and commercial concentration, but also by a concentration of ownership, and by a financial concentration, under which capitalists and banks organized and controlled whole groups of enterprises and even whole branches of industry — the "finance capitalism" of Sombart. This was especially marked in mining, the heavy iron industry, and the dye and electrical industries.

The explanation for these particular forms of industrial organization in Germany is to be found in a number of special circumstances. The presence of certain raw materials, the stage of technical development, the favorable attitude of legislators and courts, which treated cartel agreements as legal contracts, and the difficult market position of most German manufacturers do not sufficiently explain them. Von Beckerath [16] concludes that it was due "to the attitude, instilled in state and army, of disciplined union of strength and unselfish subordination of self for the general good." To this Liefman adds the old spirit of association of the Germans. The combination of a spirit of authority on the one hand and of the subordination of disciplined masses on the other gave a firm foundation for German capitalistic industry.

3. SMALL INDUSTRY SURVIVES IN FRANCE

Slow industrialization. The movement to industrialization, which was proceeding so rapidly in Great Britain, Germany and the United States during this period, was advancing at a relatively slow pace in France. It was hampered by the slight growth of the population and by the dominantly agricultural interests of the people. The widespread ownership of land disinclined the French workers to migrate to the industrial centers to the same extent as in Great Britain or Germany. If the growth of cities be taken as a measure of industrialization, France was still in 1914 predominantly rural; the percentage of the population living in towns of 2000 inhabitants or over was 32.4 in 1876 and was still only 44.1 in 1911.

The loss of Alsace and Lorraine in 1871 meant the transference

---

[16] *Kräfte, Ziele, und Gestaltungen in der deutschen Industriewirtschaft* (Jena, 1923), 5. Compare A. Marshall, *Industry and Trade* (London, 1919), 546.

of 1,500,000 people, together with important textile industries in the former and potentially valuable deposits of iron ore in the latter. Her defeat in the Franco-Prussian war lowered France's prestige and undoubtedly exercised a depressing effect on national psychology. This was followed by a long period of hard times, both for agriculture, which suffered from the phylloxera and foreign competition, and for industry, whose business was hurt by agricultural depression and falling prices. After about 1892, however, progress became more rapid and French industry became more capitalistic.

An important factor in explaining the slowness of this movement to industrialization was undoubtedly the persistence of old methods in the production of quality goods. While Great Britain and Germany were producing cheap articles for mass consumption by machine methods, France clung to lines and to techniques that emphasized manual skill and artistic workmanship rather than large scale capitalistic enterprise. But even more important, as time went on, were the character of the raw materials at the disposal of industry, and their geographical distribution.

Raw materials and their distribution. France was well supplied with iron, but lacked coal. She possessed adequate stores of some of the minor metals, such as zinc and lead, aluminum and platinum, but was without copper, of greater industrial importance. Her textile industries were well supplied with domestic wool until the sixties, but by 1914 the imports were nearly eight times the home clip. She became increasingly dependent on foreign supplies of raw silk and was wholly so for cotton. Water power was present but was largely undeveloped.

Of all the raw materials mentioned France was best supplied with iron, as the bulk of the iron ore of western Europe was concentrated in the northeastern corner of the country. The Franco-German frontier established after the war of 1870 was intended to give Germany practically all the iron deposits in Lorraine, but Bismarck's geologists made a mistake and left over half the ore on the French side.

Most of the coal was found in the north, where the coal measures were a continuation of the Belgian deposits; a smaller amount was found in the Loire district. None of it was good coking coal, the veins were narrow, and the mines generally deep, so that costs of production were high. Nevertheless, the output was creditable and increased steadily, but it was never sufficient to supply the home market.

The location of industry was determined largely by the availability of raw materials and fuel, and by the presence of markets. Consequently, industry developed principally in the north, where coal was to be had, and also in the ports, where supplies of foreign

PRODUCTION AND CONSUMPTION OF COAL

Year	Production	Consumption
	(thousands of metric tons)	
1872	16,000	24,000
1890	26,000	35,000
1900	33,400	46,800
1913	41,000	61,000

raw materials could be obtained. Paris, with its large body of consumers and workers, was always an important industrial center. The only industrially developed section in the south was the district around Lyons with its silk mills. Geographical dispersion, rather than localization as in England, was characteristic of French industry. Owing to the nature of the coal deposits, which were scattered in a large number of small beds all over the country, there was little opportunity for the development of closely grouped large industries depending on heavy use of coal. On the contrary, these local deposits afforded the basis for many scattered establishments, especially in industries that required only small amounts of fuel. A large number of small manufacturing centers therefore developed in France, especially in textiles, porcelains, and other similar products. The presence of bauxite in southern France and the availability of hydro-electric power along the upper Rhine called into being an important aluminum industry.

The structure of industry. No industrial census was taken in France during this period, but in 1896 an effort was made, on the basis of the census of population, to ascertain the number of persons in various branches of industry. Comparable figures are also available for 1901 and 1906, but they are not very satisfactory.

WAGE AND SALARY RECEIVERS IN INDUSTRY, BY SIZE OF ESTABLISHMENT *

No. of employees in establ.	No. of employees			No. of establ. 1906	Percentage distribution of employees		
	1896	1901	1906		1896	1901	1906
1-10	1,134,703	1,130,851	1,187,619	567,871	36	32	32
11-100	853,000	999,150	1,026,720	36,374	28	28	27
over 100	1,124,000	1,396,815	1,542,863	4,485	36	40	41
Total	3,111,703	3,526,816	3,757,202	608,730	100	100	100

* *Résultats statistiques du recensement général de la population effectué de 4 mars 1906* (Paris, 1908), I, 1, p. 125.

The table shows the existence of a vast number of small under-takings, which persisted almost unchanged relatively. Most of these were small workshops where textiles and clothing, artistic industries, and luxury trades were carried on by handworkers or little enter-prisers with a few helpers. The diffusion of the small enterprise is not adequately shown in the table, but may be indicated by a further breakdown of the figures for 1896. There were 1,505,800 persons working alone. Of the establishments with employees, 50 per cent had 1 employee, 20 per cent had 2, 10 per cent had 3, 5 per cent had 4, and only 15 per cent had over 4. If the number of workers be taken as the criterion, a more even distribution among the small, medium, and large establishments is shown; indeed, there was a slight gain for the large ones. The time covered is too short and the character of these statistics too unsatisfactory to warrant further analysis. It appears, however, that the typical French enterprise was that of a man working alone, with the aid of his wife, or with one or two helpers. Not until the rise of the iron and steel industry was there a strong movement to concentration and large scale en-terprise.

Handwork and house industry. The character of French indus-try, with its emphasis on artistic and quality work and luxury goods, and the multiplicity of small local trades favored the workshop and permitted its continuance in France long after it had yielded place to the factory in England and even in Germany. It stood on its own feet as an institution well suited to the individualistic attitude of the French worker; there was no system of state-supported gilds, as in Germany, to prolong its existence artificially. The last compulsory gild, that of the printers, was abolished in 1870.

House industry was also widespread in France, especially in the textile and clothing industries. There were several reasons for this. French workers did not take to the factory system as readily as did those in the neighboring countries. The absence of trade unions made it easier to use rural and urban outworkers for various lines which elsewhere were transferred to the factory. And the factory legislation of 1892 and 1900, by restricting the work of women and young persons in factories, created a reservoir of labor which could be utilized in home work. But most important of all was the exist-ence of a large peasant population who carried on home work as by-industries in connection with their small farming operations.

Official statistics of this form of industry are almost altogether lacking, but from studies of particular industries a fairly complete picture can be presented. According to the census of 1911 there were 632,338 persons engaged in house industries; most of these were to be found in the silk industry, followed by woolen and cotton weaving, and embroidery. The most important center of the silk industry was Lyons. In 1870 the mechanization of spinning was complete, but in weaving the hand loom was still almost supreme, though it too was forced to yield slowly to the power loom. The changes may be briefly shown.[17]

Year	Power looms	Hand looms, town and country	Hand looms, Lyons alone
1873	6,000	110,000	35,000
1888	19,000	75,000	12,000
1903	38,000	50,000	4,000

By 1870 the spinning of wool was being rapidly transferred to the factories, but weaving, especially in expensive novelties, which were made in small quantities and called for expert workmanship, still held its own as a house industry. Roubaix was the center of this trade. The cotton industry of Normandy, called by Audiganne as late as 1860 *la terre classique du travail à domicile*, was completely mechanized by 1914. Spinning was early transferred to the factory, and by the end of the century the hand looms had disappeared from this district. There were still, however, some 27,000 hand looms scattered throughout the country.

As the rural house textile industries were forced out, a new form developed in the urban clothing industry. The sewing machine, especially after the introduction of electricity as a motive power, made it possible for individual workers to carry on this industry outside of the factory. It was a sweated industry and developed conditions similar to those in England and Germany. Other industries which were carried on at home or in small workshops yielded cutlery, furniture, watches, toys, and a host of small but expensive goods known as *articles de Paris*. Most of these home industries produced consumption goods, often luxury goods, whose market was fluctuating and small. In an age when the tendency was towards the production of cheap wares for mass consumption or for capital goods, the hand-made quality goods of France suffered and the country steadily lost ground to her more highly industrialized rivals.

Motive power in French industry. The development of industrialism may be fairly accurately gauged by the use of non-human power. Judged by this standard it appears that France made steady though not rapid progress.

Most of these engines were used for mining and metal working, and after 1900 increasingly for the development of electricity. Both the horse power per establishment and that per machine showed a

[17] J. H. Clapham, *The Economic Development of France and Germany*, 1815–1914, 253.

STEAM ENGINES IN FRANCE *

Year	Number of establishments with steam engines	Number of steam engines	Power (1000 h.p.)	H.p. per establ.
1870	22,851	27,088	336	14.7
1880	34,063	41,772	544	16.0
1890	46,671	58,751	863	18.5
1900	57,306	74,636	1,791	31.2
1910	63,135	82,238	2,912	46.1
1913	63,113	81,740	3,539	56.1

* *Annuaire Statistique*, 1924, p. 65.

notable increase, so that the factories and mines were better equipped than the growth in the number of steam engines would indicate. The horse power per establishment grew from 15 in 1870 to 56 in 1913, while that per machine increased for the same dates from 12 to 43. In spite of this progress France lagged far behind England and Germany. Even including 750,000 horse power derived from water power, France generated only about 3,000,000 horse power in 1906, against about 8,000,000 each in Germany and England.

Textile industries. The outstanding French textile industry was silk. Under earlier conditions of production silk goods were expensive and the market was comparatively narrow. When fashion entered in new patterns had continually to be produced. This could be done by hand methods, but when machinery was introduced quantity production of the same pattern took place. Production for the masses was, however, possible only if the goods were cheap. This was not feasible with pure silk, but by mixing silk with cotton or other cheap materials popular goods at a low price, with all the lure of real silk, could be produced. And so the French silk industry was transformed from a narrow de luxe trade to one for the masses. Production and export both responded to these conditions. In 1880 France produced more silk goods than all other European states together.[18] Her best market was free trade England, which in 1913 took 65 per cent of the exports, and next the United States. This latter country was at this date also the leading producer, using twice as much raw silk as France.

A second transformation took place at the beginning of the twentieth century with the entrance of rayon into the market on a commercial scale. It was the irony of fate that an invention which was so greatly to injure the real-silk industry should have been made by a Frenchman. Chardonnet first produced rayon in 1889 and exhibited it at the Paris Exposition of that year. The first rayon factory

[18] H. Sée, *Französische Wirtschaftsgeschichte*, II, 451.

was established at Besançon, but the new industry was appropriated by the more industrialized countries, especially the United States, and the French real-silk industry suffered severely from this new competition of a cheap yet appealing rival.   Out of a world production of 12,600 tons of rayon in 1913 France consumed only 600 tons.

The woolen industry developed along much the same lines as silk.   By 1870 spinning was almost completely mechanized, but weaving did not move out of the cottages into the factories so rapidly.   There were still hand looms to be found for special fabrics in 1914.   The industry was concentrated principally in two centers: Roubaix with the neighboring city of Tourcoing in the north, which had the advantage of nearness to coal and to ports where imported wool was landed, and Reims in the east.   It showed steady progress until the eighties, occupying in France the same dominant position that the cotton industry did in England.   In 1882 the export of woolen goods reached its highest point, with 401 million francs, but after that it lost ground in the world markets.   The woolen industry proper, which used carded, not combed, wool, was slow in adopting power machinery and also suffered from changes in demand.   It produced relatively heavy goods, suitable for men's wear, such as flannels and broadcloth; but the latter went out of fashion.   The production of cheap shoddy cloth, to which the French gave the more picturesque name of *drap de renaissance*, on the other hand, increased, especially in the south.   The worsted industry, which made fabrics for women's wear, showed steady growth.   In these, distinctive patterns, artistic finish, and draping qualities gave to French manufacturers a superiority, especially in novelties, which they never lost.   About half of the output was exported to the only free market, that of Great Britain.

The growth of the modern French cotton industry may be dated from the sixties.   At that time the cheapening of transportation, both land and water, reduced costs of production, chiefly in raw materials, even more than did improvements in technique.   It also increased international competition and destroyed the isolation of local markets.   A more direct blow was the cession to Germany of the Alsatian industry with 1,500,000 spindles out of 6,000,000 and an even greater proportion of looms.   Partly as a result of the pressure of these new forces, there took place rapid changes in technical equipment, which carried spinning entirely out of the cottages and into the factories.   The transition in weaving, from hand to power looms, went on more slowly.   There were still 27,000 hand looms in use in 1914, most of these being found in Tarare; on them fine muslins and lawns were woven.

The industry as a whole showed a considerable expansion, though the number of spindles is a defective measure for due account is not taken of the speed of the machine or the fineness of the yarn. It was concentrated in three main districts: Normandy, with Rouen as the center, was the oldest seat of cotton production and at the beginning of this period had about half the spindles in France, but it had progressed least; in 1911 it had 1,670,000 spindles. The north, with Lille as the center, the home of fine spinning, especially of lace, embroidery, cambric and mixed tissues, doubled the number of its spindles between 1870 and 1911, and by the latter date had about 2,800,000. The east, centering around Épinal, with about the same number of spindles in 1911, showed an even more rapid expansion. Having developed late the industry possessed modern machinery and it had cheap labor and water power. There was a similar localization of weaving, over 87 per cent of the looms being found in the districts of Normandy, the east around Épinal, and the south around Tarare and Roanne.

Iron and steel. In 1870 France was second only to Great Britain in the production of iron and steel, with a total output of about 1,000,000 tons. Between 1878 and 1885, however, the deposits of iron ore in the central and northern districts, which had been the centers of the industry, began to approach exhaustion. The loss of Lorraine deprived France of great iron deposits in the east. The outlook was indeed dark, but the situation was saved through the discovery of immense deposits of ore on the French side of the new boundary, which were easily worked and had the precious quality of fusibility, but which had a small iron content and a large proportion of phosphorus and sulphur. It was consequently ill adapted to steel making by the Bessemer process, which requires a non-phosphoric ore. Nevertheless, French metallurgists at once adopted the Bessemer method. Indeed, they claimed that they improved upon it, by introducing manganese as a deoxidizer; this innovation, first perfected at the mills of Terrenoire in the Loire district, gave a more malleable metal, cheaper and better adapted to the needs of industry than Bessemer, which was somewhat brittle. Since, however, French ores were not suited to this process, pure ore was imported from Spain, Italy, and Algiers during the period 1864–78. Under the circumstances, the iron and steel industry could have only a restricted development.

Fortunately, two revolutionary inventions were made just at this juncture which gave a new lease on life to the French industry. In 1879 Thomas and Gilchrist invented their basic process, by which phosphoric ore could be converted into steel. Once again the door was opened for a successful iron and steel industry in France. The leading French metallurgists, Schneider and De Wendel, at once purchased licenses to use this method, and a new era began. The first Thomas converter in France was installed in the Creusot plant in 1879. In the same year Pierre Martin improved his open hearth process by introducing a basic lining of magnesite. As a result of these two inventions the steel industry took a great spurt. Indeed the development of the modern iron and steel industry in France may be said to have begun between 1880 and 1890. French metallurgists used both the Thomas-Gilchrist converter and the Martin open hearth process, but as time went on they found the former better adapted to their needs and to their ores, especially the *minette* of Lorraine. The Martin process worked less rapidly than the converter, but it yielded steel of a better quality. In 1913 the distribution of steel production by processes was Bessemer 3.2 per cent, Martin 40.6, and Thomas 56.2.

Up to this time the production and use of iron had far exceeded that of steel. In 1882 iron production reached the maximum, with 1,073,000 tons as against 485,000 tons of steel. The Eiffel tower was built of iron in 1889. But by 1900 steel had passed iron, and in 1913 had reached an output of 4,635,000 tons, while iron production had shrunk to 526,000 tons. The production of iron ore in 1913 and its conversion into iron and steel, in comparison with Great Britain and Germany, is shown in the following table: [19]

Country	Iron ore	Pig iron	Steel
		(in millions of tons)	
France	21.7	5.3	4.6
Great Britain	16.2	10.4	7.7
Germany	28.6	16.7	17.6

It is clear that France was not utilizing her great deposits of iron ore. The industry labored under serious natural disadvantages which were not alleviated by the high tariff policy. Most of the ore was located in the Lorraine basin, which was well served by transportation facilities, but lacked coal, especially good coking coal. This was met, for certain purposes, by the importation of coke, chiefly from German Westphalia, but this was expensive for the price was controlled by German interests. Since costs of production were higher in France than in other industrialized countries, she was not able to sell her products in the competitive international markets and the home industry could not absorb all the iron ore produced. Half of the ore was therefore exported, mostly to Germany. Where coal and ore are separated, it is usually found cheaper to move the ore to the coal, for in the process of coking the coal used for smelting the gases are recovered and used for heating the furnaces. Valuable

[19] P. de Rousiers, *Les grandes industries modernes* (Paris, 1927), II, 128.

by-products are also obtained both in the coking and in the smelting processes. Since German metallurgy was farther advanced than that of France, there was little doubt that the union of the ore and the coke would be effected in the former country.

The oldest iron and steel district in France was situated in the center; here were located the Creusot works. It had some good hematite ores, but lacked coal and was at a disadvantage when the new processes were introduced. Only by concentrating on quality goods was the industry in this area able to survive. "In the north and east," wrote Levainville,[20] "the high furnace gave life to the industry; in the center, the laboratory." Here Creusot turned out armament and cannons of the finest steel, electrical supplies, measuring instruments, airplane and automobile parts.

The industry of the north was based upon the coal of the Nord and Pas-de-Calais, which in 1913 together produced 72 per cent of the coal and 93 per cent of the coke of France. Favored by a good system of transportation this district drew the needed supplies of iron ore from Normandy and especially Lorraine. Its products consisted of half-finished and finished wares such as nails, chairs, machine parts, and small articles like nails, screws, and bolts; it led in iron plates and sheets.

The eastern district lacked coal, but it had deposits of iron which ranked only after the Lake Superior region in the United States. In 1913 Meurthe-et-Moselle in the heart of the Lorraine *minette* produced 91 per cent of the iron mined in France. The coal needed for the blast furnaces was drawn from Belgian and German mines, but fully half the ore was exported instead of being smelted at home. The products of this region were heavy massive wares, which found an outlet principally in the domestic and colonial markets.

Industrial combination. France was a nation of small enterprises scattered over the whole country. Not until the rise of the heavy industries was there any tendency to geographical concentration. In the textile and some other industries the development of gas engines and electric motors was even making for decentralization. Nor was there any strong movement to large scale enterprise, to concentration in big establishments, for the French types of goods were not well adapted to mass production. The statistics of steam power, already given, showed a gain in the horse power per establishment from 15 in 1870 to 56 in 1913, but even this last figure does not indicate any such striking industrial concentration as was going on in England or Germany. And finally the fact that only 15 per cent of the establishments employed over four workers each conclusively proves the predominance of the small industry.

[20] *L'industrie du fer en France* (Paris, 1922), 85.

Under such circumstances industrial combinations and cartels could not flourish, though they were not altogether absent. Not only was the industrial structure unfavorable to their development, but the law regarded them with disfavor. The penal code, practically unchanged since 1810, punished any improper fixation of prices by combination; it endeavored to secure a free competitive market. In spite of these difficulties efforts were made in most of the leading industries to stabilize prices and avoid the evils of unrestricted competition. This policy was most successful in coal mining, where the geographical concentration and limited number of producers made a unified market policy feasible. A coal cartel, bearing the innocuous name "Office of Coal Statistics of the North," was formed, embracing about two-thirds of the production in the Valenciennes district, but some of the most important and many of the little miners refused to come in. Its object was to regularize production and to stabilize prices; the net effect was apparently to steady the former and raise the latter.

Several somewhat firmer combinations were effected in the iron and steel industry, which regulated production by assigning quotas to their members, but they were unable to bring more than a tenth of the total output under their sway. Illustrations of such combinations were two *comptoirs* in the pig iron field, one of which controlled sales in France and the other in the foreign market. No restrictions were placed on the total production of members, but if they exceeded their quotas they must sell the excess outside the territory covered by the *comptoir*. Prices were nevertheless held steady and even reduced, and integration was stimulated. Integration never proceeded as far in France as in other countries, partly by reason of the geographical dispersion of the raw materials. The relationship between iron mines and blast furnaces is so close that they were generally brought under one management. Less often did they have their own coal mines. Complete integration was to be found only in the great plants of the center district, like the Creusot works under the Schneider brothers. Using, as they did, primarily the Martin open hearth process, they obtained notable technical economies by carrying the ore and fuel in an orderly progression from mine and coking plant, through the blast furnace, the steel mill, and the rolling mill, to highly finished manufactured articles and by-products such as fertilizer and cement.

In the textile industry cartels were formed only in spinning; weaving was too much in the hands of small establishments to be brought together. A few other cartels existed, in petroleum, cement, paper, glass, and some other industries, but they exercised little influence on trade.

French cartels, on the whole, endeavored to secure to old, quality industries prices necessary for their existence by regulating competition. The spirit underlying them was that of the gild and was strongly influenced by traditions of artistic enterprise. In conformity with the individualistic temper of French enterprisers, they limited the freedom of their members as little as possible and left to them the carrying through of sales and other operations connected with the business. They resembled trade associations rather than cartels of the German type or trusts on the American model. The character of French industry, with its emphasis on artistry, taste, fashion, and luxury, did not fit it for the regimentation which the mass production of other countries made inevitable.

BIBLIOGRAPHICAL NOTE

1. *Britain.* Discerning comparisons of the development of industrial organization in Great Britain, Germany, and France are scattered throughout A. Marshall, *Industry and Trade* (London, 1920). A good outline is T. G. Williams, *The Main Currents of Social and Industrial Change since* 1870 (London, 1936). On the separate industries H. S. Jevons, *The British Coal Trade* (London, 1915) is a careful study. On the iron and steel industry P. L. Burn, *The Economic History of Steel Making, 1867–1939* (Cambridge, 1940) is authoritative. J. S. Jeans, *The Iron Trade of Great Britain* (London, 1906) is informed and somewhat technical. J. C. Allen, *Birmingham and the Black Country, 1860–1927* (London, 1929) is broader than the title suggests and gives a keen analysis. G. F. H. Lloyd, *The Cutlery Trades* (London, 1913) is excellent. Two of the newer industries are treated in A. G. White, *Forty Years of Electrical Progress* (London, 1936), and S. Miall, *History of the British Chemical Industry, 1634–1928* (London, 1931). On industrial organization G. R. Carter, *The Tendency Toward Industrial Combination* (London, 1913), and H. W. Macrosty, *The Trust Movement in British Industry* (London, 1907) present a good historical survey. H. Levy, *Monopoly and Competition: A Study in English Industrial Organization* (London, 1911) is rather theoretical but penetrating.

2. *Germany.* The evolution of Germany as an industrial state is described by K. Oldenberg, *Deutschland als Industriestaat* (1897). A glorification of Germany's industrial advance is K. Helfferich, *Germany's Economic Progress and National Wealth, 1888–1913* (New York, 1914). E. D. Howard, *Causes and Extent of the Recent Industrial Progress of Germany* (Boston, 1907) is a careful survey. T. Veblen, *Imperial Germany and the Industrial Revolution* (new ed., New York, 1939) is a penetrating analysis. H. Rauchberg, *Die Berufus- und Gewerbezählung im Deutschen Reich* (Berlin, 1901) is an excellent critical analysis of the census of 1895. Handwork is described by F. Hoffmann, *Die Organization des Handwerks* (1897), house industry is described by H. Koch, *Die deutsche Hausindustrie* (München, 1913) and is defended by P. Arndt, *Die wirtschaftliche und soziale Bedeutung der Heimarbeit* (Jena, 1922). Small industry is well treated in W. Kulemann, *Der Kleingewerbe* (Göttingen, 1895). Of separate industries R. M. R. Dehn, *The German Cotton Industry* (Manchester, 1913) gives a clear but elementary description. More scholarly is G. Schulze-Gävernitz, *The Cotton Trade in England and on the Continent* (Translated from the German, London, 1895). The competitive struggles of the iron industry are well portrayed in R. Martin,

Die Eisenindustrie in ihrem Kampf um den Absatzmarkt (Leipzig, 1904). Industrial organization is traced historically in J. Strieda, *Studien zur Geschichte der kapitalistischen Organizationsformen* (Leipzig, 1914), and more theoretically in R. Liefmann, *Cartelle and Trusts* (4te Aufl., Stuttgart, 1920). Somewhat narrower is A. H. Stockder, *German Trade Associations* (New York, 1924). H. Mannstadt, *Ursachen und Ziele des Zusammenschlusses im Gewerbe* (June, 1916) is a study of monopoly.

3. *France.* A general and somewhat philosophical survey is G. Renard et A. Dulac, *L'évolution industrielle* (Paris, 1912). G. d'Avenel, *Mécanisme de la vie moderne*, 5 vols. (Paris, 1896–1911) covers the whole of French economic life. A. Aftalion, *Le développement de la fabrique dans les industries de habillement* (Paris, 1906) traces the clothing industry, and *Le développement de la fabrique et le travail à domicile* (Paris, 1906) sweating. G. Levy, *Des moyens de conserver l'industrie à domicile* (Lyons, 1914) defends house industry. The cotton industry, as the leading one, aroused most interest, and is treated in R. B. Forrester, *The Cotton Industry of France* (Manchester, 1921), a well-informed account; G. Grandgeorge et L. Tabourier, *L'industrie textile en France au* 1896 (Paris, 1897); P. de Rousiers, *Les grandes industries modernes*, 5 vols. (Paris, 1926–28). Vol. I covers coal, Vol. II iron and steel, and Vol. III the textile industries. These volumes are somewhat technical, but clear. An excellent, clear, and concise account of the iron and steel industry is J. Levainville, *L'industrie du fer en France* (Paris, 1922). The growing chemical industry is described in K. Löffl, *Die Chemische Industrie Frankreichs* (Stuttgart, 1917). Industrial organization is well treated in P. de Rousiers, *Les syndicats industriels de producteurs, en France et en l'étranger* (Paris, 1912), and in J. Chastin, *Les trusts et les syndicats* (Paris, 1909).

CHAPTER X

COMMERCE AND COMMERCIAL POLICY

1. HEYDAY OF FREE TRADE IN BRITAIN

Foreign trade. With the growth of population, the economic development of the country, and the improvement in the standard of living of the people, foreign trade came to play a larger and more vital part in the activities of the British nation. As agriculture declined relatively, the dependence on foreign supplies of food became greater. At the same time the industrial expansion called for greater quantities of overseas raw materials, both of which were paid for primarily with manufactured goods. Markets must be had for these exports of manufactures, since economical mass production of staple goods, such as Britain turned out in enormous quantities, required large outlets. Foreign trade constituted therefore a vital part of the economic structure. The basis of international trade is usually said to lie in the relative superiority of one country or region over others in the production of particular goods, or in differences in industrial or cultural developments. The superiority of the English was to be found not so much in the possession of natural resources as in the possession of technical skills, which had been developed during the century since the beginning of the Industrial Revolution. Their geographical location, on the edge of the world's busiest ocean, and close to the most advanced nations in Europe, gave them special facilities for commerce. The commercial history of this period presents a continuous series of adaptations to a widening and changing environment. Down to 1870 it may be said that most trade was carried on between undeveloped countries producing raw materials and developed countries manufacturing them. After that date, however, the trade among the industrially developed countries became more important than that between them and the newer regions. The growth of British foreign trade during this period was primarily due to the expansion of commercial intercourse with her continental neighbors and the United States rather than with more backward nations.

The expansion of British foreign commerce during the period 1870–1914 may be briefly summarized.

The important features shown in this table are the comparative steadiness of both imports and exports between 1870 and 1900 and the tremendous spurt after that date; the years 1906–10 were the most prosperous in this whole period and showed an extraordinary advance. In 1913 about 40 per cent of the world's seaborne trade emanated from or ended in British ports. Other noteworthy features were the importance of the re-export trade, and the increasing disparity between imports and exports with a resulting adverse balance of trade. Each of these points deserves analysis.

VALUE OF BRITISH MERCHANDISE IMPORTS AND EXPORTS, 1870–1914

Period	Imports	Exports	Re-exports	Excess of Imports
	(average annual in millions of pounds sterling)			
1870–79	305	218	55	87
1880–89	331	230	62	101
1890–99	375	236	61	139
1900–09	571	410	80	161
1910–14	714	570	107	144

Imports. In 1870 the principal imports were raw materials and partly manufactured goods, together with exotic products. Shifts took place between this date and 1914. The imports may be divided roughly into two main groups — food for the increasing population and raw materials for the expanding manufactures. In 1913 raw materials, consisting of iron and other ores, wood and timber, stones and slates, fertilizers, and textile materials, made up nearly one-half of all imports by weight, foodstuffs about one-third, and miscellaneous articles, such as metals and machinery, petroleum, etc., the remainder.[1] Partly by necessity and partly through deliberate economic policy, Britain allowed itself to become increasingly dependent on outside sources of supply for food, and this dependency was accentuated by the rising standard of living and the inclusion of many new items in the average citizen's diet.

Although Great Britain was well supplied with the two most essential raw materials of modern industry, coal and iron, she lacked others, in whole or in part, which were necessary for her diversified manufactures. In order of importance these were textile raw materials, especially cotton; timber, metallic ores and unworked metals, hides, rubber, and paper-making materials. The Civil War in the United States had cut off the normal supplies of raw cotton and the Lancashire industries had suffered severely, but by 1870 the production of raw cotton in the United States was almost normal. The United States had always been the main source of supply, and after 1865 rapidly regained this position. In 1871 England's total imports of raw cotton were 1778 million pounds, of which the United States supplied 1039. The pre-eminence of the United States remained undisputed until the end of the century, but after 1900

[1] Report on Shipping and Shipbuilding, by Committee on Commercial and Industrial Policy, Board of Trade (London, 1918), 76.

became less assured; the boll weevil forced diversification of crops and cut down the yield, and new areas, like Brazil, started to grow cotton.

Wool was grown at home, but the domestic supplies were increasingly inadequate to the rapidly growing demand. The estimated yield of domestic wool in 1870 was 150 million pounds and the imports were 266 million; and by 1913 they were 95 and 800. The decline in the proportion of domestic wool was in part the result of changes in the realm of agriculture, and in part because of shifts in fashion which discriminated against fabrics made of long wools, which were best grown in England.

The other textile raw materials call for little notice. Linen was a declining industry and this fact was recorded in a falling off of flax imports. Hemp was scarcely more important. Jute, however, all of which came from India, was imported in growing quantities, to supply sacking for various purposes.

Since the practical destruction of her own forests in the eighteenth century Britain had been dependent on foreign supplies of timber. Most of this came from the Baltic countries, but there were also tropical woods, and southern pine from the United States.

Even more vital than raw materials was food. By 1870 nearly half of the wheat was imported and in 1912 almost a third. Little meat came in at the beginning of the period, but at the end about 40 per cent was imported. Tea, coffee, cocoa, sugar, tropical fruits and spices, rice, and similar commodities came in increasing quantities from the warm latitudes.

Exports. As Britain became more thoroughly industrialized it was inevitable that her exports should be manufactured goods rather than raw products. Wholly manufactured goods made up three-fourths of the exports; if partly manufactured goods are added, the total was over nine-tenths. Textiles ranked first and iron and steel second. Of the textiles, cotton was far in the lead with about three-quarters of this group, on a value basis. The development of competing textile industries in other countries, especially in medium and coarse lines, forced Britain to capitalize her unique advantages of climate and skilled labor and to concentrate increasingly upon fine-quality goods. In doing so, however, she produced for a narrower and less stable market. This was true of both cotton goods and woolens. The United States, Germany, and Japan enormously increased their production of the cheaper grades of cotton goods for their own markets, which they protected by high tariffs. The woolen industry was much less important than the cotton, but in the world trade of wool tissues Great Britain's position was apparently unassailable. She sold to almost every country in the world and her exports were more than those of her two nearest competitors, Germany and France, combined.

Other textiles contributed little to the export trade, for they were more affected by fashion and by the protective legislation of other countries.

Iron and steel and their manufactures rose during this period to second place. Improvements in transportation, owing especially to the use of steam, and reduction in costs, both of transport and of manufacture, made it possible to send machinery, rails, hardware, cutlery, and other heavy and bulky commodities to distant markets. Britain supplied other nations with the materials on which their industrial structure was based.

The export of coal has had advantages not measured by its value alone, for it contributed only 4 to 5 per cent of the total exports. Many of the imports, such as grain, meat, lumber, iron ore, cotton, and wool, were bulky, while the exports of textiles, machinery, cutlery, pottery, and general manufactures had a high value in a small bulk. But coal was a commodity in general demand which could be used to fill up the waste space of the outgoing ships. It went by millions of tons to Argentina, Brazil, South Africa, the Mediterranean countries, Holland, Denmark, and Norway. The importance of this coal export lay in the fact that, with each cubic foot of cargo space filled in both directions and earning returns, it was possible for English shippers to charge lower freight rates than could competitors who had insufficient outgoing or return cargoes.

This view, as to the importance of coal exports, was clearly stated by the Royal Commission on Coal Supplies in 1905:[2] "The witnesses generally were of opinion that the maintenance of a large coal export trade is of supreme importance to the country and essential to the prosperity of the coal producing districts. It is said that the larger output rendered possible by the export trade enables the collieries to be worked regularly and to the fullest capacity, and that, since the general and fixed charges are spread over a larger tonnage, the average cost of working and consequently the selling price to the consumer can be kept lower than would be the case if the collieries were worked for home consumption only. It was pointed out by some witnesses that coal is so essential an element of outward cargoes, that any diminution of our coal export must cause a rise in the import freights on goods."

There was a dark side to this picture, however, for, as pointed out by numerous writers, Great Britain was exporting one of her greatest national resources, and depleting her limited reserves of coal. Be-

---

[2] Quoted in *Report of Committee on Shipping and Commercial and Industrial Policy,* Board of Trade (London, 1918), 4.

tween 1870 and 1910 the percentage of the British output which was exported mounted from 13 to 32. But the loss was mitigated by the fact that 50 per cent of the exported coal was sent to British coaling stations for the use of her own ships. The rate of consumption of this limited natural resource was increasing at an alarming pace, but the same thing was occurring in the United States and Germany, two of the greatest protectionist countries. The problem was one of conservation rather than of commercial policy.

Another criticism of British exports was that the character of exports was steadily degenerating and that they represented increasingly the products of slum labor. There is little statistical proof to support this assertion and it may be dismissed with the Scottish verdict of "not proven."

Alarm was also expressed over the decline in Great Britain's share in the world trade. In 1870 she had occupied a pre-eminent position, but was losing this as the United States, Germany, and other countries developed their own industries and even exported manufactures in competition with Britain. The indefinite maintenance of superiority could scarcely be hoped for as other countries grew in population, appropriated the technology of the Industrial Revolution, and exploited their own resources.

The re-export business was important throughout the nineteenth century, reaching its high point about 1870. Great Britain was the first country to develop world-wide commercial connections, and after steamers supplanted sailing vessels she established lines to the Far East, Africa, North and South America, and Europe. In addition to the goods furnished by British industry, customers could find wares from the most distant regions in London or other British ports. London became the greatest distributing center or *entrepôt* in the world. After 1870, however, other nations established distant connections and came to depend less upon London. Hamburg succeeded London and Liverpool in supplying colonial wares to the Baltic states, and the century-old British pre-eminence was lessened though not destroyed.

The final feature in British foreign trade which calls for attention was the disparity between merchandise imports and exports. The balance was "unfavorable" in every year, reaching a maximum of 184 million pounds sterling in 1902, after which it sank to a somewhat lower level in spite of the great increase in exports, for imports grew still more rapidly. The difference was met by the "invisible" items—about £90,000,000 from earnings by British ships and middlemen, and as much more from profits and interest on British foreign investments. During this period large amounts of British capital were exported to less developed regions, where it helped to build railroads and bridges, exploit mines, and open up resources. By 1914 British foreign investments were estimated at £4,000,000,000, or about one-quarter of the wealth of the British people.

The destination of the exports varied somewhat from time to time as other nations developed their own industries or closed their markets by high protective tariffs. About one-third of the exports in 1914 went to British possessions, especially India and Australasia, and from these the mother country drew a somewhat smaller proportion of her imports. Of European countries, Germany, together with Holland and Belgium, were the best customers, followed by France. The United States ranked after the colonies as a market for British goods, but was far and away the most important supplier of British imports.

BRITISH FOREIGN COMMERCE
(in millions of pounds sterling)

	Imports from		Exports to	
	1870–74	1913	1870–74	1913
Empire countries	76	191.5	62	195.3
Foreign countries	270	577.1	228	329.9

Commercial policy. The repeal of the corn laws and of the navigation acts and the introduction of free trade had been followed by an era of unprecedented prosperity, and the free trade policy was acclaimed as the best possible commercial policy for Great Britain and indeed for the whole world. Various events after 1870, however, led men to question the validity of this doctrine, and to advocate a return to protection, or at least the adoption of imperial preference. The depression in agriculture in the late seventies and eighties, involving a decline in the prices of agricultural products, in rents, and in farmers' profits, induced a numerous and influential group to demand protection against the cheap products from the new lands across the seas. The steady cheapening of the cost of transportation by land and water was reducing the natural protection of distance and high freight rates, and the remedy seemed to be to raise domestic prices by excluding some or all of the imports. Beginning in the eighties manufacturers began to make similar demands. With the progress of industrial technique and its diffusion in other countries the advantages long enjoyed by British industrialists as leaders in the Industrial Revolution were lessened and they were confronted with severe competition, especially from the United States and Germany. Prices of manufactured goods were falling as well as those of agricultural products, and business profits were declining.

The period between 1870 and 1895 was characterized by a general fall in the price level owing to a relative world-wide contraction of the money supply, but there were additional factors affecting British prices.   The more profitable branches of industry had been fully developed and new supplies of capital, which were rapidly accumulating, had to be invested in less profitable undertakings or expansions of old industries.   The law of decreasing returns was at work.   Domestic competition was consequently severe, as well as foreign.   Against the former British industry, at least in some lines, tried to safeguard itself by combination, but against the latter it saw in protection the readiest relief.   And, finally, the international situation was changing.   France and Germany and most of the European states repudiated the liberal policy of the sixties and reverted to one of high protection.   The change in British thinking and in governmental policy from free trade to protection took place slowly, but it was stimulated by the abandonment of *laissez faire* in other lines, such as the factory acts, employers' liability, compulsory education, housing legislation, and other measures which enlarged the scope of governmental functions, and accustomed the public to look to the state for the alleviation of economic difficulties.

The movement to protection took form at first in a Fair Trade League, organized in 1881.[3]   This advocated retaliatory duties on imports, to be removed in the case of any country that would admit British manufactures free.   Duties on colonial goods entering Great Britain were to be abolished, but foreign foodstuffs would be taxed. The movement was strong enough to call for a Royal Commission in 1884 which suggested duties of 10 to 15 per cent on manufactures and foodstuffs from foreign countries not belonging to the British Empire.   No official action was taken on this report and the revival of good times diverted attention temporarily to other issues.

Colonial preference.   A new turn was given to the movement for protection by the suggestion of preferential tariffs for the colonies. It was clear that Great Britain could not adopt protection without some kind of an adjustment with India and the self-governing Dominions, especially Canada and Australia.   An opportunity to discuss this and other imperial problems was afforded by a colonial conference at the time of Queen Victoria's Golden Jubilee in 1887.   This was followed by an Empire Trade Conference at Ottawa in 1894, and another at London in 1897, and thereafter this became a regular institution.   The question of drawing the mother country and the colonies closer together by fiscal arrangements was debated, and a beginning was made in the latter year by the adoption by Canada of a reciprocal tariff with Great Britain, granting that country a reduc-

---

[3] For a statement of its aims see T. H. Farrer, *Free Trade versus Fair Trade* (London, 3rd ed., 1886).

tion in the duties on British goods imported into Canada. Germany and Belgium at once claimed that, under existing treaties, they were entitled to similar concessions. In order to open the way for colonial preference, the commercial treaties with these countries were terminated in 1898, and immediately afterwards Canada adopted a preferential tariff, which reduced duties on most British goods by one-fourth (increased to one-third in 1900).

A new impetus was given to the movement by the appointment of Joseph Chamberlain as Colonial Secretary. He seems to have been converted to the idea of imperial preference as a result of a visit to the provinces of South Africa in 1903, and after his return announced his program in a speech to his constituents at Birmingham. As a part of his plan for closer imperial union he advocated a protective tariff on imported manufactures and a preferential tariff on foodstuffs. "If you are to give a preference to the colonies," said he, "you must put a tax on food." The British Empire, he argued, should constitute a self-sustaining whole and the various units should be bound together in a customs union by tariff agreements. Chamberlain seems to have been influenced by the example of the German *Zollverein*.

The question had now been made a political issue, which at once split the Unionists. The Liberals saw their opportunity and championed the cause of the workers, declaring for free food. At a general election in 1905 they won an overwhelming victory and remained in power until 1914. This ended, for the time, the prospects of a protective tariff, but political and academic discussion of the question continued. Among teachers of economics W. J. Ashley, W. Cunningham, and W. A. S. Hewins — all economic historians — were ranged on the side of protection, while C. F. Bastable, A. L. Bowley, A. Marshall, J. S. Nicholson, and William Smart defended the policy of free trade. A voluminous literature, most of it controversial, treated the subject from every angle, but the practical issue was decided by the fear of taxed food, from which there was no escape under a scheme of colonial preference.

Colonial policy. By 1870 the British flag flew over a far-flung empire, the principal units in which were Canada, Australia, New Zealand, and India, together with Cape Colony in South Africa and numerous scattered naval bases. The appropriation of enormous areas in Africa came largely after the middle of the nineteenth century and their colonization still later. The earliest colonies had been founded and administered according to the mercantilistic policy of the exclusive exploitation by the mother country of their resources and trade. This theory of a "single market," as it was called by Thorold Rogers, broke down as a result of the American Revolution and the growth of free trade in Britain. The revival of colonial

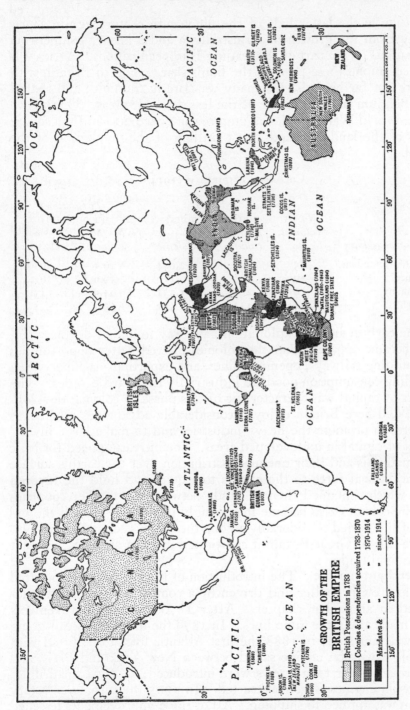

FIGURE 4.   THE BRITISH EMPIRE

From W. E. Lunt's *History of England* (Harper & Bros., 1928).   Reprinted by permission of the publishers.

expansion in the latter half of the nineteenth century resulted primarily from the growth of industrialism and a keener competition for markets on the part of the leading European nations. Africa was divided among these powers, the lion's share going to Britain, with France not far behind. Germany was late in the field, and shared with Belgium and Italy some of the less desirable areas. On the eve of the World War the colonial empire comprised 20.1 million square miles of the land area and 540.5 million of the population of the world.

COLONIAL EMPIRES IN 1914

Mother country	No. of colonies, etc.	Area (1000 sq. miles) Mother country	Colonies	Population (1,000,000) Mother country	Colonies
United Kingdom	55	121	12,044	46.1	391.6
France	29	207	4,110	39.6	62.4
Germany	10	209	1,231	64.9	13.1
Italy	4	111	591	35.2	1.4

The early policy of exploitation gave way to one of development as it became apparent that the colonies offered better opportunities for building railways, opening mines, and exporting machinery than in selling consumption goods to industrially backward peoples. The export of capital was characteristic of this phase of colonial development, and here Britain enjoyed considerable advantages as she was the first to promote the heavy industries and to make large investments of capital in undeveloped areas. The increasing need for basic raw materials and their unequal distribution over the earth's surface lent additional force to the efforts to acquire and hold the favored spots which contained them. Trade between the mother countries and the colonies also became increasingly important, though the extent of this varied considerably among the various colonizing nations. In the case of Great Britain it constituted in 1913 about 35 per cent of the total trade.

Merchant marine. The introduction of the iron steamship, fitted with a screw propeller and driven by a compound engine, was described in an earlier chapter. After 1870 further improvements were made along the same lines. In 1879 the first steel ocean-going ship was launched; in 1888 the first Atlantic liner to be fitted with a triple-expansion engine sailed between New York and Paris, and in the same year twin screws were introduced; in 1894 quadruple-expansion engines were constructed. In 1905 the turbine or rotary system was applied to shipping. All of these improvements lessened the consumption of coal, gave more space for cargo, and increased the speed. As yet, however, these improvements were confined largely to the Atlantic liners; the sailing vessel still held its own for the longer voyages, especially in the Australian trade. After 1870 there was a steady decline in the number and tonnage of sailing vessels and a much more than proportionate increase in steamers. Inasmuch as each steam ton is estimated to have four times the carrying power of a sailing ton the effective capacity of the British merchant marine was increased even more than the statistics show. This is indicated in the following table:

MERCHANT MARINE OF THE UNITED KINGDOM
(gross tons)

Year	Sailing vessels	Steamers	Total
1870	4,506,318	1,111,375	5,617,693
1880	3,851,040	2,723,470	6,574,510
1890	2,936,021	5,042,517	7,978,538
1900	2,016,490	7,207,610	9,304,100
1910	1,113,944	10,442,719	11,556,663

The next battle was between fuels. The internal-combustion engine, using petroleum, threatened the steam driven turbine, using coal. A still cheaper and more powerful oil-using motor, the Diesel engine, was invented in Germany in 1896 and applied to shipping by Russia and France in 1903. Oil was more easily handled, was cleaner, and required less storage space than coal. Its use was held back only by doubts as to sufficient supplies and adequate fueling stations, and it was only tardily taken up by British shipbuilders. By 1914 vessels with a gross tonnage of 1,310,000, or only about 10 per cent of the merchant marine, were fitted for burning oil fuel.

These technological improvements necessitated changes in shipping organization. There was first a specialization in ships, and the liner, which engaged in regular cargo and passenger traffic, was distinguished from the tramp steamer, which carried rough, bulky articles in seasonal and irregular voyages. The liners in turn were differentiated into various classes: the big, fast, luxurious passenger liner, depending primarily on the carriage of passengers and mails; the intermediate liner of slower speed, but larger cargo capacity; and the cargo liners built solely for the carriage of goods. Still another group consisted of refrigerator ships for the carriage of meat, etc., and oil tankers. Beginning in the eighties, German, French, and Scandinavian shipping began to compete vigorously with Britain for the Atlantic trade, especially the profitable emigrant traffic, while Japan contested the Oriental trade. The proportion which British shipping made of the world merchant marine declined from about one-half in 1890 to two-fifths in 1913; but they still carried over half of the world trade. Nearly half of the world's steam tonnage was British, and their cargo capacity had greatly increased. More and bigger ships were being built by all the countries, competition became severe, and rates were cut in half between 1874 and 1884. Shipping became unremunerative, and shipowners sought relief in combination. Shipping conferences or rings — the first in 1875 — were formed to stabilize rates among British companies and were finally extended to take in German and other competitors. The territory or the traffic was allocated, even the emigrant traffic being divided. By 1909 line conferences were universal, but the tramp steamers were seldom subjected to control.

2. GERMANY GOES OVER TO PROTECTION

Foreign commerce. Until the modern railway and steamship made communication easier and cheaper, nations had been largely self-sufficient. Agriculture had constituted the main industry, and life had been restricted and hard. As facilities were improved, new wants were awakened and a growing interchange of commodities was effected. Supplies of raw materials and foodstuffs were drawn from greater distances and the products of industry were poured into a world market. Interdependence took the place of economic isolation.

The rapid growth of the foreign trade of Germany during this period indicates the industrial development of that country and the extent to which it was sharing in the world economy. Improved technology made increased production possible and better transportation facilities permitted wider distribution of products. During this period Germany developed as an industrial state and this fact determined the character of imports and exports. From an agricultural country exporting raw materials and foodstuffs and dependent upon outside sources or domestic handicrafts for manufactured goods, it became a great exporter of manufactures of the most varied description, while it drew an increasing proportion of foodstuffs, raw materials, and semi-manufactured goods from distant sources. These shifts in the changing character of industry and the needs of the country are shown in the following table.

The most striking feature of this table is the enormous growth portrayed in total trade; from 5600 million marks in 1872 it expanded in forty years to over 22,000 million marks. In 1913 Germany was second only to Great Britain as an exporting nation, and not very far behind at that, while it was ahead of the United States. Partly responsible for this was the growth of population by almost 24,000,000 between 1870 and 1910; the larger numbers required

GERMAN FOREIGN TRADE, 1872–1913
(in millions of marks)

Year	Imports				Exports			
	Foodstuffs	Raw materials	Manufactured articles	Total	Foodstuffs	Raw materials	Manufactured articles	Total
1872	872	1676	710	3,258	504	787	1027	2,318
1881	793	1959	1003	3,755	457	912	2062	3,431
1890	1168	2950	1196	5,214	441	844	2482	3,767
1900	1763	2803	1200	5,766	517	1111	2983	4,611
1910	2483	5083	1369	8,935	761	1918	4796	7,475
1913	3063	5264	3039	11,366	1362	1719	7801	10,882

more agricultural and manufactured products. But at the same time there was a growth of wealth and of the standard of living of the people, which meant an increase in demand more than proportionate to the growth in numbers. More was produced and the basis for a larger domestic and foreign trade was laid.

Imports became increasingly important as Germany became industrialized, for the new manufacturers demanded enormous quantities of raw materials. This was particularly true of the metal-using industries, which required a steady flow of metallic and non-metallic minerals. Germany had plenty of coal and nitrates and a world monopoly in potash, but lacked almost completely bauxite, manganese, nickel, tin, tungsten, zinc, petroleum, phosphates, and sulphur. Supplementary imports of copper, iron, and lead were needed to eke out insufficient domestic supplies. All the cotton and silk and almost all the wool came in from overseas, as did the jute, rubber, and minerals just mentioned, while such exotic products as rice, tea, coffee, cocoa, vegetable oils, and other foodstuffs were wholly imported. The imports of raw materials grew steadily, though their proportion fell from almost three-quarters of all imports in 1870 to less than half in 1913. Imports of foodstuffs also became increasingly essential as the population grew beyond the capacity of German agriculture to support it on a high plane of living. The principal imports, at the end of this period, were, in order of importance, grain, raw cotton, wool, hides and skins, chemicals and drugs, and timber.

Exports at the beginning of this period consisted mostly of raw materials and foodstuffs, but by 1913 more than three-quarters of the exports were manufactures. The only important raw materials exported were coal and potash and the only foodstuff exported extensively was beet sugar. Germany always exported more manufactures than she imported, but the meteoric rise of the exports of manufactures began with the twentieth century. At the beginning of the period these were mostly cheap imitations of high-grade English wares. Professor Reuleaux, a representative of Germany at the Centennial Exposition in Philadelphia in 1876, reported that the products of his country were in general "cheap and nasty," *schlecht und billig;* Krupp guns were the only products of which they could be proud. Improvements in technique, and especially the development of the iron and steel, chemical, and dye industries, gradually raised the character and increased the quantity of this group of exports. Some of the industries produced primarily for the export market; thus 75 per cent of the musical instruments was sold in foreign markets, as was over half of all porcelain goods and clocks, watches, and toys, and only slightly less of the hardware. These were chiefly cheaper articles for mass consumption which were well adapted to machine processes. An export surplus became more and more necessary, in order to purchase the needed food supplies. The principal exports, in the order of their importance at the end of this period, were iron and steel and their manufactures, chemicals and drugs, cotton manufactures, machinery (including locomotives); woolen manufactures, and coal.

The balance of merchandise trade ran heavily against Germany in every year given in the table except one. This did not mean that Germans were running into debt, for the excess of imports was met and more than met, by the invisible exports — the earnings of shipping, the returns from foreign investments, bankers' and middlemen's commissions, remittances from emigrants, and other similar items. The balance of payments was increasingly in Germany's favor during this period, and enabled it to export large amounts of capital and to build up investments in many foreign countries. German foreign investments became important after 1880, and by 1914 had reached the sum of $8,000,000,000.

A great deal has been written about the German commercial organization and its success in promoting foreign trade. That it was successful is shown by the mounting figures. Care was taken to ascertain the preferences, even the whims, of foreign customers, and efforts were made to produce and pack the goods in such a way that they would meet the demand. Commercial travelers were trained in foreign languages, commercial law, and other lines needed to equip them for their task of selling their country's products. German banks gave valuable aid by facilitating the granting of long-term credits to foreign customers. The government, too, assisted by the establishment of consular representatives and the granting of special favors to exporters, such as favorable rates on the state-owned railways. And, finally, trade was helped by the development of excellent shipping facilities, which established connections with all the important markets.

That these measures aided in the development of Germany's foreign commerce is indisputable, but other factors need to be taken into account. Much of this trade consisted of new commodities and penetrated into hitherto undeveloped markets, such as those of southeastern Europe. Customers in these regions required different credit accommodations than buyers in more developed countries. German manufacturers and merchants showed great ability in adapting themselves to these requirements and in the organization of commerce, but they did not use legerdemain or steal trade from other nations. The growth of German commerce during this period may fairly be regarded as a net addition to world trade and as enriching other nations as well as Germany.

The protective tariff. The era of free trade in Europe, which had been ushered in by the Cobden-Chevalier commercial treaty between England and France in 1860, and had extended to Germany and other countries during the following decade, was brought to an end in the late seventies by a series of events which affected both manufactures and agriculture. The payment of the French indemnity stimulated speculation and overexpansion, which was followed by a severe depression. The crisis of 1873, which was world-wide, led to a dumping of British manufactures on the German market and caused German industrialists, especially in the iron and textile industries, to demand protection. The agriculturalists, especially the Junkers of the northeast, who had been free traders as long as they exported grain and wished to buy cheaply their agricultural implements and other supplies, were beginning to feel the competition of Russian rye and American wheat, and now turned to the state for assistance.

Added to these forces was the fiscal and political need of the new Empire for independent revenues, which would lessen the necessity of asking the states for contributions to support the imperial treasury. These contributions — *Matrikularbeiträge* — were raised by direct taxes, which were unpopular; but even more important in Bismark's mind was the need of freeing the imperial administration from financial subservience to the states and of giving it fiscal autonomy. For this purpose tariff duties were almost the only resource open to the Empire under the peculiar constitutional organization of a union of states (*Staatenbund*), such as Germany was. Customs duties were the most important source of imperial revenue down to 1913, when they constituted about half of the total.

These events did not cause a sudden change in commercial policy, and the movement for the liberation of trade went on unaltered down to the end of the seventies. The iron duties were lowered in 1873 in order to admit cheap agricultural machinery, and in 1877 were entirely abolished, except on fine goods. Other changes robbed the tariff of its protective character and transformed it into one chiefly for revenue. Over nine-tenths of all imports entered the country duty free in 1877, only a few highly finished commodities remaining liable to duties. This represented the high-water mark of the free trade movement in Germany and after that there was a trend towards protection.

The iron and cotton manufacturers had never ceased to agitate against the reductions of the duties, and in 1876 they united with representatives of the chemical, sugar, linen, and leather industries to form the Central Union of German Manufacturers, which constituted a powerful pressure group for protection. By 1878, when Bismark introduced a bill to raise duties, the landowners were feeling the full effects of foreign competition and were ready to unite with the manufacturers in support of such a measure. There was strong opposition from exporters, from the free cities of Bremen and Hamburg, which feared a diminution of their trade, and from many municipal councils which protested against taxes on foodstuffs. The agricultural party, however, held the balance of power and voted for the bill in return for favors to agriculture. The victory of the protectionists with the passage of the tariff act of 1879 marked the end of the liberal commercial movement, not merely in Germany, but in all Europe. Russia followed suit in 1881, France and Austro-Hungary in 1882, and other countries in subsequent years. Various conditions in Germany combined to bring about this change in attitude. There were the pressure of the world-wide depression, the increasing imports of cheap overseas foodstuffs, and the competition of British iron and steel with the developing German industry. The conversion of Bismark to the policy of protection was simply the recognition of changed economic conditions.

The general policy of the tariff of 1879 was one of moderate protection for agriculture and industry alike, but the former fared somewhat the better. Duties on grain and timber, abolished in 1864, were reimposed, as were those on iron. The taxes on coffee, tea, rice, wine, tobacco, cattle, and textiles were raised, and paper, leather, glass, rubber, and woolen goods, some metal and chemical wares, and petroleum were taxed. The chief raw materials, such as cotton, wool, ores, and earths, were left on the free list. This act was followed by the negotiation of commercial treaties with the leading countries.

From the fiscal point of view, the new tariff was most advantageous to the imperial treasury, for it brought in large revenues;

by 1883 it was possible not only to dispense with the *Matrikular* contributions from the states, but even to distribute a surplus among them.   The economic advantages were not so evident.   The large landowners, raising grain or cattle, seem to have profited, but the small farmer gained nothing.   Duties on raw materials or half-manufactured goods hurt producers who used these materials; thus the soap and perfumery industry protested the duties on tallow and oil, the metal traders those on pig iron, and the dress-goods manufacturers those on yarn.   Prices continued to decline, especially of agricultural products, and a demand was made for higher protection.   Germany was now definitely a grain-importing country and during the eighties the importation of foreign foodstuffs grew menacingly.   By 1884, the net imports of wheat were 718,000 tons, and prices for domestic grain were falling.   Revision was accordingly undertaken in 1885 and 1887 and the agricultural duties were considerably increased; additional protection was also given laces, silks, sewing cotton and some other items, but the great industries were left alone.

Bismark was dismissed from office in 1890 and his successor, Caprivi, was more conciliatory in his commercial dealings with other nations.   The commercial treaties, concluded in the early eighties, were about to expire, and new arrangements would have to be made. Some of the other countries had already announced their intention to raise their tariffs, and it was clearly a choice between retaliation or reciprocity and Caprivi chose the latter.   Meantime the alliance between the large landowners and the great industrialists to obtain protective duties had broken down as the result of a conflict of interests.   The iron industry, for instance, had conquered the domestic market, where it was able to hold up prices with the aid of a cartel, but it found its exports hindered by high duties in other countries. Austria, Russia, and the United States were among these countries and they imposed their duties in retaliation for the high German imposts on grain, which closed the German market to their exports. The industrialists now decided that the export market was more important to them than good relations with the great landowners, and they therefore demanded a reduction in the agricultural duties and a renewal of the commercial treaties.   In this they were joined by the trading classes, and, in spite of agrarian opposition, a series of treaties was made, the basis of which was reciprocal most-favored-nation treatment and reduction of duties.

The most important of the changes made in these treaties, from the German side, were reductions in the duties on agricultural products.   Unfortunately the changes occurred just at a time when prices were falling.   Thus the wholesale price of wheat in Prussia, which had reached $1.50 a bushel in 1891, fell to 90 cents in 1894.

The period which followed was one of commercial peace and of expanding trade. Agricultural duties, especially on cereals, were moderated; no further increases were made in industrial duties, and manufactures developed rapidly. By these treaties the leading countries of western Europe were bound together for a decade, and their interests were intertwined through the formula of the most-favored-nation clause. In this way they were assured of an opportunity for the orderly development of their industries. Raw materials and markets were meanwhile to be sought by investments of capital and the acquisition and exploitation of colonies.

A basic principle underlying these treaties was Germany's desire to foster exports. "We must export," exclaimed Caprivi; "either we export wares or we export men. The domestic market is no longer sufficient." There was also an effort to prevent a rise of prices and to maintain peaceful labor conditions. The government had embarked on a new social policy which it did not wish to jeopardize. The "accursed policy" of Caprivi aroused the fierce hostility of the agrarians, who ascribed the fall in prices solely to the tariff. In 1893 they organized the powerful *Bund der Landwirte,* representing the large landowners, and demanded higher protection. By 1895 they claimed a membership of 188,000, and in 1908 some 290,000, but these figures very inadequately measure the influence which their propagandist body exercised on commercial policy. Among the favors which they obtained for agriculture were a bounty on sugar, prohibition of the importation of saccharine, and restrictions on mixing and trading in grain.

The question of renewing the commercial treaties, most of which were made for twelve years, came up for discussion as early as 1897, and the government appointed an Economic Committee, representing agriculture, industry, and trade, to make recommendations. The committee was strongly protectionist and its reports recommended the protection of agriculture by excluding competitive products and assistance to industry by facilitating exports. The tariff act of 1902 was formed along the lines of this report, and came into force in 1906. The aim was the protection of both agriculture and industry, and at the same time the act sought to harmonize the interests of consumers and producers. An effort was also made to balance the conflicting demands of different industrial groups. This was a difficult if not impossible task, but it was handled shrewdly and fairly.

Duties on grain, livestock, meat and their agricultural products were greatly increased, and minimum rates were specified for cereals below which they could not be reduced by treaty. Industry was cared for by free raw materials, including wool, though in a few cases, like timber and linseed, concessions had to be made to agrarian demands by levying duties. Semi-manufactured goods were admitted at low rates of duty, but finished manufactures were heavily taxed. Exceptions were, however, made in the case of all ship-building materials and of some other essential articles, which were admitted free. Calculated on an *ad valorem* basis, the average rate of duties under the tariff of 1892 was 19 per cent; it was estimated that the duties under the tariff of 1902 would add 17 per cent to the taxation of agricultural produce and 6 per cent to that of industrial goods.[4] Compared with the rates in other European countries or the United States, this was moderate protection.

The tariff of 1902 differed from that of 1892 in two respects — the rates were considerably higher and the number of schedules and separate items was vastly increased. Since the Caprivi commercial treaties would soon expire, and it would be necessary to frame new ones, the tariff was purposely designed for bargaining purposes. Under the German system, there were two tariffs, the general and the conventional. The former applied to all nations with which Germany did not make commercial treaties; the latter applied to treaty-making states. Moreover, the commercial treaties almost always contained a most-favored-nation clause, according to which the nation making the treaty would automatically receive concessions granted to other countries. The rates were therefore raised to high levels in the general tariff, so that concessions might be made in the conventional tariff without bringing them below the desired level.

The tariff was also a highly specialized one, with 946 schedules, each of which had several subdivisions, so that a total of 5400 separate items was listed each with the rate of duty.[5] This had the advantage of restricting concessions made under the most-favored-nation clause to a single item or a few items, instead of a whole group, like woolen manufactures. For a neo-mercantilistic policy like that of Germany, commercial treaties did not fit into the picture, but by these indirect methods their disadvantages were lessened.

The purpose of the new tariff was evident to other nations and several of them in turn raised their duties in order to strengthen their own bargaining position. It is not possible to follow the diplomatic maneuverings, partly political and partly economic, which took place in framing the subsequent commercial treaties. It is sufficient to note that before the tariff went into force such treaties had been

[4] W. H. Dawson, *Protection in Germany* (London, 1904), 147.
[5] Th. Plaut, *Deutsche Handelspolitik* (Leipzig, 1924; 2ᵗᵉ Aufl., 1929), 115.

concluded with Austro-Hungary, Belgium, Italy, Switzerland, Serbia, and Rumania. Other countries with most-favored-nation agreements also received the benefit of the conventional tariff; such were Great Britain, France, and the United States. Russia did not make a treaty, but engaged in a serious tariff war with Germany, which was terminated by mutual concessions in 1894. Consequently, most of the imports into Germany came in under lower rates.

It is not easy to determine the effect of the tariff policy on German industry and agriculture or on general well-being. Even among German economists there was a difference of opinion. The free traders, led by Brentano, contended that the real causes of progress were improved technical efficiency, co-operation, and education, and that the rise in prices resulted from the growth of the population and the increased prosperity of the working classes. The protectionists, on the other hand, among whom were Schmoller and Wagner, argued that agriculture must be protected for political and military reasons; that a one-sided industrialization, such as had taken place in England, was undesirable; and that protection was necessary to meet the agricultural emergency. In general it may be concluded that protection permitted many farmers and manufacturers to continue in business who under free trade would have succumbed to the competition of cheap foreign supplies. Prices and the cost of living were raised. Most of the benefit went to the large landowners and the big industrialists.

But the tariff problem was not merely an economic one; it was also fiscal, social, and military. From a fiscal point of view it provided much needed independent revenues to the imperial government. Socially, it prevented a one-sided industrialization and maintained a vigorous agricultural population. But the main argument was political and military. "It is my unshakable conviction," said Caprivi to the Reichstag in 1891, "that in a future war the feeding of the army and the country may play an absolutely decisive part." This view found expression in all the tariff debates, which emphasized the necessity of making Germany as self-sufficient as possible in essential foodstuffs and raw materials. This very policy, moreover, gave a sense of security to the farmer, which encouraged him to continue in a business which otherwise would have been too speculative.

Merchant marine. The development of a merchant marine during this period from almost scratch to a rank second only to Britain was a noteworthy achievement. In 1870 nine-tenths of the tonnage were wooden sailing vessels. After that there was a shift and steamships were built at Hamburg, Bremen, Stettin, Danzig, and Kiel, which were producing on the eve of the World War almost 400,000 tons of merchant vessels annually, both for home and foreign account. This development owed little to government assistance, which was limited to a drawback on imported materials used in shipbuilding in 1870, to mail contracts, and to a subsidy to the North German Lloyd. The great rival steamship line — the Hamburg-American — grew even more rapidly without artificial stimulation. The German merchant marine followed the same line of development as other nations: the use of iron and steel instead of wood, the substitution of steam for sails, the increase in size, and finally the use of oil for coal as fuel. A German, Dr. Diesel, invented in 1903 a very economical motor engine which used crude oil, but the full application of this engine came after 1914.

TONNAGE OF GERMAN MERCHANT MARINE

Year	Sailing vessels	Steamships	Total
1871	900,361	81,994	982,355
1881	965,767	215,758	1,181,525
1890	702,810	617,911	1,320,721
1900	592,000	1,348,000	1,940,000
1910	503,000	2,397,000	2,900,000

Germany was more fortunate than France in the possession of good harbors and a comparatively short coast line. Its best ports, Hamburg and Bremen, were situated on rivers that penetrated far inland, and coal was easily accessible. Coastwise traffic between German ports was reserved for German ships in 1881, but the rule was modified for the vessels of other nations that admitted German ships to their coastwise traffic. Between 1870 and 1914 an increasing proportion of the traffic was between German ports and also with non-European countries. The opening in 1895 of the Kiel Canal, connecting the Baltic and the North Sea, was an important event, but its commercial significance came after the World War.

Colonial policy. "In 1878," wrote Professor Hayes,[6] "Germany possessed not a square foot of colonial domain. Twenty years later she owned huge areas in Africa, East, South West, Central, and West, and spacious islands and whole archipelagoes in the Pacific. Ten years more, she ranked third among the powers of the world in the extent, population, resources, and strength of her oversea holdings, and second in those by-products of imperialism — navy, merchant marine, commerce, and tariff protectionism: she was indeed Imperial Germany. Another ten years — not a square inch of colonial domain did she possess."

[6] C. J. H. Hayes, Introduction to M. E. Townsend, *The Rise and Fall of Germany's Colonial Empire*, 1884–1918 (New York, 1930), vi. By permission of the publishers, The Macmillan Company, New York.

This dramatic story began before 1878 and followed the usual pattern of imperialistic expansion. Owing to adverse conditions at home and promising opportunities in other countries, especially the United States, hundreds of thousands of Germans emigrated between 1830 and 1850. It was urged that if these emigrants could be directed to German colonies they would be saved for Germany. In Africa, where most of the later colonies were acquired, the missionaries paved the way, for they encouraged trade and helped colonists and travelers. More important, however, were the traders, usually organized as chartered companies. These made treaties with the natives, acquired concessions, and carried on trade between the home country and the overseas lands. Down to about 1884 these ventures were spontaneous and individual efforts, the official attitude of the German states being one of *laissez faire*.

The period between 1880 and 1884 witnessed the "international scramble" for Africa, during which other powers consolidated their colonial empires. Under pressure from the *Kolonialverein*, founded in 1882, and other pressure groups, Bismark in 1884 established protectorates over South West Africa, Kamerun, Togoland, and East Africa. He adopted, however, the cautious policy of supporting the chartered companies rather than seizing territory. By 1895 Germany had become a world power and Kaiser Wilhelm II felt strong enough to chart a "new course" of *Weltpolitik*, which was supported by his ministers and by public opinion. Although Germany obtained large but not very valuable territories in Africa, Samoa, and other regions she felt herself hampered by the entrenched special privileges of nations which had already built up colonial empires.

In 1907 the first Secretary for the Colonies, Bernhard Bernberg, was appointed, and he inaugurated an active policy of scientific colonization. The concession policy was abrogated and the state gradually took over the colonies. Railways were built and efforts were made to have the colonies contribute more to Germany's needs, especially along the lines of cotton, cocoa, tobacco, mineral resources, and other lines in which the mother country was lacking. But the African lands were unsuitable for settlement and Germany next turned to the development of the resources of the Near East. She obtained from Turkey a concession to build a railway across Turkey which would ultimately link Berlin, Byzantium (Constantinople), and Bagdad — the B B B Railway. This was actively pushed after 1906, but it was bitterly opposed by Russia, France, and Great Britain, all of whose vested interests in the Near East were threatened by this project. The conflict of interests thereby engendered must be counted as one of the major causes of the World War.

The Treaty of Versailles, in 1919, provided for the dissolution of the German colonial empire. Her colonies were distributed, for the most part to Britain and France as mandates under the League of Nations.

From a strictly economic point of view the colonies were a liability to Germany, but politically they were regarded as a symbol of imperial power. Their loss, therefore, was a source of serious discontent after the war. The cost of the colonies was large and was never compensated by the trade, which year by year showed an adverse balance. Only Togoland was self-supporting in 1913. Taken as a whole the colonial empire involved a steady drain on the German treasury.

TRADE AND COST OF GERMAN COLONIES *
(1000 marks)

Year	Imports	Exports	Excess of import over export	Total expend.	Revenues of colonies	Deficit
1907	144.1	73.8	70.3	73,130	23,580	49,550
1909	172.8	124.3	48.5	68,200	42,630	25,570
1911	257.1	178.3	78.8	96,690	53,180	43,510
1913	....	....	....	105,810	67,970	37,880

* A. Zimmermann, *Geschichte der deutschen Kolonialpolitik* (Berlin, 1914), 307-09.

3. TARIFF STRUGGLES IN FRANCE

Smallness of foreign trade. Owing to the almost stationary population, the predominance of agriculture, and widespread small industries France was more nearly self-sufficing than either Great Britain or Germany, and therefore less dependent upon foreign trade. Consequently this did not play as important a role in her national economy, and her share in world commerce showed a steady decline during this period.

DISTRIBUTION OF WORLD COMMERCE

Year	Total exports and imports (bills. of $s)	Percentage share of Gt.Britain	U. S.	Germany	France	Rest of world
1880	14,800	23	10	9	11	47
1900	20,100	21	11	12	8	48
1913	40,400	17	15	12	7	49

One explanation of France's declining share was to be found in the lessened importance of consumption goods, among which textiles used to bulk very large, as a result of the growth of local manufactures in these lines in all countries. Capital goods, on the other hand, such as machines, electrical appliances, chemical and metal products, made up a larger share of international trade. In other words, the articles in which France was strongest were less in demand and those in which she was weakest were more in demand. This was reflected in her declining contribution to world trade; it was even more clearly shown in a more detailed analysis of France's exports and imports.

FRENCH MERCHANDISE IMPORTS AND EXPORTS
(in millions of francs)

Imports

Year	Foodstuffs	Raw materials	Manufacturers	Total *
1870	802	1767	289	2858
1880	1961	2472	599	5110
1890	1445	2372	619	4589
1900	819	3035	843	4839
1910	1413	4345	1414	7351
1913	1817	4945	1658	8625

Exports

1870	648	729	1425	2802
1880	811	916	1839	3699
1890	855	897	2010	3890
1900	769	1084	2254	4308
1910	858	1930	3444	6487
1913	838	1858	4183	7165

* This column contains some additional items not covered by the preceding ones.

The imports, as in all industrial countries, were primarily raw materials, coal, coke, petroleum, wood, cotton, wool, silk, hides and skins, copper, and other essentials for manufacturing; those made up practically one-half of the total throughout this period. Wool was the most important, followed by silk and cotton. The foodstuffs were principally exotic products, such as oil-seeds, coffee, and rice, for in all the more important foods France was practically self-sufficient, though in years of crop failures cereals were imported. The large excess of imports under this head in 1880 was chiefly wheat and wine to make good the deficient home crops of 1879 and the ravages of phylloxera in the vineyards. During the seventies and eighties the importations of these two groups were very large, and continued to be substantial in the twentieth century. Manufactures made up a steadily growing proportion of the total, and consisted largely of bulky articles such as machinery of the most varied description and later electrical appliances, and the cheaper products of large scale industry.

Exports of manufactured goods made up half of the total exports in 1870 and nearly 60 per cent in 1913. Such growth as took place during this period was largely in this group. The character of these exports reflects what has already been said as to French manufactures. They were primarily articles of art, luxury, and fashion, wine, soap, perfumes, leather goods, cotton, woolens and silk manufactures, clothing, and so-called *articles de Paris* — products of French taste and artistic workmanship, in which the country was unrivaled. But more substantial manufactures also left French ports, though in smaller amount, for all the markets of the world, such as metal products, machinery and tools, automobiles, chemicals, and medicinal compounds. Of foodstuffs wine was the only one which figured importantly in export statistics. In spite of its advanced industry France managed to export some raw materials, as hides and skins, raw silk, and wool. Lacking coal, she was forced to export a large share of her great stores of iron, and in 1913 was the greatest exporter of raw iron in the world.

The balance of trade is the difference between the merchandise exports and imports, and this usually ran against France, as her imports were greater than her exports in 22 out of the 34 years ending in 1914. The French were able to import an excess of merchandise only because they rendered equivalent services to the rest of the world in one form or another. These services constituted the "invisible exports" of the international accounts and must be combined with the merchandise balance sheet to obtain a complete balance of payments. The main items of income from service were interest on foreign investment, earnings of shipping, tourist expenditures, and brokers' and insurance commissions. The receipts from these various sources increased from about 1000 million francs in the early seventies to about 2750 million just before the World War. The balance of payments was therefore largely in France's favor and this country was able to invest large sums annually in other countries. These foreign investments amounted in 1913 to about $9,000,000,000 gross. It must be said that French investors, under the guidance of the government, did not make very wise selections in the purchase of foreign securities, for about 11 per cent was sunk in Russia and about as much more in the Balkan states and Mexico. The excess payments due, above the sums invested abroad, were received, as is usual in the case of creditor countries, in the form of commodities.

Most of this trade was carried on between France and her near neighbors; only with the United States was distant trade of any magnitude. It would seem that the basis of modern commerce is not so much differences given by nature, like climate and natural resources, as those resulting from aptitude, training, education, and invention. The five nations with which France's trade was largest in 1869 were, in order of value, England, Belgium, Italy, Germany, and Switzerland. By 1909 the list and the order were somewhat different: England, Germany, Belgium, United States, and Algiers. Except for Italy in the first list and the United States in the second, France managed to sell to all these countries more than she bought from them, but the need for raw cotton was so great that the imports from the United States were double the exports to that country.

The protectionist revival. The commercial treaties of the sixties had given France the most liberal commercial policy of the nineteenth century, but the world-wide fall in prices which began in the seventies led to a demand for a change. The fall was due in part to the appreciation of gold and even more to the cheapening of transportation, but relief was sought in the exclusion of foreign goods from French markets. Dissatisfaction with the free trade policy of Napoleon III had already manifested itself before 1870 and with his fall the way was opened for a return to protection. Emphasis was given to the movement by the agricultural depression of the seventies, caused by the competition of Russia and America. Improvements in transportation and the reduction of transport charges lessened the protection of distance, and duties which previously had kept out competing products were now no longer adequate. The distress of the cereal farmers was aggravated by bad harvests, especially in 1879, but owing to the influx of foreign grain they were unable to obtain higher prices for their lessened supply. The price of wheat fell steadily during the seventies and eighties. An additional misfortune befell the wine growers, until now free traders, whose vineyards were destroyed by the phylloxera. The manufacturers were also suffering from industrial depression, and the financial needs of the government were great. These various groups joined in a demand for higher duties. This was not an isolated movement on the part of France, but was general among European countries, where similar events had produced like results. Thus Spain undertook a revision of her tariff in 1877, Italy, Austria, and Rumania in 1878, and Switzerland, Greece, and Germany in 1879.

The commercial treaties, however, which had been negotiated under the liberal policy of the Empire, and which did not expire until 1877, stood in the way. The discussion of these engagements and of the terms of their renewal afforded the protectionists an opportunity to present their views to the public and every advantage was taken of it. In preparation for a new tariff the treaties were denounced by the government and the way was clear.

The tariff system of France was a double one. The "general" tariff applied to all powers except as it was modified by treaty, and such treaty arrangements were known as the "conventional" tariff. As a result of the pressure exerted by the various protectionist groups a new general tariff was adopted in 1881, which raised the rates on manufactured goods about 24 per cent higher than the previous conventional or treaty tariffs; but as such rates were designed as a basis for bargaining and the granting of reciprocal concessions, little additional protection was actually granted manufacturers. Agriculture was practically left out of consideration, and foodstuffs and raw materials were generally unprotected. Specific duties were substituted for *ad valorem*. Commercial treaties were concluded with most European states for ten years and during the life of these treaties therefore no changes could be made in the duties on manufactures.

Since agriculture had, however, been excepted from treaty arrangement it was possible to raise the rates on its products. Agriculturists were quick to take advantage of this situation. In 1881 the importation of American pork was forbidden on hygienic grounds. Four years later moderate duties were imposed on rye, barley, and oats, which had previously come in free; that on wheat was increased. Still greater protection was given cattle, and fresh meat and spirits were taxed. But competition appeared in other fields. The production of wine fell off as a result of the destruction of the vineyards by phylloxera, and Italian and Spanish wines began to invade French markets. The competition of China and Japan threatened the silk-growing industry, and the beet sugar producers complained of the bounty-fed sugar of Germany and Austria. The sugar tax was accordingly raised in 1884 and that on wine in 1890. France, influenced in part by military considerations but more especially by the pressure of an almost self-sufficient agricultural economy, endeavored to retain the home market for domestic producers by excluding foreign competition. Agricultural interests were now protected at almost every point and were able to meet the new international competition. The duties were moderate, however, and prices remained low.

The industrialists, who had been suffering from low prices and from depression since 1882, now thought their turn had come and became louder in their demands for a change from the existing system. The election of 1889, which was fought principally on the question of the tariff and resulted in a sweeping victory for the protectionists, decided the issue. All of the commercial treaties expired in 1892, and a new tariff act was accordingly enacted in that year. This marked the beginning of the strong protectionist movement in France, the door for which had been opened in 1881. The tariff of 1892 adopted the scheme of maximum and minimum duties; the former constituted the general tariff that was to be applied to all countries which did not make special treaties or conventions; the latter was the conventional tariff and was reserved for commercial friends who made reciprocal concessions.   In this way the government would be enabled to persuade other countries to make favorable treaties, for there would be the threat of the maximum duties if they did not.   As a matter of fact commercial treaties, granting the minimum tariff, were made with all European states except Portugal.   The rates of even the minimum duties, however, were so high that they guaranteed considerable protection.

Agricultural products were given further protection, and some articles which had previously come in free, such as buckwheat, vegetables, seeds, and timber, were now taxed.   Such raw materials, however, as wool, silk, hides, flax, hemp, oil seeds, and fruit were kept on the free list, in spite of the efforts of the agriculturalists to include them in the protected list.   Other raw materials and crude products, such as coal, manganese and spiegeleisen, bricks, cement, and paving stones, were subjected to duties.   On manufactures, especially textiles, the rates were in general raised.   It was estimated that the *ad valorem* equivalent of the specific duties imposed by the tariff of 1892 averaged 34 per cent.   In order to reconcile the growers of silk, flax, and hemp to the free entry of these articles, they were given bounties.   Manufacturers using taxed materials were in some instances given drawbacks of the duties.   Bounties were also given to sugar growers and shipbuilders.

The tariff system of 1892 stood for eighteen years, the only alterations being some increases on wheat, cattle, butter, wine and meat.   During this period, however, important technological changes had taken place and new industries had come into being which were not protected.   Such were "automobiles, artificial silk, some electrical industries, typewriters and phonographs, synthetic perfumery, and machinery and mechanics' tools of all kinds.   There had been important changes in manufacturing methods also, the most conspicuous perhaps being the mercerization of cotton goods, the mineral tanning of hides and skins, numerous electro-technical processes, and the production of alloy steel by the utilization of such metals as tungsten and molybdenum.   New natural products, such as quebracho (a dyeing extract), had made their appearance in French markets." [7]

The manufacturers claimed that these new industries could not be fitted into the existing tariff, and that a thorough revision was

---

[7] P. Ashley, *Modern Tariff History* (3rd ed., London, 1926), 348.   By permission of the publisher, John Murray, London.   See also Arnauné, 338; Sée, 543; and Levasseur, II, 560.

due. They also argued that the existing tariff gave insufficient protection since the minimum rates had been extended to all the European countries except Portugal. It had originally been announced that the general or maximum tariff would be the rate and that minimum rates would be the exception, but the exact opposite had developed. Moreover, the slight spread of 10 per cent between the minimum and maximum tariffs made threats to end treaties or impose the higher rates ineffective; it was a weak bargaining weapon. And finally, other countries had been making revisions of their tariffs, which were becoming more specialized. A revision of the French tariff was accordingly made in 1910 to meet these new conditions.

The new tariff did not change the existing system, but brought only modifications of detail. Just as the tariff of 1892 had favored agriculture, so that of 1910 was predominantly in the interests of industry. Greater protection was given by raising the minimum rates on most of the manufactured imports and by taxing many new articles. Since agricultural products were already adequately protected they were left substantially undisturbed, and the free admission of raw materials was continued.[8] The bounty system was also continued. The spread between the minimum and maximum scales was raised from 15 to 50 per cent, so that the hands of the government were strengthened in making new commercial treaties. The general system of commercial treaties on the basis of reciprocal concessions was not disturbed, and treaties granting the minimum rates, in whole or in part, were made with sixty-two states. In 1913 the general or maximum tariff was applied only to Australia, Bolivia, Chile, Guatemala, and Peru.

French writers on the tariff are inclined to ascribe the industrial expansion of the two decades before the World War to the system of protection. That advance was made is undoubted; this has been described in previous chapters. Whether it might not have been greater under a freer commercial system must be a matter of opinion. It may fairly be argued that the high prices of machinery and of some partly manufactured goods prevented French manufacturers from developing a vigorous export trade along certain lines, while the dulling influence of protection on the initiative and energy of the industrialists probably encouraged them to maintain antiquated methods. The imports of wheat were checked, but the price of bread was raised and the average per capita consumption declined. The tariff increased the cost of agricultural machinery and hindered its wide use. On the other hand, some industries, notably textile

---

[8] A table giving the rates of duty on the principal articles in the tariffs of 1881, 1892, and 1910 is given in E. Levasseur, *Histoire du commerce de la France* (Paris, 1912), II, 604-05.

and metal working, would have suffered severely and possibly would not have been able to survive if they had been exposed to the full blast of international competition. The character of French products did not fit her to be a great commercial nation, and she preferred to reserve her home market for her domestic industries. National self-sufficiency was obtained but not without cost.

Shipping. The development of shipping paralleled roughly that of foreign trade. In 1870 the French merchant marine had a total tonnage of about 1,000,000, and it remained around this figure for the next thirty years except during the depression of 1893–96 when it sank below 900,000; by 1900 it had regained its former level and after that it grew steadily to 1913, when it comprised approximately 1,500,000 net tons. Relatively, however, it fell behind the other leading commercial nations, for while the French merchant marine showed an increase of 50 per cent during this period, that of Great Britain and the United States doubled, that of Germany trebled, while Japan's grew from nothing to over 2,000,000 gross tons. In 1913 France occupied sixth place, being surpassed by these four nations and by Norway. The growth and composition of the French merchant marine may be briefly shown.

FRENCH MERCHANT MARINE
(in thousands of tons)

Year	Sail	Steam	Total
1870	918	154	1072
1880	641	277	918
1890	440	499	939
1900	510	527	1037
1910	636	815	1451
1913	601	980	1581

France was handicapped during this period by a number of unfavorable conditions. Owing to the high cost of iron and steel and of machinery, she was very slow in converting her sailing vessels into steamships; in 1870 the former constituted 85 per cent of the total mercantile marine and 38 per cent in 1913. French shipping was therefore less efficient in ocean transportation than that of other nations with a larger proportion of steamships. In 1877, for instance, three-quarters of French mail was carried by the swifter British ships.

The character of French foreign trade rendered full utilization of the vessels difficult. Imports consisted largely of heavy and bulky raw materials, such as coal from England, cotton, petroleum, and copper from the United States, iron from Spain, phosphates from

Algiers, sulphur from Italy, nitrates from Chile, and tin from India. The exports, on the other hand, were valuable merchandise, light in weight and small in bulk, such as fine textiles, laces, wine, perfumes, medicinal compounds, and electrical appliances. In 1880 the imports weighed about five times as much as the exports, and in 1913 about twice as much. This meant that many ships entering French ports laden with freight had to leave in ballast, and the earnings of French shipping were correspondingly reduced.

Efforts were made to stimulate the building of ships and numerous devices were tried. In 1866, in conformity with the general free trade tendencies of that decade, protection of the mercantile marine was abolished, except that foreign vessels were excluded from the coasting trade. Materials for shipbuilding were at the same time admitted free, in the hope that French shipbuilders would avail themselves of this opportunity to construct their own vessels. Disappointed in this expectation the government next initiated a policy of state bounties. The law of 1881 granted subventions to French shipbuilders to compensate them for the higher costs of construction. It was estimated by the French Minister of Marine in 1893 that the cost of building a steamship in France was about 420 francs per ton, as compared with 300 francs in England. At the same time premiums were granted for long-distance voyages, a fixed sum for each thousand miles covered. A temporary stimulus was given to the building of steamers, at a cost of about $24,000,000, for the decade 1881–90, but by the end of that period the experiment was given up.

In 1892 a new bounty system was tried. The distance premiums were abandoned, but bounties for shipbuilding were paid as before. Preference was, however, given to sailing vessels, as the cost of constructing these was less and it was thought they would serve better as training schools for sailors. The next ten years accordingly saw the construction of 509,000 tons of sailing vessels and only 112,000 tons of steamers, at a cost in construction and navigation bounties of $30,000,000. In view of the world movement to the latter type of ship, this scheme fell into disfavor, and in 1902 a third method was tried. By this time the domestic iron and steel industry had made notable progress and preference was now given to steel steamers. At the same time distance premiums for long voyages were revived. Differential duties were also imposed on foreign ships entering French ports. Whether as a result of this bounty policy or because of the general economic improvement, the next decade saw the greatest development of the mercantile marine which it had ever experienced. The shipping of other nations grew faster, however, and the share of the French marine in the carriage of the world trade fell from 29 per cent in the decade 1867–76 to 20 per cent in 1889; it even lost in the carriage of its own foreign commerce.

The operation of French ships has come in for its share of criticism. "The navigators themselves," wrote Professor Gide,[9] "might make progress in many ways — better professional instruction, better moral conduct, better health (tuberculosis and alcoholism are very prevalent among them), better discipline, and better understanding with their employers." The merchant operators were said to lack initiative and to be too much under subordination to the navy. Owing to the system of bounties, the state interfered unduly. And, finally, freight rates were higher on French vessels than on British or German for equivalent distances, and the former lacked the profitable emigrant passenger traffic which the latter carried. Even with government support shipping did not attract capital, which sought other more profitable channels of investment.

France has nearly 2000 miles of seacoast and many harbors, but none with first-class natural advantages. No other country faces on so many waters of commercial importance. Southern France is washed by the Mediterranean, through which runs the second greatest of the ocean trade routes of the world, the route by the Suez Canal to the Far East. The opening of this route to commerce in 1869 had important economic consequences: since sailing vessels could not use it, the progress of steam navigation was hastened. It also greatly shortened the distance to the East Indies and the Orient. On the west France faces the Atlantic Ocean and on the north the English Channel which leads into the North Sea, one of the commercially most used bodies of water in the world. The supposed advantage of touching on three seas had its drawbacks, however. The large number of dispersed harbors prevented the development of a compact and concentrated traffic and the building up of a few excellent ports. Marseilles was the greatest port of France and one of the leading half dozen in the world; it was the outlet to the Mediterranean, but had only a moderately good harbor. Bordeaux, sixty miles up a rather narrow estuary, was the principal port on the Atlantic Ocean; the low sandy coast of the Bay of Biscay had no really good harbor in its 806 miles. Havre, at the mouth of the Seine, was the leading port on the English Channel; it was the harbor of Paris, and was closely followed by Cherbourg and at some distance by Boulogne and Dunkirk.

The French seaports lacked natural advantages, as the water in some of them was too shallow and they were difficult of access; this disadvantage became greater as the size and draft of the ocean-going vessels increased. They lacked protection against storms, which had

[9] Charles Gide, *Effects of the War upon French Economic Life* (Oxford, 1923), 35.

to be provided by expensive seawalls. Connections with interior railways and canals were inadequate, and equipment in the form of docks, quays, cranes, loading and unloading devices, etc., was backward.

The development of improved transportation by water and land, and of quicker means of communication by submarine cable, telegraph, and telephone, gave to this period a special character which completely differentiated it from the easier-going one that had preceded. New lands were brought into contact with international markets, and the economic structure of the industrial countries of Europe was profoundly affected.

Colonial policy. After 1870 there was a recrudescence of colonial expansion, which was especially strong in the eighties. It is not possible to trace the growth of the colonial empire in Africa, Asia, and the islands of the sea, but by 1914 it covered 3,860,000 square miles and contained 46,000,000 inhabitants. Practically all French colonies were situated in tropical regions, which were unsuited to European settlement on a large scale, or were already densely peopled by natives. Such were Indo-China, West Africa, Congo, the Pacific islands and Algeria. These were *colonies d'-exploitation,* to be retained for the benefit of the mother country and ruled by it.

FRENCH COLONIAL EMPIRE *

Area	Number of Square miles	Number of inhabitants
Africa	3,612,522	29,037,000
Asia	32,424	16,593,000
Oceania	8,376	86,000
America	35,233	418,000
	3,688,555	46,134,000

* Sée, op. cit., 557.

The basic economic motives for this expansion were the search for markets, the need of raw materials, and the desire to increase manpower. Since her home population was practically stationary, France never emphasized settlement, but looked upon the colonies as markets and as producers of exotic, non-competitive products and raw materials. In pursuance of these aims the colonial policy was one of assimilation, treating the colonies as separated parts of the mother country. French law was applied to the colonies and the natives were expected to adopt the language, the beliefs, and customs of France. The eighteenth-century view of the colonies as feeders to home trade and as areas of exploitation guided colonial policy.

Colonial interests were entirely subordinated to those of the mother country. The tariff system of France against the outside world was extended to include the colonies, but between them and France free trade existed with the exception that duties were laid upon the importation of tea, coffee, and cocoa into the latter.

The policy of assimilation, or more correctly subordination, did not produce favorable results for the colonies. The application of a unified bureaucratic administration to regions in different stages of economic development prevented natural progress. Nor did France gain commensurate advantages. Although French trade with her colonies increased, it was limited by the inconsiderable buying power of the native populations on a lower scale of living. After 1900 considerable French capital was invested in railways and mining, concessions for which were reserved to Frenchmen. From a purely economic point of view the colonies represented a liability, for colonial revenues never equalled expenditures and the deficit was met out of the French treasury.

4. DOMESTIC TRADE IN GERMANY AND FRANCE

(a) GERMANY

Importance of domestic trade. The number of persons engaged in trade increased faster than the population during this period in almost all countries. In Germany, for the twenty-five years between 1882 and 1907, the commercial group increased faster than any other group of the population; it grew 140 per cent while the population expanded only 40 per cent. The explanation of this expansion was to be found in the growth of cities, the break-up of the natural or self-sufficing economy, the increase in the volume of goods, and the lengthening of the road from producer to consumer. The growth of specialization, the division of occupations and trades, and the consequent necessity of passing goods from one group to another, facilitated as it was by improvements in transportation and the mechanism of exchange, brought about a corresponding increase in trade. The movement was not confined to Germany, and was exceeded in England and France, the proportion of the employed population engaged in trade and transportation in Great Britain (1911) being 14.4, in France (1911) 10, and in Germany (1907) 6.2 per cent. The commercial group (*Handel und Verkehr*) grew as follows in Germany:

The German statistics distinguish between the small establishments (with 1-5 persons employed), medium (with 6-50), and large (with over 50). Confining our attention only to trade, we find that in 1907 the small establishments comprised 94 per cent

TRADE AND TRANSPORTATION IN GERMANY

Group*	Number of establishments			Number of persons at work		
	1882	1895	1907	1882	1895	1907
Trade	616,836	777,495	1,088,298	838,392	1,332,993	2,063,634
Insurance	32,463	19,238	59,459	11,824	22,256	69,027
Transportation	99,321	100,646	113,713	175,246	230,421	404,768
Hotels and restaurants	257,645	278,689	374,195	314,246	579,958	803,603

* Trade included money and credit and accessory businesses; insurance included agencies which were often conducted as subsidiary to other businesses; transportation included only private companies.

of the total, medium 5.9, and large 0.1 per cent. The last group, however, had 9 per cent of the personnel and the first only 55 per cent. The modest size of the establishments may be seen from the fact that one-third of all employed from 1 to 3 persons and one-half had between 1 and 10. The same tendency towards concentration was observable in trade that was seen in industry, though to a lesser degree. There were 548 "giant" enterprises with over 1000 employees in industry and only 36 in trade and transportation. The following brief table shows the changes:

PERCENTAGE OF PERSONS
ENGAGED IN TRADE, BY SIZE OF ESTABLISHMENTS

Year	Small	Medium	Large
1882	78.9	19.6	1.5
1907	66.1	27.3	6.6

Although German statistics as to the number of establishments and personnel are probably the best, even they fail to give information as to the amount of trade. The value of the turnover was, however, estimated at about 20,000 million marks in 1895 and 30,000 million in 1907. The domestic trade was further estimated by weight at 128,000,000 tons in 1890 and 367,000,000 in 1911. However calculated, the conclusion is irresistible that German trade was advancing during this period *pari passu* with other branches of German economy.

Characteristics of modern trade. The most significant features of modern commerce are probably regularity and speed, permitting continuous operation. This was a product of improved methods of transportation and communication. Punctuality became a moral obligation, and a new concept of space developed; the world shrank. One effect of these changes was to separate trade and transportation. The ancient merchants transported their own goods, but by the middle of the century a sharp distinction arose between the two, first in the wholesale, later in the retail trade. With this separation it was no longer necessary for the merchant to keep large stores of goods on hand. Railroads, boats, and warehouses performed this function for him, and the great merchant houses with their deep cellars and high roofs disappeared.

Quicker and cheaper transportation also permitted the bringing to market of an increased quantity and variety of goods. Heavy and perishable goods alike were drawn into the vortex of trade. Specialization began and was furthered by the increased size of the turnover. At the same time competition became keener and made the task of the merchant more difficult. But quick transportation, by reducing the costs and loss of time in moving goods, aided trade. It became easier to direct the movement of large quantities of goods according to need. A new profession, that of forwarding merchants, was called into being, and they helped to develop trade. No longer was it necessary for the merchant to travel with his goods; from his office he could order, by telegraph and later by telephone if need be, the desired quantities, determine their movement, and issue selling orders to his agents or brokers. He had command over masses of goods, even in distant places, which he could draw upon as wanted. Retail trade still needed its own warehouses, but they were small. With these changes the old fairs, markets, and traveling peddlers were no longer necessary for the distribution of goods, and they steadily declined in importance. And yet marketing was made easier and the needs of the population were better cared for.

Too favorable a picture must not, however, be drawn. The apparatus of trade and distribution grew rapidly during this period, but it was only slowly perfected and rationalized. Indeed, one of the wonders of this development was the survival of over-complicated, often inappropriate, and sometimes wholly obsolete instrumentalities of trade still in use. This was especially true of domestic trade, and particularly of goods for daily consumption.

The commercial development took place under private initiative in an atmosphere of free enterprise, with little legislative interference except to trim off some harmful excesses. Thus the margarine law of 1887 required that it be labeled as such and not sold as a substitute for butter; the sale of pharmaceutical products and poisons was regulated in 1901, and peddling was restrained; and in

1896 there was a comprehensive law against unfair competition (*unlauterer Wettbewerb*).

Specialization was another characteristic of trade during this period. Although it had begun before 1870 it proceeded even more rapidly after that date. The increased domestic and foreign trade in staple goods, with their price fluctuations and changes, forced the wholesaler to devote his entire speculative foresight to a single line of goods. Importers dealt exclusively in coffee, or cotton, cocoa, rubber, guano, tobacco, tropical fruits, tea, wine, petroleum, grain, or wood. The exporters remained more versatile; they provided a South American country, for instance, with a great list of many commodities, instead of selling one kind in many different places. This was more profitable because of the wide distribution of sales outlets for manufactured goods, for which no world market was possible because of their differences in quality and design.

The most revolutionary change was probably sale by sample instead of by display or shipment of a complete stock. With the expansion of trade the latter method proved to be too roundabout and clumsy. The merchant no longer demanded actually to see the wares before purchase, to take them into his own warehouse before offering them, and then to sell in small quantities from the purchased stock. Instead of the old procedure came delivery trade according to sample (*Lieferungshandel*). The manufacturer or wholesaler let his commercial travelers lay before the retailer samples and models, and the latter ordered what he thought he could sell. Frequently, in order not to over-stock his store, he ordered for different times of delivery, with the condition that if any commodity sold particularly well he could order more and it would be delivered to him at the same price and of the same quality. By the end of the century trading by sample "had become the rule at Leipzig, for pottery and glass, light metal goods, fancy goods, hardware and toys."[10] Later it was applied to bicycles and automobiles.

Such "deliveries on time" were a real advantage for many branches of manufacture. The manufacturers were no longer required to produce great quantities of goods before sale, in order to have these ready for their customers. They undertook rather to produce samples and models and to send their travelers around with these to get orders. When the travelers sent in their orders from the customers, then the manufacturer determined how much he should produce of this or that article. For the manufacturer this meant a great reduction in production costs; the articles which did not find acceptance he did not need to produce; and those which did could

[10] Chapham, op. cit., 371.

be produced continuously. There was another advantage, that now the manufacturer or importer was frequently able through his travelers to make direct contact with the retailers, and to eliminate the wholesaler or jobber.

These changes in methods of marketing led to standardization according to form and quality; and this in turn to simplification and fixed types. Orders could be given according to samples, by telegraph if need be, with assurance of the exact filling of orders. All this facilitated trade, especially distant trade. Germany was the pioneer in establishing export sample warehouses, the first being organized in Stuttgart in 1881. Branches and other warehouses were opened in different parts of Germany and in foreign trade centers, and were soon copied by other countries.

Wholesale trade. The wholesale trade was threatened by these changes and stood in danger of being pushed out by the large industrial establishments with their own purchasing and selling organizations and bank connections. Most of the wholesale business was probably in the hands of the middle group, with 6 to 50 employees; of great businesses, with over 50 employees, there were less than 1000 in all Germany. Although the little traders, with fewer than 6 employees, made up nine-tenths of all in 1907, Sombart [11] believed that there was a tendency towards concentration in wholesale trade. The factors working for and against this movement were the following: for concentration were the advantages of large enterprises, easier credit, and the necessity of many-sidedness in the interest of safety and of serving customers better. On the other hand certain factors were working against concentration: the transfer of the burden of large capital on to associated businesses, as on to transportation agencies, warehouses, etc.; changes in the organization of the wholesale trade by which the commission business pushed back the independent operator; and the ease of establishing a wholesale business, for which often only a typewriter was necessary, and that on credit.

Retail trade. [12] The distribution of the retail stores according to the number of employees showed a somewhat greater proportion in the middle group in 1913 than was true of the wholesale houses. In that year 70.7 were classified as small, 27.9 as medium, and 1.4 as large. The retail trade showed in general a slightly greater concentration than the wholesale trade. This was rendered possible by the development of department stores, branch stores, and mail-order houses. The business of retail stores is to meet the needs of the

[11] W. Sombart, *Das Wirtschaftsleben im Zeitalter des Hochkapitalismus* (Munich, 1927), 860.
[12] This has been variously named in Germany. In contrast with *Handel en gros* it was first called *Detailhandel;* but since it was usually on a small scale, it next came to be called *Kleinhandel.* As the latter had a bad connotation, it was finally changed, about 1910, to *Einzelhandel.*

people; and as the population grew and concentrated in large cities, and as industry increased the number and variety of commodities, they had to adapt themselves to new conditions. The small trader could survive by specializing and rendering better service, or he could give way to the large establishment. Both movements took place.

Specialization took place along three lines. Some retailers concentrated on one or a few articles, which they could get cheaper becaues they bought in large quantities and sold with more assurance and expert knowledge than the little store which sold everything. Thus in the eighties special coffee stores were established, which by 1912 were handling fifty different qualities. Shortly afterwards similar stores were opened for paints, chocolate, butter, eggs, and soap. Or newly developing wares were at once displayed in special stores; so factory-made shoes found their first outlet, about 1870, in such establishments. Just before the World War a choice of over 1000 kinds was offered, and there were even special stores for orthopaedic shoes. The same development took place for sewing machines, typewriters, optical instruments, artificial limbs, and corsets. According to the census of 1882, goods and transactions in trade and transportation were classified under 1674 headings; only comparatively few of these formed the basis for specialty stores. The further the specialization proceeded the easier became the combination between the retailer and the factory. At that stage many factories established their own retail outlets, as did also dairies, coffee roasters, and other producers. The supremacy of production over trade seemed to be assured.

A second type of specialization soon followed. Coffee, for instance, did not long remain alone in the special store, but related articles, like sugar, chocolate, oils, etc., were added. Specialization according to the needs and convenience of customers took the place of specialization according to wares. It was discovered that customers objected to going to one store for one article, and to a second for another. The man who bought a suit wished not only a choice of models, but also a hat and gloves. So, out of the cloth store finally evolved the shop for men's or women's clothing; out of the yarn and ribbon store, the fashion shop. In the larger cities, where there was great disparity among income groups, a further specialization took place according to the financial ability of customers; thus there were luxury stores and 50-pfennig variety stores.

A final kind of specialization was that according to place. This took two forms. Those stores which met the daily needs of their customers, as for groceries, vegetables, meats, bakery products, tobacco, etc., opened wherever the growth of population created a market.   Other stores, which served only periodic needs, as for clothing, hats, shoes, furniture, hardware, office supplies, etc., sought out rather the places of liveliest traffic, where they would find the most customers.   A familiar phenomenon of all large cities was these "business streets," for clothes, automobiles, and other articles.

By the 1890's department stores were giving keen competition to the retailers.   Their growth meant the death not merely of some of the small retail establishments, but also of wholesalers, for they generally bought direct from the manufacturer.   They also cut into the trade of the independent artisan, who made goods on order, according to specification.   But the department stores sold especially those lines, such as clothing, underwear, shoes, furniture, etc.   These stores united in one organization a number of departments, at the head of each of which stood a well-paid specialist who was responsible for the success of his particular department.   The house of Wertheim in Berlin had 65 such departments.   Characteristic features of department stores were large and varied stock, rapid turnover, small profit on each unit sold, and cash payments from customers.   They attracted trade, not only by low prices, but by window decoration, by advertising, and by selling good wares.   The freedom of movement in such a store and the absence of compulsion to buy gave them a certain democratic aspect, and led many customers to prefer them to the smaller and more insistent specialty stores.   The principle of the department stores, as of the 50-pfennig variety stores, was that it was better to work for the million than for the millionaire.

Branch stores also developed during this period.   They usually grew out of retail stores, for the most part with Jewish proprietors, which prospered and established branches with different members of the family.   According to Grünfield 99 per cent of the large retail establishments in Germany began as very small stores.   The greatest of these stores, Kaiser's coffee business, started after 1890, but by 1896 had 75 branches, and 1402 branches by 1912 with 6 per cent of all the coffee business in the country.   Branch stores were also established for shoes, corsets, men's clothing, and small machines.   Many articles, outmoded in the large cities, found their way, through these establishments, into the provincial cities.

Mail-order houses were less important.   They did not have stores, but sent out catalogues and samples to prospective customers, and filled their orders, for the most part, by means of the post office.

One other agency of distribution may be noted, namely the peddler, who still survived amid all the commercial changes.   The census of 1882 recorded for that year in Prussia the greatest number, 65,014.   This sank to 43,947 by 1895, as a result of repressive legislation and more severe administration. Peddlers found their best opportunities in thinly settled districts among the rural population. Here they introduced for the first time numerous industrial products, such as factory-made shoes and umbrellas, fashion goods and ready-made clothing. They also provided a welcome method of disposing of goods, usable but out of fashion, which could find no outlet in the cities.

The older retailers, the embittered foes of the large establishments and especially of the department store, claimed that the latter owed its success to advertising, to cheap and therefore presumably inferior goods, to the use of loss leaders, of premiums, and of accessory services such as the sale of theater and railway tickets, or to a restaurant with music. Whatever truth such a charge might have had in the nineties, it was without foundation after 1900. The level of retail trade had by then been distinctly raised. Finding denunciation unavailing, the retailers next paid the tribute of imitation. About 1890 there was a movement among them to unite for purposes of purchase. In 1907 the dealers in colonial wares formed a union, whose turnover grew from 3.3 million marks in 1908 to 48.5 million in 1914. This was followed by a number of others. Finally the retailers demanded legislation to halt their commercially dangerous rivals. The several states responded by imposing taxation. At the head stood Prussia with a heavy tax on turnover of 1 to 2 per cent. The immediate result was a decline in the number of department stores from 109 in 1901 to 73 in 1903. But these stores either changed their organization or succeeded in shifting the taxes back in part to their weaker purveyors. By 1912 their number had grown to 121. The small retailers next demanded that the large stores should be closed on account of fire hazards and that the restaurants be prohibited, but to such extreme proposals the states turned a deaf ear. In trying to meet the competition of the large store the retailers made wide use of the instalment plan. An investigation in 1900 showed that in many branches three-fourths and even nine-tenths of all sales were made this way.

Co-operative consumer associations. The consumers finally united in co-operative associations in order to save for themselves the middlemen's profits. Their success rested not on large capital, but on the assured sale to their members, the system of fixed prices, and of cash payments. They bought in large quantities at reduced prices, their costs of operation were not high, and they succeeded in underselling even the department stores. An investigation made in 1909 showed that the addition to the original purchase price made by the latter was 27.5 per cent, while that for the consumers' co-operative associations was only 19.8 per cent. They were most successful when they confined themselves to the sale of staple articles of assured quality, such as colonial wares, foodstuffs, soap, chemicals, and coal. Their popularity was due in part to the system of distributing their earnings to their customers in proportion to their purchases, and in part to the approval of the social democrats. They frequently labored under the difficulty of obtaining good managers, and tended often to approach the status of ordinary private retail establishments by selling to nonmembers and stocking with luxury articles and similar items. Their expansion was steady and was convincing as to their social significance.

CONSUMERS' CO-OPERATIVE ASSOCIATIONS IN GERMANY

Year	No. of unions	Members	Turnover	Capital
			(in million marks)	
1900	618	522,116	108.6	26.7
1910	1506	1,492,875	513.4	137.2
1912	2118	1,753,829	....	....

Produce and stock exchanges. As the amount of goods entering the market increased and trading by sample grew, there came into being central markets at which sales and purchases could be effected without the physical presence of the commodities traded in. For this purpose, produce, metal, stock and other exchanges were established. On such an exchange a purchaser did not buy specific goods, but a specific quantity of goods of a definite character. Only commodities could therefore be traded in which could be graded and standardized, so that any unit of a given grade could be substituted for any other unit without loss. Stocks met this condition and consequently stock exchanges were the first to be organized. With the development of trading by sample, and the exact grading and classification of such articles as grain, coffee, tobacco, etc., produce exchanges followed. In the eighties exchanges for coffee and cotton were organized at Hamburg and Bremen, for grain — especially rye — at Berlin and Mannheim, and for sugar at Magdeburg. There were also general produce exchanges in a number of other German cities, on which grain, flour, potatoes, alcohol, eggs, and other commodities were bought and sold.

All exchanges were organized under the laws of the separate states. In Munich and Dresden they were organized by the merchants as private associations. In Leipzig and Hamburg they were supervised by the Chamber of Commerce, but in Prussia the permission of the Minister of Commerce was necessary for their establishment. But in all cases the members conducted their business without legislative interference. The crisis of 1890, which was attended by cases of misrepresentation, swindling, and bankruptcy, directed attention to the evils of speculation.   Imperial taxes on new issues and on transfers had existed since 1881, but now sharper control was demanded.   This was imposed by the imperial exchange law of 1896, which was amended in 1908 as some of its more stringent provisions proved unworkable.

The law of 1896 endeavored to stop speculation, and so prohibited future dealings in certain specified classes of commodities, as grain and flour, and securities.   Future markets for other commodities could be established with the permission of the *Bundesrat*, but only qualified persons, whose names were entered in a public exchange register, could engage in such transactions.   The prohibition of future dealings in grain and flour, passed under pressure from the agricultural interests, effectively killed the grain markets at Berlin and Mannheim.   Berlin ceased to be the world market for rye.   Some of the stock exchange business moved to Amsterdam and London, and the various commodity exchanges declined in importance.   The amendment of 1908 permitted future dealings in mining and manufacturing enterprises, provided that these possessed a capital of not less than 20 million marks and were officially sanctioned.   One unanticipated result of this legislation was the growth in power of the banks.   The consensus of opinion among German economists condemned this legislation.

(b) FRANCE

Chain stores made their first appearance in France, and may be dated from the foundation in 1867 of such an undertaking by the Delhaize brothers.   It was soon followed by others, which proved very successful.   The reasons for their popularity seem to have been the low prices of their goods, made possible by the saving in the investment of capital as compared with the independent retail store, their buying in large quantities with resultant savings, and the general tendency toward specialization, as well as changes in the buying habits of the people.   Most of their trade was in staple articles of food.   The number of branch stores was estimated at 12,000 in 1912 with total sales of 1200 million francs.[20]

Still another type of establishment was the single price store, of which the first was opened in Paris in 1883 by the Baud brothers. All goods were priced at .45 franc apiece, on the model of the American 5- and 10-cent store.   This type was never very popular in France, but the idea was taken over by other establishments and introduced on a small scale.

[20] A. Haase, *Der Detailhandel in Frankreich* (Berlin, 1930), 57.

The growth of internal trade was more rapid after about 1860. By this time the transportation system was adequate to the distribution of the goods which the expanding industry was pouring into the markets. The amount of this commerce cannot be precisely stated, for statistics are difficult to get. Few internal transactions come under administrative or judicial control, and hence are not recorded. Some products, consumed at home, did not come to the market, and others were transferred several times. An indication of the expansion which was taking place in internal commerce is furnished by the amount of merchandise that was transported by rail, river, and canal. This grew roughly from 1500 million ton miles in 1847 to 3000 million in 1857 and to 6000 million in 1867. Block estimated in 1875 that the internal commerce was about 35,000 or 40,000 million francs per annum, or about 1000 francs per capita. This was about six or seven times as much as foreign trade. The census of 1906 published a statement of the number of commercial establishments and of the persons engaged in retail trade.

COMMERCIAL ESTABLISHMENTS, 1906 *

Number of employees	Number of establishments	Total number of wage earners employed	Wage earners per establishment
Without wage earners	113,251	....	....
1–5	240,077	407,761	1.7
6–10	12,021 }	235,559	12.1
11–50	7,490 }		
Over 50	882	121,727	138.0
TOTAL	373,721	765,047	2.0

* *Annuaire Statistique* (Paris, 1909), 188.

According to these figures 30 per cent of the establishments were carried on by the proprietor, frequently by the wife with the assistance perhaps of members of the family. Many of the apparently independent stores were, however, in reality branches of larger organizations and the so-called proprietor was only a manager. Almost two-thirds employed from 1 to 5 helpers. The typical retail establishment was overwhelmingly a small scale affair; only slightly over 5 per cent of all establishments employed over 5 wage earners and the average number of employees was only 2 per establishment. One would expect from the preponderance of small stores to find a disproportionately large proportion of the working population engaged in trade, but the reverse was true. Only about 10 per cent of those at work were in trade, a smaller proportion than in Britain,

Germany, or the United States. This was probably owing to the agricultural character of the population.

BIBLIOGRAPHICAL NOTE

1. *Britain.* A good introduction is J. F. Rees, *A Survey of Economic Development with Special Reference to Great Britain* (London, 1933). The keen rivalry that developed with Germany is attested in R. J. S. Hoffman, *Great Britain and the German Trade Rivalry*, 1875–1914 (Philadelphia, 1933), and E. E. Williams, *Made in Germany* (London, 1896). A broader survey is J. W. Root, *The Trade Relations of the British Empire* (Liverpool, 1903). The increasing discussion of protection called forth a flood of controversial literature and a few good books. Among the latter may be named: W. J. Ashley, *The Tariff Problem* (London, 1911) and W. Cunningham, *Rise and Decline of the Free Trade Movement* (2nd ed., London, 1907), both protectionist; F. W. Hirst, *From Adam Smith to Philip Snowden: a History of Free Trade in Great Britain* (New York, 1926), free trade; G. Armitage-Smith, *The Free Trade Movement and its Results* (New York, 1904), and W. Smart, *The Return to Protection* (London, 1904), impartial. Shipping operations are covered in W. Clement Jones, *British Merchant Shipping* (London, 1922), and R. J. Cornwall-Jones, *The British Merchant Service* (London, 1898). Ships and their construction are described in J. W. C. Haldane, *Steamships and their Machinery* (1893) and D. Pollock, *The Shipbuilding Industry* (London, 1904). On colonial policy it is sufficient to cite the scholarly work of H. E. Egerton, *A Short History of British Colonial Policy*, 1606–1909 (9th ed., London, 1932), and C. H. Currey, *British Colonial Policy*, 1783–1915 (Oxford, 1926), clear and concise.

2. *Germany.* G. A. Pogson, *Germany and its Trade* (London, 1903) is popular, but makes a useful introduction. D. Bellet, *Le commerce allemand* (Paris, 1916) is careful. H. von Scheel, *Der auswärtige Handel des deutschen Zollgebietes im letzten Jahrzehnt* (Leipzig, 1892) is purely statistical. On the tariff W. H. Dawson, *Protection in Germany: A History of German Fiscal Policy during the Nineteenth Century* (London, 1904) is journalistic but good. A scholarly work is A. Zimmermann, *Die Handelspolitik des deutschen Reiches*, 1871–1900 (Berlin, 1901). W. Gerloff, *Deutsche Zoll- und Handelspolitik* (Leipzig, 1920), and H. Sieveking, *Auswärtige Handelspolitik* (Leipzig, 1905) are useful surveys. W. Lotz, *Die Ideen der deutschen Handelspolitik*, 1860–1891 (Leipzig, 1892) is theoretical. R. Weber, *System der deutschen Handelsverträge* (Leipzig, 1912), deals with legal and administrative aspects. A comprehensive account of German shipping is Aimé Dussol, *Les grandes compagnies de navigation et les chantiers de constructions maritimes en Allemagne*, 2 vols. (Paris, 1908–12). Tjard Schwartz, *Fünfzig Jahre deutschen Schiffbaus* (1909) describes shipbuilding. A clear and trustworthy introduction to colonial policy is Otto Köbner, *Einführung in die Kolonialpolitik* (Jena, 1908). D. Schäfer, *Kolonialgeschichte* (3te Aufl., Leipzig, 1910) is a concise survey. Also good is A. Zimmermann, *Geschichte der deutschen Kolonialpolitik* (Berlin, 1914). Mary E. Townsend covers the whole subject in two books: *Origins of Modern German Colonialism*, 1871–1885 (New York, 1921) and *Rise and Fall of Germany's Colonial Empire*, 1884–1918 (New York, 1930).

3. *France.* The best book on French commerce for this period is A. Arnauné, *Le commerce extérieur et les tarifs de douane* (Paris, 1911). The financial aspects of international trade are carefully covered in H. D. White, *The French Inter-*

national Accounts, 1880–1913 (Cambridge, Mass., 1933). B. Nogaro et W. Oualid, *L'évolution du commerce, du crédit, et des transports* (Paris, 1914) is a concise survey. Two other useful books are G. Lecarpentier, *Le commerce internationale* (Paris, 1910), and A. Landry, *Notre commerce d'exportation* (Paris, 1916). A good introduction to French tariff policy is H. O. Meredith, *Protection in France* (London, 1904). The development of the protection policy is described in C. Augier et A. Marvaud, *La politique douanière de la France* (Paris, 1911), strongly protectionist, and B. Franke, *Der Ausbau des heutigen Schutzzollsystem in Frankreich* (Leipzig, 1903), objective. Commercial treaties are covered in Funck-Brentano et C. Dupuis, *Les tarifs douaniers et les traités de commerce* (Paris, 1895). J. Charles-Roux, *Notre marine marchand* (Paris, 1898) describes the merchant marine, as does P. Rousiers, *Les grandes industries modernes* (Paris, 1928), Vol. IV. Two books on French ports are P. Masson, *Les ports francs* (Paris, 1904) and P. Rousiers, *Les grands ports français* (Paris, 1909). The best book on colonial policy is S. H. Roberts, *History of French Colonial Policy,* 1870–1925, 2 vols. (London, 1929). A. Girault, *The Colonial Tariff Policy of France* (New York, 1916) covers one aspect.

4. *Domestic trade.* Two excellent companion volumes on German domestic trade are H. Sieveking, *Entwicklung, Wesen und Bedeutung des Handels* (Tübingen, 1925) and J. Hirsch, *Der moderne Handel, seine Organization und Formen und die staatliche Binnenpolitik* (Tübingen, 1925). R. van der Borght, *Handel und Handelspolitik* (Leipzig, 1900) is older but good. Retail trade is covered in A. Lampe, *Der Einzelhandel in der Volkswirtschaft* (Berlin, 1930). A more specialized study is E. von Wassow, *Geschichte und Entwicklung der Warenhäuser* (1906). G. Bernhard, *Die Börse, ihre Geschichte, ihr Wesen und ihre Bedeutung* (Berlin, 1906) describes the stock exchange.

French domestic trade is well described by A. Haase, *Der Detailhandel in Frankreich* (Berlin, 1930). A general, popular account is G. Normand, *Le grand commerce de détail* (Paris, 1920). The changes that were taking place are treated in L. Duclos, *Les transformations du commerce de détail* (Paris, 1902). The development of department stores is described in H. Garrigues, *Les grands magasins de nouveautés* (Paris, 1897), and of chain stores in P. Moride, *Les maisons à succursales multiples en France et à l'étranger* (Paris, 1913), a clear and simple account. The struggle against these of the small shop is sympathetically treated in E. M. Saint-Léon, *Le petit commerce français, sa lutte pour la vie* (Paris, 1911).

CHAPTER XI

TRANSPORTATION

I. RAILWAY RULE IN BRITAIN

Development of the railway net. The rapid growth in railway building which had characterized the earlier decades slackened perceptibly after 1870. The structure of the British railway system was by then fairly well determined, and it remained only to fill in the gaps and provide extensions. Additions were continuous, though at a steadily slowing rate, and by 1914 the mileage was the greatest attained up to that time. Great Britain was now amply supplied with railway facilities.

MILES OF RAILWAY IN OPERATION IN UNITED KINGDOM

Year	Miles	Year	Miles
1870	15,537	1900	21,855
1880	17,933	1910	23,387
1890	20,073	1914	23,701

About two-thirds of this mileage, exclusive of sidings, was double track. A greater proportion of the railways in England and Wales consisted of double, treble, or other multiple track than in any other country. The percentage of single track was 33, while in Germany (entire system) it was 61.7, and in France (main lines) 57. The investment per mile of road in 1801 was £45,661 or about $225,000. This contrasted with an investment of about $60,000 per mile of road in the United States.

Service of railways. Measured by the financial returns the freight business was more important than the passenger traffic, though the disparity was not great. Freight traffic is based on the natural resources and industries of a country and upon their geographical distribution. The resources and manufactures of Great Britain were compacted into a small area. The coal fields were located largely in the northwest; cotton manufactures highly centralized in Lancashire, in the midst of the coal fields; the woolen industry, in Yorkshire, was surrounded by the Yorkshire mines; and the iron and steel industries were situated to the south near the Staffordshire coal fields. There was here no wide separation between the areas of mining and those of manufacturing and of consumption, such as existed in the United States.

The freight traffic was in consequence predominantly short haul business. The area was comparatively small, and no place in England was farther than 90 miles from the sea.   It has been estimated that the average haul throughout the Kingdom was probably not more than 30 miles for minerals and for merchandise not more than 50 miles.   The shipments were, moreover, predominantly of merchandise in comparatively small lots.   Certain marketing practices grew up during this period which emphasized this movement.   Storage of imported goods and of domestic products was made at docks and warehouses, from which shipments were made by the railways as these were needed.   With the development of the telegraph and telephone, orders could be quickly filled and merchants ceased to carry large stocks.   These facts impressed upon British railways certain distinctive features, such as the use of small cars, which carried a small load and could be easily detached from a "goods" train and left on a siding, and also speed in deliveries.   These cars were adapted to the traffic and the existing merchandising practices.   Economies were possible through increasing the trainloads and making larger shipments in bigger cars.   But the savings in freight would have been offset by higher charges in other directions, so the changes were slight.   An additional obstacle lay in the fact that nearly half the freight cars in use belonged to private owners, who were not inclined to make the large outlay which such a change involved.

The passenger traffic had always been heavy and dense.   During this period the average British citizen made more railway trips and traveled a greater mileage during the year than did the people in any other country.   To gain and hold this patronage the railways made great improvements in comfort, speed, and safety of passengers.   So comfortable and convenient were even the third class coaches made, that an increasing proportion of the passengers rode third class, the percentage growing from about 80 in 1870 to 95 in 1914.   The rates remained very stable at 2 d. a mile for class I and 1 d. for class III.   This service was much better in Great Britain than on the Continent, at about the same rates.   Other facilities were improved, dining cars were introduced, sleeping cars more tardily, and vestibuled trains finally appeared.

In the matter of safety a great advance was made.   Although the leading railway men resisted the introduction of the block system, about a fifth of the railway mileage in Great Britain was under it in 1870.   During the ensuing two decades rapid progress was made, but it was felt necessary to apply compulsion by an act of 1889 to force the laggard companies to adopt a proven safety device.   The same story applied to continuous brakes, which were also made compulsory in 1889.   No other legislation was passed along this line, however, except the Railway Employment (Prevention of Accidents) Act of 1900, which required the Board of Trade to make rules to safeguard the lives of railway employees. More effective was the Workmen's Compensation Act of 1897, which made the railways liable for personal injuries to the workers, which were not the result of their own negligence.

Improvements were also made in speed. A new interpretation was given to the term express train in the historic "race to Edinburgh" in 1888, when the Great Northern, the Northwestern, and the Midland entered into a speed contest. The distance between London and Edinburgh was 188, 196, and 202 miles respectively on the three roads, and the running time was 9 hours. The time was cut on each road in turn to $8\frac{1}{2}$ hours, to 8 hours, and finally to 7 hours 32 minutes on the Great Northern. With that achievement the contest came to an end, but the time between the two capitals was permanently reduced to 8 hours.

Electric tramways made their appearance during this period. Tramways had been introduced into England during the fifties, but they did not gain popular favor until the lines in Liverpool in 1868 demonstrated their success. London, Glasgow, Edinburgh, Dublin, and other cities rapidly followed suit. The first lines were horse-drawn, then by cable, but the great impetus to street railways came with the application of electricity as a motive power. This was introduced in Leeds in 1891, but its spread was delayed by hostile legislation. Charters must be obtained from local authorities and these often asked exorbitant sums of the companies as a condition for using the streets. The result was that private capital was discouraged from entering this field and that about two-thirds of the lines down to 1914 were built and operated by municipalities.

The advantages of electric traction were soon seen by the railways and many of these converted their suburban roads into electric lines. The Lancashire and Yorkshire seems to have been the pioneer in this field in 1902, but was promptly followed by other railways and, in 1905, by the Metropolitan District Railways in London. The traffic problems of this great city could not be cared for adequately even by this new service and beginning in 1901 underground tubes were built in all directions. About the same time motor busses began to supersede the animal-drawn vehicles, and by 1913 the transformation had been practically completed, only 142 horse-busses being then in operation. All these new services cut into the passenger traffic of the railways and many of the suburban trains were discontinued.

Rates. It was estimated in 1900 that the average receipt per ton per mile on a representative railway in England was over 2.33 cents while that of a representative American railway was .54 cent. In view of the great difference in conditions and in the character of the commerce it is very difficult to make comparisons. British shippers complained of high rates and of discriminatory rates and much legislation was passed concerning these matters.

The early charters had prescribed maximum rates, but competition, both among the railways and with water transportation, led early to a reduction of rates below the maxima. Owing to the small size of the island — Great Britain is somewhat smaller than the states of New York and Pennsylvania combined — much of the traffic was exposed to water competition, and the railways were forced to lower their rates to meet this; but these lower rates did not apply to the intermediate traffic or to that between stations not having water communication. It was estimated that probably three-fifths of the rail rates were determined by water competition. British shippers at the inland points protested at these place discriminations, but were particularly bitter against the lower rates granted imported goods. If a cargo of wheat were shipped from New York to an importer in London, it might go direct by boat to its destination, or it might be shipped to Liverpool or Southampton and then by rail to London. In the latter event the English rail rate would have to be so low that the total charge by boat and rail would not be greater than the ocean freight direct to London. Personal discriminations were rare, and the secret rebate, a flagrant abuse in the United States, was non-existent. British railways performed various services beyond haulage, and charges for these were grouped under the head of "terminals." Shippers complained that the railways were thereby enabled to charge more than the maximum rates, and these terminal charges were a frequent source of irritation.

Consolidation. In 1872 the railway companies made a determined effort to bring about amalgamation of important lines. Parliament, which had never established a definite railway policy and had vacillated between competition and monopoly, side-stepped the issue and fell back on the familiar expedient of a Select Committee. The committee made an excellent report, but out of it all there emerged only the Act of 1873, which set up a tribunal of three railway commissioners to handle complaints against railways. The larger question of sanctioning amalgamations was not touched by the Act, and from then until 1914 the amalgamation question shaped its own course.

No legislation was passed to prohibit consolidation, but the necessity of having it approved by special act of Parliament prevented any comprehensive move in this direction. Mergers, leases, and working agreements were freely permitted and pooling arrangements were declared legal. Under such circumstances actual consolidation was not a pressing problem, for rates could be controlled by agreement.   Many combinations took place, largely of lines which radiated from the larger commercial and industrial centers, but not of parallel lines.   The formation of the larger systems had been achieved in the earlier period.   There were seven great systems between 1870 and 1914, with more than 800 miles each at the end of the period — the London and Northwestern, the Great Western, the London and Southwestern, the Northeastern, the Great Eastern, the Great Northern, and the Midland — each of which had been built up by a process of absorption and amalgamation.   Although the idea of districting the country into distinct monopoly areas had been discussed no legislative steps in that direction were taken, and the railways were permitted to develop as needs arose.   Few of the larger companies established a monopoly over any considerable area, and competition was general, though this found expression in methods of speed, comfort, and service rather than rates.

Legislative control.   The early theory underlying railway legislation had been reliance on competition to safeguard public interests. Later, when the tendency toward monopoly was seen to be irresistible, Parliament undertook to control this rather than to try to reintroduce competition.   On the continent state control has usually meant state operation, but in Great Britain no attempt in this direction was made and the roads remained in private hands subject only to supervision and control.   Finding that earlier acts were not being enforced and that discriminatory and high rates were complained of, Parliament in 1873 created a Railway and Canal Commission of three to supply more effective machinery for rate regulations and to deal with railway disputes.   This legislation marks the dividing line between the early and the later attitude to the railways.   The new tribunal was established for five years, but its life was prolonged from year to year until 1888, when new legislation was passed.   It had very inadequate powers and its success was slight.   The commission was given jurisdiction over rates, terminal charges, disputes between railways, and working agreements, but its decisions could be appealed to the courts and in any case affected only the future. The railways resisted it and succeeded in nullifying its action in many cases.   One reform was effected, however, in the requirement that railway companies must keep at each station schedules of charges, which should be open to public inspection.   If complaint were made of a rate and such rate were not found in the rate book, this would be accepted as prima facie evidence of discrimination.

An important parliamentary committee made an elaborate investigation of the railway question in 1881–1882, and reported the existence of discrimination, high rates, and confusion; it recommended uniform classification of goods, and especially that the railway commission be strengthened and made a permanent court of record. Finally, in 1888, a new Railway and Canal Traffic Act was passed, providing for a revision of the entire freight rate structure and a reconstitution of the railway commission. The old board was replaced by a permanent Railway and Canal Commission of five members, whose decisions were final unless set aside by a superior court of appeal. The old maximum rates were repealed and a new rate system set up; differential rates were prohibited, as was a high charge for a shorter haul than for a long one on the same line. The railway companies were directed to submit to the Board of Trade a revised and uniform classification of merchandise traffic and revised schedule of maximum rates, differentiating haulage and terminal charges. Public hearings were held, at which objections were heard, and the schedules agreed upon were finally confirmed by law in 1892. The rate structure set up remained practically unchanged until 1913, when Parliament authorized the railway companies to raise their rates in order to recoup themselves for additional wages granted after the strike of 1911.

The system of rate control in Great Britain was very successful. "By permitting the fullest measure of co-operation in rate making among rival lines the Government has made it possible for the railways to avoid competitive struggles, and by establishing standards of reasonableness in rates together with adequate machinery for the purpose of preventing unreasonable increases or unjust discrimination, the public has been given a full measure of protection." [1] Parliament alone had the power to change existing rates, but the Railway Commission handled all complaints. The main criticism of the British system was that it tended to make rates inflexible, freezing them at the points fixed in 1892. In spite of this defect this system was the best example among European countries of private ownership and operation. Its success forestalled any movement for nationalization of the railways down to 1914.

Roads. So long as the users of the roads were horse-drawn vehicles the macadamized turnpikes and the rural gravel or dirt roads had served fairly well the needs of traffic. But towards the end of the nineteenth century two new groups of road users made their appearance, and demanded better facilities. The bicycle made its first appearance in 1867, and by 1888 had become the pneumatic-tired "safety"; by 1895 it had come into general use. But the humble bicyclists had little influence and no substantial improvements were made until motor vehicles appeared on the scene. These were introduced into England about 1894 and by 1913 numbered

---

[1] E. R. Johnson and T. W. Van Metre, *Principles of Railroad Transportation* (New York, 1920), 410. By permission of the publisher, D. Appleton-Century Company, New York.

a couple of hundred thousand. Their advent created numerous problems, not the least serious of which was their destructive effect on existing roads. Again the eighteenth-century issue was presented, whether the traffic was to be constrained to suit the road, as McAdam put it a century earlier, or whether the roads were to be constructed to suit the needs of the new users. Fortunately the latter course was adopted, though somewhat haltingly. The Locomotives on Highways Act of 1896 has been called the *magna carta* of automobiles; it sanctioned motor cars under 3 tons on the highways, but limited their speed to 14 miles an hour. The Motor Car Act of 1903 required licensing and identification plates, and raised the speed limit to 20 miles an hour.

Through a "Roads Improvement Association" the motor car owners pressed vigorously for better roads. It had become clear that the problem was a national one and that the large costs involved must be met by the national government. Accordingly, in 1909, the proceeds from increased license duties on cars and from a new tax on petrol were allocated to new road improvements. By 1914 the sums raised from these sources amounted to about £400,000 a year. Their use was, however, confined to the more important thoroughfares, and little had been done, down to 1914, towards the improvement of the rural roads.

Inland waterways. There were slightly more than 7000 miles of canals and navigable rivers in the United Kingdom in 1870, of which about 1000 miles belonged to the railways. Little change had been made in the canal map since the 1840's, and equally little change had been made in the construction or equipment of the canals. "With very few exceptions, such as the Aire and Calder Navigation, they had merely kept up the original works — with their different widths, their different depths, their locks of all sizes and occasional tunnels. The canal boat, the 'flat,' of one-horse power the wags said, was as standardized and unvarying as the state coach." [2] Traffic had gone largely to the railways. Agricultural produce and general merchandise preferred the quicker route, and only cheap, heavy, and bulky goods were left to the canals, of which coal made up nearly half. A Parliamentary report in 1906 estimated that the average haul was but 17.5 miles. The capital cost of the canal system amounted to $150,000,000, on which net returns were $642,000 for the railway canals and $1,682,000 for the independent canals. Of the latter group, the most successful were the Leeds and Liverpool Canal and the Aire and Calder Navi-

[2] J. H. Clapham, *An Economic History of Modern Britain* (Cambridge, 1932), II, 201. By permission of the publishers, Cambridge University Press and of The Macmillan Company, New York.

gation. The former crossed the Wigan coal field, from which it conveyed coal to its two important termini, and also carried local short haul traffic between intermediate points. The latter extended about 20 miles from Leeds through very productive coal fields to Goole on the Humber River, from which point the river was improved until it mingled with the salt water of the North Sea. The coal was loaded at the mines into small barges, which were hauled by trolley to the river, where they were strung into a line of perhaps 30 and drawn by tug to Goole. Both these canals had the advantage of operating over a nearly level plain, with plenty of water and few locks, and showed that inland water transportation could maintain itself under favorable conditions. Other canals, not so well situated, fell into decay, were cumbered with debris and choked with weeds.

From the Select Committee of 1872 to the Royal Commission of 1906 the canal problem had received repeated study and recommendations. Suggestions were made for resuscitation of the canals, their unification into an interior waterway system, deepening and widening the channels, and equipping them with large steam-propelled barges. Aside from the understandable desire of owners and users for their improvement, the chief argument — of doubtful validity — in favor of their maintenance was that the canals offered effective competition with the railways and held rates down. It was clear that funds to improve the canals would not be obtained by private subscription and that the government was the only agency that could finance them. Support for this view was wholly lacking in 1870. The railways had been built by private capital and it was argued that it would be unfair to subsidize a competing facility with public funds. Voices were somewhat stronger in their plans for government assistance by the end of the period, but Parliament was never convinced of the wisdom of such a course, and no action was taken.

Communication. The post office continued the expansion of its services during this period. The formation of the Universal Postal Union in 1875 was followed by the adoption of a 2½ d. charge for letters to Europe; this was later extended to the rest of the world. In 1881 came the postal order and two years later the parcel post.

The telephone, invented by Alexander Graham Bell in 1876, was introduced into England in 1878. Born at Edinburgh in 1847, Bell emigrated with his parents to Canada in 1870; it was then that he made his first experiments, but when he needed capital to develop it he moved to the United States. It was first developed in England by private companies, but these were hampered by government restrictions, as competition with the state telegraph was feared. As a result the service was poor and the rates high. A solution was

finally found in the purchase of the private companies by the state
and the establishment of a state telephone monopoly under the post
office. By 1912 there were 700,000 telephones in operation in Great
Britain.

The telephone was adopted for short distances, but distance was
annihilated by the invention of wireless telegraphy by G. Marconi
in 1896. The Atlantic was crossed in 1902 and sending and receiving stations were soon established in every country. An important
service was the equipping of vessels with wireless, which began about
1904.

2. STATE OWNERSHIP IN GERMANY

Growth of the railway net. By 1870 the domination of steam in
transportation was assured. The next twenty years constituted a
period of particularly rapid development in Germany, in response to
the economic expansion of industry. By 1890 the essential main
lines had been completed.

Part of the French indemnity went into railway construction, but
most of the new lines were built by private companies and for these
German capital was used. The expansion was too rapid and speculative for a time and railway shares fell into disrepute, but by the
eighties the development was more normal. The growth of the railway net may be briefly shown.

Year	Length (miles)	Year	Length (miles)
1870	12,137	1900	31,862
1880	20,980	1910	38,012
1890	26,579	1913	39,513

The period from 1890 to 1913 showed a steady extension of
mileage, but it was also marked by the co-ordination of the railway
net into a unified system, largely state owned, and greater efficiency
in operation. Roadbeds were improved, the installation of safety
devices was completed, existing lines extended, and other improvements made. By 1914 the German railways had a length almost
of 40,000 miles, as compared with 34,000 in the United Kingdom
and 31,000 in France; it was surpassed only by Russia.

Development of state ownership. The German railway system
was a "mixed" one in 1870 in every sense of the word. There were
70 independent administrations, partly state owned and partly private. Of the 17,333 miles existing in 1875, some 7475 were owned
by the states, 7339 were privately owned and managed, and 1916
were privately owned but under state management. In the southern

and western states of Bavaria, Wurtemberg, Baden and Oldenburg, most of the lines were state owned, in Prussia only about a third. The multiplicity of independent lines led to confusion in the rate structure, delays in transhipment, and added costs in every direction.

Bismark had in view a unified state railway system in the hands of the imperial government. The first step in this direction was taken in 1871 with the acquisition of the lines in Alsace and Lorraine. A few years later a proposal was laid before the Reichstag for the unification of all German railways as an imperial system. Financial and military considerations influenced Bismark in this proposal, but especially the belief that such a system would act as a unifying factor and would strengthen the new central government. Prussia declared itself willing in 1876 to relinquish all its railways to the Empire, but the scheme was defeated by the particularism of the southern states, which did not wish to lose their independence, and by the opposition of the private roads and of the doctrinaire free traders.

Disappointed in his plan for an imperial railway system, Bismarck next attempted to expand the Prussian state system, and in this he was wholly successful. The railway situation in Prussia was one of confusion and almost of anarchy. There was no dominating commercial center such as London or Paris, but traffic moved in all directions over many small independent lines. Rate tariffs were not uniform. Traffic crossing the frontiers was diverted to round-about routes by concessions and possibly by secret rebates, while local rates remained high and co-operation of rival roads was difficult. The country was, moreover, very unequally served. In the agricultural east local capital was lacking and the scant traffic did not attract capital from other sections for railway building. The west, on the other hand, was overbuilt and competition was keen. A strong case existed for state intervention.

The plan for the state ownership of the Prussian railways was presented to Parliament in 1879, and was accompanied by a comprehensive memorandum, which presented the arguments in its favor. The evils of private management were first portrayed: waste of capital through competitive lines, the cost of transhipment, the multiplicity of tariffs, confusion of time tables, waste in advertising, uneconomical utilization of cars, diversion of traffic, high costs of operation, and high rates. The positive advantages followed; those of military nature were placed first: the easier movements of troops, the concentration of large numbers, and the greater certainty of supplies. For the national economy the advantages were alleged to be the more rapid and even development of transport facilities, their connection with foreign railways, with inland water and ocean vessels, the greater unity of operation, the steadiness and publicity of a

uniform tariff, the equal treatment of the public, the building of
double tracks where needed, the rebuilding of depots, the construction of union stations, and finally an adequate supply of cars and
locomotives.

Although it was placed first, the military argument was not important, for the private lines had served the needs of the army satisfactorily in the war of 1870. Each of the evils of private management
and of the advantages of state ownership given in the memorandum
pointed to a lack or a positive abuse, which called for remedy.
In Great Britain the problem had been met by regulations, in
France by subsidies and control. Prussia adopted state ownership
and operation. The real reason for this seems to have been the desire to make the railways serve the economic interests of the nation.
As the industrial development of Germany proceeded, it became
clear that railway transportation was an absolute requirement for any
business. It was also urged, that the railway was by nature a monopoly. The conclusion was irresistible, to the Prussian mind, that only
the state could be trusted to administer such a natural monopoly
with fairness and far-sightedness.

The plan was approved by the Prussian Parliament, and under
the guidence of Maybach, minister of public works, a beginning was
made in the purchase of private roads by the state. Between 1879
and 1882 the state increased its holdings from 3838 to 9489 miles,
and two years later added 2480 miles more. This gave the state
control of all the main lines, though further purchases continued
until 1903. The terms of purchase were very liberal, payment being made in Prussian 4 per cent bonds in such amounts as would
ensure the owners the previous rate of return, ranging between 4 and
$8\frac{1}{2}$ per cent. Prussia bought up not only the private lines, but also
the state lines of the smaller neighboring states, and incorporated
these in the Prussian system. Meantime Bavaria began about 1875
to buy up the private roads in that state, and Saxony followed suit
after 1876. There was, however, no unified system for the whole
Empire. An event of considerable importance was the railway unification between Prussia and Hesse in 1897, as it influenced railway
policy in south Germany. That in the north was dominated by
Prussia. By 1912 the various states owned 21,182 miles of main
lines and 14,090 of auxiliary lines. There were left in private ownership only 173 miles of main and 2079 of auxiliary railways, and
these were operated in accordance with regulations laid down by the
state.

State ownership did not stop with the railways, for other important sections of economic activity were being socialized. The
federal states owned domains and forest land, mines, iron works,

and other enterprises. There was a strong movement during this period for municipal ownership of public utilities, such as electric light and power plants, gasworks and waterworks, traction companies, and slaughter houses. The states also owned the postal, telegraph, and telephone systems. Even the banking system, exclusive of the four state banks, was under strict governmental control, and practically the whole savings bank system was municipal. Nearly half of the economic activities were publicly owned and managed.

Administration of the railways. Although Germany is usually described as having a state-owned railway system, it must not be forgotten that the railways were owned by the separate states and not by the Reich. The imperial constitution conferred certain powers of regulation and administration upon the central government and an Imperial Railway Office was established in 1873 to carry out the provisions of the constitution. This accomplished considerable in the way of unifying construction, equipment, liability, signals and similar matters; rates, which were at first wholly under the jurisdiction of the several states, were finally unified and systematized for the whole country. In spite of rather large powers, the imperial government made little use of them. Not until after the World War were the railways in Germany administered as a single unified system.

With over eighty per cent of all the state railways Prussia dominated the situation and determined railway policy. At the beginning the state railways were managed on the same principles and showed the same abuses as private lines. But as the state holdings increased, the administration was improved with a view to obtaining greater efficiency. After various experiments the system of management was definitely settled in 1895. The Prussian Minister of Public Works was the titular head and the railways were administered by a railway department of this ministry. Four sections dealt respectively with management, construction, traffic, and finance. The actual operation was placed in the hands of twenty-one directories, each having charge of the railways in a particular section of the country. There was a steady movement towards unification: in 1909 a freight car association was formed which pooled all freight cars and made them available for any of the lines; the announced purpose of this was to facilitate the free movement of freight cars in order "to promote traffic and to simplify and cheapen accounting and operation." In 1907 a central railway office was established at Berlin to ensure uniformity in matters of common concern.

Rates were set by the railway directories, but these were assisted by advisory bodies, composed of merchants, manufacturers, and agriculturalists, and also by voluntary technical groups. The rate structure was extremely complicated and undoubtedly concealed many abuses. Since the railways were used to produce revenues for the state, rates were kept high, and since they were utilized to further national economic policies, such as the promotion of foreign trade and assistance to agriculture, rates were frequently discriminatory. Special rates were given to imports and exports, concessions were made to large shippers, and an unduly large proportion of the traffic was carried under low "exceptional tariffs." The Prussian rate system was usually described as one based on the cost-of-service principle, but this principle was considerably modified in application. Passenger fares were lower than the corresponding rates in Great Britain or France, but freight rates were probably higher and the facilities inferior.

Railway service. It is difficult to make international comparisons, because of the difference in conditions in the various countries. In spite of the density of traffic in Prussia less than half of the railways were double tracked and only one per cent of the mileage had more than two tracks in 1914. The government was slow to improve the roads and equipment. But by the end of this period the 20 ton cars with a dead load of 40 per cent had superseded the 10 ton and 15 ton cars with a dead load of 50 per cent. A limit was placed upon the size by an international agreement, to which Prussia was a party, limiting the maximum axle-load to $15\frac{1}{2}$ tons for freight cars crossing the frontier. In view of the character of the freight carried on German railways such small cars were probably uneconomical, for 40 per cent of the traffic consisted of coal and coke, 15 per cent of metals, cement, etc., and about as much more was of forest and agricultural products; that is, over two-thirds of the freight consisted of heavy, bulky, cheap products, which could have been more efficiently handled in large units. The tracks would, however, probably not have stood up under heavier loads.

The expansion of facilities and of the services rendered by the German railways may be shown by a few representative figures.[3]

Item	1885	1911
Locomotives	12,450	28,088
Passenger cars	22,735	59,857
Baggage and freight cars	250,640	596,763
Ton-miles (millions)	10,292	38,359
Passenger-miles (millions)	4,918	23,470
Officials and workers	333,439	713,187
Capital invested (million marks)	9,722	17,833

This expansion was sufficient to make the highly industrial district of the lower Rhineland and lower Westphalia the strongest compact

[3] Sartorius von Waltershausen, op. cit., 569. An obvious error is made in the original table.

railway unit which existed on the Continent. Close networks of railways connected this district with the iron mines of Alsace and Luxemburg, while other lines stretched across Saxony to the iron mines of Silesia. The rapid economic development of Germany would have been impossible without her railways.

Railway finances. Whatever may be said about the services of the railways there is no doubt as to their profitableness. They were operated honestly and efficiently and earned large net receipts. Between 1882 and 1914 the annual net operating income of the Prussian state railways averaged about 6.5 per cent of the capital invested. This profitable showing was made possible not only by efficient management but also by a favorable terrain, which held down costs of construction and operation. In southern Germany, where the topography is more mountainous, the financial returns were lower; in 1911 the state railways in Bavaria earned 4.5 per cent on their capital, in Saxony 3.9, and in Wurtemberg 3.1 per cent. Instead of passing on the high earnings to the users in the form of lower rates, the state government covered them into their treasuries; this rendered unnecessary the levying of heavier taxes. Critics referred to the railways as the "milch cow of the Treasury." Although this amounted in effect to taxing users of the railways for general purposes, little complaint of high rates was made by shippers. Such complaints as were made were directed rather against discriminatory rates.

Water transportation. The victory of the railroad over the slower inland water transportation had been so complete during the period 1840–1870 that the general opinion as to the adequacy of the latter was unfavorable. The giving up, in Great Britain and in the United States, of many of the canals made a deep impression in Germany; their day seemed to be over. And this view was deepened by the lack of success of those canals which were built to compete with the railroads. After about 1875, however, there was a gradual swing of public opinion in favor of inland waterways. They were favored by those who did not approve of the Prussian policy, after 1879, of using the state railways to favor exports and to hinder imports or to achieve profits, and who saw in the waterways an instrument with which to combat these policies. Water freights, especially on the so-called international streams, which were outside German jurisdiction, could be set so low as to "neutralize the tariffs," as Bismark once said. All important rivers, except the Weser, rise outside her borders, or flow across them into other countries. Moreover, after 1875, with the increasing demand for traffic facilities, especially for coal and iron and building materials, the inland waterways proved their usefulness. The great advantage of water transportation is cheapness, and this rests on the slight motive power required to convey goods. It was estimated that a horse with a speed of slightly over two miles an hour could draw 1.6 tons on a level road, 15 tons on level rails, and 60–100 tons on quiet water. The freight costs usually determined whether goods should go by railway or water, and the advantage lay with the latter.

In 1870 Germany had a comprehensive network of waterways, as most rivers were linked together by canals. But the rivers were shallow and the canals small and neither could accommodate larger vessels. The rivers had an imposing length, but they had to be canalized and regulated, at enormous expense, before they could be utilized; the several changes in depth, the rapid currents, and the probability of freezing in winter, all offered obstacles. The problem was not so much to build additional waterways as to improve existing ones. In 1878 the Prussian government undertook the improvement of the water routes in that state, especially the larger rivers, such as the Rhine, Weser, Elbe, Oder, Weichsel, and Memel. Thus the channel of the Rhine was deepened, so that Cologne, 150 miles from the sea, virtually became a seaport. In 1886 it began the reconstruction and improvement of the canals at state cost, and in 1895 it opened the Kaiser Wilhelm or Kiel Canal, which cut through the peninsula of Jutland and connected the Baltic and the North seas. Although built mainly for strategic purposes this formed an important artery for water commerce. More vessels passed through it in 1913 than through either the Suez or Panama Canal, though it was surpassed by both the others in net tonnage. Statistics for internal water transportation were not gathered until 1908, and even then they were not complete, so that it is impossible to present an accurate picture of the expansion. The usual figure given in 1870 is 6200 miles. In 1913 the situation was as follows (in miles):

Country	Rivers	Canals	Total
Germany	7242	1311	8553
France	4345	3080	7425
Great Britain	....	....	5890

The figures are not very trustworthy, owing to the different interpretations put upon the phrase "navigable waters." During this same period the German railways grew from 12,000 to nearly 40,000 miles. But the development of water transportation cannot be measured by mileage, for the rivers and canals had been vastly improved and had a much greater carrying capacity. How brilliantly the engineering problem was solved, the figures of inland ships and cargoes make clear. In 1877 cargoes of 800 tons could ascend the

Rhine up to Mannheim; in 1905 cargoes of 2000 tons. In 1877 cargoes of 500 tons could ascend the Elbe to Magdeburg; in 1905 cargoes of 1200 tons. In 1877, 80 tons were the maximum cargo on the Ems; in 1905 cargoes of 950 could get through on the Ems to Dortmund. The average canal boat cargo coming into Berlin in 1878 was 70 tons; in 1905 it was 190 tons. Or again, in 1887 there were 600 boats or barges of more than 400 tons at work on the inland waterways; fifteen years later there were nearly 4000, and of these 1200 were upwards of 1200 tons. By 1912 there were nearly 5000 boats with a capacity of over 400 tons. Between 1887 and 1912 the total cargo capacity of the boats and barges had increased from 2,000,000 tons to 7,400,000 tons. In the latter year the normal capacity of a Rhine boat was about 1500 tons.

The waterways were not merely improving their facilities; they were more than holding their own with the railways. In 1875, 21 per cent of the traffic went by water, but 25 per cent in 1913. Owing to the declining economical importance of the Baltic Sea, into which many of the German rivers empty, the traffic on these streams fell off; half of the heavy water traffic went by the Rhine, and a third by the Elbe, both of which flowed into the North Sea. The Prussian government justified its large expenditure for improvement of the waterways on the ground that the railways would thereby be relieved of the necessity of carrying the heavy traffic. There was a certain division of labor between the two systems and an increasing proportion of the coal and ore was moved by water. The total freight traffic on the waterways — 93,000,000 tons in 1912 — was, however, only one-fourth of that carried by the railways. The waterways would not have won even this modest success, moreover, if there had not been complete co-operation between the state-owned railways and the waterways. Fair joint rates, provision of transfer facilities, and practical co-ordination of the whole transportation system gave the waterways a useful place, subordinate to the railways but associated with them.

One other service of the waterways remains to be mentioned. In addition to the functions of transportation they offered storage facilities in high degree, both before and especially after the movement of commodities to market, particularly for the wholesale trade. Thus building materials for Berlin were brought to the city in barges and remained in them until wanted. Some of the smaller canals were used only for floating logs.

Communications. The development of means of communication kept pace with the industrial and commercial growth in other directions. They were almost as essential as transportation systems in carrying on domestic and foreign trade. Without the postoffice, telegraph, and telephone the great manufacturing and commercial enterprises could not have been brought together in unified concerns, nor could the railroads have been safely run. Improved means of transportation, communication, and credit made possible the industrial development of this period.

By 1870 the telegraph had spread over all western Europe, and Germany held a high though not a leading position in this movement. State ownership prevailed in Germany and in 1875 the various state systems were amalgamated under the imperial postoffice. The following year, because of the serious destruction of the lines by storms, these were laid underground. The importance of the telegraph is only partially indicated by the number of messages sent, which increased from 17,860,000 in 1887 to 52,273,000 in 1912.

The early history of the telephone was international. Charles Boursel, a Frenchman, suggested in 1854 the possibility of electric telephony, and six years later Philip Reis, of Frankfort a.M., invented an instrument based on this suggestion. The real beginning of the commercial telephone came, however, with the invention of the American, A. G. Bell, in 1876. The first telephone in Germany was installed in Berlin in October, 1877. Its use spread rapidly, as it was aided by an alert electrical industry. Like the telegraph, the telephone system was in the hands of the state. Germany led all Europe in the utilization of the telephone; the number of telephonic messages increased from 55,600,000 in 1888 to 2,326,700,000 in 1912. This was seven times as many as in France.

Down to 1872 each German state had its own postal system, but in that year they were united in the *Reichspost* or imperial post office, though some of the states still retained their own stamps. Improvements in the service were steadily made, as in greater rapidity of transmission, the introduction of telegraphic letters, automatic stamp machines, and the simplification of telegraph and telephone charges. In 1909 the postoffice check system was introduced, which facilitated the transfer of money from place to place. This was quickly adopted by the people and in 1912 the total transfers amounted to 35,535 million marks. By the end of this period the German postoffice transmitted a greater number of letters than that of any other European country. On a per capita basis, however, it was surpassed by Great Britain, which had 87; Germany had 64, and France 34.

3. FRANCE EXPERIMENTS WITH RAILWAYS

Railways. The second third of the nineteenth century saw the development of the modern transportation system. By 1870 the main lines had been laid out and it remained only to fill in the gaps, extend existing facilities, perfect methods, and determine policies. Railway building was fairly continuous, following in general the ups and downs of the business cycle. The following figures show the growth of the French railway net.

FRENCH RAILWAYS, 1870–1912
(in miles)

1870	10,835	1900	26,697
1880	16,236	1910	30,769
1890	22,889	1912	31,144

Mileage is a very inadequate measure of the efficiency of a railway system; ton-miles and passenger-miles afford a better standard of comparison. Yet the virtual trebling of the mileage in this period is a symptom of growth. At the same time the speed of the average train was increased and the comfort and safety of passengers were improved. At one time the Paris-Calais train held the record as the fastest express train in the world. On a per capita basis the population of France was better served than either Great Britain or Germany, though it was less so per square mile of territory. Owing to the sluggish industrial development of the country the services of the railways, both in the transportation of freight and of passengers, expanded slowly.

In spite of the cession of some 500 miles in Alsace-Lorraine to Germany the railway net grew between 1870 and 1875 by some 2500 miles. It was felt that the inadequacy of the transportation system had been partly responsible for defeat, and strenuous efforts were made to repair the lack. Many of the lines then built proved unprofitable and the smaller railway companies were faced with bankruptcy. The local roads were principally in the north and southwest. The former were absorbed by the prosperous Northern Company, but when the Orleans line proposed to take over the latter with a guarantee of interest the government refused unless the company would agree that the state should have absolute control over its rates. When this proposition was rejected the state in 1877 purchased this and certain other tributary lines of a total length of about 1600 miles.

The year 1878 was a turning point in French railway policy. Economic conditions were good, the war indemnity to Germany had been paid, and the treasury was in receipt of surplus revenues. De Freycinet, an engineer, at the moment minister of public works, proposed an ambitious building program which received the support of Gambetta, the president of the Chamber of Deputies, and of Léon

Say, the finance minister. The plan involved the appropriation of 3,000,000,000 francs for railway building, and was given effect by the laws of 1878 and 1879. These authorized the building of 5486 miles of state railways and preliminary work on 2574 miles additional. At the same time ten unprofitable lines, with a length of 1621 miles, were bought outright and incorporated in the state system. There was thus created a scattered governmental network of lines alongside the private roads and in competition with them. Only in the southwest were the lines sufficiently compact to be brought together into an operating unit.

The state roads proved a financial failure. Many of them had been built through remote and mountainous districts, in response to political pressure rather than commercial needs. Their cost, moreover, was double the first estimate. De Freycinet was forced out of office in 1880 and Gambetta died in 1882, thus removing two of the leading advocates of state railways from the scene. The period 1880–82 had been one of great prosperity and loans were readily placed; the private companies, moreover, were able to repay part of the advances made to them under the law of 1859. But in 1882 there was a financial crash and repayments to the government stopped, while the treasury surpluses were converted into deficits. Under the circumstances it did not seem feasible to throw the burden of completing the building plan upon the taxpayers, and the only way out was to ask the great railway companies to do so.

In 1883 the further construction of railways by the state was abandoned and an entirely different program was put into effect, which was adhered to with little change during the rest of this period; this was the old plan of granting a complete monopoly of transportation to subsidized private companies in the districts in which they operated. The state retained its system of roads in the southwest, in the triangle between Tours, Nantes, and Bordeaux, and gained access to Paris by obtaining a right of way over the lines of the Orleans and Western companies. It turned over to the six great private companies 7120 miles of new lines — the "third network" — and received from them certain small lines which might have competed with its system in the southwest. The companies agreed to issue their obligations for 2,000,000,000 francs, to complete the third network, taking over the rolling stock and works at 15,500 francs per mile. The money thus advanced was to be repaid to the state in annual installments, so arranged that the debt would be expunged by the time the charters expired. This would be between 1950 and 1960.

It will be remembered that the law of 1859 had prescribed a complicated set of financial arrangements between each separate company and the state, distinguishing the old and new networks, to which different guarantees were given. These distinctions were now swept away, and it was provided that all the financial transactions of each system were to be consolidated into a single account. Railway finance was thus greatly simplified. From its receipts each company was to pay first the interest and sinking fund charges and second a dividend to the shareholders, varying from 6 to 10 per cent according to the previous earnings of the roads. The state guaranteed these payments in case the earnings were insufficient to meet them. If, however, the earnings should exceed those sums, then the excess was to be applied to repaying advances made by the state. Whenever any company extinguished its debt to the state it could divide the excess above the guaranteed dividends between itself and the state in the proportion of one to two. This system of guarantees proved very costly to the state, especially during the next two decades, as five out of the six great companies were forced to take advantage of it. Only the Northern system stood on its own feet. Not until 1905 were payments from the companies to the state greater than those from the state to the companies. By 1914 the Eastern and Paris-Lyons-Mediterranean lines had paid back the advances; the Northern had never needed any. The Orleans system was in debt 280 million francs and the Southern 337.

During all this time the Western system had been receiving payments from the state under its guarantee, and in 1908 the government decided to exercise its option of purchase. The Western connected with the state system in the southwest and would give through lines to Paris. It seemed unlikely that the road could ever pay its debt to the state, but, on the other hand, it could be bought cheap since the price was determined on the basis of the previous earnings, which had always been low. Accordingly, in 1909 the state took over this system, thereby trebling the state-owned railway net, which now constituted one-fifth of the total railway mileage in France.

The act of 1883, nicknamed the "rascally conventions" (*Conventions Scélérats*), envisaged profits to the state, but receipts fell far short of expenses. The economic consequences were equally disastrous. For a decade it stimulated healthy railway building, nearly half of the French lines being built in that period, but by 1895 the railway net was practically completed and the Convention became the source of serious losses to the treasury. The increase of the state-owned lines was hailed as a great victory for nationalization, but the results of its operation did not augur well for nationalization in general. The state employees showed a lack of discipline, the number of accidents grew, the speed of the trains lessened, and they were less punctual. The failure of state management on the state system has often been used as an argument against railway nationalization, but in fairness it must be pointed out that this did not constitute a fair test in view of the character of the road.

The distinction between private and state railways in France is weakened by the fact that the state exercised control equally over both. According to French law the government had not only the right of supervision of the railways, but had also on all lines a legal right of decision in cases of public necessity, which justified interference of every kind. This found expression in the conventions with the private companies and in the liability for damages which cut deep into their economic freedom. The relation of state railways to the government was finally determined by the law of 1911, which abolished their autonomy and placed the whole network under the Minister of Public Works. The actual operations were superintended by a director of operation.

The making of rates remained in the hands of the private companies, but they could not exceed the maxima which were fixed by law. Changes could be made only with the approval of the Minister of Public Works. If a railway company wished to alter a rate it made application to the Minister of Railways, which transmitted a copy of the application to the prefect of the department in which the railway was located, who in turn notified the local chambers of commerce. These had one month in which to reply. On the basis of the evidence given by these various interested parties the Railway Advisory Council reported to the Minister, who then rendered his decision. Writing in 1885, Hadley concluded that the general effect of the monopolistic position of the French roads had been to prevent reductions in rates. The rates in 1881 were 1.55 cents per passenger-mile and 1.63 per ton-mile. "These rates," he wrote, "are on the whole much higher than those of Belgium, probably somewhat higher than those of Germany, and somewhat lower than those of Austria. Compared with the United States, they are, of course, much lower for passengers, and much higher for freight." [4]

One reason why French railway rates were high was because of failure to develop long-distance traffic. But the local self-sufficiency of France in respect of many products, the decentralization of industry, and the backward development, during most of this period, of the heavy industries, all militated against this. Moreover, much of French merchandise, especially for export, was of high value and small bulk and could consequently stand high rates better than cheap and heavy articles. Railway policy reflected the industrial situation and was largely determined by it, but on the other hand the rate

[4] A. T. Hadley, *Railroad Transportation: its History and its Laws* (New York, 1886), 201.

policy undoubtedly affected the development of traffic and made the roads less serviceable than they might have been.

Canals and rivers. The loss of some 250 miles of canal to Germany in 1871 destroyed the unity of some of the canals and the new boundaries cut across them. In order to meet this difficulty and establish direct connections with the Belgian coal deposits, a new canal, the Canal de l'Est, connecting the Saône and the Meuse, was authorized in 1874. The new iron and steel industry demanded that the canals be made available for the 300-ton barges from Belgium. When de Freycinet launched his building program in 1878, provision was accordingly made for improvement of the waterways; 1160 million francs were to be allocated to canal building and 532 million for river improvements. It proved impossible to carry out this plan, however, and relatively little was done in the way of new construction. At the same time the unification of the canal system was taken in hand. All waterways which would admit 300-ton barges were declared first-class; of these there were 2500 miles of canals and 2200 miles of rivers. Tolls were abolished on all state waterways in 1880, and provision made for the nationalization of all the canals, which was completed in 1898. The growth of the system of waterways and of the traffic carried upon them was slow during this period.

WATERWAYS IN FRANCE, 1876–1913

Year	Length (in miles) Canals	Rivers	Traffic (in millions of ton-miles) Canals and Rivers
1870	2830	4160	124
1880	2890	4540	134
1890	2990	4700	200
1900	3010	4530	290
1910	....	....	323
1913	3080	4345	384

France is covered with a network of waterways and all the important rivers are connected with each other by canal. Only in the industrially developed north, however, were the waterways of first-rate importance. Here the land topography of the country and the ample rainfall favored this type of navigation, especially on the Seine and the canals which connected with the northern coal fields. The usefulness of many of the canals was lessened by the large number of locks; thus, on the 257-mile stretch between Paris and Nancy there were 134, and on the 396-mile stretch between Paris and Lyons there were 229. The canals also differed in depth and in the size of the locks. Standardization of locks and of the width and

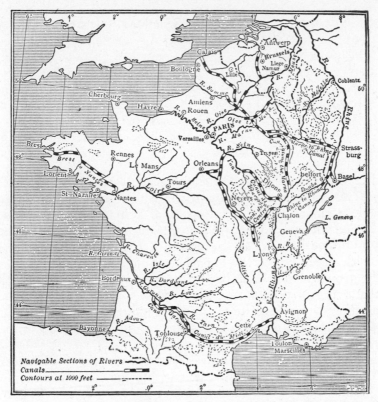

FIGURE 5. FRENCH AND BELGIAN WATERWAYS

From J. R. Smith's *Commerce and Industry* (Henry Holt & Co., 1925).
Reprinted by permission of the publishers.

depth of the canals was begun in 1879 but was not made compulsory by law until 1903. The standard depth was fixed at 6½ feet. The canals in the agricultural south were therefore doubly handicapped, by geography as well as by lack of traffic. The famous Canal du Midi was scarcely used.

The tonnage on the canals consisted of cheap, heavy articles, over a third of building materials, and about a fifth of coal, limestone, and iron. Only about 3 per cent was manufactures.

Roads. The road system of France, one of the best in Europe, was practically completed by 1870. All that was necessary was to maintain it at its existing high standard. Extensions were confined to the communal roads.

The national highways were macadamized and averaged nearly 30 feet in width; the departmental roads were about 23 feet, and the communal roads about 15 feet wide. But even the unimproved roads were kept in excellent condition. All bridge tolls were abol-

ROADS IN FRANCE *

(in miles)

Year	National roads	Departmental roads	Communal roads
1870	23,790	....	203,708
1880	23,170	...	258,323
1892	23,500	14,170	297,391
1900	23,640	10,710	316,583
1910	23,740	....	331,647

* *Annuaire Statistique* (Paris, 1924), 66.

ished in 1880, making road traffic absolutely free. Many places in France were reached only by road, which made them an indispensable element in the transportation system. Their value was heightened with the advent of motor traffic in the twentieth century.

Communications. The expansion of the postoffice did not keep pace with other aspects of French commerce, though it showed a steady growth. The number of letters handled increased from slightly over 300,000,000 in 1871 to over 1,500,000,000 in 1910. It was, moreover, a favorite medium for effecting transfers of money, the postal money orders expanding from 139,000,000 francs in 1871 to 2,619,000,000 in 1910.

The telegraph came into commercial use very late in France. In 1850 the number of telegrams sent within the country amounted to only 9000. The high cost — 13 francs for a message — was largely responsible for this, but as rates were reduced, to 2 francs in 1861, to 1 franc in 1868, and finally to half a franc in 1877, the service expanded. By 1870 over 4,000,000 telegrams were sent, and by 1910 over 45,000,000.

The telephone, invented in 1877, met with an immediate popular response. Lines were built throughout the country linking up all commercial centers. By 1910 the number of telephone calls was 264,000,000.

BIBLIOGRAPHICAL NOTE

1. *Britain.* The most informative account of inland water transportation is the *Report of the Royal Commission on the Canals and Inland Navigations of the United Kingdom* (London, 1909. Cd. 4979). An unofficial but good survey is J. E. Palmer, *British Canals, Problems, and Possibilities* (London, 1910). On railways a good book is E. Cleveland-Stevens, *English Railways: their Development and their Relation to the State* (London, 1915), though it deals only with railway consolidation. L. M. McPherson, *Transportation in Europe* (New York, 1910) traces the development in England and on the Continent as does C. L. Roper, *Railway Transportation* (New York, 1912). W. M. Acworth, *The Railways of England* (2nd ed., London, 1889) is popular and anecdotal. G. Paish, *The British Railway Problem* (London, 1902) discusses state control. On communications,

E. Murray, *The Post Office* (London, 1927), and F. G. C. Baldwin, *The History of the Telephone in Great Britain* (London, 1938) may be cited.

2. *Germany.* A sharp analysis of German railway policy is G. Cohn, *Zur Geschichte und Politik der Verkehrswesens* (Stuttgart, 1900). K. Hassert, *Allgemeine Verkehrsgeographie* (Berlin, 1913) is a geographical study but contains much historical material. Gotz, *Die Verkehrswege im Dienst des Welthandels* (Stuttgart, 1888) is historical. Br. Schultz, *Die volkswirtschaftliche Bedeutung der Eisenbahnen* (June, 1922) emphasizes their social significance. Government ownership is described and depreciated in W. M. Acworth, *Historical Sketch of Government Ownership of Railroads in Foreign Countries* (Washington, 1917); S. O. Dunn, *Government Ownership of Railways* (New York, 1913); and W. M. W. Splawn, *Government Ownership and Operation of Railroads* (New York, 1928). K. Sautter, *Geschichte der deutschen Post* (Berlin, 1928) emphasizes operating problems.

3. *France.* A careful, detailed, and authoritative study of French railways is A. Picard, *Les chemins de fer, aperçu historique* (Paris, 1918). A companion volume of documents and speeches by the same author is *Les chemins de fer français*, 6 vols. (Paris, 1884). Lord R. A. H. Monkswell, *French Railways* (London, 1911) gives an informed account. C. Colson, *Transports et tarifs* (Paris, 1910) is more technical. R. Kaufmann, *Die Eisenbahnpolitik Frankreichs*, 2 vols. (Stuttgart, 1896. Translated by F. Hamon as *La Politique française en matière des chemins de fer.* Paris, 1900) is a careful, thorough account of policy. P. Girard, *L'exploitation rationelle des chemins de fer en France* (Montpellier, 1923) is useful.

CHAPTER XII

MONEY, BANKING, AND FINANCE

I. BRITAIN THE FINANCIAL CENTER OF THE WORLD

Money. Although Great Britain had been on the gold standard since 1816, she was not unaffected by the great fall in the price of silver and the so-called scramble for gold which began in the seventies. Germany adopted the gold standard and began the sale of her silver in 1870–71, France and the other states of the Latin Union limited the coinage of silver in 1874 and discontinued it in 1878, Holland and the Scandinavian countries demonetized silver in 1875. In other words there was a great decline in the monetary demand for that metal. But more important was the increase in supply, owing to the enormous growth in silver production from newly discovered but extraordinarily rich mines in the United States, and the invention of cheaper methods of extraction from the ore by the cyanide process. As the various nations discarded or limited the use of silver for monetary purposes the demand for gold became greater. And as the populations grew and trade expanded the need for additional supplies became more insistent. Industrial uses also increased, absorbing as much as 60 per cent of the new gold in the eighties. Hoarding, especially in India, which had always been known as a "silver sink" but which now drained off the gold also, diverted some of the supplies from monetary use in Europe.

There has been much argument as to whether the fall in general prices which occurred between 1874 and 1896 was caused by the demonetization of silver and the relative scarcity of gold upon its general adoption as the standard of value by the European nations. Believers in the quantity theory of money, holding that prices varied directly with the amount of money in circulation, pointed to the rise in prices between 1849 and 1870 that followed the gold discoveries in the United States and Australia and the consequent additions to the monetary supply. Now, they insisted, there was a similar connection between the relative scarcity of gold and the fall in prices. From this fall, which was undoubted, the bimetallists drew the conclusion that the remedy to apply was bimetallism; but no European nation adopted it. The United States alone expanded its use of silver as money. Critics of the quantity theory of money, on the other hand, insisted that the general price decline was due to causes not connected with the amount of gold in circulation, and cited numerous special factors to account for it, such as improved and cheaper methods of production for silver, and of steel and manufactured goods turned out by machinery in quantity, the opening up of new lands for grain, meat, and wool, and above all the improvements in transportation which cheapened all commodities that moved to a market. The conclusion seems warranted, however, that the basic cause was the changed situation with respect to gold. During the period 1896 to 1914 the annual world production of gold was doubled, owing chiefly to new discoveries in Africa and Alaska. At the same time the general level of commodity prices rose. The Sauerbeck price index, based on the gold price of 45 commodities, showed these changes.

SAUERBECK PRICE INDEX

Year	Index number	Year	Index number
1871	100	1900	75
1880	88	1905	80
1890	72	1910	107
		1913	116

The currency in use in Great Britain in 1870 consisted of gold coin, subsidiary silver, Bank of England notes, and the notes of country banks. Since the smallest note issued by the Bank of England was for £5, it did not enter largely into circulation, being confined to the more important cities and used only for large transactions. A large circulation of gold sovereigns in the hands of the people was the ideal sought by English legislation. How well it was attained is shown by the fact that in 1875 the gold in circulation was estimated at £100,000,000 for the United Kingdom, and by 1913 had swelled to over £150,000,000.

Meanwhile the monopoly of note issue was gradually being concentrated in the Bank of England. Under the Bank Charter Act of 1844 the credit issues of the Bank, against which it held securities and not gold, were limited to £14,000,000. For all notes beyond this sum it was required to hold an equivalent amount of gold. The Act provided, however, that if any country bank surrendered its issues, the Bank of England might increase its uncovered notes by two-thirds of the amounts thus surrendered. The growth of banking after this date, which was very rapid, was all in the direction of deposit banking. Checks proved to be a more convenient means of carrying on business transactions than notes. The country banks therefore gradually surrendered their right of note issue in order that they might engage in deposit banking in London or unite with a city bank already there. The authorized country bank issues were reduced from £8,648,843 in 1844 to £2,958,900 in 1900, and were finally all surrendered in 1921. At this date the uncovered note

issues of the Bank of England amounted to £19,758,000.   Bank
notes played a relatively unimportant role in England, the elastic
part of the currency system consisting of its deposits.   It has been
estimated that over 98 per cent of the transfers of money in London
were effected by means of checks and over two-thirds in the provinces.

The banking system.   The banking system of Great Britain was
a complex, at the heart of which stood the Bank of England.   Its
peculiar and important position was emphasized by the manner in
which the other constituent elements developed.   The private banking houses steadily declined in number, most of them being absorbed
into the joint stock companies.   By 1886 there were only 251 left,
and a decade later twenty of these amalgamated to form Barclay
and Co., a joint stock bank.   The business of the private banks was
falling off and in order better to meet the competition of the joint
stock banks they combined.   The remnants of them formed, in 1914,
together with the merchant firms and accepting houses, a kind of
banking aristocracy in London.   The merchant bankers or accepting
houses, though not bankers in the strict sense of the term, were
closely allied to the London banks.   Their most important function
was that of accepting bills of exchange drawn by exporters, and
by their endorsement making them easily negotiable credit instruments.   For this service they charged a commission.   Similar in
function were the discount houses, which dealt primarily in foreign
bills of exchange and Treasury bills.   Finally, there were the bill
brokers, financial middlemen, who performed useful services in distributing commercial paper; they were peculiar to the London
money market and were not found in either France or Germany.

The banking business proper was conducted almost entirely by
the joint stock banks, which covered the whole country with a network of branches.   The number of banking offices in the United
Kingdom, that is of head offices and branches, grew from 2924 in
1872 to 7861 in 1908.   This increase in banking facilities took place
in spite of a decrease in the number of banks.   Centralization of
banking was an outstanding feature of this period and was usually
effected by the amalgamation of existing institutions.   A great impetus had been given to the growth of joint stock banks by the grant
of limited liability in 1879, and as they grew they came into closer
competition, and rivalry developed.   After about 1890 the combination movement in industry and commerce reacted slowly on the size
of the banking structure.   The leading banks wished greater geographical extension and wider spread of risks, and were also actuated
by an ambition for mere size.

A second outstanding feature of this period in British banking history, as indeed of much of the previous period, was the shifting of importance from bank notes to deposits. With this change in emphasis the monopoly of issue by the Bank of England became relatively less significant and the deposit functions of the commercial banks more so. Government legislation, as in the Act of 1844, had been confined to regulation of the note issues, so that in all other respects English banking was completely free from restriction and regulation by law. This freedom explains in part the amalgamation movement and the extension of branch banking, in contrast with American prohibitions.

The function of the banks thus far described was to create credit and provide the community with currency with which to carry on business operations. Standing somewhat apart from these, and yet performing an important service, were the savings banks. They did not discount bills nor make loans, nor issue notes, but safeguarded deposits. They were guardians rather than banks. Of these there were two classes, trustee savings banks and postoffice savings banks. The former were established originally as philanthropic institutions to encourage thrift, but in 1817 were brought under Parliamentary supervision and required to invest their funds in government securities. After the establishment of postoffice savings banks in 1861 many of the trustee savings banks were closed and those that remained grew less rapidly than their new rivals. The latter had the advantage of providing facilities for the opening of a deposit account wherever a post office was established. Both institutions paid 2½ per cent interest on all deposits, and were a valuable aid in accumulating the capital of persons of small means.

Investment and finance. The currency and banking system of Britain was not an insular affair, for it extended to all parts of the world. The soundness of British financial institutions made the pound sterling almost the equivalent of an international currency, and linked it with the currencies of many other countries. British banks had widespread international connections and carried on financial transactions that reached into every European capital and backward area. The accumulation of capital and the increasing difficulty of finding profitable use for it at home led to the export of capital and its investment in other regions that offered higher returns. Foreign investments of British capital amounted to about £800 million in 1870 and by 1914 had grown to over £4000 million, or more than one-quarter of British national wealth. By the end of this period probably half of current British savings were each year being invested abroad, nearly half of these in the Empire, and 10 per cent of the national income was being drawn from these sources. This movement of capital into other lands, together with the accompanying policy of imperialism, had the effect of breaking down the insularity of the British people and of broadening their outlook. Much more important, it required peace and orderly development for satisfactory functioning. Not only investment but also British foreign trade were intimately linked up with the economic progress of the rest of the world.

This period of prosperity and expansion was reflected in government finance. Revenues and expenditures both followed an upward curve, from about £70 million in 1870 to £190 million in 1914. This latter figure was about one-fifth of the national income, and was an illustration of the general tendency toward the expansion of governmental functions. It was possible not only to balance the budget, but also out of the annual surpluses to achieve a slight though steady reduction in the public debt. This was cut down from £791 million in 1870 to £650 million in 1914.

2. GERMAN FINANCIAL IMPERIALISM

Money. The monetary and banking system of Germany was in urgent need of reform before 1870. The northern states had the thaler system and those in the south the gulden; since the coins were of different denominations, and many of them obsolete and of different degrees of abrasion, heavy exchange charges absorbed most of the trader's profits. Silver was the standard and constituted the principal metallic stock; some gold pieces were coined but they were not legal tender. The character of the money in circulation was further confused by the existence of paper currency, which was issued by every state except the three free cities of Hamburg, Lübeck and Bremen and the principality of Lippe. Over 180,000,000 marks of this paper money was in circulation in 1873. And finally there were 33 banks of issue, with capitals ranging from 1 to 60 million marks, with varying rights of issue, and with charters running to 50 or 100 years or without limit of time. Their distribution was quite arbitrary; thus all Bavaria had only one such bank, with permissible issues of 21,000,000 marks, while Saxony had five with issues of 120 million, and little Schaumburg-Lippe, with 32,000 inhabitants, had a bank with unlimited note issue. It was estimated that 140 different kinds of state paper money and bank notes were in existence in 1870.

The reform of the coinage system was undertaken first.[1] The

---

[1] The possibility of an international currency had been discussed during the liberal sixties. By slight changes in their coinage value the shilling, the franc, and the dollar could be brought into equivalence, and it was hoped that Germany would make her currency conform to that of the Latin Union. This was not done. The gold value of the different coins in cents was: shilling, 24.3; franc, 19.3; mark, 23.8.

adoption of the gold standard and the unification of the currency had been recommended by a commercial convention in 1868, and in 1871 a law was passed providing for uniform coinage. The unit was the mark, equal to one-third of the Prussian thaler; the decimal system was adopted. The gold standard was adopted in 1873, an imperial coinage system was established, and silver coins were made token money by reducing their silver content. The coinage of silver was stopped in 1872 and two years later the old silver coins were called in; thereafter subsidiary silver pieces were coined only on government account, and by a later law were limited to 20 marks per capita. Part of the stock of silver which came into possession of the government was used for this purpose, but the greater part was sold on the world markets before 1879. The adoption of the gold standard was made possible by the payment of the French indemnity in 1871. Although the direct payments in gold by France were only 273,000,000 francs, the power of drawing the proceeds of bills of exchange on London and Paris gave the German government access to vast stocks of gold. By this act Germany ranged itself beside Great Britain, the only other country on the gold standard. It was an act of outstanding importance and led the way to the general adoption of the gold standard.

The extinction of paper currency issued by the several states was provided for in 1874. The outstanding paper was to be called in and replaced by imperial treasury notes (*Reichskassenscheine*), which were convertible into gold, but not a legal tender.

The last step in the reform of the currency system was taken in 1875 when the banks of issue were brought under the control of the imperial government. A limit of 385,000,000 marks was set for the aggregate note issues which were not covered mark for mark by gold, and this sum was allocated to the various banks; uncovered issues beyond these sums were taxed. Fifteen of the banks declined to issue notes under the onerous provisions of this law, and by 1894 ten more had withdrawn their issues. In 1914 only the four banks of Bavaria, Wurtemberg, Saxony, and Baden still retained this privilege, outside the Reichsbank.

The Reichsbank. The Reichsbank was built on the old Bank of Prussia, which in 1875 transferred its rights and privileges to the new imperial institution. As to ownership it was a private bank, but in its management it was essentially a public institution. Official control over the bank was exercised by a council of curators, composed of the Chancellor of the Empire and four other members, one named by the Emperor and three by the Federal Council. The administration was carried on by a directorate composed of a president and members appointed for life by the imperial government. Employees of the

Bank were regarded as public servants. The stockholders elected a committee of fifteen which determined the loan policy and attended to business details, subject always to the approval of the imperial authorities.

The division of the profits showed, if further proof were needed, the close association of the state with the Reichsbank. The law originally required that of all earnings in excess of a dividend of $4\frac{1}{2}$ per cent, one-fifth should go to surplus and the remainder be divided equally between the shareholders and the government; if the annual dividend reached 8 per cent the government should receive three-quarters of the excess. In 1889 the ordinary dividend was limited to $3\frac{1}{2}$ per cent, and the point at which the government should receive three-fourths was reduced to 6 per cent. Again in 1899, upon the second renewal of the charter, further concessions were exacted. Of the profits over $3\frac{1}{2}$ per cent, the state was to receive sixty per cent instead of half, and when the required surplus was accumulated it was to be paid three-quarters of all profits beyond the ordinary dividend. This arrangement was very profitable to the state, whose revenues from this source were considerable.

The note circulation was modeled after the English system, but with important modifications. The Reichsbank could issue notes on credit, without any specific security, up to an amount fixed originally at 250,000,000 marks but raised subsequently as the other banks of issue surrendered their rights. Notes beyond this uncovered circulation must be offset by an equivalent amount of cash. No limit was placed on the amount of notes that might be issued, but if any uncovered notes were issued beyond the statutory amount they were taxed. An elastic limit was thus provided which permitted the Bank to increase its issues in times of commercial pressure, but gave the profits of such transactions to the state. The tax forced the contraction of the issues when the need was over. This was a great improvement over the hard and fast requirement of the English law, and was made use of whenever it was convenient; thus in 1909 taxed notes were issued twenty-five times in normal banking procedure. The notes were not legal tender, but had a national circulation. The total Reichsbank issues, covered and uncovered, increased from 685,000,000 marks in 1876 to 1,958,000,000 in 1913. At the last date the circulation of the four other note-issuing banks was 149,000,000 marks.

Like the Bank of England, the Reichsbank had the duty of conserving the metallic reserves of the nation, but the concentration was not so great. While about half of its loans were made to banks by rediscounting their commercial paper, the Reichsbank was less a bankers' bank than was the Bank of England. The metallic reserve increased from 510,000,000 marks in 1876 to 1,200,000,000 in 1913, and the composition of the stock shifted during this period from mostly silver to mostly gold. Except for foreign exchange the demands upon the Reichsbank for gold were not important, for any increased need for currency for domestic purposes could be met by additional issues of notes. The elastic limit permitted this in effective fashion.

An important part of the Bank's activities was the transfer of cash from place to place at very low rates. This was the so-called "giro" system, which took the place of the English check system, and was preferred. Any customer who wished to make a payment to another person, whether in the same town or in some other place, would hand in to the Bank a form properly made out. If cash were wanted a different form was filled out, which would be honored by the Bank and collected from the party upon whom it was drawn. In this way transfers of money were made throughout the country, at a minimum of expense and a maximum of safety. The giro business in Germany never attained the dimensions that the use of the check did in England or the United States. The system was extended in 1909 by the introduction of the post-check, which operated in the same way through the post office, and had the advantage of rendering it unnecessary for the letter carrier to carry sums of money to and from customers and the Bank or its branches every day.

In its relations with the public the Reichsbank resembled the Bank of France more than the Bank of England. It was required by law to establish branches wherever needed, but it did not wait for official prodding. Taking over 130 branches of the old Prussian Bank, it increased these to about 100 principal branches and 400 local offices. The Bank discounted bills as low as 10 marks, and for any applicant, whether he was a depositor or not. It was forbidden by law to make a loan for longer than four months, and could not therefore accommodate the farmers and small tradesmen who wished longer credit. These were encouraged to form credit associations, whose paper was rediscounted by the Reichsbank. In this way the credit of the Bank was extended to the humblest borrower.

Commercial banks. More closely associated with the industrial growth of Germany during this period than the Reichsbank were the joint stock commercial-deposit banks, or credit banks, as they were called in Germany. The so-called *Gründerjahre* or boom years of the early seventies saw the establishment of a number of new credit banks: in 1870 there were four, among them the Deutsche Bank; in 1871 nine; and in 1872 the great Dresdner Bank was founded as well as many smaller ones. By the end of this year there were in Germany 139 credit banks with an aggregate capital of 1122 million marks. After the panic of 1873 many of these disappeared and no new banks of importance were established except the Nationalbank für Deutschland in 1881. The existing institutions were sufficient to care for the credit needs of the country.

After the early period of organization there ensued one of concentration. The large banks sought to expand their operations by increasing their capital and by absorbing the smaller banks. By 1883 the total number was reduced to 71, but thereafter new establishments kept pace with the combinations, so that in 1907 there were 144. The new banks were mostly comparatively small local institutions, for the great banks confined their activities to the important industrial and commercial cities and had few branches; toward the end of this period they established many agencies, deposit offices and branches. The five greatest Berlin credit banks finally formed an important combination by establishing a community of interest with other smaller banks, which functioned under their leadership. Thus the Deutsche Bank had twelve attached banks and a series of friendly banks, the Dresdner Bank had eight, the Discontogesellschaft had six, the Darmstädter Bank four, and the Schaffhausen Bankverein three. The movement to concentration was especially vigorous in the years 1897–1906. These groups exercised an enormous power and controlled over two-thirds of the banking capital in Germany. At the end of 1911 these groups had a combined capital of 1840 million marks with 543 million reserves, or about 2,400 million out of a total banking capital for the whole country of 3,400 million marks.

The development of these commercial banks was of great significance for the rapid industrialization of Germany as they furnished the necessary financial means for expansion and technical improvements. They carried on all kinds of credit operations, not merely normal banking functions such as discounting commercial paper and making advances on personal security or on goods (Lombardgeschäft), but also by founding industrial undertakings or selling their shares to the public. They were thus a combination of commercial bank, investment bank, and investment trust. Lacking the financial resources of Great Britain, bank credit alone could supply the enormous amount of capital needed to establish the new industries. The speculative advances made by the banks to industrial concerns on their securities as collateral violated every canon of sound banking that had been set up in Britain, but without them the rapid economic program that Germany achieved would have been impossible. There was an extraordinarily close association between the banks and industry, and bankers tended more and more to control industrial policy. The combinations of coal mines, of blast furnaces and steel works and rolling mills, or electrical companies,

and the formation of the so-called mixed works, which characterized the latter part of this period, were undertaken mostly with the
financial assistance of the great credit banks and largely through their
pressure.

While the great banks competed with each other for normal banking business each had a field of operation that was peculiarly its own
and which was respected by the others.   Thus the Dresdner Bank
was recognized as representing the Krupp interest, and the Deutsche
Bank busied itself largely with foreign investments, especially in
Turkey and Austria, while the Discontogesellschaft served the railways and the smaller banks.   As German foreign trade and investments increased, it was recognized that there existed a gap in the
organization of the German credit system, which had to be filled if
German trade were to render itself independent of English intermediation.   The introduction of the gold standard in Germany in
1873 made this easier and the other German banks began to establish foreign branches and connections.   The general adoption of
the gold standard promoted greater stability of foreign exchange
rates among gold standard countries, and this stability facilitated
international trade and international lending.   There ensued a financial penetration into Russia, Italy, the Balkan states, and South
America.   The rapid growth and extent of German foreign interests
may be gauged by the following brief table of the face value of the
securities dealt in on the German stock exchanges (in millions of
marks):

	1900	1910
German	2424	2757
Foreign	448	2242

The credit banks were an important medium for national industrial unification.   They were also a politico-economic instrument in
carrying out German power policy.   In addition to financing industry at home they facilitated the policy of economic penetration.
Despite the comparative scarcity of domestic capital, it was found
possible to make large foreign investments.   These grew from 5000
million marks in 1883 to approximately 25,000 million marks in
1914.

Concentration of banking took place during this period, especially
in the large Berlin banks.   In 1910 slightly over 40 per cent of the
deposits of all banks with at least 1,000,000 marks capital were held
by the four so-called D-Banks — Deutsche, Dresdner, Darmstädter,
and Discontogesellschaft.   These great centralized institutions, each
of which was closely associated with some leading heavy industry, used their influence to bring about industrial combinations or

cartels. Monopoly in banking led to monopoly in industry. They also exercised a powerful influence in the management of industrial undertakings, obtaining key positions, voting proxies, and in other ways determining policies.

Other banks. Industry and foreign trade were better served by these great banks than were domestic commerce or agriculture. But for the latter an excellent system already existed. Land-mortgage associations (*Landschaften*), operating on the basis of the collective responsibility of their members, permitted borrowing at low rates and gave great mobility to the securities. These served the large landowners. Credit for the owner of urban real estate was given by mortgage banks (*Hypothekenbanken*), which came into existence for the most part in two periods of expansion, 1862–72 and 1894–96. In 1913 these had issued mortgages for 11,400 million marks. Smaller borrowers with less security to offer were cared for in the cities by the Schulze-Delitsch banks, and in the rural districts by the Raiffeisen banks, both operating on the mutual system of joint responsibility of all members.

The German banking system, as it existed on the eve of the war, had developed a certain characteristic structure. The banks still united investment financing with deposit banking, but the former was tending to decline. This change was hastened by the crisis of 1906, which led to an official inquiry into the liquidity of the great banks. Berlin was the financial center, and here there was a strong concentration in a few large institutions, but the provinces were neglected. Medium and large industry looked to the credit banks for assistance, but small industry and agriculture obtained credit from mutual and savings banks. In the banking hierarchy the Reichsbank was powerful and exercised control over the money market by regulating the discount rate, which was uniformly higher than in Britain or France, owing to the greater scarcity of capital.

3. SAVING AND INVESTMENT IN FRANCE

Money. Owing to the gold discoveries the value of gold had fallen and the legal ratio of 15.5 to 1, established by the mint of France in 1803 no longer represented the market ratio between gold and silver after 1850. The mint ratio overvalued gold and this metal consequently flowed into France in enormous quantities, while even greater amounts of silver, which was worth more as bullion than for coinage, flowed out. As a result there was a growing scarcity of silver coins, and some embarrassment to retail trade. Similar conditions existed in Belgium, Italy, and Switzerland, which had adopted the French decimal system of coinage and which freely received each other's coins. Unfortunately, however, Switzerland had reduced the fineness of her small silver coins under five francs to .800, Italy and France to .835, while Belgium had left hers unaltered at .900. In order to meet this situation these four countries in 1865 formed the so-called Latin Union, joined by Greece the following year, which agreed to make all silver coins below the five-franc piece token money by reducing the amount of fine silver in them to .835, and to limit their amount according to population and also their legal tender quality. In 1867 the value of silver began to fall and soon the gold began to disappear and silver was presented to the mints of these countries for coinage in growing amounts. In order to protect their gold reserves they consequently agreed in 1874 to limit the coinage of silver five-franc pieces to comparatively small annual amounts. Silver continued to fall in price, for reasons already described, and in 1878 the coinage of five-franc pieces was absolutely suspended. Silver coin thus became token money.

During most of this period France had been on a paper money basis, to which she had been forced in 1871 as a result of the war with Germany. When she prepared to resume specie payments in 1877 she was therefore confronted with a difficult situation. Redemption of the paper money in gold or silver at the option of the holder would result in draining off the gold in the Bank of France. The policy was therefore adopted of redeeming the notes in gold or silver at the discretion of the Bank, and of charging a premium for gold. The Bank was thereby enabled to protect its gold reserve and to prevent its withdrawal for exportation. The same end was being achieved in England by permitting the Bank of England to raise its discount rate, a more flexible and less disturbing procedure than the arbitary French method. The Bank of France tried to force the silver five-franc pieces into circulation, but the public preferred notes resting on the combined security of gold and silver in the bank reserves. As trade expanded, therefore, its needs were met by larger issues of notes of the Bank of France, and little metallic money in the form of either gold or silver, except as subsidiary coins, entered into circulation. Since the use of checks and similar credit instruments was but slightly developed in France, most transactions were consummated by the actual payment of cash in the form of notes of the Bank of France.

Bank of France. The charter of the Bank of France expired in 1867, and when it was renewed for thirty years the government took advantage of the opportunity to require the Bank to maintain a branch in each department. Between 1873 and 1877 there were added 25 branches and by the end of the century the full number of 86 had been opened, together with a large number of auxiliary bureaus and banking offices. The Bank occupied a unique position in the French banking structure. It had a monopoly of note issues, which were given the legal tender quality. Its relation to the state was very close and it had rendered valuable assistance in the payment of the war indemnity in 1871. Incidentally, it had profited greatly, along with the other banks, from operations in connection with the indemnity, mostly from the transfer of securities. In return for the privileges granted it the Bank was required in 1867 to subscribe for new three per cent government bonds for which the market was unfavorable, and by the middle of 1871 it had made further loans to the government of nearly 1,500,000,000 francs. Specie payments were suspended in 1870, and the Bank greatly increased its note issues to take care of the requirements of the government and also of the needs of business. Notes as small as five francs were authorized. With the resumption of specie payments in 1874 all notes of less than 25 francs were withdrawn. The legal tender quality was not abolished until 1878.

When the question of the renewal of the charter came up again in 1897, the plan of state ownership was urged, but the Chamber decided to leave the Bank a private institution. The charter was renewed until 1920, an unusually short time. But opportunity was taken again to require some serious concessions as the price of a renewal of its exclusive privilege. The Bank was directed to increase the number of its branches by transforming 18 existing offices into branches and creating 11 new ones, and also 30 new offices. It was required to pay a tax on its productive circulation, with a minimum of 2,000,000 francs per annum; it was also forced to make permanent advances to the government of some 180,000,000 francs without interest, and to extend its services as an agent of the state in handling public funds. The total annual financial burden imposed on the Bank by the law of 1897 amounted to 10,937,000 francs in 1911.

The organization of the Bank gave further proof of its close relation to the state. Although it was a private institution the government appointed the governor and two sub-governors, and three out of fifteen of the regents, who constituted the governing board. The only shareholders entitled to vote at the annual meetings were the two hundred who held the largest number of shares. Management was thus concentrated in the hands of a small, wealthy group.

More important than the relation of the Bank of France to the state was its position in the banking hierarchy. In 1870 it was primarily a bankers' bank; it regulated the money market; it received deposits but did not allow interest on them; it discounted only bills with three signatures. Like the Bank of England it was the custodian of the metallic reserves of the country. The other banks paid attention only to the composition of their portfolios, that is the soundness of their commercial bills. If one of them needed cash, it added the bank's signature to some of its bills, thus giving them the required three signatures, and rediscounted them at the Bank of France. The cash reserves of the Bank were therefore always kept extraordinarily large. From 1,130,000,000 francs in 1870 the average metallic reserve increased to 3,975,000,000 in 1913. The proportion of gold to silver remained fairly steady until 1895, but after that date the gold steadily increased and some of the silver hoard was disposed of as opportunity arose. The proportion of cash reserve to notes was at all times impressive; in 1870 it was 74 per cent and in 1913 it was 77 per cent. This emphasizes the responsible position which the Bank held as the custodian of the banking reserves of the country. The following table shows the increase both in notes and reserves:

NOTE CIRCULATION AND RESERVES OF THE BANK OF FRANCE

Year	Average amount of notes in circulation	Average amount of metallic reserve	Coverage per cent
	(in millions of francs)		
1870	1514	1131	74
1880	2306	1974	85
1890	3060	2513	82
1900	4034	3238	80
1913	5675	3975	77

The Bank of France remained for a long time a bank for banks, but the government was determined to make it a bank for the people. In 1867 it was required to establish branches which were ultimately to reach 377; in 1895 it was obliged to handle bills as small as 5 francs; and it was made to accept private deposits. Credit was thereby democratized and the Bank became more truly a national institution. More than half of the Bank's business was carried on by the branches. That it was still largely a bankers' bank, however, was shown by the fact that as late as 1910 about 70 per cent of the commercial paper held by the Bank bore the signature of some other bank as endorser, that is to say it had been rediscounted by the Bank. But growing use of its facilities was being made directly by merchants and manufacturers. The small size of the average bill — about 600 francs for twenty days — showed that it accommodated small tradesmen and shopkeepers as well. The average bill handled for collection was between 200 and 250 francs. Fuller details of notes discounted at Paris in 1911 showed that 49 per cent of all were for 100 francs or less.

NOTES DISCOUNTED AT BANK OF FRANCE, IN PARIS, 1911

Size of note	Total amount
5 to 10 francs	237,512
10.1 to 50 francs	2,231,942
50.1 to 100 francs	1,536,126
Over 100 francs	4,218,384
Total	8,223,964

Other credit institutions. The great financial institutions, such as the Crédit Lyonnais, the Comptoir National d'Escompte de Paris, the Société Générale, and the Crédit Industriel et Commercial, played a more important part than the Bank of France in the distribution of credit. Through their numerous branches throughout France and even in Paris itself, these banks came in more intimate contact with the people, and made incredibly small loans. In 1910 the average was about 500 francs. They gradually taught the people new habits of investment and confidence in credit; instead of being hoarded, money was deposited in the banks. While deposit and discount were their main functions these banks also undertook other operations, such as stock-market orders and the flotation of securities. Loans were usually made on commercial paper, but also on securities, and in slack times treasury bills were purchased. These institutions thus served a clientele and performed functions not open to the Bank of France. The growth of the four most important deposit banks may be briefly shown.[2]

Institutions	Year	Capital & reserve	Deposits	Discounts	Number of branches & agencies
			(in millions of francs)		
Crédit Lyonnais	1880	80	133	138	99
	1900	350	490	760	170
	1909	398	825	1277	224
Comptoir National d'Escompte	1890	42	133	144	9
	1900	166	291	369	110
	1909	237	593	876	190
Société Générale	1880	73	145	112	147
	1900	99	233	317	345
	1909	263	424	857	725
Crédit Industriel et Commercial	1880	22	42	77	8
	1900	30	45	65	105
	1909	45	66	147	174

[2] B. Mehrens, *Die Entstehung und Entwicklung der grossen französischen Kreditinstitute* (Stuttgart, 1911), 254.

The network of branches of these banks spread over the whole of France, where not a town of importance nor a market with a substantial volume of business but possessed one or more branches of the great Paris banks, either as permanent establishments or as temporary business for market days.

The success of these banks attracted competitors and between 1870 and 1881 inclusive 39 new banks were founded. These tried by every means to entice customers, to whom they sold speculative securities of doubtful value. They advertised widely and established a great number of branches and agencies. Most of these new banks were venturesome and even dishonest, but their apparent success led to wild speculation in their stocks. As an example the Union Générale may serve. This gained large profits in financing enterprises in Austria and Serbia, increased its capital and tried to make itself the leading bank in France, saw its shares advance from 930 at the end of 1880 to 3450 in December, 1881, and failed disastrously the following February.[3] The depression of the next few years wiped out these speculative banks and the field was left to the older and more conservative houses.

Below the great Paris institutions stood the local banks. Their importance diminished as the large banks multiplied their branches and some of them were absorbed. They served primarily the small tradesmen and manufacturers or peasant proprietors of their districts; for the granting of personal credit they were well equipped by reason of their knowledge of local conditions. Beginning with the eighties the local banks increased in number and importance. But handworkers still resorted to private lenders or to the pawn shops, while the small retail trade was financed by its purveyors.

There was a continual struggle between the local banks and the great banks centered in Paris with branches throughout the country. Economic forces did not flow smoothly from Paris to the provinces, but the movement toward centralization seemed irresistible. The large banks had certain distinct advantages: they had large capital and widespread activities; with better credit they could get funds at lower rates, and because of their geographical spread and diversification had smaller risks. The local banks, on the other hand, could expand only as far as local opportunities for investment existed, and if their deposits grew beyond this point they were tempted to invest in fixed assets not easily realizable; on the other hand, they might prove unable to meet the credit needs of rapidly expanding local enterprises. They maintained themselves best where personal credit played an important role. There was constant criticism of the large city banks in the smaller towns, to which they sent managers to con-

[3] Mehrens, op. cit., 190-96.

duct branches after they had absorbed the local banks, on the ground that these did not know local needs or conditions. The branches of the large banks were, moreover, organized in extremely bureaucratic fashion, which left little initiative to the branch manager.

The conclusion seems justified that the available credit was not well distributed to the various branches of the national economy, largely owing to the banking concentration. "The small and medium trade, the small and medium industry do not find in France sufficient facilities of credit, and especially of long-term credit," wrote Mr. Caillaux to the President of the Republic in 1911 in a letter accompanying a project for the appointment of a commission to study the banking problem. An attempt was made by a law of that year "to facilitate the obtaining of justifiable credit by solvent industrialists and tradesmen," but mere legislation could not meet the situation.

Another criticism of the banks was that they directed the stream of national savings into foreign loans and so starved industry of needed capital. Some of the facts necessary to a judgment on this question may first be presented. By 1870 France was a capital-exporting country, her net foreign investments by that year amounting to about 11,000 million francs; by 1913 they were nearly 40,000 million. French industrial development was proceeding slowly, and foreign investments offered a higher rate of return than those at home. There was a definite bias in favor of foreign investments, created partly by the wish to cement political connections with certain countries, partly by financial considerations, but most of all by the desire on the part of the banks to earn large commissions. Practically all the larger loans were arranged through the agency of a small group of powerful banking houses with headquarters in Paris. French investors relied upon the advice furnished them by their banks, but these frequently misrepresented the soundness of foreign issues and bribed newspapers to print favorable comments. The result was that large sums were loaned to the government of Russia, and lesser amounts to the Balkans, Austria, Mexico, and Brazil, loans which later entailed serious loss to French investors. French industries, deprived of these savings, were forced to finance themselves from their earnings. The effects were bad for investors, for industry, and for the whole national economy.

Savings banks. The savings banks aided the small saver in safer fashion. Individual deposits were limited in amount, in 1881 to 2000 francs and in 1895 to 1500. Investments of these banks were limited to government bonds or to paper bearing the state guarantee. In 1881 a national savings bank in connection with the post office was established, which co-operated with the older banks. By 1909 there were 550 savings banks with 8,100,000 depositors and a balance of 3833 million francs, while the postal savings bank had 5,800,000 depositors and savings of 1707 million francs.

Agricultural credit. None of these institutions met the need for agricultural credit, for the commercial banks were restricted to discounting paper having not over ninety days to run and the savings banks could not make farm loans at all. The farmer needed a loan that ran from seed time to harvest, or about six months. The Bank of France and the other large banks met this difficulty by renewing the ninety day notes for a second period of ninety days, changing only the date of maturity. This was unsatisfactory for all purposes, however, and in 1900 a new banking organization was set up to provide more adequate agricultural credit, in the form of the Crédit Agricole. The plan was to establish in each of the 86 departments a regional bank, and in each of the 36,000 communes, except the urban ones, a local office. Any local farmer might become a stockholder by buying a 20 franc share and was then eligible for a loan. All the capital of the local offices was turned over to the regional bank, to which the government loaned, without interest, an amount four times the capital thus subscribed. Loans were made by the local offices to the farmers for productive purposes, such as the purchase of a cow, fertilizer, machinery, etc., but not for consumption goods. If the local office approved, it endorsed the farmer's note and sent it to the regional bank. If this had the money it lent it directly; otherwise the president of the regional bank signed it, and since it now had three signatures it could be discounted at the Bank of France. The regional banks loaned to the local offices at 3 per cent and the local office lent to the farmer at $3\frac{1}{2}$ to 4 per cent; the spread was sufficient to pay expenses.

The Crédit Foncier was planned to extend long-term agricultural credit. Founded in 1850 it was given a legal monopoly of mortgage operations until 1877. Although this privilege was not renewed it maintained a practical monopoly. Its purpose was to help the larger landowners, but actually most of its loans were on city property. Loans were made on mortgage up to 50 per cent of the value of the property—30 per cent in the case of vineyards and forests—and the interest rate was that paid on state bonds. Although the statutes permitted loans for seventy-five years, the average term was under twenty-five.

BIBLIOGRAPHICAL NOTE

1. *Britain.* An excellent short account of the monetary history of Britain is contained in N. G. Pierson, *Principles of Economics,* 2 vols. (transl. from the Dutch, 2nd ed., London, 1902). An important document is reprinted in R. W. Robey (Ed.), *The Monetary Problem: Gold and Silver.* A reprint of the Final Report of the Royal Commission Appointed to Inquire into the Recent Changes in the Relative Values of the Precious Metals, 1888 (New York, 1936). A good short survey is K. Mackenzie, *The Banking Systems of Great Britain, France, Germany, and the United States* (2nd ed., London, 1935). J. F. Ashby, *The Story of the Banks* (London, 1934) describes the development of the "big five" English banks. H. Withers and others present an informal but authoritative picture in United States Monetary Commission, *The English Banking System* (Washington, 1910). W. E. Beach, *British International Gold Movements and Banking Policy, 1881–1913* (Cambridge, Mass., 1935) and W. T. C. King, *History of the English Discount Market* (London, 1936) show London's position as the international money market. A careful study of foreign investment is C. K. Hobson, *The Export of Capital* (London, 1914). Somewhat broader is H. Feis, *Europe, the World's Banker,* 1870–1914 (New Haven, 1930).

2. *Germany.* K. Helfferich, *Das Geld* (6te Aufl., Leipzig, 1923. Transl. as *Money,* New York, 1927) is a general study but gives a German slant. J. Riesser, *Zur Entwicklungsgeschichte der deutschen Grossbanken mit besonderer Rücksicht auf die Konzentrationsbestrebungen* (2te Aufl., Jena, 1906. Translated for the United States Monetary Commission as *The German Great Banks and their Concentration,* Washington, 1910) is an excellent historical account. The United States Monetary Commission also published *The Reichsbank,* 1876–1900 (Washington, 1910), a good history. A study of the deposit banks is W. Huth, *Die Entwicklung der deutschen und französischen Grossbanken* (Berlin, 1918). Their operations are subjected to critical analysis in A. Weber, *Depositenbanken und Spekulationsbanken, ein Vergleich deutschen und englischen Bankwesens* (München, 1915). The legal basis is treated in W. Lotz, *Geschichte und Kritik der deutschen Bankgesetzes* (Leipzig, 1888).

3. *France.* H. P. Willis, *A History of the Latin Monetary Union* (Chicago, 1901) describes an interesting experiment in bimetallism. Of the many books on the Bank of France only a few can be mentioned. Flour de Saint-Genis, *La Banque de France à travers le siècle* (Paris, 1896) gives a snapshot. A. Neymarck, *La Banque de France de 1880 à 1905* (Paris, 1906) carries on the story. C. Lebeau, *La Banque de France: ses operations, son organisation* (Paris, 1931) describes the internal working. L. Pommier, *La Banque de France et l'état en 19e siècle* (Paris, 1904) is a slight sketch. The function of the banks in providing credit is discussed in M. Patron, *La Banque de France et le crédit national* (Paris, 1908); M. E. Kaufman, *La Banque en France* (Paris, 1914); A. Huart, *L'Organisation du crédit en France* (Paris, 1913), especially good. The deposit banks are described by A. E. Sayons, *Les banques de dépot, les banques de crédit, et les sociétés financières* (Paris, 1900), and their organization and administration in E. Kaufmann, *Das französische Bankwesen, mit besonderer Berücksichtigung der drei Depositengrossbanken* (2te Aufl., Tübingen, 1923). Savings banks are treated in A. Cormont, *Les caisses d'épargne en France* (Paris, 1922). The United States Monetary Commission published translations of several good French books: Liesse, *Credit and Banks in France;* Patron, *Bank of France;* Vidal, *History and Methods of the Paris Bourse;* Warburg, *The Discount System in Europe.* National wealth is estimated in R. Pupin, *La richesse de la France devant la guerre* (Paris, 1916).

CHAPTER XIII

LABOR AND THE LABOR MOVEMENT

I. BRITISH LABOR BECOMES CONSERVATIVE

Trade unionism. Under the leadership of the strong and well-organized unions of the fifties and sixties the labor movement was becoming conservative, favoring arbitration rather than strikes and endeavoring to correct the inequalities in labor law. An occasion for presenting these aims to the public was given in 1866, when some extremists among the workers resorted to violence and destruction of life and property during a strike at Sheffield. A Royal Commission was appointed in 1867 whose report found some unions guilty of illegal practices, but concluded that existing law, by denying legal status to the unions, tended to provoke rather than to repress violence. Although the Act of 1825 had legalized trade unions, adverse court decisions had held that, since they were restraints on the freedom of industry, they were really illegal and could neither hold title to property nor defend their rights before the courts. The Commission recommended that they be permitted to exercise both these privileges. Another grievance which the workers resented bitterly was the unequal rights of employer and employee in a labor contract. Under the existing law a workman who broke his contract by refusing to work could be arrested and sentenced to three months in prison by a single magistrate from whose decision there was no appeal, whereas an employer who broke a contract by withholding wages was liable only to a civil action to compel him to pay them. Moreover, a worker could not give evidence against his employer, although an employer could testify against a worker. This was remedied in 1867 by the passage of the Masters and Servants Act, which abolished imprisonment for breach of contract and placed the two parties on an equal footing before the law.

Scarcely had this slight success been won when a new blow fell. The Boilermakers' Society had sued their treasurer for appropriating £24, the property of the Society. The magistrate and, on appeal, the Lord Chief Justice, held that a trade union, being an instituton "in restraint of trade," was outside the protection of the law. The unions were now forced to obtain new legislation which would give them the same rights to protection as were enjoyed by other law-abiding associations. In 1871 a Trade Union Act was passed which permitted unions to register as benefit societies and thus protect their funds; and no union could be refused the right of registration because its rules were in restraint of trade. But at the same

437

time a Criminal Law Amendment Act was passed, which visited with severe penalties picketing, molesting, obstructing, threatening, and other acts which were incidental to effective combination.

The labor voters, who had been enfranchised in 1867, now turned against the Liberal Party, which had served them so ill, and elected the Conservatives to power in 1874. They accordingly passed the Employers and Workmen Act in 1875 to replace the Masters and Servants Act of 1867; this made stoppages of work actionable wrongs but not crimes. At the same time the criminal law was modified by a Conspiracy and Protection of Property Act which legalized peaceful picketing and stated that no act committed by a combination of persons in a trades dispute was to be regarded as a criminal offense unless the same act committed by one person was criminal. Picketing was expressly permitted and some of the elastic words of the previous act, such as "coerce" and "molest," which had opened the way for prejudiced decisions, were omitted altogether. Collective bargaining was now recognized as a legal method of fixing wages, and for thirty years this act was regarded as the *magna carta* of labor.

It had taken fifty years, beginning in 1825, to gain full legal rights for trade unions. They were now thought to stand on the same footing as ordinary corporations, so far as concerned their right to exist, to hold property, and to carry out the objects of their organization. This progress had been accompanied by a change in public attitude towards trade unions. The dread of working class organizations lessened as these showed themselves more conservative and as English society became more democratic. Even the employers, in many cases, modified their hostility to trade unions and found it preferable to deal with a well-disciplined group than with an unorganized body of dissatisfied laborers. The spread of conciliation, for the settlement of wage disputes and similar questions, was an indication of the new spirit. From about 1860 on, conciliation boards were formed in one industry after another, and by 1875 between two and three hundred such voluntary boards had been formed. The unions, meanwhile, had become a recognized part of the social structure, emphasizing such matters as wages, hours, factory inspection, friendly benefits, workmen's clubs and evening classes. They were practically confined to the skilled artisans, for as yet the masses of unskilled workers remained outside of their ranks.

Trade union philosophy was still dominantly individualistic. The workers thought that if they could obtain the right to bargain collectively, they could fight their own battles and obtain favorable conditions for labor without state interference in the wages contract. Unlike the trade union movement of 1833–34, which aimed to get rid of the capitalist employer, the attitude at this time was one of acceptance of the capitalist system and an effort to obtain for the workers a fair share of the enlarged national income. The growth in membership of the unions between 1872 and 1874 was extraordinary; the Trades Union Congress of 1872 claimed only 375,000, but in 1874 had delegates representing 1,191,922 members. The "new model" unions were at the height of their power in 1875 and felt confidence in their strength. Unfortunately, this year ushered in an industrial depression, and the remarkable growth of the previous half decade was now largely lost. With the revival of prosperity trade union growth as a whole was resumed, although individual unions were born and died. All through this period there was a close correlation between the strength of unionism and the fluctuations of the business cycle. The growth of organized labor is shown in the following table; the figures before 1892 are estimates.

Year	Number in unions	Year	Number in unions
1872	375,000	1902	1,953,307
1874	1,192,000	1907	2,406,746
1888	750,000	1912	3,287,884
1892	1,502,358	1914	3,918,903
1897	1,613,998		

Agricultural labor unions. The success of the trade union movement in the early seventies stirred other groups into action, and touched even the agricultural laborers. This group had not shared in the agricultural prosperity of the preceding period, and their efforts to improve their condition led to a movement new in England and without precedent in other countries. This was the organization of agricultural labor unions. Some organizations had been formed between 1865 and 1871 and had been successful in raising wages, but the date usually assigned as the birth of the new movement was February 7, 1872, when Joseph Arch founded a union in Warwickshire.[1] By May 50,000 members had enrolled and a congress was held, attended by delegates from many parts of the country. Arch was elected president and a platform was adopted. The objects were stated to be to raise wages to 16 shillings a week, limit hours to from 6 a.m. to 5 p.m. abolish payments in kind, regulate the employment of women and children, and increase the number of moderately rented allotments. They also included political and social reforms, such as the Parliamentary franchise for agricultural laborers—which the majority of industrial workers had received in 1867—changes in the land laws, the disestablishment of the church, enquiries into charitable endowments, and the creation of peasant proprietors. But they realized the need of adjusting the supply of

[1] *Joseph Arch, the Story of his Life, told by Himself* (London, 1898).

labor to the demand, and advocated migration from the congested districts to others where the demand was greater, and also emigration. In the first nine years of its existence the Union helped 700,-000 to emigrate to the British colonies and other countries.

The movement toward organization spread like wildfire, south, east, and west, and two years after its organization the Union claimed a membership of 100,000 and could already boast of its achievements; it had succeeded in raising wages by one or two shillings a week, in getting rid of the abuses of payment in kind, in working toward the limitation of women's labor, and enforcing the provisions for the education of their children. Its success alarmed the employers and in 1874 the farmers in several counties locked out all members of the Union, which had demanded an increase in wages and a shortening of hours. The best workers had migrated and now the farmers were asked to pay more for inferior labor, at the very time that prices were falling.[2] The movement spread and resulted finally in the disastrous defeat of the Union. The agricultural depression of the next few years made the position of the workers hopeless, and the Union was reduced to a mere shadow.

After a long period of quiescence another attempt was made to organize the agricultural workers and the National Agricultural and Rural Workers' Union was established. In 1890 this had a membership of 14,000.

Technological and social changes. The agricultural depression was followed by an industrial depression which reached its culmination in 1879. This year registered the low-water mark of the trade union movement, which lost in numbers and influence and saw the gains of the previous years swept away. But aside from the business depression, which threw thousands of workers out of employment, technological changes were occurring in industry which introduced new lines of cleavage among workers and led to dissension and jurisdictional disputes. When iron replaced wood in shipbuilding, the iron and steel workers came into conflict with the old-fashioned shipwrights; the former also quarreled with the carpenters and the latter with the boilermakers. New methods revolutionized processes in many lines of production, rendering certain forms of skilled labor obsolete and creating new ones, and introducing semi-skilled machine operators to replace the skilled craftsmen. Industries themselves were changing in importance; the textiles were yielding their primacy to iron and steel and the metal-working industries, and shifts in the proportion of workers in different callings were taking place. The

[2] "Labor has been more costly and less efficient, so that the average labor bill of an arable farm is at least 25 per cent higher at the present time than it was some twenty years ago." — *Report of the Royal Commission on Agriculture* (London, 1882), 26.

result of these changes was to break up the trade union world into struggling groups without any common purpose.

In the meantime, labor was tempted several times to depart from the straight path of working for improved conditions of work and higher wages into the devious by-ways of general reconstruction of the whole economic system. Two brands of socialism made their appeal: the Fabian Society, organized in 1883, believed in an evolutionary movement, which, advancing step by step, would ultimately embrace the whole economic structure; its activities were directed primarily to educational propaganda among the upper and middle classes, though it furnished frequent guidance to the British labor movement during the next two decades. The Social Democratic Federation, based on the theories enumerated in Karl Marx' *Das Kapital*,[3] was founded in 1884. Its revolutionary doctrines did not appeal to the British workingman and it remained small and without great influence during this period. Of greater immediate importance was the publication of Henry George's *Progress and Poverty*, which advocated the appropriation of land rent by taxation; so lucrative would a tax on land rent be, he argued, that it would supply all needed revenues and become a single tax. Land nationalization societies were formed and George's proposals were hailed as a new evangel, but the movement soon waned.

The period was one of intellectual and social unrest; the depressions of 1876–79 and 1884–86 created unemployment and forced economic issues to the front. Government commissions investigated housing and sweating, Charles Booth published in 1889–91 his elaborate investigation, *Labour and Life of the People*, which showed that one-third of the population of London lived permanently on the verge of starvation, and General Booth founded the Salvation Army to rescue souls and also bodies. In spite of the prickings of the public conscience over the demoralizing poverty which was revealed, the government did little to improve conditions. A partial reform in employers' liability for accidents to their workers was obtained in 1880, and employers were expected to insure their workers. The Act of 1897 provided that no civil action could be entertained against a trade union for its acts. On the whole, however, it appeared that labor would have to depend upon its own efforts to better its lot.

Trade union struggles. The old unions had been more like friendly societies than fighting organizations. They represented the aristocracy of labor, had large union funds, and sought to maintain their privileged position, paying little attention to the unskilled laborer. Beginning about 1880, however, a new type of unionism

---

[3] The first volume of this work was published in German in 1867; in 1873 a French translation was made, but not until 1886 did it appear in English.

appeared, which had strong socialistic leanings and sought to organize the unskilled. A tremendous impetus was given to this movement by the success of strikes by the London match girls in 1888 and by the dockers the following year, both groups of helpless and exploited workers. The strikes were won by good generalship and by enlisting public sympathy and support. Unions of unskilled workers now sprang up everywhere. Dockers, manual workers, agricultural laborers organized in loose unions, as well as railway employees, sailors, and firemen. A wave of trade unionism, similar to the movements of 1833–34 and 1873–74, spread into every branch of British industry. The total membership of trade unions in 1892, the first year in which official statistics were gathered, was over 1,500,000. From this date until 1914, the number grew almost uninterruptedly, reaching about 4,000,000 just before the war. The Webbs estimated that these figures represented about 20 per cent of the adult male manual working group. The strength of trade unionism was not to be explained by this proportion, however, but rather by the massing of union members in certain industries and areas, where they sometimes made up over 50 per cent of the total number of workingmen.

The labor movement showed a growing capacity for dispensing with middle-class ideas or guidance and for developing its own leaders. With the great increase in the number of permanent wage workers there emerged a definite class consciousness. An important movement was the growth of common action among the unions; in 1899 a general Federation of Trade Unions was created, with the aim of enabling labor to meet employers and employers' associations on a more equal footing. The smaller unions were consolidated into stronger units, so that the number of separate unions decreased, though the total membership grew.

The Taff Vale Case, decided in 1901, was a serious blow to the trade unions, but it proved to be only temporary. Employees of the Taff Vale Railway Company had engaged in a tumultuous and at first unauthorized strike, and in the course of the strike had destroyed railway property. The railway company sued the Amalgamated Society of Railway Servants, to which the offenders belonged, for damages, and was awarded £23,000 by the House of Lords, the highest court. The decision held that the union, as a union, could be held responsible in law for the acts of its members. This was a stunning blow to the whole union movement, but especially to the old craft unions with their well-filled treasuries. Labor now went into politics, determined to obtain an amendment of the Conspiracy and Protection of Property Act of 1835, which would render further decisions like that of the Taff Vale Case impossible. The workers helped the Liberals overturn the Conservatives in 1905, and were rewarded by the passage of the Trade Unions and Trade Disputes Act of 1906. This made peaceful picketing legal and forbade damage suits against unions because of tortious or injurious acts of members. Trade unions were now placed in a more favorable position than other organizations, for they were practically non-suable.

The political activities of the trade unions received a serious setback in the Osborne Judgment of 1909. It had been the practice of the stronger unions to use part of their funds to support labor members in the House of Commons. A member of the Amalgamated Society of Railway Servants, named Osborne, objected to this and brought a test suit to prevent it. This went to the House of Lords, which decided that no union could use its funds for this purpose nor compel its members to contribute to such funds. This was a serious blow at labor representation, for the labor members of the House of Commons were poor men. Parliament met the problem in 1911 by voting a governmental salary of £400 a year to all members and by passing in 1913 an amendment to the Trade Union Act of 1876. Trade unions were redefined as combinations whose statutory objects were trade regulation and benefits for members. It further provided that such bodies could accumulate political funds provided the purposes were decided by secret ballot and the contributions were not compulsory.

After 1910 the trade unions withdrew in large measure officially from political activities, which they left to the rapidly growing Labor Party, which had been formed in 1900. They devoted themselves to their specific aims, the improvement of the condition of labor and the raising of wages. Strikes flamed up frequently in large numbers, but at the same time there was a rapid development of the machinery of conciliation and arbitration.

Social insurance. The belief had meanwhile been growing that modern industrialism, complex and unstable, exposed the worker to many economic mischances which even a strong labor organization could not combat. During the last quarter of the nineteenth century Germany had developed a well-rounded system of social insurance, and when the Liberal Party came into power in 1905 they adopted a program which incorporated the essential principles which German experience had proven to be practicable in this field. The first evil which called for reform was the indemnification of workers for accidents suffered in the course of their employment. Prior to 1880 injured workmen had no protection except that of suing the employer for damages. But the latter had three defences — the normal risks of the occupation, the fellow-servant doctrine, and contributory negligence — which made it practically impossible for the worker to hold the employer responsible, even if he could afford the heavy expenses of bringing suit.

In 1880 an Employers' Liability Act was passed which made the employer responsible for injuries to his employees through occupational accidents in a number of lines. This left many loopholes, however, and was replaced by a Workmen's Compensation Act in 1897, which applied to factories, quarries, mines, railways, and building construction — the so-called dangerous industries. By this act the employer was made liable for compensation for all injuries suffered by workmen in the course of employment, not caused by the latters' own wilful misconduct. This principle was made universally applicable by the Act of 1906 to all workers earning less than £250 a year, and added to the former list domestic servants, clerks, sailors, and other groups, covering in all some 13,000,000 persons. Employers were not required to insure, as they were in Germany, but practically always protected themselves by taking out insurance. The whole cost was therefore borne by the employers.

Two years later a comprehensive system of old-age pensions was established. Previously the aged poor had been cared for in workhouses, or, after 1895, by outdoor relief in their own homes. It was felt, however, that these persons should be cared for by a general system which did not carry with it the stigma of public charity or residence in a workhouse. In 1908, accordingly, it was provided that all persons over seventy years of age should be given a pension, provided their annual incomes did not exceed £31 10 s. ($153). The pensions were raised entirely by taxation, and ranged between 5 s. and 1 s. a week, according to the amount of outside income. By 1914 some 984,000 persons were receiving pensions, at an annual cost of over £12,000,000.

There were still two other serious liabilities to which workers were exposed — sickness and unemployment — and these were cared for by the National Insurance Act of 1911. The provisions governing sickness and invalidity insurance required every worker to become insured, and about 13,000,000 persons came within its scope. The cost was borne by contributions from the worker, the employer, and the state, of 4 d., 3 d., and 2 d. a week, respectively. Benefits were paid for medical service, sickness, invalidity, and maternity, and varied according to sex, age, and length of disability.

The second part of the Act dealt with unemployment insurance. Previous to this time the unemployed had been taken care of by an extension of poor relief, by "distress works" of a public character, by their trade unions, or were thrown on their own resources. Labor exchanges or state employment bureaus were set up in 1909 but, although quite successful, these did not go to the heart of the problem. This Act assumed that there was work for all and that it was only necessary to bring the unemployed worker and the prospective employer together. The Act of 1911 recognized, on the other hand, that unemployment was a permanent aspect of modern industry and that the burden of supporting the unemployed should be borne by society as a whole. For the first time in history provision was made on a national scale for handling this most serious and baffling problem of modern capitalism. All workers over sixteen years of age engaged in the building or engineering [4] industries — the two groups which were most affected by depression — were required to be insured against unemployment. Contributions were made in nearly equal proportions by workers and employers, with smaller contributions by the state. The benefit consisted of a payment of 7 s. a week for a maximum period of fifteen weeks.

Social insurance is the most important and serious attempt of modern society to grapple with the problems confronting labor. For the worker it has the advantage of making the receipt of relief quicker, smoother, and a matter of right without the stigma of charity. A larger number of persons is reached, and the administration is automatic. Another important advantage is the permanency of the institution, for it is scarcely conceivable that it will be abolished after it has once been established. The employer derives from the system the benefit of a regularization and spreading of costs which are bound up in the very nature of modern enterprise. Socially, it is a recognition of the solidarity of the interests of all classes and of the responsibility of the state to interfere positively on behalf of needy groups or against industrial evils. It marks a long step away from the complacent *laissez faire* attitude of the previous century.

2. LABOR FIGHTS FOR ITS RIGHTS IN GERMANY

Character of the labor force. In 1870 the majority of the people were still engaged in agricultural pursuits; as late as 1882 almost 43 per cent of the gainfully employed were employed in farming and forestry. In the next twenty-five years there was a complete reversal in the roles of agriculture and industry, while at the same time trade and transportation gained at the expense of agriculture. The following table shows the shifts in occupation that were going on:

The purely industrial workers numbered only 4,430,000 in 1882, the remainder of those listed under industry being engaged in handwork or house industry. The proportion of factory workers grew

[4] See definition, Chapter VI, p. 209.

OCCUPATIONAL DISTRIBUTION, 1882–1907

Year	Total number gainfully employed	Agriculture and forestry	Industry	Trade and trans- portation (percentage)	Other	Without occupation
1882	18,986,494	42.5	35.5	8.0	6.9	7.1
1895	22,913,683	35.7	39.1	10.6	5.2	9.4
1907	30,232,145	28.6	42.7	12.6	4.8	11.3

steadily during this period, as the factory system established itself more fully. By 1907 there were 13,000,000 factory wage-earners. The agricultural laborers, attracted by the higher wages and by the educational and recreational advantages of the cities, streamed into the industrial centers and sought work in the factories. The small handworkers, too, left their trades and enlisted with their victorious rivals.

Over two-thirds of the workers in 1882 were men, but the proportion of women grew steadily. In 1882 slightly over one-fifth of the women in Germany were gainfully employed, but by 1907 the proportion was about one-third. These figures do not reveal the labor of women as housekeepers, wives, and mothers at home, nor in social work of all kinds, when they rendered unpaid services. The 10,-000,000 women at work in 1907 were to be found primarily in agriculture (48 per cent), then in industry (22), domestic service (13), trade and transportation (10), other services (7). Of some social significance was the decline in the proportion of domestic servants from 23 per cent in 1882 to 13 in 1907, and their transference to industrial and commercial fields. The clothing and textile industry claimed nearly half of the women in manufactures.

To the credit of Germany it should be pointed out that the number of children at work was astonishingly small, though the percentage of employed children under 14 years of age grew from 2.6 of all in 1882 to 3.8 in 1907. At the latter date 296,786 such children were at work, of whom almost three-quarters were in agriculture. Perhaps because of this fact the proportion of the total population at work was somewhat less in Germany than in other industrial countries. The percentages of the population who were gainfully employed were, in France, 68.2 (1901); in Great Britain, 64.4 (1901): in the United States, 61.3 (1900); in Germany, 61.1 (1907).

It is not possible to group under the designation factory workers all industrial wage-earners in the German economy, for some of them stood outside of the factory. The handworkers still made up a not inconsiderable though declining fraction of the workers. General causes of their diminution and unfavorable economic position were the lack of technical education, the breakdown of the apprenticeship system, and the movement of handworkers to the cities where they found it difficult to set up for themselves because of lack of capital and credit and of local restrictions, but easy to become factory workers.[5] Other factors gave advantages to large industry which the independent handworkers could not meet, such as economies in production, credit, marketing and similar things, and standardization. The personal service group held its own, but many of the others became mere outworkers at piece rates for larger industrialists. Another group was the domestic or home workers, who also tended increasingly to become outworkers in accessory lines organized by factories or *Verleger*. In 1907 there may have been 1,000,000 handworkers and 500,000 home workers out of a total industrial working force of 14,000,000.

The workers in the German economy differed as to ability, training, and economic opportunity. The German workman was characterized by a friendly English critic [6] as dependent, but industrious and plodding. "He is not quick, yet no one can turn out better work, if the right tools, material, and time are allowed him." On the other hand, a German writer [7] noted certain moral defects: bad housekeeping and family life, due to thoughtless early marriages and to poor dwellings, inadequate training of the housewives and frequently the employment of married women away from their homes, resulting in poor bringing up of the children. Still other faults were a lack of thrift, drunkenness, irreligion, mistrust of employers, misuse of the freedom of combination, hatred of the propertied classes, and a revolutionary spirit. Such sweeping generalizations can scarcely be accepted as a fair characterization of all German workmen, though they doubtless applied in numerous instances.

Labor organization. The legal status of labor organizations was defined by the liberal legislation of 1869, which permitted coalitions of employers and employees for the purpose of improving their economic conditions. But agricultural laborers, seamen, and domestic servants were forbidden to combine. Strikes and lockouts were legalized, though striking was actually impeded by the conspiracy laws; and the use of physical force, threats, abuse, and intimidation of any sort was forbidden. This liberty of action and of association was limited, moreover, by the reactionary legislation in the various states, the hostile attitude of the police, and the interpretations of the courts, so that the workers had a hard struggle. The nascent unions received a hard blow by the anti-socialist act of 1878, which

[5] O. Thisson, *Beiträge zur Geschichte des Handwerks in Preussen* (Tübingen, 1901), 66.
[6] W. H. Dawson, *The Evolution of Modern Germany* (London, 1907), 149.
[7] G. von Schönberg, in *Handwörterbuch der Staatswissenschaften* (Jena, 1890), I, 390, s.v. "Arbeiter."

was passed after two attempts had been made on the life of the Emperor. This was an exceptional measure, expressly directed "against the subversive efforts of the social democrats." It forbade all associations, meetings, and publications having for their object "the subversion of the social order." It gave the police power to seize socialistic publications and to prohibit or disperse socialist meetings. Although, in the debate on this law, the Government promised that it would be used only against political and not against labor organizations, in practice it resulted in an almost complete destruction of the trade union movement. By the end of 1878, sixteen of the existing unions were dissolved, and a number of others disbanded or reorganized themselves, like the book printers, into trade associations (*Fachvereine*). The example of the printers was followed by the shoemakers, the woodworkers, masons, metal workers, and others. The Social Democrats seized every opportunity to organize the workers, and the trade union idea of association for the protection of their interests was widespread. When the socialist law lapsed in 1890, in spite of the fact that the Government had dissolved 109 trade unions, there were 53 unions still in existence with a membership of 227,733.

In spite of undoubted development during the period of repression, the trade union movement was small and weak when the socialist law was repealed. The existing unions were local affairs which were not united and had no organized method of exchanging views. In order to promote greater unity a conference was held in Berlin in 1890, at which a central organization was created, — the General Commission of German Trade Unions. A struggle now ensued between the trade unionists led by Karl Legien, the head of the Woodworkers' Union, and the Social Democrat Party, led by F. A. Bebel, a convert of Marx. The socialists feared that they would suffer from a strong trade union development, and did not interest themselves in this movement. As proof of this Cassau cites the curious fact that the Socialist Party organ, *Neue Zeit*, founded in 1883, did not include the word "trade union" (*Gewerkschaft*) in its index until fourteen years later.[8] The members of the unions were themselves weak in their support of the movement, and were unwilling to assume any financial burdens; the average assessments in most of the unions ran between 2 and 4 cents a week for qualified workers. But in spite of all difficulties the trade union movement proceeded.

The depression of the early nineties slowed up the growth, but tested the real strength of the movement. The industrial recovery brought with it a corresponding expansion of labor organizations.

[8] T. Cassau, *Die Gewerkschaftsbewegung*, 22.

The number of members, which had been 277,000 in 1891, declined to a low of 269,000 in 1895, and then rose rapidly, passing the 500,-000 mark in 1899, that of 1,000,000 in 1902, 2,000,000 in 1906 and 3,000,000 in 1909.   This was a larger number than were organized at that time in Great Britain, France, or the United States. The growth in strength and activity was traceable less to new ideas or energetic leadership than to the industrial development of Germany.   The concentration of factory workers in the industrial centers furnished new members, who feared the economic changes going on around them.   In spite of strong class consciousness and socialistic principles the trade unions of the early twentieth century were governed, not by the will to build a new economic world, but by the practical exigencies of the daily struggle.   They worked for better living conditions and supported this aim by social-political measures, as well as by usual trade union weapons.

Among the objectives of the unions were the shorter working day and the passage of social legislation.   They established workers' secretariats and legal aid bureaus, commissions to protect building construction workers and children, industrial schools, employment offices, statistical bureaus, and other welfare agencies.   Above all, they sought to put through a general wage regulation which would compel employers' associations to make wage agreements with them. A noteworthy feature of trade unionism in Germany up to this time had been the slow progress of collective bargaining.   The workers wished agreements in which an exact determination would be made of wages, work, time, payment for overtime, Sunday and night work, vacations, and similar matters.   But the employers, imbued with a medieval philosophy and united in trade associations, refused to recognize or negotiate with the trade unions; they used the blacklist and boycott against both unionists and socialists.   It must be recognized, however, that collective bargaining was scarcely feasible until the unions grew to a point where they fairly represented labor. This point was not reached until the beginning of the twentieth century.   The real growth of collective bargaining may be dated from the negotiation of an important wage scale for the building trades in Berlin in 1896.   After this, similar agreements spread to other handicrafts and to the factory workers.   By 1912 there were 10,739 agreements in force, which established wage and working conditions for 1,574,285 persons in 159,930 establishments.

The growth of trade unionism and the situation toward the end of this period may be briefly shown.

Over 60 per cent of all trade union members in 1913 were enrolled in the free or Social-Democrat organizations.   These were strongest (in the order named) in the building, metal and mineral,

TRADE UNIONS IN GERMANY

(Number of members in thousands at end of year)

Unions	1891	1900	1910	1913
Free	278	682	2017	2553
Hirsch-Duncker	63	92	123	107
Christian	0.5	77	295	343
Peaceful	....	....	121	231
Independent	....	5.5	264	310
Total	341.5	856.5	2820	3544

wood, transportation and trade, textile, mining, clothing, and food and drink industries. While most of the members were socialists, the unions as such had no direct connection with the political movement. There was a definite division of labor between the Social Democrat unions, which devoted themselves to the bettering of wages and general working conditions, and the Social Democrat Party, whose task was the political education and organization of the workers. Owing to this close relationship there was no pure and simple trade unionism in Germany, but a combination of industrial and political aims. These unions were thoroughly class-conscious and believed that there was an unbridgeable gulf between the workers and the capitalist employers, and that lasting peace could be obtained only by abolishing the wage system. In the meantime, however, they aimed to improve the position of the worker. In the work of organization and agitation the free unions were assisted by very efficient newspapers, to which most of the members subscribed.

The Christian unions were founded to provide an organization through which the church could maintain a hold on the workers. Although formed in protest against the Social Democrat unions, they were nevertheless a replica of the latter in their organization. As time went on they broadened the basis of their platform and undertook more aggressive activities, even engaging in strikes and labor propaganda. They were strongest in the mining industry. The Hirsch-Duncker unions grew more slowly than any other group. A split occurred in 1890 between the old guard, which emphasized the idea of self-help and absolute independence of the state, and a new group which wished more agitation and finally political action. After the death of Hirsch in 1905 the latter group grew stronger and undertook many new activities, which clearly showed a swing to the left. They gave up the original idea of a harmony between labor and capital, but had nothing to present like the class struggle of the socialists or the religious connection of the Christian unions. They were strongest in the metal and metal-working industries.

Later developments in the trade union world included the independent unions, local societies with broader social interests, and peaceful unions. The latter, dubbed "yellow unions" by their opponents, were founded and financed by employers as a measure of defense against the militant socialist organizations and corresponded to the company unions of the United States or the free labor associations of Great Britain. There were also numerous associations of clerks, commercial travelers, officials, and others, having a total membership in 1911 of 822,600. These were more in the nature of professional societies than trade unions.

Although the trade union movement in Germany was complicated by politics and hampered by the hostility of employers and the lukewarmness of the government, it nevertheless made substantial progress during this period. By its activities it helped to raise wages and to improve the general conditions of labor; without the pressure of strong organizations these gains would not have been won so soon and perhaps not at all. But the unions were not merely fighting organizations; they devoted large sums to education and the press, to advice bureaus, labor registries, etc., as well as to the ordinary expenditures for sick pay, unemployment pay, strike pay, and similar benefits. The funds of all the unions were estimated at 99,956,000 marks in 1912.

The growing power of labor called forth a corresponding organization of employers, especially after 1890. In that year an employers' association was formed in Hamburg, which was the forerunner of a strong movement. By 1913 nearly 158,000 employers, employing over 4,500,000 workers, were members of such associations.

Labor legislation. Before 1870 the legislative protection of labor vested with the separate states. Of these only Prussia, Saxony, Wurtemberg, and Baden had passed such legislation, but as these were the industrially most developed states, the majority of the factory workers were covered. Establishment of the North German Confederation in 1867 was shortly followed by the enactment of a general industrial code of national scope, modeled after the Prussian legislation. This, however, was unequal in its application to different industries and did not go far enough in the clauses affecting women and children to give them the protection they needed under the new conditions that were developing. Upon request of the Reichstag the Chancellor instituted an elaborate inquiry whose report formed the basis for the act of 1878. This regulated apprenticeship and the employment of children, forbade the truck system, and made the inspection of factories, mines, and docks compulsory on a national scale.

During this period the factory system was developing rapidly in Germany and the industrial workers were being concentrated in larger establishments and in urban centers. Women and children were increasingly employed, accidents became more frequent and wages were held down. It was a time, moreover, of labor organization and of socialist agitation. The social insurance legislation did something to meet the new problems but did not satisfy the demands for an adequate labor code.

Working conditions. The working day was extremely long at the beginning of this period, not only for agricultural laborers and independent peasants but also for industrial workers, especially the handworkers and home workers. The first comprehensive picture of the situation was presented in the reports of the factory inspectors in 1888. At that time the average working day was between 10 and 12 hours for factory workers. The 10-hour day was usual in Berlin, Bremen, and some other urban centers; but it lengthened to 12 hours in the rural districts. The worst conditions were found in the house industries, especially the textiles, where a 14- to 16-hour day was usual. The handworkers and small industrialists too, beset by the superior competitive strength of the factories, sought to offset this advantage by working long hours. The best conditions were found in the factories and especially the large establishments, but even there they were unsatisfactory.

Efforts were made to establish a normal working day of 12 hours, but they shattered on the resistance of a small minority of employers. The legal fixation of a maximum period was made first for women; in 1900 this was 65 hours per week. This was reduced to 60 hours in 1908. Men's working hours were not restricted and varied greatly, being shortest in those industries in which labor organizations were strongest. The limitation of the working hours of women, however, tended to fix the length of the day for men also, especially where they worked together, and consequently by the end of this period the 10-hour day had become the general rule.

Social insurance. In the industrial state that Germany was fast becoming the worker was exposed to vicissitudes which neither the industry and thrift of the individual, the combined action of trade unions, nor labor legislation could meet satisfactorily. In an economy of self-sufficing agriculture and independent handworkers, the problems of old age, invalidity, accident, and unemployment were handled by the family or by the local community. But with the introduction of the factory system, the increasing specialization and division of labor, and above all the growth of large groups wholly dependent on money wages, these problems became more pressing and wider in scope. Some attempts to meet them by various methods of mutual insurance and legislation had been made in the separate states, but these were manifestly inadequate.

The principle of employer's liability had early been established in Prussia with respect to accidents to railway employees, and had later been extended to factories, mines, and quarries, by imperial law. But the difficulty of proving his case and the legal expense of collecting damages made this method unavailable to the average worker. The gilds had long extended relief to sick members and buried the dead. Benefit societies were general in many of the states. A report to the Reichstag in 1876 listed for the country as a whole over 5000 burial clubs with 1,600,000 members, nearly 400 invalidity, old age, and widows' clubs with 62,000 members, and 1000 mixed clubs with 172,000 members. But these various mutual insurance schemes barely touched the fringe of the labor problem, and it became evident that this must be handled on a national scale.

The factor which, more than any other, brought about the adoption of a comprehensive plan of national social insurance was the desire on the part of the Government to win the workers from socialism by removing one of their grievances against the capitalist system. Bismark, the Chancellor, first tried the method of repression, but the socialist law of 1878, forbidding all socialistic meetings and publications, proved a failure and was repealed in 1890. In the meantime, however, he offered an olive branch to labor in the form of state social insurance. In proposing this plan, which was a radical departure from the private scheme which had previously existed, Bismark sought first of all to justify the Government's adoption of state socialism. In arguing for the first accident insurance bill in 1881 he presented the theoretical basis for this position. "That the state," he said, "should interest itself to a greater degree than hitherto in those of its members who need assistance is a duty not only of humanity and Christianity — by which state institutions should be permeated — but of a state-preserving policy, whose aim should be to cultivate the conception, especially among the non-propertied classes who form at once the most numerous and the least instructed part of the population, that the state is not merely a necessary but also a beneficent institution." The old police state, whose functions were negative and limited to the protection of life and property and the enforcement of contracts, was to be replaced by a welfare state, whose functions were positive and directed to the general raising of the standard of living of the less fortunate members of society. The first step in this direction was social insurance.

The sickness insurance act was passed in 1883; this was followed by an accident insurance act in 1884, and five years later by one providing for old age and invalidity. These all rested on the principle of compulsory insurance of the workers by a state-administered system, in which the workers, the employers, and the state contributed in varying amounts. The costs were distributed approximately as follows:

DISTRIBUTION OF COSTS OF INSURANCE

	Sickness	Accident	Disability and Old Age
employers	$\frac{1}{3}$	all	$\frac{1}{2}$
workers	$\frac{2}{3}$	....	$\frac{1}{2}$
state	cost of admin.	....	50 marks annually

*The original sickness insurance law applied only to industrial workers, but the revision of 1911 extended it to practically all workers with annual earnings of less than 2000 marks. Insurance was administered through local societies of insured persons, and for this purpose the existing sick-benefit societies (*Krankenkassen*) were utilized as far as possible. The benefits included free medical care, sickness allowance of usually one-half the average wage up to six months (if the illness continued longer, subsequent payments were made out of the accident funds), and burial costs in case of death. By 1910 the number of insured persons was over 13,000,000 representing one-fifth of the entire population.

The accident insurance law of 1884 applied to only a few especially dangerous industries, but subsequent legislation, ending with the codification of 1911, brought in workers in agriculture, forestry, railways, marine navigation, and practically all others with annual earnings of less than 5000 marks. The system was administered by mutual associations of employers in the same general industry, which all persons entering that industry were compelled to join. Contributions to the insurance funds were made in proportion to payrolls and the hazards of the industry. The benefits to the injured included free medical and surgical treatment, and a cash benefit graded according to the disability suffered. In case of death there were a burial benefit and provisions for widows and children and other dependents. The number of persons covered by accident insurance was 21,000,000 in 1907.

The invalidity and old-age insurance applied, with few exceptions, to all persons over sixteen years of age working for wages, and to salaried persons with annual earnings of less than 2000 marks. The system was administered by the Government. Benefits to the insured included an invalidity annuity in case of serious permanent disability and old age pensions to all persons who had passed their seventieth year. The number of persons insured under this law reached 15,000,000 in 1907. Survivors' insurance was added in 1911, which provided for widows and orphans. By another act of the same year all salaried employees whose yearly salaries did not exceed 5000 marks were included within the invalidity and old age insurance.

Unemployment insurance on a nation-wide basis was discussed, but the imperial government did not see its way clear to undertake this. The various states also declined to do so. A number of cities, however, beginning with Cologne in 1894, organized plans of purely local scope. The problem of unemployment was handled principally by public employment bureaus and relief stations. More important was the unemployment assistance granted by trade unions to unemployed members, which in 1913 amounted to 11,500,000 marks.

Conclusion. The labor movement in Germany was never so strong during this period as that in Britain. The German workers were not so independent or aggressive as the British and were less accustomed to self-help. Many of the most important reforms were instituted by the government; they proceeded *von oben herab* — from above down — as the Germans were accustomed to say. This was particularly true of the most important of all, that of social insurance, which was at first opposed by the social democratic trade unions. In this field Germany was a pioneer; social insurance, it has been said, was "made in Germany." It gave to the workers a security which had disappeared with the decline of the gilds and the introduction of new forces of competition in markets which were rapidly becoming international in scope. While employers at first feared that the additions to the costs of production involved in the burden of insurance payments would handicap them in the world markets, they soon adjusted themselves to the new conditions. The weaker, marginal concerns, which had existed only by the exploitation of their workers, were forced out. The better ones modernized their plants, introduced labor-saving machinery, and effected economies by greater specialization and in other ways. Labor legislation, however, lagged behind and offered less protection to the German worker than was afforded at the same time to British wage-earners.

3. LABOR BECOMES RADICAL IN FRANCE

The labor movement. The French labor movement had certain features which differentiated it from the contemporary developments in Great Britain and Germany and gave it a unique character of its own. The existence of a large middle class of small property owners and independent producers and shopkeepers made the wage-earners a relatively smaller proportion of the population than in those countries where the development of a large scale factory system had produced a broad group of dependent wage workers. Wealth was more evenly distributed and appeals to the expropriated proletariat met with less response. Industrialism had, however, proceeded sufficiently far in France to call into being a distinct wage earning class, and working conditions were sufficiently bad to lead these to organize for their improvement.

The orderly development of the French labor movement was interrupted by the Franco-Prussian war and the excesses of the Commune. The latter were attributed to the machinations of the communist International, founded by Karl Marx in 1864, and summary punishment was meted out to all those suspected of having had a hand in it. The error of this view seems to have been recognized by the pardon, eight years later, of all offenders still surviving. The establishment of the Third Republic did not immediately alter the position of labor. In 1868 the Minister of Commerce and Public Works had announced that workers' organizations would be "tolerated" on the same terms as organizations of employers, without, however, modifying the laws on coalition. Exercising this privilege, the workers organized trade unions, or syndicates [9] as they were called after 1867, in growing numbers. The movement was especially strong in Paris and in 1875 there were 135 unions in the capital city.

Syndicates were sufficiently numerous in the country by the following year to hold the first French labor congress. This gathering was moderate in its demands, looking to co-operation for a solution of social problems and repudiating socialism. When the third congress was held in Marseilles in 1879 the socialists gained the upper hand and the gathering adopted the name "Socialist Labor Congress." This meeting was of great significance in the labor movement for it began the control of trade unionism by the socialists, a control which continued throughout the rest of this period.

Socialist groups. The decade of the eighties was one of struggle for leadership by various factions and groups. The moderates withdrew at the Havre congress in 1880 and the predominant socialist group, led by Jules Guesde, a follower of Marx, organized the French Labor Party (*Parti Ouvrier Français*). Two years later this party split and a moderate, opportunist group, led by Brousse, organized the Federation of Socialist Workingmen of France (*Fédéra-*

[9] The words syndicate and syndicalism may be accepted as roughly synonymous with union and trade unionism, although they have taken on new meanings in France, peculiar to the temperament and philosophy of the French workers.

tion des Travailleurs Socialistes de France). The Broussists soon split in turn, and two new parties were formed. The quarrels of these various groups belong to a history of socialism rather than to one of the labor movement and need not be recounted. Suffice it to say that finally, in 1905, the long-deferred fusion of the warring groups was accomplished by the establishment of the Unified Socialist Party (*Parti Socialiste Unifié*). In 1910 the popular socialist vote was 1,200,000 and the party elected 105 candidates to the chamber. The practical accomplishments of socialists in France did not, however, measure up to their political power or their party programs.

Trade unions. The legitimate trade union movement in France was distracted by the struggle of the various socialist factions for control, and was weakened by the opposition of employers and the government. The year 1884 is generally signalized as marking the beginning of a new era. In that year trade unions or professional associations of more than twenty persons were given the legal right to organize and to combine in federations. But even then certain conditions were attached: the unions could be for economic interests only, they must record their by-laws and the names of their officers with the government; if a federation were formed, the name of every separate union must be given. The effect of such legislation was to arouse the hostility and distrust of the workers and to give a left turn to the labor movement.

Labor organization became at once livelier and more complex, and federations of crafts and industries multiplied. In 1887 the first Labor Exchange (*Bourse du Travail*) was opened in Paris, followed by others throughout the country, and in 1892 a Federation of Labor Exchanges was organized. The *bourse du travail* was a unique French institution. It combined all the workers' syndicates of the same village, serving as a center where all the syndicates had their headquarters, giving out information, acting as an employment office, organizing educational courses, and maintaining libraries. By this means the local groups of workers were more closely associated than was the case in either Britain or Germany.[10] By 1902 there were 96 such exchanges in France. In forming these the initiative was taken by the workers, though they asked subventions from the municipalities. Their program embraced friendly aid, education, propaganda, and resistance. Between 1887 and 1902 this was the strongest syndical organization in France, but in the latter year it entered the General Confederation of Labor and ceased to have a separate existence.

General Confederation of Labor. The General Confederation

[10] P. Louis, *Histoire du mouvement syndical en France*, 1789–1906 (Paris, 1907), 207.

of Labor (*Confédération Générale du Travail*), commonly referred to as the C.G.T., was formed in 1905 as a central agency of all the syndicates in the country, and speedily became one of the largest and most important labor associations in the world. The C.G.T. consisted of two independent sections, that of the federation of labor exchanges, and that of the federations of craft or industrial syndicates. Except in rare cases, a syndicate did not belong directly to the confederation, but to one of the subordinate groups. Each of the exchanges and federations was represented at Paris by a delegate, and these delegates constituted the confederative committee. A national congress was held every other year. Although a union of all labor organizations had been effected, there were still two distinct groups. The moderate one, made up of labor exchanges, followed a realistic policy, like that of the British trade unions or the German *Gewerkschaften*. The other group was more radical and socialistic. A test vote at the congress at Bourges in 1904 put the latter group in complete control, and the movement thereafter became steadily more radical.

Syndicalism. The next few years constituted a formative period during which the C.G.T. perfected its organization and developed its functions. By 1902 it was sufficiently strong to announce its program, which was that of revolutionary syndicalism; its weapons were the general strike, boycott, trade union label, and sabotage. The fundamental idea was the Marxian concept of class struggle — the workers with empty hands against the employers who controlled the means of production. The syndicate was the natural organ of the workers in carrying on this struggle, direct action was the normal form, and the general strike the best means of winning it. By direct action, which became the slogan of the syndicalist movement in France, was meant the application of economic pressure, as by a strike, in contrast with parliamentary action, which was indirect, proceeding by delegation or by intermediaries. The syndicalists therefore rejected legislative reforms, such as old age pensions, since they would only delay the final revolution of the proletariat. Sabotage (poor work for poor pay) was like the Scottish "ca-canny" (slow work for low pay). Although the idea was not necessarily violent or destructive, it soon became a name of dread in France. Its scope was probably accurately defined by an anti-strike law passed in 1910 as "the wilful destruction, deterioration, or rendering useless, of instruments or other objects, with a view to stopping or hampering work, industry or commerce."

The organized workers distrusted the political parties, and in 1906 adopted the so-called "Charter of Amiens," which stated the determination of the C.G.T. to free itself of all political action or domination by political parties and to continue the policy of direct action. The duty of the worker, said Georges Sorel, was "to destroy the existing political organization and to deprive the state and all local authorities of all their functions in order to transfer them to the syndicates." Syndicalism was revolutionary rather than evolutionary socialism, and the final goal was the "violent expropriation of the capitalist class." The immediate aim of the syndicates, however, was the defense of the wage scale, that is to prevent wages from being lowered in bad years and to obtain an increase in good years. This they tried to obtain by negotiation with the employers, but if this failed then by the strike. The most usual cause of strikes was the question of wages, but hours, piece-work, the dismissal of a foreman, or the return of a worker also figured. They were most frequent in the textile industry, in which there were relatively few syndicates — perhaps a proof that they were not primarily fighting organizations.

Syndicalism is not to be confused with socialism, although they had many points in common. Both believed in the class struggle and in the emancipation of the proletariat by its own efforts, but in most other respects they differed. Syndicalism expected to attain its ends by the action of a determined minority, socialism by a mass movement. Syndicalism was opposed to the state, which was a bourgeois invention, and to parliamentary government because this admitted other groups; socialism proposed to make use of both these agencies to reach its goal. Syndicalism was impatient of reforms but wished complete reorganization by direct action; socialism — at least the moderate wing — was willing to proceed in evolutionary fashion, a step at a time. The radical view was stated by Léon Jouhaux, for many years secretary of the C.G.T. — "it is necessary that the proletariat should know that between parliamentary socialism, which is tending toward a simple democratization of existing social form, and syndicalism, which pursues the aim of a complete social reorganization, there is not only a divergence of methods, but especially a divergence of aims." Syndicalism never lost sight of its final goal, which was the overthrow of existing society. It would seem that syndicalism was a cross between anarchism and communism; it was at all events distinctively French.

Strength of Syndicalism. In spite of the noise which they made and the deep influence which they undoubtedly had upon the French labor movement, the syndicates contained only a fraction of the working population. The latter was given in the census of 1906 as 10,000,000, but the total number of organized workers was only about 1,000,000. Of these approximately 600,000 were in member syndicates of the C.G.T., and within these there was always a moderate group. It appears, therefore, that a small minority determined the platforms and policies of French labor organizations, and that the total membership was small. The individualistic attitude of the French worker has always disinclined him to enter into associations; other reasons given were indifference, timidity, satisfaction with existing conditions, but, above all, opposition of women, and the unwillingness to pay regular dues. These latter were always kept low and as a result the syndicates were unable to accumulate benefit or strike funds. The growth of the trade union movement is shown in the following brief table:

Year	Number of syndicates	Number of organized workers
1884	68	....
1890	1006	139,692
1900	3287	491,647
1910	5325	977,350
1913	4846	1,026,303

About a third of the organized workers were in mining, in spite of the large number of foreigners employed in that industry; then followed the chemical industry, and transportation and trade. These were not the industries in which the workers were being exploited by the new industrialism. In the metal-working and textile industries, in which the worst conditions prevailed, less than 20 per cent of the workers were organized.

Other organizations. There were also some organizations outside of the C.G.T. Catholic unions had been formed among the manual workers, but these were weak; more successful was a union of clerical workers, which was organized in 1887 and formed a federation in 1913. Another group was the "yellow" unions, which repudiated socialism and emphasized agreements with the employers; they hoped eventually to control industry through purchase by the workers of the means of production. At first quite successful, they were without much influence at the end of this period; in 1914 there were 233 yellow syndicates with about 50,000 members. Least important were the remnants of the old *campagnonnages,* which had survived, in spite of industrial changes that robbed them of all significance. Outside of industry two other groups of workers had organized.

The agricultural laborers took advantage of the act of 1884 to establish unions and by 1914 some 1300 agricultural syndicates existed. The comparatively small number of French agricultural laborers and their wide dispersion made combination among them difficult, but the twentieth century saw them organized and employing the same methods as the city workers. Augé-Laribé [11] criticized their intransigence. "Conscious of their importance, they show themselves often demanding, undisciplined, and difficult to manage. The agricultural proletariat is organized; it belongs to the *Confédération Général du Travail*. It practices sabotage and direct action." This statement was, however, exaggerated, for most of the agricultural laborers remained unorganized; only a few specialized groups, like gardeners and woodmen, formed unions. But even among the unorganized groups the rise in prices, which began with the turn of the century, and unsatisfactory rural conditions, together with the spread of socialist doctrines, led to strikes. Wages were raised somewhat, though the low productivity of French agriculture prevented a satisfactory solution of this problem. The small proprietors were, however, more interested in matters of agricultural technique, credit, and mutual insurance than in questions relating to wages or hours.

State employees also formed associations, primarily for mutual benefit purposes. The syndicalists insisted that these be permitted to join the C.G.T., but this was denied by the government on the ground that state employees did not have the right to strike. This contention was soon put to the test. In 1909 the postal employees struck and in 1910 the railway employees. In both cases the government stood firm and in the railway strike called out the reserves (to which most of the strikers belonged). In spite of the fact that the prime minister, Aristide Briand, was himself a socialist, the movement was effectually crushed and severe punishment was meted out to the leaders of the strike. Thereafter state employees were restricted to associations for friendly or educational purposes only.

The organization of employers was not as strong or as general as was that of the workers. Such organizations as existed were of the type of American Chambers of Commerce. Relieved of the burden of serious labor problems by the weakness of the syndicates and the peculiar character of French industry, they were able to devote most of their attention to matters of production and marketing. Their sessions dealt with general questions concerning the industry as a whole or with questions of trade. Most of them supported technical schools and laboratories, published bulletins, and frequently undertook social welfare work. In 1914 there were in existence 4967 associations with 403,000 members.

[11] Op. cit., 153.

BIBLIOGRAPHICAL NOTE

1. *Britain.* A good introduction is furnished by G. D. H. Cole, *The World of Labour* (2nd ed., London, 1915) and G. D. H. Cole and R. Postgate, *The British Common People*, 1746–1938 (London, 1939). More conservative is W. T. Leyton, *The Relations of Capital and Labour* (London, 1915). A sympathetic discussion is G. Drage, *The Labour Problem* (London, 1896), as is his *Trade Unions* (London, 1904). Two books by a trade unionist are G. Howell, *Conflicts of Capital and Labour* (London, 1878; 2nd ed., 1890) and *Trade Unionism, New and Old* (3rd ed., London, 1900). G. D. H. Cole, *Introduction to Trade Unionism* (London, 1928) is a more thoughtful discussion. H. H. Schlosser and W. S. Clark, *The Legal Position of Trade Unions* (2nd ed., London, 1913) is useful. B. G. Montgomery, *British and Continental Labour Policy* (London, 1922) is a careful study.

2. *Germany.* An English view of the German worker is W. H. Dawson, *The German Workman* (London, 1906). A somewhat prejudiced picture is presented in J. Kuczynski, *Labour Conditions in Western Europe*, 1820 *to* 1935 (London, 1937). A good introduction to the trade union movement is A. Braun und R. Seidel, *Die Gewerkschaften, ihre Entwicklung und ihre Kämpfe.* 2 Bde. (Berlin, 1925). P. Umbreit, *25 Jahre deutscher Gewerkschaftsbewegung*, 1890–1915 (Berlin, 1915) traces the history of trade unionism. Th. Cassau, *Die Arbeitergewerkschaften* (Halberstadt, 1915) is also good. A special phase is treated in A. Wende, *Die Konzentrationsbewegung bei den deutschen Gewerkschaften* (Berlin, 1913), and another by W. Kulemann, *Die Berufsvereine* (Jena, 1908). The social democratic unions are described in O. Heilborn, *Die freien Gewerkschaften seit* 1890 (Jena, 1907), and the Christian unions in A. Erdmann, *Die Christlichen Gewerkschaften* (Stuttgart, 1914). Two popular socialist pamphlets are K. Legien, *Die deutsche Gewerkschaftsbewegung* (2te Aufl., Berlin, 1911) and W. S. Sanders, *Trade Unionism in Germany* (2nd ed., London, 1916).

3. *France.* A general sketch is E. Tarle, *Geschichte der Arbeiter in Frankreich* (1905). A very good introduction to trade unionism is L. Levine, *Labor Movement in France* (New York, 1912); a second edition was published under the title *Syndicalism in France* (New York, 1914). Two excellent books are P. Louis, *Histoire syndical en France*, 1789–1906 (Paris, 1907; 3rd ed., 1924), and G. Weill, *Histoire du mouvement social en France*, 1852–1910 (Paris, 1911; 3rd ed., 1924). Also useful are A. Clay, *Syndicalism and Labor* (London, 1911); J. A. Estey, *Revolutionary Syndicalism: an Exposition and a Criticism* (London, 1913); and R. Garmy, *Histoire du mouvement syndical en France des origines à* 1914 (Paris, 1933). Employers' associations are discussed in W. Lexis, *Gewerkvereine und Unternehmerverbände in Frankreich* (Leipzig, 1879).

CHAPTER XIV

POPULATION AND WELFARE

I. IMPROVING STANDARD OF LIVING IN BRITAIN

Population. Between 1871 and 1911 the population of England and Wales increased sixty-three per cent. The growing productivity of the industrial state, and the ability to draw upon the rest of the world for supplies of food, made it possible to support an ever larger population and at the same time for them to raise their standard of living. Owing, moreover, to the increasing industrialization of Great Britain, the town population grew continually at the expense of the country. Both these movements are shown in the following table:

GROWTH AND DISTRIBUTION OF THE POPULATION, ENGLAND AND WALES

Year	Total population	Urban *	Rural
		(Percentage)	
1871	22,712,000	61.7	38.3
1881	25,974,000	67.9	32.1
1891	29,002,000	74.7	25.3
1901	32,527,000	76.8	23.2
1911	36,070,000	78.1	21.9

* Beginning with 1871 the census counted as urban all communities with over 2000 inhabitants, even if they were not charted as towns. The figures of urban and rural population given here consequently do not correspond with those on p. 229, which are calculated on the old basis.

The urbanization of the population went on at an extraordinary rate and by 1912 practically four-fifths of the people were town-dwellers. The towns, however, were by now safe places in which to be born and live, for the unsanitary and disease-breeding conditions pictured in a previous chapter had been pretty well abolished, though housing still called for improvement. The success of the fight for public health was shown in the steady decline of the death-rate; after the turn of the century this fell rapidly. The birth-rate was also falling though not so rapidly, so that the net additions to the population showed a decline. The decennial changes are shown in the following table:

Working conditions. The average working week in 1870 was about sixty hours, somewhat less for the building trades and others of the well-organized industries, and more for the unprotected and unorganized workers. The program of the seventies was a fifty-four hour week — $9\frac{1}{2}$ hours daily and a Saturday half holiday.

Annual Birth-rate and Death-rate
(per 1000 of the population)

Year	Birth-rate	Death-rate	Excess of births over deaths
1871	33.8	21.5	12.3
1881	32.5	18.7	13.8
1891	30.4	20.0	10.4
1901	28.0	17.1	10.9
1911	24.4	14.8	9.6

This seems to have been realized by 1880, for Mulhall reported that the average weekly number of hours for all workers in that year was fifty-two in Great Britain, as against sixty in France and Germany. This permitted a half holiday on Saturday — *la semaine anglaise* — which was thereafter solidly established in British industry.

The age at which children might go to work was steadily raised during this period. It stood at nine years in 1870, but was raised to ten in 1874, to eleven in 1891, and to twelve in 1901. These were the ages fixed by the factory acts, but outside of the factories there were many industries in which very young children were employed, though the growth of heavier jobs in the iron and steel and related industries tended to decrease the demand somewhat. A long step forward was taken by the Factories and Workshops Act of 1878 which applied the provisions of the factory legislation to all workshops. In 1895 the weekly limit of working hours was fixed at thirty for children below thirteen. By this legislation a steady reduction in the number of children at work was effected.

The restriction of child labor had been effected by the factory acts down to 1870, but in that year the real cure of compulsory education was applied. All children below the age of thirteen were compelled to attend school, though this was slightly relaxed in 1876 by allowing children below that age engaged in agriculture to work for six weeks a year. This met the objections of the strongest group of opponents of compulsory education. The Elementary Education Act of 1880 permitted a certificated child of ten and any child of thirteen to go to work. A government report of 1901 estimated that in 1898 about 300,000 children combined school attendance with paid employment, of whom about two-thirds were employed in street-trading, agriculture, and various forms of home work and casual work. The number of schools grew rapidly, and the quality of instruction was steadily improved. From about 1,000,000 children in school in 1869 the number grew to about 6,000,000 in 1913. As a result of the spread of education, illiteracy (among males) declined from 19.4 in 1870 to 1.4 per cent in 1907 in England and Wales.

Wages. Money wages, which had been steadily rising since the repeal of the Corn Laws, continued their upward movement at a somewhat accelerated pace. Between 1870 and 1900 money wages increased about thirty-five per cent and between the latter date and 1914 by another six per cent. Real wages did not present so favorable a picture, since prices moved in the same direction during the latter part of the period. The long period of falling prices came to an end in 1896, and after that a slow rise set in, retail food prices going up about twenty-five per cent between that date and 1914. The combination of these factors was carefully worked out by two statisticians,[1] whose conclusions may be considered authoritative. Their conclusions for the period 1880–1913 are presented in the following table:

WAGES AND COST OF LIVING

Year	Average of wage incomes	Cost of living	Real wages
1880	100	100	100
Average, 1881–85	101	96	105
Average, 1886–90	104	89	117
Average, 1891–95	110	88	125
Average, 1896–1900	115	87	132
Average, 1901–05	121	91	133
Average, 1906–10	126	94	134
1913	134	100	134

From this table it is evident that a very considerable improvement took place in the real wages and the standard of living of the working class, but that this was achieved during the latter part of the nineteenth century. After 1900 the cost of living returned to the level of 1880, and real wages remained nearly stationary. Broadly stated, the incomes of the generation before the war were one-third greater at the end than at the beginning of their lives. It is, however, not possible to include in a statistical table all the factors which make up a people's well-being, and further interpretation is necessary.

In the first place, wage-rates do not represent earnings, for no account is taken of unemployment or slack time. Averages, while presenting a correct broad picture, may not portray accurately the condition of any individual or group, for wages rose and fell un-

[1] A. L. Bowley, *The Changes in the Distribution of the National Income, 1880–1913* (Oxford, 1920), 18. He combines the conclusions of J. H. Wood with his own. By permission of The Clarendon Press, Oxford.

evenly in different lines of work. After the introduction of compulsory education there was a growing tendency for the more intelligent to transfer from manual labor to clerical work, teaching, and other professional occupations in which wages were generally higher. The length of the working day was steadily decreasing during the whole of this period, and consequently total wages did not go up as fast as rates per hour. And finally wages were not the only determinant of the standard of living; the worker was the beneficiary of a century's technological advance in a hundred additions to his comfort, which were now within reach of his purse. Improved sanitation and medical progress increased his health and prolonged his life, while the decrease in the size of the family permitted a higher standard of living. The extension of governmental functions gave to the urban factory worker, and in less degree to the agricultural laborer, a multitude of social services, such as police and fire protection, parks, libraries, and free schools, public baths, sanitation, public hospitals, and the newer measures for workmen's compensation, oldage pensions, and health insurance. Even the agricultural laborer shared in the general progress. "The general condition of agricultural labor," said a Royal Commission in 1893, "judged by appearances, has greatly improved. His standard of life is higher; he dresses better, he eats more butchers' meat, he travels more, he reads more, and he drinks less." The next two decades certainly saw no deterioration in these conditions, but rather an improvement.

Consumption. No adequate statistics exist of consumption, except in the case of articles which are supplied wholly from foreign sources or for which a domestic excise permits fairly accurate estimates. The increase in the consumption of semi-luxuries in general use revealed in such statistics throws light upon the general upward movement in the standard of living of the British people. This may be briefly shown.[2]

ANNUAL PER CAPITA CONSUMPTION IN THE UNITED KINGDOM
(five-year averages)

Article	1883–87	1888–92	1893–97	1898–1902
Tea, lbs.	4.9	5.2	5.6	6.0
Coffee, lbs.	.9	.8	.7	.7
Cocoa, lbs.	.4	.5	.6	.9
Sugar, lbs.	72.0	76.0	83.0	86.0
Meat, lbs.	110.0	119.0	123.0	133.0
Beer, gals.	27.3	29.3	30.0	31.3
Tobacco, oz.	23.0	24.0	27.0	30.0

[2] A. L. Bowley, *National Progress in Wealth and Trade* (London, 1904), 28. By permission of The Clarendon Press, Oxford.

Taking all these articles together there was an increase in their consumption of about twenty per cent. The consumption of wheat and flour per head remained about the same during this period, seeming to indicate that the great bulk of the population was adequately supplied with bread, since a fall in price did not lead to larger purchases. The consumption of imported butter, bacon, cheese, and eggs also increased, although, since large quantities of these articles were produced at home, it is not possible to state the per capita consumption. Meat entered into the dietary of the British worker in larger amount than in other countries; in Germany the per capita consumption was estimated at seventy-five lbs. and in France at seventy lbs., or not much over half as much as that in Britain.

Robert Giffen wrote [3] in 1886 of "the great progress of the working classes in the last half century" and summed up his conclusions as follows: "The great rise of money wages among labourers of every class, coupled with stationary or even falling prices of commodities on the average, the all but universal shortening of hours of labour, the decline of pauperism, the enormously increased consumption of the luxuries of the masses, the improvement in the rate of mortality — these and other facts combine to prove that there has been a general advance in well-being among the masses of the community."

Fifty years later another eminent statistician asked the question whether there had been similar progress during the period 1886–1936, and answered it in much the same way. "In a large measure the answer is yes," he wrote.[4] "Wages have increased more than prices, and the rise was greatest in the classes where improvement was most needed. The hours of labour have greatly diminished; the so-called masses consume more of what Giffen termed luxuries (sugar, tea, tobacco), and have a greatly increased variety of amusements, many of them of recent invention, on which the increased margin of income over necessaries can be spent. The rate of mortality has fallen till there seems to be little room for it to fall further."

Co-operation. During this period the workers endeavored to improve their position as consumers by co-operation. The number of societies and their activities grew greatly between 1870 and 1914, as is shown by the table on page 468.

The size of the average society expanded considerably, though the sales per member remained very steady. Some amalgamation took place toward the end of the period. The strength of the move-

[3] *Essays in Finance, Second Series* (London, 1890), 409. By permission of the publisher, George Bell and Sons, London.

[4] A. L. Bowley, *Wages and Income in the United Kingdom since* 1860 (Cambridge, 1937), xii. By permission of the publisher, Cambridge University Press, and of The Macmillan Company, New York.

RETAIL CO-OPERATIVE SOCIETIES IN GREAT BRITAIN

Year	Number of societies	Total membership	Total sales (£)	Total capital (£)
1881	971	547,212	15,411,185	5,380,246
1900	1439	1,707,011	50,053,567	20,566,287
1914	1385	3,053,770	87,978,898	39,537,049

ment was to be found in the industrial and mining districts, where trade unionism was stronger; in the agricultural and middle class residential districts it was weak. The development of retail co-operative stores made desirable the establishment of wholesale organizations for joint purchasing of commodities, and in 1863 a wholesale society was established in England, followed five years later by one in Scotland. The sales of these wholesales to the retail societies, their only clients, expanded from £783,000 in 1870 to £40,000,000 in 1913.

Even more significant in the development of co-operation was the extension of activity from merchandising to production, which was undertaken both by the retail and wholesale societies. The English Wholesale Society began with the acquisition of a biscuit factory in 1873, and extended its enterprises until in 1914 it had about fifty factories, producing such staple commodities as flour, soap, machinery and hardware, clothing, etc. The Scottish Society entered the field a decade later, but in 1900 the two organizations established a joint committee to manage their tea, cocoa, and chocolate enterprises, and at the same time purchased plantations of their own in India and Ceylon. The value of goods produced grew from £4,000,000 in 1900 to £30,000,000 in 1913.

As the wholesale societies grew they undertook still other activities. Thus in 1913 they took over the Co-operative Insurance Society, which had been organized in 1867 to insure the properties of the retail societies, and had later entered the general insurance business. Banking had been added in 1872, when the Wholesale Society began to accept deposits from the retail societies, but after 1910 individual members and trade unions were urged to open accounts. For advisory, propaganda, and educational purposes all the co-operative societies in Great Britain were federated in 1869 in the British Co-operative Union. It succeeded in enlisting less than ten per cent of the population in the movement.

Producers' co-operation was of slight importance and made little headway. Somewhat over one hundred small undertakings carried on a precarious struggle just before the war.

2. BETTER CONDITIONS IN GERMANY

Population growth and distribution. The new Reich in 1871 had a population of 41,000,000, of whom 2,000,000 had been added by the accession of Alsace and Lorraine. The railways were the first factor in stimulating the growth of population, which increased six millions between 1850 and 1870. The next twenty years added another eight millions, but the greatest upsurge in numbers occurred in the twenty-five years ending in 1915, when there was an increase of over eighteen millions. The maximum population, 67,900,000, was reached in the last year. The great industrial and commercial expansion of this period, accompanied by improvements in agriculture, had removed a check to population growth. Immense resources, especially in the form of coal and iron, were opened up, and science devised new ways of utilizing them. Industrially, Germany was in the position of a young country, in which restraints on the growth in number were weak. The ability of German industry and trade to absorb these large additions was the more remarkable in that emigration fell off after 1890 until it became a mere trickle at the end of the period. The changes are shown in the following table:

GERMAN POPULATION, 1871–1914

Year	Total population	Rural per cent	Urban per cent
1871	41,058,792	63.9	36.1
1880	45,234,061	58.6	41.4
1890	49,428,470	57.5	42.5
1900	56,367,000	45.6	54.4
1910	64,926,000	38.3	61.7
1913	66,978,000	....	....

The increase was due less to an increasing birth-rate, for this was steadily declining, than to a still more rapid fall in the death-rate. The number of births per 1000 inhabitants declined from 40.7 for the decade 1871–80 to 27.8 for the period 1911–14. But at the same time the mortality fell from 28.8 to 16.0, so that the excess of births over deaths remained stable. The decline in the birth-rate was especially marked after 1900, during the very period of Germany's greatest industrial expansion. This took place, not only among the well-to-do groups, but also among the clerical workers and the laboring population; it was most marked in the large cities, and was lowest of all in Berlin.

This tendency, which was considered alarming for a militaristic nation such as Germany had become, called forth a voluminous literature which offered various explanations. An obvious one was the notable decline in infant mortality. A second, more disputable, theory was the lessened fertility of marriages resulting from the mixture of races and racial groups which was taking place. Similar to this was the idea that the spread of venereal disease lessened the fertility of women thus affected. More important was the increasing use of contraceptive devices, as the result of unwillingness of couples to endanger their improving standard of living by burdening themselves with children. Beginning with the well-to-do these practices spread down even to the working classes. The growing industrialism and independence of women also militated against large families.

Even more striking than the fall in the birth-rate was the rapid decline in the death-rate. This was the result of improved medical science and a better standard of living. The most striking gain was in child mortality, where these factors were especially important. The death-rate of infants during their first year was reduced from 20.7 in 1901 to 15.1 in 1913. The changes in population growth may be stated briefly.

POPULATION GROWTH

Period	Birth-rate *	Death-rate *	Excess of births over deaths
1871–80	40.7	28.8	11.9
1881–90	38.2	26.5	11.7
1891–1900	37.3	23.5	13.9
1901–10	33.9	19.7	14.3
1911–14	27.8	16.0	11.8

* Births and deaths both include stillborn. If these were omitted the figures in both these columns would be slightly lower, but the net gain would remain unchanged.

Along with the growth in numbers there was taking place a steady urbanization of the population, which was especially marked after 1890. This is shown in the table on p. 469, which lists as urban all persons living in communities of 2000 and over. From a predominantly rural nation in 1871 Germany had become predominantly urban in 1910. The number of large cities with over 100,000 inhabitants grew from eight in the earlier year to forty-eight in the latter; over one-tenth of the people lived in such cities in 1890 and over one-fifth in 1910, while over one-third were to be found at the last date in towns of over 20,000. This urban concentration was caused primarily by the industrial development which brought together huge masses of men and women in factories and workshops. Germany had few good seaports and the commercial expansion of this period led to a building up of only a few such cities as Hamburg, Cologne, and Breslau, each of which could boast of a population of over 500,000 in 1910. The extension of governmental activities also required the services of a vast army of officials who tended to concentrate in the more important centers.

Living conditions. The standard of living of the German people was being raised steadily and considerably during this period. A generally accepted measure of this is the consumption of food and semi-luxuries, and judged by this standard there could be no question of the improvement which was taking place. Wheat bread was slowly pushing out rye bread, though the latter still remained the staple in 1913. The diet of a German workman was composed largely of eggs, vegetables, farinaceous food, and fruit, but the consumption of meat, though behind that of the British, showed a marked gain, from 65 pounds per capita for the year 1873 to 95 for 1912; there was, on the other hand, a decline in the consumption of herrings ("the poor man's meat"). Such things as coffee, cocoa, tea, and sugar, rice, spices and tropical fruits entered more abundantly into the dietary of the common man. Beer and brandy failed to advance in the twentieth century, owing to the temperance movement. On the other hand the growing consumption of such things as petroleum, cotton, and wool indicated greater comfort and better clothing; leather boots supplanted wooden shoes, and silk goods were sometimes worn.

While the consumption increased quantitatively, the quality was also being improved and articles bearing the same name were greatly superior in 1913 to what they had been in 1870. There was also going on a democratization of needs; great quantities of staple goods were produced at moderate prices and entered into general consumption. This in itself was an indication of improved economic conditions. The improvement was especially marked after 1890: imported cigarettes and fruit preserves, sofas, carpets, glass windows, gas stoves, electric lights, improved sanitary appliances, bicycles and automobiles were a few of the commodities which came into fairly general use during this period.[5] The simple and frugal economy of 1870 had by 1913 become more complex and profuse.

Housing failed to keep pace with the general advance. The use of cellar dwellings, overcrowding, and other evils presented themselves. This condition had not been wholly remedied by 1914, but improved transportation facilities were leading to decentralization of the population and the building of garden cities. At the same time the equipment of the homes was being made more sanitary and comfortable. Gas in the cities and lamps in the country had previously

[5] For a lively description of the changes that were taking place, see Sartorius V. Waltershausen, op. cit., 390-98.

furnished illumination, but electricity offered them a fierce competition after 1870.   Even the rural districts shared in these improvements.

The higher standard of living reflected the greater prosperity of the people.   Some scattered statistics may be offered in proof. The annual income of the people was estimated by Helfferich at 22,-000 million marks in 1895 and at 40,000 million in 1913, the average income growing from 884 to 1334 marks.   At the same time there was a better distribution of the augmented income.   Incomes in Prussia showed the following changes between 1895 and 1911:

PERCENTAGE DISTRIBUTION INCOMES IN PRUSSIA

Annual income	1895	1911
Under 900 marks	68.7	41.2
900–3000 marks	27.7	52.1
Over 3000 marks	3.6	6.7

There is indicated here a remarkable shift from the small incomes to those of higher brackets.   The industrial development had called into being a new middle class, in the persons of foremen, overseers, inspectors, as well as a large clerical force.   In the same way the peasant middle class increased.   There was a growth also in the number of persons living on their incomes with no gainful occupation from 5 per cent of the population in 1882 to 8.4 per cent in 1907. These figures probably reflect not so much the rise of millionaires as the influence of the insurance and pension system and the increase in the number of students.   The total deposits in banks, savings banks and co-operative societies tell the same story of growing prosperity: from 6500 million marks in 1888 they swelled to 30,000 million in 1913.   The statistics of wealth are estimates and can be regarded as only approximately correct but the trend is unmistakable: from about 200,000 million marks in 1895 the national wealth increased to between 300,000 and 400,000 million in 1913.

Wages.   German wage statistics for the early part of this period are almost altogether lacking.   A proposal to gather such information in connection with the occupation census of 1875 was given up as impracticable, but statistics of the daily wages of ordinary laborers began to be collected in the eighties by the officials administering the sickness and accident insurance.   For the decade 1870 to 1880 the yearly wages of workers in the repair shops of the Upper Silesian railway may be taken as showing the general trend; these rose from 958 marks in 1870 to 1072 in 1875 and fell again to 964 in 1880. A German student, Paul Göhre,[6] who worked in a machine shop

[6] *Drei Monate Fabrikarbeiter und Handwerksbursche* (Leipzig, 1891), 17.

in Chemnitz, Saxony, in 1890, reported an average annual income for most of his fellow workers of 800-900 marks; with such an income they "could live without serious anxiety if they did not have too many children." It was otherwise if there were sickness, death, accident, long military service, or unemployment.

A table giving relative money wages, cost of living and real wages at decennial intervals may be presented for the purpose of showing the general trends.

WAGES AND COST OF LIVING IN GERMANY *
(1900 = 100)

Year	Money wages	Cost of living	Real wages
1870	64	83	77
1880	78	99	79
1890	92	98	92
1900	100	100	100
1910	119	120	99
1914	132	130	102

* J. Kuczynski, *Labour Conditions in Western Europe*, 1820–1935 (New York, 1936), 93. By permission of the publisher, International Publishers, New York.

The great increase in money wages was partly nullified by a concomitant rise in prices, but still the period ended with real wages 30 per cent higher than they had been at the beginning. The skilled workers fared somewhat better than the manual laborers, and there was also a relative strengthening of the proportion who belonged to the skilled groups.

Co-operative associations. The aim of trade unions is to raise the wages and improve the working conditions of their members. The object of consumers' co-operative associations is to increase the real wages by enabling their members to obtain commodities at lower prices. The co-operative movement developed later in Germany than in England or France, but just before the World War had more associations than the former and more members than the latter.

The first co-operative associations in Germany were formed in the late forties among handworkers, for the purpose of buying their raw materials more cheaply. In 1848 a bread-buying society was established in Berlin and in 1852 one in Hamburg, for the distribution of the necessaries of life. Other societies were formed for the co-operative purchase of clothing and cigars. They were organized for the most part by the workers themselves with the occasional assistance of members of the middle class, and there was a good deal of confused experimenting, though English experience had already pointed the way. A famous quarrel broke out between Hermann Schulze, the founder of the workers' credit institutions, who favored the principle of self-help, and Ferdinand Lassalle, who advocated state assistance. Perhaps because of the advertising it received the movement expanded rapidly in the decade 1865 to 1875, from 6600 to 98,000 members. The statistical growth is shown in the following table:

CONSUMERS' CO-OPERATIVE ASSOCIATIONS IN GERMANY *

Year	Total number of associations	Total number of members (in thousands)	Total sales (in million marks)
1870	354	45	9
1880	645	94	30
1890	984	215	57
1900	1528	522	125
1910	2311	1474	407
1913	2417	2115	637

* *Handwörterbuch der Staatswissenschaften* (Jena, 1892), IV, 843, for 1870 to 1890; and Woytinsky, op. cit., V, 158, for 1900 to 1913.

The real movement began after the law of 1867 fixed the legal status of co-operative associations, and became unusually rapid after 1889, when they were given the privilege of limited liability. Most of these societies were small neighborhood unions, though in the cities larger associations were formed. The most important group was the socialist workers' consumers' unions. As they grew in numbers and size, the value of a central purchasing agency became apparent, and in 1893 the Co-operative Wholesale Society was organized. By 1913 the local associations were buying about one-third of their supplies from the central agency, which now operated a considerable number of factories for the production of foodstuffs, clothing, tobacco, matches, cabinet wares, and other articles of general use. The turnover was largely limited to the relatively cheap goods of daily consumption.

Even more numerous and active were the co-operative associations of producers, especially among the peasants. They soon learned the advantages of joint purchase of fertilizer, implements, and other articles, and of joint agencies for the sale of agricultural products. Most popular of all were the credit unions, by means of which the peasants, small industrialists, and handworkers could obtain the necessary capital. The relative importance of these groups may be shown for 1908 in the table on page 475.

3. STATIONARY POPULATION IN FRANCE

Population. The transition to a stationary population was particularly marked after 1870. The cession of Alsace-Lorraine brought

CO-OPERATIVE ASSOCIATIONS IN GERMANY

		Associations	Members
A.	Co-operative associations of producers	23,811	2,905,955
	Industrial	3,253	1,037,709
	Agricultural	20,558	1,868,246
B.	Co-operative associations of consumers	2,282	1,402,250

with it a loss of 2,000,000 persons, which it took a quarter century of population growth to recover. The slowing up of the rate of growth was a phenomenon which was already apparent in other countries, but which had been carried farthest in France. Many of the middle class, of the peasants, and of the industrial workers wished to secure for themselves and their children an assured position and to improve their standard of comfort. "The real cause of the diminution of our birth-rate," wrote A. Dumont,[7] "is the decision to have no or few children, and this decision is determined by the working together of intellectual, moral, and esthetic considerations, which are peculiar to our nation." The effects were particularly noticeable in the rural districts, which lost not only by decline in population growth, but also by migration to the cities. The changes in the number and distribution of the population are shown in the following table:

THE POPULATION OF FRANCE

Year	Total population	Percentage distribution Rural	Urban
1871	36,102,921	68.9	31.1
1881	37,672,048	65.2	34.8
1891	38,343,192	62.6	37.4
1901	38,961,945	59.0	40.9
1911	39,601,509	55.9	44.1

The movement of the population to the cities was not as pronounced in France as in Britain or Germany, owing to the wide distribution of small farms, but it was nevertheless concentrating a greater proportion of the people in large cities. In 1871 there were 9 cities with over 100,000 inhabitants, and in 1913 there were 14. By the latter date 44 per cent of the population lived in towns of 2000 or over.

In other countries the slowing up of the birth-rate had been more than offset by the still greater decline in the death-rate. In France, on the other hand, the decline in the death-rate was accompanied

[7] *Dépopulation et civilisation* (Paris, 1891), 97.

by an exactly equal decrease in the birth-rate, so that the population remained practically stationary. This phenomenon of a stationary population alarmed a good many French writers and a vast literature on the subject was produced, most of it unscientific and alarmist. The main causes and results pointed out may, however, be briefly summarized.

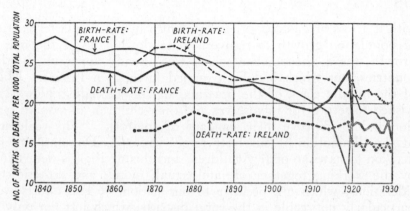

FIGURE 6.   BIRTH-RATES AND DEATH-RATES IN FRANCE AND IRELAND, 1840–1930

A. M. Carr-Saunders, *World Population* (Oxford, 1936), 90. By permission of the publishers, The Clarendon Press.

The fundamental factor, it was generally agreed, was economic — the desire for comfort.[8] While this was general in western Europe, it proceeded farthest in France, and produced there a distinct mentality on the subject. The fairly even distribution of wealth and the existence of large numbers of small industrialists, peasant proprietors, and governmental functionaries reinforced this attitude. The birth-rate was lowest in the richest districts, in departments where savings bank accounts were numerous, or where peasant proprietorship was widespread; it was highest in very small rural communities and in purely factory towns. Comfort, or the hope of attaining it, reduced the number of children. The age of marriage was steadily pushed up (in 1884 it was thirty years for men and twenty-five for women), owing partly to excessive formalities concerning marriage contracts, to the laws of inheritance, to the difficulties in finding lodgings and sometimes employment which confronted people with children, and partly to other factors. In no other country was birth control so generally used. Some writers detected greater sterility among the women as a result of these practices. The lessening of religious faith was also alleged as a cause.

[8] J. Bertillon, *La population de la France* (Paris, 1911), 102.

The results were painted in still darker colors. At the beginning of the nineteenth century France had 40 per cent of the population of the great European powers; in 1914 only 7 per cent. From a military standpoint France had become a second-rate power. The French language was losing ground as the universal language of diplomacy and polite intercourse. The peopling of her colonies by France became impossible; on the other hand France itself was being increasingly populated by foreigners. In 1896 there were 1,130,000 foreigners living in France, but only 517,000 Frenchmen living abroad. Industrial development was checked by an insufficient supply of labor. Especially serious was the effect on the national character, which became less enterprising. The majority of the causes of depopulation, said one writer,[9] "group themselves about the desire for an easy life, which modern parents have now, for themselves and their children. . . Formerly the characteristic French quality was daring (*audace*); today the Frenchman seeks above all to assure himself of well-being." The statistical basis for these conclusions may be briefly shown.

BIRTH-RATE AND DEATH-RATE IN FRANCE

Period	Average annual birth-rate	Average annual death-rate	Excess of births over deaths
1871–80	25.5	23.7	1.8
1881–90	23.8	22.1	1.8
1891–1900	22.2	21.6	0.6
1901–07	20.9	19.7	1.2
1908–13	19.3	18.5	0.8

Labor legislation. Interventionism on the part of the state on behalf of the workers scarcely existed in the beginning of this period. It was distrusted by the workers and opposed by employers, and regarded with indifference by the general public. No legislation for the protection of labor had been passed since 1841. The establishment of the Third Republic in 1870, however, created a spirit more sympathetic to the claims of labor and thereafter France slowly but steadily enlarged the scope of state action. The act of 1874 raised the minimum age for child labor to twelve years, and limited the work day to 12 hours including rest periods; night labor was prohibited for boys under sixteen and girls under twenty-one; girls, women, and boys under twelve were forbidden to work in mines; and school work was required for children under twelve. Exceptions were made in the case of indispensable labor in establishments with continuous fire. For the enforcement of the act 15 division

[9] R. de Félice, *Les naissances en France* (Paris, 1910), 337.

inspectors were to be appointed by the government.   In their reports the inspectors complained of constant violations of the act.   In the metallurgical works, where continuous fire had to be kept up, the employers ignored the law and imposed a 13 hour work day. But the worst abuses were found in non-profit charitable establishments; these were exempt from the law by a decree of 1881 and in them children of seven to eight years of age were found working from five in the morning to four in the afternoon.   In spite of abuses the number of children under twelve years employed in industrial labor fell from 6.5 per cent in 1876 to less than one per cent by 1885.[10]

Another step forward was taken in 1892.   A new act in that year raised the minimum age for work to thirteen years; young persons between thirteen and sixteen years could work only 6 hours a day, between sixteen and eighteen a total of 60 hours in the week; girls of more than eighteen and women were limited to 11 hours a day. This law proved difficult to apply, and led to extraordinary complications.   Instead of reducing the work day for all laborers to 10 hours, it had the effect of raising it to 11 hours.   Violations of the law were constant.[11]   It was consequently modified in 1900.   The maximum work day of 12 hours, which had remained unchanged for men since 1848, was now reduced to 11 hours; to $10\frac{1}{2}$ in 1902; and to 10 in 1904.   The distinctions between children, young persons, and adults were abolished and all alike were subjected to the law.   Night work was absolutely forbidden.   A weekly day of rest was made obligatory in 1906.

These laws dealt with the age of workers and the hours of labor, but they were supplemented by a vast number of other acts touching every phase of labor.   Dangerous trades were regulated and medical inspection was required; the conditions of women's work in stores and shops were fixed; the hated *livret ouvrier* was abolished; an employment service was set up; the exemption from seizure of a worker's estate, up to 8000 francs, was introduced in imitation of the American homestead law; machinery for conciliation and arbitration was provided; and a Ministry of Labor was established.   But the most important acts were those dealing with social insurance.

Social insurance.   The *laissez faire* policy of France had little room for compulsory insurance or for a state system.   A breach was made in this attitude first by compelling the communities to care at public expense for the insane (1838) and for children (1869), and finally in 1893 to recognize the right of the poor to free aid in case of sickness.   The application of this principle was, however, left to

---

[10] P. Louis, *Histoire de la classe ouvrière en France* (Paris, 1927), 168-70.
[11] *Ibid.*, 232.

private voluntary sickness insurance organizations, which were brought under government supervision. These were mutual societies of workingmen, supported by small monthly contributions, usually one franc, from their members, and sometimes by gifts from employers. In 1912 there were 21,240 such societies, with 5,117,-000 members. Only in the case of miners and sailors was a system of compulsory insurance, supported by both employers and workers, set up.

Accident insurance was also placed on a voluntary basis. The civil code had limited the responsibility of employers so narrowly that little protection had been given the workers. Under the Employers' Liability and Workmen's Compensation Act of 1898, however, employers were made liable for all occupational accidents to their employees. Accidents causing an interruption of work of more than four days gave rise to an indemnity, paid by the employer, not to exceed 2400 francs. For absolute and permanent disability the worker received two-thirds of his annual wage, and corresponding sums for temporary disability or death. Employers were not compelled to insure, but the heavy charges in case of accident led most of them to do so. Before the war probably three-quarters of the workers within the scope of the law were protected by insurance.

Old age insurance on a voluntary mutual basis had been provided as early as 1850 by the *Caisse Nationale des Retraites pour la Vieillesse*, which sold annuities at very low rates. In 1905 the state assumed the burden of a modest old age pension system, paying to all persons seventy years of age or over and to infirm persons an annual pension of 60 to 240 francs. This system was expanded and made compulsory in 1910. All wage-earners employed in industry and trade, agriculture, domestic service, the liberal professions and governmental service, whose annual wage was less than 3000 francs, were covered, but not miners, sailors, or railway employees, for whom a separate compulsory system was provided. Employers and employees contributed to a fund, to which the state added a subsidy. Insured workers could claim a pension when they reached the age of sixty or sixty-five, in the latter case at a somewhat higher rate. Certain other groups, as artisans, small employers, tenants, and wage-earners receiving between 3000 and 5000 francs annually, were permitted to contribute under the act, but in those cases there was no contribution from employers. By 1914 the total number of those insured under the Old Age Pensions Act was 7,710,000.

The French system of social insurance differed from both the British and the German systems by leaving the administration for the most part in the hands of voluntary organizations. It thus avoided a bureaucratic centralization. But, on the other hand, the system suffered from faulty management and lack of comprehensiveness.

Wages and standard of living. Labor made great progress during this period, not only in legislative protection, but also in wages and a higher standard of living. The following table gives a brief summary of the important changes: [12]

WAGES AND COST OF LIVING IN FRANCE
(Non-agricultural workers. 1895 = 100)

Year	Money wages	Cost of living	Real wages
1870	79	102	77
1880	93	115	81
1890	99	104	95
1900	108	99	109
1910	120	102	118
1914	123	110	112

Money wages rose steadily during this period, reaching their highest level just before the war. Prices fluctuated, but did not advance greatly beyond the level of the seventies. Real wages consequently moved up, almost parallel with money wages, though lagging slightly behind. The rise in wages in France was not due primarily to the strength of the trade unions, as in Britain, nor to state socialism, as in Germany, but to the stationary population, which gave labor a semi-monopolistic position. Whatever disadvantages a low birth-rate may have had from a military or moral point of view, there is no doubt that the relative scarcity of labor, in the face of an advancing industrialism, led to a rise in wages and kept them high. Labor recognized this situation and did not oppose the introduction of labor saving machinery, nor the application of methods of rationalization and efficiency.

State intervention was invoked in the case of the sweated labor of women in home work, where wages of three and four cents an hour were prevalent. A minimum wage law was passed in 1911, which applied primarily to women home workers in various branches of the clothing industry. Wages customarily paid to factory workers in the same lines and of average skill were to be ascertained by wage boards, created by an act of 1908. On the basis of this information minimum wage rates were to be fixed that would "enable a female worker of average ability to earn in ten hours a wage equal" to this average wage.

It is difficult to measure the improvement in the standard of liv-

[12] J. Kuczynski, *Labour Conditions in Western Europe*, 1820–1935 (New York, 1936), 105. By permission of the publisher, International Publishers, New York.

ing, for there was not only a gain in the purchasing power of wages,
but the quality and variety of goods available increased greatly.   On
the other hand, home production for home use had given way to cash
purchases, so that money wages now covered articles of consumption
which were formerly not counted in.   The improvement in the
standard of living may fairly be gauged by the consumption of certain semi-luxuries, all of which were bought with money.

CONSUMPTION OF SEMI-LUXURIES IN FRANCE *

Year	Tea	Coffee	Cocoa	Sugar	Beer (qts.
		(lbs. per capita)			per cap.)
1871	1.5	244	49	17	....
1881	2.6	378	72	22	25
1891	3.5	402	83	26	23
1901	4.6	488	104	24	39
1910	7.3	617	151	35	41

* *Annuaire Statistique de la France* (Paris, 1910), Vol. 30.

The consumption of these typical semi-luxuries more than doubled during this forty year period, and that of staple articles also
increased.   Between 1885 and 1913 the consumption of cotton in
France rose from 290 million pounds to 596 million; wool increased from 440 million to 590 million.   Other indices, such as
savings bank accounts, size of estates, and the increase in national
wealth, all point to the conclusion that the standard of living of the
whole nation, including that of the wage-earners, showed remarkable
improvement, and had probably reached the high point when war
put an end to peace and prosperity.

Co-operation.   The beginning of the co-operative movement in
France is usually dated from 1880, although some earlier societies
had already been established.   Various experiments had been made
with producers' associations, which wished to free themselves from
the exploitation of capitalism, along the lines of socialism expounded
by Fourier or Blanc.   Consumers' co-operative societies also appeared in 1865, but all of these were swept away by the crisis of
1870.   The ensuing decade followed without any action, but in 1880
some 22 distributive co-operative societies were established, followed
by 21 more the next year.   After this the growth was slower.   Influenced by events in Britain, the retail societies in 1887 organized
a Co-operative Union and also a Wholesale Society, to act as central
purchasing agent.   This struggled along until the early nineties
when a split occurred between two rival movements: the "bourgeois" co-operatives, who opposed the entrance of the co-operatives
into politics, and the socialist co-operatives, who advocated a militant

policy. The latter finally withdrew, forming a separate union and in 1906 establishing a rival wholesale society. This grew rapidly, but with success came moderation, and in 1912 it was ready to unite with its rival. The two unions amalgamated as the *Fédération nationale des Coopératives de Consommation* and the wholesalers merged under the name of the *Magasin du Gros*. The pact adopted the Rochdale principles and announced as its aim "to substitute for the present competitive and capitalist regime, a regime where production will be carried on for the collectivity of consumers and not for profit." The development may be briefly shown.

CONSUMERS' CO-OPERATIVE SOCIETIES IN FRANCE

Year	Number of societies	Number of members	Annual turnover (million francs)
1865	3	....	....
1880	50(?)	....	...
1895	1221	300,000	100
1910	2882	800,000	250
1913	3261	880,000	320

BIBLIOGRAPHICAL NOTE

1. *Britain.* An excellent study of urbanization of the population is M. P. Meuriot, *Des agglomérations urbaines dans l'Europe contemporaine* (Paris, 1898). Not quite so good is A. F. Weber, *The Growth of Cities in the Nineteenth Century* (New York, 1899). On wages there are three excellent studies by A. L. Bowley, the outstanding authority in this field: *National Progress in Wealth and Trade* (London, 1904); *The Changes in the Distribution of the National Income 1880–1913* (Oxford, 1920); *Wages and Income in the United Kingdom since 1860* (Cambridge, 1937). The subject is also handled, though less satisfactorily, in J. Kuczinski, *Die Entwicklung der Lage der Arbeiterschaft in Europa und Amerika, 1870–1933* (Basel, 1934), and in R. R. Kuczynski, *Arbeitslohn und Arbeitszeit in Europa und Amerika, 1870–1909* (Berlin, 1913). An excellent study of unemployment is W. H. Beveridge, *Unemployment; a Problem of Industry* (London, 1909; rev. ed., 1930). A pioneer work on co-operation is G. J. Holyoake, *History of Co-operation*, 2 vols. (London, 1875–79; rev. ed., 1908). Somewhat more critical, though sympathetic, is B. Potter (Mrs. Sidney Webb), *The Co-operative Movement in Great Britain* (London, 1891). An official history of the wholesale society is P. Redfern, *The Story of the C. W. S.* (Manchester, 1913). The best general study is C. R. Fay, *Co-operation at Home and Abroad; Description and Analysis.* Vol. I, *Pre-War* (4th ed., London, 1939). A narrower field is covered by Benj. Jones, *Co-operative Production*, 2 vols. (Oxford, 1894).

2. *Germany.* A sketch of the population question is Otto Most, *Bevölkerungswissenschaft* (Berlin, 1927). A sympathetic account is W. H. Dawson, *The German Workman* (London, 1906). F. C. Howe, *Socialized Germany* (New York, 1915) writes approvingly of welfare institutions. W. J. Ashley, *The Progress of the German Working Classes in the Last Quarter of a Century* (London, 1904) is somewhat too favorable. A longer and more balanced view is Frege, *Zur Lohn-*

bewegung der letzten hundert Jahre (Berlin, 1911). J. Kuczynski, *Löhne und Konjunktur in Deutschland*, 1887–1932 (Berlin, 1933) paints a darker picture. Social insurance is exhaustively covered in three books: W. H. Dawson, *Social Insurance in Germany*, 1883–1911 (London, 1912); L. K. Frankel and M. M. Dawson, *Workingmen's Insurance in Europe* (New York, 1916); United States Bur. of Labor, *Workingmen's Insurance and Compensation Systems in Europe*, 2 vols. (Washington, 1911). T. O. Cassau, *The Consumers' Movement in Germany* (Manchester, 1925) is good for co-operation.

3. *France.* A general survey of labor conditions is E. Levasseur, *Questions ouvrières et industrielles sous la troisième République* (Paris, 1917). The slow growth of the population called forth a voluminuous literature, mostly alarmist. J. Bertillon, *La dépopulation en France* (Paris, 1911) is scholarly and careful, as is P. Leroy-Beaulieu, *La question de la population* (2e ed., Paris, 1913). More pessimistic are R. de Félice, *Les naissances en France* (Paris, 1910), and M. Huber, H. Bunle, et al., *La population de la France* (Paris, 1937). J. Goldstein, *Bevölkerungsprobleme und Berufsgliederung in Frankreich* (Berlin, 1900), discusses the distribution of the population. Wages and the well-being of the workers are well treated in P. Louis, *Histoire de la classe ouvrière en France de la Révolution à nos jours: la condition matérielle des travailleurs, les salaires et le coût de la vie* (Paris, 1927). On co-operation two books by B. Lavergne, *Régime coopératif* (Paris, 1908) and *Les coopératives de consommation en France* (Paris, 1923) are useful. Chas. Gide, *Consumers' Co-operative Societies* (Translated from the French, Manchester, 1925) is an enthusiastic advocate. Other good studies are J. Corréard, *Des sociétés coopératives* (Paris, 1908) and P. Hubert-Valleroux, *La coopération* (2nd ed., Paris, 1904).

Part III: Economic and Commercial Rivalries.
1914-1939

CHAPTER XV
THE CAUSES AND CONSEQUENCES OF THE WORLD WAR

Causes of the war. The dictum of Aristotle that though wars may have small occasions great wars have always proceeded from deep-seated causes was significantly illustrated by the World War and the peace treaties which followed it. The basic causes of this struggle have been listed by Professor Fay [1] under five heads: secret alliances, nationalism, militarism, economic imperialism, and the press. Of these he thought the most important single underlying cause was the system of secret alliances, which united the leading nations of Europe into two opposing camps, the Triple Alliance of Germany, Austria-Hungary, and Italy, formed in 1882, and the Triple Entente of Britain, France, and Russia, finally consummated in 1907. Britain, which had hitherto stood aloof, tipping the scales in the European balance of power, now became a part of the system. These two hostile groups were increasingly suspicious of one another and steadily built up greater and greater armies and navies. Another important underlying cause was militarism, with its standing armies, powerful cliques of military and naval officers, and the pressure of the munition makers. Nationalism was probably the oldest of the underlying causes, but it received a new impetus after 1870, and was especially strong in Germany. The newspapers and periodical press inflamed national feeling and contributed powerfully to the enthusiasm for war which made it possible.

The economic motives, which became prominent during the last quarter of the nineteenth century, may be summed up as a struggle for markets, raw materials, fields for investment, and colonies.

With the growth of large scale machine industry, producing articles for mass consumption, adequate markets for these goods were vital to the prosperity of the industrial nations. These were sought first of all at home, and, except in free trade Britain, the domestic markets were reserved in large part for home producers. High protective duties shut out competing foreign goods. But these tariffs, and the retaliatory measures to which they gave rise, created

[1] S. B. Fay, *The Origins of the World War* (2nd ed., New York, 1930).

friction among the various countries. More important for Britain and Germany, and to a less degree for France, were foreign markets, as the swelling volume of the exports from these countries abundantly shows. The struggle to win and hold these markets gave rise to endless international jealousies and frequent questionable maneuvers. Since the development of foreign trade is described in a later chapter, this mention must suffice at this point.

Of even more fundamental importance in the economic development of any country is the possession of certain essential raw materials, especially minerals. Fortunately for the human race, minerals exist throughout the world in abundant quantity, great variety, and in widely distributed locations. But unfortunately they are very unequally distributed. North America and Europe produced about 90 per cent of the coal and iron, and in the United States, Britain, and Germany the metallurgical industries were highly developed. But they lacked other essential key raw materials, such as the ferro-alloys, which were located in other less developed countries. In their efforts to obtain these the leading industrial European nations appropriated the territory in northern Africa for the sake of the mineral wealth located there, and, with Japan, sought the partition of China to obtain interests in the coal and iron deposits of that country. Germany and France came into conflict over the coal and iron resources of the Rhine region. With the growing use of oil for ocean transportation and industry, attention was next directed to petroleum deposits. The United States, Mexico, and Russia controlled over 40 per cent of the estimated oil reserves of the world, while Persia and Mesopotamia had nearly 15 per cent additional. Of these latter Britain gained control of the Persian oil fields, but those in Mesopotamia (Irak) were sought by both that country and Germany, thus providing another cause of international friction, and Germany also cast a longing glance at the Caucasus.

The search for investments in foreign countries characterizes an advanced stage in the capitalistic development of a country. In an earlier stage goods were exported, but as wealth accumulated beyond the point of continued profitable investment at home, the export of capital took place. Britain had reached this position a century earlier, France attained it more tardily, and Germany was entering this stage of the export of capital at the beginning of the twentieth century. British investors, themselves business men, placed their capital directly in industrial undertakings or bought the bonds of railroad and mining corporations, and of manufacturing and commercial enterprises. Much of the economic development of the backward regions of the world had been carried on with British capital. Being first in the field they not unnaturally sought out the

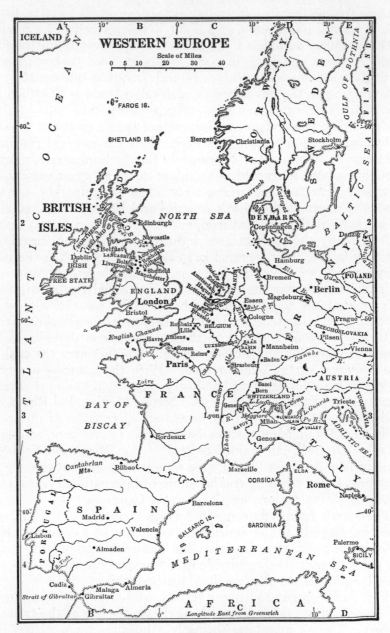

FIGURE 7.   EUROPE IN 1920

From J. R. Smith's *Commerce and Industry* (Henry Holt & Co., 1925). Reprinted by permission of the publishers.

best investments, and may be said, speaking somewhat figuratively, to have obtained first mortgages for their outlays.

The French, with their customary preference for government bonds, invested chiefly in the public securities of Russia, Turkey, Rumania, and Mexico. That such an unwise choice should have been made by the French investor must be charged against the French bankers, who let themselves be influenced in the advice they gave their clients by the size of their commissions or by political considerations.

Germany, aided by the enormous productive capacity of her people, was passing from the stage of export of commodities and search for markets to that of export of capital and search for investments about the opening of the twentieth century. But here, as before in her commercial expansion, she found in Great Britain her greatest rival. The favored spots had been appropriated, the best investments had been taken up, and German expansionists and foreign investors had to content themselves with the neglected remnants of Africa and other available countries as colonies, and with second mortgages or with investments in more doubtful enterprises and in less promising countries. Some of these enterprises, like the British Cape-to-Cairo railway or the German Berlin-Bagdad railway, had serious political repercussions. On the eve of the World War German foreign investments were estimated by the Federal Trade Commission to have amounted to nearly $8,000,-000,000;[2] those of France were about $8,500,000,000; and those of Great Britain some $20,000,000,000.

The population of Europe grew from about 165,000,000 in 1790 to nearly 465,000,000 in 1914, and in some countries this led to a pressure of population on the means of subsistence. The pressure was relieved primarily by improvements in the means and methods of production and transportation and to a less degree by emigration. Nevertheless some 50,000,000 left their homes for oversea lands during this period. The desire to retain political control over these emigrants was undoubtedly one of the motives in the movement for colonial expansion, but other factors, described in other chapters, were more important.

Cost of the war.[3] In spite of a generation of armament and war talk the actual outbreak of war on August 1, 1914, fell on an unprepared world. The intricate interlacing of international trade and of foreign investment would, it was believed, prevent a general

---

[2] The McKenna Committee reported to the Committee of Experts (Dawes Plan) that the foreign investments of Germany in 1914 amounted to 28 billion gold marks, or about $7,000,-000,000.

[3] For a detailed account of this subject see my *Direct and Indirect Costs of the Great World War* (2nd ed., Washington, 1920), and *War Costs and their Financing* (New York, 1921).

struggle, while the enormous costs envisaged would either preclude it or limit it at most to a few months. Neither of these factors, however, proved a deterrent. Economic ties did not determine the line-up for war nor prevent former friends from fighting. The costs of a general European war had been estimated by several experts, but every guess fell far short of reality. The total costs of the more important wars of the nineteenth century, including the Napoleonic, Crimean, American Civil, Franco-Prussian, Boer, and Russo-Japanese wars, amounted to $18,330,000,000, but this figure was equalled in the first year of the World War and exceeded in each subsequent year. The explanation of these enormous expenditures was to be found in the improvements that had been made in the machinery of destruction, the possibilities of airplanes and submarines, and the economic mobilization of whole peoples for "total war." It was the first war in which modern technical science pitted machines and the output of factories against the forces of the enemy, and the instruments and munitions of warfare were produced and destroyed with a reckless prodigality which ran the costs up to incredible figures. From the standpoint of expenditures the World War established a new record.

In the last analysis it was of course the production of these instruments of war that decided the outcome, and not the financial mechanism. But since the activities of the three leading nations in the fields of agriculture, industry, commerce, transportation, banking, and labor during the struggle will be described later, attention will be confined here to the financial aspects. It must be remembered, moreover, that the normal procedure of a capitalist economy was followed in raising and expending the sums required by the war budgets. It remained for a later struggle to subordinate finance to a minor position and to organize the productive resources of the belligerents under direct government management.

The following table is an estimate of the direct money costs of the war to the principal active belligerents.

These were the direct money outlays by the governments of the belligerent nations, but in addition there were enormous indirect costs. Among these may be mentioned destruction and damage to civilian property on land, losses of merchant ships and cargo, production losses through non-economic production or failure to produce, and loss of human life. A fairly prophetic quotation may be made from a study of this subject, written shortly after the war.[4]

"The figures . . . are both incomprehensible and appalling, yet even these do not take into account the effect of the war on life, human vitality, economic well being, ethics, morality, or other

[4] See my *Direct and Indirect Costs of the Great World War* (2nd ed., Washington, 1920), 299.

Money Cost of the World War
(in millions)

Country	Gross cost	Advances to Allies	Net cost
United States	$ 32,080	$ 9,455	$ 22,625
Great Britain	44,029	8,695	35,334
Rest of Brit. Empire	4,494		4,494
France	36,400	1,547	34,853
Russia	22,594		22,594
Italy	12,314		12,314
Other Entente Allies	3,964		3,964
Total	$155,875	$19,697	$136,178
Germany	$ 40,150	$ 2,375	$ 37,775
Austria-Hungary	20,623		20,623
Turkey and Bulgaria	2,245		2,245
Total	$ 63,018	$ 2,375	$ 60,643
Grand total	$218,893	$22,072	$196,821

phases of human relationships and activities which have been disorganized and injured. It is evident from the present disturbances in Europe that the real costs cannot be measured by the direct money outlays of the belligerents in the five years of its duration, but that the very breakdown of modern economic life might be the price exacted."

There were three methods open to the governments for raising these vast sums — taxation, borrowing, and the issue of paper money — and it is a matter of record that all three were used, though in varying degrees by the different countries, the United States and Great Britain being the only countries that succeeded in raising by taxation any part of war expenditures. The United States raised about a third and Great Britain about a quarter of the costs of the war by vigorous and sustained taxation. In every belligerent European country the tax revenues were insufficient to meet the civil budget and the interest charges on the mounting debt. On the part of the Continental nations the feeling was general that the war itself constituted a sufficient burden without adding that of taxation. Some new taxes were introduced, such as the war profits, the excess profits, and the sales tax, and old ones were stepped up. Import duties proved non-dependable, especially for the blockaded countries. This was serious for Germany, whose peculiar constitutional structure had allocated this source to the Reich as almost its sole source of revenue.

The continued reliance of Germany upon borrowing is probably traceable, in part at least, to this fact.

Loans were of preponderant importance in war finance, for over four-fifths of the expenditures were met by borrowing. Every nation made use of this method. Except for about $3,000,000,000 borrowed in the first two years in the United States by Britain and France, each nation was forced to rely upon its own citizens to buy its bonds. By this mechanism titles to wealth and current production passed from private hands to the governments, and capital was diverted from normal peace-time enterprises to the prosecution of the war. The public debts of the various nations increased enormously. This is shown for the three leading belligerents (in millions, converted into dollars at pre-war values).

NATIONAL DEBT AT END OF FISCAL YEAR

	United Kingdom	France	Germany
1914	$3,248	$6,708	$1,273
1918	36,357	30,224	33,600
1920	40,385	46,025	49,250 *

* 1919, exclusive of indemnities. The debt for 1920, including payment for the railways and compensation to German citizens for war losses, was estimated at over 100,000 million marks.

A second form of borrowing was from the banks. Whether the advances were received by the governments in the form of bank notes issued by the central bank, as in France and Germany, or in the form of deposits, as in Britain, the universal result was an expansion of the means of payment beyond the normal needs of business — in other words, inflation — and a rise of prices.

A third method of meeting the costs of the war was by the direct issue of fiduciary paper money by the government. Great Britain authorized the issue of currency notes in denominations of one pound and ten shillings, and made them unlimited legal tender. By December 31, 1918, there were oustanding $1,616,205,000 of these notes. Although a small metallic reserve was held against them, it was so small, amounting on the date named to only 8.9 per cent, that they may fairly be regarded as primarily fiat money. France did not make use of this device, relying wholly upon bank notes issued by the Bank of France. Germany issued Imperial Treasury notes (*Reichskassenscheine*), which were payable to bearer on demand, exchangeable at the Reichsbank for bank notes, and acceptable at all public offices for public dues. On July 23, 1918, the amount in circulation was $86,000,000.

There was still a fourth way of meeting war costs and that was by the loan or gift of advances from other nations. Thus Great

Britain advanced huge sums, $8,695,000,000 in all, to France, Italy, Russia, the Dominions, and other allies. France, in turn, helped to finance Russia, Belgium, and Serbia. Germany granted financial assistance to Austria-Hungary, Turkey, and Bulgaria. After the entry of the United States into the war, that country made advances of about $9,500,000,000, mainly to Great Britain, France, and Italy. The presence of these inter-Allied loans greatly complicated post-war finance and introduced a disturbing factor in the settlement of the reparation problem.

The burden of war costs did not end with the termination of hostilities, for interest on the war debts had to be met. How serious this was may be seen from the fact that in Great Britain, France, and Germany the interest charges on the public debt for 1919 were alone greater than the entire pre-war civil budget. If the debt could be reduced the situation would be greatly eased. A capital levy on all wealth sufficient to expunge the national debt in a single operation was suggested but everywhere rejected, and less drastic methods were followed. Britain did not reduce the principal but succeeded, by a series of bond conversions, in somewhat alleviating the burden of interest charges. France wiped out four-fifths of her debt by devaluing the franc, and Germany got rid of hers altogether by the inflation of 1923. The concept of the sacredness of property rights was given a hard jolt by these actions.

Reparations. Both the Central Powers and the Entente Allies had signified during the struggle their intention of demanding reparations from their enemies if they were successful, and when the Allies won the war they lost little time in translating their threats into action. According to the pre-armistice declaration of November 4, 1918, which Germany accepted, she agreed to make compensation "for all damage done to the civilian population of the Allied and Associated Powers by aggression by land, by sea, and from the air." This phrase was literally interpreted by the American delegation at the Peace Conference, but upon the insistence of Clemenceau and Lloyd George it was stretched to cover pensions and allowances and other claims. It thus became possible to demand practically unlimited reparations from Germany. Opinions as to Germany's capacity to pay varied from the American estimate of $15,000,000,000 to that of the French of $200,000,000,000.

When the Treaty of Versailles was made with Germany it proved impossible for the Allies to agree upon the amount of reparations, so this point together with the method of payment was referred to the Reparation Commission, which was set up for that purpose. By the Spa agreement of July, 1920, the distribution of the reparations receipts among the creditors was fixed, but the total was still left undecided. Germany at first made a valiant effort to meet the terms of the Treaty, but, finding this nearly impossible, offered in 1921 either a capital sum of $12,500,000,000 or annuities totalling $50,000,000,000. This offer was indignantly rejected and instead the Reparation Commission that same year fixed the total bill at 132,000,000,000 gold marks or about $32,000,000,000. The next two years saw a steady deterioration in Germany's economic and financial condition and a falling off in reparations payments. Finally, in 1923, the Reparation Commission declared Germany in default, and French troops occupied the Ruhr in an attempt to obtain reparations by force. It soon became evident that this method offered no solution of the problem and finally the question was removed from the political sphere by the appointment of a committee of experts to bring in recommendations. Their report, known as the Dawes plan,[5] from the name of the American chairman, was made in April, 1924.

This plan, wrote Josiah Stamp, "was not a solution of the Reparation policy, but it was a substantial step away from lunacy." It did not fix the total reparations bill, but instead set up a schedule of annuities which for the first time represented a sincere effort to adjust reparations to Germany's capacity to pay. The annuities began with 1000 million gold marks in 1924–25 and rose to 2500 million in 1928–29, which was designated as the standard year. Half of this sum was to be obtained from general taxes, 290 million from a special transport tax, 660 million from bonds of the Imperial railway system, which was transformed into a joint stock company, and 300 million from a blanket mortgage placed on industry. All sums raised were to be paid into the Reichsbank, and credited to the various claimants. The creditors were to use the moneys in Germany or convert them into foreign currencies. Provision was made, however, to limit the accumulation of unused funds or their transfer if this would endanger the stability of the currency. In order to safeguard the carrying out of the plan an agent general for reparations payments was appointed, as were also a trustee for the railway and industrial bonds and three commissioners for railways, the Reichsbank, and the controlled revenues, all of whom were foreigners.

The inauguration of the Dawes plan ushered in a period of remarkable prosperity in Germany. The currency was stabilized, foreign capital flowed in to rehabilitate industry, and general business rapidly revived. By 1928 Germany had again attained her pre-war economic strength. The Dawes plan, however, provided

[5] This report is reprinted in full in C. G. Dawes, *A Journal of Reparations* (London, 1939), 278-511. It may also be found in *Current History*, May, 1924, in *World Peace Foundation*, Vol. VI, No. 5, 1923, and in H. G. Moulton, *The Reparation Plan* (New York, 1924), 139-308.

only a breathing spell and was not a final solution, for it did not fix the total amount of reparations which Germany was obligated to pay. After five years of successful operation, accordingly, the time was thought ripe for a more definitive solution of the reparations problem.

The Young plan [6] of 1930, made retroactive from September 1, 1929, was next put into force. This provided for annuities to run for fifty-nine years, totaling $28,800,000,000. The present actuarial value of these annuities was calculated as $9,250,000,000, which was somewhat less than the amount offered by Germany in 1921. The full and final responsibility for the payment of these annuities was placed upon Germany, and the whole apparatus of foreign control was swept away. A Bank for International Settlements was set up at Basle, which was to handle reparations payments and transfers. Provision was also made for the "commercialization" of a part of the reparations payments, that is the delivery of bonds which could be sold in the open market. The Young plan was a great advance over the Dawes plan, though it failed to constitute "a complete and final settlement of the reparation problem," as its framers hoped it would.

Accompanying the Young plan, though for obvious reasons not a part of it, was a so-called Concurrent Memorandum. In this the four chief creditor countries and Germany agreed that "any relief which any creditor power may effectively receive, in respect of its net outward payments on account of war debts," should be applied to reduce Germany's reparations payments. During the first 37 years Germany was to benefit to the extent of two-thirds of such net relief and during the last 22 years by the whole of it. Since what were diplomatically called "out-payments" were exactly the sums due the United States on its loans to the Allies, the Concurrent Memorandum attempted to tie up the war debts to reparations. The United States, however, refused officially to admit that there was any connection between them.

Before the Young plan had been in operation a year the world crisis and depression prevented its successful execution. Severe runs on German banks occurred, foreign capital was withdrawn from the country, and the government was compelled to restrict foreign exchange transactions and to enforce standstill agreements on its short term obligations abroad. So serious was the situation that President Hoover proposed a moratorium to run for one year from June 30, 1931, on both reparations and inter-Allied debts. This was agreed

---

[6] This report is reprinted in full in my *Young Plan and Other Papers* (Claremont, 1931), pp. 100-50. It may also be found in *Current History*, July, 1929, and in *Federal Reserve Bulletin*, August, 1929.

to, but the end of the year found international financial relations in an even more critical situation. Consequently in July, 1932, a new agreement was made between Germany and her principal reparations creditors, known as the Lausanne Agreement. This drastically reduced the reparation obligations to a total sum of $750,000,000, but this diminution was not to be effective unless the claimant nations were able to effect similar reductions of their war debts to the United States. As the latter country never agreed to any modification in the debts due it, the reparations owing by Germany were still legally those fixed by the Young plan. Practically, however, all payments ceased with the Hoover moratorium and were never resumed.

BIBLIOGRAPHICAL NOTE

The most scholarly and comprehensive study of the causes of the World War is S. B. Fay, *The Origins of the World War*, 2 vols. (2nd ed., New York, 1930). A brief dispassionate account is K. Page, *War: its Causes, Consequences and Cure* (New York, 1923). More economic are J. Bakeless, *Economic Causes of Modern War; a Study of the Period 1878–1918* (New York, 1921), and L. Robbins, *The Economic Causes of War* (London, 1937). A penetrating analysis is O. T. Crosby, *International War, its Causes and its Cures* (London, 1919). A French defence is R. Poincaré, *The Origins of the War* (London, 1922) and an English one is H. H. Asquith, *The Genesis of the War* (London, 1923). Imperialism is brilliantly sketched in A. Viallate, *Economic Imperialism and International Relations during the Last Fifty Years* (New York, 1923). Leonard Woolf, *Economic Imperialism* (New York, 1920) is a damning indictment. P. T. Moon, *Imperialism and World Politics* (New York, 1926) is a careful appraisal. The costs of the war are estimated in E. L. Bogart, *Direct and Indirect Costs of the Great World War* (2nd ed., Washington, 1920) and *War Costs and Their Financing* (New York, 1921). E. M. Friedman, *International Finance and its Reorganization* (New York, 1921) is a careful study. The economic and financial provisions of the Treaty of Versailles are thoroughly described in B. M. Baruch, *The Making of the Reparation and Economic Sections of the Treaty* (New York, 1920). A caustic criticism is J. M. Keynes, *The Economic Consequences of the Peace* (New York, 1920). J. F. Bass, *The Peace Tangle* (New York, 1920) shows some of the results. The most elaborate and careful account of the reparations plan is K. Bergmann, *Der Weg der Reparation* (Frankfort a.M., 1926. Translated as *The History of Reparations*. Boston, 1927). A later account, also by a German, is E. Salin, *Das Reparationproblem*, 2 Bde. (Berlin, 1929). An impassioned attack is M. Sering, *Deutschland unter dem Dawes Plan* (Berlin, 1928. Translated as *Germany under the Dawes Plan*. New York, 1929). E. L. Bogart, *The Young Plan and Other Papers* (Claremont, 1931) describes the later plan. A general survey is given in A. Philips, *Economic Aspects of Reparations and Allied Debts* (Leyden, 1930). The various aspects of reparations are carefully traced in a number of volumes published by the Institute of Economics: H. G. Moulton and C. L. McGuire, *Germany's Capacity to Pay* (New York, 1923); H. G. Moulton, *The Reparation Plan* (New York, 1924); H. G. Moulton and C. Lewis, *The French Debt Problem* (New York, 1925); H. G. Moulton and L. Pasvolsky, *World War Debt Settlements* (New York, 1926); H. G. Moulton and L. Pasvolsky, *War Debts and World Prosperity* (New York, 1932).

CHAPTER XVI

AGRICULTURE

I. THE GOVERNMENT RESCUES AGRICULTURE IN BRITAIN

Agriculture during the war. By 1914 British agriculture had adjusted itself to the world market and to the economic organization at home, and was enjoying a quiet prosperity. The nation depended upon imports for over half of its food, paying for them with exports of home manufacture. The merchant marine had in part supplanted the farmer. With the outbreak of war the situation changed. The long duration of the struggle and the German submarines made it increasingly necessary for Great Britain to augment the supply of food raised at home. But the urgency of the problem was not at first recognized and the early efforts to stimulate production were limited to education and administration. The prevailing *laissez faire* attitude opposed government intervention in the highly individualistic business of farming, and only gradually was there developed a vigorous policy to deal with the situation. This took two forms: stimulus to domestic production and control over consumption.

During 1914 no organized efforts were made, though as a result of higher prices and appeals to patriotism a larger area of land was sowed to winter wheat in the fall. There seemed no reason for worry, for bumper crops in North and South America more than made good the loss of Russian supplies, and there was abundance of food to be had. This situation held through 1915 and limited the activities of the government to appeals. The following year saw a change for the worse in almost every direction. The potato crop failed and the yield of wheat fell off a quarter, American crops were short, and finally in the spring of 1917 the submarine warfare interfered seriously with imports of food from overseas. At the same time the withdrawal of some 300,000 men from agriculture for army service created a serious labor shortage. This was met in part by the release of some men from the army for spring plowing and for harvesting, and by the employment of boys. In 1917 the government actively intervened, granting aid for fertilizer and agricultural implements and furnishing tractors to make good the labor shortage. This was also met by the use of prisoners, interned enemy aliens, boys, and for the first time women, who proved unexpectedly efficient.

Under the *laissez faire* policy before the war British farmers had turned from the raising of wheat, in the production of which they

495

could not compete with the virgin lands of North and South America, to livestock and perishable articles. Since 1870 the tillage area had decreased 3,375,000 acres: about 36 million acres were devoted to stock and 3 million to wheat and potatoes. But now the country needed the largest possible production of food in the shortest possible time. Since arable farming will support at least four times as many persons as the same area devoted to livestock, there could be no question as to the policy to be pursued in order to stimulate production.

The policy of subsidizing agriculture was introduced in 1917. By the Corn Production Act minimum prices were guaranteed for wheat and oats for the next six years, but at the same time maximum prices were fixed. Minimum wages were also guaranteed and restrictions were placed on raising rents. Tractors, reapers and binders, and other agricultural machines were furnished by the government, allotments were encouraged, permanent pasture was plowed up and planted in crops, and advice and encouragement given to the program to increase the home supplies of food. As a result of these efforts the production of wheat was increased in 1918 over 60 per cent, oats 50 per cent, and potatoes 40 per cent beyond the average of the decade before the war. Of the 1,400,000 allotments in cultivation in 1918 over 870,000 had been created since the war began; these gave employment to the industrial population and yielded valuable additions to the food supply, mostly in the form of vegetables. The most criticized part of the policy was the plowing up of some 2,500,000 acres of grass land and its use for crops. So eminent an authority as Sir Henry Rew stated that the total amount of food produced had been decreased — "cereals had increased, but meat and milk had decreased." Measured in terms of calories, however, the shift from meat to wheat was a gain, and, even more important at a period when cargo space was scarce, it successfully met a serious situation by freeing some three million tons of shipping for the transport of troops and munitions.

The second part of the war program was the conservation and rationing of the food supply, which was placed in the hands of a Food Controller. In order to make the best use of existing supplies certain industries, like brewing, were severely restricted, and the manufacture of such articles as flour, chocolate, and candy had to be carried on in prescribed ways; certain grains were limited to human food, and starch all but disappeared from the laundries. The government took possession of the flour mills and extracted a higher percentage of flour from the wheat, and also mixed the grains to make a coarser loaf. Foreign trade was taken in hand and the export of needed articles was forbidden, while only essential imports were admitted and these could be requisitioned by the government. Rationing was adopted as a method of assuring fairness in distribution as well as because of scarcity. This was begun in 1917 with an appeal to the nation, requesting every one to limit the weekly purchases of bread, meat, and sugar to specified amounts. Later meat, sugar, butter, margarine, and lard were rationed by the ticket system. Bread was not rationed as the supplies of wheat were sufficient at all times. The adequacy of the program seems to be evidenced by the fact that food prices rose less in Great Britain than in most of the European countries. For a great many articles prices were regulated, but there was a tendency for these to rise to the maximum; market prices were always higher than the minimum where this was guaranteed.

Post-war adjustments. The policy of war subsidies to agriculture was ended in 1921, and the British farmer was again exposed to international competition. During the war the United States, Canada, Argentina, and Australia had vastly expanded their wheat acreage — from 80 million acres in 1913 to 112 million in 1919 for these four countries — and when the European belligerents undertook again to supply their own needs for food, the augmented output glutted the markets. Prices fell more than half between 1920 and 1923. At the same time increased imports of meat, butter and eggs, and even fruit from abroad began to challenge British farmers in fields in which they had felt fairly secure. Under similar circumstances in 1815 the landowners had been able to pass a Corn Law to exclude foreign grain, but this was not possible now. The agricultural producers were consequently forced to adopt those lines which were most sheltered and would yield the largest returns. There was again a quick shift from arable to grass farming and by 1923 three-quarters of the 3,000,000 acres which the war needs had brought under the plow had reverted to grass. The decline was greatest in the south-midland and southern counties where new industries were springing up, and least in the north, owing possibly to the introduction of improved breeds of grains and plants. There was a geographical shift in land use, and arable farming retreated to those sections of the country most suited to it. Another shift was the concentration on special crops whose prices did not fall so rapidly as that of grain, such as fruits and vegetables.

Previous to the war the British farmer had used his grass land primarily for the production of beef cattle and sheep, but the importation of improved chilled beef from Argentina and of mutton from New Zealand now made this less attractive. To some extent the farmer held the domestic market by improvements in feeding which permitted him to bring "baby beef" to maturity in less than two years, but for the most part he turned to dairying and used the land for his milk herd.   Dairy cows and the output of milk both showed a large increase.   Sheep grazing fell off, the production of pigs was relatively unimportant, but poultry and eggs about doubled in the decade 1924–34.   By 1939 only 6,500,000 acres out of 25,-000,000 were planted in crops, the rest of the cultivable area being used for permanent grass or clover and rotation grasses for stock feeding.   A driving force in this agricultural readjustment was the steadily increasing cost of labor, which led to the selection of those lines requiring the least labor and which had a quick turnover.   The number of agricultural laborers fell from 643,000 in 1911 to 511,-000 in 1831, but by 1939 had increased with the general expansion to 606,000.   Such readjustments are, however, always painful and slow, and meanwhile a further disastrous fall in world agricultural prices in 1929 plunged the British farmer in still greater difficulties. Between 1928 and 1931, the price of wheat, which had recovered somewhat in the past half decade, fell almost half.

Return to protection.   In 1931 free trade was abandoned and for the first time in eighty-five years protection was extended to agriculture in peace time.   By the Ottawa Agreement of November, 1932, Great Britain taxed imported foreign food, but admitted Empire food free.   This arrangement minimized the protection given British farmers, but it especially hurt producers outside of the Empire.   The aim was to give first claim on the British market to British and Empire producers.   The causes of this movement were numerous: farm prices of most agricultural products were falling, imports were increasing — 60 per cent of all foodstuffs came from overseas, — industrial exports were declining, so that the balance of payments was becoming adverse, and the marketing system was ineffective.

Instead of a rigid Corn Law a mixed system of assistance was introduced, varying according to circumstances, composed of tariffs, subsidies, import quotas, and minimum prices.   A preliminary step had already been taken in 1924 when a subsidy was granted to factories on beet sugar refined by them.   It was hoped that the growing of sugar beets would provide a useful root crop in a system of rotation, and would also yield valuable feed for livestock.   Employment would be provided and the nation made more self-sufficient. The experiment was successful, and the home production of sugar increased from 24,000 tons in 1924 to 615,000 a decade later, but the cost to the government and to the consumer was heavy and the industry failed to become self-supporting.   In 1935 the scheme was reorganized and a Sugar Commission established, which was empowered to grant a subsidy, varying according to market prices, adequate to call forth a domestic output of not over 560,000 tons of refined sugar. Meanwhile the cost of producing cane sugar in other countries was halved, and a heavy burden was imposed on British taxpayers to support an uneconomic industry.

More important was the Wheat Act of 1931 which was designed to protect the British farmer against the disastrous fall in cereal prices, and to make the nation more self-sufficient. A standard price of 45 shillings a quarter ($1.37 a bushel) was guaranteed, and the difference between this and the market price, if lower, — a so-called "deficiency payment" — was paid to the wheat grower by the government. The funds were collected from the millers by an excise on flour. The policy was successful in stimulating wheat growing, though the increased acreage was offset by a decline in that devoted to oats and barley. Claims for similar assistance to these cereals were soon put forward and in 1937 the price guarantee was extended to oats and barley, but in this case the cost was borne wholly by the government. As a method of attaining national self-sufficiency in cereal production the system was unimportant, and the food bill of the nation was raised. Nor did it offer a solution of the problem of unemployment, for cereal growers tended to use machinery and to economize on labor whenever possible.

Beef producers had meanwhile been hit by increasing importations from Australasia and Argentina, and in 1932 steps were taken to restrict imports by a system of quotas. These were designed to favor Dominion trade, but quotas were applied even to them. When these mesaures failed to check the fall in meat prices, a subsidy policy was introduced in 1934 as a temporary measure. In 1937 this was made permanent. The purpose was not to guarantee a minimum price, as in the case of the cereals, but to grant assistance to a hard-pressed industry. From a national standpoint it is difficult to justify such a burden on the taxpayers, for it simply delayed an inevitable readjustment to world conditions. Still another branch of animal husbandry was meanwhile clamoring for protection. Imports of pork products had been steadily increasing and by 1930 about 85 per cent of the bacon and ham and 50 per cent of the pork consumed in Great Britain were being imported. Two years later imports were reduced by voluntary agreement with the exporting countries, and in 1934 a quota system was introduced designed to stabilize the total bacon and pork supplies at a point corresponding to normal consumption.

In one way or another the producers of the staple food products were protected against foreign competition. Certain other lines were, however, able to survive without protection and even to expand; such were potatoes, vegetables, fruit, poultry and eggs, and

milk. They occupied a somewhat sheltered position, for most of
these products could not stand distant transportation. This probably points the way along which British agriculture will make further
adjustments if the policy of protection is ever reversed.

In addition to assistance by tariffs, quotas, and subsidies, efforts
were made to improve the ineffective marketing system. Marketing
acts of 1931 and 1933 covered hops, bacon, fluid milk, and potatoes,
and aimed to secure orderly marketing and stable prices. A hog-
marketing scheme, introduced in 1933, was discontinued three years
later. Taken as a whole the program succeeded in checking the increase in grass land, raising agricultural prices, curtailing imports,
and improving the marketing organization. On the other hand
the cost of living index rose and the consumer helped pay the farmer's
bill.

Land holdings. The census of 1930 listed 294,292 farmers in
Great Britain and a somewhat greater number of holdings. After
eliminating scattered holdings under a single ownership and those
used for non-agricultural purposes a recent careful study[1] estimated
the following distribution in round numbers:

DISTRIBUTION OF AGRICULTURAL HOLDINGS IN GREAT BRITAIN, 1931

Size-group	No. of holdings	Percentage of total agricultural acreage in each size-group
150 acres and over	55,000	53
50–150 acres	110,000	35
1–50 acres	134,000	12

The 55,000 medium and large scale farmers cultivated slightly
over half of the acreage, but produced somewhat less than half of
the agricultural output. In their hands lay most of the production
of cereals and beef. Here the economies of large scale production
and of machinery gave them an advantage over their smaller rivals
and even enabled them to meet foreign competition. Most of the
110,000 medium holdings were devoted to mixed farming, in which
the cheap family labor played an important role. The small holdings of less than 50 acres contained only 12 per cent of the acreage
but produced 17 per cent of the output; they were able to hold their
own in certain lines like fruit growing, market gardening, and dairying, but those under 20 acres were generally unprofitable and were
to be justified on social rather than on economic grounds. As British
agriculture became more mechanized, employed more capital, and
concentrated on the production of high quality foodstuffs in bulk, the
advantages were all on the side of the large holdings.

[1] Viscount Astor and B. S. Rowntree, *British Agriculture, The Principles of Future Policy*
(London, 1938), 359.

The size of the holding is an economic and technical problem, that of land ownership is more social. Unfortunately no official survey has been made since the *New Domesday Book* of 1873, and today it is not known who owns the land or how much land is farmed by tenants. The changes that have taken place in the past sixty years and especially since the war have undoubtedly increased the number of proprietors and brought about a wider distribution of land ownership. Many farmers bought their land at inflated prices in 1920 and others after that time. With the increase in taxes and the rise in wages and other costs absorbing most of the rents, landowners were glad to sell their properties. It has been estimated that in 1921 there were 21,000 more landowners than in 1913. There was also an increase in occupying ownership, the number of tenant farms falling from about 90 per cent around 1913 to about 67 per cent in 1938, according to an estimate of the Ministry of Agriculture. A generation ago this shift would have been hailed by the advocates of peasant proprietorship as a great gain. Today, in view of the violent price fluctuations and the increasing dependence of the farmer on the market rather than upon agricultural technique, the advantages of ownership are not so obvious. Indeed, as a result of legislation regarding compensation for improvements, the tenant occupies a preferred position. In spite of minor shifts the main structure of the British land system remains essentially unaltered.

2. "BLOOD AND SOIL" IN GERMANY

German agriculture during the war. The chief food problem for Germany during the war was that of stretching insufficient and dwindling supplies to meet the irreducible needs of the nation. The seriousness of the problem was not at first recognized, for the war was expected to be short, and the food resources of the Reich were overestimated. Actually about one-quarter of the grain was imported, one-third of the feedstuffs for cattle, two-fifths of the fats, and a large proportion of the artificial fertilizers. Other foods, such as vegetables, fruits, rice, eggs, fish, and tropical products, were also drawn in still larger measure from other countries. The blockade, when it became effective, cut off about a third of the food supplies for humans and cattle upon which the German economy depended. Until 1916, however, existing supplies, the produce of German farms and purchases from neighboring neutral states were sufficient to prevent any scarcity from being felt. But beginning with that year and especially after the entrance of Rumania into the war and tightening of the blockade, supplies from them steadily fell off and Germany was thrown back upon her resources. And the longer the war lasted the more serious became the situation. In 1916 the total food imports amounted to 1685 thousand tons, in 1917 they were 574 thousand. Under these circumstances there were only two paths open: one was to stretch existing supplies by careful utilization and rationing, and the other to increase domestic production.

The first steps in the former program were taken in 1914 when it was prescribed that a larger percentage of wheat and rye must be converted into flour, and potatoes must be added before it was baked into bread. This was the so-called K-bread. The following year the percentage of flour to be obtained from the grain was raised, rye must be mixed with wheat flour, and the proportion of potatoes was doubled. The resulting coarse loaf was called KK-bread. In 1917 beets were added to the mixture. Meanwhile the bakers had been forbidden to use whole milk or cream in baking bread or cake.

The supplies of meat could not be stretched, like those of bread-stuffs, but they could be spread. In 1915 meatless and fatless days were introduced. Restaurants were forbidden to serve meat two days in each week, and on two other days they were severely re-stricted in the use of fats. In order still further to utilize to best advantage the inadequate supplies of meat and other food communal kitchens were established which served meals at reasonable prices. By the end of the war some 3000 such kitchens existed which sup-plied nearly 4,000,000 guests with food daily.

In the case of some articles, like coffee, existing supplies were ex-hausted by 1914 and for them substitutes (*Ersatz*) were invented. Roasted barley, rye, wheat, chicory roots, figs, and acorns served as substitutes for coffee, and for other semi-luxuries a multitude of substitutes were put on the market. It was estimated that by July 1919 there were 11,000 food substitutes on sale.

It was not enough to stretch or to spread existing supplies, but waste must be prevented. It was argued that the land devoted to raising sugar, half of which was exported before the war, could be better used for growing crops; beer and brandy were luxuries and the barley and potatoes used in their production were needed for food; and cattle consumed materials that would serve for human con-sumption. The efforts made to carry out these ideas ran into unex-pected difficulties. In the case of sugar a shortage showed itself in 1915 as a result of the decline in beet acreage, a decrease in the yield per acre, and the fall of the sugar content of the beets. The further reduction of production was prevented by the clamor of consumers for sugar, which even the general use of saccharin could not satisfy. When an effort was made to divert corn, potatoes, and other mate-rials from the manufacture of alcohol to human consumption, it was discovered that alcohol was necessary for industrial purposes, such as the manufacture of powder and ether, and for internal-combustion engines. To handle this problem an imperial liquor monopoly was established in 1916, which shut off the supply of alcohol for drinking and used it henceforth only for military, industrial, and medicinal purposes. To conserve the barley utilized for beer the amount which could used by breweries was in 1915 reduced to about two-thirds of the average before the war; by 1918 it was down to between 10 and 15 per cent, at which time the total output was only a third of what it had been.

The most serious problem was presented in connection with animal husbandry. The consumption of meat had been increasing markedly before the war, but this was now threatened since the feedstuffs, largely drawn from abroad, were cut off by the blockade. Domestic supplies were insufficient to support the existing herd of cattle and especially of hogs, and food fit for human consumption could not be diverted to their support. It seemed clear therefore that the number of livestock in the country must be reduced. In pursuance of this plan a wholesale slaughtering of hogs took place, which reduced these from 26 million in 1913 to 17 million in 1915. After various experiments with maximum prices and other schemes the slaughter of cattle was made an imperial monopoly in 1916, to be administered through local organizations.

Rationing was introduced early in 1915, at first for bread, but was soon extended to all sorts of food, and finally to other articles. The technique was that of ration cards. The actual distribution under this system varied according to the harvests and other conditions, but there was a steady reduction. The daily ration of bread was 7.9 pounds of flour daily at the beginning of 1915 and 5.6 pounds in 1918; fat fell from about a third of a pound daily in 1916 to slightly over a quarter in 1918. The most tragic restriction of all was that of milk, which was $\frac{1}{10}$ of a quart daily in 1917 and $\frac{1}{11}$ in 1918.

The second method of meeting the food problem was that of increasing domestic production. During the generation before the war Germany had made extraordinary increases in the yield per acre along many lines. In 1914 the per acre yield for rye, wheat, barley, oats, potatoes, and meadow hay was higher in Germany than in England, France, Italy or Russia, with the single exception of potatoes in which England had a slight lead. It was scarcely credible that this peace-time performance could be bettered during the war, and as a matter of fact there was a serious decline in every line.[2] The labor force was drained by the army, 1,000,000 horses were taken

[2] See table on p. 506.

for war service, artificial fertilizers, whose liberal use had been chiefly responsible for the great increase in yields, were cut off by the blockade, and in other ways the productivity of agriculture was lessened. The scarcity of labor was in part made good by the use of school children, convalescent soldiers, women, and prisoners. Of the latter 700,000 were employed in 1916, 800,000 in 1917 and 900,-000 in 1918. At certain crucial times, as during the harvest, agricultural workers were temporarily released from military service and sent back to the farms. An effort was made to increase the use of farm machinery to offset the labor shortage, but without much success.

Scarcely less important was the shortage of artificial fertilizers. Of potash Germany had ample stores, since she possessed almost a world monopoly of this resource, but nitrates and phosphates, the other two members of the fertilizer trinity, had come largely from abroad. The imports of phosphates fell to a fifth and of nitrates to a third of the pre-war amounts. The use of the latter would have stopped almost completely if the Haber-Bosch process of the fixation of the nitrogen of the air had not been invented. Without adequate supplies of these fertilizers, the yield of the naturally infertile soil of Germany fell off markedly.

Animal husbandry was equally hard hit by the cutting off of imports of feedstuffs and the necessity of using domestic crops for human consumption. Cattle, and especially hogs, were slaughtered in order to equalize the livestock with the available fodder. Efforts were made to utilize the land hitherto planted with grain for the growing of potatoes, which would yield larger returns both for humans and cattle, but these shattered on the lack of labor and fertilizer. The situation was a difficult one. If the number of animals were decreased in order to raise more crops, there would be a shortage of meat and milk, and also of animal manure. If, on the other hand, the animals were not slaughtered, they could not be properly fed. The average milk production per cow sank by a third, and the weight of animals slaughtered fell off. The weight of dressed cattle declined from 550 pounds before the war to 287 at the end of 1918, that of sheep from 48 to 35, and of pigs from 187 to 130.

Textile raw materials, such as flax, jute, and wool, had declined greatly before the war, as Germany depended increasingly on imported supplies. It was not possible suddenly to increase the production of these articles and for them substitutes must be found, as well as for cotton, whose supply was wholly cut off. Here science was called upon and paper made out of wood pulp was used for clothing and other purposes. Gardens, as in England and the

United States, were encouraged, and needed supplies of vegetables were grown. Potatoes and vegetables were dried in order to spread their use over the lean winter months. The treatment of sugar, alcohol, and beer, as part of a program of land utilization has already been described.

A careful study [3] of the food problem in Germany concluded that during the last two years of the war "The greater part of the civilian population were in a state of chronic starvation." The soldiers and munitions workers received adequate rations, and the farmers held back food sufficient for their own needs, but the urban professional and clerical workers were undernourished. For them the normal ration of 3200 calories per day of the pre-war period had been cut to between 1500 and 1600 calories by the end of the war. This undoubtedly contributed to the breakdown in morale which led to the armistice.

Agriculture after the war. The governmental control of agriculture continued until 1923, when all war measures were repealed. During this interval few changes took place in agricultural practice. The inflation period permitted the reduction of the mortgage debt on the land from 16,000 million marks to 4000 million, but this gain was offset by the fact that agricultural prices lagged behind others during the inflation boom. The fluctuating and usually low price of rye especially hit the Junker class, whose great estates in the northeast raised most of this crop. In all the reforms of this period they formed an intransigent group. Labor relations and wages underwent the greatest changes. The revolution of 1918–19 swept away the remnants of the patriarchal system, and in its place established one of equality. The legal and material position of labor improved. The agricultural workers were given unrestricted rights of combination and machinery was set up for collective bargaining and arbitration. By 1921 over 7600 agricultural organizations had been formed with 991,000 members. Minimum wages were set by law, though the powerful employers' organization managed to construe these in practice as maximum rates. Wages had lagged behind prices during the war, but after peace was declared they rose more rapidly, so that by 1921 both nominal and real wages were higher than they had been in 1914. In spite of higher wages, the movement of labor from the land to the cities, which had slowed up during the inflation period, began again after 1924. The large holdings were hard hit by labor shortage and high wages, and peasant holdings were increased by purchases from the owners of estates. The movement of labor out of agriculture was a natural adjustment to

[3] E. H. Starling, "The Food Supply of Germany during the War," in *Journ. Roy. Stat. Soc.*, March, 1920, 226.

conditions of non-expanding agriculture and developing industry, but by the Junkers, who wished cheap labor, it was regarded as a personal grievance.

The changes of territory brought about by the Treaty of Versailles reduced especially the areas devoted to rye and sugar beets, and to a less extent meat. Since there was an equivalent loss of population the main result was a shift in emphasis. The chaotic economic conditions following the war, the currency inflation, and the influx of cheap agricultural products from overseas, caused German farmers to reduce the production of marketable surpluses and to restrict their operations to their own needs. There was a great decline in the areas sown to cereals and root crops and a corresponding increase in the area under grass. The deficit of the early years could not be met by largely increased imports because of the lack of foreign exchange, and the result was inadequate supplies of food for the urban population and a decline in the standard of living.

At the same time there was a decline in the yield per acre, the nadir being reached in 1922. The following table shows the high point of 1913, the low of 1922, and the recovery after that date:

AVERAGE ANNUAL YIELD PER ACRE IN BUSHELS

Period	Rye	Wheat	Oats	Barley	Potatoes
1909–13	28.9	31.9	55.0	38.6	203.6
1922	18.2	19.2	31.6	23.6	201.6
1925–30	23.4	27.1	46.1	31.4	190.3
1936	26.3	31.3	56.2	38.5	246.4

After the restoration of the currency in 1924, conditions began to improve. The ten-year shortage of operating capital was gradually made good through farm credit organizations (whose resources were provided largely by foreign loans), although interest rates were 7 to 9 per cent. Mortgage and intermediate credits rose between 1925 and 1928 from 1 billion marks to nearly 4 billion, and millions of marks were invested in stock, machinery, and improvements. In 1925 essential foodstuffs, whose entry into the country had been free since 1914, were again protected by a tariff, but even more important were import quotas, import monopolies, and exchange controls, which developed later. By 1929 German agriculture had largely recovered from the effects of the war, but it was once more plunged into distress by the world agricultural depression. Prices fell disastrously and the government attempted to meet the situation by various measures. The tariff was raised, wheat flour must be 97 per cent from domestic wheat, a corn monopoly was established to limit imports, an import quota was set for butter, compulsory mixing of domestic potato alcohol with motor fuel was ordered, and hops used by brewers must be at least 75 per cent domestic. The home market was to be reserved to domestic producers and Germany was to be made as self-sufficient as possible.

Just prices were to be maintained by an elaborate system of regulation. All producers, distributors and processors were organized in market associations, on a regional basis. Such associations were set up for grain, livestock, dairy produce, eggs, sugar, potatoes, flour, feed, and other articles. Price control rather than price fixing was the central feature, and for this purpose the market associations fixed prices, regulated supplies, and prescribed charges for the various phases of processing. Imports and import prices were all closely regulated. Because of the scarcity of foreign exchange importers were required to obtain a foreign exchange certificate before being permitted to bring goods into the country. The efforts to make agriculture profitable to farmers and yet keep prices to consumers low, to adjust the production of grain as against livestock, to iron out shortages or surpluses, all gave rise to administrative difficulties. Through 1934 the main problem was to maintain minimum prices to aid producers, but after that maximum prices were fixed in the interest of consumers. Production, selling, and processing were brought under ever stricter control, extending even to quantities, kinds, and technical methods.

Agriculture under National Socialism. By the law of September 13, 1933, — the First Four-Year Plan — there was effected a complete reorganization and assimilation of German agriculture into the Reich Food Estate (*Reichsnährstand*) on a strictly co-operative basis. All producers, agricultural co-operative associations, and dealers in and processors of agricultural products were made compulsory members and previous organizations were dissolved. The announced aims were stability of tenure, just prices, and increase in production, and to achieve these a number of measures were put in force.

The Hereditary Farm Law of 1933 established over 700,000 "hereditary" farms — all those between 19 and 309 acres — in order to ensure a permanent agricultural class. Such farms provided an inflexible form of tenure, since they could not be sold, subdivided, or mortgaged. These farms made up about 44 per cent of the arable and forest land of Germany, and were especially important in Bavaria and western Germany. The owner must be of Aryan descent and upon his death only one child (usually the oldest) could inherit the estate. Neither a tenant nor a landlord could have a hereditary farm, but only an operating owner. The peasants were thereby to be transformed into a "new nobility," which would serve as a blood reservoir for the German people, in accordance with the slogan of *Blut und Boden*. Tenancy had never been very important in Germany, owing to the highly developed farm credit system, and had remained almost stationary at about 10 to 12 per cent of all land. It had, however, permitted poor but efficient farmers to climb the agricultural ladder and to become farm operators. After 1933 it was hampered by strict regimentation, although compensation for betterments was provided in order to encourage tenants to build silos and make other improvements.

The question of optimum size of the agricultural holding is of such interest that a slight digression may be made to examine the results of the agricultural censuses of 1925 and 1933. Since the latter did not include farm units of less than $1\frac{1}{4}$ acres, the following table has been constructed to show comparable data at those two periods and in 1907:

DISTRIBUTION OF AGRICULTURAL HOLDINGS, BY SIZE

Size in acres	Per cent of holdings			Per cent of cultivated acres		
	1907	1925	1933	1907	1925	1933
5–$12\frac{1}{2}$	43	43	34	18	12	9
$12\frac{1}{2}$–50	45	46	49	33	39	37
50–250	11	10	15	29	29	35
250 and over	1	1	2	20	20	19

Little change occurred between 1907 and 1925, but between the latter date and 1933 a small revolution took place. The number of holdings below $12\frac{1}{2}$ acres fell off 25 per cent and the land in these small farms declined over 1,000,000 acres. On the other hand, the medium holdings, from 50 to 250 acres, increased both in numbers and land area. These were the holdings on which improved technique and agricultural machinery yielded the largest returns and whose owners were the best educated. This was a reversal of the movement that had been recorded between 1882 and 1907, and seemed to indicate a new orientation of the peasant farmers. These were much readier to adopt new methods and to utilize machinery than they had been before the war. A comparison of farm equipment in 1906–10 and 1924–25 showed that at the former date 23 per cent of the small farms between 5 and $12\frac{1}{2}$ acres used agricultural machinery, and 66 per cent at the latter; for the next group, between $12\frac{1}{2}$ and 50 acres, the figures were 65 and 90 per cent. Half of the farms had electric motors in 1933, and haymowers, reapers, seed drills, and potato diggers were in general use. Mechanization had been adopted as a method of meeting the scarcity of labor.

The final goal was an increase in production in order to attain self-sufficiency. It was dramatized, as in Italy, by the so-called

"Battle of Production," which was launched in 1934. This aimed especially at increasing the production of articles which were largely imported. Toward the attainment of this end every possible means was employed — tariffs, subsidies for oilseeds and textile fibers and fruit trees, reclamation, drainage, improvement of breeds, larger use of fertilizer, economical feeding, elimination of waste, rational farm management, and constant propaganda. The success of these measures may be briefly recorded. Germany had produced relatively large quantities of the more staple and coarser foods, such as rye, potatoes, sugar and pork products, but lacked the lighter foods such as fresh vegetables and fruits. More attention was now paid to these.

The area of the land used for agriculture decreased slightly from 52,858,000 acres in 1913 (post-war territory) to 52,811,000 acres in 1937. Somewhat over three-fifths of the arable land at the latter date was under the plow and less than two-fifths was grass land. There was a decrease in the land devoted to oats and rye, but an increase in wheat growing; potatoes remained the same. The yield per acre, which had seriously declined during and after the war as a result of lack of fertilizer and of poor tillage, came back in part but failed to reach again the high point (except in the case of potatoes).[4]

There was a decided gain in the use of artificial fertilizers by the end of this period, compared with pre-war conditions.

CONSUMPTION OF ARTIFICIAL FERTILIZERS IN GERMANY
(pounds per acre of arable and grass land)

Year	Phosphates	Nitrates	Potash
1913–14	17.6	5.7	15.4
1936–37	19.1	17.8	29.5

A somewhat better showing was made in animal husbandry, both as to numbers and quality. Cattle fell from 18,474,000 in 1913 to 16,317,000 in 1922 and rose to 19,911,000 in 1938, and swine fluctuated even more, from 22,533,000 to 14,679,000 and to 23,-545,000, for the same three years; sheep and goats declined. But, taken as a whole, the destruction of the war years had by now been repaired. Weights were greater and the yield of milk was raised from an annual average of 490 gallons per cow in 1909–13 to 550 in 1937. German agriculture had, however, not recovered its pre-war efficiency and the country was less able to support itself in 1936 than it had been in 1913. The upper limit of land that could be profitably tilled had been reached, but the population was increasing at nearly the pre-war rate. Self-sufficiency for all requirements in

4 The table on page 506 shows the yield of the principal foods.

food, which was possibly 85 per cent in 1913, was about 75 per cent in 1933, and by 1936 it had been raised to 81 per cent. But this was not enough.

The Second Four-Year Plan. In 1936 there was launched, under the leadership of Hermann Goering, a comprehensive scheme whereby control over the whole German economy was centralized in the Four-Year Plan Organization. "In four years' time," said Hitler in explaining the purpose of the plan to the Nuremberg Congress in September, 1936, "Germany must be completely independent of foreign countries for all materials which can be produced in any way by German skill, chemistry, engineering or mining." The production of foodstuffs was especially emphasized even though profits disappeared. In order to supply the necessary stimuli for private producers and to prevent wasteful consumption the prices of rye and potatoes were increased to industrial users, the prices of artificial fertilizers were reduced, and subsidies were granted for the construction of farm buildings and improvements, including the purchase of farm machinery for general use. Credits were granted through the rent bank for mechanization to relieve the labor shortage. And finally all land available for agricultural use must be brought under cultivation; fallow had been reduced to less than two per cent of all land in 1931, but this was now put under the plow. But the slight gain was more than offset by the additional land used for military purposes, highways, and other needs, and for the growing of industrial fibers. There was actually a net loss in land used for food production.

Another step in planning of production and tighter consumption control was taken in 1937. As a result of the growing scarcity of bread grain consumption was restricted, the feeding of bread grain to livestock or its use for distilling was forbidden, and an effort was made to accumulate supplies in government hands. The mills were ordered to raise the extraction of wheat and rye flour from 75 per cent to 80, and to mix 7 per cent of corn flour with wheat, and 6 per cent of potato flour with rye flour. Truck crops were put under control to prevent over-production, but, on the other hand, high prices were guaranteed oilseeds in order to stimulate their production. The growing and marketing of hogs were closely regulated, and butter, lard, bacon, and tallow were rationed. Specified quotas for deliveries of grain were set up for each farm. The whole system was one of regimentation and planning to increase production and conserve supplies.

The effects of the second Four-Year Plan are difficult to gauge, for it was interrupted by war before the four years were over. Production in some lines was stimulated; root crops increased at the

expense of peas and beans and fallow. But the burden on consumers
was a heavy one. Domestic prices of important agricultural products, such as wheat, rye, butter, sugar, and wool, were 200 to 300
per cent above world prices. Rye bread was kept cheap by subsidies,
as was low-quality margarine. The food bill of the industrial workers and of the non-agricultural middle class was nevertheless raised
to privation levels. The total supply of foodstuffs in 1938 was
about equal to that available in 1929, but as the population had increased by 3,000,000 persons, consumption, especially of fats, had
to be reduced. An estimate of German self-sufficiency in respect to
foodstuffs and agricultural raw materials in 1935 showed that about
80 per cent of domestic needs of foodstuffs could be produced at
home; not so much of raw materials.

PROPORTION OF HOME PRODUCTION TO HOME CONSUMPTION *

Articles	Per cent
Cereals, potatoes, meat (exclud. pork), liquid milk, hops	98–100
Bacon, fresh-water fish, vegetables	90–97
Pork, fruit	80–90
Fowls, eggs, timber	70–79
Sea-fish	60–70
Total fats (incl. margarine and lard), hides and skins	50–59
Leguminous products	40–49
Tobacco	20–30
Flax, tannin	10–19
Wool	5–9
Oilseeds, oilcakes, vegetable oils	1–4

* Institut für Konjunkturforschung, April 17, 1935.

A limiting factor in all the plans to increase production was the
shortage of agricultural labor. The measures taken to create employment under the First Four-Year Plan had even accelerated the
rural exodus. In 1936, therefore, provision was made to prohibit,
without special permission, the engagement of workers trained in
agriculture for employment in non-agricultural undertakings. An
important step in building a closed occupational organization of agricultural workers was taken in 1937 by the establishment of an apprenticeship system for farm laborers. A boy worked for two years
on a farm and then took an examination in general farm duties; after
two more years on another farm he took a final examination and
became a qualified agricultural laborer and was entitled, after 1938,
to higher wages. Those workers who had already spent four years
on a farm qualified automatically. Agricultural labor was thus recognized as skilled labor and given a higher social status.

In other ways also efforts were made to render conditions more attractive for the agricultural worker. Long-term contracts were introduced in order to make employment permanent and not seasonal. Subsidies were given for housing and loans for furnishing were granted to newly married couples. In 1938 more positive measures were taken to ensure an adequate supply of farm labor. Individual youths, not trained in agriculture, were allocated to various farms (auxiliary land workers without allowances), organized groups of auxiliary workers (land service) were established, and settlement of agricultural workers' families (family rural aid) was encouraged. A year of compulsory service in agriculture was also established for women, and no woman under 25 years of age could be employed in industry unless she could show from her workbook that she had spent a year in agriculture or domestic service. In the planting and harvest season, when there was need of additional labor, men were sent to the farms by the Labor Front, by private and public enterprises, and even the students helped. Direct pressure was exerted at times by refusing unemployment relief to men capable of working at agricultural pursuits.

Efforts were also made to stimulate production, especially of those articles in which there were shortages. Interest rates on mortgages were compulsorily lowered, and mortgage indebtedness was reduced. Agriculture was burdened with a mortgage debt of about 12,000 million marks, the interest on which absorbed one-seventh of all agricultural income. The owners of "hereditary" farms, however, which could not be mortgaged, found it difficult if not impossible to obtain credit and were frequently unable properly to stock or equip their holdings. The main effects of this much publicized law were an enormous increase in the number of landless younger sons, the breakdown of the highly organized mutual agricultural credit system, and the promotion of a certain laxness since the farm could not be sold for debt.

Campaigns were started among consumers, entitled "Fight that Waste" and "Consumption Steering." The former is self-explanatory; the latter was designed to shape and direct consumer demand to available food supplies and market conditions. It emphasized especially the savings which could be effected by a vegetarian diet. The resulting shortage of labor forced an increasing mechanization of agriculture, though this was somewhat impeded by the relatively small size of the average holding. Parcellization was never so serious as in France and after 1933 regrouping of scattered holdings was hastened; between that year and 1937 about 1,000,000 acres were regrouped in compact holdings. Almost nine-tenths of the land was owned by cultivators; a larger proportion than in France and much more than in Britain.

3. PEASANT PROPRIETORSHIP SURVIVES IN FRANCE

The problems that confronted agriculture in France upon the outbreak of war in 1914 were different from those presented in either Great Britain or Germany. Only in France was there an actual decrease of arable, but here over 6,000,000 acres of cultivated land was occupied by the enemy until 1918, a reduction of 11 per cent below 1913. But the figures of acreage do not give an adequate idea of the loss involved, for among the invaded departments were some of the most productive areas of France. These had produced one-fifth of the wheat, one-quarter of the oats, and over half of the beets for sugar and distillation. The result of this loss of territory, together with other factors, was a serious decline in the output of practically all farm products, as indicated by the following figures:

| | Yield of certain crops (percentage of aver. of 1904–13) | | | | | Number of animals (percentage of aver. of 1913) | | |
	Wheat	Potatoes	Sugar beets	Wine	Milk	Horses	Cattle	Pigs
1918	69	48	20	81	52	70	83	57

The most serious loss was in beet production, which was concentrated largely in the northern invaded departments, but even wine showed a reduction, although the wine area was scarcely touched by the invasion. More serious from a nutritional standpoint was the reduction in potatoes and milk (which included its products, cheese and butter). Aside from the loss of territory the chief cause of the lessened production was scarcity of labor. It has been estimated that there were 5,200,000 men engaged in farming in 1913 and that 3,700,000 of these were mobilized during the course of the war. The remaining labor supply left on the farm was composed of those too old or too young for military service. This meager force was supplemented by over 3,000,000 women, who took the men's places, though they did not constitute a net addition as they were a normal part of the active agricultural population. Efforts were made to bring in immigrants, especially Spanish and Italians, of whom about 150,000 came in during the war. Prisoners of war, school boys and girls, and disabled soldiers were also drafted for service, and during the seasons of sowing and harvesting some agriculturalists were temporarily relieved of military duty and sent back to work in the fields. In addition to the scarcity of labor, agriculture was hampered by lack of fertilizers, never adequately applied in France, by the decline in animal power on the farms, by difficulties of transportation, and by the slight use of farm machinery. As a result there was considerable increase in the amount of uncultivated land, rising to 20 per cent of all by the end of the war. Prices of almost every item that entered into production increased greatly, while those for farm produce were held down by law.

French agricultural policy during the early years of the war was dominated by the desire to protect consumers from extreme increases in prices of foodstuffs. Imports were encouraged by the suspension of duties, while the export of articles necessary for the nation's food supply was prohibited. The reduction of supply, however, led to an upward movement in prices and this the government hastened to check. Prices of cereals, milk and its products, meat and live cattle, and a number of other commodities were fixed by law from time to time. In spite of legislation, prices continued to rise during the war, partly because of insufficient supply and partly because of inflation.

Efforts were also made to encourage production. The increase of motor tractors and other farm machinery was urged, but the unfamiliarity of French agriculturalists with these implements made their introduction difficult. Fertilizers were purchased and distributed during the last year of the war, uncultivated land could be requisitioned and put to use, and in other ways assistance was given to agriculture. These methods were not very effective, and crop yields and livestock showed a steady decline, reaching their lowest levels in 1918.

The control and rationing of food were undertaken in France as in other belligerent countries, though the practical self-sufficiency of the country in respect to the essential foodstuffs did not at first seem to warrant drastic measures. As the home supply fell off, however, and it became increasingly difficult to meet the deficiency by importation, the government intervened more vigorously. The percentage of extraction of flour from grain was compulsorily raised, in the case of wheat from 70 to 85, and wheat flour had to have fixed percentages of from 15 to 25 per cent of rye, barley flour, bean and other flours mixed with it. In 1917 the situation became so serious that the government set up a monopoly of cereals, taking over the domestic crop at a fixed price, and arranging for foreign purchases. The distribution of the supplies was effected through the flour mills, which were in turn subjected to strict control. Bread cards were issued entitling the holder to a specified ration of bread; in 1918 the card system was extended to all foods. As the home-grown supplies fell off the imports became more vital, but at the same time the intensified submarine warfare made it increasingly difficult to obtain these. In 1916 a wheat executive was set up in London, composed of representatives of France, Great Britain, and Italy, with wide powers to purchase needed supplies abroad, to ship, and to distribute these in agreed-upon proportions.

Meat consumption was not taken in hand until 1917, but then two meatless days each week were prescribed, which were raised to three the following year. At the same time the imports were taken over by the government and inter-Allied machinery for their joint purchase, similar to that for cereals, was established. The same procedure was followed in the case of sugar. Different measures were taken in respect of wine, oil, potatoes and dried vegetables, beer and cider, pastry, confectionery, cheese, and other articles, varying from stimulation of imports to limitation of consumption.

The object of all these measures was to obtain the principal commodities that the country needed and to effect their proper distribution. While the full amounts needed to maintain the high standard of living that prevailed before the war were lacking, and some semi-luxuries like cake and chocolate disappeared from general consumption, there was at no time a failure in the supply of essential foodstuffs. The determination to hold down the price of bread to consumers involved a heavy loss to the treasury, which bought foreign wheat at high prices. Down to the end of 1918 the excess of expenditures over receipts for grain and flour cost the Food Department about 2500 million francs. This may be regarded as a bread subsidy, and was about the same as the cost to Great Britain of a similar policy.

Agriculture after the war. Decontrol of agriculture was begun soon after the armistice, but it proceeded slowly and was not finally accomplished until August, 1921. Prohibitions of imports and exports were gradually canceled and it was hoped that pre-war conditions would be restored. Agriculture was, however, confronted by a serious situation. Over 8,000,000 acres of land had been devastated, dug up by trenches, torn by shell holes and traversed by miles of barbed wire, over 300,000 farm buildings had been damaged and destroyed, and nearly 2,500,000 head of livestock had to be replaced. By 1923 most of this damage had been repaired, but the productivity of the devastated area was still only about 85 per cent of what it had been before the war.

Advantage was taken of the situation to reorganize the scattered holdings. In a considerable number of communities the boundaries of individual properties were suppressed and by a law of 1919 the conditions of rearrangement were fixed. Such operations showed the peasants the advantages of co-operation, and were particularly successful in those regions where associations for joint purchase or use of agricultural implements had been created. The lease for livestock (*cheptel*) too was reduced; at the time of the armistice it was only a tenth of that in 1913, and in the next twenty years this amount was halved.

The shift from cereal production to animal husbandry, which had been proceeding before the war, was greatly accelerated by that event. Crops which required much labor were largely abandoned. The amount of plowland showed a great decrease, while grass land and forests increased. Permanent pasture pushed down the mountain sides and forced crops onto more fertile land. At the same time, owing to the scarcity of labor and also its diversion to other uses, the amount of land not used in agriculture grew considerably. The character of animal husbandry was itself changing. The world market was now being flooded, not only with cheap grain, but with frozen beef, mutton, and pork, and the French farmer again showed his adaptability, in the face of changing economic conditions, by giving more attention to dairy production. Between 1913 and 1936 the number of swine and goats remained practically stationary, and that of horses increased slightly, but there was a decline of almost half in the number of sheep. Only in the case of cattle was there an appreciable gain, from 14,788,000 to 15,762,000.

Agricultural policy. The French government did not regard the decline of the arable land with equanimity, and after 1919 developed an active agricultural policy designed to maintain diversified farming in spite of adverse conditions. This took three lines. In the first place imports of competitive articles were restricted. Tariff rates were practically doubled, but even more effective were import quotas, which were imposed on livestock and meat, butter and cheese, grains, truck crops such as potatoes, dried beans and peas, certain fats and oils, and fruits. The policy was successful in curtailing drastically the imports of the major agricultural products. In the second place, grants and subsidies were given to certain distressed crops, which suffered severely from international competition. The purpose was to maintain prices at a point that would make domestic production profitable. At times direct price fixing was employed. As a case in point, the domestic price of wheat was raised to $1.72 a bushel, almost double the world price. Milk prices, which slumped badly with the increase in production, were held up by higher tariffs, import quotas, and finally export subsidies. Wine was helped by a reduction in output and regulation of sales and a vigorous export propaganda.

The third line of attack was educational and social. The organization of agricultural credit and insurance associations, both mutual and co-operative, was stimulated, and co-operative marketing and purchasing associations were formed. In 1935 there were 1800 co-operatives for threshing and using agricultural machinery. In order to make country life more attractive, the government undertook road construction, rural electrification, improvement of rural water supply, more satisfactory schools, and other betterments.

These various efforts did not materially affect agricultural production, but they undoubtedly helped prices, and possibly prevented a decline in the lines selected for assistance. The cost to the government was, however, a heavy one and the burden upon consumers was still greater if measured by the difference between prices in France and those in the world market.

In spite of legislation the area planted in cereals fell off. Between 1913 and 1938 there was a decline in wheat from 16,439,000 acres to 12,474,000, in rye from 3,000,000 to 1,640,000, in barley from 2,000,000 to 1,889,000, and in oats from 10,000,000 to 8,096,000, or a total for these four crops of about 7,500,000 acres. The loss in acreage was, however, in part made good by an increase in yield per acre in every case. Thus, between 1913 and 1935, the average number of bushels per acre for the same four crops rose as follows: 19.7 to 29.8, 17 to 19.2, 26.6 to 30.9 and 36.5 to 46.2. Of other crops, potatoes were the most important, about half of the product being used for human consumption and a third for fodder.

The causes of the shift from arable to grass were numerous, but the most important was the greater relative profit to be obtained from livestock. Prices of meat did not fall as rapidly as did those of bread. The shortage of labor and the lack of adequate working capital favored animal husbandry, and on the other hand there was an increasing demand for meat from urban and industrial centers, while the consumption of wheat bread remained about the same and that of rye decreased rapidly. The French farmer followed the example of British and Danish agriculture and concentrated upon dairy and high-priced animal products and depended less upon the production of grain. More than 70 per cent of the farmer's income came from the sale of livestock and animal products. Agriculture in France tended to become intensive, leaving the extensive production of cereals to new lands and power machinery.

Unlike the Danish or Dutch farmers, however, who specialized in dairy farming, few French peasants carried on dairying as a business. Cows were widely scattered and each peasant owned one to three. There was little scientific breeding, and the animals were badly housed and insufficiently fed. The result was a very low yield of milk per cow — only 380 gallons in 1929, according to the census of that year. Compared with the annual yield in Germany of 550 and in Denmark of 700 gallons per cow, this was a poor showing. About half of the milk was converted into butter and cheese, which were produced principally on the farms.   Milk separators were in general use, and some 2200 co-operative dairies were established, but these treated only one-seventh of the French output.

Ownership.   The question of ownership of the land does not arouse such excited debate among French writers today as it did before the war, perhaps because agricultural changes have pushed the peasant proprietor up in the economic scale.   During the war prices had been held down, but when price controls were removed they shot up as a result of market conditions and of the rapidly mounting inflation.   Many of the peasants, thinking that prices would remain high, hastened to buy land, which owners sold without reluctance. *Métayage* declined, as the share renters purchased the land they were farming.   As more land changed hands, the parcellization of the holdings became worse.

It is dangerous to generalize about this period, for no agricultural census was taken after 1892 until 1929, but a comparison of the findings of these two reports reveals some interesting changes.   Although there was an increase in total acreage, due to the incorporation of Alsace-Lorraine, the number of holdings shrank by almost a third.   The greatest fall occurred in the small holdings up to 25 acres.   The medium holdings of 25 to 125 acres showed the greatest expansion both as to number and acreage.   It seems evident that these shifts reflected the changes in the types of farming that were taking place in France.   Three-quarters of the farmers in 1929 were proprietors cultivating their holdings, for the most part with the aid of the family.   *Métayers* made up only 5 per cent of all.   The changes as to land holdings are shown in the following table:

LAND HOLDINGS BY SIZE IN FRANCE—1892 AND 1929

Size of holding	No. of holdings (in 1000)	Per centage	Acreage in 1000	Per centage	No. of holdings (in 1000)	Per centage	Acreage in 1000	Per centage
Less than 2.5 acres	2235	39.2	3,072	2.7	1015	25.6	1,791	1.6
2.5–25 acres	2618	45.9	25,657	22.8	1864	47.0	23,603	20.7
25–125 acres	765	13.4	34,376	30.9	973	24.6	55,422	48.6
Over 125 acres	85	1.5	45,525	43.6	114	2.8	33,263	29.1
Total	5703	100	106,630	100	3966	100	114,079	100

Productivity of agriculture.   French peasants have always been reluctant to spend money for fertilizers and agricultural machinery;

and while the census of 1929 showed an improvement over 1892, the returns were discouraging. In that year there were in all France only 1,389,000 mowers, 739,000 horse rakes, and 354,000 hay makers, though the expansion of grass land and of animal husbandry would seem to have required larger numbers. Even if only the 1,087,000 holdings of 25 acres and over used these implements, they were poorly equipped. Machines for arable farming were still fewer: 322,000 drills, 420,000 reapers, and 204,000 threshing machines. There was thus one hay mower per holding, only one half of the operators had reapers, and still fewer the other machines. The peasants were equally backward in the use of fertilizers, and used less per acre than any other country in Europe. There had, however, been a great improvement in this respect since before the war.

CONSUMPTION OF ARTIFICIAL FERTILIZERS IN FRANCE
(lbs. per acre of arable land)

Year	Phosphates	Nitrates	Potash
1909	70	12	4
1929	117	32	9

In spite of improvement and of the fact that agriculture was the most important French industry, it lagged behind other countries in western Europe in efficiency and productivity. Responsible for this was primarily the fact that agriculture was chiefly in the hands of peasants, who cultivated small farms cut into tiny strips, used little agricultural machinery or fertilizer, and were slow to adopt the best practices in cropping, animal breeding, or scientific agriculture. Only his indomitable industry and thrift enabled the French farmer to make progress behind a high tariff wall.

Agricultural organization. The farmers pursued their efforts at organization after the war with considerable success. In 1925 there were about 10,000 agricultural syndicates with 1,250,000 members, which was 25 per cent more than in 1913. About 4000 of these were producers' co-operatives, especially dairies, associations for the utilization of agricultural machinery, and wine growers. Since the local groups could not defend their interests effectively, national associations were formed. By an act of 1919 regional and departmental offices were created to facilitate contracts between the government and the co-operatives. A decade later chambers of agriculture were created to represent this interest and to give advice.

Mutual agricultural credit had been established by local and regional banks twenty years before the war, and in 1920 the structure was completed by the creation of a national bank of agricultural credit. This bank distributed the subsidies received from the Bank of France and an equal sum from the government; by the end of 1933 these together amounted to 1500 million francs. The long-term loans, up to a maximum of 25 years, were of great assistance to the small proprietors and enabled them to make the necessary transformations in the methods of production. Even M. Augé-Laribé, the ardent proponent of these associations, was forced to admit, however, that "the advantage of organization has not been understood as rapidly as one could have wished." [5]

Conclusion. Agriculture may be regarded, from a national point of view, as a source of the food supply of the nation, or from a private point of view as a business enterprise run for the sake of profits. In a Europe torn by war or the fear of war the first view has largely determined recent agricultural policy, and each nation has striven to make itself agriculturally self-sufficient, at least for the main staples of life. While absolute independence of outside supplies, or *Autarchie*, is impossible, the desirability of lessening such dependence was vividly illustrated during the World War. Indeed the final outcome was determined in large measure by the inability of the German people to obtain outside supplies adequate to maintain even a minimum standard of health and efficiency. Consequently government policy during the next twenty years was directed to meeting this danger, though methods differed greatly from one country to another.

Protection to agriculture was generally adopted, even Britain deserting her free trade policy in 1931 to extend much-needed aid to agriculture. This was not new, but now its scope was broadened and it was raised to new heights, even to the point of absolute exclusion of foreign products in some cases. New techniques were, moreover, adopted, and, in addition to customs duties on imports, quotas, fixed prices, clearing agreements, and other devices were used to control and direct international trade in agricultural products. The repercussions on food-exporting countries were severe and, as these saw their markets closed, they were in turn forced to manufacture for themselves goods which they had formerly imported and paid for with their agricultural products. The former international territorial division of labor was upset and new adjustments had to be made both in Europe and the newer countries of the world.

Increase in production was sought by various methods. It was not enough merely to exclude foreign competition, but domestic production must at the same time be stimulated. This was dramatized by the "Battle of Wheat" in Italy in 1925 and a decade later by the somewhat broader "Battle of Production" in Germany. For this

[5] *Syndicats et coopératives agricoles*, 155.

purpose subsidies, reclamation, drainage, improvement of seeds and breeds, rationalization, and constant propaganda were utilized. The results were, however, somewhat disappointing and new disequilibria were introduced into traditional methods of farming. Soviet Russia sought to attain the same end by the more radical program of establishing highly mechanized collective farms, on which large scale operations with the most modern farm machinery would cut costs and increase the yield. The results of this experiment in communism were still uncertain when they were interrupted by war.

Science and education were also invoked to solve the problems of production. Physics, chemistry, biology, entomology, and other sciences were used to determine the nature of the soil best adapted to particular crops, the character and amount of fertilizers that would produce the best results, the propagation and selection of improved strains of seeds and livestock, and the prevention of disease. Farmers were taught better methods of farm management, accounting systems were devised and introduced, and agriculture was transformed from an art to a science.

Except in Russia, farming was left in the hands of private enterprisers and the profit motive was supposed to supply the necessary stimulus to production. Unfortunately, however, this was no longer as powerful as it had been, and for the change a number of factors played their parts. Agriculture in Europe was in an almost constant state of depression during the twenty years following the World War. Primarily responsible for this was the competition of overseas products, whose production had been enormously increased during the war. Prices fell disastrously, especially for cereals. The first reaction of European farmers was to retreat to those fields in which competition was least severe, such as the raising of livestock, dairying, fruit growing, and similar lines. But this demanded a radical readjustment, and was a painful and slow process. Another factor was the inelasticity of demand for most agricultural products. In the case of industrial articles a fall in price usually taps lower strata of demand and an increased supply is thus taken off the market. But in the case of foodstuffs the human appetite is not elastic and an increase in supply is apt to leave an unwanted surplus in the hands of the producers. The state, however, did not sit idly by in this emergency, but endeavored by every means in its power to bolster agricultural prices — by tariffs, subsidies, loans, and the fixation of prices at remunerative levels.

Another difficulty which the farmer faced was the disparity between the prices for agricultural products and those for manufactured articles. He could no longer buy as much as he had formerly, nor could he pay wages comparable with those earned in the factories. His standard of living declined, and labor deserted the farm and flocked to the cities. It was not always possible to make good this loss by the use of machinery, for frequently his farm was too small, or his crops of a nature that did not permit its use. In spite of these adverse conditions there was an increase in ownership of farms during this period, which in Germany was even prescribed by law.

The European farmer in 1940 stood in a very different position than that which he had held in 1914. He was much less independent, much more under the tutelage of the state, and more inclined to look to the state for help. The distinction between agriculture as a national agency and as a private enterprise was much less clear. Political rather than pecuniary considerations increasingly dominated agricultural policy, and the farmer tended to become a servant of the state.

BIBLIOGRAPHICAL NOTE

1. *Britain.* The food problem during the war is discussed in B. H. Hibbard, *Effects of the Great War upon Agriculture in the United States and Great Britain* (New York, 1919), a preliminary sketch; T. H. Middleton, *Food Production in War* (Oxford, 1923), an authoritative study; and H. Rees, *Food Supplies in Peace and War* (New York, 1920), a good summary. A careful general survey is P. L. Yates, *Economics of Food Production* (London, 1940). J. A. S. Watson and J. A. More, *Agriculture; Science and Practice of British Farming* (3rd ed., Edinburgh, 1933) describes farm management. O. W. Wilcox, *Reshaping Agriculture* (London, 1933) and A. D. Hall, *Agriculture after the War* (London, 1920) describe changes. J. A. Venn, *The Foundations of Agricultural Economics, together with an Economic History of British Agriculture during and after the Great War* (2nd ed., Cambridge, 1933) is a scholarly work. W. A. Astor and K. A. H. Murray, *The Planning of Agriculture* (Oxford, 1933) is a preliminary survey of an ambitious and careful study: W. A. Astor and B. S. Rowntree, *British Agriculture: the Principles of Future Policy* (London, 1938). A valuable official report is Great Britain, Agriculture and Fisheries Board, *Agricultural Output and Food Supplies of Great Britain* (London, 1929).

2. *Germany.* Two excellent studies of food conditions during the World War are A. K. F. Skalweit, *Die deutsche Kriegsernährungswirtschaft* (Stuttgart, 1927), and F. Aeroboe, *Der Einfluss des Krieges auf die landwirtschaftliche Produktion in Deutschland* (Stuttgart, 1927). A broader study is K. Hanefeld, *Geschichte des deutschen Nährstandes* (Leipzig, 1935). Two careful general surveys are O. S. Morgan (Ed.), *Agricultural Systems of Middle Europe* (New York, 1933) and L. G. Michael, *Agricultural Survey of Europe: Germany* (U. S. D. A., Dept. Bull. No. 1399. Washington, 1926). The efforts to settle peasants in East Prussia are described in H. Schnee, *German Colonization, past and present* (London, 1926), and C. Turnor, *Land Settlement in Germany* (London, 1935). M. Sering, et al., *Deutsche Agrarpolitik auf geschichtlicher und landeskundlicher Grundlage* (Berlin, 1922) is more technical than historical. J. B. Holt, *German Agricultural Policy, 1918–1934* (New York, 1936) gives the history. J. Müller, *Wirtschaftskunde von Deutschland auf wirtschaftsgeographischer und wirtschafts-*

geschichtlicher Grundlage (Leipzig, 1936) attempts to justify Nazi policies on geographic and historical grounds. An excellent statistical survey of German economic life from 1913 to 1923 is *Deutsche Wirtschaftskunde: Ein Abriss der deutschen Reichsstatistik. Bearbeitet im Statistischen Reichsamt* (2te Aufl., Berlin, 1933).

3. *France.* There are two good studies of French agriculture during the World War: M. Augé-Laribé, *L'agriculture pendant la guerre* (Paris, 1925), and M. Augé-Laribé and P. Pinot, *Agriculture and Food Supply in France during the War* (New Haven, 1927). A general survey is D. Zolla, *L'agriculture moderne* (Paris, 1917). A. Garrigou-Lagrange, *Production agricole et l'économie rurale* (Paris, 1939) gives a clear description of French agriculture and economic organization. C. Rist, G. Pirou, et al., *De la France d'avant guerre à la France d'aujourd'hui* (Paris, 1939) give a penetrating interpretation. B. Nogaro, *Les prix agricoles mondiaux et la crise* (Paris, 1936) is a specialized study.

CHAPTER XVII

INDUSTRY

I. BRITAIN STRUGGLES FOR LEADERSHIP

Industry during the war. Like any organism upon which a serious wound is inflicted, the British economy suffered a severe shock from the outbreak of the war, but, like a living organism, it adjusted itself more or less quickly to the new conditions. Of all the belligerents Britain experienced the greatest difficulty in making the necessary readjustments, largely because of its high industrialization and specialization, and also because of the prevailing economic philosophy of non-governmental interference. There were two obstacles to a speedy and complete adaptation of peace-time industry to war conditions. One of these was the very general belief that the war would be over in a comparatively short time, and that therefore it would not be necessary or desirable to make radical changes in the industrial organization. The other was the general insistence that there should be no interference with normal business. It was thought that private industry could meet the new war demands without sacrificing normal production. Months of stress were required to force home the grim lesson that modern war is fought not only by the soldiers at the front but by the whole national economy. It was estimated that for each man in the trenches, six were needed in the rear to provide food, munitions, clothing, and other supplies. For the first time in military history modern technical science pitted machines, the output of factories, and other resources of the belligerents against one another. Peace-time industry was consequently utterly deranged; the normal functioning of supply and demand was abrogated, land transport was upset, shipping was short, and labor was constantly drained from industry. New methods of organization and control were necessary.

The munitions industry was the first to call for attention. Neither government munition plants nor private armament firms were in a state of readiness in August, 1914, but by the following April were able to supply the British demand and in part that of the Allies. The Defence of the Realm Act (nicknamed D O R A), passed in March, 1915, gave the government wide powers of control. These were needed. Labor was restive, strikes were frequent, and trade union restrictions held down production. The co-operation of the workers was won by Mr. Lloyd George, as Minister of Munitions. Labor was "diluted" by the use of women and unskilled labor, plants were reorganized, specialized, and expanded, and priority regulations regarding raw materials, transportation, labor, and credit assured the war industries essential supplies. This was especially true of metallurgy. Probably no other industry underwent such profound modification during the war. A sufficient supply of raw materials was guaranteed by placing pig iron and steel on the list of prohibited exports. Between June 1915 and June 1916 the production of rifles was trebled, of machine guns it was increased fourteenfold, of bombs it was thirty-three times greater, and of high explosives sixty-six times. Industries not considered essential to the winning of the war, on the other hand, were pushed to the wall. By the spring of 1917 the government was in practical control of the production of munitions, and especially of the supply of iron and steel.

The control of coal production was taken over very tardily, though the problems in this field were serious. Production, and with it exports, was falling, prices were going up, and labor was intransigent. The difficulties which confronted the industry were serious. Half a million men were drawn from the mines for military services, or practically half the pre-war labor force, so that there was a continuous labor shortage. Under the Conscription Act, however, coal miners were protected against enlistment. There was also a shortage of mine timber, of machinery, and of other equipment. Price fixing was adopted for inland consumption, the miners were partly cajoled and partly threatened, and the export trade was regulated. In February, 1917, the entire mining industry was brought under state control. A campaign for economy in residential consumption of coal was inaugurated, and finally rationing was put in force. The production of coal for the war years was as follows: 1914, 266 million tons; 1915, 253 million; 1916, 256 million; 1917, 249 million; 1918, 227 million.

The textile industry presented different problems, for much of the wool and all of the cotton and silk were imported. The government was first of all concerned to maintain in the country an adequate supply of wool. Restrictions upon the export of certain kinds of wool and cloth were established in the fall of 1914, but the growing scarcity caused a rise of prices and in 1916 the government took over the entire wool clip of the United Kingdom, and the following year purchased the crossbred wool from Australia and New Zealand. This was sold to manufacturers at fixed prices. Manufacturers were classified into three groups, producing respectively for military requirements, export, and civilian needs, and priorities were granted in this order.

Cotton and hides and leather were also put under government control and systems of rationing were put in effect, but interference with private industry was not carried as far as it had been in the case of wool.

Industry after the war. The damage inflicted on British industry by destruction during the war was negligible, but that caused by dislocation was serious. The industrial plant had been enormously expanded along some lines, and this must now be converted from military to peace-time purposes. Other lines had been permitted to run down and these needed rehabilitation. New industries had sprung up and old ones had lost their importance. Shifts in industries occurred in response to political and social changes, which would have been accounted a revolution before the war. Some idea of the movements may be obtained by comparing the results of the census of 1911 and of 1921:[1] the number of workers in domestic service declined 300,000 and those in agriculture 100,000, but on the other hand those engaged in the iron and steel and metal-working industries increased by 321,000, in mining by 160,000, and in civil service by 230,000.

The world which post-war British industry confronted was very different from that of the pre-war period. Peoples were impoverished by the long struggle and their buying power was lessened, currencies were disturbed, banking and commercial relationships broken, and trade was disorganized. New states had been created, and in these even more than in the older states, the spirit of nationalism led to high tariffs and the establishment of competing industries. Demand for British products fell off and markets shrank. While demand was less the productive efficiency of industry was increased by changes in technique and industrial organization. The war stimulated the use of labor-saving devices, new machinery and new methods were introduced, and science was applied to industry. New processes, new metals, new chemicals, new machines revolutionized manufacturing. Many new products were introduced, such as aluminum, rayon, synthetic dyes, radio, airplanes, and still others. And in 1921 this changing scene was still further complicated by a financial depression. Britain's early pre-eminence was lessened in some of her leading industries, such as coal, iron and steel, cotton textiles, and to a less degree shipbuilding and woolen textiles. The developments can probably best be traced by a survey of some of the most important industries.

Mining. Coal and iron were the basic resources upon which were built up Britain's major industries. From 1900 to 1913 Great Britain produced annually more coal than all the rest of Europe together, and today is estimated to possess one-third of all the reserves in Europe. These are calculated at about 193,000 million tons.

[1] Committee on Industry and Trade, *Report*, II, 9.

The other principal mineral produced in Great Britain was iron ore, but here her position was much less satisfactory. Although there are vast deposits — 1000 million tons or more — most of them are low in iron content and contain much phosphorus. No other minerals of outstanding importance are produced.

The stormy career of coal during and after the war illustrates vividly the vicissitudes of British industry. The year 1913 marked the greatest production, but after that it fell off steadily, with a slight recovery in 1937. Annual production in million tons was as follows: 1913, 287; 1924, 267; 1934, 221; and 1938, 232. The chief cause of the slump was the decline in exports, due in part to the disorganization caused by the war and in part to the depression in trade. Before the war France was Britain's best customer, but after peace she obtained German reparation coal, and the same was true of Italy, Britain's second best customer. And even after reparation payments ceased Germany retained these markets. Between 1913 and 1936 Italy's imports from Great Britain fell from 900,000 tons to 60,000. Exports to Germany, Britain's third best customer, declined over forty per cent, and smaller countries also bought less. The home consumption remained fairly steady at around 180 million tons annually. Expansion in the demand for coal was checked, among other things, by the increasing use of oil, and by greater economies in the use of coal. The wasteful bee-hive oven was supplanted by by-product plants, whose gases were used for heating purposes, thus saving fuel; boiler and furnace designs were improved, and central power stations built. The difficulty and cost of mining were also increasing as the mines were sunk deeper and wages went up. Mechanical equipment to cut and carry the coal was used only in the best mines. The combination of decreased exports, increased costs, and improved technique in the utilization of coal at home had disastrous effects upon the coal industry and it cried to the government for relief.

In 1919 a Coal Industry Commission was appointed to investigate the causes of unrest among the miners and to make recommendations as to the reorganization of the industry. This broke with liberal English tradition and recommended state ownership of the coal mines. The government, however, rejected nationalization, but provided for higher wages and shorter hours. In spite of this a serious strike occurred in 1921, and another still more disastrous one in 1926. The owners asserted that they were producing at a loss and demanded a reduction in wages, while the miners protested that the decentralized and unco-ordinated nature of the industry — over 3000 mines were operated under separate ownerships in 1921 [2] —

[2] R. A. S. Redmayne, *The British Coal-Mining Industry during the War* (Oxford, 1923), 270.

made for inefficiency, particularly in the smaller undertakings, that private management was incompetent, and demanded state ownership and operation. Although this was not done, the government granted assistance and the industry struggled on under private ownership, always on the edge of bankruptcy.

The best hope for the coal industry seemed to lie in the development of new processes and uses, especially the carbonization of coal and the sale of its products. These included gas, coke, coal tar, ammonia, and sulphur. Upon coal tar alone were built important chemical industries. The larger use of electricity, obtained from the use of coal as fuel, also offered an outlet. The immediate problems, however, could not be met by the slow development of new processes and coal mining remained a "sick" industry. Finally, in despair, the nationalization of the coal mines was decided upon. A Coal Commission was set up under an act of 1938, which was to have vested in it after July 1, 1942, the ownership of all coal and certain associated minerals, and was to promote the efficiency and better organization of the coal mining industry. The compensation to the private owners was fixed at £66,500,000.

Iron and steel. The war forced a modernization of the British iron and steel industry by cutting off the supplies of rich foreign ores. Upon them and the non-phosphoric British ores had been built up the converter acid process of steel making. Great Britain had practically inexhaustible supplies of iron ore, phosphoric in nature and with a low iron content, but conveniently located. When it became necessary to fall back upon these resources, the open hearth basic process of converting the resulting pig iron into steel was adopted. The changes are shown in the following table:

PRODUCTION OF STEEL IN GREAT BRITAIN, BY PROCESSES
(in 1000 gross tons)

Year	Converter		Open Hearth	
	Acid	Basic	Acid	Basic
1913	1049	552	3811	2252
1918	755	551	3881	3986
1928	477	....	2169	5669
1937	254	418	2215	9660

The new developments in technique, indicated by these shifts, temporarily handicapped British industry. The replacement of the Bessemer acid process by the open hearth basic process necessitated extensive changes in British plants. The larger use of scrap steel reduced the output of the blast furnaces, and the substitution of steel for wrought and cast iron, on which Britain had specialized, reduced the demand for the latter. War forced improvements that the conservative manufacturers, steeped in tradition and with a heavy investment in (sometimes obsolete) plant, had been unwilling to initiate. The most striking change in the British iron and steel industries after 1917 was the increase in productive capacity in certain branches. The increase in efficiency was least in the blast furnaces. These lagged behind Continental and American practice, many of them being below the standard of size required for efficient working. The average weekly output of British blast furnaces was somewhat over 1000 tons, although there were American and Continental furnaces capable of producing that amount daily.

FURNACES IN BLAST AND PIG IRON PRODUCED

Year	Average furnaces in blast	Pig iron make (tons)
1913	337	18,260,315
1918	317	9,107,384
1928	140	6,611,300
1939	....	9,183,000

Steelmaking and rolling mills practice made a much better showing, largely owing to the scrapping of relatively inefficient small plants during and after the war, and their replacement by more modern types. Coking plants did not show much improvement.

The close association of blast furnaces and steel works, which is so striking a feature of American practice, made more headway. Localization of different branches of the industry was, however, still predominant. The movement toward combination, which had begun before the war, received a great impetus during the years 1916 to 1920, when steelmakers saw the desirability of assuring themselves raw materials and finishing works. A small number of vast undertakings were formed on vertical lines, from coal mines to merchant houses. In spite of this the official Committee on Industry and Trade was able to make in 1928 the following caustic criticism: [3] "Few British works, if any, are modern throughout in equipment and practice, with coking ovens, blast furnaces, steel furnaces and rolling mills adjacent to one another, and making full use of waste gases." There was considerable improvement after this, but it was not possible to start with a clean page. Rationalization might go too fast, as it did in Germany between 1926 and 1933, but it did not go fast or far enough in Britain. Since the products of this industry were so heavy the location of the works was important. The early practice had been to base the industry on coal and to locate near the coal

[3] Committee on Industry and Trade, *Report* (London, 1928), Part IV, 27.

mines, but as coal deposits were diffused this resulted in scattering the plants. As technological improvements reduced the amount of coal needed for smelting, the industry moved to the vicinity of iron. This resulted in a considerable concentration in the Midlands and also near the sea, where foreign ore was landed and from which exports could be easily shipped.

The total foreign trade in iron and steel, both imports and exports, declined from about 6,000,000 tons in 1913 to slightly over 3,000,-000 tons in 1936, but the exports fell much more rapidly than imports. The imports were mostly crude or semi-finished products, while the exports consisted chiefly of finished iron and steel products. The year 1913, a boom year, saw the highest exports in the history of the country, and they did not again regain that level. The imports of African, Spanish, and Swedish non-phosphoric ores were very important for the manufacture of fine products, of which Sheffield was the center. The competitive position of Great Britain in the iron and steel industry was made difficult by the expansion of the industry in other countries. Recent changes are shown in the accompanying table.

RELATIVE POSITION OF FIVE IRON AND STEEL PRODUCING COUNTRIES
(per cent of total production)

	Pig iron			Steel		
Country	1913	1929	1939	1913	1929	1939
United Kingdom	14	8	9	12	9	10
France	7	10	8	7	9	6
Germany	15	13	23	25	14	20
United States	42	44	33	48	48	36
Russia	6	4	16	....	4	14
All others	16	21	11	11	16	14
World production (million tons)	74	97	108	68	118	147

The most striking feature of the table is the expansion of Russia, but Germany also forged ahead, while France lost ground. Britain just about held her own. British producers endeavored to meet the situation by co-operative action; in 1929 they formed the British Steel Export Association to centralize the selling of plates, sections, and joints, and in the same year they organized the British Steelwork Association to promote the use of constructional steel and steelwork. But now they were threatened with the loss of their home market, as foreign products invaded Britain itself, and they clamored for protection. In 1932 duties of 33⅓ per cent were imposed on pig iron and on semi-finished steel and most finished products.

Textiles. Although second in importance to the metal industries, the textile industry employed more people and contributed more to foreign trade than any other. Including allied industries it employed over 1,000,000 workers and accounted for over a quarter of the country's exports in 1937. The cotton industry still ranked first, followed by the wool industry, and rayon. Since the various branches differed so in their characteristics and problems they must be treated separately.

The outstanding features of the cotton industry were the extreme specialization of its constituent parts, the high degree of localization, and the slight development of integration of any kind. Including the merchants and finishers, the industry in 1924 contained over 3000 small, highly specialized undertakings. The economies of integration and mass production were impossible in such an unorganized industry. The localization in Lancashire was originally due to its damp climate and the proximity of coal fields, and, after the importance of these was lessened by new techniques, the eminence of this area was perpetuated by the inventiveness, industry, and thrift of those engaged in the industry. No marked changes seem to have taken place since the war, and the technical equipment, which had been raised to a high degree of efficiency before that event, remained practically unaltered for a quarter century. The result was that most of the factories were equipped with relatively old machinery; the "mule" spindle was still used largely instead of the faster "ring" spindle, and few automatic looms were employed. The industry was very strongly unionized and it was difficult to introduce improvements. There was a slight increase in the number of spindles and a decline in the number of looms after 1913. The supreme position which the country had once held gradually slipped away. In the eighties Britain had one-half of the world's spindles, in 1914 about one-third, and in 1936 slightly over one-quarter. Of the looms in the world Britain had eighteen per cent in the last year.

These shifts do not reveal the changes that were going on within the industry. Owing to the rise of cotton mills in new producing areas British manufacturers concentrated more and more on the finer "counts" in yarn and on superior quality in piece goods. Consequently there was not so great a shrinkage in value as there was in quantity. The cotton industry probably suffered more from the effects of the war than any other industry, the decline beginning in 1913 and accelerating rapidly after 1929. For this there were several reasons. As additional countries developed their own industries, the international market shrank. And of this shrunken total Britain's share became smaller. The changes in production and export may be briefly shown.

PRODUCTION AND EXPORT OF COTTON YARN AND PIECE GOODS *

Year	Cotton yarns (1,000,000 lbs.)		Cotton piece goods (1,000,000 yards) †	
	Production	Export	Production	Export
1910–13	1922	1432	8044	6673
1924	1352	942	5426	4625
1930	1047	137	3320	2407
1937	1350	159	3386	1922

* British statistics of the textile industry are most unsatisfactory. Even in official publications figures differ from table to table, and in some cases are quite irreconcilable.

† Before 1930 the figures are for linear yards, in 1930 and thereafter in square yards. Since a linear yard is slightly more than a square yard the earlier figures are somewhat exaggerated.

In addition to the severe international competition, especially from Japan and China, other factors contributed to the terrific decline. The disturbed state of the world, the depression of 1930 and subsequent years, and changes in demand affected the industry adversely. Under the last head may be mentioned the lessened use of lining in clothes, changes in women's dresses, and a tendency to spend on amusement and recreation rather than on clothing.

The characteristic feature of the wool textile trade was the small size of many of the industrial units. Small scale undertakings were prevalent in nearly all branches of industry, and on the whole the operating unit was distinctly smaller than in the cotton industry. Most of the mills were owned by individuals or private firms. There was little standardization because of frequent changes in demand and the requirements of the export market. Mass production scarcely existed. The woolen and worsted branches of the industry were differently organized. In the woolen branch it was quite common for a single firm to carry on all the processes from the preparation of the raw material to the weaving and frequently the dyeing and finishing of the cloth. In the worsted branch, on the other hand, many firms confined themselves to a single process, as buyers, combers, spinners, weavers, or dyers. Such an organization permitted the formation of a monopolistic combination at any particular stage, and some developed from time to time. The reasons for this striking difference were partly historical and partly technical and need not be retold here. Comparatively little improvement in the mechanical equipment of the spinning and weaving sections of the industry seems to have been made since 1913, but the combing section was making larger use of machinery. The industry as a whole was highly concentrated in Yorkshire. The production and export of woolen and worsted goods were as follows:

Production and Export of Woolen Goods in Great Britain *

	Production of woolen and worsted tissues	Exports	
		Woolen tissues	Worsted tissues
Year	(1,000,000 square yards)	(1,000,000 square yards)	
1909–13	550	127	98
1924	443	165	57
1935	408	110	42

* Since 1913 the unit of quantitative measurement has been square yards, whereas before the war it was linear yards.

The decline in the industry as a whole was due in part to a shift of demand to other textiles and in part to a decline in total world trade. In the world market Britain maintained her leading position. Strong light is thrown on the difficulties confronting the industry in a report by the West Riding Chamber of Commerce, giving the reasons for the decline in the export of worsted stuffs, such as dress goods and linings.[4] Among these were the following: (a) Changes of fashion, such as preference for cotton, silk, and rayon wear, and for knitted rather than woven garments, and the lessened amount of material and of linings per dress. (b) The high cost of production, owing to the highly specialized nature of the product and of the processes. As a result of changes in demand the nature of the cloth changed; tissues were of lighter weight, cotton, silk, or rayon were mixed with the wool, fancy designs in delicate colors or intricate patterns were common. The industry became increasingly one of specialties, involving a greater risk of fluctuations, because of changes in fashion. (c) More intensive competition from the Continent, accentuated in some cases by depreciating exchanges.

The home market also declined and for this the following reasons were assigned:[5] (a) Reduced spending owing to a decline in real wages or to unemployment, and to heavy taxation. (b) A diversion of spending from clothing to other articles, as motor cars, motor bicycles, radio, cinema, and other amusements. (c) The high retail price of wool textile goods.

Changes in the structure of industry. An effort may now be made, on the basis of this survey of individual industries, to describe the general changes that were occurring in industry. A striking and disturbing factor was instability of demand. This was in large part the result of the shift in demand from staple goods to semi-luxuries, itself a result of a higher standard of living and a partial redistribution of the national income. Since the demand for

[4] Quoted by Committee on Industry and Trade. *Report*, III, 212.
[5] Ibid., 213.

conveniences and luxuries is more elastic than that for necessities, industry became more speculative and business fluctuations more severe. This was accentuated by changes in fashion, which introduced a new element of uncertainty in already speculative enterprises. We have already seen the operation of these forces in the textile industries. Some writers have distinguished between "old" and "new" industries, the former group, which produced staple goods, having declined since the war, and the latter or semi-luxury group having expanded.

OLD INDUSTRIES

Year	Pig iron	Steel	Coal	Export cotton piece goods	Export woolen and worsted goods
	(production in million tons)			(million linear yds.)	(million sq. yds.)
1910–13	9.64	6.80	270	6673	226
1932	4.12	7.00	207	2032	94
1939	9.18	15.12	232 (1938)	1922 (1937)	....

This slowing down of the production of staple goods was a world-wide phenomenon, and seems to have resulted from changes in habits and tastes. Responsible for this were shifts in the age-composition of the population as the birth-rate slackened, cheapening of the staples which set free a larger proportion of the incomes for other things, a changed psychology which preferred present goods to future goods, and technical improvements. The effects of these various changes gave new opportunities to some industries, but hurt others, especially those engaged in mass production. These were further hit by the shrinkage of foreign markets.

Between 1913 and 1929 there was a considerable increase in the total physical volume of production, in spite of the decline in most of the staple goods. The explanation is to be found in the expansion of numerous industries which before the war were of minor importance. Such were the motor, cycle, aircraft, electrical apparatus, radio, chemical, canned goods, rayon, hosiery, and the newer non-ferrous metal industries. Motor vehicles, electrical apparatus, and rayon may be cited as outstanding examples.

NEW INDUSTRIES, PRODUCTION

Year	Motor vehicles (1000)	Rayon (million lbs.)	Electrical machinery and apparatus (1000 £)
1913	44	3	14,000
1935	399	113	83,000 *

* 1930.

These shifts in production reflect the changes in the consumption of goods which have occurred within the past generation. Food is demanded in greater variety rather than in increased quantity. Clothing has shifted from woolens and cheap cottons to more aesthetic materials such as rayon. And the growth of leisure together with larger purchasing power on the part of the manners of the people has called into being entirely new industries, such as motor vehicles, radio, motion pictures, electrical appliances, and others. The relative decline of the old or staple industries did not imply the industrial decadence of Great Britain, but rather that she was adjusting herself to new conditions. In any dynamic society it becomes possible to produce the grosser necessities of life with a smaller expenditure of labor and resources, and to devote the surplus to the gratification of wants of a higher order. Such changes make for progress, even though they are attended by pains of readjustment.

Industry also suffered from difficulties on the side of supply. Changes in technique and organization increased productive efficiency. Standardization, with a view to eliminate waste caused by unnecessary multiplication of different patterns and to ensure interchangeability of parts, was widely introduced. An illustration of waste caused by failure to standardize, cited by the Committee on Industry and Trade,[6] was that of pit tub wheels: one firm had 3000 patterns in stock, whereas in their opinion fifty would meet the needs of the whole country. An obstacle to standardization in British industry existed, however, in its dependence upon foreign markets, with their uncertain and fluctuating demands. Mass production of standardized articles meant competition with the other industrialized countries and the probability of over-expansion. The production of quality goods seemed to offer more promise for the future than quantity goods.

Combination. One method of escape from these perplexities seemed to be along the line of combination. The growth of this movement may be regarded as one aspect of the profound transformation that was taking place in the organization of British industry. It had received a great stimulus during the war, but many of the combinations formed during that period broke down when industry was decontrolled. In the earlier post-war years many vertical combinations were formed for the purpose of ensuring supplies of raw materials and outlets for the finished goods. The Committee on Trusts compiled a list in 1919, not complete, of thirty-five combinations in the iron and steel industry, and stated that in the matter of iron castings used in building houses the combine controlled

[6] *Report,* Part I, p. 32.

ninety per cent of the total industry, all of the galvanized sheet iron, and eighty per cent of the metal bedstead firms. Two great consolidations controlled most of the chemicals made in the country; the electric industries, soap, tobacco, wallpapers, salt, cement, and textiles were also objects of combination. It was particularly marked in the basic industries, but it showed itself to some extent in nearly every industry. "We are satisfied," stated the Committee on Trusts,[7] "that Trade Combinations and Combines are rapidly increasing in this country, and may within no distant period exercise a paramount control over all important branches of British trade." The movement proceeded at so rapid a rate that the Balfour Committee [8] a decade later called attention to the "tendency for separate productive undertakings to associate themselves with other similar enterprises with a view to regulating output, prices, marketing, or other matters."

The causes of this movement were not so much the desire for monopoly profits as the necessity of obtaining productive economies. The committee just quoted believed [9] that "the first step towards putting British industries in a position to compete successfully in overseas markets is to subject their organization and equipment to a thorough process of reconditioning. . . The reconditioning of British industry," they went on to say, "will undoubtedly involve a great deal of scrapping and replacement of plant, and enlargement of the industrial unit, both by growth and by the re-grouping of units through consolidation or other forms of association, so as to obtain the full benefits of large-scale production, elimination of waste, standardization and simplification of practice."

The method pursued was largely that of self-regulation by the industry concerned, with a minimum of government interference. Governmental action was mostly confined to specific authorization of combination, as in agriculture, coal, and cotton, or of encouragement, as in the case of iron and steel and chemicals. Most of the combinations were, however, entirely voluntary, and were designed to curtail capacity, to integrate industry, to unify selling, or to control prices and output. The legal attitude towards combination in Great Britain was liberal, though not so much so as in Germany. In the case even of complete consolidations there were no legal obstacles to their growth and no special conditions were imposed, except those applying to joint stock companies in general.

The results of the combination movement may be noted in two or three typical industries. The iron and steel industry, as recently

[7] *Report* (London, 1919), 11.
[8] *Final Report* (London, 1929), 176.
[9] Ibid., 297.

reorganized, was probably the most completely controlled British industry. It sought technical reorganization through integration and the formation of larger producing units, and the suppression of competition. Behind the tariff wall a federated organization of some thirty-five price-fixing and quota associations was formed, covering practically every iron and steel material and finished goods produced in Great Britain. In the case of coal mining the total output was fixed and each mine was assigned its share. Prices were fixed by district committees. In the textile industry very different degrees of combination and control existed in the various branches. The wool industry achieved least, but even here prices were fixed and surplus wool-combing machinery was scrapped. The cotton industry went much further and during the single year 1937 destroyed 1,900,000 mule-equivalent spindles, reducing the total from 58,000,000 in 1913 to 43,000,000 in 1937. Prices were fixed by an industrial association, without government supervision.

The development of private control in British industry was essentially a depression phenomenon and rested upon the assumption that free competition had failed. Collective control, designed to stabilize production or prices, was substituted for *laissez faire* in one sphere after another. The policy of protection encouraged the growth of trade associations and combinations in a large number of industries, and even in non-protected industries a similar movement showed itself. There was, however, the danger that this development might lead to private monopoly and to monopolistic control over prices, and accordingly the government intervened directly in an increasing number of instances and assumed new economic responsibilities. A profound change was evidently taking place in the British economic structure and in the relation of the state to industry.

2. GERMANY'S RECOVERY

Industry during the war. The outbreak of the war, in combination with the disturbances in trade and transportation, the disorganization of credit, and other disarrangements of the industrial system, brought about a sharp reduction in the volume of production. The output of coal sank within a month to one-half of the pre-war production, and other branches were similarly affected. Unemployment increased as factories and mines closed down. The first effect of war on the national economy was one of disorganization and panic. Gradually, however, industry was reorganized on a war basis. It took about eight months to effect this transformation. The whole constitution of industry was changed. Since the state had not accumulated supplies for war, it drew upon the resources of private industry, generally by purchase but sometimes by confiscation. Thus, in Germany, the state took over the harvests and the stores of metal. It also regulated labor, transportation, the use of capital and credit, and other activities. Modern war is a struggle between national economies, involving the entire population, on the basis of universal military service, the production of highly technical equipment, attempts to weaken the enemy, and other factors. The immediate effect of the war was to make the conditions of production worse. A vivid illustration of this is furnished by the gradual drying up of the supplies of raw materials, many of which came from abroad. Foreign trade statistics are not available for the war years, but the movement of freight upon the railways gives a clear picture of the shrinkage of these supplies.[1]

MOVEMENT OF IMPORTANT RAW MATERIALS UPON GERMAN RAILWAYS
(1913 = 100)

Year	Cotton	Jute	Wool	Dyewoods	Skins	Iron ore
1913	100	100	100	100	100	100
1914	82	73	100	90	97	70
1915	65	18	69	120	107	65
1916	19	4	48	50	84	77
1917	13	4	42	20	68	71
1918	10	3	33	35	65	69

The growing shortage of labor also contributed to the decline in production. As more men were called to the colors, the labor force was diluted by the employment of more women. These had constituted one-third of the working population in 1913, but by 1918 they made up one-half. The proportion of unqualified workers also grew. At the same time food conditions became much worse and malnutrition reduced the productivity of the workers. The index figure of industrial production sank steadily during the war years, and in 1918 it was only 57 per cent of the volume of 1913. Moreover, substitutes had frequently taken the place of the original articles, so that there was a qualitative as well as a quantitative decline.

The peculiarities of war consumption contributed also to the disorganization of industry. The normal process of production reproduces capital or finished goods as these are consumed, and their consumption creates a further demand. But war consumption represents pure loss and is without an economic equivalent. This was somewhat modified by a drastic restriction in private consumption, but as the drain of war became greater even this could not offset

[10] R. Wagenführ, "Entwicklungstendenzen der deutschen und internationalen Industrieproduktion 1860 bis 1932." In *Vierteljahrshefte zur Konjunkturforschung.* Sonderheft 31 (Berlin, 1933).

the destruction that was taking place. The men in the army were consumers only and not producers, and they consumed not only consumption goods but also capital goods. Existing supplies of raw materials and finished articles were used up, capital equipment was not replaced as it wore out, transportation facilities and other agencies were not repaired, and the whole industrial machine became less efficient.

As industry was increasingly organized to meet war needs, different branches were affected quite differently. The industries which primarily served war needs, such as chemicals, coal, iron, and metals, held their own best, and some of them, like chemistry, even earned enormous profits. Those industries which served purely private needs, as housing, furniture, and similar lines, suffered the greatest decline, as they were denied materials, labor, and other facilities, and at the same time demand fell off owing to the general impoverishment. A third group which served both war and private needs, as textiles, clothing, food, etc., stood between the two extremes. Taken as a whole, however, the economic and technical effects of the war upon industrial production can only be described as unfavorable. The maintenance and renewal of productive equipment were neglected, the productivity of the workers sank, the relations between separate groups in industry were completely destroyed, and the total volume of production steadily diminished. Germany's share in world industry, which had been 15 per cent in 1913, fell to 7 per cent in 1919.

The strong concentration upon war production affected the organization of industry. Scattered private demands for such things as clothing and food were now concentrated in large part in the army, while the production of munitions called for the closest coordination. A planned economy replaced in part the normal price and profit system. At first private organizations were combined and the combine was charged with the necessary production. Good prices were paid by the state for the products which it purchased and the administration was left in private hands. Later the state took part in the management.

Industry after the war. During the twenty years following the armistice German industry underwent such kaleidoscopic changes that it will be necessary to trace these by periods. The first period was that of the conversion of industry from a war to a peace basis. The demobilized soldiers had to be re-incorporated into the industrial system. This could not be done quickly, and unemployment followed; by January, 1919, there were about six and a half million unemployed, but this figure was gradually reduced. The deferred demands for consumption goods of every description called for satis-

FIGURE 8.   RUHR COAL AND IRON FIELDS

From Blanshard and Visher's *Economic Geography of Europe* (McGraw-Hill Book Company, Inc., 1931) as adapted from Brooks and LaCroix's *U. S. Geological Survey Bulletin* 703. Reprinted by permission of the publishers.

faction, and the supplying of these needs provided work, while the apparatus of production, which had suffered serious injury during the war, had to be repaired and replaced.

The Treaty of Versailles deprived Germany of vital parts of her pre-war resources. On the basis of 1913 production Germany surrendered 19 per cent of her coal, 74.5 per cent of her iron ore, 26.7 per cent of her blast furnaces, 19.2 per cent of her raw iron and steel, 15.8 per cent of her rolling mills, and 68.5 per cent of her zinc foundries.[11] The most serious loss was the iron ore of Lorraine, from which Germany had drawn about 75 per cent of the supplies used in the Ruhr iron and steel district before the war. This highly integrated industry was now broken up, for France received the iron ore, while Germany retained the coal; mines, cokeries, blast

[11] J. W. Angell, *The Recovery of Germany* (New Haven, 1929), 363.

furnaces, and rolling mills were separated from each other by national boundaries. The cession of Alsace brought with it also the loss of highly developed textile mills. As a result of these and other factors industrial production fell off greatly, and in 1919 the country was producing approximately the same quantities of goods that it had turned out in 1888.

The year 1919 marked the lowest point in industrial production, and after this the situation gradually improved; by 1922 the industrial index was about 70 per cent of 1913. The mild inflation of this period acted as a stimulus, especially for the capital goods industries, and the owners profited greatly. Wages lagged behind prices, and the saving to manufacturers on this account has been estimated at between 24 and 28 billion gold marks, much of which was used for plant expansion. At the same time the inflation permitted the enterprisers to pay off mortgages and other indebtedness at a fraction of the original amount.

The fall of 1922 saw a turn for the worse. Inflation proceeded at an increasing tempo, prices rose to unbelievable heights, and normal conditions of supply and demand, of wages and costs of production, became unpredictable. By 1923 production had fallen a third below that of the previous year, though it did not reach the low level of 1919. This abnormal period was brought to an end by the "inflation crisis," which was followed by stabilization of the currency and recovery.

The six year period 1924–29 witnessed a remarkable rehabilitation of German economy from a condition which appeared almost hopeless. Several factors contributed to this end. There was first of all the pressure of necessity. The loss of territory and of resources compelled a better utilization of those remaining. The industrial plant had, moreover, run down during the war and was in many respects impaired and obsolete. A thorough reconstruction was necessary, and advantage was taken of the situation to build the new plant on the latest lines and to equip it with the most modern machinery. This was made possible by the aid of foreign, largely American, capital, to which German industry had ready access after stabilization had placed credit on a sound basis. As a result the German industrial plant became one of the most modern in Europe.

This movement of reorganization has been called rationalization, a word that was used in a variety of senses.[12] Perhaps the best definition was given by the World Economic Conference at Geneva in 1927, which described it as "the methods of technique and organization designed to secure the minimum waste of either effort or

---

[12] An excellent analysis of this movement is given in *Handwörterbuch der Staatswissenschaften, Ergänzungsband* (4 Aufl., Jena, 1929).

material. It includes the scientific organization of labour, standardization both of material and products, simplification of processes, and improvements in the system of transport and marketing." Rationalization was applied in varying degrees to different industries. In machine building, for instance, a comprehensive reorganization was effected in most of the plants, the system of progressive assembly and series manufacture, modeled on the Ford and other American plants, was introduced, and the costs of production were diminished. The same thing was true of electro-technical products, and to a less degree of highly finished iron and steel products, such as cutlery, tools, and household utensils, and especially fine instruments. But it was in coal mining that it found its fullest application. Taking industry as a whole there was an undoubted gain in the productivity of labor. The census returns of 1907 and 1925 had shown a gain, after making allowance for the shortening of hours in 1919, of 11 per cent; between 1925 and 1929 there was a further increase of 25 per cent.

The rationalization of German industry during this period involved concentration of establishments in larger units. A smaller number of plants turned out a larger proportion of the output; thus in 1927 about two-thirds of the industrial wares were produced by 1.5 per cent of the establishments. The mechanization of industry also made rapid progress. Between 1907 and 1925 the horse power employed in industry increased 70 per cent, and between the latter years and 1929 there was a further gain of 38 per cent. In addition to mechanization and concentration, rationalization also involved standardization, simplification, and reduction in the number of types. This was, however, less easily accomplished in Germany than in the United States, because of the great variety of and frequent changes in demand, both at home and abroad. The Taylor system of scientific management was in part adopted and adapted to German conditions, and industries were better organized, so as to eliminate duplicate plants, cross freights, and other wastes. The thorough-going mechanization of all German industry was, however, restrained by two factors, the low price of labor and the high price of capital, which made a large investment in machinery of doubtful advantage.

The brilliant achievements of these years were, however, partially counterbalanced by less favorable factors. Interest payments on borrowed capital amounted to almost 900 million marks in 1929, whereas in 1913 the returns from foreign investments of German capital had been 1000 million marks. The picture of these years usually presented is confined largely to the mining and metal working industries, and a large group of so-called "young" industries, in which the development was rapid. But many "old" industries did not show similar expansion and some of them declined. They were under heavy pressure, both from taxation and from changes in demand. Recovery operated very unevenly. The following table shows the situation in 1928, on a percentage basis:

COMPARATIVE PRODUCTION OF SELECTED INDUSTRIES IN 1928
(1913, old boundaries = 100)

"Old" Industries		"New" Industries	
Iron ore	25	Lignite	190
Zinc	38	Aluminum	657
Gas mantles	26	Automobiles	1010
Linen, spinning	36	Rayon	633
Pianos	58	Rubber	228
Sugar	61	Chocolate	155
Beer	80	Electricity	412

The most rapid progress was made in the heavy industries, in the production of capital goods. These were most urgently needed for the economic rehabilitation of Germany, and they were obtained, even at the cost of a continued low standard of living for the mass of the people. By 1928 Germany had practically regained the productive capacity of the old Empire of 1913. Taking industry as a whole the aggregate physical volume of production was up to the pre-war level, but the composition of this aggregate showed many changes, as indicated in the previous table. The fluctuations in physical production are clearly shown in the following table:

INDUSTRIAL PRODUCTION INDEX
(1913 = 100)

Year	1914	1919	1924	1928	1932	1935	1938
Index	83	37	69	102	59	93	126

The rationalization and development of the twenties had resulted in an over-expansion of certain lines, especially of capital goods. When the crisis of the early thirties broke out, there was an immediate contraction of production. This was especially marked in luxury goods and household supplies, in such production goods as iron and steel, auto trucks, and machines, and least so in the food industries. By 1932 industrial production was back on the level of 1897. Production fell off in all the important industrial countries, but the decline was greatest in Germany, which now took fourth place, being outranked in order of importance by the United States, Soviet Russia, and Great Britain; she was, however, still ahead of France.

No industrial census was taken in Germany after 1907 until 1925;

the next was in 1933. The two latter were confined largely to the working population and consequently only meager information as to production can be obtained from them. The changes in the number of industrial establishments, and of their personnel and power, are shown for industry as a whole and also for iron and steel and textiles.

Occupation	Year	Number of establishments (in 1000)	Persons employed (in 1000)	Horse power used (in 1000)
Industry and handwork	1907 *	2251	10,702	7,200
	1925	1917	13,098	19,780
	1933	1918	9,152	24,636
Iron and steel	1907 *	158	772	....
	1925	152	906	1,043
	1933	157	598	1,650
Textiles	1925	123	1,215	1,773
	1933	68	857	1,033

* Boundaries of 1920.

The Weimar Constitution had contained a vague promise of the socialization of industry, but this was not carried out. Governmental control of business was, however, expanded, and the state railways were transferred to Reich ownership. The few remaining private gas works, waterworks, street railways, subways, and bus lines were taken over with few exceptions by the municipalities, and a vast housing program was undertaken by various public authorities. Although the socialist program was not carried out, there was undoubtedly a strong swing in that direction. In order not to put too great a strain on the state administrative machinery, most of these industries were organized as separate units run by the methods of private business. Stock companies were formed and all their stock held by a Reich-owned holding company, while the Reichs-Kreditgesellschaft acted as banker. Price control was extended to most of the important commodities produced by private industry. If not socialization, the policy approached it.

Industry under National Socialism. The First Four-Year Plan initiated in 1933 was designed primarily to end unemployment and a vast scheme of public works was instituted. Industry and commerce were organized into regional groups, at the head of which stood a National Economic Chamber which exercised far-reaching control over economic affairs. Compulsory cartels were set up in a number of industries and production of consumption goods went on more rapidly than of capital goods, but as public works began to be subordinated to rearmament in 1935 the heavy and metal industries expanded rapidly and greatly.

The Second Four-Year Plan, launched in 1937, had as its main objective the economic independence of Germany with respect to essential foodstuffs, raw materials, and manufactured products needed in war time. She wished especially to free herself from the handicap of depending upon imports for iron ore, coal and oil, textile fibers, and rubber. National self-sufficiency or *Autarchie* involved the greater utilization of domestic supplies, which could be used to produce synthetic materials instead of natural products. Accordingly German timber was increasingly used for paper, cellulose, and other products; the exploitation of low-grade iron ore was undertaken; lignite was used more largely; synthetic oil was distilled from coal; staple fiber (*Zellwolle*) was made from wood; and artificial rubber was produced. Other raw materials were made by new or improved processes, such as rayon, aluminum, synthetic resin, and plastic materials. Science and technology were harnessed to industry on a scale never before witnessed, and the result was a notable increase in production. It was true that all these synthetic materials were considerably more costly than the imported natural products, but they were produced at home. Taking 1928 as 100, the total index of production had reached 126 by 1938, but the output of production goods expanded about four times as rapidly as did that of consumption goods. The energies and resources of the German people were being devoted to rearmament rather than to raising the standard of living. "Guns for butter," said Goering truly.

Among other pre-election pledges the National Socialists had promised to nationalize big industry. This was not done; but, although the titles of private ownership were not disturbed, other methods brought about the practical socialization of industry. The organization of industry was prescribed by the law of 1934 on the Organic Constitution of the German Economy. Faintly resembling the corporative state in Italy, this organized the whole economy functionally and regionally into groups, which were subordinated to the Minister of Economics. Every business man must belong to a group and was subject to all the regulations imposed by government. He was told what he might produce and how to produce it, what raw materials he might obtain, the buying and selling prices, and the persons to whom he might sell or through whom he might buy. It seems a misnomer to apply the term free capitalist system to such a planned economy.

A clearer idea of the changes in industry that occurred during this period will probably be obtained if the leading branches of the producers' goods and of the consumers' goods industries are presented in greater detail. For this purpose the coal and metal-working and textile industries are selected.

Coal. During the war period many new mines were opened, but as these were less productive and the efficiency of labor was decidedly lower the annual output per worker steadily declined. From 287 in 1913 it fell to 176 tons in 1919 and four years later it reached an all-time low of 78 tons. In no field was there a greater need for rationalization and nowhere was it more vigorously applied. The demand for coal was falling off as a result of changes in the coal-using industries. There was a greater use of oil and of hydro-electric power; furnaces and firing methods had been greatly improved so that the amount of coal necessary to produce a given amount of steam had been reduced by 40 per cent, and many old furnaces were being scrapped and replaced by the new fuel-saving types. And most important there was an increased use of lignite or brown coal, which could be more easily mined and was cheaper when used at the mine for the generation of electricity. Lignite was rich in bitumen and as coal came to be used increasingly for the production of chemical intermediates it was preferred to the so-called stove coal.

Between 1924 and 1929 the coal industry was thoroughly reorganized. The mines were mechanized as far as possible, though the thinness of the seams and their frequent faulting made this less successful than in many American mines where the coal deposits are thicker and straighter. Nevertheless, nearly 78 per cent of the coal in Germany was machine-cut in 1928, compared with 26 per cent in Great Britain. Improved mechanically operated transportation facilities were introduced, both in the mines and above ground, automatic loading and unloading equipment was installed, and other labor-saving devices were utilized. By 1929 the annual output per worker had been raised to 315 tons, compared with about 175 in 1921.

On the coal-using side the changes were equally comprehensive. Every mine was treated as a coal-using as well as a coal-producing enterprise, and coking, by-product, and power establishments were linked together in a vast undertaking. The production of coke increased from 32 million tons in 1913 to over 40 million in 1937. Even more striking was the production of by-products: between 1913 and 1937 tar and pitch increased from 1000 to 1600 thousand tons, benzol from 176 to 529, and ammonia from 421 to 536. It was estimated that by 1927–28 nearly 60 per cent of the coal was chemically treated. The ideal utilization of coal, as envisaged by German chemists, was through by-product coke ovens, only coke and gas being used for fuel while the by-products would yield a wide range of organic chemicals. Germany was well suited to such a chemical industry, for the large deposits of bituminous and brown coal assured a long-time sufficiency of raw materials. But even more important were the production and utilization of gas from the cokeries. A large surplus was being produced in excess of the needs of industry, especially as the iron and steel plants were depending more and more on blast furnace gas. In order to dispose of this excess gas a vast system of interconnected pipe lines was built, which supplied gas to industrial establishments, municipalities, and private consumers. Between 1913 and 1937 the production of gas from the cokeries alone grew from 150 million cbm to 17,000 million; there was another 3000 million from the gas works. The production of coal and lignite for a few selected dates was as follows:

PRODUCTION OF COAL AND LIGNITE
(in million metric tons)

Year	Coal	Lignite
1913 *	190	87
1913 †	141	87
1925	133	140
1929	163	175
1933	104	122
1938	186	195

* Old boundaries.
† New boundaries.

A striking and important development was the scientific exploitation of the once despised lignite. Upon it was built up the manufacture of synthetic nitrogen and later of synthetic gasoline, and from it was developed cheap power for long-distance transmission. For this adjustment of industry to the new conditions imposed by the Treaty of Versailles credit must go to science and research.

In addition to the technical improvements in the industry a structural change was also taking place. There was a strong concentration of ownership in the hands of a few large concerns, and of production in the best mines. The smaller and badly located mines, whose geographical situation and geological formation made production costs high, were closed down. Thus, whereas in 1900 about one-fourth of the coal mined was produced in large mines with annual production of over 500,000 tons, in 1928 the proportion was three-fourths. At the same time the various concerns were combined in a cartel. Such a combination had been formed first in 1893 as the Rhenish-Westphalian Coal Syndicate, which continued on a voluntary basis, with varying fortunes, until 1919. In that year the government provided for a compulsory syndicate of the coal industry by the Law Regulating the Coal Industry. By this act coal and lignite were declared to be affected with a public interest and hence were subjected to governmental supervision. The members of the syndicate were free to combine their properties and to determine production and price policies, but the government shared the management. At the time of its passage the act was called "socialization," but private ownership and operation still prevailed. The cartel system was recognized as best suited for purposes of regulation and was therefore made compulsory.

Iron and steel. During the period between 1870 and 1913 Germany had built up a closely-knit iron and steel industry, based on Lorraine ore and Ruhr coal. Blast furnaces and steel mills were built in Lorraine, to take advantage of geographical specialization and to reduce transportation charges. The Treaty of Versailles broke up this integrated industry, and with the cession of Lorraine deprived Germany of three-quarters of her iron ore reserves and part of the various processing plants. The owners of these plants were indemnified for their loss by the German government, which, however, stipulated that the money received must be used in reconstructing old plants or building and equipping new ones on German soil. By 1924 steel production was up to 80 per cent of 1913 and by 1927 had surpassed the pre-war figure. Other nations had at the same time increased their capacity and production and the over-expansion disorganized the markets of Europe. This difficulty was met in Germany by regrouping and combining establishments, closing high-cost, obsolete and badly located plants, and concentrating production in the most efficient ones. Each plant tended to specialize on particular products instead of making all types, and there was a better adjustment among the different steps in the industry between the iron ore and the finished product.

Integration, or vertical combination, resulted in great economies. A blast furnace combined with a coking plant had the advantage of cheaper and better-handled coke. If converters or open hearth furnaces were connected with rolling and tube mills, it was possible to pass the molten metal, without reheating, from the steel mills to the others for further processing. The structural changes in the industry permitted these economies to be effected, as well as other improvements such as standardization and reduction in the number of types. These improvements were not new, but they were now applied more generally and on a larger scale. There was a strong geographical concentration in the Rhenish-Westphalian and Upper Silesian districts; by 1929 the former was producing 82 per cent of the pig iron and 81 per cent of the steel. The center of manufacture was determined by the supply of good coking coal, which was located principally in the Ruhr district. The production of iron and steel fluctuated greatly, but over the years there was a steady gain in productive capacity. The actual output may be shown for a few selected dates.

PRODUCTION OF IRON AND STEEL
(in 1000 metric tons)

Year	Iron	Steel
1913 *	16,800	17,147
1913 †	10,730	11,768
1920	6,388	6,300
1929	15,344	18,273
1932	5,281	7,115
1938	18,655	22,991

* Old boundaries.
† New boundaries.

Technical improvements were also made in the industry, though these were not as important as the structural reorganization. The first problem was that of ore. Domestic production fell from 29 million tons in the former Reich in 1913 to 6 million in the new in 1929, but the deficiency was in part made good by imports from Sweden, Spain, France, and smaller amounts from Newfoundland and Algeria. There was a greater use of scrap iron, as a result of which the Siemens-Martin process, which could best utilize this, was preferred to the Thomas process. It was estimated that in 1930 half of the total iron content of the raw material required by the iron and steel industry took the form of scrap, one-third of foreign ore, and one-sixth of domestic ore. Blast furnaces were rebuilt, many old ones being replaced by larger and more efficient types, as a result of which the average pre-war capacity of 160 tons was raised to over 300 in 1929. At the same time the operation of the furnaces was mechanized by the introduction of mechanical transportation and charging equipment, costs were cut by the use of waste furnace gas for preheating the blast, and other economies were instituted.

The conversion of pig iron into steel, the second step in the industry, was also reconstructed by a similar process of structural reorganization and technical improvement. Obsolete plants were scrapped and new mechanized ones built at strategic points, fuel consumption was decreased, and the quality of the product raised. Rolling and tube mills were also reorganized, but here the progress was less pronounced.

Textile industry. Measured by the value of the product, the textile industry was the most important in Germany, but such a rating is somewhat misleading since the industry comprised half a dozen different branches, and many subdivisions. The cotton industry just about held its own. The number of spindles and looms remained practically stationary,[13] but their capacity increased, owing to improvements in design and to greater speed, so that the output per machine was practically doubled. In contrast with the mining and metallurgical industries, cotton manufacturing was carried on in many small scattered establishments. The woolen industry had a hard struggle, largely because of changes in demand and the competition of cheaper materials. The number of spindles and looms and the physical volume of production fell below the pre-war level. This too was widely dispersed in small establishments, especially over central Germany. The linen and jute industries declined in Germany, as they did in other countries.

In contrast with these branches the rayon industry expanded rapidly. Germany was the largest producer in the world in 1913, but after the war the United States, Great Britain and Italy enlarged their output faster than Germany. Nevertheless, production was increased from 3500 metric tons in 1913 to 28,000 tons in 1932, and to 67,000 in 1938. Since rayon production is essentially a chemical industry it was in a state of flux, as improvements were rapid and different methods were being tried out. The most extraordinary development was that of staple fiber or wood-wool (*Zellwolle*). This was very different from the perishable paper clothing of the World War period, and proved an acceptable substitute for cotton and wool. Its production rose sharply from 2650 metric tons in 1932 to 91,900 in 1936 and 162,000 in 1938. So great was the demand that it was necessary to ration it in 1936. If the textile industry as a whole be taken as typical of the consumption industries, it is evident that during this period the labor and capital of Germany were being devoted primarily to the production goods industries. The country was developing its internal resources, building up its industrial and particularly its munitions plants, and denying itself consumers' goods.

Chemical and electro-technical industries. In order to appreciate better the close linking of science and industry in Germany a brief glance may be given at two other industries in which that country was pre-eminent. Before the war Germany had produced about 80 per cent of the world's production of aniline dyes, but after that it fell to less than half. This loss was made good by the development of a wide range of new chemical products, such as the manufacture of synthetic nitrates, rayon, synthetic alcohol and the hydrogenation of coal to obtain gasoline and lubricating oil. The first of

[13] Spindles in 1909, 10.1 million; in 1937, 10.3 million.

these was due to the invention in 1913 of the Haber-Bosch ammonia
fixation process, which soon superseded other processes. The production of synthetic nitrates, which were used mainly as fertilizers,
soon became the most important branch of the chemical industry.
In no industry have the contributions of science and research been
so important.

Except in the south, Germany was not able to produce hydro-
electric power, but made good this lack by a development of thermo-
electricity. The amount of coal required to produce a given quantity of power was cut from 6 lbs. in 1900 to less than 2 lbs. in 1930.
Three-quarters of the power used in German industry at the latter
date was supplied by electricity. Cheap and easily mined lignite was
burned at the mines and used to supply current as well as to produce
valuable by-products. Electric power was distributed by a network
of high-tension lines to every part of the country, over half of it being produced by publicly owned central stations. Germany also
manufactured electrical machinery for her own needs, but did not
regain the export markets she had supplied before the war.

Industrial combination. Three types of combinations in Germany may be distinguished. The cartel was a temporary association
for the purpose of controlling prices and increasing the profits of its
members. It may be defined as a voluntary combination among enterprises in the same kind of business, each of which retained its
independence, for the sake of monopolistic control of the market.
They were wholly concerned with the market, either with the regulation of buying conditions for their members or with sales. Prior
to the war the cartel or horizontal combination was the generally
accepted form of combination. One reason for its rapid development was the practically unlimited freedom of association under
German law, as contrasted with the Roman or the English common
law. Cartel agreements were not only permissible, but were also
enforcible at law.

A second type of combination was the permanent amalgamation or
complete merging of two or more enterprises in a single unit. The
usual form of these was the vertical combination or integrated industry. For these the object was economic and technical rather than
financial, to reduce costs rather than to hold up prices. These were
called *Konzerne*. The third type was the pool or trust or holding
company, a permanent union in which the members sacrificed their
financial independence but retained varying degrees of managerial
autonomy.

During the war there was a shift from cartels to vertical combinations. War conditions favored centralization and strict organization, and government orders provided markets for large quantities

of standardized commodities which could best be produced by large concerns.   When the war was over the growing scarcity of raw materials gave to the owners of the remaining resources increased power.   There seemed to be no place for the cartels, whose main function was the control of prices, and these declined in number and influence.   The period was called that of *Kartellsterben.*   On the other hand, the outstanding phenomenon of the period from 1918 to 1924 was the development of vertical combinations, especially during the inflation period.

The most extreme example was the Stinnes *Konzern,* which began as an integration of iron and steel plants with coal and ore mines on the one hand and with machine works and other finished products on the other.   To these were added automobiles, petroleum and paper, lumber and textile mills, sugar factories, farms, hotels, electric power, ocean transportation, foreign trade companies, insurance, and banks.   This unwieldy combination, which had been built up largely on borrowed funds during the inflation period, went to pieces after stabilization of the currency.   It lost liquidity and could not meet its obligations as money rates were high; parts of the combination went bankrupt and it was finally dissolved in 1925.

In 1924 the movement known as rationalization began, in which emphasis was placed on efficiency of production and distribution. The enormous inchoate combinations of the inflation period, like the Stinnes concern, were replaced by more homogeneous vertical combinations which had an economic justification.   This type of organization, however, did not sufficiently take into account the relation between production and sales.   It was necessary to adjust production, which had greatly expanded, to the market, with respect both to amount and to price.   For these purposes the horizontal combination or trust, comprising a number of previously competing producers, was found to be better adapted.   They could control a larger proportion of the output of industry, and, through the consolidation of selling organizations, could better develop market outlets and adjust the volume of production to market demand.   The horizontal combinations could effect economies by bringing together in one organization the lowest-cost plants and processes and by closing unprofitable plants.

The most important of the new combinations were the *Vereinigte Stahlwerke A.G.* (United Steel Works Corporation) in the steel industry, the *I. G. Farbenindustrie A.G.* (literally, Community of Interest Dye Industry Corporation), composed of six great firms in the heavy-chemical industry, and the *Allgemeine Elektricitäts-Gesellschaft* (General Electric Company) in the electro-technical field.   There was little close organization in the textile industry, though there were a good many loose cartels or agreements. The general tendency in the formation of these great combinations was for the owners of the primary stages of production to consolidate into larger units and then to secure stable and concentrated outlets for their products. Added force was given to the movement where monopoly was possible, as in the iron and steel industry.

Various estimates were made from time to time of the number of cartels or associations like cartels.[14] Their number was estimated by Tschierscky in 1911 at 550 to 600, and by Liefman in 1922 at 1000. Metzner, the director of the *Kartellstelle des Reichsverbandes der deutschen Industrie*, gave a round 1500 for 1923. Two years later the Reich Economic Ministry estimated a total of 3000, of which 2500 were to be found in industry. Of all the estimates that of Metzner was probably the most reliable at the time it was made.

Under National Socialism there was a vast expansion of cartels, for their price-fixing machinery lent itself admirably to the state control of prices. A compulsory cartel law was passed in 1934, and a cartel census the following year showed that over 1600 new cartel agreements affecting prices had been made since June, 1933. They included such goods as soap, glass, cigarettes, playing cards, porcelain wares, radio sets, gas stoves, enamelled goods, and other articles. By 1936 it was estimated that 66 per cent of all German industry was cartellized. Although the cartels were given a large measure of independence in price fixing and the management of industry, they were hampered by an interminable amount of red tape in the hands of a vast bureaucracy. There was also a growth of so-called "mixed" enterprises, that is organizations in which public and private interests were combined. Such units dated from the beginning of the twentieth century, but they assumed new significance under National Socialism, as the state extended its economic power. It was a mere matter of administrative efficiency and of political expediency whether the state should directly carry on production or should use the former private entrepreneurs as its agents.

3. FRANCE MISSES HER OPPORTUNITY

Industry during the war. The invasion of France disrupted industry to an extent not approached in either Britain or Germany. The invaded districts were industrially among the most important in the country, particularly in those lines that were most essential for an effective prosecution of war. This is clearly shown by noting a few of the more important ones.[15]

---

[14] See K. Wiedenfeld, *Gewerbepolitik* (Berlin, 1927), 113.
[15] A. Fontaine, *L'industrie française de la France pendant la guerre* (Paris, 1925), 40.

PRODUCTION IN 1913

Item	Total production tons	Percentage in invaded departments	Item	Total Spindles	Percentage in invaded departments
Coal	40,844,000	74	Wool	2,700,000	81
Pig iron	4,027,000	81	Cotton	7,500,000	29
Steel	5,207,000	63			
Beet sugar	786,000	76			

The outbreak of war was followed by a short period of complete disorganization and unemployment, occasioned not only by invasion, but also by the mobilization of able-bodied men, from which a slow recovery was made in succeeding years. The output of coal fell in 1915 to less than half the figure for 1913, and did not again reach the pre-war production, though it was increased during the next three years. The shortage was made good by increased importation of British and American coal and larger use of hydro-electric power, which was almost doubled between 1914 and 1919. This, in brief, was a picture of the changes in French industry as a whole — prostration, partial recovery, and assistance from the Allies.

The production of pig iron showed the greatest decline of all, that for 1915 being only 585,000 tons, scarcely more than a tenth of the 1912 output. Although there was a recovery from this low figure, iron production suffered seriously throughout the war from lack of fuel and transportation difficulties. Steel production did not show so great a falling off, while the consumption was actually greater in 1917 than it had been in 1913, thanks to increased imports. As this was a key industry every effort was made to develop it. When it became clear that the war was to be a long one and that munitions were to play an all-important role, skilled workers were sent back from the front, new blast furnaces and steelworks were built, and output was increased. The open-hearth basic process was especially developed, as this was best suited to the French phosphoric ores. It was estimated that by July, 1918, the establishments at work represented 92 per cent of those operating in 1913, while the number of workers was 50 per cent greater.

The condition of the textile industry was fairly satisfactory on the eve of the war.[16] In some localities the machinery was antiquated, but in others both the equipment and organization were excellent. The industry supplied the home market, thanks to the high tariff which kept out imports, and exported considerable quantities of fine manufactures. It was wholly dependent upon outside sources for cotton and jute, and largely so for wool, silk, and flax. Taken as a

[16] A. Aftalion, *L'industrie textile en France pendant la guerre* (Paris, 1925), 3.

whole the imports of textile raw materials fell from 880,000 metric tons in 1913 to 243,000 in 1918. As will be seen from the table, the woolen industry was especially hard hit by the invasion. Over four-fifths of the spindles fell into the hands of the enemy; the situation was not quite so bad for the wool-weaving industry, although two-thirds of the looms were in war territory. In addition to this the woolen textile industry was disadvantageously affected by the shortage of fuel, the disruption of transportation, and the scarcity of labor. After 1917, when the submarine menace grew serious, and shipping was scarce, imports of wool, especially from Australia, fell off markedly.

The cotton industry fared better, since it was not so localized in the war territory. The imports of raw cotton held up well until 1918, but much of this was used for the manufacture of gun-cotton. There was an increase in the demand for cotton cloth, because of the scarcity of woolen and linen goods, but this was met by increased imports rather than by an expansion of domestic production. An important reason for this was the disinclination to use precious shipping space for bulky raw materials. A preference was given to compact manufactured goods, such as cloth or yarn, instead of raw cotton or wool. The silk industry was not directly affected by the invasion, by reason of its localization, but, since silk goods were a luxury, their consumption fell off markedly. Toward the end of the war the demand for silk by the aviation industry revived it somewhat.

The industry which, next to metallurgy, showed the greatest development during the war was the chemical. At the beginning of the war the effective personnel was cut in half, but by 1918 it was 20 per cent greater than it had been in 1913. The need for various chemical raw materials for munitions, which had previously been obtained from Germany, forced the country to develop its own sources of supply. Nitrates, drawn from Chile before the war, were produced by hydro-electric power in the region of the Alps. Cyanamide production, raised from 7500 tons in 1913 to 100,000 in 1918, was another new war industry.

The really remarkable achievements of France during the war, in spite of enormous difficulties, were due in no small part to changes in the organization of industry. There were a wider application of scientific method and scientific discoveries to industry, and a multiplication of research laboratories. War materials, by reason of the vast quantities needed and the small number of types, lent themselves admirably to mass production and the assembly line, which had been made familiar by American practice. These methods, together with the Taylor system, standardization and interchangeable parts, and other improvements, were gradually introduced and led to a technical transformation of French industry, although in many cases this was not fully realized until after the war. The very demands of war itself speeded up the industrialization of the country. The development was, however, very uneven, for while war industries advanced, the non-essential industries suffered a severe setback. The pre-war equilibrium was completely upset.

The state did not stand by as a powerless spectator, but intervened actively to promote those industries which were needed to prosecute the war and to repress those that were regarded as non-essential. The co-operation of the Allies for the utilization of their material and financial resources, which took form under the pressure of necessity, forced the government to regulate the economic life of the country on a growing scale. Requisitions, government purchasing, priority orders, rationing, and restrictions on imports and exports followed the lines already described for Great Britain. In 1915 the importation was forbidden of goods whose origin was Germany or Austria and in 1916 the importation of sugar, alcohol, and a large number of non-essential articles. In 1917 import quotas were authorized, according both to kind and origin, and the admitted quotas were distributed among the different industrial and commercial groups according to their indispensable needs. For this purpose so-called consortiums, or associations of producers in the same field, were established which handled primarily raw materials, such as coal, cotton, wool, jute, flax, and hemp.

Industry after the war. After the armistice it seemed as though a new era of prosperity might return. The feeding of central Europe and the satisfying of the accumulated needs of all the countries promised busy times for agriculture and industry. But this hope was short-lived. It was impossible for industry, geared to a war economy, suddenly to transform itself. Moreover, a war-uneasiness diminished the output of labor, the demobilization and diversion of the soldiers to new tasks created disorganization, and unemployment and production fell off. The urgent necessity for reconstruction, however, soon provided employment, and the 48-hour week, introduced in 1919, spread it. The material damages which France had suffered, due primarily to the enemy occupation, were momentous. These were officially estimated, with an eye on possible reparations, at 100,000 million francs. But, even allowing for an undoubted exaggeration, the losses in men, in capital, and in resources were serious.

The restoration of the devastated areas was a laborious task. More than half of the population had been evacuated, over four-fifths of the cultivated area had been devastated, many villages had been destroyed, mines had been wrecked, and machinery destroyed.

The work of reconstruction was vigorously prosecuted and the government advanced some 60,000 million francs for this purpose, an inflated figure which represented both extravagance and the depreciation of the franc. But by 1927 the work was practically completed. The population of the invaded departments was larger than it had been in 1913, nearly all of the devastated land, thought to be irretrievably ruined, had been restored to cultivation, and the villages rebuilt in better locations and with better sanitary arrangements. The mines were re-opened and the factories reconstructed. At the same time they were supplied with new and up-to-date equipment which was more efficient than the antiquated machinery which it replaced. The permanent plant was improved, electric and mechanical appliances were installed, larger and newer types of machines were introduced, and factory locations and layouts were more efficient. In spite of the enormous losses of the war France emerged a decade later with a more diversified and productive industrial plant than before. Although she had not caught up with her industrial rivals, she at least lessened the great gap which existed in 1913 between herself and Britain and Germany.

The treaty of peace, which restored Alsace and Lorraine to France, added some 3 per cent to the area and over 4 per cent to the population of the country. The mineral resources of Lorraine gave France some coal, in which she was sadly deficient, and doubled the reserves of iron ore, making her the richest country in Europe in this regard. She also obtained a little petroleum and rich beds of potash, while Alsace brought a well-developed textile industry, especially in cotton, woolen, and rayon.

The co-operation of experts and the spread of new scientific techniques during the war had as a consequence the acceleration of industrial change after that event. The industrial revolution at the end of the eighteenth century had been based upon a series of mechanical inventions and the utilization of steam as a motive power; that of the twentieth century was characterized by the use of electricity and the development of the chemical industries. This necessitated profound changes in industrial organization and even affected economic life in general. The changes were not new, but they were greatly accelerated after the war. Concentration, integration, and the use of scientific methods were the principal ones. The war industries had learned the value of research, of improved factory layout, of standardization, of machinery and machine tools, and now these spread to other branches.

These changes can best be traced in particular industries, and for this purpose the leading capital goods and consumer goods industries may be studied in more detail.

Iron and steel. The lack of coal had always hampered the industrial development of France, and this was increased by the destruction of her mines in the north. By way of compensation the mines of the Saar basin were given to her for a period of ten years, and Germany was forced to deliver a certain amount of coal and coke by way of reparation. The Saar coal was not good for coking, but the French mines were restored sooner than was anticipated. They were, moreover, equipped with the most modern machinery, such as mining shafts and hoisting and conveying machinery, power houses, and ventilating systems. The average annual output per worker, which was 279 metric tons in 1913, was raised to 314 in 1933. This latter figure may be compared with 732 gross tons in the United States for the same year.[17] The per capita consumption of coal was increased considerably, though it was still below that of Britain and Germany, and it was necessary to import some 30 million tons annually.

By the treaty of peace the iron resources of the French were greatly increased. With the cession of Lorraine she obtained reserves estimated at 5000 million tons, the greatest iron reserve in Europe and the second in the world, being exceeded only by the Lake Superior region in the United States. The iron and steel industry, which had been almost transformed during the war, was further improved by introducing the latest developments. The plants in the north were rebuilt with modern machinery, and those of the interior, which had been the backbone of the industry during the war, underwent a thorough conversion. There were three main areas of production. The region of the East, which turned out 78 per cent of the pig iron and 68 per cent of the steel, devoted itself largely to finished products. The North, with 13 per cent of the pig iron and 18 per cent of the steel, served local markets; and the Center, badly situated with respect both to fuel and raw materials, concentrated on specialties, especially high-grade steel tools, automobiles, and similar things.

The average French blast furnace before the war was a small affair, turning out in 1912 an average daily output of only 89 tons, as compared with 170 in Germany and 254 in the United States. After the war missions of experts were sent to other countries, especially to the United States, to study the best ore-mining, coke oven, blast furnace, and steel mill practices. As a result of their recommendations the average daily output of blast furnaces was raised to 179 tons in 1927 and 300-450 tons in 1934. The newer furnaces were equipped for mechanical charging of ore and coke, and for the recovery of the by-products. French ironmasters de-

[17] A gross ton contains 2240 pounds, a metric ton, 2204.

cided not to adopt the 1000-ton furnaces in favor in the United States and Germany, but purposely kept the French furnaces smaller since they could not produce on so large a scale as their competitors. The development of the iron and steel industry is shown in the following table:

METALLURGICAL PRODUCTION IN FRANCE *
(in 1000 metric tons)

	Iron ore	Pig iron	Steel	Coal
1913	21,714	5,311	4635	40,844
1919	....	1,333	1293	22,400
1929	51,000	10,360	9717	48,884
1937	33,208	8,200	7800	46,147

* P. de Rousiers, *Les grandes industries modernes,* 5 vols. (Paris, 1926–28), II, 133. The figures for 1913 do not agree with those in the table on p. 554, given by Fontaine.

In the production of both iron and steel France lagged far behind both Germany and Britain. The chief explanation of this must be found in the lack of fuel for smelting and subsequent operations, for France did not lack iron ore. So long as Germany was forced to deliver coal to France by way of reparations the industry flourished, but when these shipments ceased it reverted into its old channels. Since it is cheaper to ship iron ore than coal, after 1929 the former was exported to Germany there to build up a vigorous iron and steel industry. Of the iron converted into steel in France over two-thirds was produced by Thomas open-hearth basic process, which lent itself best to the phosphoric French ores. These open-hearth furnaces were lined with dolomite, where the phosphorus, having a great affinity for lime, abandoned the iron to incorporate itself in the chalky elements of the lining.

A weakness of the French metallurgical industry lay in the impracticability of concentrating on a few standard types and of realizing the economies of mass production. For this the lack of an adequate market was largely responsible. France could not hope to compete with the United States, Germany, or Britain in heavy industries, but was compelled to confine herself primarily to a widely diversified list of quality products. Owing, however, to the acquirement of large supplies of iron ore in Lorraine and the renovating of her industrial plant, France was able to increase her share of world production of iron between 1913 and 1932 from 7 to 21 per cent and of steel from 5 to 16 per cent, but by 1937 she was turning out only 12 per cent of the world production of iron and 6 per cent of steel. Integration was never carried as far in France as in the three countries just named. There was little integration of blast furnaces and foundries, because of the irregular demand of the latter for iron. According as the foundry produced large or small pieces, it required more or less iron, and it was difficult, if not impossible, to maintain a constant equilibrium between the capacity of the furnace and that of the foundry. This obstacle disappeared when production was confined to one or a few uniform types, as was done in a few of the larger plants. The integration of blast furnaces and steel works was more common, and in some instances there were added iron mines, if conveniently located, and at the other end rolling mills and other processing plants.

Textiles. The textile industries still constituted the most important industrial group in France, both because they employed the largest number of workers and because they contributed most to the export trade. The leading place was held by the cotton industry, in which France ranked third, being surpassed only by the United States and Britain. The return of Alsace, in which this branch was highly developed, together with the expansion of the industry in other parts of France, raised the number of spindles from 7,500,000 in 1913 to nearly 12,000,000 in 1931; of looms from 141,000 to 208,200. Of the latter, over 8000 were still handlooms. The equipment was modernized, but small scale establishments predominated, and these retained a family character. There was little concentration in spinning and weaving, but the finishing branches were highly integrated, both technically and financially. Since production was of specialties rather than of staple goods, a vast variety of yarns in spinning and of short runs in weaving were required. Under such circumstances mass production was uneconomic and hand labor still played an important part, though spinning was done almost entirely by automatic machinery. The depression following the crisis of 1930 reduced production in 1934 to two-thirds of the 1913 figure. It was less seriously affected than silk, as most of its product was consumed at home and domestic consumption did not fall off as much as did foreign trade, which had to meet the severe competition of Japanese manufacturers.

The woolen industry showed only a slight growth, in spite of the addition of Alsatian establishments. Localized largely in the north, it suffered severely during the war, but the reconstituted industry was much better equipped and more efficient than that of 1913. There was some shifting from north to south to take advantage of the new water power as well as to be in a safer position. It remained, however, a small scale industry for much the same reasons that affected cotton. Medium and small establishments, of a family character, predominated. Wool combing was performed entirely by automatic machinery, but further processes in which taste and craftsmanship counted were carried on by small machines or even by hand. The number of spindles grew from 2,700,000 in 1913 to 3,300,000 in 1931, but the number of looms remained practically stationary at 65,000; of these, 10,000 were handlooms. The woolen industry enjoyed remarkable prosperity after reconstruction down to 1930, but the depression of that and the following years ushered in a period of crisis. Primarily responsible for this was the fall in prices, but other factors contributed. The excessive equipment in France and other countries produced more than the markets could absorb at prevailing prices, and high tariffs closed many of these to French producers. Changes in fashion which shifted demand from French staples to sports goods, a greater use of mixtures, and the advent of rayon also played their part. Dependent on exports for the disposal of half of the output, the shrinkage of foreign markets was particularly disastrous.

The silk industry, subject to changes in fashion and catering to a luxury trade, suffered most. But even more than these factors, the rise of rayon or artificial silk threatened the real-silk and cotton industries.

Organization of industry. War needs for standardized products on a large scale gave an impetus to mass production of munitions and to the creation of great establishments in the metallurgical industries. After the war many of these plants continued in operation and concentration in large establishments was marked; five concerns were said to produce four-fifths of the Lorraine pig iron and all of the Lorraine steel. Similar concentration in large establishments and in a few companies existed also in the coal, aluminum, tin plate, machinery, automobile, electrical, and chemical industries. It would be misleading, however, to conclude that large scale operations were characteristic of French post-war industry as a whole. When we turn to the textile industries a very different picture is presented.

The individual cotton factory employed a relatively small number of persons. The 335 spinning mills recorded in the 1926 census showed an average of 210 employees, and the 989 weaving establishments an average of only 128. Automatic machinery was not generally adopted because the price of such machines was high and they were profitable only when used for mass production. But this was not feasible because of rapid changes in fashion in the lines upon which French manufacturers concentrated. Standardization and specialization were therefore rare and small scale operations and family character of the industry were the rule. This was especially true of the weaving industry, where the tastes and needs of the market ran almost into infinity. Only in the finishing sections was concentration marked.

The woolen industry, like the cotton, silk, and other branches of the textile industry, was also organized on a relatively small scale in comparison with Britain or Germany. The 1926 occupational census showed that of the 798 establishments in the preparatory processes (washing, combing, spinning, etc.) just half had 1-20 employees, while 81 per cent had fewer than 100. Of the 1481 weaving establishments 56 per cent had 20 employees or less. The small scale of operations is also shown by the machine equipment, the average number of spindles per establishment being 4100 and of looms only 50. The industry retained essentially its pre-war family character. The technical causes leading to industrial concentration operated with varying intensity in different branches. It was more marked in spinning than in weaving, more in cottons than in woolens, more in both of these than in hemp or linen, and least in silk. If the cotton and woolen industries were used as illustrations of decentralization rather than of concentration, no exaggeration could be charged.

Capitalistic organization. A survey of French industry as a whole shows a growing tendency toward capitalistic organization. The average number of employees in 593 manufacturing establishments, in 1906, was 480 and in 1926 a comparable group of 512 establishments employed an average of 760. These were, however, exceptional; probably nine-tenths of the manufacturing establishments did not employ over 20 workpeople each. At the same time the motive power increased from 2,565,000 to 6,917,000 horse power. The use of machines and of power grew more rapidly than the labor force, clear evidence of industrialization. France was not able to escape the pressure of modern capitalism.

Two or three different types of industry must be distinguished if the picture of recent trends is to be complete. A group of new industries sprang up, largely after the war, which were located in the most advantageous spots, near sources of raw material, markets, and labor. Unhampered by tradition or custom they adopted the best equipment and most efficient forms of organization. They represented modern capitalism. Among these were the electrical, chemical, automobile, and rayon industries.

A second type consisted of industries which felt the pressure of the new forces but were not able to change their old methods completely. They stood midway between the highly mechanized and power-driven industry of modern capitalism and the more primitive of the French pre-war period. The metallurgical industries were an illustration.

A third group was made up of industries which, so far as form went, were carried on in small dispersed establishments, and even by the family. It presented every appearance of small scale organization, but in reality was organized on a capitalistic basis, the home workers being merely outworkers for a central enterprise. The best example of this type was the textile industries, especially in weaving and garment making. It was found in rural and mountainous districts, as in the silk industry about Lyons, or in large cities where it took the form of sweated industries. Evidently no broad generalization can be employed to describe the industrial development of France, or to picture the future of French industry. The problem is still unsolved as to whether France will follow the lead of Britain and Germany and engage in mass production of cheap standardized goods, or confine itself to the production of high-quality, high-priced articles, such as wines and jewelry, perfumes and cosmetics, lingerie and laces, fashionable gowns and millinery, and high-grade metallurgical and electrical products. The choice seems to lie between quantity and quality.

Combination. Combination was not carried as far in France as in either Britain or Germany. This was owing in part to the highly individualistic character of the average French enterpriser, and in part to the absence of any legal method by which a majority could enforce a recalcitrant minority to comply with agreements. Vertical combination or integration took place in a few industries, notably the metallurgical. Thus a few firms, like Wendel, Schneider and Creusot, owned coal and ore mines, blast furnaces, steel works, and manufacturing plants.

The metallurgical industry also furnished illustrations of horizontal combination. After the war coal mine owners combined for specific business purposes, such as purchase of mine props, production of electricity, working up by-products, and sales. Between 1919 and 1925 working agreements were made among various iron and steel firms as to the nature of the future output in works to be built, and as to the pooling of interests in coal and ore mines or in processing plants. The crisis of 1930 forced a closer agreement and in the following year the largest steel producers agreed to apportion future output among the plants on the basis of their production for 1929 and 1930.

Conclusion. The World War marked the end of one era and the beginning of another. It acted as a catalyst on economic forces, producing new combinations and accelerating existing trends. The destruction and waste of the war itself and the dislocations of industry caused by the territorial changes prescribed by the Treaty of Versailles involved a considerable reorganization and reorientation in all the major industrial countries. The main movements may be briefly summarized.

Britain, Germany, and France were highly industrialized by 1914, but after the war the agricultural countries entered upon an industrial revolution.   Such states as Russia, the Scandinavian and Baltic states, India, and still others began to exploit their resources and to manufacture goods for themselves.   Since they developed their industries so late they were able to equip their factories with the most efficient machinery and to adopt the latest methods of organization.   This was facilitated by the fluidity of modern industrial capital, always seeking for profitable investments.   And since their standard of living and consequently their wage scale were low, they were able to supply their own markets in competition with the older producers.   Nationalism, which was stirred to fever heat during this period, was a strong factor in this movement.   Because of patriotism, fear of war, or desire to diversify industries, each little state sought to make itself as self-sufficient as possible.   As a result the old territorial division of labor was broken down, and the major industrial countries found their markets shrunk and themselves forced to a reorganization of their own industries.

Private capitalism seemed to have broken down, and in this emergency two methods of rationalization were put in practice.   The first was self-regulation by industry itself, in the form of combinations, cartels, and similar trade associations.   The second was control and economic planning by the state itself.   This found most drastic expression in the communist state of Soviet Russia, but underlay also the organization of Fascist Italy and Nazi Germany.   Even in individualist Britain and France there were a vast extension of government control and even some economic planning.

Changes in industrial structure and output paralleled the changed attitude of the state.   Recent industries, producing for the most part consumers' goods, expanded enormously, while the older staple industries barely held their own.   At the same time science was creating entirely new synthetic products, either as substitutes for those already in use or as fresh contributions to human welfare.   In ingenuity of invention, in rapidity of progress, in extent of command over the forces of nature, and in altered relations to the state, industry witnessed even greater changes during this period than had marked the Industrial Revolution one hundred and fifty years earlier.

BIBLIOGRAPHICAL NOTE

1. *Britain.* Two books deal with British industry in war: H. L. Gray, *War Time Control of Industry* (New York, 1918), good though early, and C. W. Baker, *Government Control and Operation of Industry . . . during the World War* (New York, 1921), sketchy. A general outline is G. P. Jones and A. G. Pool, *A Hundred Years of Economic Development in Great Britain* (New York, 1940). A good though brief summary is A. Wilmore, *Industrial Britain: a Survey* (new ed., London, 1939), as is also G. D. H. Cole, *British Trade and Industry: Past and Future* (London, 1932). Hugh Butler, *The United Kingdom* (Washington, 1930) provides excellent statistical material. The [Balfour] Committee on Industry and Trade, *A Survey of Industries*, 4 Parts (London, 1927–28) and *Final Report* (London, 1929), is a careful and thorough investigation. This was answered by the Liberal Industrial Inquiry, *Britain's Industrial Future* (London, 1928), a critical and constructive report. L. D. Stamp and S. H. Beaver, *The British Isles* (2nd ed., London, 1937) gives the geographical setting. Of the different industries most attention was given to coal, as this was a "sick" industry. The Royal Commission on the Coal Industry, *Report* (London, 1925) is a careful study. This was followed by numerous books, of which two may be mentioned: A. M. Neuman, *Economic Organization of the British Coal Industry* (London, 1934) and R. C. Smart, *The Economics of the Coal Industry* (London, 1930). A very thorough account of the war period is R. Redmayne, *The British Coal Mining Industry during the War* (London, 1923). There was also a flood of books on oil, of which L. Fischer, *Oil Imperialism* (New York, 1926) may be cited. M. W. Murray, *L'industrie cotonnière anglaise*, 1913–1923 (Lille, 1925) gives a partial picture. The growth of public ownership is described in W. A. Robson (ed.), *Public Enterprise: Developments in Social Ownership and Control in Great Britain* (London, 1937). On industrial organization an excellent study is A. F. Lucas, *Industrial Reconstruction and the Control of Competition: The British Experiments* (New York, 1937). Also good are G. C. Allen, *British Industries and their Organization* (2nd ed., London, 1935) and H. Levy, *Monopolies, Cartels, and Trusts in British Industry* (2nd ed., London, 1927).

2. *Germany.* A good description of industry during and immediately after the World War is H. v. Beckerath, *Kräfte, Ziele, und Gestaltungen in der deutschen Industriewirtschaft* (Jena, 1922). An excellent survey is R. Wagenführ, "Entwicklungstendenzen der deutschen und internationalen Industrieproduktion 1860 bis 1932" (in *Vierteljahrshefte zur Konjunkturforschung*, Sonderheft 31, Berlin, 1933). W. Meakin, *The New Industrial Revolution; a Study for the General Reader of Rationalization and Post-War Tendencies of Capitalism and Labor* (London, 1928) describes changes after the war. J. W. Angell, *The Recovery of Germany* (New Haven, 1929) is an excellent account of the period 1924–1929. P. Dawson, *Germany's Industrial Revival* (London, 1926) is largely political and journalistic. R. A. Brady, *The Rationalization Movement in German Industry* (Berkeley, 1933) is a careful account of the development of economic planning. The National Industrial Conference Board, *Rationalization in German Industry* (New York, 1931) deals mostly with the cartel movement. On separate industries M. Beaumont, *La grosse industrie allemande et le charbon* (Paris, 1928) treats coal; M. Meisner, *Weltmontanstatistik, Die Versorgung der Weltwirtschaft mit Bergwerkserzeugnissen*. Bd. I, 1860–1926; Bd. II, 1926–1930; Bd. III, 1930–1935 (Stuttgart, 1925–36), iron; and M. Köpke, *Probleme der Elektrizitätspolitik in Deutschland* (Eberwald, 1931), electricity. On industrial organization a pio-

neer work is R. Liefmann, *Kartelle, Konzerne und Trusts* (9te Aufl., Stuttgart, 1934. English translation, *Cartels, Concerns, and Trusts.* New York, 1932), mainly descriptive. H. v. Beckerath, *Industrielle Kartellprobleme der Gegenwart* (Berlin, 1926) is more theoretical. Slighter, but useful are D. Warriner, *Combines and Rationalization in Germany, 1924–1928* (London, 1931) and R. K. Michels, *Cartels, Combines, and Trusts in Post-War Germany* (New York, 1928). H. Levy, *Industrial Germany. A Study of its Monopoly Organizations and their Control by the State* (Cambridge, 1935) is good.

3. *France.* A. Fontaine, *L'industrie française pendant la guerre* (Paris, 1925. English translation, *French Industry during the War.* New Haven, 1926) is excellent. Somewhat more sketchy is C. Gide, *Effects of the War on French Economic Life* (London, 1923). W. MacDonald, *Reconstruction in France* (New York, 1922) is an informed account. Slightly broader is E. Théry, *Consequences économiques de la guerre pour la France* (Paris, 1922). W. F. Ogburn and W. Jaffé, *Economic Development of Post-War France* (New York, 1929) is a careful study of production. A good, though brief, description of industry is P. George, *Géographie économique et sociale en France* (Paris, 1938). Excellent statistical tables may be found in *L'évolution de l'économie française, 1910–1937: tableaux statistiques publiés par l'institut scientifique des recherches économiques et sociales* (Paris, 1937). On separate industries A. Aftalion, *L'industrie textile pendant la guerre* (Paris, 1925) is a brief account. More specialized is P. Despature, *L'industrie lainière* (Paris, 1935). The developing chemical industry is covered in P. Baud, *L'industrie chimique* (Paris, 1931) and K. Löffl, *Die Chemische Industrie Frankreichs* (Stuttgart, 1917). A. Boutaric, *Les grandes inventions françaises* (Paris, 1932) is informative. L. Guillet et J. Durand, *L'industrie française* (Paris, 1920) gives a cross section.

CHAPTER XVIII

COMMERCE AND COMMERCIAL POLICY

1. BRITAIN DESERTS FREE TRADE

Commerce during the war. In its commercial aspects the struggle between Britain and Germany was not unlike that between England and Napoleon a hundred years earlier, although the weapons had altered. Again the effort was made by each belligerent to prevent the other side from obtaining needed supplies from overseas, and, while most of the blows were aimed at the opponent, neutral trade was also seriously affected. Britain had long been dependent for much of her food and raw materials upon outside sources, but during the war she was forced to rely upon these sources in ever-increasing measure for food, munitions, and other supplies. The German submarine campaign, on the other hand, sought to prevent these supplies from reaching Britain or her Allies. The amount, character, and direction of foreign commerce during the war were determined by other than purely economic considerations and were wholly abnormal. The following table shows the general course of trade.

BRITISH FOREIGN COMMERCE, 1913–1920

(in million £)

Year	Net imports	Domestic exports	Re-exports	Excess of imports
1913	659	525	110	134
1915	753	385	99	368
1918	1285	501	31	784
1920	1710	1334	223	376

These figures do not give an accurate picture of the actual quantities of goods exchanged, for prices increased greatly during this period. The Board of Trade price index rose from 100 in 1913 to 315 in 1920. Measured in 1913 prices, the value of the domestic exports of 1920 was only £423 million, so that there was a fall rather than an increase. This is more clearly shown if some of the important items are presented in terms of quantity. Thus the export of cotton piece goods fell from 7000 million yards in 1913 to 3700 million yards in 1918, woolen and worsted goods from 168 to 98 million yards, iron and steel products from 5 to 1.6 million tons, and coal from 73 to 25 million tons. Exports decreased greatly, since the productive resources of the country were devoted to war industries rather than to the production of articles for sale. Imports, on the other hand, tended to increase as Britain sought to meet immediate needs by purchases abroad. The principal imports were food (rice, wheat, flour, bacon and hams, cheese, milk, cocoa) and those for military purposes (oil, gasoline, copper, arms and ammunition, chemicals). There was at the same time a shift from Europe as a source of supplies to British possessions and also to the United States, especially after the latter entered the war. Trade with the Baltic practically ceased, as did that with the Central Powers. The re-export trade of foreign and colonial goods showed the greatest loss.

Restrictions of both exports and imports were imposed during the war. The importation of raw materials, especially wool and some metals, not of Empire origin, was forbidden unless specifically licensed; later numerous other commodities were added to the list. These regulations were designed to give priority to the movement of foodstuffs and munitions, but as the submarine warfare reduced the amount of available tonnage, it became necessary to exclude bulky and less essential commodities. The re-export trade, by which the goods of foreign countries were distributed throughout the world, was practically destroyed. The system of licensing and prohibition was finally abolished in September, 1919.

Commerce after the war. Britain's dependence on foreign trade was probably greater after the war than it had been before, but she faced a world less willing and less able to buy her goods, while her own purchasing power had been seriously impaired. The depression of 1920 had a dulling effect, but there was a steady recovery after that until 1929. The fluctuations may be shown by citing a few selected years.

BRITISH FOREIGN TRADE

(in million £)

Year	Total imports	Total exports	Excess of imports
1913	769	635	134
1929	1221	839	382
1933	675	417	258
1938	920	532	388

The imports were chiefly foodstuffs and raw materials, as is shown by the list of the first ten imports in 1938 in order of their monetary value: foodstuffs, wood, non-ferrous metals, wool, cotton, oil, hides and skins, machinery, iron and steel manufactures.

Exports consisted mainly of manufactured goods — 79 per cent in 1928 — and coal. Since these were used to purchase food and other articles for home consumption, exports indicate roughly the prosperity of the British people. If 1913 be used as a basis of comparison, the exports since the war averaged only about three-quarters of the earlier period, after making allowance for the higher price level. It was small consolation, in view of the actual fall, to be told that Britain had not fared worse than other countries. The decline extended to all the principal articles of export, and was also widespread geographically. Mr. J. A. Hobson estimated in 1922 that it would be necessary for Britain to increase the export of manufactures by £100,000,000 annually in order to pay for imports needed to restore the pre-war standard of living.[1] The causes of the falling off of British exports were stated by the Balfour Committee on Industry and Trade [2] to have been the decline of purchasing power of importing countries, the growth of manufactures in such countries, or the displacement of British goods by imports from other sources. As illustrations they cited the decline of cotton goods exports to India, as a result of the poverty of that country, of the development of her own iron resources by that country, and finally the loss of various textile markets, due to the rise of Japan as a competitor. In 1934 for the first time Japanese cotton exports exceeded those of Great Britain.

Other factors also contributed to worsen Britain's position as an exporting nation. The return to the gold standard in 1925, with its deflationary effects, discouraged exports while it encouraged imports. The costs of production did not fall as rapidly as the value of the pound rose, wages especially declining less than the level of general prices. Taxation was steadily growing more burdensome as the government assumed new social services. More fundamental, however, was the rigidity of organization in British industry, the persistence of tradition, antiquated equipment, slowness in adopting new methods and processes, the opposition of labor to changes, and the extreme individualism of the average manufacturer.

In a word Britain, as an "old" industrial country with an established economic structure that was not easily changed, suffered from the competition of countries with newer plants and methods and in some cases with lower standards of living. Coal and textiles — two of the leading exports before the war — had slumped badly, largely because of changes in technology and the introduction of substitutes. Other industries, such as iron and steel, machinery, and shipbuilding, found their foreign markets blocked by quotas, clearing agreements, and other obstacles to international trade. The general movement

[1] "Britain's Economic Outlook on Europe," in *Journ. Pol. Econ.*, Aug., 1922.
[2] *Survey of Overseas Markets* (London, 1924), 5.

away from the relatively free, automatic international economy of pre-war days to the strict control of totalitarian governments threatened Britain's commercial dependence.

As a creditor nation Britain had long enjoyed a favorable balance of payments. The balance had been re-invested in foreign countries where it exercised a powerful influence in gaining orders for British machinery and other goods, and thus increased British exports. After the war the amount available for foreign investment fell, and after the crisis of 1930 it sank to still lower levels. The following table, based on estimates by the Board of Trade, pictures the changes clearly.[3]

BRITISH BALANCE OF INTERNATIONAL PAYMENTS, 1913–1938

| | Debit | | Credit | | |
Year	Excess of imports over exports	Earnings from shipping	Net income from investments	Earnings from other sources	Estimated balance
1913	158	94	210	35	181
1924	324	140	220	50	86
1929	366	130	270	104	138
1935	261	75	185	38	37
1938	318	100	200	35	17

Commercial policy. The period after 1914 saw the revival of a mercantilistic commercial policy in Europe. Great Britain, the citadel of free trade for eighty years, abandoned that policy and returned to one of protection. During the war imports and exports were subjected to drastic control, most of which was protective in effect. In England the first breach with the existing system of free trade was made in 1915 when the McKenna duties of $33\frac{1}{3}$ per cent ad valorem were laid upon certain manufactured luxuries (private motor cars, clocks, watches, motion-picture films, and musical instruments). This was regarded as a temporary war measure and was designed to restrict luxury consumption as well as to produce needed revenue. In 1919 the principle of imperial preference was introduced by granting a rebate of one-sixth of existing revenue duties on goods imported into Great Britain from Empire countries. Another step to protection was taken in 1921 with the adoption of the Safeguarding of Industries Act, intended to help manufacturers through the difficult post-war period. This imposed duties of $33\frac{1}{3}$ per cent ad valorem for five years upon the imports of certain "key" industries, such as scientific instruments, optical glass, some chemicals, magnetos, etc., which were considered essential to national defense, and to which were later added other articles which it was

[3] C. Day, *A History of Commerce* (4th ed., New York, 1938), 632.

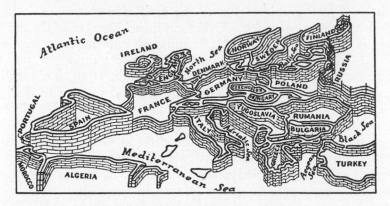

FIGURE 9.   EUROPEAN TARIFF WALLS

Reprinted by permission of the Carnegie Endowment for International Peace, publishers.

desired to protect for industrial reasons.   In 1926 the five-year period expired, but it was extended for another ten years.

The definite adoption of protection and abandonment of the time-honored system of free trade was taken in 1932, when the Import Duties Act was passed.   British industry was suffering from the "distress dumping" by other countries in the one remaining free trade market and from the competition of countries with depreciated currencies.   This Act was designed to give protection to domestic industries, and to provide a basis for imperial preference and for reciprocal arrangements with foreign countries.   It imposed 10 per cent duties on imports, with the exception of certain foods and raw materials, but higher duties under previous acts were retained. Higher duties were also authorized upon luxury goods, and upon articles which could be produced in Britain at reasonable cost and in adequate quantities if granted protection.   The far-reaching effect of this act is evident when it is noted that at the end of 1932 only 25 per cent of the imports entered Great Britain free of duty, as compared with 83 per cent in 1930.

This break with the system of free trade was not made without a struggle, which was particularly fierce over the iron and steel schedules, for protection to this industry broke two general rules: not to tax important raw materials or to hamper the export trade. But crude iron and steel products were raw materials for many other industries and more than 70 per cent of the industry as a whole was exported.   The protectionists won, however, largely on the ground that an adequate iron and steel industry was needed for defense, though only on conditions that they reorganize the industry and not raise prices unduly.   The export trade fell off after this date, but it would be unfair to blame the tariff for this since so many other factors were at work.   Other countries like Japan, India, and Australia were becoming more self-sufficient and imported less from Britain.   This was reflected in the fall of the total world trade in iron and steel products from 15 million tons in 1929 to 9.5 million in 1936.   The movement to protection tended in turn to diminish the importation into Britain of various manufactured and semi-manufactured articles from foreign countries and to stimulate their increased production at home.   Protection in Great Britain was in fact the result of a general breakdown of international trade.   Free markets and private initiative were swamped by the growing spirit of nationalism, and foreign trade was increasingly controlled by totalitarian governments and manipulated for political ends.   Britain did not stand aloof from this movement, but concluded a long series of trade agreements with foreign countries, using the tariff as a weapon to obtain enlarged outlets for her exports.   She thus became a partner to arrangements for "bilateral balancing" of her trade with particular countries, not very dissimilar from those carried out by Germany and Italy.

In the summer of 1932 the Ottawa Agreements provided for more trade and freer trade throughout the Empire.   The Dominions agreed to give preferences to a wide range of British commodities, and Britain accorded Empire products free entry.   These Agreements were valid for five years.   The practical effects of imperial preference were an increase in the percentage of imports from Empire countries from 25 of the total in 1913 to 35 in 1935; in the same two years the percentage of exports to these countries rose from 33 to 40.   At the latter date four out of the six leading suppliers of Britain's needs, and four out of the six best customers for British products were in the Empire.

It is difficult to measure the effect of protection and imperial preference upon British commerce and industry, for there were so many other complicating factors.   The British share of world trade, which had fallen from 15 per cent in 1913 to 12 in 1930, recovered to almost 14 in 1938.   Empire trade grew faster than that with foreign countries, and there was a gratifying increase in the exports of manufactured goods, which had slumped badly.   In 1938 over 40 per cent of British imports came from Empire countries, while half of the exports went to those countries.

The British Commonwealth of Nations.   This name, as a designation of the British Empire, came into use about 1914 and was given official approval in 1921 by its use in the Irish Treaty of that year.   It signified a new conception of the relationship between Great Britain and the self-governing Dominions and the colonies.

The idea was not new, for Chamberlain, influenced by the events of the South African war, had urged that the larger units of the Empire should be drawn closer together and suggested preferential trade arrangements as a basis of union. This fell through because it involved a tax on food imported into Britain. Informal co-operation had meanwhile been achieved through the Colonial Conference, a body organized in 1887 and composed of the secretary of state for the colonies and official representatives of each dominion, which met to discuss matters of common concern. In 1907 the name was changed to Imperial Conference.

The idea of establishing a supreme imperial government was given a new impetus by the war and the important part played in this by Australia, Canada, India, New Zealand, South Africa, and other parts of the Empire. This was given expression by a resolution of the Imperial Conference in 1917 that "any readjustment of constitutional relations . . . should recognize the right of the Dominions and India to an adequate voice in foreign policy and foreign relations." The conception of the Empire as a group of equal nations dated from this time, and the government of Britain no longer directed exclusively the whole foreign policy of the Empire. When the League of Nations was established after the war the self-governing Dominions entered it as equal partners.

Merchant marine. The maintenance of communication with outside sources of supply is a primary condition of existence for the British Isles, and during the war this was seriously jeopardized. Just as Britain by blockade endeavored to cut off supplies from the Central Powers, so Germany by her submarine campaign attempted to prevent overseas trade from reaching Britain. The marine struggle therefore centered on the ability of Britain to maintain her supremacy on the seas.

In July, 1914, there were in the United Kingdom 8587 steamers of 100 tons and over, with a gross tonnage of 18,892,000. But of these only 3888 were of 1000 tons or over, which were practically the only ships engaged in ocean commerce. The outbreak of war temporarily paralyzed shipping. German raiders, like the *Emden*, rendered distant trading hazardous, and underwriters practically refused to insure vessels or their cargoes. But without adequate insurance shipowners will not risk their vessels on the seas. By the end of July tramp chartering, which made up nearly half, had virtually come to a standstill. At this juncture the government came to the rescue, and undertook to insure both hulls and cargoes; compensation to the men was later added.

The next problem concerned the amount of merchant shipping available. Almost half a million tons were immobolized in enemy and neutral ports, and the government immediately requisitioned over 1000 ships with 4,000,000 gross tonnage for the B.E.F. The withdrawal of so much tonnage from merchant service produced a relative scarcity, and freight rates began to rise. The situation was made more serious by submarine sinkings. Submarines began effective operations as commerce raiders early in 1915, wrought serious havoc during 1916, and by "unrestricted" warfare in 1917 created terrible losses. The climax was reached in April of that year with sinkings of 545,000 gross tons. By 1917 there was a shipping famine, to which a number of causes contributed. These were listed as follows:[4] (1) Submarine sinkings. (2) Increased need for ships, since many merchant vessels had been directed to war use. (3) Necessity of a longer haul; nearby supplies from the Baltic and Black seas were cut off and must now be brought from Australia, the Americas, etc. (4) Shipyards were so crowded that repairs to damaged ships could not be made. (5) Long detours were necessary to elude the submarines; in 1917 the convoy system was adopted, but this also slowed the time. (6) Amateur administration made for delays. (7) Some ships were detained in enemy or neutral harbors. (8) Port congestion greatly slowed up turnaround, especially in French and Italian ports.

The solution of this problem was undertaken very tardily. At first the shipowners were permitted to take their profits, which averaged about 15 per cent during the first two and a half years of the war, according to an estimate of Bonar Law. But this method did not produce new ships to offset losses from submarine warfare. In 1916 more direct control of shipping was undertaken by the establishment of a Shipping Control Committee, and later by the appointment of a Shipping Controller, who was given wide powers. Ships that were not requisitioned for military or naval service had to obtain licenses for each voyage, and place part of the cargo space to and from certain ports at the disposal of the government at fixed rates. But not until 1917 was the decision made to build, buy, and run ships on government account. Standard fabricated ships were built, with standardized hulls and engines, as these could be constructed more rapidly and cheaply than specialized types. Work progressed very slowly, however, because of shortage of men and materials, and the clogging of shipyards by repair work on damaged vessels. New construction continued below war losses during 1918. The race between shipyards and submarines is clearly shown by statistics.[5]

[4] J. R. Smith, *Influence of the Great War upon Shipping* (New York, 1919), 34.
[5] C. E. Fayle, *The War and the Shipping Industry* (London, 1927), 415.

Year	United Kingdom gross tonnage steam and motor vessels over 100 tons	United Kingdom ships launched over 100 tons	War losses British shipping, including fishing and Dominion vessels
		(1000 gross tons)	
1914	18,892	1683	241
1915	19,236	651	856
1916	18,825	608	1238
1917	(not available)	1163	3730
1918	(not available)	1348	1695

These losses were made good by new building, by purchase, and after the war by the cession of enemy ships as reparation payments. The demand for shipping continued after the cessation of fighting. The repatriation of troops employed many vessels for a while and there was also a revival of trade. Immediate decontrol was considered inadvisable for fear of violent fluctuations of freight rates and prices. The licensing system was therefore continued as a method of control until 1920. In spite of the heavy shipping losses certain gains resulted from the war. The economic position of merchant seamen was substantially improved, better relations between employers and workers were established, and machinery was set up for settling disputes. The disappearance of sailing vessels was accelerated; the losses of these had been heavy and they were replaced by steamers.

By 1920 the feverish efforts of British and especially American shipyards to meet the challenge of the submarines had resulted in overbuilding. At the same time a depression occurred which lessened the amount of freight to be carried. The result was a slump in freights, a reduction in profits and wages, and a decline in the amount of new construction. Some recovery occurred during the relatively prosperous period of the late twenties, but the depression beginning in 1930 introduced new difficulties. The government finally came to the aid of British shipowners in 1935 by granting subsidies, but this was discontinued two years later. The decline of sailing vessels continued, but now the supremacy of the steamers using coal began to be threatened by oil-burning motor vessels. Whereas in 1914 nearly 97 per cent of the steamers burned coal, by 1935 the proportion had fallen to 51 per cent. The use of oil freed additional space for cargo, for it was not so bulky, and it was more easily handled and cleaner. The following brief table shows the shift that was taking place.

The increase in the size of ships and in the bulk of machinery and of the component parts of which they were built led to a con-

BRITISH MERCHANT MARINE
(in thousand gross tons)

Year	Steam		Motor		Sailing		Total	
	No.	Tons	No.	Tons	No.	Tons	No.	Tons
1925	10,526	18,517	1965	817	5785	559	18,276	19,893
1930	9,729	17,959	3237	2373	5098	500	18,064	20,832
1935	8,306	14,258	4494	3040	4351	459	17,151	17,738
1937	7,702	13,697	5294	3749	4185	441	17,181	17,887

centration of the shipbuilding industry upon the largest streams adjacent to the steel-producing regions, such as the Tyne and Clyde. British supremacy was being threatened during these years by the United States, Japan, Holland, and Sweden, all of which built actively. As a consequence the British percentage of the world's new shipbuilding fell from 58 in 1913 to 36.5 in 1939. Britain could, however, solace itself with the fact that the new luxury liner *Queen Mary* held the transatlantic speed record.

2. GOVERNMENT TAKES CHARGE IN GERMANY

Commerce during the war. Germany lay in the center of European economic activities. She might be "ringed about by enemies," but she was also surrounded by customers. Thirteen nations touched her borders, which she supplied with manufactures, fuel, fertilizers, and other goods. No other country in Europe was so well situated for peaceful and profitable trade. Like Great Britain, Germany depended for much of her food and raw materials upon imports from other countries, which she paid for with finished manufactures. By subsidies to certain industries and by favorable rates on government-owned transportation systems, as well as by vigorous efforts to win and hold foreign markets Germany had built up a far-reaching external commerce. In 1913 she carried on 13 per cent of the world's trade.

This peace-time edifice was completely shattered by the war, and later by the blockade. In its place was erected a war-time structure which was military and the effort was made to control trade in such a way as to assist in winning the war. An ordinance of August 4, 1914, permitted the free entry of 49 groups of commodities or schedules in the protective tariff. Export was forbidden of all articles which would serve military purposes, especially food and animal fodder. To these were soon added articles of which Germany held a near-monopoly and which were needed by other industrial nations. It was hoped by this procedure to force the neighboring neutral nations to buy of Germany. The plan miscarried, however, for the neutrals were able to draw upon other sources of supply or to use substitutes.

A second stage in the control of foreign trade developed as a shortage of the most necessary articles of daily consumption became evident. Just before the war, it was estimated, there had been a deficit of about 16 per cent in agricultural foodstuffs, including not only cereals, meat, vegetables and fruit, but also animal fodder. Dependence on foreign sources was still greater in the case of raw materials. Germany had few of these except coal, potash, ceramic clays, and building materials. Almost everything else was imported, in whole or in large part — cotton, hides and skins, wool, wood, copper, iron ore, mineral oil, raw silk, rubber, jute, flax and hemp, to name only the important items. The textile, leather, and printing industries were wholly dependent on imports, and metallurgy, electro-technical industries, and food, were largely so. Only coal, sugar, and most of the chemical and ceramic industries were independent of foreign supplies. It was essential to safeguard the meager domestic supplies and to stretch their use as far as possible. Many industries had supplies of raw materials for only two months, and few for more than six. The prohibition of exports was gradually extended until it embraced almost everything. At the same time domestic production was subjected to control. The administration of internal commercial policy was guided by only one standpoint, namely the maintenance of the national well-being.

As control was extended to the whole economy, private rights were more and more restricted. The housing legislation almost abolished private property in urban real estate, while freedom of movement of the individual was seriously limited. Several stages may be noted in the subordination of commerce and industry. First was the fixing of maximum prices, which began immediately upon the outbreak of the war and was extended until it covered practically all articles. This policy was not successful, for illicit trading immediately developed; if the fixed prices were too low, products were not brought to market, production of under-priced articles ceased, and the purpose of the legislation was completely defeated. This was followed by rationing and finally by control of production itself, including that of substitutes. By the time the war ended the entire mechanism of production and distribution had been placed under the regulatory power of the state.

The actual course of foreign trade was one of great shrinkage. Exports contracted to a third of the pre-war total, and imports fell to about two-thirds. Direct overseas commerce was of course almost completely destroyed, but considerable supplies leaked in through the neighboring neutral countries. After the entry of the United States into the war, the blockade was tightened and few overseas goods were received. Toward the end of the war it was impossible to obtain necessary supplies of food and primary raw materials, such as textile materials, rubber, and certain metals. The trade of these years is briefly shown:

SPECIAL FOREIGN TRADE OF GERMANY

(in millions of marks)

Year	Merchandise imports	Merchandise exports	Excess of imports
1913	10,770	10,097	673
1916	8,400	3,800	4600
1918	5,900	3,000	2900

Commerce after the war. Germany emerged from the war crippled commercially in several ways. The merchant marine, which had ranked second only to Great Britain, was now lost. Foreign commercial and financial connections had been broken and foreign markets lost, at least temporarily. The occupation of the German territory west of the Rhine and of the bridgeheads of Mainz and Cologne by Allied troops opened a "hole in the west," through which foreign goods found their way into all Germany without paying duties. Until 1925 German trade was hampered by import and export license systems, supervision of the movement of goods by various inter-Allied commissions, and other disturbing factors.

Inflation and the depreciation of the currency had profound effects upon foreign trade. According to a well-known economic principle, it acted as a premium on exports and a protection against imports. The price level within Germany was held at an artificially low level for domestic reasons and did not adjust itself to the world market. Germany was a good place in which to buy, and so great was the transfer of securities and commodities into foreign hands that it seemed as though a national sell-out (*Ausverkauf*) threatened. The increasing exports and the declining imports gave a fictitious appearance of prosperity, and for some industries and commercial interests brought in considerable profits. But for the national economy it was a losing game. Though this danger was met by a rigid regulation of both imports and exports, it was not brought wholly under control until the summer of 1923. With the stabilization of the currency in November of that year, the necessity for artificial measures disappeared and foreign trade was partially decontrolled.[6] The experiences of these years had, however, materially modified the conditions and the mechanism of external commerce.

Stabilization of the currency placed international trade between Germany and other nations on a stable basis, the Dawes Plan, adopted in 1924, gave a guarantee of financial order, and the introduction of rationalization made the industries of the country more efficient and productive. Foreign capital began to flow in to assist in the work of rehabilitation, but this was distributed unevenly. Those industries which were well and favorably known abroad were able to obtain credit or to sell their bonds on foreign markets, while other types of industry were able to reach the international capital market only through German banks, so that for them credit was more expensive. Imports jumped at once and by 1925 had passed the high peak of 1913, and, except for a temporary fall in 1926, continued to rise until 1929. Exports also increased, though not so rapidly.

SPECIAL FOREIGN TRADE OF GERMANY

(in millions of marks)

Year	Merchandise imports	Merchandise exports	Excess of imports
1923	6,150	6,102	48
1925	12,362	8,799	3563
1927	14,143	10,219	3924
1929	13,447	13,483	36 *

* Excess of exports.

The Treaty of Versailles had forced Germany to grant most-favored-nation treatment to all the Allied and associated nations for five years, whether they made reciprocal concessions or not. This treatment was extended by Germany to other nations. Of the 946 schedules in the tariff 47 were entirely free and 9 partially free of duties, aside from those normally on the free list. The five-year period expired on January 10, 1925, and Germany proceeded to reimpose protective duties. The threat of the removal of the freedom of importation gave occasion to an extraordinary rush of imports which were conveyed across the border in all haste before the new duties became effective. This is shown clearly in the sudden jump in imports, which was followed by a corresponding though smaller increase in exports. Even more important, however, in explaining the rise of imports were the vast loans and extension of credits which were being made to Germany during this period, es-

[6] According to Harms, of the 946 schedules in the tariff 457 schedules were still under import prohibition and 33 under export prohibition at the end of 1924. B. Harms, *Die Zukunft der deutschen Handelspolitik* (Jena, 1925), 80, 82.

pecially by United States investors, manufacturers, and merchants. These took the form of food, raw materials, manufactured goods, and machinery, and of course appeared on the merchandise balance sheet in the form of imports. During the five-year period, 1924–28, the excess of imports over exports amounted to over 12,000 million marks.

A clearer idea of the changes in foreign trade may be obtained by breaking down the totals into groups. For this purpose the usual classification may be given:

SPECIAL TRADE BY GROUPS OF COMMODITIES
(in millions of marks)

Group	1913 Imports	1913 Exports	1929 Imports	1929 Exports	1938 Imports	1938 Exports
Foodstuffs	3,049	1,080	3,967	723	2125	63
Raw materials	6,242	2,270	5,966	2,799	1963	464
Partly manufactured goods			1,239	6,310	980	446
Finished manufactures	1,479	6,750	2,263	3,649	381	4284
	10,770	10,100	13,435	13,481	5449	5257

The two important import groups in all three years were foodstuffs and raw materials. These made up 82 per cent of the imports for the period 1896 to 1913 and were 93 per cent in 1938. And while the proportion increased, there was also a shift within the group. Foodstuffs, such as fruits, oil fruits and seeds, coffee, tea, and cocoa, made up a growing percentage. Imports of staple agricultural products like bread, grains, and dairy products declined as domestic production increased. This was limited, however, by a rise in the margin of agricultural production, and by the doubling of interest rates and higher taxation. The largest groups of imports at all three dates consisted of raw materials and partly manufactured goods, mostly the former. The dependence of Germany upon foreign sources of supply had grown greatly as a result of the loss of deposits of coal, iron, lead and zinc, and other items. Upon a ready supply of these depended the development of the German industrial system, and if they were not to be had at home, they must be bought.

The importation of manufactured articles showed a significant increase up to 1929. A further breakdown discloses that many of these were luxuries. The states and municipalities, having got rid of their pre-war debts, used their new-found credit to build athletic fields, swimming pools, war memorials, and other similar objects. After the depression of 1932, however, and the cessation of foreign credits, these imports sank to negligible proportions. The actual course of trade is shown in the following table:

SPECIAL FOREIGN TRADE OF GERMANY
(in millions of marks)

Year	Merchandise imports	Merchandise exports	Excess of exports
1930	10,393	12,036	1643
1932	4,667	5,739	1072
1934	4,451	4,167	284 *
1936	4,218	4,768	550
1938	5,449	5,257	192 *

* Excess of imports.

When the world depression began in 1930 German trade was at once affected. Imports and exports fell to a third of the high point reached during the previous decade of expansion, and remained on a premanently lower level. Imports, however, fell more rapidly than exports, so that the nine years, 1930–38, showed a favorable merchandise belance for every year but two, giving a total for the period of over 7000 million marks. But it must not be assumed that this spelled prosperity. The returns from invisible items, which had paid for large advance balances during the twenty years ending in 1913, had disappeared. An annual credit balance of 1000 million marks from foreign investments was transferred into interest charges on borrowed capital, amounting in 1929 to 873 million marks. Foreign trade had depended largely on foreign credits, and when these dried up with the outbreak of the depression it also declined.

Foreign trade under National Socialism. The dominant trend under the National Socialist regime was concentration on domestic problems, accompanied by an intensification of state control and regulation of all forms of economic activity. The shortage of foreign exchange necessitated a drastic restriction of the import trade (except raw materials), modified to some extent by an extensive and somewhat fluctuating system of clearing agreements and barter transactions. There was a strong effort to achieve bilateral balances, that is to make the import and export trade with each country equal, instead of conducting foreign trade on the basis of multilateral exchanges. As a result of the growing shortage of basic raw materials, especially textile fibers, there was a strong trend toward the establishment of economic self-sufficiency (*Autarchie*). The government stimulated this by granting financial assistance, restricting the importation of certain dispensable raw materials, and compulsory cooperation by private industry to develop the production of substitutes under state supervision. In a number of cases the clearing arrangements served merely to cut down or to eliminate the favorable trade balance with certain countries, as with Great Britain and the United States.

An analysis of the geographical distribution of German trade showed some significant shifts. Of the European countries Britain and France decreased their shares of exports to Germany, while an increase took place from Belgium, Czechoslovakia, Holland, Spain, Switzerland, and some of the Balkan states. Trade was directed to those countries which made favorable clearing agreements and barter arrangements with Germany. This was especially true of Argentina and Brazil, whose foodstuffs and raw materials were eagerly received in Germany and in payment for which they received German manufactures, machinery, and supplies of various sorts. Nevertheless, in 1937 Great Britain still remained Germany's best customer, receiving 7.3 per cent of her exports, while France ranked second (5.3 per cent). The largest share of Germany's imports also came from Great Britain (5.6), closely followed by Argentina (5.4) and the United States (5.2).

The adoption of the New Plan governing foreign exchange in September, 1934, signalized a new intervention by the state in foreign trade. The whole import trade was placed on a license basis under the control of 25 boards. The government sought to adjust imports to the amount of available exchange, to harmonize them with its nationalistic policy, and to facilitate its trade relations with particular countries by means of clearing and barter agreements. That is, every country wishing to sell to Germany must take German goods in return. By 1938, fully four-fifths of German foreign trade was carried on under such arrangements, which were largely dictated by political considerations. Countries with clearing and payment agreements furnished 78 per cent of Germany's imports and received 84 per cent of her exports. The importation of non-essentials was permitted only where it was absolutely necessary as a *quid pro quo* for German exports. But above all, as time passed, foreign trade was made to serve the task of rearmament, as was domestic industry. Under the circumstances it was not easy to promote the export trade, which suffered from the competition of countries with depreciated currencies and from the reservation of the domestic market for home producers and for nationalistic aims. Another obstacle to the expansion of exports was the boycott of German goods by foreign nations in protest of the treatment of the Jews by the Nazi regime. This was especially strong in the United States, Holland, Poland, the Baltic states, Palestine, and South Africa. It affected most those goods whose origin could be easily determined, and was not so effective against raw materials or half-finished goods.

Foreign trade and the balance of payments. Before the World War Germany was a creditor nation and was in receipt of an annual import surplus of about 1000 million marks. During the war the foreign investments were practically wiped out, and after stabilization Germany borrowed huge sums from other nations, especially the United States. At the same time she was forced to pay reparations. As a debtor nation the only way to meet this double obligation was to develop an export surplus. According to classical foreign trade theory this might be achieved by deflation through heavy taxation, by the export of gold, or by the manipulation of credit, but none of these policies was effectively pursued. Or a drastic curtailment of imports might have produced an export surplus; but down to 1929 imports remained on a high level, and exceeded merchandise exports. Consequently she met her foreign obligations by borrowing. When foreign credits ceased to flow into Germany after 1929 it became impossible for her to continue to meet reparations payments, or even the interest charges on the privately borrowed capital. The result was virtual cancellation of the former and postponement and reduction of the latter by so-called "standstill" agreements.

Although there was a small export surplus in 1929, this was more than exhausted by the excess of imports during the next two years. To meet these German importers borrowed heavily abroad or bought on credit. When the financial crisis of 1931 broke out some of these short-term credits were withdrawn from Germany — 2900 million reichsmarks in the first seven months of 1931. But nearly 12,000 million still remained, whose withdrawal would bankrupt the country. To meet this emergency an arrangement was made between a creditors' committee, representing the creditors in eleven countries, and a debtors' committee, representing German business men and the Reichsbank, by which the former agreed to maintain their existing credits for a period of six months, subject to certain conditions. This was known as the "standstill" agreement. It was renewed each year to 1939, but in the meantime the debts were gradually being repaid. The original credits had been converted into so-called "blocked" marks, which could be spent only in Germany. This meant that if a foreign creditor wished to collect his loan he must accept German goods; he could not obtain cash. Owing to the depreciation of the blocked marks in Germany the liquidation of the "standstill" credits involved a considerable loss to the creditors. By February, 1939, only 780 million reichsmarks remained of the credits covered by these agreements.

The balance of payments is shown for three years on page 584.

Tariff changes. At the very beginning of the war freedom of entry had been decreed for a large number of foodstuffs for military

BALANCE OF PAYMENTS
(in millions of marks)

| | 1910–13 | | 1927 | | 1935 | |
Items	Credit	Debit	Credit	Debit	Credit	Debit
Merchandise	8,250	9,750	11,072	13,899	4335	4338
Services, tourists, etc.	1,000		729	2,099	937	541
Interest, dividends, etc.	1,500			430	100	650
Movements of capital		1,000	5,386	759	871	714
Total	10,750	10,750	17,187	17,187	6243	6243

reasons; after the cessation of hostilities the needs of the people forced a continuation of the policy. The Treaty of Versailles prevented a revision of the tariff for five years, but when this period was up, in 1925, a new general tariff act was passed. The rates were very moderate, but a license system was introduced and the import of certain foodstuffs was forbidden. In 1929 an agricultural crisis appeared for the grain-growing farmers of eastern Germany. Cheaper wheat from America was pouring into the market, Russia was dumping considerable quantities of grain, there was a steady shift from rye to wheat bread, and there were bumper crops in Germany. The producers of rye were particularly hard hit, for the price of rye was little above that of fodder. The agrarians clamored for higher duties and the old issue of *Agrarstaat* versus *Industriestaat*, which had been debated thirty years before, was again brought out. This time the government, inspired, no doubt, by the desire for economic self-sufficiency, decided to protect agriculture by every means in its power. Duties on all kinds of grains were raised, German mills were forced in 1929 to use a certain percentage of domestic wheat, and a national advertising campaign in favor of rye bread was launched. By 1933 the duties on wheat and rye were almost 300 per cent of the world price, and those on other grains, animals, and dairy products were equally prohibitive. The internal market for agricultural products, and especially for cereals, was now completely divorced from the world market. The cost of the system to consumers was heavy, but it did succeed in making Germany practically self-sufficing in the provision of bread grains.

The world crisis of 1931 altered the methods of protective intervention by the state without reducing its magnitude. It was discovered that the flow of international trade could be controlled by currency manipulation, foreign exchange control, quotas, and in other ways. Beginning in 1931 a severe foreign exchange control (*Devisenzwangswirtschaft*) was established, according to which every importer was assigned a certain quota of the available foreign

exchange.   The import trade was thereby held within strict bounds.
Exports, on the other hand, were stimulated by a different device.
Under standstill and other agreements with foreign creditors Germany had agreed to pay a certain proportion of the debts owed
abroad in so-called "blocked" marks, which had to be spent in
Germany.   But the blocked marks had a lower value than the free
marks.   The discount on blocked marks reflected the possibilities for
their employment within Germany and the eagerness of creditors to
dispose of their holdings.   By January, 1939, the discount on the
registered marks had risen to 63 per cent.   A German exporter,
who was paid for his goods in blocked marks which then became
free marks in his hands, received an export bounty amounting to the
difference in value between the two.   The attractive feature about
this scheme, from the German point of view, was that the bounty
was borne by the foreign creditor.   The same principle underlay
the use of "conversion" marks, which were issued in connection with
foreign loans and were similar to the blocked marks, and of Aski
marks (*Ausländer Sonderkonto für Inlandszahlungen*) which could
be used only for the purchase of German goods.   The latter, at a
discount of 20 to 35 per cent below the official par, were given in
exchange for coffee and cotton in South America.

Finished manufactures made up two-thirds (66 per cent) of exports in 1913, almost three-fourths (73 per cent) in 1929, and over
four-fifths (82 per cent) in 1938.   In addition to these the main
items were such raw materials as coal, potash, and wood.   But while
the exports of manufactures had increased, a change had taken place
in their character.   Before the war German manufacturers had produced high-quality specialties for foreign markets; but these needed
agents abroad to watch the demand, to furnish information to provide substitute parts, and in other ways to promote their sale.   The
war destroyed this mechanism and broke up foreign connections.   As
a result the export trade tended to shift from special types of manufactures to staple articles turned out by mass-production methods,
which entered the world markets in general competition with similar
articles from other industrialized countries.   It was not so easy to
produce the finer types and specialties by large scale methods, and
they could consequently be sold only at relatively high prices.   During this period other nations had in many cases developed their own
industries and were no longer dependent on German supplies; this
was particularly true of the dyestuffs industry.   High tariffs and
nationalistic policies shut out German goods from their former
markets.

Merchant marine.   In 1914 Germany had a merchant marine
second only to that of Britain, with 4935 ships having a gross ton-

nage of 5,200,000. This fleet comprised 11 per cent of the world's shipping. Many of these vessels were destroyed or captured during the World War and the peace treaty at the end handed over the remainder to her conquerors. Germany was compelled to cede all merchant ships of 1600 gross tons or upwards; one-half of the tonnage of ships between 1000 and 1600; and one-quarter of the steam trawlers and fishing boats. She was left with an insignificant fleet of small boats, totalling 500,000 tons.

During the next twenty years Germany rebuilt her merchant marine along the most modern lines. Sailing vessels over 100 tons all but disappeared, over 95 per cent of such tonnage consisting of steam and motor ships. At the same time the latter were larger and faster. In 1939 the number of merchant vessels was only 2466 but their gross tonnage was almost equal to the pre-war figure, being 4,492,708 gross tons. Since other nations, however, had meanwhile been increasing their merchant fleets, notably the United States, Norway, and Japan, Germany now had only about 6.4 per cent of the world's shipping, and ranked fifth among the nations, instead of second.

3. QUOTAS AND PROTECTION IN FRANCE

Foreign trade. The disruption of commerce which followed the outbreak of war clearly evidenced the economic interdependence of the nations. All nations suffered from its effects; there were only differences of degree as to the extent to which they were damaged. Of the three countries under review France was the hardest hit. The invasion of the northern provinces destroyed the equilibrium of domestic commerce, and the war itself broke up the international exchange of goods. Like England, France had been accustomed, for years, to enjoy a surplus of imports which were paid for by the proceeds from foreign investments, tourist travel, and other invisible items in the international balance sheet. Now the profits from these sources abruptly ceased, labor was diverted from the export industries to military activities, and the basis of foreign trade was wholly changed.

The difficulty of marine transportation, which was later aggravated by the submarine warfare, forced France to reduce its importations to a minimum during the war, especially as the still greater decline of exports created a serious trade deficit. Calculated by weight, the exports of 1917 were only one-seventh those of 1913, but according to value they were nearly equal, owing to the rise of prices. The deficit in the commercial balance was 60,000 million francs for the four years of war, 1915–1918. By the end of 1917 the situation in France was tragic. The supply of steel was sufficient for only eight days, powder would be exhausted by the end of January, and nitrates, wheat, cannon, and coal were all running low. Under these circumstances the economic co-operation of the Allies became a military necessity.

An Inter-Ally Food Commission had been established toward the end of 1914, when it became apparent that the war would be protracted, but this was a mere organ of information. A year later the joint purchase of frozen meat from Australia and Argentina was undertaken, and in 1916 this was extended to wheat. Later the purchase of all needed supplies was centralized, marine transportation was pooled, joint credits were arranged, and finally the armed forces were brought under a single supreme command. Joint action by the Allies ceased after August, 1919, when the United States withdrew.

The return of Alsace and Lorraine with their textile and metallurgical resources profoundly affected the industrial organization of France and also her foreign trade. She became an exporter of iron ore, steel, and potash, while her textile industries sought enlarged markets at home and in the colonies. Owing to the currency fluctuations statistics of imports and exports according to value are almost meaningless. They showed an enormous expansion when expressed in depreciated francs, but when these are reduced to a gold basis the course of foreign trade revealed only a slight though steady growth from 1921 to 1930. After that there was a serious decline.

THE SPECIAL TRADE OF FRANCE
(in billions of francs)

Year	Imports	Exports	Excess of imports
1913	8.4	6.9	1.5
1918	22.3	4.7	17.6
1922	24.2	21.3	2.9
1929	58.2	50.1	8.1
1935	20.9	15.5	5.4
1938	45.9	30.6	15.3

The imports into France in 1913 were distributed as follows by classes — foodstuffs, 23 per cent, raw materials and partly finished articles, 58 per cent, and manufactures, 20 per cent. By 1938, foodstuffs had risen to 27 per cent and raw materials remained at 58; manufactures fell to 15 per cent. This reflected changes in French agricultural practice and the lessened need for certain raw materials, now produced at home. Exports were chiefly manufactured goods — about 60 per cent at each date. Exports of foodstuffs were about 13 per cent and of raw materials about 27 per cent. According to value the principal imports were wool and cotton, but measured by weight coal came first and cereals second. Similarly the leading exports by value were textiles and machinery, including automobiles, while by weight they were iron and chemical products. The appearance among the exports of such things as automobiles and chemical products indicated the ability of the French to adopt new processes and to assume a stronger position in the world market.

The balance of trade ran heavily against France during most of this period, though in the four years, 1924–1927 there was a slight excess of exports. The trade deficit was very serious, for it was no longer offset, as it had been before the war, by large receipts from foreign investments, tourist travel, and other items in the balance of payments. The foreign investments were for the most part lost or liquidated, tourist travel did not regain its pre-war level, and other services were no longer performed. The course of foreign trade was, however, but slightly altered; most of France's commerce continued to be with her European neighbors, though the United States remained her greatest provider and best customer as a single country. The character of the exports, goods of high quality, stood in the way of any great expansion, and domestic producers along other lines felt foreign competition keenly. This led to a revival of the protectionist movement.

Commercial policy. No change was made in the existing tariff system through 1914 and 1915, except to prohibit the importation of imports from enemy countries. A modification was made in 1916 by the promulgation of a law which authorized the government to regulate commercial matters by decree, instead of being obliged each time to present a law for vote by the Chambers. The long duration of the war led the following year to the adoption of a new policy; instead of levying duties on imports these were forbidden, and the prohibitions were applied to Allies and neutrals as well as to the enemy. The purpose was to facilitate the prosecution of the war by giving priority to imports needed for war purposes. Imports were divided into three categories: (1) indispensable, upon which no restrictions were placed; (2) necessary up to a certain point, after which they were regarded as dispensable; (3) unnecessary — these could be forbidden. In order to administer such a system it was necessary to determine the total amounts in each group and then to allocate them. But individual derogations were permitted which introduced discrimination, and made the system ineffective and unpopular.

Another compelling factor for restricting imports was the scarcity of foreign exchange. Gold was shipped abroad and foreign credits obtained, and advances were received from Britain and, after its entrance into the war, from the United States, amounting to about 1000 million francs a month.   But the franc continued to fall and the rise of prices made the existing tariff inadequate.   The system of priorities, quotas, and prohibitions was therefore pushed to the extreme.   Finally, in 1918, the government, foreseeing the economic disequilibrium after the war, denounced all the commercial treaties then in force.

After the armistice the system of prohibition was abolished, and instead surtaxes of 5 to 20 per cent over and above the existing customs duties were imposed.   These were intended to offset the rise of prices and to restore the former rates.   This policy was, however, short-lived, and in 1920 a new system was introduced. The most-favored-nation clause was abolished and the government was authorized to apply to certain countries an intermediate tariff consisting of percentages of the difference between the general and the maximum tariff.   The aim was to protect "key" industries and to prevent dumping by countries with depreciated currencies.   Rates in the existing tariff were increased according to specified coefficients for a number of products, that is existing rates were multiplied by 2 or 3 or 5.   In this way the rates were adjusted to fluctuating prices.   This law was modified in 1926 by a decree stating that in future percentages would be calculated as a function of the general tariff alone.

The period between 1925 and 1930 was a fairly liberal one, especially at the time of the World Economic Conference in 1927, when hopes ran high of modifying the existing barriers to international trade.   This idea was ended by the depression and by the extraordinarily high rates of the Hawley-Smoot tariff of 1930 in the United States.   This was the signal for increases in almost all countries, partly by way of reprisal, and a general tariff war ensued. Britain passed a new tariff act in 1931, raising the rates.   France, however, adopted the import quota as an instrument of trade policy. It seems to have been established because other methods were not adequate to meet rapidly changing conditions or because the hands of the government were tied by the most-favored-nation clause in commercial treaties.

The quota system was designed first of all to protect French agriculture against the flood of cereals, meat, and other products which was pouring into the domestic markets.   French internal prices were higher and it was felt that the home producer must be protected. Exchange dumping, so-called, was another menace. The currencies of China, Spain, Australasia, and many of the South American countries had depreciated in value and against the artificially cheap products of those countries the bars were raised.   The quota system was intended to protect agriculture and industry and also to safeguard the currency. It was simple and supple, could be authorized by decree, and was quickly applied. Definite quantities were established which could be imported. During 1931 the system was applied to agricultural products, and in the following year it was extended to manufactures; a year later numerous raw materials were brought within the scope of the system. By 1936 quotas had been applied to over 3000 tariff items, which comprised nearly two-thirds of the total value of imports. The imports of food products decreased from 10 million tons in 1931 to 6.5 million in 1934 and those of manufactured goods fell from 9 million francs to 2 million. Exports, on the other hand, declined from 30 million francs to 18 million. After the devaluation of the franc in 1936 the system was modified, but the growing uncertainty in international affairs during the next two years prevented any reform of the tariff.

Merchant marine. The total French merchant marine in 1913 consisted of 17,719 vessels, of 2,448,000 gross tons; but of these only 196 steamers and 60 sailing vessels were over 2000 tons. During the war the merchant marine was sacrificed almost entirely to the exigencies of war, and the shipyards were diverted largely to the construction of arms and munitions. The losses through enemy action or otherwise were 1019 ships with a gross tonnage of 1,059,-000, of which less than a quarter was made good by new building. In order to centralize the work of marine transportation the government in 1916 requisitioned 60 per cent and two years later the entire fleet, and operated the vessels as a state enterprise. These, together with vessels bought at high prices from neutrals and even from Allies, made up a fleet of 800,000 tons. In 1919, when a shipping slump occurred, the state fleet was sold and returned to private ownership. From a financial point of view the venture placed a heavy burden on the treasury. The loss from operation was placed at 608 million francs, and only 136 million francs were recovered from the sale of the ships. As in Australia, Canada, and the United States, so also in France, the experiment of a state fleet involved a very heavy financial loss.

After the war the allocation of enemy ships, captured by the Allies or in compensation for war losses, the purchase of others from Britain, and the revival of shipbuilding at home brought the merchant marine up to 3,846,000 tons in 1922. This gave France third place among world powers, after Britain and the United States. The next decade was one of severe international competition, and the maritime expansion of Japan, Germany, and Norway, coupled with a slackening of her own efforts, pushed France down to sixth place. An effort was made in 1928 and 1929 to stimulate the shipbuilding industry by the establishment of the *Crédit Maritime,* the guarantee of interest on new construction, and the granting of privileges to French-built vessels. A further law of 1934 revived the old system of subsidies, based upon tonnage, speed, and the right of the state to arm the ships in the event of war. After a brief spurt, however, the total tonnage steadily declined to 3,268,000 tons in 1938. A strong but costly effort was made to attract tourists to the great luxury liners which were built to maintain French prestige, such as the *Normandie,* which was the largest ship afloat and for a time held the transatlantic record for speed.

Most of the French merchant vessels were old and slow, nearly half of them being over 20 years old. They were backward in utilizing turbines or oil-burning engines, and consequently made a poor showing in international commerce. They did little business for other nations, and carried only slightly over one-third of French imports and slightly under two-thirds of their own exports. Most of the traffic was in the hands of some very large companies with numerous banking and industrial connections, which also administered the chief ports. About half of the merchant marine was controlled by three companies, which allocated the traffic and fixed rates. Complaints were frequent as to high rates and slow service. An excuse for such monopolistic practices might possibly be found in the unremunerative character of French foreign shipping. The imports were heavy bulky articles like cereals, coal, wood, etc., while the exports were primarily manufactured goods of high value but small bulk. Vessels were therefore compelled to leave French ports without equivalent return freights, and this raised the cost of carriage in both directions.

The ports enjoyed before the war absolute autonomy and liberty in administration except for some simple and liberal police regulations. The war compelled a strict discipline by the state and military considerations forced a concentration of traffic at a few strategic ports, especially Havre, Rouen, and Bordeaux, which were greatly improved. After the war it was impossible to return to the anarchic conditions of pre-war days, and a regime of "organized liberty" was adopted. The regulation of the ports was entrusted to regional economic groups, organized by local Chambers of Commerce, but under the Minister of Public Works. In addition to the three ports just named, Dunkerque and Marseilles were great shipping points and Cherbourg ranked high as a passenger port.

Domestic trade. The period after the war showed little change in the general conditions of French retail trade, though the lack of official data in this field makes factual statements little better than guesses. There was apparently a considerable increase in the number ᴏf retail establishments, and in the severity of competition. It was estimated [7] that in 1928 about 85 per cent of the retail business was carried on by small independent concerns, about 6 per cent by department stores, 5 per cent by chain stores, 1 per cent by consumers' cooperatives, and 3 per cent unknown. The small establishments were not merely numerous, they were often incompetently run, without sufficient capital, and unable to find an adequate market. The crisis of 1929 and the ensuing depression put many of them out of business. The French legislation and literature were, however, apparently less concerned with the competence of the small retailer than with the competition which he faced from other forms of organization. The most violent attacks were made on the co-operatives, and next to these on the one-price stores. A law was passed in 1934 to restrict the operations of the former by taxing all sales made to non-members. Department stores, confined mostly to the large cities, were accepted as a matter of course, and the chain stores were comparatively free from criticism. These had been taxed in 1912 on a graduated scale according to the number of their branches, and in 1917 a special tax was imposed on a total annual turnover exceeding one million francs. Mail-order houses were never important in French retail trade.

The retailers were united in a *Fédération des Commerçants d'Étaillants de France*, which published a monthly magazine and constituted a fairly effective pressure group. The following list of achievements was given at the end of 1935: the almost complete assimilation of consumers' co-operatives into normal retail trade, one single tax on all foodstuffs, the regulation of peddlers, prohibition of public officials carrying on trade, the reduction of the tax on commercial profits from 15 to 12 per cent, and forbidding the launching of any new traveling stores in trucks. The catalogue is not an impressive one and suggests that the consumers were fairly well satisfied with the existing organization.

More significant from an economic viewpoint than this semi-political organization was the banding together of small retailers in associations for the common purchase of their wares. These were especially numerous in the food trades. By establishing joint purchasing agencies they obtained the advantages, which the department and chain stores enjoyed, of lower prices for large orders, of better credit facilities, and of saving the middleman's profits. A large number of such organizations existed before the war, but multiplied rapidly after it; these were grouped in regional associations and about a quarter were organized in a federation, the *Union Nationale des Sociétés d'Achats en Commun*.

[7] F. Simonet, *Le petit commerce de détail* (Paris, 1938), 251.

Conclusion. The period between 1914 and 1939 witnessed a tremendous shrinkage in the volume of world trade and also a decline in Europe's share in that trade. The war destroyed commercial and financial connections, closed markets, and disorganized the marketing organization which had been developed through almost fifty years of peace in Europe. And the treaty of peace introduced new disequilibria which made a return to the old system impossible. Other factors, too, contributed to cause the decline in international trade. Reparations distorted the normal flow of goods, inflation and devaluation of currencies disturbed values and artificially restricted or stimulated imports or exports according to circumstances, and the swelling tide of nationalism placed further obstacles in the way. New theories of state power in Germany, Italy, and Russia subordinated trade to national interests, and made it serve the demands of the state rather than the well-being of individuals.

The method by which foreign trade was manipulated was primarily the protective tariff, which was raised to prohibitive heights in most countries, even Britain deserting free trade after eighty years and joining the ranks of the protectionist states. But because of fluctuations in values occasioned by currency changes, the customs tariff was found to be too slow and often ineffective, and accordingly other techniques were introduced. Exchange control, quotas, and bilateral trading agreements were used to bring about a balance between imports and exports. While these methods helped to equalize the two sides of the trade balance, they had a restrictive influence and held down the total amount of trade.

It is difficult for the moment to see any escape from the present *impasse*. Economic nationalism is deeply rooted in present trends and represents an attempt to control international economic relations in much the same fashion that domestic social welfare legislation aims at internal regulation. It is a vigorous reaction against individualism and economic liberalism. Its restrictive influence is partially mitigated by the creation of great trading blocs, such as the British Empire, within which there is comparative freedom of exchange. The revival of international trade on a world scale by international agreement can be only a hope of the future.

BIBLIOGRAPHICAL NOTE

1. *Britain.* As a result of the decrease in foreign commerce attention was increasingly diverted to methods of preventing further loss and of augmenting Britain's share in world trade. A general survey is the *Report of the Committee on Industry and Trade, Survey of Overseas Markets* (London, 1925); this "Balfour Report" contains rich factual material on world markets. Commercial policy is discussed in E. V. Francis, *British Economic Strategy* (London, 1939); J. H.

Richardson, *British Economic Foreign Policy* (London, 1936). H. Heuser, *Control of International Trade* (London, 1939) describes methods of quotas, exchange clearing, and other devices. J. B. Condliffe, *Markets and the Problem of Peaceful Change* (Paris, 1939) is a thoughtful analysis. An interesting experiment is described by A. S. C. Carr and D. R. Evans, *The Lure of Safeguarding* (London, 1929), and A. Ramsay, *The Economics of Safeguarding* (London, 1930). The tariff is variously viewed. R. M. Findlay, *The British under Protection* (London, 1934) describes the transition; E. B. McGuire, *The Bitish Tariff System* (London, 1939) is an excellent concise account; F. Benham, *Great Britain under Protection* (London, 1941) carries the story down to date. On shipping during the war a careful account is C. E. Fayle, *The War and the Shipping Industry* (New Haven, 1927); J. R. Smith, *Influence of the War upon Shipping* (New York, 1919) is written too early. W. C. Jones, *British Merchant Shipping* (London, 1922) is a good account for the general reader. A. C. Hardy, *Seaways and Sea Trade* (London, 1934) is a detailed study of cargoes, routes, and services. A useful survey is C. E. Fayle, *A Short History of the World's Shipping Industry* (London, 1933). Colonial policy is described in H. D. Hall, *The British Commonwealth of Nations: a Study of its Past and Future Development* (London, 1920), thorough; A. E. Zimmern, *The Third British Empire* (2nd ed., London, 1927) good; J. A. Williamson, *A Short History of British Expansion*, 1066–1920 (London, 1922), a general sketch; A. P. Newton, *A Hundred Years of the British Empire* (New York, 1940), useful.

2. *Germany*. A study of the war period is J. Hirsch, *Deutschland's Aussen- und Innenhandel unter den Wirkungen des Krieges* (Berlin, 1923). H. Sieveking, *Grundlagen der Handelspolitik* (Berlin, 1927) provides a foundation. W. Ropke, *German Commercial Policy* (London, 1934) is good, as is A. Robinet de Clery, *La politique douanière de l'Allemagne depuis l'avènement de Caprivi jusqu'en 1925* (Paris, 1935). H. Lupmann, *Tariff Levels and the Economic Unity of Europe* . . . 1913–1931 (New York, 1938) is a broader study. A. T. Bonnell, *German Control over International Economic Relations*, 1930–1940 (Urbana, Ill., 1940) is primarily interested in exchange control, as is H. S. Ellis, *Exchange Control in Central Europe* (Cambridge, Mass., 1941). B. Heilinger, *Der Schutz der mittelständischen Detailhandels gegen Warenhäuser* (Bern, 1937) deals with retail trade.

3. *France*. A popular text on foreign trade is E. Rachinel, *Commerce* (23e ed., Paris, 1937). Tariff policy is described by A. Landry, *La politique commerciale de la France* (Paris, 1934); C. J. Gignoux, *L'après la guerre et la politique commerciale* (Paris, 1924), a concise survey; B. Nogaro and M. Moye, *Le régime douanier de la France* (Paris, 1931), a slight sketch; R. Hoffherr, *La politique commerciale de la France* (Paris, 1939); F. A. Haight, *History of French Commercial Policies* (New York, 1941), a useful outline. J. Naudin, *Les accords commerciaux de la France depuis la guerre* (Paris, 1928) describes commercial treaties. The quota system is thoroughly handled in F. A. Haight, *French Import Quotas* (London, 1935), and J. Lautman, *Quelques aspects nouveaux du protectionisme* (Paris, 1923). Shipping is covered in G. Candace, *La marine marchande française et son importance dans la vie nationale* (Paris, 1930), a plea for its revival; L. Roux, *La marine marchande* (Paris, 1923), a well-informed survey. Retail trade is treated in J. Valmy-Baysse, *Les grands magasins* (Paris, 1927); A. Guibert, *Les tendances modernes du commerce et le commerce de détail* (Paris, 1931); F. Simonet, *Le petit commerce de détail, sa lutte avec le grand commerce de détail* (Paris, 1938).

CHAPTER XIX

TRANSPORTATION

I. RAILWAY CENTRALIZATION IN BRITAIN

Railway transportation during the war. On the day after war was declared the government assumed general control of the British railway system and administered the various lines as a unit; their working management was, however, left in the hands of the technical staffs of the companies. A General Executive Committee, made up of the chief executives of the important roads, determined general principles and co-ordinated the several railway organizations into an efficient whole. The necessity of transporting troops and military equipment of all kinds, as well as the normal traffic, made it imperative that the railways should be at the disposal of the government. Unified operation was ensured by pooling the traffic and to a less degree the rolling stock of all the lines. Passenger traffic was discouraged by restricting the speed of passenger trains, reducing the amount of luggage that could be carried, and raising fares. A territorial grouping of the railways was made, cross freights were eliminated, and considerable economies effected by better organization. The government agreed to make full compensation for any loss or injury to the railways during the period of war control, and to pay to them each year during such period an amount equal to their net incomes for the year 1913. Subsequently, certain modifications were made in this financial arrangement. Under government control the railways were efficiently and economically run, and made a valuable contribution to the conduct of the war.

The Railways Act of 1921. The problem of what to do with the railways became a political as well as an economic issue after the armistice. Ever since the Taff Vale strike in 1900 there had been a growing demand for nationalization of the railways. This view, however, was rejected by Parliament, and they were returned to their private owners in 1921 together with compensation for losses suffered while under government control. The conditions under which they were to be operated in the future were laid down in the British Railways Act of 1921, and differed vastly from the regime of private competition which had existed before the war.

Part I of the Act, entitled Reorganization of the Railway System, dealt with grouping. There were 214 separate railway undertakings in Great Britain, and 121 of these were now combined into four systems. The experience of the war had shown that great economies in operation and administration could be effected and at the same time facilities increased, if a number of separate companies were operated as a unit. Such amalgamation had been discouraged or forbidden by Parliament before the war, but now they were given the sanction of law. Four large systems were created, even the old names disappearing, with one exception. This was a compromise between two divergent views; it made no provision for nationalization, but imposed strict control and by amalgamation laid the basis for possible future nationalization. Reliance was still placed upon competition, which was expected to continue between London and the main industrial centers, for freight if not for passenger traffic. Such competition as existed after the new grouping took the form of improved facilities and advertising, rather than of physical duplication of plant. Somewhat illogically, the railway companies were not permitted to allocate or pool traffic among themselves, except with the consent of the Ministry of Transport. Subsequently this prohibition was modified and traffic pooling was permitted on competitive routes.

BRITISH RAILWAY SYSTEMS, 1921

	Constituent companies (amalgamated)	Subsidiary companies (absorbed)	Mileage
London, Midland and Scottish	8	27	7750
London and Northeastern	6	27	7750
Southern	5	14	2150
Great Western	7	26	3750

Part II of the Act, entitled Regulation of Railways, empowered the Railway and Canal Commission to require reasonable services, facilities, and conveniences. This authority was used to effect a long-overdue standardization of track, plant, and equipment. The lack of uniformity in the most essential matters had long been a matter of criticism. The loading gauge varied, different styles of automatic brakes were used, the driver's position was sometimes on the left-hand side and sometimes on the right-hand side of the locomotive, signalling practices varied, freight cars were of different sizes, and even the permanent way was not uniform. The way was now open for reform of these practices, but progress was painfully slow.

By the end of the period the height of platforms, at least for new or rebuilt stations, had been standardized. Automatic train control was still being urged by the Royal Commission of 1930, but the Great Western was the only road that developed automatic signalling extensively. One of the great difficulties with this system in Great Britain is that few signal boxes can be eliminated because stations, cross-overs, etc., occur at such frequent intervals. British railways, alone of the important railways in the world, still retained loose-link coupling for freight trains. Automatic airbrakes were generally introduced for passenger trains, but in connection with freight trains two difficulties were met: the large number of privately owned cars and the short haul character of much of British freight traffic. The freight cars retained their standard size of twelve tons, although larger ones would be more economical for coal, stone, and similar heavy traffic. A peculiar feature of the British railway system was the large number of private owners' freight cars — 638,000 in 1937 as against 646,000 owned by the railways themselves. These varied in capacity from eight to twelve tons, were of older types, and were not adapted to rapid haulage. Their existence complicated the railway problem. Some electrification took place on suburban lines, but not much was done on main lines. Taken as a whole, however, the British railway system, both passenger and freight, met the requisites of a good service, namely frequency, speed, comparatively low cost, and comfort.

Part III of the Act, entitled Railway Charges, established a Railway Rates Tribunal, which was empowered to fix rates, fares, and other charges at such a level as would provide the new companies with a "standard" income. This was to equal the aggregate net revenue of the constituent and subsidiary companies in each system in 1913. The freight classification of 1891 was altered and a new rate schedule was adopted. As finally made effective in 1928 this fixed freight rates at about sixty per cent above the pre-war level, and raised passenger fares. It was hoped to simplify the rate structure and to abolish the thousands of exceptional rates that then existed, but the advent of motor vehicle competition prevented this and even led to an increase; in 1939 probably two-thirds of the traffic was carried at exceptional rates. The year 1913 was regarded as the measuring stick of railway prosperity, and the rates fixed were designed to bring in revenues comparable with that year, amounting in all to about £50,000,000. But the early estimates of savings from amalgamation were over-optimistic, competition and depression reduced earnings, and the goal was never reached. A vicious circle developed: the loss of rail traffic prevented the lowering of rates, but unless rates were lowered, especially on heavy traffic, water and motor transportation threatened to make further inroads.

Part IV of the Act of 1921, Wages and Conditions of Service, attempted to meet a labor situation aggravated by price fluctuations and the presence of three powerful railway unions. A complicated system of joint tribunals was set up, which were to adjudicate wages and other matters in disputes.

The evolution of railway regulation in Britain has been succinctly summarized by a careful student as follows: [1] "The earliest regulation related primarily to construction of the lines, later abolishing abuses which arose from financial mismanagement. By the seventies the question of safety was foremost, both for passengers and staff (probably caused by the increase in speed and density of traffic). At the commencement of the eighties rates and fares became the main subject of railway regulation, and still are. In the late nineties the conditions of work were the important feature; and more recently machinery to deal with wage disputes."

Inland waterways. At the beginning of the war the canals owned by railways passed, together with the railways, under the control of the government, and in 1917 the remaining waterways were added, making a total of 2251 miles. The primary purpose was so to organize the traffic on the canals as to relieve the congestion on the railways, and a considerable increase in traffic was achieved, especially in coal, grain, foodstuffs, and munitions.

At the conclusion of the war the canals reverted to their former owners, but conditions were now worse than they had been. Repair and maintenance had been neglected, wages had risen, and much skilled labor was lost. A report of the so-called Chamberlain Committee recommended the amalgamation of the canals into seven large systems, but no action was taken, and the depression of the following year prevented the making of needed improvements. The canal system suffered from divided ownership and the consequent difficulty in quoting through tolls and also from the fact that the canal owners were not operators of the boats. Traffic fell off, from 32,000,000 tons in 1913 to 18,530,000 in 1937.

Motor transportation. The railways had enjoyed a virtual monopoly of inland transportation from the middle of the nineteenth century to about 1910. The war had revealed the possibilities, but the full strength of motor vehicles as competitors of the railway was not realized until about 1922. Any expansion of their use depended, however, upon improvement of the roads.

Little increase in the length of roads had been made; there were 175,000 miles in 1900 and 178,900 in 1939, of which only 44,000 were "main" roads. The cost of maintaining the roads was at first met by a road fund derived from motor licenses, but after 1937 by direct Parliamentary grant. The first improvement took the form of surfaces better adapted to motor vehicles. These proved very destructive to the ordinary macadamized road, and most of them were surfaced with tar in the next few years; concrete was little

[1] C. E. R. Sherrington, *The Economics of Rail Transport in Great Britain* (3rd ed., London, 1937), II, 301. By permission of the publisher, Edward Arnold and Company, London.

used. More difficult was the problem of road layout. Existing roads were quite unsuited to motor traffic, for they were too narrow, had too many corners, cross-roads, and railway level crossings, and passed through too many towns. Improvement of these defects proceeded very slowly. One difficulty lay in the fact that highway administration was in the hands of small local units and there was little co-ordination. But in spite of difficulties the motor vehicles began to cut heavily into rail traffic.

For passenger traffic the chief advantage of both the private car and the motor bus was their mobility. They could pick up and drop their passengers at any point, and they had a low operating cost. Some railways introduced a light rail-motor car to meet the latter point, but this could not be a general solution of the problem because of varied conditions. In 1927 the railways demanded road powers to meet this competition, which was conferred upon them by the railway acts of 1928. They invested large sums in motor buses and united with existing bus and truck companies. A considerable amount of co-ordination was thus achieved. In 1939 the railways were operating some 10,000 motor road vehicles. Competition between road and rail for passenger traffic was fairly well stabilized after 1930, and tended to be divided according to distance travelled and relative convenience. By 1938 there were 3,000,000 motor vehicles licensed in Great Britain.

Competition for freight, on the other hand, remained keen, and the motor truck proved more of a menace than the bus. Motor haulage had distinct advantages: it was more suitable for certain types of traffic, like household removals, confectionery, eggs, etc.; transhipment was avoided; one- to three-ton loads, too small for a low rate by rail, could be efficiently handled; rates were frequently lower, since the road was free and only part of the cost of maintenance was paid by the truck owners. As a result of these and other factors, the motor trucks tended to attract the valuable small traffic paying high rates, and to leave to the railways the heavier and less remunerative traffic. The average railway haul was about sixty miles, but motor competition was effective up to seventy-five miles with no return load and double that distance with a return load. There could no longer be talk of a railway monopoly.

The decade of the thirties had seen a steady extension of state regulation over the road transport industry, but the railways still felt that they were being discriminated against, and in 1938 demanded what they called a "square deal." They asked for greater freedom in quoting freight rates, since no restrictions in this regard were placed upon the road companies. This request was seconded by the Transport Advisory Council the following year, and in May,

1939, the Minister of Transport announced that appropriate legislation would be introduced in the next session of Parliament.

Aviation. The military use of airplanes during the war showed the possibilities of commercial air transport, and in 1919 the first regular service was opened between London and Paris. For the first decade progress was slow, but after two noteworthy trans-Atlantic flights in 1927 a new impetus was given the industry.

BRITISH CIVIL AVIATION

Year	Miles flown (1000)	No. passengers	Tons cargo
1919	104	870	30
1928	916	27,300	813
1937	10,773	244,400	3961

Owing to the small size of the British Isles and the excellence of the railway express service, internal air transport was slow in developing. A couple of experiments in the twenties failed, and it was not until the late thirties that any considerable development took place, but by 1937 some fourteen companies were operating 4500 miles of route, among them the railways themselves. Most of the air services transcended the limits of Britain, and reached out in every direction. The Imperial Airways Limited, formed in 1924 by an amalgamation of several competing companies, developed a world-wide system of aviation. It was subsidized by the government for political and military reasons.

2. RAILWAY UNIFICATION IN GERMANY

Railways during the war. It has often been asserted by foreign critics that German railways were planned with a view to military requirements. German writers, on the other hand, claim that the main task of the railway system has always been to serve the economic needs of the country, and that military considerations played a minor part. Be that as it may, it is a matter of historical record that the role played by the railways in the Franco-Prussian war was carefully studied by military experts and that after 1871 von Moltke insisted upon close co-operation between the army and the railways. Accordingly, when war was declared in 1914 careful plans had already been formulated for the railways' part in military mobilization. Since the war was fought on two fronts and outside the borders of Germany, they were called upon to render extraordinary service in moving troops and materials. In addition to this the chief tasks of the railways were to convey war supplies and foodstuffs and to sustain the morale of the people. To these major needs all other considerations were subordinated.

As in other countries the operating personnel was greatly reduced, perhaps by a third, and at the same time skilled operatives were being replaced by unskilled. Maintenance of track and equipment suffered severely. There was a shortage of essential materials and substitutes had to be used which greatly reduced the efficiency of the equipment and made the whole system less serviceable. Between 1913 and 1918 the number of locomotives in use fell off 12 per cent, and this was typical of all branches. Total railway traffic fell from 501,000,000 tons in 1913 to 368,000,000 in 1915; the vigorous "Hindenburg program" of the next year moved it up somewhat, but by the end of the war it was down nearly to the low point. Attempts to relieve the railways of their burden by utilizing other agencies of transportation met with only meager success. Road traffic was out of the question, because horses were lacking. Canals were used for heavy goods, but they could not be counted on for regular service, since many of them suffered from ice in winter and low water in summer. Canal traffic declined steadily, from 100,000,000 tons in 1913 to 43,000,000 in 1918.

Efforts were made during the war to unify the various state railways into a single whole, but these shattered on the refusal of the separate units to give up their independence. The system remained a federal one, though the administration was somewhat centralized after 1916 by the creation of an operating division on the Prussian system, to which all the other state railways and the army were asked to send representatives. It proved impossible to achieve even a unified management during the war.

Unification of the railways. Under the terms of the Versailles Treaty Germany was compelled to deliver to the Allies 5000 locomotives, 150,000 freight cars, and 5000 motor trucks; in addition to these she was forced to replace the rolling stock which the German armies had seized when they invaded Belgium and France. Both the permanent way and equipment were in a very low state of efficiency. By 1920 the locomotives and freight cars in working condition were each about 25 per cent less than in 1913 and passenger and baggage cars were off 35 per cent.

The Weimar Constitution provided for the nationalization of the state railways and in 1920 they were taken over by the Reich at a valuation of 25 billion marks. This proved to be a poor bargain for the Reich, for the states seized the opportunity before transfer to load the railways with new burdens. Much new construction was begun which the Reich was obligated to finish. About 200,000 employees were added between 1918 and 1919 of whom nearly

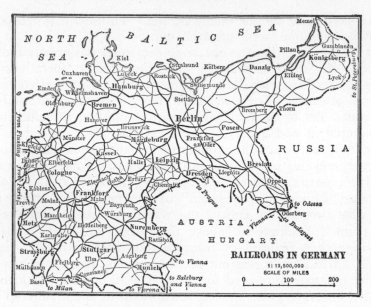

FIGURE 10.   RAILWAYS IN GERMANY

From C. C. Adams' *A Text-Book of Commercial Geography* (D. Appleton &
Co., 1909).   Reprinted by permission of the publishers.

100,000 of the non-official ratings (*Arbeiter* and *Hilfsbeamter*)
were promoted to the rank of officials (*Beamter*) on the eve of the
transfer; in other words they were made permanent and practically
irremovable employees.   The officials from the imperial railways
in Alsace and Lorraine had also to be cared for.   The railways were
thus enormously over-staffed, but the new government, depending
upon popular support for its existence, did not dare take the risk
of wholesale dismissals.

The financial results of the purchase were very unfavorable for
the Reich and came at a most unfortunate moment.   As the central
government could not pay cash for the railways it assumed an
equivalent portion of funded and floating indebtedness of the states.
It was expected that the consolidation of the railway system would
permit important economies to be effected, but little was accomplished along that line.   The introduction of the eight-hour day
also added to the labor costs.   For 1920 the total railway deficit
was 15 billion paper marks, and for 1921 the operating deficit was
7 billion marks, exclusive of interest charges.

During the period of inflation the railway debts were extinguished.   This placed the railways in a better financial position,
though it was purchased at the expense of German citizens who
held the securities.   But the gain was offset by enormous expendi-

tures for rehabilitation. Between 1918 and 1924 over 18,000 locomotives, 26,000 passenger, and 453,000 freight cars were purchased, handsome new stations were built, automatic brakes were installed, the permanent way was improved, and to some extent double-tracked and electrified. By 1924 the German railway system was the best equipped and most efficient in Europe.

The railways under the Dawes and Young plans. In 1924 the Dawes plan, providing for reparations payments by Germany, was put into effect. Under this plan the Reich railway system was converted into a joint stock company for administrative purposes. Bonds to the amount of 11 billion marks, representing the average net earnings for several years before the war capitalized at 6 per cent, were issued and placed in the hands of the Agent General for Reparations. Interest on these at the rate of 3 per cent for the first, 4 per cent for the second, and 5 per cent for the third and subsequent years was paid into the reparations fund. In addition to the bonds, seven per cent preferred stock to the amount of 2 billion marks was issued for general sale, and common stock to the amount of 13 billion marks was given to the German government. The administration was placed under the direction of a board of eighteen directors, half chosen by the German government and half by the trustees of the reparations bonds. A German general manager was put in charge of operations, and at the head of the whole system stood a railway commissioner, chosen by the foreign members of the board of directors. The control of the railways was thereby vested in the Allies though the fixation of rates remained in the hands of the Reich.

The guiding principle in German railway policy and practice had been the development of the economic life of the country; net revenue was regarded as of secondary importance. In pursuance of this policy low rates had been granted imports of raw materials and exports of manufactured goods. To this the reparations experts took exception, declaring that the railways should be run on commercial lines and should be made to yield a profit. It is incorrect to say, however, that they were run purely for profit, for national interests were still held in view and followed. But it was no longer possible for the railways to use their rate policies for the encouragement of agriculture, the stimulation of exports, or similar nationalistic ends. During the five years of administration under the Dawes Plan the profit objective was constantly kept in view, and in spite of political and commercial difficulties was realized in practice.

The personnel was reduced by 277,000 superfluous employees in 1924, and by an additional 60,000 the following year, and other economies were effected. In the period from October, 1925, to

December, 1929, the German Railway Company was enabled to earn a net profit of 436 million marks in addition to payments of 2880 million on the reparations bonds and the accumulation of a legal reserve of 500 million. The Railway Company was compelled by Reich legislation to increase wages and salaries, and was saddled with additional pensions and social charges. In order to meet them it was necessary, in spite of a reduction in staff, to raise passenger fares and freight rates, and also to cut down capital expenditures. These had been planned on a grandiose scale under the former regime, but now were restricted to "such works as are really essential to the development of traffic and for keeping level with technical progress." [2] All in all the administration and operation of the railways under foreign control were business-like and efficient, and when they were handed back to the Reich at the end of the Dawes Plan they were in sound financial and technical condition. The economic advantages of a unified system for the whole Reich, which had cost so much in 1920, were moreover now being realized.

The financial success was achieved in spite of the fact that railway freight traffic in 1925 was less by 14 per cent than it had been in 1913. Most of this loss occurred in the movement of iron ore and raw iron and of lignite, due in part to the cession of Lorraine and in part to technological changes in industry which were diminishing the movement of goods. Lignite was being utilized increasingly in the vicinity of the mines for the generation of electricity, which was transmitted by wire. There was also a greater use of hydro-electric power. The change from raw coal to coke for metallurgical operations reduced the weight carried. There was, moreover, a smaller consumption of coal, due to improved heating facilities in dwellings, and a lessened demand for iron and steel in the shipbuilding industry, usually one of the principal consumers.

The status of the Railway Company was completely altered by the Young Plan. All foreign participation in the railways came to an end, and the commissioner and foreign members of the board of directors ceased to function. The Company continued, however, as a private and autonomous organization, subject only to the control of the German government. The reparation bonds amounting to 11 billion marks were cancelled, and the annual charges of 660 million marks were converted into a tax. The change in legal structure had little effect on the traffic, which remained practically stationary during the rest of this period. The imperial railway system, with a length of about 42,300 miles in 1938, maintained the rolling stock on a constant level, but by better organization and larger use

[2] *Report of the Agent General for Reparation Payments*, December 22, 1928 (Berlin, 1929), 37.

for vacation travel increased considerably the amount of passenger traffic; freight traffic grew very slightly. In 1939 the Reich instituted a four-year replacement program, to cost 3500 million marks, providing for the purchase of 10,000 passenger cars, 112,000 freight cars, and 17,300 automobile trailers.

Inland waterways. Germany had a longer mileage of rivers than either Britain or France, and these were being canalized and improved and linked together by a comprehensive system of canals. A lively debate was carried on in the early twenties over the rescuscitation of the canals. This revealed a double conflict of interests. Western Germany favored canals, for most of the projected waterways ran through this section, while the east saw little advantage in them. The canal advocates urged that the railways should cease taking traffic from the canals, but should rather divert some of their traffic to the canals. The Imperial Railway refused to accede to this demand, but agreed to make through rates via rail and canal, and to care for the interests of the shipper. The position of the Reichstag was that only such canals should be built whose developed traffic could support them. The most ambitious project was the 375-mile Rhine-Main-Danube canal, as part of a water route of over 2000 miles across Europe from the North Sea to the Black Sea.

In 1913 the canals in Germany were carrying 17 per cent of the combined water and rail traffic, and in 1925 still held the same proportion; at the latter date the canals in France were carrying 14 per cent, and in Great Britain only 6 per cent. After this the waterways gained at the expense of the railways, though both lost to the fast-growing motor transportation. Most of the traffic was coal, ore, sand, stone, and wheat, in order of importance. Self-propelled boats, larger and faster, gradually took the place of the old barges, which fell off by half between 1913 and 1938.

Motor transportation. The large use of motor vehicles during the World War and their usefulness both at the front and behind the lines led to a better appreciation of their potentialities. After the war many military automobiles were set free for commercial use and they began to compete with the railways for traffic. The private passenger car remained a luxury; as late as 1938 there was only 1 car for every 54 persons in Germany, compared with 23 in Britain and 20 in France. Travelers seemed to prefer the railways, on which it was possible to read or sleep and to travel without strain. The autobus, however, competed vigorously with the railways for short and medium distances. It had a monopoly of traffic to places without rail connections, and had the advantage of using the public roads, provided at public expense. At junction points it stole some of the railway traffic.

The motor trucks offered even more serious competition. Up to 30 miles they practically controlled the field. Between 30 and 60 miles the competition was fairly even, except for those goods which were sent in car-load lots, which went to the railways. For distances between 60 and 250 miles the struggle centered mainly on the valuable and light goods, which the railways endeavored to retain by favorable rates. Heavy goods were moved almost entirely by rail, except in neighborhood traffic. The German Imperial Railway estimated in 1930 that the losses sustained by the railways in 1928 through competition of motor trucks were 200,000,000 marks.

The construction of arterial motor highways, free from level crossings or cross-roads, was undertaken largely for military reasons. The first stretches were opened in 1935 and three years later about 2000 miles were completed. These highways had slight commercial significance, except as they prevented congestion of troops and military supplies on the ordinary roads. The total mileage of highways of all classes in 1938 was about 150,000 miles, of which 25,000 were imperial roads.

Under *Wehrwirtschaft*, as developed by the Nazi regime, roads were very important, for they could be easily repaired if bombed. Railways, while more efficient, were more vulnerable. With the development of motorized and mechanized warfare great attention was devoted to the building and improvement of roads.

Aviation had a remarkable development after the World War. It was of especial importance for foreign travel and for long distances. In combination with ocean steamers it was also used by the post office. In 1937 German airlines flew 11,000,000 miles. As rearmament came to assume greater importance, more attention was devoted to fighting airplanes and less to purely commercial ones. By 1939 Germany was the leading country in the world in the former type.

Transportation was still in flux at the end of this period, though the tendency was evident for each class of traffic to move by that agency which offered the best service. Petroleum and gas went by pipe line. Electricity, transmitted by wire, presented primarily problems of organization and control rather than of transportation. The possibilities of its use for water craft and land vehicles was still undeveloped. The division of the field among the other agencies was still uncertain. One other contender remains to be mentioned — the humble bicycle. The number of these was rapidly increasing in the cities and by 1936 there were 17,000,000 or one to every four persons.

3. NATIONALIZATION OF THE RAILWAYS IN FRANCE

Railways during the war. The five private railway systems in France in 1913 were autonomous and highly particularistic. They had built up powerful internal organizations, and among them there was an absolute lack of co-ordination. Different types of rolling stock on the roads made it impossible to transfer cars from one line to another. There were different methods of signaling, and other diversities in practice. When war broke out the diversity among the railways forced the government to place them under state control. The immediate task was to transport troops and supplies, and to this everything else was sacrificed. Commercial traffic was completely subordinated to military needs at first, but it soon became apparent that the maintenance of industry was equally important and freight traffic was gradually restored. In the face of a national emergency the railways showed a spirit of co-operation, but the system was bad. Co-ordination and centralization of authority were needed, and they were obtained by the creation of a governmental *Direction générale de transports et importations* in 1916. The following year the powers of this office were transferred to the Ministry of Public Works, which administered the railways until they were decontrolled in 1921.

The enormous load placed upon the railways impaired the permanent way and reduced the rolling stock. Before the war the French railways had 14,000 locomotives, 31,000 passenger cars, and 375,000 freight cars, but in 1918 there were only 11,000 locomotives, 25,000 passenger cars, and 280,000 freight cars. In spite of these losses the movement of tonnage held up fairly well; in 1915 it was down to two-thirds of the 1913 figure, but by the end of the war the roads were carrying 80 per cent of the pre-war volume. Passenger traffic, which was discouraged by the military authorities, fell off more and did not recover so fully. The personnel was reduced by calling workers to the colors and by the imprisonment of those employed on the captured lines in the north. The gap was filled, however, by the employment of women, wounded, foreigners, young persons, and qualified men who were sent back from the front, and by 1918 the personnel was practically equal to that of 1913.

The financial position of the railways was especially unsatisfactory. Expenses mounted and receipts fell off. The Treasury helped by paying 40 per cent of the cost of new equipment purchased abroad and by paying for the transportation of military supplies. But repairs, new materials, and especially personnel cost more; between 1913 and 1919 the expenses of operation increased 300 per cent while receipts grew only 50 per cent. The deficit of the six great railway companies in 1920 amounted to 5573 million francs.

Railways after the war. A strong movement for nationalization developed in France, as in England, after the war. The financial arrangements by which the government guaranteed a minimum return on railway securities had always been unpopular. Only two of the five private companies had been able to make expenses in 1913, and the financial burden upon the state treasury had long been heavy. By nationalization and centralized administration it was thought these deficits might be wiped out. As in Britain, however, this view was rejected by the Chambers, and in 1921 the railways were returned to their private owners in the same condition that existed on August 2, 1914.

A Convention was concluded between the state and the railways which was designed to liquidate the past and to give assurance for the future. The guarantee of interest was considered as having stopped at the end of 1913, the state thus erasing the war-time debt. The companies were reimbursed for all damages caused by the war, and for debts created during the war. The companies, on their side, abandoned every demand for abnormal interest, losses, or failure to profit during the war. The concessions of the companies were extended to dates between 1950 and 1960, at the expiration of which the government would have the right to buy the railways, and the old arrangements as to guarantee of interest were continued. Although private operation was continued, an obligatory co-operation, administrative and financial, was established between the five private companies and the state, and the state railway and that of Alsace-Lorraine were placed under the authority of the Minister of Public Works. An Advisory Council was set up, which the Minister was obliged to consult on matters of general interest, and a Management Committee of experts, which saw that policies were carried out in practice. An important fiscal change was the pooling of all guarantees of interest in a common fund, so that the surpluses of the profitable roads could be set off against the deficits of the unprofitable ones. Tariffs were unified, services to the public were improved, and about one-third of the railway mileage was electrified. But French railways lagged behind those of other nations.

RAILWAY TRAFFIC, 1937

Country	Length (miles)	Freight (million tons)	Passengers (1000)
France	25,900	180	582
Germany	34,500	308	1500
England	19,200	271	1179

The five years following the agreement of 1921 resulted in deficits amounting to nearly 5000 million francs, but the activity of the next three years brought in surpluses of almost 1000 million. The upward trend was, however, sharply reversed by the depression beginning in 1930; and the railways demanded an increase in rates and a reduction in the heavy taxes on transportation, together with a simplification of the conditions of operation. But the government, fearing the necessity of a general reorganization, preferred a policy of waiting. Events moved too fast for this to be successful. Between 1921 and 1933 inclusive the accumulated deficits owing to the state amounted to over 25,000 million francs. The socialists seized upon this to demand the nationalization of the railways, but the government refused. An amendment to the Convention of 1921 was accepted by the seven great companies and became law in 1933, which strengthened the control of the state, but retained private operation.

The basic problem was not so much the administration of the railways themselves, as the competition of new transport agencies, especially the motor vehicles. An arrangement on this point was finally made, which allotted to the railways the transport of passengers between the main centers served by them, and to the automobiles that between local points. The merchandise traffic remained competitive. But the financial problem of over-capitalization of the railways and the impossibility of maintaining high rates, which were feasible only so long as the railway retained its monopoly position, pointed to a complete reorganization. This was effected in 1937.

The demand for nationalization of the railways continued and the socialists and the C.G.T. each submitted plans to obtain this. The government proposed a scheme which represented a compromise between private ownership and direct state operation, and this was enacted into law in 1937. A National Railway Company was created, co-ordinating rail and highway transport on a national basis, and combining the operations of the principal privately owned and publicly owned lines. The plan was one of centralization rather than of nationalization, but there was a shift to complete state control. The financial situation of the railways had, however, been made more difficult by the introduction of the 40-hour week in 1937, which increased costs of operation. An effort was made to meet this by abandoning unnecessary railway mileage and by better co-ordination of the railway and the motor traffic. But the real hope lay in increasing receipts from increased industrial activity.

Meanwhile the railways were becoming more deeply indebted to the state as a result of the recurring deficits. By 1938 they owed

25,000 million francs, which was more than three times their total capitalization. It was therefore a purely formal procedure for them to become state property on January 1, 1938. Thus one more step was taken toward the realization of the socialist ideal.

Motor vehicles. The roads were seriously damaged by the heavy traffic during the war, and little was done at the time to repair the injury. They were taken in hand after the armistice as part of the general scheme of reconstruction and were put in good condition. An especial impetus was given by the rapid growth in the number of motor vehicles. This new means of transport, slightly developed on the eve of the war, was given an incomparable test during that struggle, in which it played a decisive role. After the war it showed itself equally valuable for industry. Motor vehicles increased from 362,000 in 1922 to 2,065,000 in 1936, placing France ahead of all other European countries. About a quarter of these were trucks. For the latter year the road traffic was estimated at 6000 million ton-miles as compared with 18,000 million for the railways. Large trucks, carrying about 20 tons, made long trips, as from Paris to Rouen, Bordeaux, or Lyons, at 30 to 35 miles an hour, and crowded the roads. Able to make door-to-door hauls they offered serious competition with the railways, causing the abandonment of certain little-used lines.

Aviation made extraordinary progress during the war, and after peace was declared its advance was even more rapid. The five leading companies received postal subventions from the government amounting to 200 million francs yearly. In spite of this they fell into financial difficulties, and in 1932 were fused into a single company, the *Compagnie Air-France*. The subventions were continued for enterprises of a general interest. In 1938 the air traffic covered 10 million miles.

Water transportation. Of the French rivers only one — the Seine — is truly navigable; the others, with their irregular or torrential streams, required expensive works of improvement to make them usable. After the war, efforts were made to improve the waterways and to facilitate traffic on those that served industrial centers, such as the mines of the north, the port of Strassburg, the Parisian area, and others. The internal navigable waterways comprised 7565 miles of river and 3317 miles of canal, but only about two-thirds were used, and the principal stretches with regular traffic did not exceed 4000 miles. The tonnage transported, which amounted to 42 millions of tons in 1913, fell to half that figure in 1920; during the following decade it rose to 53 million in 1930, but the depression caused a slight reduction. In 1936 it was 50 million tons.

Although a good deal of traffic went by water the agencies handling it were still rather primitive. Of the 5700 proprietors of river vessels, 5300 were boatmen possessing one boat each. There existed only five companies with more than 100 boats and only one with over 500. The boats were undergoing steady improvement, resulting in a decrease in number and an increase in size, a tendency to substitute iron for wood in construction, and a larger use of vessels with mechanical propulsion. The modes of traction varied. Upon the large streams of the northern half of France, towing by steamboats was the general practice. Upon the canals all forms of haulage were used: caterpillar tractors, electric or Diesel engines on rails, sometimes horses, and even men in certain sections. But there was a steady tendency to replace animal traction by mechanical power. Water transportation profited by these technical improvements, and made a breach in the ancient monopoly of the railway. A law of 1934 provided for a co-ordination of the two services.

Conclusion. There was little physical growth in the railway net of Europe during this period, though there was constant improvement in facilities and in efficiency. The unification of the railways in each country into co-ordinated systems went on apace, and to a lesser extent these were allied with the water and motor vehicle traffic. State ownership continued to grow and where this was not realized, as in Britain, government control was so strict as to leave little choice. Other public utilities were in general owned by the central or local governments. Private initiative and enterprise still prevailed in the domain of inland water transportation, where it failed signally, and in those of motor transportation and aviation, where it achieved brilliant success.

The World War demonstrated the value of motor cars for mobile transportation and also for military purposes, and after the war technical improvements greatly increased their efficiency. Their use grew with astonishing rapidity and they began to dispute for traffic with the railways. Military tactics were altered with this new agency and warfare became motorized. The latest entrant in the transportation field was the airplane, whose influence both in peaceful commerce and in war has been enormous. Transportation as a whole has been in flux: each new agency supplements but never supplants the older one, and the movement is one of steady advance.

BIBLIOGRAPHICAL NOTE

1. *Britain.* Roads are described in R. M. C. Anderson, *The Roads of England* (London, 1932), and K. G. Tenelon, *The Economics of Road Transport* (London, 1925), a good account. G. Cadbury and S. P. Dobbs, *Canals and Inland Waterways* (London, 1929) is satisfactory. On transportation during the war F. H. Dixon and J. H. Parmelee, *War Administration of the Railways in the United States and Great Britain* (New York, 1918) gives a brief preliminary survey, and E. A. Pratt, *British Railways and the Great War*, 2 vols. (London, 1921) provides a very full account. H. C. Kidd, *A New Era for British Railways* (London, 1929) presents a study of the Railway Act of 1921. The Royal Commission on Transport, *Report* 1930 (London, 1931) gives a careful picture of the whole situation. K. G. Tenelon, *British Railways Today* (London, 1929) and V. Sommerfield, *English Railways* (New York, 1938) are good short accounts. Motor traffic is covered in C. T. Brunner, *Road vs. Rail, the case for Motor Transport* (London, 1929) and D. N. Chester, *Public Control of Road Passenger Traffic* (Manchester, 1936). On air transport H. E. Brittain, *By Air* (London, 1933) and H. Bouché, *Economics of Air Transport in Europe* (Geneva, 1935) may be cited.

2. *Germany.* A brief account of German waterways is O. Most, *Binnenwasserstrassen und deutsches Wassertstrassensystem* (Leipzig, 1938). The war period is treated in Baur, *Deutsche Eisenbahnen im Weltkrieg, 1914–1918* (Stuttgart, 1927), and in A. Sarter, *Die deutschen Eisenbahnen im Kriege* (Stuttgart, 1930), a detailed account. A good general picture is given in B. Harms, *Strukturwandlungen der deutschen Volkswirtschaft* (Berlin, 1928). R. Giese, *Hauptfragen der Reichsbahnpolitik* (Berlin, 1928) discusses administration. W. Hufner, *Die Neuordnung der deutschen Verkehrswirtschaft unter dem Einfluss der Arbeitsbeschöpfungsmassnahmen* (Berlin, 1936) describes the use of transport construction to provide work. The rise of auto traffic is covered in E. Merket, *Der Lastkraftwagenverkehr seit dem Kriege* (Berlin, 1926), and W. Bade, *Das Auto erobert die Welt* (1939). H. M. Bongers, *Deutschland's Anteil an Weltluftverkehr* (Leipzig, 1938) discusses aviation.

3. *France.* Railroads during the war are described briefly in G. Lefon, *Les chemins de fer françaises pendant la guerre* (Paris, 1922), and fully in M. Peschaud, *Politique et functionment des chemins de fer pendant la guerre* (Paris, 1926). A slight critique is P. Girard, *L'exploitation rationelle des chemins de fer en France* (Montpelier, 1923). The competition between the railways and motor vehicles is described in P. Cavie, *La concurrence du rail et de la route* (Lyon, 1933); M. Reverend, *La co-ordination des transports ferroviares et routiers* (Paris, 1934); and E. de la Rochefoucauld, *La co-ordinations des transports ferroviares et routiers* (Paris, 1934). A general survey is C. Dollfus et E. de Geoffroy, *Histoire de la locomotion terrestre*, 2 vols. (Paris, 1933).

CHAPTER XX

PRIVATE AND PUBLIC FINANCE

I. STRUGGLES WITH THE GOLD STANDARD IN BRITAIN

Currency. At the beginning of August, 1914, there was considerable withdrawal of gold from the Bank of England, much of which was hoarded. This, combined with the interruption to normal credit operations on the outbreak of war on August 1, created a critical monetary situation. To meet this the Currency and Bank Notes Act of August 6 suspended the Bank Act and authorized the issue by the government of currency notes for one pound and ten shillings which were made legal tender and were convertible into gold by the Bank at its discretion. These measures were taken to safeguard the gold reserve of the Bank from a run, which would have dissipated it. A year later the public was requested to pay gold to the post office and banks and to use notes in the payment of wages and other disbursements. While the export of gold was not specifically prohibited, it was generally regarded as unpatriotic to demand gold from the Bank for use in foreign transactions for fear it might find its way to Germany.

The currency notes, which were of convenient denominations, found their way into general circulation and gradually took the place of gold, for which there was no domestic demand. While there was no definite legal abandonment of the gold standard, the link with gold was slowly destroyed and Britain was actually on a paper money basis. Although a small gold reserve was set aside the currency notes were practically inconvertible government paper money, and remained so until 1928, when they were amalgamated with the Bank of England notes, and the exclusive right to issue such notes was given to the Bank.

The demand for gold in international transactions was on a different footing. Since Great Britain depended so largely upon foreign sources of supply for food and for many of the materials of war, it was essential that foreign exchange be stabilized and that the goods be obtained with as small an export of gold as was possible. American securities owned in Britain were sold in the United States and loans were placed there, but these were not sufficient to meet the steadily growing international balance against Britain and to maintain the normal rates of foreign exchange. The government also endeavored to meet the situation by restricting the importation of unnecessary goods and by encouraging the exportation of British manufactures. But after all these expedients had been exhausted there was still a balance against Britain which would have drained off the reserve of the Bank of England had shipments of gold been permitted to follow their normal course. In this juncture an arrangement was made between the British government and J. P. Morgan and Co. in New York, according to which the latter was authorized to buy all exchange offered on London at $4.765. Foreign exchange between the two countries was thus pegged at this point and remained so until March, 1919.

The currency notes were issued in excess of the needs of trade; by 1917 they were three times the total Bank note issue on the eve of the war and by 1919 they were six times as much. As a result of the monetary inflation and of speculation prices had doubled by the end of 1917 and were trebled by 1920. But other factors besides inflation contributed to the rise of prices. The scarcity of labor owing to the withdrawal of men for war purposes led to an increase in wages, thus raising labor costs. Raw materials cost more owing to the dislocation of foreign trade, the scarcity of shipping, and high freights. Food prices rose because of a shortage of the world's crops and difficulties of distribution. The effects of inflation on the price level were reinforced by factors of supply.

The pound was unpegged in March, 1919, and immediately the dollar rate of exchange, which had been held steadily at 4.76 since 1915, began to fall. Pegging had obscured the decline in the value of the pound during this period, but now it was revealed and the rate of exchange found its proper level. The pound oscillated around the purchasing power parity, that is the rate determined by the relationship between the values of the respective currencies in terms of goods in their own countries. The export of gold was prohibited in 1919 and the formal suspension of the gold standard was thus put into effect. It was later decided, following the recommendations of the Cunliffe Committee in 1918, to restore the gold standard by bringing the value of the pound up to the pre-war dollar rates of 4.86, and a policy of deflation of prices was begun, whereby the pound would gain in purchasing power. Within three or four years the value of the pound sterling had been brought close to its pre-war parity with gold, and in 1925 restoration of the gold standard was finally achieved.

The Gold Standard Act provided that Bank notes and currency notes should cease to be convertible on demand into gold coin, but should nevertheless remain legal tender. This was done to prevent unnecessary drains of gold from the Bank of England. The notes could, however, be exchanged for gold bullion under certain conditions. In other words, the standard that was set up was a gold bullion and not a gold specie standard. Gold coins no longer circulated and the notes were virtually token money as they could not be redeemed in gold coin; but nevertheless the gold standard existed. The freedom of export of gold was restored. This act was hailed as a step toward "liquidating" the war and as an indication of Britain's financial strength. "The pound could now look the dollar in the face." Some thirty other countries, which were closely linked with Great Britain by trade, also went back to the gold standard, though most of them devalued their currencies. Britain, however, clung to the pre-war parity. But this overvalued the pound by about 10 per cent in comparison with other currencies and made gold costs for British producers relatively high. That is, Britain was a good place to sell in, but a poor place in which to buy, and consequently imports increased, but exports fell off. Profits were reduced and unemployment remained at a high level. The trade slump, which had prevailed between 1919 and 1925, was aggravated by the adoption of the gold standard. No serious proposals, however, were made to devalue the pound or to abandon the gold standard. The Balfour Committee, in their Final Report in 1929, said: "It is unthinkable that any appreciable body of opinion would favour a fresh departure from the gold standard," and the Macmillan Committee in June, 1931, recommended that "this country should continue to adhere to the international gold standard at the existing parity."

Even while these pronouncements were being made, events were taking place in other countries which were to force an abandonment of the gold standard in Britain. The crash of 1929 was followed by a world depression. By 1931 the situation was serious. In the summer of that year Austria, faced with a banking crisis, forbade gold exports, but could not prevent the failure of the Kreditanstalt, one of its leading banking institutions, which had borrowed heavily abroad. The freezing of these foreign credits affected Germany, which followed Austria's example. Great Britain, which had made large loans in both these countries, was next drawn into the circle, as her credits became frozen. Foreign banks drew gold from London to strengthen their own position. The cumulative effect was a run on the pound during the summer of 1931, more than £200 million being withdrawn from the Bank of England in about two months. By September the Bank's gold reserve was down to £130 million and the government was forced to suspend the gold standard. This action was quickly followed by other countries. During 1931 some 16 countries suspended the gold standard, 12 in 1932, and 6 in 1933. France, Belgium, Holland, and Switzerland — the old Latin Union, — together with a dozen other minor countries, alone remained faithful.

After 1931 Britain had the managed paper pound. The Ottawa policy of cheap and abundant money, aiming at a rise in prices and the maintenance of price stability on a higher level, had favorable results. The depreciation of the pound brought a reduction of the British manufacturers' costs in terms of gold. A substantial lowering of interest rates, permitting the conversion of government and corporate bonds at a considerable reduction, brought relief to public and private debtors. The foreign exchange value of the pound was, however, subject to fluctuations which disturbed trade, and to meet this difficulty the British authorities in 1932 devised a new system known as the Exchange Equalization Account. This was designed to steady without stabilizing the foreign exchanges and to protect internal trade from the fluctuations of foreign exchange. The business of this agency was to buy and sell sterling in the foreign exchange markets in such a way as to steady it in terms of the leading foreign currencies. In other words it bought and sold sterling in exchange for foreign currencies. Any foreign currencies acquired were exchanged for gold. Until March, 1933, the Account operated in dollars since these could always be exchanged for gold, but when the United States in effect went off the gold standard in 1934, it operated in francs until October, 1936, when France also deserted the gold standard. At this point these three countries, each of which had similar equalization funds, agreed to buy from each other for gold any of their own currencies acquired by either of the others. By this means the pound, the dollar, and the franc were held at a fairly steady relationship, though complete equilibrium was not achieved.

The British currency was now "managed," and the automatism of the old system disappeared. The price level depended on the prudence and intelligence of bankers rather than on the movement of gold. Government transactions, now vastly greater than before the war, were of more consequence in shaping monetary affairs. New instruments of monetary policy were developed, and the determination of such policy rested with the government rather than with the Bank of England. The British monetary system had undergone a revolutionary change.

Banking. One of the outstanding features of the World War was the great extent to which the central banks of the belligerent countries extended financial assistance to the government, directly and indirectly. Almost without exception the government of each country involved turned to its great central banking institution for immediate advances to meet the costs of mobilization and the first military operations. The problem presented to the banks was twofold: in the first place they must provide the industrial and commercial world with needed accommodations, and in the second place they must give to the government all assistance possible for the vigorous prosecution of the war. Owing to the peculiar international position of Britain as the world center of international trade and finance, the first of these was more immediately urgent.

To carry on this international trade there had grown up in Great Britain a complex credit organization of bill brokers, discount and acceptance houses, and joint stock banks, with the Bank of England at the head. Exporters of goods from foreign countries were in the habit of selling their goods for bills of exchange drawn on London. Similarly exporters of British goods discounted bills drawn on their customers with the acceptance houses, which in turn rediscounted them with the joint stock banks or other institutions. When the outbreak of war interrupted the shipment of goods and also of gold with which the debts could have been met, all these bills were "frozen." To meet this situation the Bank of England agreed to discount the frozen bills, under government guarantee against loss, and large amounts of credit were thus released.

The Bank of England also lent its assistance to the government in financing the war by direct loan of its credit through the purchase of short-term Treasury bills. There was a gradual change in the portfolios of the banks, and they came to hold fewer private bills and a larger proportion of government obligations. After the war a reverse movement set in and the banks assisted in the rehabilitation of industry and trade. The banking structure remained practically unaltered, as the movement to amalgamation seemed to have run its course. The position and power of the Bank of England had, however, been profoundly affected by the war and it no longer exercised its former domination over the international money market. Because London had been the outstanding financial center and Britain held a position of international commercial supremacy, the Bank of England had been able, by regulating the discount rate, to control the flow of international credit and the movement of gold. After the war many new central banks were established with rationalistic policies, Britain lost its supremacy, and the Bank of England was no longer able to control the situation. When the gold standard was abandoned it lost its most effective regulatory tool. It was perforce compelled to devote its attention to domestic problems.

During the depressed period after the restoration of the gold standard in 1925 various efforts were made to bring industry and finance into closer relations. In 1926 the government arranged to guarantee exporters against loss up to 75 per cent of the credits granted by them to approved foreign purchasers. The joint stock and other banks agreed to accept bills guaranteed by the government as a satisfactory form of security for advances to the exporters. Two years later another depressed industry was given aid by the Agricultural Credits Act, which made provision for both long-term and short-term credits to farmers. Loans were made for long periods on mortgages for improvements, buildings, and similar capital outlays, or for shorter periods on the security of livestock and other agricultural assets for the purchase of agricultural machinery, stock, seed, etc. Again, in 1929 the Bank of England organized the Securities Management Trust to take over the work which the Bank had instituted of assisting industrial reorganization. The Bank had already given assistance to the steel industry and had contributed to the rationalization of the textile industry, but it was now proposed to carry the work farther. A year later the Bankers Industrial Development Company was organized, whose purpose was to examine rationalization schemes submitted by basic industries, and to assist an industry whose scheme it approved to obtain the necessary capital through normal banking channels. A further step toward industrial banking was taken in 1934 by the organization of the Credit for Industry, which was to provide long-term loans for small and medium-sized concerns. Increasingly the commercial banks subscribed to stock issues of industrial companies, in violation of early standards of liquidity. There was here an approximation to the pre-war German method of linking government, finance, and trade in an effort to promote the last, and of using the central bank for the attainment of objectives of national interest.

Meantime certain changes were occurring in the structure of British banking. The amalgamation movement continued, some of the greatest consolidations taking place in 1918. Out of this process of absorption emerged the so-called "Big Five," which did five-sixths of the British banking business. These were Barclays, Lloyds, London City and Midland (shortened to Midland in 1923), National Provincial, and Westminster. This movement was part of the reconstruction which followed the war and was motivated by the desire to create banks of national and even international scope to meet foreign financial competition. After that the movement slackened decidedly. Certain advantages were obtained by the establishment of strong centralized banks, such as the increased facilities through the multiplication of branches, the resulting growth of discounts and deposits, and the greater stability of the banking system. On the other hand, there was the danger of over-expansion and too large size; as a bank grew larger its expenses of management increased relatively. It may fairly be concluded that by 1939 the British banking structure had attained a position of comparative stability.

Public finance. Government finances were thrown into disorder by the World War, but taxation was resolutely employed to meet the costs of war, about one-third of the expenditures being met in this way. The war, however, left a heavy legacy of debt, and taxation continued on a high level, both to meet the interest on the debt and to defray the costs of expanded social services. The proportion of the national income taken for public purposes grew from somewhat over 10 per cent in 1913 to 25 per cent in 1921 and to about 40 per cent in 1939. During the fiscal year 1938–39 taxation took on the average £100 yearly from every family in Britain or about £2 every week. Between 1921 and 1936 the budget was balanced every year except four, but after the latter year the rapidly increasing expenditures for armament demanded such large sums that they could no longer be met out of ordinary revenues and resort was had to borrowing. The growth of defense expenditures was universal and may be shown for the leading countries.

DEFENSE EXPENDITURES
(in millions of dollars)

	1932	1936	1939
Great Britain	426.1	846.9	1817.1
France	509.2	834.4	1800.2
Germany	253.5	3600.0	4500.1
Italy	270.6	916.1	873.4
U. S. S. R.	282.5	4002.4	1500.1

The growth of these expenditures was reflected in the public debt. This amounted to £706 million in 1914 and by 1919, when it reached its peak, it was £7832 million. After this the conversion of the debt at lower rates of interest permitted a reduction of the interest charges and a slight amortization, so that by 1931 it had been reduced to £7413 million, but after this it mounted again. By March 31, 1940, it was £8931 million, or over one million pounds higher than it had been at the end of the World War.

2. INFLATION IN GERMANY

Currency. On the eve of the war Germany had a currency circulation of about 6000 million marks, of which about 3500 million marks were notes issued by the Reichsbank and four state-note-issuing banks and the rest mostly gold coin and fractional money. By the Act of August 4, 1914, specie payments were suspended and imperial treasury notes (*Reichskassenscheine*) were made legal tender; notes of the Reichsbank were already so. Gold disappeared from circulation, about half of the 2000 million estimated to have been in circulation before the war being hoarded, and the remainder being turned over to the Reichsbank in exchange for notes upon the request of the government. As a result of this the gold reserve of the Reichsbank was raised from 1253 million marks on July 31, 1914, to 2533 millions on June 15, 1917, the peak holding.

The system of German financial preparation and mobilization for war was based on three assumptions: a short war, victory, and an indemnity. Taxation was therefore neglected and the government relied for immediate needs upon advances in the form of notes from the Reichsbank and upon the issue of short-term Treasury bills. Both of these entered into general circulation. Another form of currency, peculiarly German, was the loan bureau notes (*Darlehns-kassenscheine*). These loan bureaus, based essentially on the principle of the pawn shop, were authorized to loan to small traders, merchants, and others upon merchandise, securities, and other collateral which might not be acceptable at commercial banks. The purpose of these bureaus was to mobilize a large part of the invested wealth of the country by coining it into immediate means of payment, and thus to avoid the appearance of a moratorium. Supplementary to these were the municipal loan offices which made loans to small retailers and handworkers upon similar collateral. All of these loans were made in the form of notes, which entered into circulation and resulted in an increase in the volume of currency, without regard to the needs of trade.

Before the loan bureau notes could be printed a temporary issue of emergency money (*Notgeld*) was issued, in small denominations from 5 pfennige to 3 marks. Later, the withdrawal from circulation of fractional silver and even of nickel and copper coins led to further issues and they became a permanent part of the currency. By the end of the war this emergency paper was being put out by some 2251 municipalities, districts, savings banks, industrial companies, chambers of commerce, and other organizations.

Germany was now clearly on an inconvertible paper basis. Alarmed by the expansion of note issues the government sought to restrict the use of paper money by encouraging the habit of settling accounts by means of checks and postal money orders. In consequence the amount of checking deposits at the Reichsbank increased over eightfold between 1914 and 1918. The note issues of the state banks which had this privilege remained fairly steady. In estimating the extent of inflation in Germany all these credit instruments must be taken into account. The expansion may be given as follows for July of 1914 and 1918 (in millions of marks):

Kind	1914	1918
Reichsbank notes	1892	12,570
Deposits at Reichsbank	944	7,910
Treasury notes	138	344
Loan bureau notes	....	7,586
Emergency notes	....	1,000
Notes of other banks	1560	1,620
Total	4534	31,020

During the first two and one-half years of the war the additions to the currency were not abnormal, having about doubled between July, 1914, and the end of 1916. Much of this merely filled the gap occasioned by the disappearance of gold and fractional coins. Some was issued for use in occupied enemy territory, some was undoubtedly hoarded, and as a result of the slowing up of the velocity of circulation a larger amount of currency was needed to perform the money work. The inflationary effects of these additional issues, moreover, did not become fully obvious during the war because of the government regulation of prices, especially of house rents. But during the next two years inflation went on rapidly, so that by the time of the armistice the currency was seven times the pre-war amount.

Inflation. The story of the French assignats had always served to point the moral when economists recounted the evils of inflation. But the excesses of the French Revolution were put in the shade by the events of the next four years in German monetary history. The greatest expansion in note issues came after the war. Defeat, demobilization, and payments under the peace treaty created large demands on the government which it did not meet by taxation or from other revenues. Owing to the peculiar structure of the German financial system, which was based upon a division of sources of revenue among the Reich, the states, and the municipalities, the Reich was practically limited to tariff duties, which dried up almost completely during and for some time after the war. But Germany depended on a loan policy to finance the war and did nothing serious to obtain additional revenue during the struggle and little after it. During the years 1918, 1919, and 1920 the Reich did not increase its income, although expenditures rose enormously. An attempt by Chancellor Erzberger to impose heavier taxation led to his assassination. The government was therefore forced to continue its policy of depending upon the Reichsbank for advances, and note issue followed issue. It was natural that the mark should fall in value. The following table shows briefly the progress of inflation:

CIRCULATION OF MONEY IN GERMANY [1]
(Yearly average, in billions of marks *)

	1920	1921	1922	1923
Reichsbank notes	54.0	81.0	339.7	74,941,738,917.4
State bank notes	.2	.3	.6	13,063,445.5
Other credit media	13.4	9.2	11.4	....
Total paper money	67.6	90.5	351.7	74,954,801,362.9
Metallic money	.8	.4	....	....

* Owing to the difference between American and French nomenclature on the one hand and British and German on the other, the astronomical figures used in discussing inflation frequently prove confusing. The American notation is used throughout this book.

Number	American and French	British and German
1,000,000	Million	Million
1,000,000,000	Billion or Milliard	Milliard
1,000,000,000,000	Trillion	Billion
1,000,000,000,000,000	Quadrillion	Thousand Billion
1,000,000,000,000,000,000	Quintillion	Trillion

The German billion is one million raised to the second power, and a trillion is a million raised to the third power.

The nominal value of the Reichsbank notes on November 15, 1923, the day on which inflation ended, amounted to 92,800,000,-000,000,000,000 marks. As issue followed issue prices skyrocketed. The last quotations of the paper mark, when the final smash came in November, were 75 trillion times the 1913 average. Or, to put it differently, the paper mark was then worth .000,000,000,043 of a cent. The most striking commentary on the mad orgy of paper money is furnished by the fact that two thousand printing presses, running day and night, could not keep up with the demand, so fast did the paper depreciate. In the last days the gold value of the mass of paper currency shrank rapidly, from 596,000,000 gold marks on September 30 to 16,000,000 two months later.

As in France during the issues of the assignats and in England during the restriction period, so now in Germany the inflation of the currency was stoutly denied and other explanations were adduced to account for the fall in value of the mark and for the rise in prices. "Throughout the period of the inflation the theory held by the Reichsbank,[2] by successive German Governments, by the great bankers, by great industrialists, by German officials, and by a great part of the Press, was that the depreciation of the mark was caused by the state of the balance of payments."[3] The most authoritative exponent of this theory was Helfferich, who was Secretary of the

[1] *Material für ein Studium von Deutschland's Wirtschaft, Währung und Finanzen* (Berlin, 1924), 21.
[2] Not until 1920 did the Reichsbank admit that inflation existed, and not until 1921 that inflation was the cause of high domestic prices. — H. S. Ellis, *German Monetary Theory*, 1905–1933 (Cambridge, Mass., 1934), 247.
[3] C. Bresciani-Turroni, *The Economics of Inflation* (London, 1937), 42.

Imperial Treasury and Vice-Chancellor during the war. It may be briefly stated in his own words.[4]

"The increase of the circulation has not preceded the rise of prices and the depreciation of the exchange, but it followed slowly and at great distance. . . The causes of the collapse of the money are independent of the conditions of the paper circulation. The causes are obvious: on a country whose balance was passive by about three milliards of gold marks, there was imposed the burden of the reparations bill, amounting annually to about 3.3 milliards of gold marks; to that were added the payments for the redemption of short-term debts; for the costs of occupation, etc., etc. . . . Inflation is not the cause of the increase of prices and of the depreciation of the mark; but the depreciation of the mark is the cause of the increase of prices and of the paper mark issues."

A more correct explanation was advanced by the Reparations Commission, according to which the fundamental cause of the depreciation of the mark was the budget deficits which provoked continued issues of paper money. Caused at first by the loan policy of financing the war and inadequate revenues from taxation, these were later aggravated by the burdens imposed by the Treaty of Versailles. Means of payment were obtained by advances in the form of notes from the Reichsbank, which was little more than a government department acting under orders of the Chancellor. Since these were issued without regard to the monetary needs of the country inflation resulted. This caused a rise in the prices of commodities and a fall in the rate of exchange. The adverse balance of payments undoubtedly contributed to depreciation, but was certainly not the primary cause.

The effects of inflation in Germany during this period confirmed the conclusions drawn from similar episodes elsewhere. The rise in prices gave a fillip to industry and there was an expansion of plant and of production. This was greater in capital goods than in consumption goods and was especially marked in the iron and steel industries and in shipbuilding. There was "a flight from the mark to the machine," an effort to transform the rapidly depreciating paper money into material goods. The instability of trade and the advancing prices offered extraordinary opportunities to the entrepreneurial class, of which full advantage was taken. There was a strong impetus to industrial concentration, especially in the form of vertical combinations, and great firms were established. These were most noticeable in the mining, iron and steel, shipbuilding, electrical, chemical, and potash industries.

Foreigners seemed to have a clearer understanding of the trend

[4] K. Helfferich, *Das Geld* (6th ed., Leipzig, 1923), quoted by Bresciani-Turroni, 44, 45.

of events in Germany than the Germans themselves, and the purchasing power of the mark was lower abroad than in Germany. In other words it paid the foreigner to convert his dollars or pounds into marks and use these to purchase goods in Germany. What was described as a "general liquidation" took place, because every kind of product was exported. Even necessary capital goods began to be removed from the country, and 25,000 houses in Berlin alone were bought by foreigners. By 1923 it was officially estimated that one-tenth of the total value of the share capital of German businesses was owned by foreign capitalists.

The financial effects of inflation showed themselves in the disappearance of the working and liquid capital of monetary institutions and of the reserves of insurance, co-operative, and similar companies. Schacht calculated these as follows: [5]

TOTAL RESOURCES OF GERMAN MONETARY INSTITUTIONS
(in millions)

	End of 1913 (pre-war marks)	End of 1923 Rentenmarks
Savings banks	19,700	100
Commercial banks	13,400	2700
Co-operative credit societies	4,600	400
Insurance institutions	6,300	1200
	44,000	4400

More important and far-reaching than the economic or commercial effects of inflation were the social consequences. Inflation produced violent and profound changes in the social structure and effected a radical redistribution of wealth. The big industrialists, merchants, and landowners (especially if the land was mortgaged) materially improved their position, while the rentier group and the middle class were practically wiped out. The war had furnished opportunities for exceptional profits to those who were able to use them, in munitions, financial transactions, the plundering of occupied territories, and foreign trade; but even more the disturbed conditions of the inflation period between 1919 and 1923 opened the way for the amassing of huge fortunes. In such periods, wrote Professor Schmoller, "the strong recovered their primitive habits as beasts of prey." Before the war the great leaders in industry, commerce, and finance had been creators, and had helped to develop the German economy, but the new men of the war and post-war period were speculators and traders. These profiteers, shrewd and relentless, took advantage of the swift price changes to obtain control of

[5] *The Stabilization of the Mark* (London, 1927), 190.

industrial undertakings, to buy industrial shares, and to appropriate the wealth of the more ignorant or helpless groups. Borrowing heavily from the banks, they were able later to discharge their debts with depreciated paper.

The professional class — doctors, private teachers, artists, and other intellectual workers — as well as government officials, and those who lived on incomes from investments suffered severely. Their position was even more serious than that of the wage-earners, whose status improved after the revolution of November, 1918. The real wages of this group remained fairly steady during the first stage of inflation, but fell decidedly during 1922 and 1923. Although nominal or money wages were steadily increased, they never caught up with the rapidly falling purchasing power of the depreciating mark. Tragic light is thrown on the desperate plight of the poor by the increase in the consumption of horse meat and dog flesh and the decline in that of pork, and by the increase of such diseases as acne, scurvy, and tuberculosis.

Stabilization. The stabilization of the currency was effected with surprising suddenness by the decree of October 15, 1923, which created the Rentenbank. This issued a currency secured by real estate mortgages. These notes were not legal tender, but were acceptable at all public offices, and were put into circulation by their use in the payment of salaries, etc., by the Reich and the states and in other ways. Their value was declared to be that of the pre-war gold mark, but most important of all their issue was limited to 3200 million Reichsmarks — a tacit acceptance of the quantity theory. The Rentenbank began business on November 15, 1923, and the new notes were accepted with confidence by the people. The old paper money was revalued at the rate of one trillion paper marks for one Reichsmark, or, for purposes of foreign exchange, at 4.2 trillion paper marks to the dollar. The inflation money only gradually disappeared, for it continued to be used until the new system could be put in running order. Emergency money was also issued temporarily by various organizations, but had entirely disappeared a year later. At the same time the old national metallic money, which had been hoarded, together with foreign money, entered the circulation.

With the establishment of the new Reichsbank, on October 11, 1924, the Rentenbank was liquidated and the currency was placed on a stable basis. The notes of the Reichsbank were, however, not redeemable in gold, and Germany was still on an inconvertible paper basis internally. The stability of the notes externally was maintained by foreign exchange operations of the Reichsbank, so that actually the German monetary system was on a gold exchange standard.   Not until 1931 were the notes made convertible into gold.

After the accession of the National Socialists to power a purely inflationary policy was adopted to finance public works and later rearmament.   The Nazis claimed, however, that since additional issues of money were made only when orders for the production of new wealth were placed, no inflation occurred.   The increase was made almost wholly in notes of the Reichsbank.

Year	Reichsbank notes (in millions of Reichsmarks)	Total currency
1933	3,364	5,190
1936	4,232	6,135
1940	11,798	14,000

The expansion of the currency alone was no longer so important a criterion of inflation as it was before the war, since in the meantime there had been a great increase in the use of deposits by German business men.   When this is taken into account the conclusion is irresistible that a considerable inflation had in fact taken place.   The evil effects of inflation were, however, minimized, if not wholly obviated, by a strict system of control.   The rate of interest was reduced to a level which was low in relation to the returns on borrowed capital, and was held at that level by manipulating the money and capital markets.   Profits were at the same time limited to six per cent, and new investments and plant expansion were carefully regulated.   Prices of commodities were also stabilized.

The Reichsbank.   Before the war the Reichsbank was required to maintain a gold reserve of one-third of the outstanding notes and to hold commercial paper for the other two-thirds; if excessive issues of notes brought the reserve below the required minimum, the excess was taxed progressively.   By the law of August 4, 1914, the Bank was relieved of all responsibility for the stability of the currency and the door was opened for inflation.   Specie payments were suspended and imperial treasury notes and loan bureau notes were counted as cash, and the term "commercial paper" was extended so as to include both Imperial bonds with a maturity of three months and Treasury bills maturing in 30 days.   The soundness of the bank notes was thus made dependent upon the government debt.   The fundamental principle of the basic law of 1878, namely "to regulate the circulation of money within the Reich and to facilitate settlement of payments," was subordinated to war needs.   The Reichsbank now became an institution whose main task was that of providing financial assistance to the government.   It played only a small part during the war as a source of credit for industry.   Even at the end of 1921 the advances to industry amounted to only 1 billion marks as compared with 1000 billion to the Reich.

The Bank was subjected to severe criticism for its leniency in granting advances to the government during the war, but it must be remembered that it was wholly under the control of the Treasury. Not until 1922 did the Bank regain its independence by a law which restored the conduct of business to the directors. It was, however, without power to regulate the currency or to control the money market. The former was effected by the establishment of the Rentenbank on November 15, 1923, and the latter by changes made in the law governing the Reichsbank which gave it almost dictatorial powers over German currency and credit, placed in its hands the entire control of foreign exchange, and entrusted it with the task of rehabilitating the monetary system. But the most decisive relief to the Bank was the cessation of the Reich's demands for credit. Meanwhile, however, the Bank was increasing its credits to private business and by its inflationary policy was facilitating the speculation and profiteering of this period. Even more objectionable was the low interest rate, which was held at 5 per cent until the middle of 1922, and a year later, in the midst of the wildest inflation, was still only 30 per cent. Any one who could borrow of the Bank on these terms and invest in physical values could make a fortune.

The Reichsbank had been the dominant financial institution during the war and the inflation period, and after stabilization it was again forced to assume leadership. Interest rates were fantastically high in 1924, the annual rate for monthly money rising to 30-40 per cent in July and twice as high for day money. The Bank, however, announced a policy of credit restriction and parceled out the available credit to "desirable" objectives. This deflation policy maintained the stability of the mark, but it also resulted in a ruthless weeding out of weak industries. The period was one of readjustment from inflation to currency stability, and called for economy and efficiency. Here was the impetus to the rationalization movement of these years. By the end of the purification process in 1926 a firm basis had been laid for the advance of the next few years.

The Reichsbank was reorganized in 1924 under the Dawes Plan. It was declared to be a private institution and advances to the Reich were limited at any time to 100 million marks, which moreover must be paid off by the end of each fiscal year. The Bank's charter was renewed for fifty years, and it was granted the sole right of emission, except for the four state banks; the Reich was forbidden to issue any kind of paper money. The administration of the Bank was left in the hands of a German managing board, but above them was placed a general board of fourteen members, of whom half were foreigners, while at the head stood a foreign commissioner. In other respects the organization of the Reichsbank conformed to the lines laid down in the original bank act of 1875.

The experts who drew up the Dawes Plan deemed it essential that the new Bank be freed from government influence in order that it might ensure the stability of the currency and also serve better the needs of industry. Although the foreign influence in the policy and management of the Bank was bitterly resented, the results were good. It took an active part in the recovery movement of the next five years, but maintained a sound position. On May 15, 1930, the date of the last report under the Dawes Plan, it held a gold reserve of 2578 million reichsmarks, which was 68.5 per cent of the outstanding notes, as against a legal requirement of 40 per cent. Under the Young Plan, which went into effect that same year, the notes of the Reichsbank became fully convertible into gold.

The Young Plan swept away the entire apparatus of foreign control and the Reichsbank became completely independent. Its freedom, however, did not save it from the consequences of the depression which soon involved the western world, nor from complete domination by the Nazi government after 1933. It was called upon to help finance most of the public works between 1932 and 1935, from which the credit banks stood aloof, but after that government pressure forced the commercial banks to extend their credit also for this purpose and for rearmament. The capital market was practically monopolized for these purposes between 1933 and 1938; out of a total of new domestic capital issues amounting to 17,400 million reichsmarks during this period, no less than 15,000 million consisted of public loans, mostly to the Reich. Owing to the adverse balance of international payments and the use of its funds for state needs, the gold reserve of the Reichsbank was steadily reduced; by the end of 1939 it amounted to only 77 million reichsmarks or about two-thirds of one per cent of the notes in circulation.

Other banks. Stabilization and revaluation of the currency involved corresponding changes in other financial fields. Down to 1923 the decisions of the courts regarding monetary contracts had rested on the principle that "a mark is always equal to a mark," but the great fall in the value of the mark made its further application unjust and impracticable. Attempts were now made to repair some of the evils that had befallen the creditor class, both individual and institutional, who held bonds and mortgages. The law of July, 1925, revalued government debts at $2\frac{1}{2}$ per cent of their original value, industrial bonds at 15 per cent, and private mortgages at 25 per cent, and made other adjustments. Company balance sheets were changed from paper to gold marks, and the deflated statements revealed clearly the financial and industrial losses which German economic life had suffered. The capital structure of even the strongest banks was shown to be impaired and many of the weaker ones were wiped out. The banking system was nevertheless forced to supply the monetary and capital needs of the country.

The decade 1924–33 was characterized by three important changes: [6] (1) the entrance of all types of banks into the commercial credit field and the resulting expansion of short-term credits; (2) rapid integration and centralization in each bank group; (3) the growth of public credit institutions. The former specialization broke down and practically all banks, to a greater or lesser degree, engaged in all kinds of banking, in deposit and short-term lending, brokerage, and investment banking; even savings banks entered the short-term personal loan business, while other banks competed for savings deposits. A policy of retrenchment, consolidation, and centralization was followed. The number of branches in the provinces was reduced and banking became increasingly centered in Berlin. There was also a great increase in government ownership of the great joint stock banks and of participation in management. By the middle of 1933 the government owned 91 per cent of the stock of the *Dresdner* Bank, and 70 per cent of the *Allgemeine Deutsche Kredit Anstalt* and of the *Commerz und Privat Bank*.

A significant movement was the growth of public credit institutions which paralleled the spread of government ownership. Such were the German Building and Real Estate Bank, to furnish intermediary building credits, and the Reich Transport Company, to handle the government railway funds and to extend freight credits to large shippers. The *Reichs-Kredit-Gesellschaft* was founded in 1922 for the special purpose of watching over the interests of the Reich in industrial undertakings; the Gold Discount Bank in 1924 placed its resources at the service of the agricultural credit policy of the government; the Rentenbank was made over into the *Renten Kredit Anstalt* for the purpose of granting credits to agriculture on the ground that agriculture was a public institution. There were also public savings banks, municipal banks, state land and agricultural banks, note banks, and central clearing associations (*Girocentralen*). The state held a leading position in German banking.

The basis of the German banking system remained the privately owned deposit banks. Of these the most important group was the joint stock banks, of which there were nearly 3000 in 1924. After stabilization they quickly recovered their strength and with the aid of foreign funds were able to help finance the industrial recovery of Germany. They borrowed short-term funds in foreign markets

[6] M. B. Northrop, *Control Policies of the Reichsbank, 1924–1933* (New York, 1938), 115.

and used them as the basis of long-term industrial loans, and even risked their depositors' money. When the day of reckoning came in 1931 these loans were found to be frozen, and the condition of the banks was thoroughly illiquid. A run on the banks, of both foreign and domestic creditors, took place and on July 13 the Darmstädter Bank was forced to suspend payments. This bank had been the largest investor on short-term credits in risky enterprises and was particularly vulnerable. But the others were not much better.

Of the four great credit banks, two were at the end of their liquid resources and the other two would have been forced to suspend if the run had continued. At this juncture the government declared a moratorium which prevented a collapse, but the banks lost the larger part of their capital. The government also granted aid to the distressed banks through the public banking institutions which secured to the latter practically complete or partial ownership of the great private deposit banks and of some of their industrial foundations. The complete control thus obtained rendered it unnecessary for the National Socialists later to demand state ownership. Never did the great credit banks regain the dominant position they had enjoyed before the war. Private banks were not subject to regulation until 1933, and little is known of their activities, but their number decreased from 36 per cent of deposit and lending banks in 1913 to 23 per cent in 1933. The number of state banks increased from 4 to 9, but they were comparatively unimportant, and after January 1, 1936, they lost the privilege of note issue. Co-operative banks, on the other hand, played a steadily larger role in the national economy, and became more centralized.

The law of December 5, 1934, regulating credit policy, was the beginning of an elaborate system of control by the state. All credit institutions, numbering about 36,000, were placed under new official organs, which limited credit and decreed that there must be no competition between private and state needs, preference being given to the latter. In order to make certain of obtaining credit the government established numerous public banks for special purposes and extended its control of the stock exchanges. Savings were directed increasingly into public instead of private investments. As a result of these changes the importance of the credit banks steadily declined. Their loans to industry fell from about 4000 million reichsmarks in 1932 to 3000 million in 1937, partly as a result of liquidation and repayment of debts, and partly because the state granted public credit. Owing also to the still stand agreements with foreign creditors, the debts owing them were reduced. As the amount of commercial paper in the portfolios of the banks declined, they invested in state securities. In other words they used their credit for long-term investment rather than for short-term self-liquidating loans to industry, thereby rendering their position much less liquid. Their solvency came increasingly to depend on that of the state. The former role of the credit banks, as directors of industry, was now assumed by the state, and the chief functions of the banks were to effect transfers of money and credit and to place public loans. The direction of industry and the determination of what, how much, and by whom goods should be produced were increasingly taken out of the hands of producers and their bankers and were assumed by the state. Banking policy became an instrument of a planned economy and was entirely subordinated to the requirements of public finance.

Nazi public finance.[7] The development of German public finance went through four stages between 1933 and 1939. The first phase was characterized by the issue of Work Creation bills, which were financed primarily by the Reichsbank and its subsidiaries. During the second phase, from 1935 to April, 1938, the government issued "special" bills, to finance which it drew upon three sources: further short credits from the Reichsbank and the commercial banks; growing utilization of the rapidly increasing accumulations of private capital, which it obtained by means of the $4\frac{1}{2}$ per cent Reich loan and treasury bond issues; and expanding tax revenues. The third phase, from April, 1938, to April, 1939, differed little from the preceding one, except in the larger use of short-term government bills to provide additional Reich "foredrafts" (*Vergriffe*), and the further expansion of taxation.

The fourth stage, that of the New Financial Plan, began on May 1, 1939. In spite of the fact that tax revenues had increased from 6600 million reichsmarks in 1933 to 17,700 in 1939, they were insufficient to cover the financial needs of the Reich, now greatly swollen as a result of armament and war. The additional expenditures were met not only by absorbing the funds at the disposal of the capital market, but also by greatly expanding the issues of short-term "foredrafts." The change in method consisted in the fact that these latter were in the form of tax certificates, issued in anticipation of future tax revenues. These certificates were non-interest-bearing, but were acceptable at a premium for all Reich taxes if held a certain length of time, and were legal tender. They might be issued by the Reich, the National Socialist Party, the post office, the imperial railway, and local authorities. All of these organs were limited in paying commercial and industrial accounts to 60 per cent in cash and were required to pay the balance in these tax certificates. The

---

[7] This is well described in a report by the Reichs-Kredit-Gesellschaft: *Germany's Economic Development. In the Middle of the Year* 1939 (Berlin, 1939), 42-46.

Plan was explicitly designed to divert part of the liquid resources of commerce and industry to the needs of the government. The state also laid hands on the reserves of the insurance funds, savings banks, other financial institutions, and local and municipal funds by forcing them to subscribe to Reich loans and treasury bonds. Between 1935 and 1939 issues of about 8500 million marks were thus placed. It is evident that the whole financial structure of the German economy was inextricably intertwined with the solvency of the Reich. This seems to be one of the rules of *Wehrwirtschaft*.

It was not enough to control the sources of credit and capital. The Nazi state also regulated production and consumption directly. Instead of trusting production to the profit motive of private enterprisers the government allocated raw materials, capital, and labor, and pre-empted the output. Consumption also was controlled by rationing rather than trusting to the reduction of incomes through taxation to curtail demand. Taxes were moreover increased to the breaking point. It has been estimated [8] that the percentage of the private national income absorbed by taxes increased from 18 in 1929 to 25 in 1936. If to taxation were added payments to unemployment and other social insurance, forced contributions, and subscriptions to public loans, not less than 47 per cent of the national income in 1938 was spent according to government fiat rather than by the free choice of the individual. At the same time there was a rapid increase in the officially declared public debt of the Reich. In 1924, after inflation had wiped out practically all the war and pre-war debt, it amounted to only 3917 million reichsmarks; by 1929 it was 8228 million. The burden of relief expenditures and public relief works during the next six years brought it up to 12,525 in 1935, an increase of 4000 million. But the rearmament program of the following four years involved a 250 per cent growth so that on November 1, 1939, it stood at 38,180 million. In itself this was not exorbitant. It was not much more than the German pre-war total governmental debts of 32,000 million, and was less than the British national debt of £8000 million, of the French debt of 340,000 million francs, and of that of the United States of $40,000 million. But the speed of its growth was ominous and the large percentage in short-term loans was a weakness. What proportion of the taxes and of the new debt was being applied to what was euphemistically called "Defense" in all state budgets it is impossible to state authoritatively, for no budget has been published in Germany since 1935. But it has been estimated that in the budget year ending March 30, 1934, about one-third of all expenditures went for that purpose, and for the budget year 1936–37 about two-thirds.

[8] K. E. Poole, *German Financial Policies, 1932–1939* (Cambridge, Mass., 1940), 146, 172.

3. DEVALUATION IN FRANCE

Money. The money of account in France on the eve of the war consisted almost entirely of notes of the Bank of France and subsidiary silver coins. Gold to the amount of 3500 to 4000 million francs was estimated to be in the hands of the public, but most of this was hoarded and not in general circulation. The first effect of the war was to drive the gold and silver out of circulation; after July, 1914, specie disappeared from use as money. The withdrawal of subsidiary silver coins caused considerable inconvenience to retail trade and they were replaced by various makeshift forms of small notes.

By act of August 5, 1914, specie payments were suspended, and the Bank of France was freed from the obligation to redeem its notes in specie; at the same time they were made legal tender for all debts, public and private. Exports of gold were forbidden, and an appeal was made to the public to bring hoarded gold to the nearest branch of the Bank and exchange it for notes. Before the war was over some 2500 million francs had been received. By this and other means the gold reserve of the Bank, which was 4150 million francs on the eve of the war, was raised to 4840 million by the end of 1915, and stood at 3320 million at the end of 1918. During the war the country was on an inconvertible paper money basis, and all the familiar accompaniments of such a regime appeared in due order — over-issue, depreciation, rise of prices, and devaluation.

The war was financed in France very largely by advances from the Bank to the state, which were funded at irregular intervals by enormous public loans. When the government received a credit from the Bank, it drew out bank notes and paid them out for purchases of war supplies and wages. Since the check-deposit system was not developed in France, the note issues increased *pari passu* with the Bank's advances to the state.

Date	Advances	Note issues
(end of December)	(in millions of francs)	
1913	....	5,665
1914	3,900	10,043
1915	5,200	13,310
1916	7,400	16,679
1917	12,500	22,337
1918	17,150	30,250
1919	25,500	37,275

Individual business men also borrowed from the private banks, which in turn borrowed from the Bank of France, thus expanding the volume of currency. In spite of the increased need of trade for additional media of exchange as war industries expanded, the note issues ran far ahead of commercial requirements. The increase in notes was moreover not made in response to the monetary needs of business, but rather to meet the fiscal needs of the government. Failure to distinguish between these two requirements led to a large and dangerous inflation of the currency with consequent depreciation of the monetary unit and rise in prices. The magnitude of the advances to the state was a measure of the inflation of the French currency. The effect of inflation was accentuated by the scarcity of many articles, by rising wages, and by increased costs of production generally. By 1920 the wholesale price index had risen to over five times that of 1913.

Foreign exchange was stabilized or "pegged" in April, 1916, through huge extensions of credit by Great Britain, and later by the United States after that country entered the conflict. Exchange rates were thus held steady during the war. In March, 1919, the franc was "unpegged," that is freed from artificial control and allowed to find its natural level in the market. As a result the exchange rate for the franc fell from about 18 cents in March, 1919, to less than 6 cents a year later.

The explanation of the depreciation of the French franc cannot be found alone in the inflation of the currency, though that was undoubtedly the most important cause. There were other factors at work. The post-war trade boom collapsed in 1920 and a period of commercial deflation set in. There was an insistent and politically imperative demand for the restoration of the devastated areas, and the government spent for this purpose not less than 100 billion francs or over three times as much as the total internal debt in 1913. This was almost as many francs as were spent during the war. Relying upon the receipt of reparation payments from Germany, the government borrowed huge sums from the Bank of France, and created the *Crédit National* to manage the loans. The pressure of this internal debt and the impossibility of balancing the budget led to persistent demands for reparation payments, and resulted in the desperate hazard of the Ruhr invasion.

Another factor was the adverse balance of trade. This ran heavily against France during the war, but reached the highest point in 1919 and 1920, with a deficit of over 23 billion francs each of these years. The government showed inability or unwillingness to impose adequate taxation, and the people developed a profound distrust in the stability of the franc. This period, which really was part of the war period, ended in 1922.

The next four years saw little improvement in either the financial or the political situation, and by 1926 France had reached the brink of the precipice. Lack of confidence led to a flight of capital, amounting to about 37 billion francs in the three years 1924–26. The gold value of the franc fell to less than 2 cents in 1926. Further decline was stopped by a change in the political front and the firm attitude of M. Poincaré, the new premier. The result was a sudden and complete return of confidence; the expatriated capital flowed back, the government for the first time since 1924 managed to balance its budget, and the balance of trade ran in France's favor. At the same time the Bank increased its gold reserve. The franc recovered somewhat and in 1928 the actual devaluation was legally recognized and the gold content of the franc was changed to one-fifth of its former weight. The gold standard was thus restored with a franc equivalent to 3.93 cents or 20 per cent of its pre-war value. The gold reserve of the Bank was revalued in accordance with this change. This act effected a reduction in the internal debt, since it cut the real worth of government and other securities to one-fifth of their former value. The capital levy thus became a reality.

The crisis of 1929 affected all countries. Great Britain went off the gold standard in 1931 and the other nations which were tied to sterling soon followed suit. By 1935 only four countries of the so-called gold bloc, namely France, Belgium, Holland, and Switzerland, still struggled to maintain their currencies. But meanwhile internal difficulties were accumulating in France. Reparations payments had stopped, returns from foreign investments fell off one-half, and expenditures of tourists by a third. The gold reserve of the Bank of France fell from 82 billion francs in September, 1935, to 50 billion a year later. Export industries restricted their operations and unemployment became serious. A Popular Front government was increasing the costs of production by measures of social reform and was unable to balance the budget. Finally, in 1936, France went off the gold standard.

The laws of 1936 suspended the convertibility of the bank notes, which thereupon became inconvertible paper money.[9] The Bank of France was forbidden to pay out gold or to sell it to individuals, and the export of gold was forbidden. The gold content of the franc was reduced from 65.5 milligrams of gold to an amount between 43 and 49 milligrams to be fixed by the government. This was between two-thirds and three-fourths of the previous weights. An exchange stabilization fund was created, to which 10,000 million francs were allocated. Using this fund the Bank attempted to stabilize the franc by buying gold on the open market, though it let

[9] A. Aftalion, *L'or et la monnaie* (Paris, 1938), 74 ff.

the franc oscillate between the two limits set by the law of 1936. Agreements were made with Great Britain and the United States to maintain the existing parity of the currencies of the three countries. The stabilization fund was unable, however, to stay the fall of the franc, which continued to depreciate through 1937. Public confidence was undermined by continued budgetary deficits, adverse balances of trade and of payments, and the heavy governmental expenditures for social purposes. Once again, in 1938, the franc was devalued, its legal weight now being fixed at 27.6 milligrams of fine gold.

Banking. The Bank of France occupied an intermediate position between a private bank of the type of the Bank of England and a state bank, like the Imperial Bank of Russia. During the war its relations with the government became closer, though it retained its independence and never became an organ of the state. At the outbreak of the war the government declared a moratorium for one month on all negotiable instruments, which was later extended to other liabilities and was continued to 1919. The Bank rediscounted most of these "frozen" credits, though it was not, like the Bank of England, guaranteed against loss by the government. It also made fresh loans to commerce, industry, and individuals, and helped to revive the economic life of the country. Its most important services, however, were rendered to the government. Not only did it make advances to the state, amounting by the close of the war to more than 26 billion francs, but it assisted in the flotation of government loans and sales of treasury bills. It also negotiated large commercial credits in London and New York, and by shipping gold abroad obtained important credits for government account. The invaluable assistance thus rendered was rewarded in 1918 by the extension of the Bank's charter to 1945.

In order to carry out these vast transactions the Bank was compelled greatly to increase its note issues. The gold reserve, however, did not keep pace with this expansion, so that the ratio of gold to paper fell to about 15 per cent in 1920. It will be remembered that the gold reserve of the Bank of France was not held solely for the redemption of notes, but covered deposits as well. Against these two items the reserve amounted to less than 14 per cent. This was a decline from 63 per cent on the eve of war. The Bank, however, maintained its traditional function of issuing and regulating the fiduciary currency of the nation and of maintaining the gold reserve, though during the war this was almost obscured by the paramount necessity of aiding the national treasury. It also acted as a bankers' bank, and granted credit to individuals.

After the war the Bank continued its assistance to the government, which failed to levy adequate taxes or to balance the budget, but relied on credit advances. It had always been the policy of the Bank to maintain a steady discount rate, and during the period of large loans to the government it was necessary to hold this at a low level. The discount policy of the Bank, as a means of controlling the credit situation, thereby lost much of its pre-war importance. The number of branches was greatly expanded, so that its facilities were available throughout every part of France.

A peculiar feature in the management of the Bank was the fact that only the two hundred largest stockholders had a voice in the administration or election of representatives on the administrative council, although they owned only one-seventh of the shares. The state exercised close supervision and the governor and two subgovernors were appointed by the president of the Republic, but the Bank was a private institution wholly owned by the stockholders. In 1936, the Popular Front government proclaimed its intention of democratizing the administration of the Bank by admitting the whole body of the stockholders to the annual meeting. This privilege was, however, largely illusory, for they were permitted under the new arrangement to elect only 2 out of 20 members of the administrative council, the others being appointed by the Minister of Finance or officially representing state interests.[10] The government also appointed the governor. The control of the state was thereby greatly extended, and the Bank became practically a public institution, though its ownership remained private.

The credit structure of the Bank is given for a few selected years.

BANK OF FRANCE

(in billions of francs)

Year	Circulation	Deposits	Gold reserve
1913	5.6	.8	4.1
1918	30.2	3.2	3.3
1929	67.8	....	41.5
1939	123.3	21.5	92.2

Commercial banks. In addition to the Bank of France there was a large number of commercial banks. The most important group was the credit companies, which corresponded to the national and state banks in the United States and to the joint-stock banks in England. Their operations covered not only the discounting of ordinary commercial paper, but also advances against collateral security, advances on bills of exchange arising out of shipment of goods, acceptance of such bills, and the granting of agricultural

[10] G. Pirou, *La Monnaie Française de 1936 à 1938* (Paris, 1939), 21.

credits of somewhat longer term. Since they could obtain gold at any time by rediscounting their paper at the Bank of France they did not keep large reserves on hand. These were held by the Bank of France. Commercial banking in France was controlled mainly by six large companies with head offices in Paris and innumerable branches throughout France. The four largest, which carried on about half of the commercial banking business, were the *Crédit Lyonnais, Société Générale pour le Developpement du Commerce et de l'Industrie,* the *Comptoir National d'Escompte de Paris,* and the *Banque Nationale de Crédit.*

A second group consisted of the business or finance banks (*banques d'affaires*), most of them small private institutions closely linked with the industry of the neighborhood. A smaller number of larger institutions had their headquarters in Paris, where they participated in promotions of industrial companies or underwrote new issues of stocks and bonds. Neither of these types met the needs of the situation after the war when it became necessary to revive French economic life. Accordingly the *Crédit Lyonnais* and the *Comptoir d'Escompte* together established the *Union pour le Crédit à l'Industrie Nationale,* which financed commercial operations for a longer term than was permissible for credit banks. In 1928 and 1929 two more similar banks were founded by other groups.

France was probably better provided with banks adapted to various needs than any country in Europe. There were mortgage banks, agricultural credit banks, savings banks, popular banks for small traders and producers, banks for co-operative societies, and finally a state bank (*Caisse des Dépôts et Consignations*). With resources of almost 100 billion francs in 1935 the last was one of the most powerful institutions in the country. Two-thirds of its loans were made to the state or minor divisions for long or short term, and through it the state could actively intervene in the administration of private enterprises.

Public finance. France had managed by strenuous efforts to balance her national budget in 1913, but the World War threw the finances into new confusion. Owing partly to faulty financial methods and partly to the disorders caused by invasion, the cost of the war was met entirely by borrowing. The enormous debt thus piled up was drastically reduced by devaluation of the franc, but continued budget deficits increased it again. In 1932 it was ten times the figure for 1914. France suffered from chronic budgetary deficits, and when defense expenditures rose to new highs after 1938 they became appalling. In 1939 government revenues amounted to only one-third of the expenditures, the military budget being met entirely by loans.

Conclusion. The gold standard, which had maintained a fairly firm position for fifty years, received a serious setback as a result of the World War. It was outlawed in all the European belligerent countries, which replaced it with bank notes, government paper money, and other financial devices. These lent themselves readily to inflation which occurred in every country, but reached its height in Germany. Even after stabilization Italian currency had lost 70 per cent of its gold value and French 80 per cent, while Germany and Russia were compelled to repudiate their discredited currencies and establish new ones. After the war gold was restored to its old position rather hesitatingly and on different terms by most of the governments, but the depression of 1930 drove it once more off its pedestal. After that the countries of Europe made shift with "managed" paper currencies. A major difficulty in maintaining the gold standard was the debtor position of most of the states on international balance, which drained off their gold. This accumulated in the hands of the United States, the major creditor nation, which by 1939 had 60 per cent of the world stock.

Banking during this period was characterized by further amalgamation of commercial banks and growing power of the central bank, which increasingly became an agent of the government. The state extended its control over banks and financial institutions, as it discovered in them a powerful weapon for the manipulation of money and credit in carrying out its political program. This was particularly true of Germany.

Public finance also reflected the growing power of the state over economic activities. More and more of the individual's income was spent for him by the state, often for desirable ends, but increasingly for the wasteful purposes of war.

BIBLIOGRAPHICAL NOTE

1. *Britain.* The gold standard came in for a large share of attention during this period. R. G. Hawtrey, *The Gold Standard in Theory and Practice* (4th ed., London, 1939) is a good historical account of international gold movements; his *Currency and Credit* (3rd ed., London, 1928) is more general. T. E. Gregory, *The Gold Standard and its Future* (New York, 1932) is theoretical. S. E. Harris, *Exchange Depreciation* (Cambridge, Mass., 1936) is a technical explanation. On banking R. S. Sayers, *Modern Banking* (London, 1938) is a clear description of the present system. W. J. Weston, *Economics of the English Banking System* (London, 1931) is a useful account. L. A. Harr, *Branch Banking in England* (Philadelphia, 1929) is a slight sketch. L. L. M. Minty, *English Banking Methods* (London, 1925) describes internal administration. R. W. Jones, *Studies in Prac-*

tical Banking (London, 1935) is a legal study of banking practice. R. J. Treptil, *British Banks and the London Money Market* (London, 1936) is a description of various agencies. P. Ripley, *Short History of Investment* (London, 1934) and D. H. Macgregor, *Public Aspects of Finance* (Oxford, 1939) are good on other phases.

2. *Germany.* A scholarly work is H. S. Ellis, *German Monetary Theory*, 1905–1923 (Cambridge, Mass., 1934). The best study of inflation is C. Bresciani-Turroni, *The Economics of Inflation: a Study of Currency Depreciation in Post-War Germany* (London, 1937). An optimistic interpretation is F. D. Graham, *Exchange, Prices, and Production in Hyper-Inflation Germany* (Princeton, 1930). F. Hesse, *Die deutsche Wirtschaftslage von* 1914 *bis* 1923: *Krieg, Geldblähe und Wechsellagen* (Jena, 1938) is a detailed study. H. Schacht, *Die Stabilisierung der Mark* (Stuttgart, 1927. Translated as *The Stabilization of the Mark*, London, 1927), is by the president of the Reichsbank. The entire story of inflation and stabilization is told in K. Elster, *Von der Mark zur Reichsmark, Geschichte der deutschen Währung,* 1914–1924 (Jena, 1928). S. Flink, *The German Reichsbank and Economic Germany* (New York, 1930) is a general account. M. B. Northrop, *Control Policies of the Reichsbank,* 1924–1933 (New York, 1938) is a careful study, as is F. Somary, *Bankpolitik* (2te Aufl., Tübingen, 1930). A good general survey is P. B. Whale, *Joint Stock Banking in Germany* (London, 1930). Somewhat broader is H. F. Geiler, *Die zentralen Kreditinstitute Deutschland's* (Berlin, 1935). W. Hagemann, *Das Verhältnis der deutschen Grossbanken zur Industrie* (Berlin, 1931) deals with an important phase. P. P. Rheinhold, *The Economic, Financial, and Political State of Germany since the War* (New Haven, 1928) is a sketch. German finance under the Nazis is described approvingly by W. Prion, *Das deutsche Finanzwunder* (Berlin, 1938), and critically by N. Mühlen, *Hitler's Magician: Schacht* (London, 1938). K. E. Poole, *German Financial Policies* (Cambridge, Mass., 1939) is confined to financing public relief works. A difficult subject is well handled in C. R. S. Harris, *Germany's Foreign Indebtedness* (London, 1935). C. T. Schmidt, *German Business Cycles,* 1924–1933 (New York, 1934) is a brief sketch.

3. *France.* A theoretical study is A. Aftalion, *L'or et la monnaie* (Paris, 1938). Currency history is clearly treated in G. Pirou, *La monnaie française depuis la guerre,* 1914–1936 (Paris, 1936) and *La monnaie française de* 1936 à 1938 (Paris, 1938). Inflation is carefully traced in J. H. Rogers, A. Maffry, and R. E. Landman, *The Process of Inflation in France,* 1914–1927 (New York, 1929), and in Eleanor Dulles, *The French Franc,* 1914–1928 (New York, 1929). The latter author followed the process in *The Dollar, the Franc, and Inflation* (New York, 1933). A general sketch is B. Nogaro, *Modern Monetary Systems* (London, 1927). A brief account of French banking is K. Le Cheminant, *Colonial and Foreign Banking Systems* (London, 1924). The war period is covered in G. Ramon, *Histoire de la Banque de France* (Paris, 1929). G. Guerser, *Le marché monetaire français et son controle par la Banque de France* (Paris, 1938) deals with the money market. France's growing financial power is described in G. Schmolders, *Frankreich's Aufstieg zu Weltkapitalmarkt* (Berlin, 1933). A popularly written book on financial history is G. Martin, *Histoire économique et financière de la France* (Paris, 1927). B. Nogaro, *La crise économique dans le monde et en France* (Paris, 1936) is a sketch. R. M. Haig, *The Public Finances of Post-War France* (New York, 1930) is a careful study.

CHAPTER XXI

LABOR AND THE LABOR MOVEMENT

I. LABOR COMES INTO ITS OWN IN BRITAIN

Labor during the war. On the eve of the war the condition of industry in almost all lines was one of prosperity. Unemployment — a fair gauge of the labor market — had reached a minimum during 1913 and was still very low in July, 1914. Trade union membership had doubled since 1900, and the organizations were strong and active. The outbreak of war fell like a blight upon all of these conditions. Industry was thrown into a state of uncertainty, unemployment increased, and labor faced new problems which threatened the stability of their organizations. After a brief panic stage readjustment took place rapidly in most industries. Fortunately it happened that many of the chief exports of Britain, which would normally have been depressed during the war, were just those commodities most needed, such as coal, ships, iron and steel, and machinery. Government orders for war materials created a great demand for labor along these lines, which filtered down into accessory industries, and the labor surplus was soon changed into a labor shortage. By December, 1916, the percentage of trade unionists out of work had declined to .3, an all-time low. Military service reduced the number of available workers, especially in agriculture, but also in shipbuilding, coal mining, iron and steel, and other vital industries. The unwisdom of withdrawing men from such lines through the operation of a system of voluntary enlistment led later to the substitution of a selective draft for military service.

When war broke out there was a great reduction, almost a cessation of labor disputes. An agreement was made with the Treasury in August, 1935, by the leaders of the trade unions and of the Labour Party that existing disputes would be terminated and future ones submitted to arbitration before resorting to a strike or lockout, that restrictions on output and limitations on employment would not be practiced, that overtime and dilution of labor would be permitted. In a word, they sacrificed many of the protective devices which they had developed through years of struggle to safeguard their standard of living. The government decided to act positively to prevent interference with the work of production for war needs, and in 1915 created a Ministry of Munitions, to which Mr. Lloyd George was appointed, and passed the Munitions of War Act. This was the most important piece of labor legislation enacted during the war. It authorized the government to take possession of and use for military or naval service any factory or plant and to regulate the carrying on of any work or the employment of any workmen with a view to increasing the production of munitions. While this was declared to be emergency legislation, to remain in force only for the duration of the war, it extended far-reaching control over labor. Restrictions were placed on the mobility of labor, strikes were prohibited in munitions works until the dispute was referred to the Board of Trade, and efforts were made to get rid of restrictions on output. Railway workers and coal miners became virtually state employees, and in agriculture as well as in the munitions industries government regulations superseded private arrangements. The old form of collective bargaining was preserved, for example, on the railways, but neither employers nor workers were free to act as they had before the war. As a result of the intervention of the government there was a tendency to treat labor problems on a national rather than on a local basis, and there was a decline in the close contact between trade union officials and employers, which had previously made collective agreements easier.

Another problem that the trade unions had to face was the "dilution of labor." Because of the shortage of skilled workers, and in spite of the protests of the closely organized craft unions, it became necessary to introduce women and unskilled workers into practically all industries, where they could perform quickly-learned tasks, and to restrict the skilled operatives to tasks that required long training. As the war went on the number of men available for industry steadily declined, while the number of women employed as steadily increased. By 1918 it was estimated that nearly 5,000,000 women were employed and that almost a third of them had replaced men. Over half were to be found in industry, especially in munitions, but large numbers had gone into commercial occupations, government positions, transport, and practically every gainful pursuit. The entrance of women into the industrial field proved to be permanent; after the war they made up an increasingly larger proportion of members in the trade unions. In addition to women, the shortage of labor was partially made good by the employment of men beyond military age and of lads below it who were not at work, of invalided soldiers and sailors, and finally of prisoners.

The trade union movement. The trade union movement was given a new recognition at the hands of the state during the war, and after a momentary setback the membership increased steadily. As new groups of unskilled workers were employed, and as clerical and commercial employees increased, they too were organized. Unions of these general workers were formed, and by the end of the war the National Federation of General Workers was the largest labor federation in Great Britain. Agricultural laborers also flocked into the unions, as did the clerical and white collar workers. By 1919 the former group was estimated to have 300,000 and the latter 750,000 members. British trade unionism reached its maximum strength in 1920, but after that fell off rapidly, the membership of the unions affiliated with the Trades Union Congress declining to less than 4,500,000 in 1923. It was estimated that at the height of its power it included sixty per cent of the adult male workers of the country. The following table shows the growth of trade unionism in selected years:

MEMBERSHIP IN BRITISH TRADE UNIONS

Year	Number of members	Year	Number of members
1913	4,135,000	1930	4,839,000
1917	5,288,000	1935	4,842,000
1920	8,337,000	1938	4,250,000
1925	5,522,000		

Trade union organization was meanwhile undergoing certain changes. After 1917 there was a rapid consolidation of small unions into large and powerful bodies. By 1924 almost half of the trade union members belonged to ten big unions, each with over 100,000 members. A further wave of amalgamation followed during the next decade as a result of the rationalization of industry. A second change was the growth of industrial unionism in place of the old craft unions. This was especially prominent in those industries which employed large numbers of general unskilled workers without any craft allegiance, as in the mining and railway industries. A third change was a shift in the relative strength of the different interests. There was a decrease in the old strongholds of trade unionism, among the miners, shipbuilders, iron and steel workers, cotton operatives, and an increase in rayon, printing, paper, glass, pottery, and distributive industries, among which trade union traditions were not so firmly rooted. This shift, together with the increase in the number of women members, weakened the movement.

Other events outside the trade union movement affected the fortunes of organized labor. The extension of the franchise in 1918 to include practically all adults raised the number of voters from about 8,000,000 to over 30,000,000, nearly all of those added being in the wage-earning class. This was described as an acknowledgment of the public service rendered by this group during the war. Another noteworthy event was the Education Act. All school exemptions under the age of fourteen were abolished, local authorities were empowered to raise the age to fifteen, and young people were to have a minimum of 280 hours' education between the ages of fourteen and sixteen.

Promises had been made during the war of shorter hours and better conditions for labor — Britain was to be made a "land fit for heroes to live in" — and now the labor organizations pressed for fulfilment of those provisions. But in reality the fortunes of labor were tied to the business cycle. In the brief boom period of 1919–20 wages rose and six million wage earners obtained substantial reductions in their hours of work. The sharp depression of 1920–22 ushered in a period of mounting unemployment and of wage reductions. The years 1924–29 were marked by stable equilibrium in most countries of the world, but Great Britain did not share fully in this prosperity, owing largely to the return to the gold standard at the old parity. This depressed prices, held down wages, and contributed to unemployment.

The coal strike. In 1926 a strike occurred among the coal miners, which had momentous consequences. Mining was a "sick" industry, characterized by overproduction, unemployment, vanishing profits, and low wages. The main cause of these difficulties was a decline in demand owing to greater economy in the use of coal in industry and domestic heating, and the substitution of oil and hydro-electric power for coal. When the employers' Mining Association gave notice that the wage scale of 1921 would be withdrawn and a lower one substituted, the miners refused to accept it. The Trades Union Congress decided to support the miners and declared a general strike. Strictly speaking it was a sympathetic, rather than a "general," strike, in the sense in which the French syndicalists used the word. Railway men, transport workers, engineers, iron and steel workers, electricians, shipbuilders, and printers walked out. The government, however, opposed the general strike, and managed to keep the various affected industries going. After nine days the strike was broken, and the miners were forced to accept the eight-hour day and a reduction of wages. The struggle had brought the country almost to the verge of ruin, and resulted in a serious setback to the labor movement.

The Trades Disputes Act of 1927 was passed as a result of the experience with a general strike. This declared that "any strike having any object beyond the furtherance of a trade dispute within a trade or industry in which the strikers are engaged is an illegal strike, if it is designed to coerce the Government or to intimidate the community or any substantial part of it." No member of a union was to be liable to expulsion for refusing to join a strike. Intimidation by pickets was forbidden, intimidation being broadly defined as any action causing "in a person's mind a reasonable apprehension of injury to his person or his dependents." The sympathetic strike, and even more the general strike, was declared illegal. Civil servants were forbidden to join any union affiliated with the Trades Union Congress or the Labour Party, but public authorities were forbidden to make trade union membership a condition of employment.

A serious blow at the political activities of trade unions was struck by the provisions relating to funds raised for this purpose. The Labour Party had been financed largely by an annual levy of about one shilling on trade union members. The Osborne Judgment of 1910 had removed the obligation to pay this, but the Trade Union Act of 1913 had legalized it on condition that a majority of members in a union voted for it. The Act of 1927, however, provided that no member of a union was to be liable for a political levy unless he gave written notice that he was willing to pay it; and the political expenditures were to be limited to money so raised, of which a separate account was to be kept. The first effect of this Act, as well as of the failure of the general strike, was a reduction in the membership of the unions, and in their political funds. There was a return to more moderate policies and to Parliamentary action, and a sharpening of the antagonism against the left-wing members, who were forced out and who joined the Communist Party.

Reform movements. Meanwhile the industrial and financial situation was growing more serious. The value of the pound in international exchange was falling, and by 1931 had reached $3.40. It was clear that the gold standard could no longer be maintained and in 1931 it was abandoned. In spite of the relief afforded by this action, the years from 1930 to 1933 constituted a period of acute depression, marked by wage reductions and unemployment. By 1933, however, there was an industrial recovery and wage increases became numerous. The period from 1933 on was remarkable for the prevalence of industrial peace. Partly responsible was the reaction against National Socialism in Germany, but even more important was the effort of the government, by the Coal Miners Act of 1930, and by its tariff and subsidy policy, to tie wages and prices together and to assure the workers of a fair share in national prosperity. By the Factories Act of 1937 the regulation of the hours of labor was extended so as to cover practically all industries. The Act abandoned the old distinctions between factory and workshop and defined the former so as to include all premises in which persons were engaged in manual labor, thus applying to shipyards and docks, laundries, printing works, and buildings under construction. For women and young persons the maximum working week was fixed at forty-eight hours, and for children under sixteen at forty-four. But the legal restriction of the hours of male workers, as a general principle, was still not admitted into British law. As a matter of fact, however, the limitation of the hours of women and children held down those of men; an investigation by the Ministry of Labour in 1935 reported average hours per week of 47.8.

Certain short-lived movements, designed to better the position of labor, occurred during this period. One was gild socialism, which was characterized as "a half-way house between socialism and syndicalism." This proposed that society should be organized into workers' gilds for productive purposes, and that the political state should limit its functions to matters affecting the consuming population generally. Some experiments were made along this line, notably in the building trades, but the idea did not permanently influence the labor movement. Another innovation was the shop stewards' movement. This was designed to afford the workers an organized channel through which they might express their views on questions of management and working conditions. Opposed by the employers, this movement also died out. Mention may also be made of the system of joint industrial councils, known as Whitleyism, which aimed to bring the unions into some kind of organic relation with the administration of industry and public services. A few councils were set up, notably in flour milling, the furniture and pottery industries, and the civil service, but most of the industries refused to have anything to do with the movement. Although it had the blessing of the government, it was opposed by both employers and organized labor, and soon died out.

While the Labour Party was quite distinct from the trade union movement, the fortunes of the former cannot be omitted in a history of the latter. The Labour Party had been broadened in 1918 to include brain-workers as well as hand-workers, and the extension of the franchise in that year had brought it new strength. It began to take a more active part in the interest of trade unions. In 1924 it reached the height of its power when it formed a Labour government with Ramsay MacDonald as Prime Minister. In spite of a good though purely negative administrative record the Ministry was forced out of office in October of that year, but in 1929 it returned to office with augmented strength and MacDonald was again appointed Prime Minister. Shortly after its accession the depression began, and it was confronted with the problem of caring for the unemployed. Unable to handle the situation, it was finally forced out of office in 1931, and the Conservative Party assumed control.

Trade union policy. A number of the older and more conservative trade union officials had been appointed to positions under the first Labour government, and the leadership of the labor movement had passed largely into the hands of more militant younger men. Their unfortunate experience with the general strike of 1926 made them more cautious, and after that year the trade union movement adopted a more conservative policy. The alternatives were well presented in a report to the Trades Union Congress in 1928. The workers might attempt to break down the existing capitalistic system; they might endeavor to improve conditions sectionally; or they might acknowledge that they were concerned with the prosperity of industry, but insist on having a voice as to how it is carried on. The first of the three policies received some support after the war and there were widespread strikes in 1918–19 and again in 1926. But the failure of the latter cooled the revolutionary fire. The third policy of co-partnership with capital completely dominated the movement after 1926, although it failed to obtain the support of the left-wing members.

The need for general organization had resulted in the foundation of the Trades Union Congress in 1868. In order to obtain further centralization of control as the trade unions grew in membership and diversity of interests a general council of the Trades Union Congress had been established in 1920. This grew steadily in prestige and power, and in 1938 was a closely knit organization, with eight departments and nine advisory councils. It assisted in the administration of social insurance and workmen's compensation, determined the demarcation between unions, and strongly influenced the local trades councils. The powers of the Trades Union Congress itself, with which four-fifths of British trade unionists were affiliated, were strengthened and centralized. Although this body, in the words of the Webbs, was "rather a parade of Trade Union forces than a genuine Parliament of Labour," it did act effectively as a spokesman for labor and settled jurisdictional disputes among rival member unions.

The older conception of trade unions as organs of class struggle gradually yielded to a more realistic attitude, and the unions tended more and more to emphasize their functions as justifiable institutions for the regulation of wages and working conditions within the existing capitalist system. The trade union movement, through organized consultation and sometimes through administrative or controlling bodies, came to exercise definite and constructive functions. Operating, as it did, in an industrial system increasingly interpenetrated with state power, it also came to be more definitely socialistic as time went on.

Unemployment insurance. Until the war labor supply and labor demand had maintained a fairly steady relationship with the latter running from ninety to ninety-five per cent of the former. This indicated a "reserve army" of about 500,000 permanently unemployed. There was an increase in unemployment as a result of the war, which Professor Clay [1] estimated as $7\frac{1}{2}$ per cent or the equivalent of 900,000 persons. The depression of 1921 brought the figure up to 23 per cent in May of that year, but that was the peak for a decade. With the improvement in the industrial situation down to 1928 the percentage of unemployment remained around $8\frac{1}{2}$ to 9 per cent, representing somewhat over 1,000,000 persons. The long low swing of the business cycle in the next five years brought tragic suffering to the workers; during 1932 and 1933 one British worker in four was without work or wages, and between six and seven million people, including dependents, were "on the dole." After 1934 the industrial sky brightened and the number of unemployed steadily fell, reaching a level of about 1,700,000 in 1938.

It is evident that the problem was so serious in nature and wide in scope, that neither the individual worker, the trade unions, nor local agencies could successfully cope with it. To the normal causes of unemployment such as disorganization of the labor market, the seasonal character of many industries, and deficiencies of training of workers, the war had added changes of industrial structure. Industries serving war needs were expanded beyond peace-time demands while others were restricted, and the necessary readjustments for both capital and labor were slow and painful. Especially serious was the great decline in the export trade, which reduced production and employment in some of the leading industries, and may be counted the principal cause of continuing unemployment.

The British attack on unemployment consisted of "a network of devices which include contributory unemployment insurance; noncontributory relief to members of the insurance scheme; poor relief; a wide-flung system of employment exchanges; relief works; and elaborate machinery for retraining the unemployed, for moving them from depressed to more prosperous areas, and for stimulating their migration overseas." [2]

Compulsory unemployment insurance had been introduced in 1911 for some 2,500,000 persons. Its success encouraged the government to extend the system in 1920 to practically the entire body of industrial wage earners, a total of nearly 12,000,000 workers. Unfortunately the depression of 1921, followed by chronic unemployment much greater than before the war, placed a staggering burden on the insurance fund, and the system was saved only by heavy advances from the Treasury. The decade of the twenties

[1] H. Clay, *The Post-War Unemployment Problem* (London, 1929), 29.
[2] A. C. C. Hill, Jr., and I. Lubin, *The British Attack on Unemployment* (Washington, 1934), 5. By permission of the publisher, The Brookings Institution, Washington.

saw many changes in contributions, benefits, and methods of administration, but the "means test" in 1921 and the condition of "genuinely seeking work," imposed in 1924, held the number assisted within reasonable limits.[3]   In 1930 a new Unemployment Insurance Act was passed which suspended these conditions, and altered the rules in favor of claimants.   Benefits were paid for unlimited periods as a legal right to all unemployed claimants who had ever been employed in an insured industry.   The depression of this and the following years, however, forced economies and in 1931 insurance benefits were reduced by ten per cent and in duration to twenty-six weeks per year.   Every claimant moreover had to prove thirty contributions in the two years preceding his date of claim.   These restrictions excluded over 1,000,000 persons, who were forced to seek poor relief if they were in need.   Finally, after several investigations and committee reports, a new act was passed in 1934 which extended the system to some 13,000,000 workers.   The 1931 cuts were restored and the steady contributor could draw a maximum of fifty-two weeks' benefit.

The changes in unemployment insurance between 1920 and 1934 had been stigmatized by an able student [4] of the subject as a retrogression "from insurance by contract to relief by status," but now administrative order was introduced.   Unemployment insurance was sharply distinguished from unemployment assistance.   The former was placed on a sound actuarial basis, and benefits were conditioned upon contributions.   The able-bodied unemployed who were not eligible for unemployment benefits were transferred to a newly organized unemployment assistance service, which was administered with a "needs test."   The scheme was still further enlarged in 1936 by the establishment of unemployment insurance for agricultural workers, and in 1938 by a voluntary pension scheme for "black-coated" workers earning less than £400 a year.   The voluntary scheme was also open to small business men as well as workers, provided their annual income did not exceed £400 for men or £250 for women.

A novel feature of the 1934 act was the establishment of a new national service, under the direction of the Unemployment Assistance Board.   This took over from local committees all duties in regard to transitional payments in the insurance system, and, secondly, the ordinary poor law functions in respect of practically all able-bodied poor, which had for centuries been a traditional local duty.   The handling of poverty resulting from unemployment was thus centralized on a national basis, while poverty resulting from

---

[3] The "means test" reduced benefits to those who had private resources.
[4] W. H. Beveridge, *Unemployment* (London, 1930), 88.

sickness, old age, or incapacity was left to local authorities. It was also provided, for the first time, that young people in industry between the ages of fourteen and sixteen should be included. Accordingly all persons normally engaged in an occupation, between the ages of fourteen and sixty-five, and earning less than £5 per week, were included in the scope of the act — well over 16,000,000 persons. In 1936 a new Act brought in agricultural workers, but with special rates of contribution and benefits. The only persons not covered were non-manual workers earning over £250 a year, domestic servants, and employees of railway or other companies having approved schemes of their own. Centralization of the poor law administration, with a uniform national scale, proved difficult, and various compromises had to be made, yet the system finally was put in working order and the relief of unemployment was handled more scientifically.

The attack on unemployment was not limited to insurance. An integral part of the system was the unemployment exchanges, which endeavored to place those out of work in new positions. The success of these exchanges is shown by the fact that in thirteen years, 1921–1933, over 18,000,000 vacancies were filled by them. In bad times, however, there were not enough jobs to go around and other means had to be found for providing employment. Extensive relief works were therefore set up in 1921 for the registered unemployed. Subsidies were granted to local authorities, primarily for roads, parks, and drainage, for the purpose of providing work. This plan proved costly to the Treasury — £103,000,000 by 1931, — contributed little to the solution of the problem, and was finally discontinued. Transference of unemployed workers from heavily depressed areas to more prosperous centers of industrial activity in Great Britain was begun in 1928, following a scheme of assisted emigration after 1922, but neither produced results commensurate with the outlay. More promising because more fundamental was the setting up of training establishments to fit men and women better for vocational work. By 1934 over 12,000 occupational centers had been established, and by 1937 about 250,000 men and women had received training during unemployment, while about 1,400,000 juveniles had passed through junior instruction centers.

Helpful as some of these devices were, unemployment insurance overshadowed every other measure. Its scope had increased until it included practically every group except domestic servants. The weekly contributions of employers and workers had grown with some fluctuations, from 2½ pence in 1911 to 9 pence in 1937 (that of the state from 1⅔ to 9 pence); but the weekly benefits had also risen, from 7 shillings for a man, his wife, and two children in

1911 to 38 shillings in 1938. Great Britain thus reaffirmed the doctrine of state responsibility in meeting the problem of unemployment. It recognized the social character of this evil and placed its relief on a national basis.

Social insurance. The war and the disorganization and poverty which followed it led to a wider application of the principle of social insurance. The National Health Insurance Act of 1911 received many amendments, mostly in the direction of a relaxation of regulations. Person between sixteen and sixty-five engaged in any contractual employment whose annual pay did not exceed £250 (raised from £160 in 1919) were included in the system. There were 17,000,000 insured persons in Great Britain in 1931. Contributions were 4½ pence weekly from the employer and an equal sum from the worker. The ordinary benefits to which insured persons were entitled were medical, sickness, disablement, and maternity benefits, but under certain circumstances there were also additional benefits consisting of cash, dental and ophthalmic treatment, surgical appliances, hospitalization, and nursing.

This scheme was greatly extended in 1925 by adding a contributory pension system to that of health insurance. This gave pensions for life to the widows of insured men, with temporary allowances for their dependent children, and old age pensions for life to insured men, and their wives, upon reaching the age of sixty-five. All persons insured under the health system came under the new act. Contributions were the same as for health insurance from both employers and workers. Pensions to widows amounted to 10 shillings weekly, with additional weekly allowances of 3 shillings for each dependent child under fourteen. Orphans received 7½ shillings weekly up to the age of fourteen (or to sixteen, if the child remained in school). Insured men and women received pensions of 10 shillings a week upon attaining the age of sixty-five; when they reached seventy they came under the Old Age Pension system.

The Old Age Pension Act of 1908 was a non-contributory scheme, and granted pensions of 5 shillings a week to all persons of seventy years of age or over whose annual income did not exceed £21. By 1931 the weekly pensions had been raised to 10 shillings, and were given to all persons upon reaching the age of seventy, without regard to means, residence, or nationality.

Accident compensation dated from 1880, with the passage of the Employers' Liability Act. No essential change was made in the system, but in 1923 the schedule of payments for injuries was raised considerably. Where death of the worker resulted the total maximum payment to the dependents was raised from £300 to £600. In cases of injuries resulting in disablement the allowance of a totally disabled workman was raised to 30 shillings a week, and the lower-paid workers were allowed up to seventy-five per cent of their weekly earnings. More generous treatment was also accorded the partially disabled and those suffering from industrial diseases.

The account of social insurance would not be complete without noting the spread of industrial insurance carried on by private companies. This was brought under strict governmental control in 1923 and may fairly be regarded as part of the general system. Policies were issued for life insurance, funeral expenses, and children's endowments. By 1930 some 80,000,000 small policies were in force, belonging to the working class and covering about three-quarters of the population.

The various social insurance acts possessed an importance far transcending the concession of claims for assistance on the part of the workers. They placed the state in a new role. Having witnessed what the state could do in the emergency of war, the workers demanded that it use its powers for social improvement in time of peace. State socialism and the nationalization of various industries were demanded. But, above all, security in his job and after his working days were over was claimed as labor's due. The unions were linked more closely to the state by the ingenious device of associating them in the administration of the state insurance funds. The state became the protector of labor, though always safeguarding the interests of private property. Increasingly it was forced to interfere in industrial disputes as conciliator and arbiter, and at the same time sought to raise the general status of labor.

2. LABOR BECOMES A SERVANT OF THE STATE IN GERMANY

Labor during the war. The immediate effect of the war was to disorganize industry and to throw men out of work. This was well shown by the jump in the trade union index of unemployment from 2.9 to 32.4 per cent. As war industries, especially of munitions, expanded, the labor surplus was turned into a labor shortage, and this was aggravated as more men were drafted into military service. By the end of 1916 almost two-thirds of the members of trade unions had been withdrawn from the labor market. Some of these were brought back into industry, as the need of the munitions and other war industries for skilled workers was better recognized. As in other belligerent countries increased use was made of women, of young boys, and old men. A measure of the "dilution" of labor is indicated by the increase in the women employed in the metal industries from 6.6 per cent in 1914 to 32.5 per cent in 1917. The lack of labor was also in part made good by bringing in Belgian and

Polish workers and by the immigration of skilled craftsmen from Denmark and Switzerland. The German male working population up to the age of sixty, in so far as they were not drafted into military service, were organized in 1916 under military direction as the Fatherland's Labor Service. Although the Social Democrats accepted the measure they realized that it signified, at least for the duration of the war, the loss of freedom of movement on the part of workers and other rights won during the labor struggles of the past decades.

Labor exchanges, to facilitate the placement of unemployed workers, had been highly developed before the war. Employment bureaus and lodgings for wandering workers were provided by the government, and gilds, trade unions, chambers of commerce, and other organizations co-operated. Shortly after the beginning of the war an imperial office was established to centralize the work and a semi-weekly information sheet was published. In order to bring into the system the skilled craft workers in the villages, joint bureaus of employers and workers were established in every district in 1915, and in 1916 the number of offices was greatly increased.

There were some advances in the position of the workers between 1914 and 1918, such as the shortening of the working day, especially in the textile industry, the abolition of night work in bakeries, the establishment of minimum wages for wide groups of home workers and for agricultural laborers, the establishment of arbitration committees, the improvement of safety, sanitation, and working conditions in factories, and other gains. On the other hand there developed such evils as the spread of women's work into unsuitable and dangerous lines, and the malnutrition of millions of working men and women.

Trade unions. Before the war broke out the trade unions had feared dissolution. The government was preparing in 1914 a new law against the right of workers to combine in trade unions. This was now dropped and the right of labor to organize was openly recognized. The unions changed their attitude of hostility and entered the war in support of the state; and in response the government ceased its opposition to the right of combination, its unfavorable administration of the law, its policy of excluding trade unionists from public affairs, and other methods of suppression. Labor agreed not to strike during the war, the employers refrained from lockouts, and the civil authorities abstained from interference. But, though the trade unions were freed from the pressure of the police, they fell under that of the military. No new impulse was given to growth in numbers during the war, though the idea of discipline was strengthened and the organizations became more bureaucratic.

In 1918 occurred the revolution which swept away the old imperial regime and set up a republic. A naval mutiny at Kiel, only two days before the armistice, was followed by an uprising of sailors, soldiers, and workers, who formed workers' councils on the model of those recently established in Soviet Russia. Control soon passed, however, into the hands of the older union leaders who favored a republican form of government. Unfortunately there were no strong leaders, and there were disagreements among the socialists themselves. Those in control were vacillating and followed the mass instead of leading them. There was thus a strong move to the left, for the workers were hungry, embittered, and disillusioned. Among the salaried workers, too, there was a strong radical feeling, a result of reaction against the oppressive policies of many short-sighted employers during the war.

The Weimar Constitution, upon which the new Republic was based, was probably the most liberal in the world in recognizing the right of wage earners to have a share in determining working conditions and in shaping the general economic policy of the country. It put labor under the special protection of the state and guaranteed the right of combination to safeguard the position of the workers. Trade unions were given the right to participate on an equal basis with employers' organizations in the determination of working conditions, in collective bargaining, and in arbitration. Provision was also made for social insurance, works councils, an eight-hour day, and other long-standing demands of labor. The new constitution made no break with the past, but rather represented a culmination of certain trends; it accepted the deeply rooted concept of the subordination of the individual to the group and the supremacy of the state.

One of the first fruits of the new order was the famous agreement of November 15, 1918, between the leaders in German industry and the largest trade unions, called at the time the "Magna Charta" of labor. Labor was accepted as an equal partner with the employers in framing working arrangements, and the unions were recognized as official representatives of the workers and salaried employees. There was to be equality in the administration of labor offices and the principle of collective agreements was adopted as the normal procedure. The eight-hour day was made applicable to all German industry, the independent unions were alone recognized as having collective bargaining and contracting power, and the yellow or company unions were thereafter to be left to themselves without support from the employers. Even more radical was the provision for works councils in all establishments employing over nineteen persons, to be elected by the workers, and to discuss with the employers such matters as accidents, health, and questions of unfair dismissal. These various provisions were enacted into law in March, 1919, and remained substantially unchanged until 1933. The most important legislation of the years immediately following the war was the establishment of works councils and machinery for conciliation and arbitration in industrial disputes.

Membership in the trade unions had fallen off greatly during the first two years of the war, that of the Social Democratic or "free" unions declining from 2,574,000 in 1913, to 945,000 at the end of 1916. In such luxury trades as those of painters, upholsterers, and barbers, the losses ran to over 80 per cent. By 1918, however, the total membership was back to normal, and in the next two years the growth of the trade unions was phenomenal. The "free" unions grew to 8 millions in 1920; the Christian unions from about 350,000 in 1913 to one million; and the Hirsch-Duncker unions from 100,-000 to 150,000. A new group, which had been developing since 1907 but which became prominent only after 1918, was that of the salaried employees (*Angestellte*), the so-called "white collar proletariat"; by 1925 they had a membership of 1,500,000. Agricultural workers, forbidden to organize before 1919, formed local unions, of which there were 9000 in 1920, with a membership of about 700,000. The total strength of all these organizations was around 11,000,000.

The next step was the federation of the various unions into strong centralized bodies, and this was taken in 1919. All the Social Democrats or "free" unions were federated in 1919 into a single large central organization known as the *Allgemeiner Deutscher Gewerkschafts-Bund* (the A.D.G.B.). In the same year the independent Catholic unions merged with other Christian labor organizations to form the *Gesamtverband der Christlichen Gewerkschaften*. The third group of trade unions, the Hirsch-Duncker or "liberal" unions, united as the *Deutsche Gewerksvereine*. Each of these new organizations was federal in character, the membership consisting of local unions, which were left with complete independence as to their internal organization and policies.

The period between 1919 and 1924 was one of industrial unrest, of inflation, of rapidly shifting values, and of wage struggles. The necessary adjustment of wages to prices was very slow, as the idea prevailed that higher wages would raise prices further, and produce a vicious circle. The result was that real wages fell steadily. Strikes became more numerous. Between 1899 and 1913 the annual average number of workers participating in strikes was 235,000 and they lost an average of 8,000,000 working days each year. During the war strikes sank to a minimum. But between 1919 and 1924 the annual average number of participants was 1,633,000 and of days lost 25,367,000. The years 1923–24 saw a shift in the labor situation. Lockouts by employers were frequent, unemployment became severe, the eight-hour day was disavowed, and some 5,000,000 workers deserted the unions. By 1926 there were 10,000,000 persons receiving public aid. The yellow or company unions, thought to be dead, reappeared under a new name, that of *Werkgemein-schaften*. After this there was a decade of comparative peace, the low point of labor conflicts being reached in 1931 when 178,000 workers lost only 2,000,000 days.

Labor peace was promoted by the wide extension of wage agreements. Before the war these covered only about 10 per cent of the workers, but by 1922 over half and by 1931 four-fifths of the wages and salaries were determined by collective agreements or by law. An individual bargain between employer and employee was an unusual circumstance. Agricultural strikes had been unheard of before the war, but in the hunger years after its end they grew rapidly, reaching a maximum in 1923. After that the new machinery for settlement became effective and they all but disappeared. In 1920 about 300,000 enterprises had collective agreements affecting nearly 6,000,000 workers, but by 1931 there were 805,000 contracts covering over 10,000,000 workers. Collective bargaining had become a general and legally recognized practice. The scope of an agreement could moreover be greatly extended by the government, by declaring it "generally binding," that is applying to the whole industry in that district. Even where no voluntary agreement was achieved, the mediator's decision, if accepted by either party, became binding on both. Industrial relations were thus increasingly subject to state control.

Meanwhile there had been developing a system of arbitration and conciliation to deal with industrial disputes. During the war conciliation bodies had been established, with army officers as chairmen, and these were retained under the Republic but with civilian chairmen. These boards had only powers of persuasion and when these proved inadequate in the face of revolutionary upheavals, the element of compulsion was added in 1919. The procedure was simplified in 1923 and three years later labor courts were established. After this the chief function of arbitration was to facilitate a "continuous network of collective agreements" and to regulate working conditions. The following years were relatively quiet, wages rose, and the arbitration system functioned effectively. When, however, the trade unions were destroyed in 1933 and the employers' associations dissolved, the basis of a system of collective agreements and

arbitration ceased to exist.   Henceforth there was authoritarian regu-
tion of labor conditions.

The membership of the unions reflected the changes in the business cycle, the strength of the government, and the power of the
employers.   The total numbers in all the unions grew from about
3,000,000 in 1913 to over 9,000,000 in 1922, when persons of all
descriptions, including brain workers and civil servants as well as
manual workers, flocked in.   This rapid and unsought addition weakened rather than strengthened the labor movement, for it represented divergent views and interests.   From this maximum the
membership fell off to 5,000,000 in 1931.   As before the war there
were three principal central organizations, but with different names.
Of them the A.D.G.B. was by far the most important, and claimed
to be the spokesman for organized labor.   It was a federal organization, composed, like the British T.U.C. and the French C.G.T., only
of national unions.   Its functions were agitation, research, education,
adjustment of difficulties among constituent unions, and arbitration
in cases of conflict.   The following table shows the fluctuations in
membership and the distribution of strength among the three central
groups:

TRADE UNION MEMBERSHIP

Year	A.D.G.B.	Christian	Hirsch-Duncker	Total
1913	2,574,000	343,000	107,000	3,024,000
1922	7,895,000	1,049,000	231,000	9,175,000
1932	4,569,870	1,283,270	573,950	6,427,000 *

* There were in addition about 500,000 members of Independent, Peaceful, and Communist
unions.

At the last date the trade union membership in Great Britain was
about 4,400,000, and in France slightly over 1,000,000.

Unemployment.   Unemployment presented a serious problem in
every country after the war and nowhere more so than in Germany.
To the difficulties of demobilization was added the unsettlement
caused by political revolution.   A systematic organization of labor
exchanges for the whole country, including municipal and inter-
municipal public placement offices, was established in 1922 under
the Ministry of Labor, but this could not solve the problem.   The
situation was somewhat alleviated during the spurious boom of the
inflation period, but by December, 1923, it again assumed serious
proportions, when 28 per cent of trade union members were reported to be wholly unemployed; the average for the year was 10
per cent and the total number out of work was reported as 1,500,000.

During the next few years conditions were made worse by the rationalization movement, which was extraordinarily rapid and replaced men by machines faster than they could be absorbed back into industry. It was officially estimated that at least 2,000,000 workers were rendered unemployed between 1925 and 1930 by this movement.

To blame rationalization for all this unemployment is to assign it too much significance and to overlook other factors. More important was the pressure of the trade unions, through collective agreements, to increase or maintain wage rates at a high level when prices were falling and industrial activity was diminishing. Under such circumstances producers were forced to cut their costs, including wages, or to curtail output. Since they were prevented from reducing wages, they were forced to restrict operations and throw men out of work. The pressure in this direction was accentuated by the scarcity of capital and its high cost — interest on mortgages was over 8 per cent — and by the increasing burden of the unemployment insurance contributions. From 3 per cent of the wage bill they were raised to $3\frac{1}{2}$ in January, 1930, to $4\frac{1}{2}$ in August, and to $6\frac{1}{2}$ in October.

UNEMPLOYMENT IN GERMANY, 1929–33

Year	Percentage of trade unionists wholly unemployed	No. of unemployed reported at the labor offices
1913	2.9	....
1929	12.5	1,843,000
1930	21.6	3,008,000
1931	33.5	4,465,000
1932	43.9	5,561,000
1933	46.4	5,855,000

A "reserve army," in Marx's phrase, of unemployed workers had always existed in pre-war Germany, which had at times run up to 1,500,000. But here was an unprecedented situation which demanded immediate relief. In January, 1933, there were 6,014,000 names on the official unemployment registers and nearly 1,000,000 additional non-registered unemployed. When the National Socialists took over the reins of government in the spring of that year they faced the problem of carrying out their pledges to cure unemployment. They attacked the problem vigorously from two sides, by increasing the demand for labor and by decreasing the supply of labor on the market. The policy was outlined by Hitler in May in the First Four-Year Plan and was put into effect by the Law for the Reduction of Unemployment the following month.

To increase the demand for labor a system of public works was inaugurated, comprising housing, road building, including a grandiose scheme for 4300 miles of motor roads, river regulation, public utilities, agricultural and suburban settlement, and other works. At the same time private individuals were encouraged to employ labor by exempting replacements and renewals from taxation and by allowing abatements in income taxes when additional female domestic servants were employed. To take workers off the market marriage loans were made, and women in industry were urged to return to the "three Ks" (*Kinder, Küche, Kirche*) and let men have their places. Such organizations as the Labor Service (*Arbeitsdienst*) absorbed a good many and the Land Help (*Landeshilfe*) took many young people out of the industrial areas to work on the land. The Labor Service compelled every young man to work six·months before his military service on land reclamation, soil improvement, and forestry; and a similar organization existed for girls. The Land Help was designed to settle juvenile unemployed on the land. Together they gave employment in 1924 to about 200,000 persons, who received full maintenance, but not money wages. The various military and political organizations and the army also gave new employment. By such methods the number of unemployed was reduced steadily from an all-time high of 6,014,000 in January, 1933, to 1,170,000 in July, 1936, and to 74,000 in July, 1939, a record low.

Beginning with 1935 there was a shift from public works to rearmament. Munitions factories were built, barracks and airports constructed, and armament supplies were manufactured on a huge scale. Unemployment not only fell to negligible proportions, but there developed a serious shortage of labor. Some of the former policies were reversed and women were recalled to industry. Production was shifted from consumption to capital goods, especially in the building, metal-working, and automotive industries. But these required imports of raw materials of every sort, not needed under the earlier policy, and called for new extensions of state control. The First Four-Year Plan had solved the problem of unemployment, but in doing so had produced a new set of difficulties. These were met in characteristic fashion.

A Second Four-Year Plan was outlined by Hitler in September, 1936, which was designed to make Germany self-sufficient, industrially and agriculturally. The necessary raw materials were to be produced or invented, the supply of foodstuffs was to be increased, waste was to be prevented, and foreign trade was to be manipulated so as to assure those goods which could not be produced at home. The carrying out of such a plan accentuated the shortage of labor, especially in highly skilled trades and in industries in which the Second Four-Year Plan called for increased production. Measures were taken to increase the number of apprentices, especially in the metal-working and building industries. Priorities were established to determine the placement of workers; rearmament stood first, followed by food supply, domestic raw materials, exports, and building. To decrease the turnover of labor each worker was compelled to have a workbook, without which he could not obtain fresh employment. A black mark in the book was practically a death sentence. The mobility of labor was thereby greatly restricted and whole sections of workers were prevented from leaving their occupations in order to find others. Agricultural workers were not allowed to leave the country and move into the cities. In 1936 the metal workers, and in 1937 masons and carpenters were forbidden to change their occupations or working places except by permission of the Labor Exchange Office. And finally, in 1938, the drastic step was taken of putting all Germans under industrial conscription, by which they must work at an assigned job, or undergo training for a certain occupation.

These measures effected primarily a redistribution of the existing labor force. The supply increased slightly by the use of immigrant labor, primarily in agriculture, by deferment of retirement for older men, and by greater employment of women. The "hidden reserve" of women workers was systematically tapped by prescribing a year of compulsory service for them, primarily in unskilled or short-time work. The working day was also lengthened, especially in the armament industry, and attempts were made to increase the productivity of labor by the larger use of machinery. Between 1932 and 1937 the productivity of labor increased about 11 per cent.

Labor under National Socialism. It is evident that there had been built up, under the Weimar Republic, a political and economic system under which the workers enjoyed considerable power, if not domination. Yet it was wholly destroyed by the rise to power of the National Socialist Party under the leadership of Adolf Hitler in 1933. What were the causes of this revolution? No single explanation will suffice, for many factors contributed to the change. Among these were the political failure of the Republic to solve existing problems, resentment over the treatment of Germany by the Allies, hostility of reactionary groups such as the Junkers, the big industrialists, and the military, to the growing power of labor, and diversity and lack of vigorous leadership in the labor movement. But the decisive factor was the depression. The curve of the rise of National Socialism closely paralleled that of unemployment.

There was no place for trade unions in a totalitarian state and these were suppressed in May, 1933, when all Social Democratic or A.D.G.B. trade union buildings were occupied, their leaders arrested, and their property confiscated. The following month the Social Democratic Party was prohibited. The remaining trade unions — Christian and Hirsh-Duncker — seeing the handwriting on the wall, did not wait to be dissolved but voluntarily joined the new organization set up in place of the unions. This was the Labor Front, which took over the functions and funds of the unions.

The Labor Front differed from the trade unions in that it included employers as well as employees. According to National Socialist ideology brain workers and hand workers formed parts of a common structure. Membership was theoretically voluntary, but the pressure to join was strong, and non-members did not find it easy to obtain employment. It had about 26,000,000 members in 1938. Although it was supposed to be independent of the National Socialist Party, it was closely linked with it. The Labor Front was therefore a very powerful organization, and its activities were varied. It granted relief to needy members, subsidized housing, inspected factories and suggested improvements, and developed vocational training on a large scale. But its most spectacular activities were comprised under Strength through Joy (*Kraft durch Freude*). This was designed to provide recreation for the workers' leisure time, and organized dances, concerts and theatrical entertainments, encouraged sport, and provided cheap holiday excursions. Six million persons are estimated to have gone on these trips in 1936. Not all of these activities were new, for many of them had been carried on by the trade unions, workingmen's clubs, and similar organizations, but the propaganda value of the Labor Front was undoubted, and it afforded a method of maintaining a centralized control over the workers.

The position of labor in the economic and political structure of the Third Reich was determined by the law of January 20, 1934, for the Regulation of National Labor. This was based on three principles:[5] unity of employers and workers instead of class conflict; the leadership principle of "full authority downwards, full responsibility upwards"; and strict state control over industrial relations. The interests of capital and labor were held to be harmonious since they were both working for the common good. Each factory community (*Betriebsgemeinschaft*) consisted of the leader, or employer, and the followers or employees, but the leader was "master in his own house." He managed his business and decided questions of wages, hours, and working conditions, but these must be stated in writing. The state, however, exercised final control and set up three bodies to protect the interests of the workers and of society.

Every business employing more than 20 persons had a Confiden-

[5] H. A. Marquand (Ed.), *Organized Labour in Four Continents* (London, 1939), 110.

tial Council (*Vertrauensrat*), consisting of the employer and 2 to 10 employees, who must, however, be loyal Nazis. The Councils, which were merely advisory, were supposed to improve mutual relations, increase efficiency, and prevent or settle minor disputes. They were emasculated substitutes for the former works councils but were devoid of any significant power or function. Collective agreements were outlawed, and strikes and lockouts were prohibited. Ultimate authority in industrial relations was vested in the fourteen Labor Trustees (*Treuhänder der Arbeit*), who were state officials. They had absolute powers to fix wages and hours, to draw up rules for framing works regulations, and to decide in cases of dispute not settled within the factory. Finally, Social Honor Courts (*Soziale Ehrengerichte*) were established to try cases where either employer or worker offended against "social honor." Most of the cases which came before the Court were complaints against employers.

3. THE POPULAR FRONT IN FRANCE

Labor during the war. The outbreak of war caused a great dislocation in the labor market. About 3,500,000 men were at once called to the colors, as a result of which nearly half of the factories, stores, and offices were closed, and some 2,000,000 workers were thrown out of employment. The situation clearly called for action on a national scale, as neither the employment bureaus of the labor syndicates nor the public employment offices in the cities could cope with the problem. Accordingly, on August 20, 1914, the government created a National Employment Fund and later a Central Office for the Placing of Unemployed Workers and Refugees, which was useful in redistributing the labor force.

As the highly mechanized character of the new warfare became apparent it was necessary to direct more workers into munitions plants. At the beginning of the war these employed about 45,000 workers, but at the end 2,000,000. To obtain these skilled operatives, men were called back from the army, but there were not enough of these to meet the expanding demand. Consequently, civil workers, both men and women, and finally immigrants and colonials, were drawn upon. The policy of a selective draft was gradually developed, and a classified catalogue of some 700,000 industrial workers was made. Men qualified for military service were divided into two groups: (1) skilled workers, who might be assigned to factory jobs, but who still were under military jurisdiction, and (2) laborers without special skill, who were subject to call if needed.

There was also a "dilution of labor" by the more general employment of women. The ratio of women to men in private industry rose from 33 per cent in July, 1914, to 40 per cent in July, 1918. The women proved unexpectedly efficient, especially in the operation of automatic machinery and in the inspection of products. In order to make the employment of women possible manufacturers found it necessary to change their equipment and methods, and to introduce mechanical contrivances to lighten labor, such as hoisting apparatus, travelling cranes, cutting machines, and so on. There was also more division of labor, the organization of production in series, and extreme specialization. The hours of labor, which had been jumped to 11 and 12 hours a day immediately after the outbreak of war, were modified, hygiene improved, and even recreation, lunch rooms, etc., provided. The exigencies of war forced a rationalization of industry which economic forces had not been able to accomplish in time of peace.

Labor organization. During the war, the military power became the supreme authority, and the acquired liberties of the workers, such as the rights of association and coalition, were greatly restricted. The press was subjected to censorship and syndical action became difficult.[6] The unions, however, loyally supported the war, and abandoned their pacifist and internationalist attitudes. The doctrines of class struggle and direct action were tacitly renounced, strikes were few, and organized labor lent its assistance to the government. It thus abandoned the social philosophy of pre-war syndicalism, which was based upon the theory of class struggle, direct action, and overthrow of the bourgeois state.

When the war ended the General Confederation of Labor (C.G.T.) experienced a rapid growth in numbers and in influence. From 600,000 in 1914 it jumped to a claimed membership of 2,-000,000 in 1919. These new accessions weakened rather than strengthened the C.G.T., for they were impatient for immediate reforms and also irritated by concrete grievances. A list of "minimum demands" was put up to the government, which included a general eight-hour day, recognition of collective agreements, the reconstruction of the devastated regions by organizations of producers, consumers, and officials, and the expropriation by the state and transfer to decentralized and independent groups organized in the same way of all enterprises exploiting essential national resources, such as mines, power, and railways. The first demand was granted by the eight-hour law of 1919; the legal 48-hour week thus prescribed was soon reduced in practice to 44 hours by the general adoption of a Saturday half holiday, the so-called *semaine Anglaise*. This reduction of working time does not seem to have been followed by a falling off of production.

[6] P. Louis, *Histoire du socialisme en France,* 1789–1936 (Paris, 1936), 352.

The years 1919 and 1920 were marked by many strikes, most of them over the question of wages; it was a period of prosperity and readjustments were called for. In 1920 a conflict occurred which led to a serious setback to the trade union movement. It began with a strike by the railway employees on the P. L. M. Railway Company over the discharge of a union man. The adjustment made in this case was unsatisfactory to the workers, and, under pressure from the radical groups, the C.G.T. decided to call a general strike on May 1, with a demand for the nationalization of the railways. The railway men went out, supported by a sympathetic strike of a select group of key industries, the marine, port, and dock workers, and the miners. Later the workers in the metal, building, and transport industries were called out. Employers, the press, and the government opposed the strike, consumers were incensed by the interruption of travel and supplies, and there were defections among the workers themselves. The government managed to maintain railway and other services, and finally ordered the dissolution of the C.G.T., and arrested the revolutionary leaders. On May 22 the strike was called off and the men returned to work. The strike was a complete failure and resulted in greatly weakening the C.G.T., whose membership declined in the following year to 600,000. It also accentuated the factional bitterness and schism in the C.G.T.

There were fundamental differences in aims and methods among different groups in the French labor movement which made harmony practically impossible. The communist group, in close association with the Moscow International, sought to wrest control of the C.G.T. from the moderate or reformist group. By 1922 the communists had been expelled by most of the syndicates in the C.G.T. and they formed a new central body, the C.G.T.U. (*Confédération Générale du Travail Unitaire*), with a membership of about 400,-000. The C.G.T., having got rid of the radical elements, abandoned its previous revolutionary principles and turned towards immediate reforms in working class conditions. Their chief demand was for a social insurance law, which was finally achieved in 1930, but they also concerned themselves with working class education, the organization of leisure time, and other methods of improving the status of labor within the existing capitalist system.

The C.G.T.U., which was at first torn by dissensions between the communist and anarchist elements, expelled the latter from their ranks in 1924 and thereafter received their inspiration, and apparently orders, from Moscow. It was a militant order, interested in fomenting strikes and class conflict, and had considerable influence among the unorganized workers. This split in the union ranks crippled the trade union movement for the next decade and a half. But finally, after long effort on the part of the leaders, a fusion of these two groups, the C.G.T. and the C.G.T.U., was effected in 1936. Other smaller organizations existed, such as the Christian Confederation (*Confédération française des travailleurs Chrétiens*) and the company or yellow unions, but neither of these claimed as many as 500,000 members, while the C.G.T. had over 5,000,000.

The deepening of the depression and the Fascist menace called for active measures and in 1934 the C.G.T. united with the political parties to carry through a plan of economic reorganization. The coalition was known as the *Front Populaire*. This issued a program in January, 1936, demanding certain reforms: effective disarmament and dissolution of the fascist leagues, reduction of working hours to forty a week without reduction of wages, old age pensions, a national unemployment fund, public works for the unemployed, assistance to the peasants, taxation of large incomes, reform of the Bank of France, and prohibition of the export of capital. These were "urgent and therefore limited demands," which were to be supplemented later by "measures of a deeper nature in order definitely to remove the state from the influence of industrial and financial feudalism."

The spring elections returned a Popular Front majority and some of these demands were enacted into law. The 40-hour week was introduced without reduction of wages, and fifty-four additional annual holidays on full pay were granted the workers. As a result of this legislation the number of working days in the year was reduced from 305 to 251, while the average weekly duration of work, which had been 45.8 hours, was reduced to 40.4 in 1937 and to 38.7 in 1938. A special motive for the 40-hour week was the hope that by it the unemployed, whose number had increased greatly since 1932, might be absorbed into industry, and this was accomplished. At the same time the so-called Matignon agreement was negotiated, by which the wages of industrial workers were raised 10 per cent; another similar increase was granted in 1937. Unfortunately these changes were followed in 1938 by a reduction in output 30 per cent below that of 1930. The reduction of hours in 1919 had been salutary, for prior to that time the working day had been unduly long, but the further reduction in 1936 was disastrous for the whole national economy. Other factors undoubtedly affected production, such as the depreciation of the currency, strikes, etc., but the lessening of the number of working days and the shortening of the daily working time were primarily responsible.

Collective bargaining had developed before the war, but it was not significant and during the war fell into abeyance; in 1915 only one agreement was made. Further legislation in 1919 and 1920 legalized collective agreements as binding contracts, and made them enforceable.   But their fulfilment was guaranteed only by the rules of private law, especially by a suit for damages.   Consequently such agreements were not numerous or important.   They were found primarily in coal mining and maritime transportation and to a lesser extent in the building and leather industries, and were largely confined to questions of wages.   In 1936 a new law was passed which greatly strengthened the position of the syndicate and practically lent to a collective agreement the force of public regulation.   Procedure for the settlement of disagreements was made obligatory in all collective bargaining.   Further legislation in 1938 provided for conciliation and arbitration.   There was also a change of attitude on the part of employers, many of whom had been hostile to agreements with the unions, but who now accepted the new order.   The number of collective agreements rose sharply from 29 in 1935 to several thousands in the following years, and the institution of shop stewards, representing the workers in the factories, lessened the fear of dismissal and raised the status of labor.   The C.G.T. was officially recognized as the representative of the interests of the workers, and was accorded a position of importance and power.

The attitude of the C.G.T., formerly strongly hostile to the state, now became friendly and co-operative.   It concerned itself first of all with defending from attacks by employers the new social legislation, strove to secure its enforcement, and attempted to obtain further laws favorable to the working class.   It stood for centralization and stability.   French labor leaders recognized that syndicalism, as practiced before the war, meant instability, and they therefore forsook this philosophy and endorsed collective bargaining, benefit features in the unions, and similar reforms.   One of the secretaries of the C.G.T. described the new orientation as follows: [7] "French trade unionism is no longer in opposition; it is no longer an outlaw; it accepts the idea of a system of labour law; social reforms no longer seem unclean to it; it submits to arbitration; it makes collective agreements; it places itself under the power of the law, which demands subjection, but gives protection."

The membership of the C.G.T., which is fairly typical of the French labor movement as a whole, reflected the fluctuations of the business cycles, the shifts in political power, and the internal dissensions of the organization.   The numbers for a few selected years may be given.

Labor legislation.   Part of the labor legislation enacted during this period has already been described, but some other measures may be briefly mentioned.   Sickness and accident insurance had been developed before the war on a voluntary basis; it was estimated that

[7] Quoted by H. A. Marquand, op. cit., 153.

MEMBERSHIP OF THE C. G. T.

Year	Number of members
1913	1,026,000
1919	1,581,000 *
1927	897,000
1932	250,000
1938	5,000,000

* There were also 400,000 organized civil servants.

in 1914 about 70 per cent of industrial workers were protected by insurance policies taken out by their employers entitling them to compensation. A state system of old-age pensions also existed. Not until 1928 was a comprehensive system of social insurance established, but in that year a law was enacted which covered sickness, invalidity, old age, death, maternity, and unemployment. It applied compulsorily to all workers whose annual earnings did not exceed 18,000 francs.[8] Equal contributions of 5 per cent of the wages were made by workers and employers. All persons who reached the age of sixty and who had worked 30 years were to receive a pension of 40 per cent of their average annual earnings. In case of sickness medical treatment was given, and in case of incapacity a pension which varied according to the number of years the worker had contributed to the insurance fund, but with a minimum of 1000 francs a year after six years. Of the money received by the fund one per cent was set aside for unemployment insurance. The state had subsidized the trade union unemployment funds since 1905, and since 1914 had given direct aid through municipalities and departments, but now took over the relief of unemployment on a national basis.

In addition to the legislation covering hours, collective bargaining, and social insurance, the Popular Front demanded the nationalization of armament manufactures and of the Bank of France, the establishment of a Wheat Office to organize the market for agricultural produce, and other measures.

Conclusion. Labor shared the vicissitudes of this period in common with the other factors in the economic system. The war introduced disorganization and the trade union movement was temporarily weakened, while some of the hard-earned gains of labor seemed lost. The restoration of peace, however, and of more normal activities brought to the unions new accessions of numbers and increased power. Labor assumed a more responsible position both in determining industrial policy and in shaping public affairs. But its status was precarious and was weakened by several conditions. In the first place there was disagreement within the ranks of labor itself as to the

[8] The franc was then worth slightly over 6½ cents, so this sum represented about $1200.

objective to be aimed at and the methods to use in order to attain it. The conservative right wing was content to work for reform within the existing capitalistic system, but the radical left wing wished a radical reorganization of society and saw in Sovietism the answer to their dreams.

The fortunes of labor were intimately tied to the business cycle, and price movements were of more immediate significance than social philosophies. Numbers and powers fluctuated with the ups and downs of business, as did employment and wages. But labor was also affected by the political cycle. The rise of authoritarian states, which had no place for a strong trade union movement such as was possible in a democratic society, crushed the unions and placed labor under the control of the government.

Unemployment was a problem common to both totalitarian and democratic countries and called urgently for solution. It was met in democratic Britain by unemployment insurance, in which she was the pioneer, in Nazi Germany and Fascist Italy by economic planning and practical conscription, and in Soviet Russia by assignment of workers to definite places in the communist economy. Nowhere was the remedy wholly satisfactory, and the case of John Doe, unemployed, still waits for a final decision at the bar of social justice.

BIBLIOGRAPHICAL NOTE

1. *Britain.* The war period is covered in P. U. Kellogg and A. Gleason, *British Labor and the War* (New York, 1919), and M. B. Hammond, *British Labor Conditions and Legislation during the War* (New York, 1919). Conditions at the end of the war are described in National Industrial Conference Board, *Report of the European Commission: Problems of Labor and Industry in Great Britain, France, and Italy* (Boston, 1919). Post-war conditions are treated in A. Hutt, *The Post-War History of the British Working Class* (New York, 1938), a communist appraisal, and J. Kuczynski, *Condition of the Workers in Great Britain, Germany, and the Soviet Union* (London, 1939), a socialist view. R. H. Tawney, *The British Labor Movement* (New Haven, 1925) gives a very general account. W. Milne-Bailey, *Trade Unions and the State* (London, 1934) is a philosophical appraisal. J. T. Murphy, *Modern Trade Unionism* (London, 1935) is a socialist approach. H. Marquand and others, *Organized Labour in Four Continents* (London, 1939) contains essays by eleven specialists. L. Wolman, *Union Membership in Great Britain and the United States* (New York, 1937) estimates the numerical strength of the unions. D. E. McHenry, *The Labour Party in Transition, 1931–1938* (London, 1938) deals with political aspects.

2. *Germany.* A glimpse of post-war labor conditions is afforded in R. R. Kuczynski, *Postwar Labor Conditions in Germany* (Washington, Bur. of Lab. Stat., 1930). Trade unionism during the war is treated in P. Umbreit, *Die deutschen Gewerkschaften im Kriege* (Stuttgart, 1938), poorly organized but informative. Other books on the labor movement are S. Nestriepke, *Die Gewerkschaftsbewegung,* 2 Bde. (2te Aufl., Stuttgart, 1923), of which Vol. II covers the period 1914–1922; T. O. Cassau, *Die Gewerkschaftsbewegung* (Halberstadt, 1925), an objective analy-

sis; A. Braun and R. Seidel, *Die Gewerkschaften, ihre Entwicklung und ihre Kämpfe*, 2 Bde. (Berlin, 1925), historical; R. Goetz, *Les syndicats ouvriers allemands après la guerre* (Paris, 1934). N. Reich, *Labor Relations in Republican Germany* . . . 1918–1933 (New York, 1938) is a summary. F. Wunderlich, *Labor under German Democracy: Arbitration*, 1918–1933 (New York, 1940) describes efforts to improve these relations. Legislation to save handwork is described in W. Heller and F. W. Karzwelly, *Die Handwerkerversorgung nach dem Gesetz*. . . . *von 21–12–'38* (1939), and W. Wernet, *Soziale Handwerksordnung* (Berlin, 1939). Nazi philosophy is expounded in G. Feder, *Das Programm des N.S.D.A.P. und seine weltanschaulichen Grundgedanken* (München, 1933), and G. Starke, *N.S.B.O. und deutsche Arbeitsfront* (Berlin, 1934), an official publication.

3. *France*. Labor conditions are set forth in A. M. Wergeland, *History of the Working Classes in France* (Chicago, 1916); P. Louis, *Histoire du socialisme en France depuis la Révolution jusqu'à nos jours*, 1789–1936 (3rd ed., Paris, 1936), by a socialist. The war period of the labor movement is covered in P. Paraf, *Le syndicalisme pendant et après la guerre* (Paris, 1923), and R. Picard, *Le mouvement syndical pendant la guerre* (Paris, 1927), a detailed account. J. German, *La C.G.T.* (Paris, 1921) describes the situation after the war. M. R. Clark, *A History of the French Labor Movement*, 1910–1928 (Berkeley, 1936) is a clear outline. D. J. Saposs, *The Labor Movement in Post-War France* (New York, 1931) is a scholarly analysis. L. Jouhaux, *Le syndicalisme, ce qu'il est, ce qu'il doit être* (Paris, 1937) and *La C.G.T., ce qu'elle est, ce qu'elle veut* (Paris, 1937) are an exposition of aims by a syndicalist. M. Thorez, *France Today and the People's Front* (New York, 1936) describes the political organization. H. Dubreuil, *Employeurs et salaires en France* (Paris, 1934) is useful.

CHAPTER XXII

POPULATION AND WELFARE

I. BRITISH ATTACK ON UNEMPLOYMENT

Population. In spite of losses during the war of about 600,000 men and of nearly as many non-combatants from disease and other casualties, the population of Great Britain grew at almost a normal rate. The exact figures were as follows:

POPULATION OF ENGLAND AND WALES

Year	Population	Percentage Rural	Urban
1911	36,070,492	21.9	78.1
1921	37,885,242	20.7	79.3
1931	39,947,031	20.0	80.0
1935	40,645,000	....	....

The birth-rate and death-rate both continued to fall during this period as they had during the pre-war period. Immediately after the war, however, the number of marriages increased and the birth-rate for 1925 reached the high figure of 25.5 per thousand. But this was exceptional and the general trend downward continued practically without interruption. The birth-rate fell faster than the death-rate, so that the annual excess of births over deaths fell to new lows.

ENGLAND AND WALES

Period	Annual birth-rate	Annual death-rate	Excess of births over deaths
1911–20	21.8	14.3	7.5
1921–30	18.3	12.1	6.2
1934	15.2	12.0	3.2
1938	15.5	11.8	3.7

Wages and wage regulation. "Among the minor revolutions that the war brought about in England," wrote Professor Clay,[1] "was an almost complete reversal of the traditional attitude of Government to wages." Before the war governments were careful never to fix a wage rate, but at the end they were directly or indirectly fixing the wages of a majority of the wage earning population. Although the primary object of wartime wage regulation was the control of the labor supply and the stimulation of production, and the adjustment of wage rates was incidental to these, the latter was

[1] H. Clay, *The Problem of Industrial Relations* (London, 1929), 20.

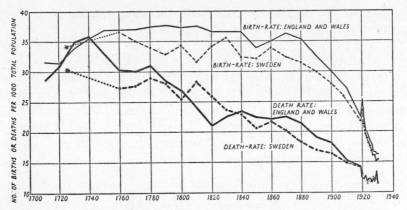

FIGURE II. BIRTH-RATES AND DEATH-RATES IN ENGLAND AND WALES
AND SWEDEN: 1710 to 1930

A. M. Carr-Saunders, *World Population* (Oxford, 1936), 61. By permission of the
publishers, The Clarendon Press.

widely extended. A Committee on Production was appointed early
in 1915 "to ensure that the productive powers of employees . . .
shall be made fully available in the present emergency," but for a
time it left the fixation of wages to the usual bargaining procedure.
After the passage of the Munitions of War Act later in the year it
was committed to continuous and growing interference. The Committee settled industrial disputes submitted to it for arbitration and
awarded advances to meet the increased cost of living. It thus
assumed a general responsibility for wages. Two points in its system of control carried over into post-war wage negotiations, namely
the treatment of industry on a national rather than a local basis and
the basing of wage changes on the cost of living.

After the war industry was dislocated and the labor market disorganized. The pre-war bargaining procedure could not be trusted
to secure justice as between employers and workers, and among different classes of workers. At the same time labor organizations had
grown greatly in power and stoutly resisted any efforts to reduce
wages. The drastic fluctuations in the price level, however, the decline of the export trade, and other economic forces compelled
changes and gradually wages were adjusted to the capacity of industries to pay them.

During the war money wages rose, but they lagged behind prices,
so that the cost of living increased and real wages declined. By
1919, however, money wages caught up with the cost of living and
real wages were higher. The highest point in the wholesale price
index was reached in March, 1920, when it was 299½, but within
the next two years it fell to half that figure. These were extraordi-

nary fluctuations and made impossible the maintenance of the pre-war currency system, or of stable wage rates.

The cost of living seemed to have settled on a level fifty per cent higher than before the war. This was not wholly due to a higher price level, but was in large part the result of a higher standard of living of the working classes. Desirable as this was, it was unfortunately not attended by a corresponding increase in the productivity of labor, so that labor costs rose. This in turn caused increases in retail prices, in which labor is an important element. The following table shows briefly the changes.

BRITISH WAGES AND THE STANDARD OF LIVING (1914 = 100)*

Date	Money wages	Cost of living	Real wages
1914	100	100	100
1915	110-115	135	83
1920	270-280	265	104
1925	175	175	100
1930	159	153	104
1935	163	147	111
1938	172	154	111

* Based on G. D. H. Cole, *A Short History of the British Working Class Movements*, 1789–1937 (2nd ed., London, 1937), II, 228, 232.

A general table does not disclose the changes that were occurring as between different groups of wage earners. In general, it may be said that the unskilled workers and those with lower wages gained most in the upward movement, and that the skilled artisans did not improve their position much, except by a reduction of working hours. But the working class as a whole gained a larger proportion of national income. "The general result of the whole system of taxation, wage adjustments, and social expenditure," wrote Bowley,[2] "has been a very marked redistribution of the National Income. . . The very rich have less than half their pre-war income (allowing for taxes and change of prices); the least well-off of the working class have gained most."

Concrete cases frequently convey a clearer picture than general averages, and the increase in wages of agricultural labor, of unskilled urban labor, and of skilled artisans may be cited.[3] Between 1913 and 1936 the average weekly wages of agricultural laborers rose from 18s. to 32s., those of builders' laborers from 27s. to 52s., and those of bricklayers from 40s. to 69s. The money wage of the agricultural laborer, though increasing seventy-eight per cent, remained on a very low level, while that of the unskilled urban worker almost doubled.

[2] A. L. Bowley, *Some Economic Consequences of the Great War* (London, 1930), 160.
[3] Astor and Rowntree, op. cit., 313.

Legal protection was also given to the workers, to enable them to receive in practice the wages fixed in collective agreements. Until 1934 these were not in general enforceable in the courts and individual employers not infrequently ignored such agreements. To prevent such unfair practices the Cotton Manufacturing Industries Act was passed in 1934, authorizing the Minister of Labour to make collective agreements in this industry legally binding on all employers. Similar legislation was passed in 1938 for the road transport industry. Another stone in the temple of individualism was thereby removed.

Consumption. Further light may be thrown on the well-being of the people by noting changes in the consumption of staple articles of food. The following table [4] shows the estimated annual consumption per head of the population in the United Kingdom of the most important ones.

Article	1909–13 (lbs.)	1936 (lbs.)
Wheat flour	211	212
Potatoes	208	213
Meat	135	148
Butter	16	25
Sugar	79	94
Fruit	61	114
Vegetables	60	126

People in Britain, according to these figures, were eating less bread and potatoes, but were consuming increasing quantities of fruit, vegetables, and dairy products. At the same time they were drinking less beer and wine. The consumption of milk, on the other hand, remained pitiably small, amounting on the average to about one-third of a pint per person per day. The shift on the whole was toward foods containing a larger proportion of vitamins.

In other lines too there was improvement. Better housing was provided by the construction of 3,500,000 new houses in Great Britain between 1920 and 1937; the census of 1921 had recorded only slightly over 9,000,000. Education was more widespread and the standard was being raised; the number of secondary school pupils almost trebled between 1913 and 1935. Hours had been reduced and real wages increased. But the rate of unemployment was higher than it had been before 1914, and it was still legal for children of fourteen years of age to work. The political power of the workers had increased and their social position improved. Professor Cole [5]

---

[4] "Problem of Nutrition." *Third Report of League of Nations* (Geneva, 1936).

[5] G. D. H. Cole, op. cit., III, 223. By permission of the publisher, George Allen and Unwin, Ltd., London.

summed up the changes as follows: "The workman of 1937 certainly dressed better, probably ate better, was sometimes (though by no means always) rather better housed, than the workman of 1900. He was on the whole healthier, and his children considerably so. He amused himself more, especially with the cinema and the wireless, and was altogether less distinguishable in manner, appearance and habits from large sections of the middle classes. It follows that he saved less."

Increased leisure through shorter working hours may also be noted among the social gains of this period. Immediately after the war nearly 7,000,000 workers had their hours of labor shortened, the average reduction being about six hours a week. In the depression of the early twenties some of these gains were lost, but on the whole the work-week remained fairly stable until 1936. In that year a new movement for still shorter hours was initiated, in common with similar moves in France and the United States.

Co-operation. During the war consumers' co-operation held its own, but showed no growth of membership. Sales, on the other hand, showed an enormous apparent expansion owing to the inflation, reaching over £250,000,000 for the retail societies in 1920, and £137,000,000 for the wholesale. If, however, these swollen values be converted into 1913 values, they would shrink to £100,-000,000 and £54,000,000, showing merely a normal development. A considerable expansion came in the thirties, and by 1935 the retail societies could boast a membership of 7,600,000. This was nearly one-fifth of the population. Few changes took place in the organization, but production by manufacturing and agricultural undertakings expanded steadily. The co-operative movement had become more than a distributive enterprise. By the end of this period it sold more goods than any private company; it manufactured more products and employed more workers than any private employer; and owned more land than most private landlords. It also carried on banking, insurance, mining, farming, and other activities. The following table presents a brief statistical picture of the recent growth of the movement:

Retail societies	*1913*	*1935*
Number	1387	1096
Membership (in millions)	2.8	7.6
Sales (in millions)	£83	£218
Wholesale societies		
Sales (in millions)	£30	£117
Production (in millions)	£11	£40

2. PUBLIC RELIEF WORKS AND ARMAMENT IN GERMANY

Population. The turn of the century saw the same decline in rate of population growth in Germany as in Britain and France, though not quite so pronounced. Nevertheless by 1913 the Reich numbered 66,978,000 persons. This figure declined to 59,853,000 in 1919, as a result of war deaths of 1,691,841 men and of the loss of 6,500,000 persons in the ceded territories, which was only slightly offset by new births. After this the population mounted again, although at a slackening rate, until by 1936 it had passed the pre-war figure. This growth took place in spite of a steadily falling birth-rate, which was not wholly compensated by a decline in the death-rate as a result of the progress of medical science and of hygiene. The fall in the birth-rate was greatest in the largest cities, and in Berlin and Hamburg there was even an excess of deaths over births in some years. Partly responsible for this was probably the lack of housing after the war, and partly the general poverty. The purposeful limitation of the number of children, which had previously been confined largely to the more well-to-do classes, now spread to the industrial and even the agricultural workers. The higher age of couples at time of marriage also served to restrict the size of families.

When the National Socialists came into power they immediately put into force measures designed to stimulate the marriage rate and the birth-rate. In addition to several minor methods they passed an act in 1933 providing for marriage loans and also encouraging women to withdraw from the labor market. Loans up to 1000 marks were made to married couples to furnish a home, repayable in small monthly instalments. One-fourth of the loan was remitted on the birth of each child. The response was immediate, and there was a striking increase in marriages and births. The marriage rate jumped from 7.9 in 1932 to 11.1 in 1936, and the birth-rate from an all-time low of 14.7 in 1933 — which was below even the rate of 16.4 for the war years 1915–19 — to 19.0 in 1936. The recovery was only temporary, however, and in 1939 the birth-rate was down to 17.1.

POPULATION GROWTH IN GERMANY, 1913–39

Year	Total population	Birth-rate	Death-rate	Excess of births over deaths	Per cent urban
1913	66,978,000	27.5	16.1	11.5	61.7
1920	61,797,000	25.8	14.4	11.4	....
1925	63,411,000	22.1	12.0	10.1	64.6
1930	64,294,000	17.5	11.1	6.4	....
1936	67,346,000	19.0	11.8	7.2	67.2 *
1939	69,200,000	17.1	12.1	5.0	...

* 1933.

The age distribution of the population was very different after the war from what it had been before that event. Owing to the absence of so many men at the front during the war the birth-rate fell to half what it had been — 14 per thousand in 1917 as against 28 in 1911. It was estimated that during the five years 1915 to 1919 there was a deficiency of births below normal of about 3,000,000. As a result there came to be a disproportionately large number of older persons and a smaller number of young persons born since 1914. This is not revealed in the table of population growth, but is clearly shown in the following graph.

The movement toward the cities continued, though somewhat less rapidly, but by 1933 over two-thirds of the population were to be

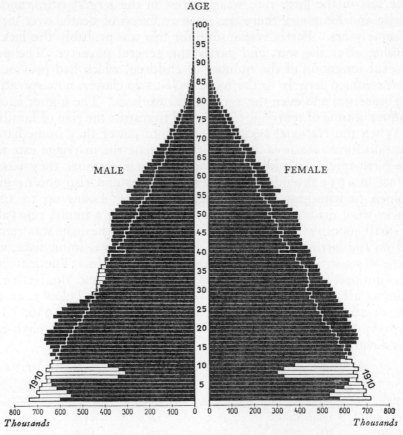

FIGURE 12.   DISTRIBUTION OF THE POPULATION IN GERMANY BY AGE, 1925

Deutsche Wirtschaftskunde (Berlin, 1933), 13.

found in urban communities of 2000 or more inhabitants. The large cities of 100,000 or over grew fastest and by the end of the period housed over 30 per cent of the population. Such strong urbanization may be accepted as evidence of a highly developed capitalistic economy. Further proof is found in the fact that three-quarters of the employed workers were engaged in industry and handwork.

Social insurance. The main features of social insurance had been pretty well developed by 1911, and little was done between that year and 1927, when the structure was completed by adding insurance against unemployment. A beginning had been made before the war with unemployment-relief systems operated by local authorities, of which there were two main types: the Cologne system, in which the state administered the fund and assumed the financial responsibility, and the Ghent system, in which the trade union administered the fund with a state subsidy. These local agencies proved inadequate to meet the problem of unemployment after the war and the task of caring for the unemployed demobilized soldiers fell to the Federal Office for Economic Demobilization, which was created on November 12, 1918. It ordered the communes to grant unemployment benefits to needy war workers who could not find jobs, the expense to be shared by the federal government, the states, and the municipalities. The increase of unemployment a year later shifted emphasis from relief to provision of work. Productive unemployment relief was instituted, according to which a job paying prevailing wages was offered in place of monetary assistance. This program of public works fitted into Germany's need for extensive construction to compensate for the absence of building activity during the war. These various experiments made clear certain essentials of unemployment assistance. Local assistance was less satisfactory than national; insurance was preferable to relief; unemployment exchanges were a necessary part of the system and should be integrated with insurance. All these principles were embodied in the Employment Exchanges and Unemployment Insurance Act of 1927.

The cost of the system set up by this Act was met by equal compulsory contributions of employers and workers, which ran up to 3 per cent of the wages. Wage earners receiving less than 6000 marks and salaried employees receiving up to 8400 marks annually, who were regularly employed, were eligible. To enjoy the benefits a person must have been employed 26 weeks in a compulsorily insured occupation during the year. Benefits were calculated upon the remuneration received during the last six months of employment, and ran from 35 per cent of the highest wage to 75 per cent of the lowest, for a period of 20 weeks. The further burden of support of an unemployed person, after 20 weeks, was placed upon the poor relief fund.   The number of workers insured against unemployment under the German compulsory system was 17,920,000 in 1935, or 57 per cent of the working population.   This was less comprehensive than the British system under which 67 per cent were insured. The increase in the number of unemployed and the resultant rise in expenditures led in 1931 to a reduction in the period during which the standard benefit was payable from 26 to 20 weeks.   And in the following year an average reduction of 23 per cent was made in the scale of benefits.   Those insured against sickness numbered 20 million, against accident 24 million, against invalidity 18.5 million, while about 500,000 received old age pensions in 1930.

The financing of this vast system presented difficulties, especially after the fading away of the reserves during the inflation period. And when these were partially restored, they were "borrowed" by the Nazi government.   Still the claims of the insured had to be met, especially for old age and invalidity.   Accordingly the state took over the insurance system in December, 1937.   The former independent insurance agencies were combined with the Treasury, and a system of general public insurance was instituted.

Conditions of work.   Germany had developed a comprehensive labor code before the war, which remained substantially unchanged until 1933.   Child labor was forbidden in general for children under thirteen years of age, or over thirteen who were still obliged to go to school, in establishments where ten persons were employed. Such a law, of course, permitted their employment in domestic industries and agriculture.   But the hours of labor were restricted to 6 daily for children under fourteen.   Other provisions in the labor code regulated the length of the working day for young persons and adults, granted rest periods and Sunday holidays, prohibited truck payments for wages, and guarded the labor contract.   The great expansion of the insurance system led to the enactment of measures to forestall illness and accident by preventive measures and by hygiene and medical care.

Under National Socialism the old labor code was replaced by new labor legislation.   This abolished collective agreements between employers and workers and replaced them by collective regulations whose terms were fixed by the state.   An ordinance in 1934 codified all existing legislation on the hours of labor, placing in the hands of governmental authorities the power to regulate the hours and conditions of work according to the variable situations in each industry.   The average work-week was increased from about 42 hours in 1932 to 48 hours in 1938.   When Goering launched his Second Four-Year Plan in 1936 he made the ten-hour day legal in the building trades and relieved armament manufacturers of all restric-

tions. Under the armament program, moreover, the intensity of
work was greatly increased, and, while production was expanded, the
number of accidents grew — from 3.4 per cent of the workers in
1932 to 5.7 per cent in 1937.

Wages. In spite of every effort during the war to adjust labor
supply to labor demand, there was a growing scarcity of skilled
workers for the expanding war industries, and wages rose. This
tendency was met by the fixation of wages, with the co-operation of
the trade unions, at a point about 30 per cent above the pre-war
level. At the same time efforts were made to eliminate the middlemen and small masters. At first, with the expectation that the war
would be a short one, it was provided that the wage tariff should not
be changed during the war, but as this was prolonged and prices rose,
it became necessary to increase wages also. Prices, however, rose
faster than money wages and real wages fell. By 1918 the whole-
sale-price index was 216 and trade-union wages were 190. In the
unorganized and non-military trades wages were much lower. By
1920 it was estimated that real wages were only about two-thirds
those of 1913. The inflation period brought still greater hardship
to the working classes, for all contractual payments rose less rapidly
than the rapidly advancing price level. At times wages dropped to
less than half the estimated minimum of subsistence. The physical
weakening of the country's labor power was quite as serious during
this period as it had been during the war. After stabilization wage
rates increased and by 1928 real wages were back on the 1913 level.
The trade unions claimed credit for this advance and they undoubtedly contributed to its realization by their ceaseless struggles, especially by means of collective agreements.

German labor policy was dominated by the theory of a "living
wage" rather than by a productivity theory, and it was difficult to
link wages payments to productive efficiency. During the war labor
performance fell off sharply, but this was due in large part to lack
of materials and malnutrition, and towards the end to a general war
uneasiness. But the shortening of the work day to eight hours in
1919 was not accompanied by an increase in production. After the
war, under the pressure of domestic and reparation needs, piece rate
wages were largely used. But the so-called Taylor system, especially the premium wage, which might have called forth greater efforts, penetrated only slowly into German industry. Only in highly
mechanized establishments, or where the assembly line was introduced, did the productivity of the workers increase. The lack of a
close relationship between wages and output is indicated by the fact
that, whereas wages increased some 80 per cent between 1924 and
1928, the general volume of production rose only 40 per cent.

Earnings declined steadily after 1928. In addition to that there was a great increase in unemployment and short time was more general. In 1932 an emergency decree cut all wages by 10 to 15 per cent, irrespective of collective agreements setting higher rates. But from the actual earnings serious deductions were made for the wages tax of 1925, social insurance payments, trade union dues, and illness. After 1933, under National Socialism, wage rates were stabilized and unemployment and short time were eliminated. Every effort was made at the same time to hold prices steady. The official statistics therefore show that real wages remained on a very even level. The Nazi policy was to hold wages down, for higher wages would have increased the demand for consumers' goods, and by so much would have reduced the labor and raw materials for the production of armament. But the official statistics make no allowance for deductions for social insurance, winter relief, "Strength through Joy," and similar purposes, amounting to as much as 25 per cent of the wages received. When these are taken into account the conclusion is inevitable that there was a decline in real wages, and if to these be added the deterioration in the quality of manufactured consumers' goods and the shortage or absence of others (eggs, butter, edible fats, etc.), there seems ample ground for believing that the standard of living of the worker declined between 1913 and 1938, though it doubtless improved between the low point of 1932 and 1938. It was certainly lower than that of the contemporary British worker.

Consumption. During the war consumption fell off, but by 1924 had pretty well caught up with pre-war levels. There were some shifts, such as the partial substitution of cocoa for coffee, and the larger consumption of vegetables and dairy products instead of bread and potatoes, and the partial substitution of fish for meat. By 1928 production was on a high level both for capital goods and consumers' goods, but the crisis years brought them both down sharply. Under National Socialism the efforts, first to combat unemployment, and secondly to push rearmament, placed increasing emphasis on production goods and the output of consumption goods remained nearly stationary. The changes may be shown for a few foodstuffs.

CONSUMPTION OF FOODSTUFFS PER HEAD
(in pounds)

Year	Rye	Wheat	Potatoes	Sugar	Fish	Coffee	Meat
1913	337	211	1540 †	42	6	5.3	96
1922	202	105	1261 †	46	4	....	58
1929	114 *	123 *	378	51	20	4.2	99
1938	121 *	123 *	389	54	26	3.5	105

* Flour only.
† Including industrial uses.

After 1933 the consumption of some luxury items, such as wine, brandy, and tobacco, as well as radios and automobiles, available only to the rich, actually increased, but the consumption of such staple commodities as fruits, fats, and eggs declined. An effort was made to foster the consumption of cabbage, pork, and fish, while the manufacture of whipped cream, fatty cheese, and rye brandy was forbidden. Certain *Ersatz* foods were produced to take the place of those not readily obtainable. Thus sugar was extracted from wood, "pumpkin" milk competed with cow's milk, potato starch was used in bread, and "fish sausage" vied with real *Wurst*.

3. HIGHER WAGES IN FRANCE

Growth of population. The population trends, evident in France for a century, did not change during this period. Both birth-rate and death-rate continued to decline and the population to grow at a rate slower than in any other country in Europe. Indeed, if it had not been for the purely statistical gain of 1,700,000 inhabitants by the accession of Alsace-Lorraine, the population would have remained practically stationary between 1911 and 1936. This addition somewhat more than offset the 1,400,000 men who were killed during the war. Important changes in population growth and distribution may be indicated.

Year	Population	Rural	Urban
1911	41,479,000 *	55.8	44.2
1921	39,210,000	53.7	46.3
1931	41,860,000	51.0	49.0
1936	41,906,000	47.7	52.3

* Boundaries of 1921.

Several unfortunate results followed from this practically stationary population. The slow but steady movement from country to city continued and gained in momentum, drawing off needed agricultural labor which was no longer recruited from large rural families. The age distribution showed a larger proportion of older persons of sixty years of age and over, and a smaller proportion of children, than in Britain, Germany, or the United States. This was a disquieting situation, whether regarded from an economic or a military point of view. Finally, it became necessary for France to rely increasingly on foreign labor, in order to make up the domestic shortage. Even before the war there were over 1,100,000 foreigners in France and during that struggle about 400,000 Algerians and Chinese were brought in chiefly to assist in agriculture. After the war there was a great shortage of labor, especially in view of the work of reconstruction, and the immigration of Italians, Belgians, Swedes, Portuguese, and Spanish laborers was encouraged. It is estimated that about 300,000 foreigners immigrated into France during 1921–26, and that by 1931 there were some 1,600,000 of these domiciled in the country. There was particularly a shortage of skilled labor, which was especially unfortunate since France had acquired large mineral resources in Lorraine and was developing her iron and steel industry.

When the depression began this policy of encouraging immigration was reversed, and in 1932 a law was passed to preserve the home market for French labor. Foreigners were required to obtain work permits and these were granted only if there were no unemployment in that occupation. Renewals of work permits was denied to aliens who had been in France less than two years. It was expected by these methods to force the immigrants to return to their homes, but funds to deport them were lacking and many of them remained. The need of agriculture for seasonal workers was, moreover, too strong to prevent the entry of thousands of Belgian, Polish, and other farm hands each year.

Primarily responsible for these changes was the declining birth-rate, with which improved medical science and hygiene could scarcely keep pace by bringing down the death-rate. The relationship may be shown for selected years, according to official French statistics.[6]

Year	Birth-rate	Death-rate	Excess (+) or deficit (−) of births over deaths
1913	18.8	17.7	+ 1.1
1915	11.8	26.2	−14.4
1920	21.4	17.2	+ 4.2
1925	19.0	17.4	+ 2.6
1930	18.0	15.6	+ 2.4
1935	15.3	15.7	− 0.4
1938	14.6	15.4	− 0.8

The war period from 1914 to 1918 was of course wholly abnormal. If the addition from Alsace-Lorraine be omitted, there was a loss of 2,100,000 in population between 1911 and 1921. In addition to those killed, it has been estimated that there were about 900,000 fewer births during the war than might reasonably have been expected, and that it would require some seventy years to replace the war casualties at the existing rate of population growth. After the war the death-rate continued high for a few years because of increases in infant mortality and the influenza epidemic. After

[6] *Statistique générale de la France* (Paris, 1937), 13.

1922 previous tendencies again asserted themselves, and both the birth-rate and the death-rate fell to the lowest levels on record. The chart on page 476 shows the changes during the past century.

French leaders were fully aware of the dangers inherent in this stationary population, and a flood of books and articles deplored the situation. Emphasis was laid primarily on the military and political weakness of the country, but also on the economic, social, cultural, and biological perils. Positive measures were also adopted to combat the evil. By means of prizes, propaganda, day nurseries for working mothers, and other devices private individuals and foundations sought to stimulate larger families. More important but almost equally ineffective were governmental efforts. Anti-birth control laws were passed in 1920 and 1923, prohibiting propaganda for contraceptive devices and abortions. The extension of the latter practice may be gauged by the fact that abortions were about half as frequent as births. In 1932 the family wage system was made compulsory on all employers, according to which an addition to the wage of the parent must be made for each child under fourteen. As the allowance was less than the cost of caring for a child, the law had little effect. Although the attention of French writers has been directed almost entirely to the falling birth-rate, it should be pointed out that the fundamental cause of the slow population growth was the high death-rate. The former phenomenon was observable in all highly industrialized countries, but elsewhere it had been offset by greater reductions in the mortality rates.

Wages. The fixation of wages during this period was in general left to the usual bargaining process of a competitive capitalist country, but the government moved to protect one particularly helpless class. This was the domestic women workers in the sweated industries. A law of 1915 established a minimum wage for women outworkers in any branch of the clothing industry. It is difficult to follow wage movements during the war, but in general it may be said that the wages of unskilled workers and of women rose faster than those of skilled workers, while the salaried groups lagged behind the other three groups. But changes were uneven, both by groups and geographically. By 1919 real wages, measured by purchasing power, were slightly above the pre-war level. After the war the problem was complicated by the growing inflation and the advance in prices, which gave rise to serious conflicts as labor demanded higher wages to meet the mounting cost of living. A trial was made of adjusting wages according to changes in the cost of living, but the unsatisfactory price statistics made this impracticable. The following table shows the general movements: [7]

[7] A. Viallate, *L'activité économique en France* (Paris, 1937), 371, 430.

INDEX OF WAGES AND COST OF LIVING

Year	Money wages	Cost of living	Real wages
1914	100	100	100
1921	398	381	104
1925	489	447	109
1930	707	621	114
1935	672 *	484	136

* Miners only.

Nominal money wages rose steadily until 1931 after which there was a decline to 1935, but the resistance of wage rates to pressure was strong and they yielded only slightly. It was quite otherwise with prices, which moved upward less rapidly during the twenties, and fell disastrously during the depression years of the thirties. The result of these two movements may be seen in the column of real wages which, except for the year 1926, rose pretty steadily during the whole period. Although the statistics are somewhat doubtful, the picture of the general trend is without question correct as to daily wages. But it leaves out of account the question of unemployment. During the latter part of this period the number of days worked, both for workers in general and for individuals, was considerably reduced by the spread of unemployment, and the total earnings of the workers suffered serious reduction.

Scarcity had characterized the labor market during the war and after peace was declared the work of reconstruction of the devastated areas gave abundant employment. It was possible to absorb the demobilized soldiers back into industry and agriculture without serious difficulty. Except for a short depression in 1920, the number of unemployed down to 1924 did not exceed 30,000. The census of 1931 recorded slightly over 400,000, but the deepening crisis of the thirties brought the number up to 1,250,000 in 1934 while the number of the partially employed oscillated between 1,500,000 and 2,000,000. After this there was a decline of the state-assisted unemployed to 302,000 in 1939. The combination of unemployment and the rise in the cost of living swept away the greater part of the wage increase under the Matignon agreement. French workers, however, did not suffer in these regards as much as those in other industrial countries, and on the whole improved their condition during this period.

Co-operation. On the eve of the war the consumers' co-operative societies had a unified national organization, which was aggressive and enthusiastic. During the war they performed useful services in distributing foodstuffs, but their number declined. After the war they revived and the government, in recognition of their services, assisted them with loans and other favors. But the development of chain stores and of large department stores with branches forced the co-operatives to reorganize their methods. The separate neighborhood stores, each selling perhaps one commodity, were replaced by great regional societies, whose branches handled a wide range of foodstuffs and general merchandise. Control was centralized and modern technique of retail marketing, based on the model of the chain stores, was adopted. In this way they were able to cope with large private retail businesses. Their growth may be briefly shown.

CONSUMERS' CO-OPERATIVE SOCIETIES

Year	Number of societies	Number of members	Annual sales (million francs)
1914	3156	894,000	316
1920	4790	2,498,000	1840
1929	3296	2,288,000	3831
1933	2902	2,573,000	3800

The Wholesale Society showed a less rapid growth, since not all the buying was concentrated in their hands. They succeeded, however, in increasing the number of affiliated retail societies from 309 in 1913 to about 1500 in 1926. Their sales grew between the same two years from 12 to 457 million francs, but the latter figure was inflated by depreciation. An important expansion in their activities was taken in 1922 when a bank was organized, whose main functions were to act as a savings bank for co-operators and to supply the wholesale and retail societies with short-term funds. It was very successful and by 1934 had about 3000 branch offices and deposits of 385 million francs. Contrary to its statutes it had unfortunately loaned 117 million francs to private capitalistic enterprises, most of which was lost in the panic, and the bank was compelled to close. With the aid of the government, however, an agreement was reached with the bank's creditors by which the debts would be paid off in fifteen years, and the bank resumed operations. As a result the control of the whole movement was further centralized and sharpened.

Co-operation of producers was less important than that of consumers, but it showed some growth, especially in processing foodstuffs and in agriculture. Some 400 societies were listed in 1937 but many of them were small groups of handworkers; it was difficult to meet the competition of large scale capitalistic industry. They claimed to have 9 per cent of the grocery and 4 per cent of the bakery business of France.

Consumption. One final test of national well-being, the consumption of semi-luxuries, showed that the mass of the French people were slightly improving their standard of living. The decrease in the consumption of potatoes and the increase in that of sugar and coffee are particularly significant, and bear out the statistics of wages.

CONSUMPTION PER CAPITA

Article	1913	1925	1935
Potatoes (lbs.)	752.4	827.2	737.0
Sugar (lbs.)	39.8	44.0	51.0
Coffee (lbs.)	6.4	9.2	9.9
Wine (qts.)	105.7	138.5	124.7
Beer (qts.)	35.2	30.5	30.4
Tobacco (lbs.)	2.3	2.8	2.7

Conclusion. Certain population movements were common to all European countries during this period. Among them were a decline in both the birth-rate and the death-rate and the movement from the country to the city. None of these was new but they gained in momentum. The "retreat from parenthood" with its smaller families caused especial alarm in the more militaristic countries, such as Germany, Italy, and France, and these all sought to reverse the trend, but without much success. The fall in the mortality rate was of course an unmixed blessing. The more far-reaching effects of a shift in age distribution, resulting in a population with a smaller proportion of young and a larger proportion of old persons, seems to have been appreciated only by the statisticians. Each year saw a growing percentage of the people concentrated in towns, a movement which called for better housing, town planning, the provision of municipal utilities, and other facilities, which were met in increasing measure.

Wages, both nominal and real, followed on the whole an upward trend. The regularity of wages did not present as favorable a picture as their amount because of recurrent unemployment, but this was increasingly met by insurance and public relief works. Society recognized its responsibilities to workers and extended protection to them by legislation and positive acts. The addition to money wages contributed by various social services, such as insurance, pensions, medical care, low-cost housing, education, etc., probably amounted to from 20 to 25 per cent.

The material well-being of the mass of the people was undoubtedly higher in all the countries under discussion than it had been in 1914. Absolute destitution was almost unknown, and for large groups the standard of living was improved. Unfortunately war and the shadow of war during the next few years diverted the capital and labor of the leading nations into unprofitable armaments at the expense of individual welfare. It appeared as though the gains of a century and a half were to be sacrificed on the altar of power politics.

BIBLIOGRAPHICAL NOTE

1. *Britain.* On population it is sufficient to cite three books: A. Andréadès, *La population anglaise avant, pendant, et après la guerre* (Ferrara, 1924); A. M. Carr-Saunders, *World Population; Past Growth and Present Trends* (New York, 1936), very general; S. V. Pearson, *Growth and Distribution of the Population* (London, 1935), a sociological approach. H. A. Mess, *Factory Legislation and its Administration* (London, 1926) is good. Most attention was directed to the problem of unemployment. F. Morley, *Unemployment Relief in Great Britain* (Boston, 1924) discusses one method of handling it. Unemployment insurance is treated in J. L. Cohen, *Insurance against Unemployment* (London, 1921) and *The British System of Social Insurance* (London, 1932); H. Clay, *The Post-War Unemployment Problem* (London, 1929); A. C. Hill and I. Lubin, *The British Attack on Unemployment* (Washington, 1934); R. C. Dawson, *British Unemployment Policy: The Modern Phase since 1930* (London, 1938). A constructive critique is W. H. Beveridge, *The Past and Present of Unemployment Insurance* (London, 1930). The text of the laws is given in A. Crew, R. J. Blackham, and A. Forman, *The Unemployment Insurance Acts, 1920-1930* (London, 1930). Wages are covered authoritatively in A. L. Bowley, *Prices and Wages in the United Kingdom, 1914-1920,* and *Some Economic Consequences of the Great War* (London, 1930); and in A. L. Bowley and M. H. Hogg, *Has Poverty Diminished?* (London, 1925). A. G. B. Fisher, *Some Problems of Wages and their Regulation in Great Britain since 1918* (London, 1926) discusses wage regulation, as does H. F. Hohman, *Development of Social Insurance and Minimum Wage Legislation in Great Britain* (Boston, 1933). Along the same line is G. Williams, *The State and the Standard of Living* (London, 1936). On co-operation S. and B. Webb, *The Consumers' Co-operative Movement* (London, 1921) is a careful study. F. Hall and W. P. Watkins, *Co-operation . . . in Great Britain* (Manchester, 1934) is semi-official. H. J. Twigg, *The Economic Advance of British Co-operation, 1913-1934* (Manchester, 1934) is mainly statistical. S. R. Elliott, *The English Co-operatives* (New Haven, 1937) is a popularly written account. A. M. Carr-Saunders and others, *Consumers' Co-operation in Great Britain* (London, 1938) is a good survey. C. R. Fay, *Co-operation at Home and Abroad*, Vol. II, *Post-War* (London, 1939) is the best work.

2. *Germany.* Two careful studies of the effect of war upon the population are R. Meerwarth, *Die Einwirkung des Krieges auf Bevölkerungsbewegung* (Stuttgart, 1932) and *Die Entwicklung der Bevölkerung während der Kriegs - und Nachkriegszeit* (Stuttgart, 1932). A thorough specialized study is C. Lorenz, *Die gewerbliche Arbeit der Frauen während der Krieges* (Stuttgart, 1928). C. Neuhaus, *Die Bewegung der Bevölkerung im Zeitalter des Kapitalismus* (Berlin, 1925) covers a longer sweep. The subject of unemployment naturally produced a number of books, of which only a few can be cited. K. I. Wiggs, *Unemployment in Germany since the War* (London, 1923) is a slight sketch. The effect of rationalization is discussed in H. Hagen, *Der Einfluss der Maschine auf die Arbeitslosigkeit* (Stuttgart, 1935). The early methods of combating unemployment are described in O. Weigert, *Administration of Placement and Unemployment*

Relief in Germany (New York, 1934). W. S. Woytinsky, *Three Sources of Unemployment: The Combined Action of Population Changes, Technical Progress, and Economic Development* (Geneva, 1935), and *The Social Consequences of the Economic Depression* (Geneva, 1936) give a scholarly analysis. M. R. Carroll, *Unemployment Insurance in Germany* (2nd ed., Washington, 1930) and F. Goldmann and A. Grotjahn, *Benefits of the German Sickness Insurance System* (Geneva, 1928) are sympathetic studies. A. Egger, *Die Belastung der deutschen Wirtschaft durch die Socialversicherung* (Jena, 1929) is severely critical. W. Zimmermann, *Die Veränderungen der Einkommens- und Lebensverhältnisse der deutschen Arbeiter durch den Krieg* (Stuttgart, 1932) is a careful study. J. Rosen, *Das Existenzminimum in Deutschland: Untersuchungen über die Untergrenze der Lebenshaltung* (Zurich, 1939) is an investigation of living conditions among the unemployed in Berlin in 1933. Co-operation is described in T. O. Cassau, *The Consumers' Co-operative Movement in Germany* (London, 1925), and W. Wygodzinski, *Das Genossenschaftswesen in Deutschland* (2te Aufl., Von A. Müller, Leipzig, 1929).

3. *France.* An elaborate study of population during the war is M. Huber, *La population de la France pendant la guerre* (Paris, 1931). This is supplemented by M. Huber, H. Bunli, et F. Boverat, *La population de la France, son évolution et ses perspectives* (Paris, 1938). A pessimistic analysis is given in J. J. Spengler, *France Faces Depopulation* (Durham, N. C., 1938). H. Harmsen, *Bevölkerungsprobleme Frankreichs'* (Berlin, 1927). A statistical study of wages is J. Kuczynski, *Die Entwicklung der Löhne in Frankreich, 1895–1933* (Berlin, 1934). G. Letellier, et al., *Le chômage en France de 1930 à 1936* (Paris, 1926) is a thorough study. Also useful is E. Poisson, *La politique du mouvement coopératif français* (Paris, 1929).

CHAPTER XXIII

NEW FORMS OF ECONOMIC ORGANIZATION

I. SOVIETISM IN RUSSIA

Most of the readers of this book have been brought up in a school of thought which believed in political democracy and economic liberalism, that is, a representative government determined by the will of the electorate and an economic system based on free initiative and independent enterprise. But after the World War, three of the leading countries of Europe successively moved away from both democracy and *laissez faire* and toward systems of economic planning and collective control. These assumed different forms in these countries, as Sovietism in Russia, Fascism in Italy, and National Socialism in Germany, but fundamentally they were alike in being systems of state-controlled and managed economies. In order to understand present conditions, it is therefore necessary to trace the development of these new economic orders. We shall begin with Russia.

The peasant under serfdom. The population of Russia in 1861 comprised some 70,000,000 people of about two score nationalities and differing languages. They were overwhelmingly rural, only 8 per cent living in urban communities. Most of the people were concentrated in the central or black earth region, as neither the cold and inhospitable north nor the treeless and almost rainless south could support any considerable number. The rural population consisted almost entirely of peasants, of whom nearly three-quarters were serfs. The system of serfdom was similar to that which had existed in eighteenth century France or Germany, the typical form being one in which the lord cultivated half of the land on his estate with the labor of his serfs, who owed him so many days' work each week. In the less fertile regions, the serfs paid a quitrent, partly in kind and partly in money. Here the land exploited by the lord seldom formed more than a fourth of the estate, and the peasants developed various handicrafts in addition to agriculture.

The land was owned almost entirely by the crown and the nobility and held in large estates. Those portions cultivated by the serfs were held under various forms of feudal tenure, but were not owned by them. The serfs lived in small village communities called mirs, and each community regulated the cultivation of the land held by it. The prevailing organization of agriculture was the three-field system, the land being divided into strips with one-third remaining uncultivated or fallow each year. Since the proprietors needed labor for the cultivation of their land, legislation and practice forbade the serf from leaving the estate upon which he was born. He was tied to the soil and passed with it to the new proprietor if the land were sold or changed ownership.

As in Prussia in 1807, the reform of this system was brought about largely by non-economic factors. Growing unrest among the serfs, the development of an abolitionist sentiment among the more enlightened of the nobility, and finally the defeat of Russia in the Crimean War showed the need of a thorough-going reorganization of the country's social and political structure. From a purely economic point of view, moreover, the rigidity of the system prevented the development of industry or the most effective utilization of the land. The formal abolition of serfdom was undertaken by Czar Alexander II, culminating in the Edict of Emancipation, in 1861.

Emancipation of the serfs. The first step was the liberation of some 25,000,000 serfs on the crown estates, to whom personal freedom was granted as well as ownership of their homesteads and some arable land. More difficult was the freeing of the serfs on the estates of the nobles, but this was finally achieved. The nobles were the legal owners of the land and clung to their vested rights in the labor of the serfs with the usual persistence of a privileged class. They were, however, persuaded to grant the 25,000,000 serfs on their estates their personal freedom and part of the land, for both of which they demanded full compensation. "The right of bondage over the peasants settled upon the landlord's estates, and over the courtyard people, is forever abolished," declared the first article of the Edict of Emancipation. But a mere grant of personal freedom was insufficient; the former serfs must also be endowed with land. This was accomplished by having them buy the land from the nobles. But since few of the peasants could pay the purchase price, which was fixed by law, an arrangement was made whereby the government paid the landlords in full with bonds, and then collected these sums from the peasants in annual instalments spread over a period of 49 years — the "redemption payments." In this way practically half of the agricultural area of the Empire passed into the hands of the peasantry.

In spite of the undoubted social gain from the abolition of serfdom, two main criticisms have usually been directed against the land allotment scheme which accompanied it. In the first place, the allotments to the peasants were too small in size for their support. The average for the former serfs on the crown lands was about 23 acres and for those on the noble estates it was slightly over 9 acres. Since 14 acres were estimated to be the minimum holding adequate to support a family, it appears that at least half the peasants did not receive sufficient land to feed them or to give full employment. They were therefore compelled to supplement their income by domestic industries or by working for the lords as agricultural laborers. Some writers have even contended that the allotments were purposely kept small in order that the lords might have an adequate supply of cheap labor.

The second criticism was the crushing financial burden imposed upon the peasant by the redemption payments and taxes. The peasants seem to have been grossly overcharged for the land which they bought. A careful student presents the following picture: [1]

Value at market prices of 1863–72 of land under redemption   647,000,000 R.
Original redemption loans of government to the landlords (to be
    recovered by the government from the peasants)....................   866,600,000 R.
Excess of redemption loans over market value of land................   218,800,000 R.

In fairness it must be said, however, that other factors entered into the picture besides the land. The lords surrendered their claims to the unpaid labor of the serfs, and the latter on their part gave up their rights of grazing cattle on the landlord's pasture, of gathering wood in his forest, and of help in time of need. It is impossible to say how far these claims offset each other and whether after balancing they created a credit on the landlord's side, compensation for which was included in the redemption payments. But whatever the justice of the payments, they were beyond the capacity of the peasants to meet. Just as the Prussian land allotment scheme of 1810–11 fell far short of the French distribution of 1789–93, so the Russian plan was a mere travesty of the Prussian. In Russia the peasant nowhere received a free piece of land for his own cultivation, as in the other two countries, but was forced to pay an exorbitant price for it.

The origin of the Russian mir or village community has been a matter of dispute, but it offered at this time a convenient administrative unit for the collection of the redemption payments, and was accordingly utilized for this purpose by the government. For purposes of collection the village commune was treated as a unit and all the members of it were made jointly responsible for dues and taxes, but the system met this function very inadequately, and on the other hand introduced obstructive rigidity into the peasant economy. As a member of the mir, the former serf was compelled to accept his allotment of land with all the obligations attaching to it; and, to make sure that he would not escape them, his mobility of movement was seriously limited. The peasant, it was said, became a "serf of the state." But even the power of the state could not collect payments in bad years, and arrears began to pile up. By 1900 they were

[1] G. T. Robinson, *Rural Russia under the Old Regime* (New York, 1932), 88. A ruble was roughly 50 cents.

150,000,000 rubles. Some relief was granted in 1881 when the redemption payments were reduced by a fourth, and in 1904 the arrears were cancelled.

Even more accountable for the lack of progress was the organization of agriculture. The open-field system, with its compulsory common rotation and periodical redistribution of the land, prevented personal initiative and held down the crop yields. The average annual yield of wheat per acre was given as 6 bushels on peasant holdings in 1861–70 and 10 bushels forty years later. While this shows some improvement the returns at both dates were incredibly low. Partly responsible also were ignorance, obstinacy and poor equipment of the peasant. His farm implements were of the most primitive type and his work animals few. He was always so near the border line of poverty that any untoward incident, such as a crop failure or illness, could push him over the line. In such cases he was likely to come under the control of the village usurer or *kulak*, who exacted harsher terms than the lord or the state. Economic inequality developed even under the egalitarian conditions of land division, the shrewd and thrifty rising in the scale and the weak and improvident sinking.

By the beginning of the twentieth century the seriousness of the agricultural problem was finally recognized. Attempts were made to increase the yield by the introduction of better seeds and implements, a more scientific rotation of crops, and the introduction of improved livestock. But these did not remedy the fundamental evils, which were finally attacked by the government only after serious peasant disturbances forced the issue. The peasants demanded more land; and, although by 1905 the nobles had sold about half of their land, the cry was for still more. In this same year the government cancelled all the redemption payments still due, and soon after passed legislation designed to eliminate the mir and to promote individual ownership of land. In those communes where periodical redistribution of the land had not taken place — about half of all — holders were recognized as owners of their holdings. And in the other communes every member was given the right to claim his share of the common land as his individual property. Enclosure of the land and rearrangement of scattered strips were also provided for. Substantial progress was made in carrying out these reforms, but they were still far from complete when the World War broke out.

Industrialization. The agrarian organization has been described at some length because the vast majority of the population lived in rural districts and derived their living from agriculture, but a word may be said about industrial conditions in the towns. Although factories existed before and after emancipation, the industrial revolution began in the last two decades of the nineteenth century. It was due largely to the efforts of Count Sergey Y. Witte, Minister of Finance from 1892 to 1903, who promoted a vigorous railway building program, supported industry by a policy of tariff protection and subsidies, and introduced the gold standard. Other factors contributed to the movement, such as the freeing of the serfs and their greater mobility, which provided a supply of cheap labor. Capital was scarce, but this was obtained by foreign loans, chiefly French and Belgian, which were the more readily obtained because the crisis of 1893 in the United States discouraged investment there. The necessary technical personnel was also brought in, mainly from Britain and Germany. This dependence on outside sources, necessary as it was, had the drawback of making Russia peculiarly vulnerable when war broke out in 1914.

Since the industrial development came so late, Russia was able to avail herself of the latest machinery and processes. The new factories were therefore equipped and organized on thoroughly modern lines. Nearly half of the three million factory workers, on the eve of the war, were concentrated in some 450 enterprises with more than 1000 employees each. Alongside of the developing factories, however, the domestic system of manufactures persisted, in which about four million peasants produced some 30 per cent of the total output. Wages of the factory workers were extraordinarily low and living conditions were atrocious, but labor costs were high because of low productivity. Trade unions were prohibited by the government until 1906, but, though legalized, they were prevented from developing a vigorous labor movement after that by the hostile attitude of the authorities and the ignorance and apathy of the workers. At the peak of trade union development, in 1907, there were only 650 unions with a membership of about 250,000. The rapid industrial advance of Russia from 1890 to 1913 may be shown in the case of a few leading branches (in thousand short tons for all commodities):

Industry	1890	1900	1913
Pig iron	991	3,192	5,110
Iron and steel	937	2,392	4,452
Petroleum	4,080	11,395	10,134
Coal	6,630	17,802	39,970
Cotton textiles	142	289	468
Sugar		885	1,957
Railway building (mi.)	18,480	32,670	42,108
Workers in factories (thousands)	1,425	2,373	2,931

In spite of this rapid development, Russian industry compared unfavorably with the same lines in other countries, and was extremely backward from the technical point of view. Only 2.2 per cent of the world output of mechanical power units was utilized in Russian industry, agriculture and transport, and the comparative average output per industrial worker was 9, compared with 26 in France, 65 in Germany, and 80 in Britain.

Industrialization was followed by social as well as economic changes. A new middle class or *bourgeoisie* developed, consisting of big bankers and industrialists whose economic interests committed them to the existing regime, and small merchants, technicians, and the liberal professions who were liberal if not radical in their views. Parallel to this movement was the rise of an urban proletariat, composed largely of peasants who moved to the cities. Here they suffered all the evils incident to an unregulated industrial revolution — long hours, low wages, indescribably bad housing conditions, and brutal treatment by employers and by the police. The prohibition of organizations to protect the interests of labor led to an underground revolutionary movement, which became the basis of the Bolshevist Party.

Revolution of 1917. The orderly transformation of agriculture and industry, which had made considerable progress, was rudely interrupted by the World War. Other changes were also taking place, which gave promise of raising the standard of living for the mass of the people. A step toward constitutional reform had been taken in 1905 with the establishment of a Duma or popular assembly, and a beginning was made in popular education, while a vigorous co-operative movement started, growing to 31,000 societies by 1914. The war disorganized all activities. The mobilization of 15,000,000 men, many of them skilled workers, created a serious labor shortage, which was reflected in a falling off of production in agriculture, industry, and mining. The interruption of ocean shipping, resulting in a veritable blockade of Russia, prevented the importation of machinery, raw materials, and munitions, for which the country was dependent on foreign sources of supply. These difficulties might have been overcome, and were in fact being successfully met by 1917, had not the political situation become so serious, resulting in the complete breakdown of the old regime. A weak and obstinate Czar, a reactionary court dominated by the monk Rasputin, and ignorant and selfish ministers were utterly unable to cope with the new forces. As a result of the March revolution of 1917, a Provisional Government replaced the imperial regime, but it was unable to hold control in the face of growing discontent and in November was overthrown by the Bolsheviks, who established in its place a Union of Soviet Socialist Republics.

The changes which took place under the Soviet regime were so kaleidoscopic that a brief chronological chart may be given before they are described.

1917–1920	War Communism
1921–1928	New Economic Policy
1928–1932	First Five-Year Plan
1933–1937	Second Five-Year Plan
1938–	Third Five-Year Plan

War communism. "The war communism of 1918–20," wrote Professor Dobb,[2] "was the formal embodiment of the communist dream." Lenin hoped, by the "dictatorship of the proletariat," to transform the existing organization into a communist state, but three years of foreign intervention and civil war prevented the carrying out of any comprehensive plans. The Bolshevists took over an economic system which was already thoroughly disorganized. Their first task was to establish themselves in control, which they did by a policy of terrorism. The socialization of all branches of national economic life proceeded slowly. Banks and transportation were first nationalized and foreign trade was declared a state monopoly. The estates of the large landowners, the Czarist family, and the church were confiscated, and the title to all land was vested in the state. In practice, however, the peasants were left in possession of the land which they had seized during the revolution. Industrial establishments were left in private ownership, but workers' committees were given certain rights of consultation and control.

This compromise system soon broke down. The peasants held back grain from the market and forced the government to adopt a policy of requisition, but this in turn led the peasants to restrict the area sown and to slaughter their livestock. By 1920 agricultural production was only slightly over half of the pre-war average, and the drought of 1921 brought a terrible famine. Industrial output fell to one-seventh of that of 1913, and the average productivity of the industrial workers was only a third of what it had been. The system of workers' control in the factories broke down completely. There was at the same time a shortage of imported goods, of raw materials, and of fuel. Transportation was disorganized and it was difficult to make the necessary repairs. The Commissariat of Finance estimated in 1923 that half of the 5 billion rubles of fixed capital in large industries before the war had by now been lost. Steps to

[2] M. Dobb, *Russian Economic Development Since the Revolution* (London, 1928), 7.

remedy these difficulties were begun in 1918 when the state nationalized all industrial plants with over 1 million rubles capital, and were concluded in 1920 by the nationalization of all enterprises with mechanical power employing over five persons and those without mechanical power which employed ten or more. The government also tightened its grip over the workers, first by denying them the right to strike, and then by a system of labor conscription. After this, "war communism," as a series of opportunistic measures to meet rapidly changing conditions, came to an end.

The New Economic Policy. The growing poverty and unrest in the country made necessary a new procedure that would increase production, and this was attempted in the New Economic Policy. War communism had represented a concession to the left, but the NEP was a swing to the right, justified by the Soviets as a necessary breathing spell. It was a system of state capitalism. Agricultural production was encouraged by abolishing the state grain monopoly and substituting a tax (first in kind, later in money) for requisitions, and by granting the peasants a free market in the towns. The highly centralized state industries were placed under the control of some 486 trusts, employing nearly three-quarters of all industrial workers and administering groups of factories, which were given greater independence. Private shops and markets were re-opened, labor conscription was dropped, and a stable currency system was established. As a result of these changes, together with better harvests and cessation of war, an improvement took place in the economic life of the people. By 1926–27 the production of both agriculture and industry had passed the pre-war level.

The new policy was hailed abroad as a restoration of capitalism, but this conclusion was soon seen to be too hasty. The state still retained in its grasp industry, transportation, banking, and foreign trade. Peasant holdings were left undisturbed, but the prohibition of the sale or purchase of land prevented the rise of a landlord class. Individual initiative was restricted largely to the field of retail trade, which could at any time be taken over by the state. Little foreign capital, which was essential to the development of private industry, flowed into the Soviet Union during these years, owing to political uncertainties. The period of the New Economic Policy, from 1921 to 1928, must be regarded, not as a return to capitalism, but as a temporary retreat from communism, which enabled the government to consolidate its internal position and to effect the necessary economic reconstruction before embarking upon a more definite system of state planning.

The "classless" state, hailed as the ideal by Lenin, was abandoned under the NEP, for social stratification developed both in the city and on the land.   The former saw the rise of small manufacturers, shopkeepers, commission men, and others who operated with private capital, though the great majority of city dwellers were workers in state establishments.   There was also a differentiation in the villages into the three elements of rich (*kulaks*), middle, and poor peasants. Not only did all these groups operate on a profit-making basis, but even the government enterprises were placed on a "commercial basis" under NEP.   The opposition, led by Trotsky, criticized this policy as a drift toward capitalism, but Stalin and his followers defended their position and in 1927 expelled Trotsky and about one hundred other leaders of the opposition from the Communist Party.

The First Five-Year Plan.   By 1928 the output in agriculture and industry had passed the 1913 level and the Soviet leaders felt strong enough to put into effect more thorough-going measures designed to transform Russia into a modern industrial state on a socialist basis.   They aimed to make the country industrially independent and at the same time to show that a socialist state could surpass the achievements of capitalist states.   Stalin expressed this view in 1931: "Either we die or we overtake and outstrip the advanced capitalist countries.   We are fifty to one hundred years behind them.   We must cover this distance in ten years."   It was necessary to make haste, both as a measure of military preparedness and also to meet the demand for a higher standard of living.   The most important feature of the new measures, however, was the fact of governmental planning in itself, for this involved the abandonment of the easygoing policy of the NEP and the incorporation of private trade and individual farms into a state planned economy.

The First Five-Year Plan, which had passed a preliminary trial in the field of electrification, was drawn up by the State Planning Commission (*Gosplan*), and was launched on October 1, 1928.   Since it was held essential that the country must first of all be equipped for the manufacture of means of production, resources and labor were concentrated on the development of the heavy industries.   Any increase in the production of consumption goods was temporarily to be delayed until the more important goal was achieved.   Foreign critics pointed out, correctly enough, that during this period the standard of living of the Russian people was not improved, and that they suffered from serious shortages of prime necessities, such as shoes, clothing, housing, and manufactured foodstuffs.   The explanation was to be found in the urgent necessity of diverting social capital into the heavy rather than the light industries.   A curious parallel existed between the situation in Russia and that in Britain at the time of the Industrial Revolution.   In both cases, wages were held down and capital was accumulated by compulsory saving at the cost of a low standard of living. Stalin explained the accumulation of capital more euphemistically by stating that it came "from light industry, agricultural economy, and budget reserves." The accumulated capital was plowed back into industry, but in the one case it was done by private entrepreneurs and in the other by the power of the state. The purpose and the result were identical, namely the increase in productive power.

A great amount of new industrial construction was completed under the first Five-Year Plan. Tractor plants were built at Stalingrad, Chelinbinsk, and Kharkov; the largest agricultural machinery factory in Europe was established in Rostov; a factory with an annual capacity of 140,000 automobiles and trucks was set up at Nizhni Novgorod; and two large steel plants were erected, one in Magnitogorsk in the Urals and the other in the Kuznetzk Basin, in Siberia. Blast furnaces with a daily capacity of 1000 tons — double that of the average American furnace — were built. A number of electric power plants were constructed, the most important of which was the Dnieprostroi hydro-electric plant on the lower Dnieper. Roads, and especially auto roads, more than doubled in length. Railway expansion lagged behind, but a significant project was the Turkestan-Siberian Railway, which provided needed transportation facilities for new grain, lumber, and cotton regions. Never had so furious a drive been made for industrialization as took place in Soviet Russia during this period.

An immense increase in production was envisaged by the Plan, and almost fantastic estimates were made. While these were not met, the industrial output was roughly doubled between 1928 and the end of 1932, when the Plan was officially declared to be completed. It was claimed that this part of the Plan was fulfilled to the extent of 96.4 per cent, a claim which is scarcely borne out by the few figures available. The Soviet Union officially claimed the leading rank in the world in the production of agricultural machinery, tractors, and peat. By 1932 the country had been largely transformed from an agrarian into an industrial state.

The agrarian problem was more difficult. The NEP had given new life to the *kulaks*, who expanded their operations, renting land and hiring labor, until they controlled about a third of the grain production. It became evident that the perpetuation of this "private sector" in agriculture jeopardized the success of the communist state, and in 1929 a drive for collectivization in agriculture began. The first step was to "liquidate" the *kulaks*, who were deprived of their land and equipment and were barred from entering the new collective farms. They retaliated by slaughtering their cattle and burning state granaries. These acts, combined with a drought, resulted

PRODUCTION *
(in million tons)

Industry	1913	1927–28	Estimated output, 1932	Actual output, 1932
Coal	28.9	35.4	75	64.2
Oil	9.3	11.8	22	21.4
Pig iron	4.2	3.3	10	6.2
Steel	..	3.9	10	5.9
Cotton cloth (million meters)	2300	2871	4,700	2,540
Tractors (number)	..	3200†	53,000	49,700
Electric power (million kw. hrs.)	1945	5007	17,000	13,576

* League of Nations, *World Economic Survey*, 1933–34 (Geneva, 1934). Most of the Russian statistics of production are given in rubles, which are misleading since the value of the ruble fluctuated greatly.
† 1928–29.

in a serious famine in 1932–33, during which a loss of life took place which was estimated at from two to five millions. The *kulaks* were shipped off by the hundreds of thousands and were forced to work in lumber camps, on the canals, and in new construction. This forced labor was an important factor in the industrial expansion of this period. The terrible internal struggle that went on between the individualistically inclined peasants and the state were reflected in the decline of livestock, which was probably paralleled by humans.

LIVESTOCK
(million head)

	1916	1929	1933	1938
Horses	35.1	34.0	16.6	17.5
Cattle	58.9	68.1	38.4	63.2
Sheep and goats	115.2	147.2	50.2	102.5
Pigs	20.3	26.0	12.2	30.6

Collectivization, however, went on. By March, 1930, it was announced that 55 per cent of all peasant farms had been collectivized, which was raised to 62 per cent by the end of 1932. Collectivization and mechanization were the basic features of the new plan.

The usual type of collective organization was the *artel*, which combined communal ownership of land and equipment and individual ownership of homes, personal property, and minor implements for personal use. Only a few collective farms were organized on the "commune" basis, where everything was held in common. Each collective farm was required to deliver to the state all produce not needed for consumption on the farm. This system worked badly, for the peasants had no incentive to increase production, and in 1932 it was changed to a grain tax, fixed before planting. At the same time, stricter control by the government over collective farms was obtained through the machine and tractor stations. Since these were a government monopoly, the collectives, which made large use of farm machinery, were thus made dependent upon the state. By the end of the first Plan over 200,000 collective farms had been formed. There were also about 5000 state farms, operated by the state and intended to serve as models of management and technique, but they were too large — 150,000 acres on the average — and were inefficiently run.

To prove that the first Five-Year Plan was a success statistics of production along carefully chosen lines and of the increase in the number of collective farms and of their equipment were usually cited. But such figures did not reveal the darker side of the picture. Results differed widely, from striking success to dismal failure. Increased production in factories was offset, in part at least, by the decline of the domestic industries. Industrial production in the new mechanized establishments was inefficient and wasteful, and the labor required to produce a given result was much greater than in any capitalist country. Labor productivity was low and costs were high. The concentration on heavy industry involved a distressing shortage of even staple consumption goods, while the quality of those that found their way to the market was poor. Owing to the great increase in population, the movement to the cities, and other causes, the per capita consumption of grain was actually less than under the Czarist regime and there was also a diminution in the supplies of meat, milk and dairy products. The heavy hand of a huge bureaucracy held down improvement, and the enormous amount of paper work involved in a planned economy meant delay and added expense. Nevertheless, it was officially proclaimed that the share of the public sector in the total national income of the U.S.S.R. had increased during this five-year period from 44 per cent at the beginning to 93.6 per cent by the end. The latter figure, however, represented in large part a transition of industries from non-enumerated private enterprise to government enterprise, where they were recorded in official figures, rather than a real increase.

Second Five-Year Plan. Only an imaginary line separated the first and second Five-Year Plans, for they were successive steps in a single movement. The first over-ambitious plans for industrialization were, however, modified as experience showed the dangers of too great haste. The grandiose schemes for quantity output and new construction gave way to greater emphasis on quality and to the more efficient operation of the new giant establishments. The framers of the first Plan suffered from megalomania — the belief that large size connoted superiority — and overestimated the productive capacity of the people. Compared with the fantastic preliminary estimates of production that were set up in 1931 for the second Plan, the final figures for 1937 were very restrained. The preliminary and final estimates and actual production may be given for a few leading industries.

SECOND FIVE-YEAR PLAN FOR 1937

Item	Preliminary estimate	Final estimate	Actual production
Coal (million tons)	650	152	123
Pig iron (million tons)	62	16	14.4
Steel (million tons)	10	19	17.7
Oil (million tons)	125	46.8	30.4
Electric power (billion kw. hrs.)	100	38	36.4
Tractors (thousands)	173	88.5	..
Freight cars (thousands)	..	118	59
Railway track (miles)	10,540	6570	4348
Automobiles (thousands)	200	200	181
Cotton fabrics (million meters)	..	5100	3447
Footwear (million pairs)	..	180	164
Soap (1000 tons)	..	1216	495
Housing (million square yards)	74.4	76.8	..

The second Plan embodied two fundamental changes. The first was a policy of decentralization; newly projected factories were to be located near sources of raw materials, and they were to be more moderate in size. In this Plan, said Stalin, "the ardor for new construction must be supplemented by the ardor for mastering the new plants and new technique." The second was the promise that more attention would be given to the production of consumers' goods, new and modern housing, and a chance to play. Political and military considerations, however, compelled a postponement of this aim, and the second Plan, like the first, was characterized by a feverish expansion of heavy industries, and especially an effort to modernize Soviet armaments and to build an adequate air force and a navy. In fact, the disproportion between the output of producers' and consumers' goods grew greater; in 1933 the latter constituted 58 per cent of the total national production, but in 1936 only 39 per cent. Although industrial production in no case met the goal set by even the modified estimates for 1937, there was a substantial increase in most lines over 1932. But the quantitative increase was purchased at the expense of quality, while the efforts to speed up production resulted in defective goods, deterioration in machinery, and waste of materials. Costs, therefore, remained high. Consumers' goods were not only scarce, but were high priced and poor in quality. In spite of "planning," complementary industries did not keep pace with each other; coal and raw materials fell short of industrial demand, and agricultural production fluctuated greatly.

The integration of the peasantry into the socialist state was being accomplished by a steady expansion of collective farms. It was estimated that at the end of 1937 the 243,000 collective farms contained 93 per cent of all the peasants and 99 per cent of the country's cultivated area. Such a comparison was, however, not a fair test between collective farms and individual farms, for credit of any kind was withheld from the latter and they were denied the use of tractors and other agricultural machinery controlled by the state machine-tractor stations, and were discriminated against in the delivery of seed, in access to pasture, in taxation, and in other ways. The tractor stations, which in 1938 had 367,000 tractors, 104,600 harvester combines, and 67,000 trucks, served only the collective farms.

Third Five-Year Plan. The year 1938 saw the launching of a third Five-Year Plan. Sobered by the failures of the speed-up tactics of the first and second Plans, Stalin and his advisers now adopted a policy of "deceleration," and declared that any plan must conform to the normal capacity of industry. This declaration was attended by a wholesale purge of "wreckers," who, it was contended, had sabotaged production at every stage and prevented plans from being realized. Industry thus lost thousands of experienced managers and technicians, while those who remained feared to take the initiative and sought safety in inaction. The results of the third Plan were little publicized because it emphasized defense production. From the few figures released, however, it is clear that Soviet output no longer was making the spectacular showing it did after depressed 1932. Production was slowed up by rapid depreciation and lack of repairs. When a factory manager's position, and often his life, depended on his fulfilling the Plan, he dared not stop for overhauling and repairs. The result was a steady deterioration of plant and equipment. The presence, moreover, of so many "wreckers" and "shirkers," who had to be purged, suggests serious disaffection among the workers.

Population and labor. The rapid increase of the population cramped the efforts to improve the condition of the people, for it was difficult to absorb the annual accretion into the industrial organization and they were not needed on the mechanized farms. The growth of the population may be briefly shown.

POPULATION IN RUSSIA

Year	Absolute numbers	Per cent		Birth-rate	Death-rate
		Rural	Urban		
1870	71,900,000	92.0	8.0	49.2*	34.1*
1913	139,300,000	86.8	13.2	45.0	25.0
1928	154,300,000	82.1	17.9	42.7†	23.2†
1939	170,467,000	67.1	32.9	..	..

* Average, 1891–1900. † 1924.

The rapid growth was the result of an unusually high birth-rate, higher than that of any other country in Europe. The "fertile marriage beds" of Russia had not yet felt the restraining influences which in western Europe were causing a decline in the rate of growth. In spite of the fact that the utmost freedom was given to birth control, this affected only a small section of the population. Although the death-rate was also the highest, the excess of births over deaths yielded an enormous annual increment.

As industrialization proceeded there was an increasing movement of the population from the country to the city, from agriculture to industry. This was welcomed by Soviet leaders, since a shortage of labor showed itself when the government embarked on its intensive program of industrialization. Unemployment disappeared in the cities, but there was still a "disguised unemployment" in the country owing to the existence there of a surplus rural population, estimated at between 20 and 30 million persons. When machines were substituted for hand labor on the collective farms these agricultural workers were no longer needed. This fact explains the efforts to transfer the population from agriculture to industry as rapidly as possible. This movement, however, brought other problems in its train. Housing did not keep pace with the growth of the cities, and accommodations for the workers remained inadequate and bad. Even more difficult was the transformation of farm laborers into industrial workers. The magnitude of this task may be illustrated by a single example: of the 15,000 employees in the Stalingrad tractor plant in 1931, nearly one-half of the workers had less than six months' experience in any form of industrial production and 80 per cent had less than one year.

The low productivity of labor was the Achilles heel of the Soviet system and various methods were adopted to increase this. At first these took the form of "shock troops" of picked workers who were moved from place to place to bolster up the weak spots, and of bonuses and honors to "heroes" among the workers who exceeded the normal performance. After 1931 piecework rates were generally substituted for time wages and efficiency was rewarded by higher monetary rewards. In 1934 about 70 per cent of the total hours worked were paid on a piecework basis. Great results were anticipated from the Stakhanov movement, launched in 1935 by a miner who increased his output by rationalizing his work, but it was soon found that the extraordinary records achieved by individual workers were purchased at the expense of overexertion and deterioration of machinery.

Another weak point in the Soviet economy was the constant shifting of workers from factory to factory in search of higher wages and better conditions. In coal mining, for instance, the annual labor turnover exceeded the average number of those regularly employed. Stringent measures were taken to discourage labor migration, first by the introduction in 1939 of labor books, which contained the worker's record and reasons for change, and second by denying the right to a paid vacation and of other social benefits to those who moved too often. The free movement of labor, guaranteed by the Labor Code of 1927, was thus abrogated. In spite of all these efforts, the labor productivity of a Soviet worker was estimated in 1935 at less than half that of a comparable American worker. Stalin himself, in reporting to the Party Congress in 1934, complained of "the continued lag in the increase of the productivity of labor, in the reduction of the cost of production, and in the establishment of cost accounting."

The hours of labor had been fixed by the Labor Code at seven per day "for the overwhelming majority of the workers," and at the same time the work-week of five days followed by a day of rest on the sixth was established. As a result of these changes, the average number of work-hours in a year fell from 2553 in 1913 to 1828 in 1936. In an effort to increase the industrial output changes were made in both of these points in 1940: the seven-hour day was lengthened to eight hours and the six-day week was replaced by the seven-day week. At the same time the number of "revolutionary holidays" was reduced to five per annum. By these methods the number of work-hours in a year was raised to 2464, or to practically the pre-war level.

Trade unions and co-operative associations, institutions which in capitalist countries had done much to improve the working and living conditions of the working classes, call for a word of explanation. Both of them continued to exist in the Soviet Union, but their functions were greatly changed. During the period of war communism membership in a trade union was made obligatory for all industrial workers. Under the easy-going NEP policy, the trade unions became somewhat independent of the government, and membership became voluntary. But the government feared their growing power, and moved to bring them under Party control. A three-sided control of industrial plants was instituted, consisting of factory committees of workers, Party committees, and management, but gradually the once absolute powers of the workers' committees were cut down until by 1937 they were merely consultative. The trade unions became state agencies, whose officials were appointed by the Communist Party and whose function was the surveillance and disciplining of the workers. They were left with little independent scope except in social, educational, and recreational activities. Nevertheless, about six-sevenths of the industrial workers were members of trade unions.

Consumers' co-operation had a vigorous development in pre-war Russia, and supplied practically all the agricultural population and a large section of the urban proletariat with wares, but after the revolution they became largely state enterprises. As the state distributing system expanded, the co-operatives became less important and by 1934 they handled only about 60 per cent of the total retail turnover. By the end of 1935 they had lost most of their original independence and became state organizations in all but name. They bought their goods from state industries, used state transportation agencies, and obtained their capital by means of state credits.

Wages are particularly difficult to estimate, both because of the fluctuating value of the ruble and because the Soviet worker, in addition to his money wage, received "socialized wages," which included social insurance benefits, paid vacations, and sometimes reduced rent and free light and fuel. The Moscow Institute of Conjuncture estimated that the real wages of urban workers in 1926–27 were 17 per cent above those of 1913. The economic position of the rural workers had, however, seriously deteriorated. Soviet money wages followed on the whole a rising curve after 1928, but the high cost of consumers' goods made the gains illusory. It was estimated that between 1914 and 1940 wages increased five-fold but food prices rose ten- to fifteen-fold. The Marxist ideal, "from each according to his ability, to each according to his needs," was necessarily scrapped in favor of the capitalist system of "to each according to his work." Moreover, when the longer hours were introduced, piecework rates were scaled down to keep monthly earnings at the former level.

Prices of all manufactured goods were fixed by the government. After 1936, in an effort to make each branch of industry self-supporting, prices were fixed at the average cost of production. Those establishments whose costs were above the average were compensated by the more capable, whose costs were low. Since prices and costs were based upon uncertain data, an element of arbitrariness was introduced into the price structure which weakened the supposedly scientific objectivity of economic planning.

Consumption probably constitutes a better criterion of a people's well-being than do money wages, for after all the wages must be spent for food and other necessaries. The following table [3] brings together some recent careful estimates of food consumption in the U.S.S.R.:

CONSUMPTION IN OUNCES PER HEAD PER WEEK

Article	Russia			Britain 1934
	1933	1927–28	1934	
Wheat and rye (expressed as bread)	152.5	144.0	150.0	61.0
Potatoes	80.0	80.0	80.0	64.0
Meat and fat	16.8	18.6	6.9	44.3
Pork	..	..	0.8	5.8
Beef	..	..	1.6	17.0
Milk and milk products (expressed as milk)	112.5	128.0	76.0	254.0
Butter	..	..	0.4	7.8
Cheese	..	..	0.4	3.2
Sugar	9.0	8.3	8.0	17.8
Tea	..	..	0.02	2.8
Eggs (number)	0.9	1.1	0.05	2.9

Conclusion.   It is clear from even this brief sketch that the communism of Marx and Lenin has not been established in Soviet Russia. Although the 1936 constitution declared that the economic basis of the U.S.S.R. was the socialist ownership of the means of production, "firmly established as a result of the liquidation of the capitalist system of economy, the abolition of private ownership of

[3] Colin Clark, *A Critique of Russian Statistics* (London, 1939), 10, 21. By permission of the publisher, The Macmillan Company, New York.

implements and means of production, and the destruction of the exploitation of man by man," private property is permitted. Small peasant farms and handicrafts, provided they do not involve the use of hired labor, are allowed, although these have been reduced to the vanishing point. And every Soviet citizen has the right to own personal property, such as a house, furniture, books, domestic articles, and even a savings account. The value of such a privilege depends, however, upon the ability of the Soviet economy to provide the desired consumers' goods and upon the wage scale. So far the average worker has been able to obtain only the most urgent necessities.

The non-material values, such as freedom of speech, religion, choice of occupation, and freedom of movement, have been sacrificed in the effort to raise the general standard of living. It is true that literacy has been raised, according to official estimates, from 32 per cent of persons over seven years of age in 1897 to 81 per cent in 1939. That it has failed to achieve general well-being on a scale comparable with that attained under capitalism, seems abundantly proved.

The Soviet experiment has shown that a socialist economy can maintain itself and it has accumulated a store of experiences that may serve as a guide or a warning to similar experiments in the future. It has developed considerable industrialization, has introduced a more scientific mechanized agriculture, and has maintained economic relationships with capitalistic countries. But, on the other hand, it has failed to convince other countries of the superiority of communist organization, and has suffered from the same problems that confront democratic countries. Industrial efficiency is woefully backward and the productivity of the individual worker, in spite of constant appeals to his social duty, remains low. The "dictatorship of the proletariat" has become the absolutism of a few, maintained in power by terroristic methods. Sovietism has signally failed to demonstrate that it is more equitable or more efficient than a system of capitalism based on private property and individual initiative.

2. FASCISM IN ITALY

Fascism and Sovietism are apparently diametrically opposed to each other. Sovietism rests, theoretically at least, upon internationalism. Fascists oppose internationalism and therefore resist communism and those forms of socialism which rest upon Marx's cosmopolitan philosophy. Fascism also denies the existence of the class struggle, upon which Marxian socialism rests, and insists that class conflict can be abolished by a better organization of economic society within the framework of the totalitarian state. It refuses to recognize any claims to loyalty other than those to the state, and thus sees only danger in the allegiance owed by Marxian communists to class and to internationalism. And yet in one respect Fascism and Communism are similar — they both embody a system of economic planning and of centralized control. Politically, they both oppose Democracy, which dignifies the individual, while Fascism and Communism exalt the community. Economically, both the latter treat property as a community interest, while Democracy guards it as a private right. There is, however, at this point a difference between the two opponents of individual enterprise: the communist state owns and operates all enterprises directly, while the Fascist state does so indirectly, permitting individual entrepreneurs to conduct the businesses under strict government supervision. The right of the owner under Fascism is not only seriously impaired by government-controlled syndicates and cartels, but is completely subordinated to the final authority of the state.

Fascism dates back to 1919, when some forty young men of the proletariat and middle classes gathered around Mussolini and founded the new Fascismo. Italy at that time was in a state of political turmoil and economic disorganization. To dissatisfaction over the peace settlement, which was called a "mutilated victory," the vacillating impotence of the government, and revelation of fortunes made by graft in war contracts, were added the influence of the Russian revolution, widespread unemployment, and the rapidly rising cost of living. The Socialist Party had quadrupled its membership since before the war and in the 1919 elections its candidates received one-third of all the votes cast. The trade unions also greatly increased their numerical strength. The General Confederation of Labor, which had 300,000 members in 1914, grew to 2,300,000 in 1920, while the Catholic unions had nearly 2,000,000 at the latter date, and the lesser unions claimed 700,000. Nor was organization confined to the industrial workers, for a quarter of the members of the G.C.L. were peasants.

There was a wave of strikes in industrial establishments in 1919 and 1920, and of seizure of landlords' estates by the peasants. The number of working days lost in strikes, which had averaged only 4,000,000 annually in the years before the war, rose to 22,000,000 in 1919 and 30,000,000 in 1920. By the use of mass pressure the unions were able to push up wage rates, shorten the hours of labor, and exact better working conditions. Business and property rights were also being attacked by the workers. Perhaps a third of the country was "red" and many of the local governments and the industrial establishments were in the hands of communists. The socialists might have used the opportunity to seize power and restore order, but they were unwilling to use force and depended on democratic processes. The situation, however, called for immediate and forceful action, for the continued disorder under communist instigation was leading to further confusion. At this juncture the Fascist Party intervened to cope with the emergency and succeeded in restoring order.

The policy of the new party was at first aggressively socialist and combined a demand for the entire reconstruction of the Italian state with a radical economic program. It was strongly influenced by Syndicalism, which proposed direct action and violence in order to gain political and economic control. In the face of the communist danger, however, the Fascists appeared next as the champions of order and in opposition to strikes. They were able to reduce the number of strikes in 1921 to only half of those of the previous year and the number of working days lost was cut to 8,000,000. A vigorous campaign was carried on against both socialists and communists. The "march on Rome" in 1922 put the Fascist group in control, and in October of that year Benito Mussolini was appointed prime minister.

The main strength of Fascism came originally from the small bourgeoisie or lower middle class, made up of merchants, artisans, and peasant farmers, all of whom disliked large scale capitalism, but even more feared socialism or communism. Its rise to power undoubtedly resulted from the support of the big industrialists, who were less afraid of the anti-capitalist platform of the new party than they were of the menace of communism. It benefited also from the support of the civil servants, army officers, and judges, and from the failure of the more moderate groups, the Socialists and Catholics, to offer a unified resistance. The Fascists promptly paid their political debt to those who helped them to victory. Industrialists and landowners were relieved of various burdens; taxes were removed from capital issues of corporations and from family inheritances, and were changed as far as possible from direct to indirect. The peasants were ousted from estates they had seized and financial assistance was withdrawn from the workers' co-operatives. The government retired largely from the economic field, which it left to private enterprise.

At the basis of Fascist theory lies the conception of the totalitarian national state. "All within the state, all for the state, none against the state," is a slogan which sums up the idea that the state embraces all activities of individual citizens and subordinates them to national ends. The state is the ultimate social organism and claims the complete allegiance of its citizens. Fascism therefore opposes democratic liberalism on the one hand and Marxian socialism on the other, for they would set up other allegiances. It also rejects the idea that the individual is the unit, for whose sake the state exists, which it exactly reverses. Under a free constitution the citizens have rights, personal and political, but under a fascist dictatorship such rights are defined by the Fascist Party, which alone is allowed to exist. Fascism denies likewise the validity of any international superstate, for it is based on a fervid nationalism. "The state must be absolutely sovereign," wrote a defender of the system,[4] "and must dominate all the existing forces in the country, coordinate them, solidify them, and direct them towards the higher ends of national life." A more authoritative exposition of Fascist doctrine was given by Mussolini himself in his "Doctrine of Fascism," published in 1932, from which a few sentences may be quoted:[5]

"Outside the state there can be neither individualism nor groups (political parties, associations, syndicates, classes)."

"The nation as a state is an ethical reality which exists and lives in so far as it develops."

"The Fascist state, the highest and most perfect form of personality, is a force, but a spiritual force, which takes over all the forms of the moral and intellectual life of man."

Such abstract statements sound rather vague, but applied under the circumstances of Italian economy they acquire a definite meaning. Italy was a poor country, with limited natural resources, especially in coal and iron; if she were to take high rank among industrial nations, every effort must be directed to utilizing these resources in such a way as to reduce her dependence on the outside world and yet to assure to the Italian population a decent living. This task involved the complete subordination of individual and class interests to those of the state, as determined by the Fascist Party.

The economic theory of Fascism can be understood properly only if this idea of the totalitarian state be held in mind. It rejected *laissez faire* and unrestrained competition as undesirable and as abstractions that never really existed. On the other hand, it opposed the comprehensive governmental control that characterized Sovietism and all socialistic and communistic schemes. State production and distribution are wasteful, said the Fascists, and lead to economic disorganization and bureaucratic inefficiency. Fascism held, on the contrary, that private initiative is the most efficient instrument yet devised for achieving the economic ends of the state. The role that

4 T. Sillani, *What is Fascism and Why* (New York, 1931), 18.
5 This is conveniently found in M. Oakeshott, *The Social and Political Doctrines of Contemporary Europe* (Cambridge, England, 1939), 166-68.

was assigned to private enterprise under Fascism was a restricted one, but an understanding of this is essential to a comprehension of Fascist economic theory and organization. But Fascism went through several stages, both in its economic and its political program, before it finally developed its present form and structure. These have been listed as follows: [6]

1922–26. The government policy was that of encouraging industrial expansion and private enterprise. Easy money was provided by inflation and there was an industrial boom. The index of industrial production rose from 81 to 127 between 1922 and 1928.

1927–29. The monetary policy was reversed and the lira was stabilized at a high rate, which resulted in falling prices and lessened business activity. By 1929 the index of industrial production was down to 109. To meet the lower prices rationalization was introduced into industry and mergers and consolidations took place. There was also an increase of government assistance and of direct state intervention in the economic system.

1929–32. This was a period of world-wide depression, by which Italy was particularly hard hit. The industrial production index fell to 73, and unemployment increased from 319,000 to 1,085,000. Foreign trade dropped 60 per cent and domestic trade 40 per cent. To meet the unemployment problem the government undertook a vast public works program. Increasing assistance was given to industry and government domination increased.

1933–. This period saw the development of the corporative state with full control over the economic system. Economic self-sufficiency or autarchy in essential commodities became the aim of the state in a program that was increasingly one of armament and war.

Syndicates of employers and employees were first set up and these were organized vertically in unions, federations, and confederations, each of these in turn representing larger geographical groupings. Theoretically all the confederations were linked together in the Ministry of Corporations, but this scheme remained largely a paper organization, for no corporations were established until 1930. Fascism was still in what Mussolini called the "syndical phase." The "corporate" organization of the Fascist state was effected by the law of February 5, 1934, which provided for a horizontal structure of connecting links by establishing twenty-two "category corporations." Their task was to unite the corresponding employers' and employees' syndicates into single organizations, culminating in the National Council of Corporations. Above this stood the

[6] H. W. Schneider, *The Fascist Government of Europe* (New York, 1936), 101.

Fascist grand council and party organization, and over all the Duce. As thus organized Italy became a complete totalitarian state, thoroughly united under the absolute authority of the leader.

One of the early aims of the Fascist state was to make Italy agriculturally self-sufficient, and to achieve this a two-fold program of increasing production and of land reclamation was launched. The most spectacular exhibition of the former was the so-called "battle of wheat" which was designed to "free Italy from the slavery of foreign bread." Begun in 1925 this became an annual feature of Italian rural life, including visits by Mussolini to the fields, in which he was invariably photographed taking part in the wheat harvesting. As a result of government stimulation the area under cultivation was enlarged above the pre-war average and wheat production was increased. The larger use of silos, farm machinery, and fertilizer was encouraged and the prices to the farmer of fuel oil and artificial fertilizer were held down by subsidies. Every effort was made to raise the average yield by the distribution of better seeds, more fertilizers, improved methods, and scientific research. As a result the average yield of wheat was raised from 15.5 bushels per acre in 1909–13 to 23.8 in 1937, and the total production from 198 million bushels in 1921–25 (the half decade before the "battle of wheat" began) to 293 million in 1937. Since the normal annual consumption of wheat in Italy was about 275 million bushels, Mussolini proclaimed that the battle had been won.

But victory in wheat involved losses along other lines. The balance in Italian agriculture was upset, for wheat diverted attention from livestock and tree crops, in which Italy enjoyed climatic advantages, and involved the plowing up of grass land. Thus, between 1926 and 1937 the number of horses and mules fell off nearly a quarter, sheep nearly a third, and goats almost half; only hogs increased. An especially heavy burden was placed on consumers, since almost prohibitive import duties were imposed on wheat, as well as on wheat flour, corn, and other breadstuffs. Since bread was literally the staff of life in Italy, living costs were raised to the mass of the workers. The per capita consumption of cereals was less in 1937 than it had been a decade earlier, as well as of meat, fruits, vegetables, sugar, coffee, milk, cheese, wine, and beer.

Another part of the agricultural program for making Italy more self-sufficient was land reclamation. This had the double purpose of abolishing malaria and of making unusable land available for cultivation. About half of the land in Italy was in the possession of some 25,000 families, and it was hoped by this method to expand peasant proprietorship, which was regarded as more in harmony with Fascist ideas of home than life in the industrial cities. Nearly half of the population was engaged in agriculture, most of them eking out a bare subsistence on "dwarf" holdings. Over a third (35 per cent) of the holdings were 2½ acres or less and over half (55 per cent) were between 2½ and 25 acres. The remaining 10 per cent, however, contained over two-thirds of the land.

The land reclamation program included drainage, irrigation projects, reservoirs, road building, schools, and rural electrification. About 5,700,000 acres, or 7 per cent of the total area, were too swampy for cultivation and those were drained and settled by peasant farmers. Projects for land reclamation had to be approved by the government and, if regarded as urgent, might be undertaken directly by the government or carried out by private organizations which were subsidized by the state. Thus far neither expropriation (even with compensation) nor land nationalization has been applied to the great estates, though a thorough-going application of the Fascist program would seem to call for one or both of these methods for bringing about a better distribution and perhaps a better utilization of the limited land resources of Italy.

In spite of early Fascist pronouncements there was no general movement to nationalization of the means of production; aside from a small number of fiscal monopolies and state-owned enterprises, industry in Italy remained in private hands. Drawing its support largely from small industrialists and peasant farmers, Fascism was under the necessity of retaining the institutions of private property and individual enterprise. Any factory owner or farmer was theoretically at liberty to produce on his own responsibility, but as time went on this liberty was severely circumscribed. Private interests were regulated by the government in order that they might not run counter to the interests of the state. Emphasis must be placed, according to Mussolini, not on individual profits, but on collective welfare.

Industry flourished during the rather speculative period down to 1926, but the stabilization of the lira the following year ended inflation and checked the industrial expansion. This was followed by a further decline during the world depression. The government was forced to come to the aid of industry and intervened in three ways.[7] Positively, it extended assistance to desirable undertakings which it wished to stimulate by lending state credit and in other ways. The most outstanding example of this was the development of the hydro-electric industry. Italy had only limited supplies of lignite of low heating capacity and imported most of its coal from England.

---

[7] "Intervention," declared the Charter of Labor of 1927, "may take the form of encouragement, regulation, or direct management."

In order to lessen its dependence on foreign supplies and also to reduce its imports Italy greatly expanded its water power resources. Hydro-electric production increased, under government encouragement, from 6 billion kilowatt hours in 1923 to 14.4 billion in 1937.

The iron and steel industry, together with the shipbuilding industries, was promoted in order to furnish the country with the industrial basis for the armament program, which was increasingly emphasized after 1934. As a result of this stimulation production along these lines was more than doubled between 1913 and 1937 (iron and steel from 989 to 2087 thousand tons and the merchant marine from 877 to 1772 thousand net tons). Aid was also given to the silk and sugar beet industries. Every effort was made to ensure self-sufficiency, especially in essential industries in the event of war.

State intervention was sometimes negative or purely regulatory, if private initiative seemed to be developing in undesired directions. The fact that Italy was poor both in raw materials and in capital was never lost sight of. If either of these was wasted in one industry other industries were starved. The government therefore endeavored to prevent speculation, overproduction in any particular branch, or other misdirection of the country's resources. All enterprises were compelled to obtain licenses before they could start new industrial plants or enlarge old ones. Some radical Fascists advocated the substitution of state operation for private initiative in industry, but the big industrialists were able to maintain the institutions of private property and free enterprise, subject, however, to rather serious limitations. Theoretically capital was privately owned and was free, but its use was severely restricted. Every owner of property was supposed to use it not only for himself, but also for social ends. Fascism, declared Mussolini, placed the emphasis on national welfare rather than on individual profits. Practically, this led to a limitation of profits to 6 per cent.

The third form of intervention, by state ownership and operation, would seem to be unnecessary, since control has been made complete by regulation and subsidies.

Population and labor. A basic principle in Fascist economic policy was population growth, which was especially necessary if Italy were to carry out its imperialistic ambitions by force of arms. The birth-rate was declining and was not offset by a corresponding reduction in the death-rate, so that the annual additions to the population were becoming smaller. To meet this situation the government first of all encouraged the growth of large families by a series of measures: taxes on bachelors (1926), tax reductions to large families (1928), preferment in civil service for married men (1929), loans to couples intending to marry (1937), and restrictions on employment of women in industry (1938). Strict laws were also passed against birth-control propaganda and the sale of contraceptives. Migration, both internal and external, was controlled in order to prevent the loss of farm labor by exodus from the rural districts to the cities or the loss of Italian citizens to foreign countries. As a result of the latter policy emigration was reduced from over 1,000,-000 annually before the war to an average of 134,000 for the years 1921–27, and to 23,000 in 1937. The effects of these various measures may be seen in the following table:

Year	Population	Birth-rate	Death-rate
1913	36,120,100 *	31.7	18.7
1920	36,147,400	31.8	18.7
1925	38,973,600	28.3	17.1
1930	40,762,700	26.7	14.1
1935	43,009,000	23.3	13.9
1937	44,557,000 †	22.9	14.2

* 1915. † 1939.

The role of labor under Fascism was even more restricted than was that of capital. This was defined in the Charter of Labor, adopted in 1927, which laid down the basic principles governing labor relations, wages, social insurance, and social welfare. "Labor in all its forms, intellectual, technical, and manual," declared the Charter, "is a social duty." Nominally free, labor was actually under stricter control than was enterprise. Since maximum production was desired, both for the welfare of consumers and for national power, every effort was made to prevent interruptions. Consequently, strikes and lockouts were alike forbidden. The conflict of interests between labor and capital was recognized, but this must be subordinated to the higher national interest of efficient production, which was declared to be a "unitary" process, bringing together the different factors. Industrial peace was to be obtained by regulating the relations of workers and employers through collective labor contracts. The Charter of Labor set up elaborate machinery by which the two parties, organized into syndicates, made collective agreements covering questions of hours, wages, and conditions of work. The chief function of the syndicates was the negotiation of such agreements, which, when completed, became binding on all persons in the respective occupations.

The old trade unions, standing outside the Fascist organization, were not suppressed as they were in Nazi Germany. Workers might belong to them, but the unions were reduced to impotence by being denied the right to bargain collectively with the employers.   Only the Fascist unions or syndicates had this power, and, since their agreements became binding on all workers in an occupation, even if only ten per cent of those employed agreed to them, the old unions were in fact almost completely liquidated.   The introduction in 1933 of a compulsory workbook for all employees further tightened the reins about labor.   The labor movement was thus brought completely under the control of the Fascist Party. Nevertheless, in 1938, over one-quarter of the workers remained outside of the Fascist unions.   Much working class discontent undoubtedly remained, but it was inarticulate and without means of expression.

Since disputes were inevitable and strikes and lockouts were barred by law as criminal offenses, provision for the settlement of industrial disputes by arbitration was necessary.   Such disputes were referred in the first instance to the federations of syndical associations.   If they failed to reach a settlement, the matter was next taken to the Ministry of Corporations.   The few disputes that failed of settlement here were finally submitted to the governmental labor courts, which were first established in 1926.

This syndical and corporative system of collective bargaining and arbitration, proclaimed by the Fascist Party as the solution of the problem of industrial relations, has evoked equally warm criticism by its opponents.   In the first place, they assert that the free association of workers for their class interests has been replaced by a bureaucratic organization under the control of the state, and that as a result the workers have been left practically helpless.   It is also urged that collective labor contracts, dictated largely by the government and interpreted by labor courts under Fascist influence, simply perpetuated existing inequalities and maladjustments and prevented labor from sharing in social and economic progress.

To these arguments the Fascists reply that the conflict of interests between workers and employers cannot be permitted to disturb the economic equilibrium of the state, and that syndical organization has the merit of maintaining a balance between the two groups.   A competent critic [8] of the Fascist system gives his conclusion as follows: "In reading the decisions of the Italian labor courts one gains the impression that the decisions are fair and that the courts are inclined to consider sympathetically every legitimate demand of the workers."   More fundamental is their insistence that only one allegiance can be recognized and that is to the Fascist state; all other considerations must be subordinated to its interests.   Class struggle therefore cannot be tolerated.   The purpose of the corporative sys-

[8] W. G. Welk, *Fascist Economic Policy* (Cambridge, Mass., 1938), 85.

tem, declared Mussolini, is to achieve "a higher social justice for all the Italian people" and to strengthen Italy "for expansion in the world." Social justice was defined as "secure work, a fair salary, a decent home . . . and the opportunity to develop and improve incessantly." How far this aim has been achieved in terms of material well-being is not easy to ascertain.

The Charter of Labor re-introduced the medieval concept of a "just wage," and declared that wages must be adjusted to "the normal requirements of life, the possibilities of production, and the productivity of labor." This eclectic theory would seem to have placed a maximum beyond which wages could not advance, but gave no guarantee of minimum wages. In practice these were determined by agreement between the parties to the collective contracts. Fascist wage policy is roughly divisible into two periods: 1923–34 and 1934– . In the first of these periods the government's monetary policy was a determining influence in fixing wages, while in the second external factors were of more importance.

Money wages and prices both rose gradually up to 1926, but fell rapidly after the revaluation of the lira in 1927, reaching their lowest point in 1934. Since prices fell more rapidly than nominal wages, however, real wages increased for industrial workers between 1927 and 1934, though they declined somewhat for agricultural workers. After 1934 nominal industrial wages rose, but real wages remained steady on a somewhat lower level. Comparable statistics for agricultural laborers after 1934 are lacking. The statistical basis for these statements is presented in the following table, although any conclusions on the basis of official Italian statistics are open to doubt.

INDEX OF WAGES AND COST OF LIVING IN ITALY *

Year	Nominal hourly wages Agriculture (men)	Industry	Cost of living	Real hourly wages Agriculture	Industry
1928	102.0	101.6	100.0	103.7	103.4
1929	100.0	100.0	101.2	100.0	100.0
1930	94.8	100.4	97.7	98.0	103.9
1931	85.1	93.7	88.3	97.4	107.4
1932	77.1	92.6	84.1	92.8	111.5
1933	74.7	89.9	80.5	94.1	113.1
1934	72.3	87.2	76.4	95.8	115.4
1935	70.4	83.0	77.5	90.8	107.1
1936	....	88.1	83.5	....	105.5
1937	....	98.9	91.7	....	107.8
1938	85.4	113.1	98.7	86.5	114.6

* Based on various tables in W. G. Welk, op. cit., 234-41.

In pursuance of its policy to stabilize the lira on a high level in 1927 the government pursued a policy of deflation and made drastic cuts in wages, prices, and rents. Wages were officially reduced in 1927 by 20 per cent, in 1930 by another 12 per cent, and in 1934 by from 6 per cent in the lowest grade to 20 per cent in the highest. Most of these decreases were directed at government employees, but private employers lost little time in following suit. At the same time the government endeavored to ensure corresponding reductions in prices, rents, and other charges, by a vigorous policy of price control. This was successful in holding the purchasing power of wages at a fairly even level.

The hours of labor were reduced by a law of 1923 to 48 a week in all occupations, and eleven years later the 40-hour week was established by agreement between the Fascist confederations of workers and employers. This was a work-sharing program and was accompanied by a proportional reduction of pay, suppression of overtime, and decrease in the number of women and children employed. Family allowances to heads of families were introduced for industrial workers and in 1937 were extended to all occupations. Unemployment had increased steadily since 1925, and the years 1932 and 1933 saw over 1,000,000 unemployed, but the introduction of the 40-hour week in 1934 brought some relief. The various governmental free employment offices assisted in placing and distributing the workers. Unemployment insurance helped to tide the worker over short periods; an insured worker who had contributed for 48 weeks received unemployment benefits for 90 days, amounting to from 6 to 20 cents a day. Social insurance was developed under Fascism, but Italy was far behind Britain and Germany, and even France, in this regard. In 1938 every Italian worker was compelled by law to carry accident, sickness, old-age, tuberculosis, and unemployment insurance.

A more unique contribution of Fascism to the welfare of labor was the institution in 1925 of *Dopolavoro* or National Leisure Time Organization. This body, which was open to all workers and had only nominal membership dues, grew rapidly and in 1937 had over 3,000,000 members. It offered its members a wide variety of recreational facilities and provided the workers with opportunities to employ their leisure time in various athletic, artistic, and cultural pursuits, such as sports events and camping trips, dramatic and choral societies, public libraries and vocational instruction. It also secured reductions for its members in the cost of medical and hospital care, and assisted in the organization of home-building societies. In any computation of labor's share in the national income these non-monetary benefits must in fairness be included.

Conclusion. From even this brief survey it is clear that, while Fascism has preserved the forms and methods of capitalism, this has been greatly modified and restricted. Fascism has retained certain features of capitalistic economy, such as private property and the private operation of most business, but has rejected the principle of *laissez faire*. Business is theoretically competitive and prices are fixed in most cases by market conditions, but there has been increasing government interference and control of prices since 1926. Wages are set by collective contracts under government auspices, and not by demand and supply or bargaining. The standard of living is distinctly lower than it was before the war. Both employers and workers have been regimented in syndical organizations, which are wholly under the control of the Fascist Party and do not enjoy self-regulation. The employing group, however, exercises a much stronger influence than do the workers in the determination of policies and wage contracts. But the interests of both groups are subordinated to those of the state, which they are made to serve by a system of strict economic discipline.

3. NATIONAL SOCIALISM

National Socialism did not begin with the rise of Adolf Hitler in 1933, for it ran back much earlier than that. The ideology and philosophy of the movement had their roots in the history of the German people. Nationalism, though late in developing, had been growing since the foundation of the Empire in 1871, and socialism was accepted as a normal procedure. Socialism is often used as a term of opprobrium, but in Germany it was a symbol of social progress. "National Socialism" was a sublimated, fervidly patriotic, anti-Semitic movement, which intensified the underlying forces of German history. As a movement it began in 1919, when six men organized the National Socialist German Workers' Party (N.S. D.A.P.). Hitler joined the group later in the year as its seventh member. From this small beginning grew one of the most portentous movements of modern history. The fortunes of the new organization fluctuated with the ups and downs of the business cycle, remaining at a low ebb in good times and showing strength in periods of depression. Its final and complete victory came after the crisis of 1931 and as a result of the growing misery and discontent of the mass of the people.

It will be remembered that after the defeat of Germany and the flight of the Emperor the Social Democrats took over the government, framed the Weimar Constitution and established a republic, which made Germany, they boasted, "the most democratic state in the world." This change was greeted with enthusiasm in other democratic countries and was hailed as the beginning of a new and enlightened era for an oppressed people. What was not realized then and is scarcely understood now is that the German nation did not wish to be free. "This excellent people has no real sense of freedom," wrote Walter Rathenau in 1914; "it loves authority, it desires to be governed, it resigns itself and wants only to obey." The new constitution imported its leading characteristics — parliamentary democracy, liberalism, and individualism — from abroad, and they never took root in German soil or in the German soul. Indeed, they were resented as antagonistic to the true German traditions. The Republican rulers during the next decade, moreover, bore all the blame for the ignominy of the Ruhr occupation, the ruin of the inflation period, and the burden of reparation payments under the Dawes and Young plans. By 1932 they were thoroughly discredited, and were repudiated by three Germans out of four in the April elections of that year. The following year saw the Nazis entrenched in power.

Important economic changes were also occurring. Capitalism in Germany was never characterized by unlimited free competition among unorganized small enterprisers. The Reich owned and operated the railroads, the several German states owned or had large investments in coal and potassium mines, nitrate and aluminum production, lead and silver mining, and forests, and the municipalities owned most of the public utilities. Private enterprises were coordinated by a widespread system of cartels, which were compulsory in the coal and potassium mining industries. This state control of industry was greatly extended as a result of the financial crash of 1931, during which the government was forced to take over some of the banks and extend loans to others. Through the credits which the banks had extended to industrial concerns, the government came, indirectly, to control these also. State money was also advanced to the Steel Trust and to shipping companies. As a result of all of these events the control of the state over banking and industry was enormously increased. Capitalism in Germany was therefore characterized by an extension of state ownership and control which in other countries would be considered inconsistent with a system of free enterprise and initiative. It was, in a word, State Socialism.

Agriculture in Germany suffered greatly, as in all other industrial countries, from the catastrophic changes which followed the World War. State assistance had been granted in the form of high protective tariffs, and to the large agriculturalists of East Prussia loans of public funds were made, although 6000 of these estates were hopelessly bankrupt and unable to cover the costs of production at the price of grain in the world markets. But in spite of this aid the farmers were dissatisfied.

The position of the worker under the Weimar Republic was one of security. He had obtained the right of collective bargaining and the arbitration of labor disputes under governmental sanction. He enjoyed the advantages of an elaborate system of social insurance and other services in addition to his money wages. If to all this there be added the improvement in his social status and the liberalization of the educational system, it may be concluded that the worker had attained a position of some power, if not domination, in the economic system. Unfortunately some of the labor groups had used their power to exact concessions from the employers which the latter considered unjustifiable. Among the larger industrialists there existed therefore a deep-seated hostility to labor and to the government which they supported.

One other group remains to be described — the lower middle class, made up of shopkeepers, small business men, white-collar employees, independent peasants and farm laborers, and persons living on their savings and pensions. These people were ruined by the inflation and reduced to destitution by the depression. Their life-savings wiped out, their security for old age gone, they had become practically a proletariat. They feared socialism, disliked the Republic, and were strongly nationalistic, but were bewildered by the breakdown of their world. The system of private capitalism had failed them and they were ready for new leaders.

Even more bitterly hostile to the existing economic system was the younger generation, especially the students of the universities and technical schools. Students are apt to be radical, but there was an economic basis for the radicalism of the German student. Owing to the overcrowding of the professions and to the depression he could see no opportunity of finding employment in his chosen field; indeed he could not count upon finding employment at all.

The existence of these various discontented groups gave an economic basis for National Socialism. The lower middle class and the youth especially rallied to Hitler out of despair. Hatred for the Treaty of Versailles, which was fanned to fever heat by the National Socialists and which gave a nationalistic turn to the movement, undoubtedly played an important role also. To the discontented Hitler offered hope and comfort. Like Mussolini, Hitler was a consummate organizer and showman, who understood how to arouse loyalty and enthusiasm. To a people accustomed to the pomp and circumstance of the Empire he gave again the spectacle of uniforms, of marching, of music, and of flags, and to the young the opportunity of playing at being soldiers. But he also attracted the big industrialists who saw in this movement a chance not only of crushing communism but also of destroying the trade unions.

It is not easy to describe the economic organization of Germany under National Socialism, first because it was overshadowed largely by politics, second because economic practice did not coincide with promised economic reforms, and third because it was finally subordinated to rearmament. The original program of twenty-five points was proclaimed in 1920 and six years later was declared by the constitution of the party to be unalterable. Of these the two main ones, strongly emphasized by Hitler, were the Common Interest before the Interest of the Individual (*Gemeinnutz vor Eigennutz*) and Abolition of the Thralldom of Interest.

The lower middle class had been won to Hitler by the promise that "slavery to interest" would be broken, and that production would be directed to supplying the necessities of life rather than gaining the largest possible profits. Small shopkeepers had been assured that the large department stores would be forced out of business, and that the trusts would be nationalized. Although the National Socialists, like the Communists, asserted that interest is usury and therefore immoral, they did nothing to change the institution. The attitude of the government towards big stores vacillated between radicalism and conservatism. At first violent propaganda was launched against the department stores and the public was urged to boycott these and patronize the small shopkeepers. Hardly was this under way when the official policy underwent a change and the big stores were permitted to carry on business as before.

The interpretation of the other point was equally difficult and open to change. Its practical application meant the subordination of individual interests to what the government at any time might decide to be the interests of the community. This left the door wide open to unlimited interference with personal freedom of action, in both the political and the economic sphere. The German government exhibited a concentration of power unequalled in any other country and with the fewest constitutional restraints. All legislative and executive power was centered in the cabinet, at the head of which stood the Leader. The principle of leadership, introduced by the Nazis, was basic in their philosophy and was carried into every sphere of action. Authority was concentrated in the National Leader and was delegated by him to other persons. "The national state," wrote Hitler in *Mein Kampf*, "must work untiringly to set all government, especially the highest — that is, the political leadership — free from the principle of control by majorities — that is, the multitude — so as to secure the undisputed authority of the individual in its stead." Democratic freedom he stigmatized as "licentiousness" and condemned parliaments as talking clubs without power to act.

The state thus set up was a "totalitarian state" (*Totalstaat*), and the government was that of a dictatorship, involving propaganda, the spy system, and the denial of free speech and assembly. No aspect of life was free from government interference. Individualism and personal rights had no place in the Nazi scheme; the so-called community of the people (*Volksgemeinschaft*) was proclaimed as the aim. Economic self-sufficiency (*Autarchie*) was sought so far as possible, for only in a wholly nationalistic and centralized state could economic planning be successful. In order to accomplish this it was necessary to unify the German people and to overcome the particularism of the separate states. This was achieved, not only by changes in the political organization, but also by the creation of a new national ideology. To effect the latter powerful psychological appeals had to be used, and these were found in attacks on the Treaty of Versailles, the demand for breathing space (*Lebensraum*), and the policy of anti-Semitism. The people were told that the Fatherland had been stabbed in the back during the war and betrayed in the framing of the peace treaty by Marxists and Jews, most of whom were communists and internationalists. The country must therefore be cleared of all non-Nordic elements, internationalism must be crushed, and truly national aims set up. All parties except the National Socialist Party were suppressed, unsympathetic persons were removed not only from political office, but also from the civil service and from educational institutions, and if actively hostile were sent to concentration camps. A new history, literature, and religion were presented to the young, designed to make them thoroughly nationalistic. After about 1936 a new turn was given to the theory of economic organization — the so-called Defense Economy (*Wehrwirtschaft*). This directed all economic activities in peace time towards complete military preparedness and subjected the whole German people to the regimentation and privations of a war economy.

BIBLIOGRAPHICAL NOTE

1. *Russia.* No experiment in social organization has ever aroused such widespread interest or called forth such a flood of books as has that in Soviet Russia, but only a few of those of economic significance can be cited. Two good economic histories of Russia provide the background: Jas. Mavor, *An Economic History of Russia,* 2 vols. (2nd ed., London, 1925), and L. Lawton, *An Economic History of Soviet Russia,* 2 vols. (London, 1932). A useful general survey is F. E. Lawley, *The Growth of Collective Economies* (London, 1938). An excellent account of conditions in old Russia is G. T. Robinson, *Rural Russia under the Old Regime* (New York, 1932). M. S. Miller, *The Economic Development of Russia, 1905–1914* (London, 1926) is a careful study, based on statistical material. Conditions after the Revolution are pictured in M. Dobb and H. C. Stevens, *Russian Economic Development since the Revolution* (2nd ed., London, 1929), a keen economic analysis; C. D. Hoover, *Economic Life of Soviet Russia* (New York, 1931), objective; G. S. Counts and others, *Bolshevism, Fascism, and Capitalism* (New York, 1932), a good account. After the Five-Year Plans were launched the emphasis was upon economic planning. A clear description of the system is W. H. Chamberlin, *Soviet Planned Economic Order* (Boston, 1931); his *Russia's Iron Age* (Boston, 1934) is severely critical but informative. S. and B. Webb, *Soviet Communism: A New Civilization?* (New York, 1926) is highly favorable. A. R. Williams, *The Soviets* (New York, 1937) is laudatory and uncritical. Official accounts of the first two Plans are State Planning Commission of the Union of Soviet Socialist Republics, *The Soviet Union Looks Ahead; the Five-Year Plan for Economic Construction* (New York, 1929); and *The Second Five-Year Plan for the Development of the National Economy of the U.S.S.R., 1933–1937* (New York, 1937). No report was published on the Third Plan. The following books are adverse: M. T. Florinsky, *Toward An Understanding of the U.S.S.R.* (New York, 1939), well-informed; M. Gordon, *Workers before and after Lenin* (New York, 1941); C. Clark, *A Critique of Russian Statistics* (London, 1939), keen analysis. A specialized study is L. E. Hubbard, *Soviet Trade and Distribution* (New York, 1938). A useful survey is E. Lamb, *The Planned Economy in Soviet Russia* (Philadelphia, 1934). W. N. Loucks and J. W. Hoot, *Comparative Economic Systems* (New York, 1938) is a text book and impartial.

2. *Fascism in Italy.* The two best books in English on the early period are A. Rossi, *The Rise of Fascism: Italy from 1918 to 1922* (London, 1938), and F. Pitigliani, *The Italian Corporative State* (London, 1933). A clear general survey is H. W. Schneider, *Making the Fascist State* (New York, 1928). H. E. Goad, *The Making of the Fascist State: a Study of Fascist Development* (London, 1932) is a defense of Fascism. C. Haider, *Capital and Labor under Fascism* (New York, 1930) is more specialized. C. E. McGuire, *Italy's International Economic Position* (New York, 1927) is informative. For an understanding of later developments events after 1934 must be studied. B. Mussolini, *Fascism: Doctrine and Institutions* (Rome, 1935) presents Fascist ideology. One or more of his addresses are reprinted in R. E. Westmeyer, *Modern Economic and Social Systems* (New York, 1940). A good collection of documents is M. Oakeshott, *The Social and Political Doctrines of Contemporary Europe* (Cambridge, 1939). A very good comparative study is E. Colton, *Four Patterns of Revolution* (New York, 1935). M. T. Florinsky, *Fascism and National Socialism: a Study of the Economic and Social Policies of the Totalitarian State* (New York, 1936) is an excellent introduction. M. Ascoli and A. Feiler, *Fascism for Whom?* (New York, 1938) is a penetrating analysis. G. Gaddi, *The Workers in Fascist Italy* (London, 1939) discusses

the legal position of labor. G. L. Field, *The Syndical and Corporative Institutions of Italian Fascism* (New York, 1938) is a scholarly study. C. T. Schmidt, *The Plough and the Sword* (New York, 1938) describes agriculture and labor; his *The Corporate State in Action: Italy under Fascism* (New York, 1939) has good economic material. G. Tassinari, *Fascist Economy* (Rome, 1937) is a concise favorable account. W. G. Welk, *Fascist Economic Policy: an Analysis of Italy's Economic Experiment* (Cambridge, Mass., 1938) contains valuable economic data.

3. *National Socialism in Germany.* A good general survey is W. F. Bruck, *Social and Economic History of Germany from William II to Hitler, 1888–1938* (Cardiff, 1938). The development of National Socialism is described in K. Heiden, *History of National Socialism* (Translated from the German. London, 1934). A clear picture of conditions on the accession of Hitler to power is given in C. B. Hoover, *Germany Enters the Third Reich* (New York, 1933), and E. A. Mowrer, *Germany Puts the Clock Back* (New York, 1933). To get Hitler's own ideas, one should read Adolf Hitler, *Mein Kampf* (40te Aufl., München, 1936. English translation, *My Battle*, New York, 1939). Other semi-official pronouncements are H. Goering, *Aufbau einer Nation* (Berlin, 1934), and G. Feder, *Hitler's Official Programme, and its Fundamental Ideas* (translated from the 5th German ed., London, 1934). Two other favorable accounts are P. Blankenburg and M. Dreyer, *Nationalsozialistischer Wirtschaftsaufbau und seine Grundlagen* (Berlin, 1934), and H. Brautigam, *The National Socialist Economic System* (3rd ed., Berlin, 1936). W. F. Bruck, *The Road to Planned Economy* (Cardiff, 1934) is a keen analysis. F. Ermarth, *The New Germany: National Socialist Government in Theory and in Practice* (Washington, 1936) is useful. V. Trivanovitch, *Economic Development of Germany under National Socialism* (New York, Nat. Ind. Conf. Bd., 1937) is an objective survey. S. Roberts, *The House that Hitler Built* (London, 1937) is careful and impartial. H. Lichtenberger, *The Third Reich* (Translated from the French by K. S. Pinson. New York, 1937) is an excellent objective study. C. W. Guillebaud, *The Economic Recovery of Germany from 1933 to the Incorporation of Austria in 1938* (London, 1939) is a scholarly analysis, authoritative and clear.

INDEX OF NAMES

INDEX OF SUBJECTS

J.